R
813.52
F263r

**FOR REFERENCE**

**Do Not Take From This Room**

**Renner Learning Resource Center
Elgin Community College
Elgin, IL 60123**

*A Reader's Guide
to the Short Stories of*
WILLIAM FAULKNER

*A
Reference
Publication
in
Literature*

Everett Emerson
Editor

# A Reader's Guide to the Short Stories of
# WILLIAM FAULKNER

Diane Brown Jones

G.K. Hall & Co.
An Imprint of Macmillan Publishing Company
*New York*

Maxwell Macmillan Canada
*Toronto*

Maxwell Macmillan International
*New York   Oxford   Singapore   Sydney*

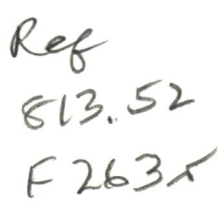
Ref
813.52
F263r

Copyright © 1994 by Diane Brown Jones

All rights reserved. No part of this book may be reproduced or transmitted in any form or by any means, electronic or mechanical, including photocopying, recording, or by any information storage and retrieval system, without permission in writing from the Publisher.

G.K. Hall & Co.  
An Imprint of Macmillan Publishing Company  
866 Third Avenue  
New York, NY 10022

Maxwell Macmillan Canada, Inc.  
1200 Eglinton Avenue East  
Suite 200  
Don Mills, Ontario M3C 3N1

Macmillan Publishing Company is part of the Maxwell Communication Group of Companies

Library of Congress Catalog Card Number: 93-36283

Printed in the United States of America

printing number 1 2 3 4 5 6 7 8 9 10

Library of Congress Cataloging-in-Publication Data

Jones, Diane Brown.
   A reader's guide to the short stories of William Faulkner : tales from "The country," "The village," "The Wilderness," and "The middle ground" in The collected stories / Diane Brown Jones.
      p.  cm. — (A Reference publication in literature)
   ISBN 0-8161-7272-2
   1. Faulkner, William, 1897-1962—Criticism and interpretation. 2. Short story. I. Title. II. Series.
PS3511.A86Z8586 1994
813'.52—dc20                                                               93-36283
                                                                                                     CIP

The paper used in this publication meets the minimum requirements of American National Standard for Information Sciences—Permanence of Paper for Printed Library Materials. ANSI Z39.48-1984 ∞ ™

For Earl

# Contents

*The Author*   ix
*Foreword*   xi
*Introduction*   xiii
*Abbreviations*   xvii

*The Country*   1
    Barn Burning   3
    Shingles for the Lord   32
    The Tall Men   43
    A Bear Hunt   54
    Two Soldiers   64
    Shall Not Perish   73

*The Village*   85
    A Rose for Emily   87
    Hair   142
    Centaur in Brass   154
    Dry September   169
    Death Drag   204
    Elly   221
    Uncle Willy   237
    Mule in the Yard   248
    That Will Be Fine   260
    That Evening Sun   267

*The Wilderness*     317
    Red Leaves     319
    A Justice     342
    A Courtship     362
    Lo!     375

*The Middle Ground*     385
    Wash     387
    Honor     402
    Dr. Martino     411
    Fox Hunt     422
    Pennsylvania Station     432
    Artist at Home     440
    The Brooch     453
    My Grandmother Millard and General Bedford Forrest and the Battle of Harrykin Creek     466
    Golden Land     476
    There Was a Queen     487
    Mountain Victory     515

*Index of Faulkner's Works*     531
*General Index*     537

# The Author

Diane Brown Jones is a Lecturer at North Carolina State University in Raleigh. She has published on Elizabeth Peabody in *Studies in the American Renaissance*, written on Elizabeth Blackwell for the forthcoming *Oxford Companion to Women's Writing in the United States*, and presented papers on William Faulkner and other Southern writers. Jones recently completed her Ph.D. at the University of North Carolina at Chapel Hill where she received the C. Hugh Holman Fellowship for her dissertation project on Faulkner.

# Foreword

As with the entire Reader's Guide to the Short Stories series, Diane Brown Jones's volume provides a great quantity of useful information. As short fiction begins to receive the critical attention it merits, particularly in the study of American letters, this meticulous compilation of fact, critical opinion, and historiography will increase in use. No other kind of publication provides so much sheer help about the way an author wrote a story, the way that story was received by the reading and the scholarly public, and the assessment of various controversies that sift down through time. Jones has taken on one of the American writers most difficult to interpret—William Faulkner. In the often murky patterns of his writing and publishing, patterns sometimes obscured intentionally by the writer himself, Jones manages to bring a clear and concise view of many central Faulkner stories. She has necessarily limited this book to coverage of some of Faulkner's most often taught short fiction, including the works from "The Country," "The Village," "The Wilderness," and "The Middle Ground" of his *Collected Stories*. Here the reader will find a compendium of sound information about "Barn Burning," "A Rose for Emily," "Dry September," "Mule in the Yard," "That Evening Sun," "Red Leaves," "Wash," "Dr. Martino," "The Brooch," "There Was a Queen," "Mountain Victory," and as many more. Both useful and perceptive, Jones's work deserves our commendation.

Linda Wagner-Martin
Hanes Professor of English and Comparative Literature
The University of North Carolina at Chapel Hill

# Introduction

*These 13* (1931), *Doctor Martino and Other Stories* (1934), *Knight's Gambit* (1949), *Collected Stories of William Faulkner* (1950), *Big Woods* (1955), *Uncollected Stories of William Faulkner* (1979), *Mayday* (1977), *The Wishing Tree* (1967), and *New Orleans Sketches* (1958)—beyond a specialized few, most readers do not recognize this list of short fiction collections by the author now regarded as one of the greatest writers of the twentieth century. But Faulkner excelled not only as novelist but also as short story writer. A substantial proportion of his literary output is short stories, the total number exceeding one hundred.

*Collected Stories*, which includes all of the stories from *These 13*, most of those from *Doctor Martino*, and several other previously uncollected stories, constitutes the most significant gathering of Faulkner's short pieces. These forty-two stories— what could be called the master's selection—demonstrate the fullest expression and variation of Faulkner's short fiction. The stories range from early to later works, Yoknapatawpha to non–Yoknapatawpha settings, comic to tragic visions. Any study of William Faulkner that seeks to trace transtextual patterns of theme and style across the canon should include *Collected Stories*.

Faulkner's view of the book was that it was "to be comprehensive," excluding, however, those short works "previously allotted to other complete volumes in future" (*SL* 280). Most of the forty-two stories take their final form in *Collected Stories*. Three of them—"A Bear Hunt," "Red Leaves," and "A Justice"—were later revised for inclusion in *Big Woods* (1955); "Centaur in Brass" and "Mule in the Yard" were subsequently incorporated in *The Town*. Earlier, "Wash" had been made part of *Absalom, Absalom!*, and the events of "Barn Burning" were retold in *The Hamlet*. As Faulkner became involved in selecting the stories, his correspondence reveals renewed pleasure in some stories and scarce acknowledgment of others. He did not think "The Brooch," "Pennsylvania Station," and "Shall Not Perish" were particularly good. He liked "Uncle Willy," though, and after rereading "Mule in the Yard" and "Shingles for the Lord," he declared, "I spent a whole evening laughing to myself" (*SL* 274, 304).

Faulkner not only carefully selected the stories to be included in collection, he also sought an ordering strategy. With his characteristic interest in structure, he wanted to give the "volume an integrated form of its own" that was "single, set for one pitch, contrapuntal in integration, toward one end, one finale" (*SL* 273, 278). The sectional arrangement of the volume reflects that intent, as do the sectional titles. Faulkner wrote to editor Saxe Commins about his concern for the titles, especially the suggested use of the word *Indians* to follow *Country* and *Village*: "Then I thought, not *Indians* but *Wilderness*, and then suddenly the whole page stood right, each noun in character and tone and tune with every other . . ." (*SL* 277). Faulkner's design was set: "The Country," "The Village," "The Wilderness," "The Wasteland," "The Middle Ground," and "Beyond." Each of the six sections possesses geographical and/or thematic unity, though the last two sections, "The Middle Ground" and "Beyond," present a greater challenge to that intention.

This Reader's Guide includes discussions of thirty-one of the forty-two stories in *Collected Stories*. Because all the stories could not be covered in the volume, a most difficult step was determining which ones to eliminate. My regard for the collection as a cohesive unit is so great that I committed myself to maintaining the integrity of the sections. Consequently, this volume takes up all the stories in "The Country," "The Village," "The Wilderness," and "The Middle Ground." While these sections include the stories recognized as Faulkner's best, the decision has meant omitting stories from "The Wasteland" and "Beyond," and these are not insignificant texts. "Carcassonne," for example, represents Faulkner's portrait of the artist, and the five stories of "The Wasteland" make a substantive contribution to the modernist temper of the post–World War I writers. Nevertheless, the decision facilitates extensive consideration of "Barn Burning," "A Rose for Emily," "That Evening Sun," "Red Leaves," and "Wash."

This volume has been designed in accordance with the goals of the Reader's Guides to the Short Stories series, specifically, to be useful to anyone who would be an informed reader of fiction in an age when the amount of scholarship, analysis, and criticism is more than anyone except the learned specialist can accommodate. Each story is treated in a separate chapter that assimilates and presents everything substantial that has been written about that story. Each chapter includes sections headed Publication History; Circumstances of Composition, Sources, and Influences; Relation to Other Faulkner Works; Interpretation and Criticism; and Works Cited.

Given the size of the critical canon on Faulkner, the following qualifiers apply: the criticism reviewed is restricted to published work in English. Although making the project more manageable, this tactic has the disadvantage of eliminating the excellent body of international criticism. A cursory review of *American Literary Scholarship* can attest to this claim. Works that offer synopses or character lists are included only when they also offer an evaluation or when the summary becomes part of a dialogue between critics. Reviews of the short story collections appear only occasionally, again, typically when a comment has become a point of entry for critical discussion of a story. Dissertations on the short stories are not included.

Locating the criticism for the short stories has presented its own challenge. A large body of writing on the stories appears in periodicals, and references to them, usually by way of comparison, also appear in longer studies of particular novels or topical studies. Faulkner bibliographies have been invaluable in identifying those books and articles pertinent to each story. I have relied especially on the following bibliographies:

Bassett, John E. 1972. *William Faulkner: An Annotated Checklist of Criticism*. New York: David Lewis.
———. 1983. *Faulkner: An Annotated Checklist of Recent Criticism*. Kent, OH: Kent State University Press.
———. 1991. *Faulkner in the Eighties: An Annotated Critical Bibliography*. Scarecrow Author Bibliographies, No. 88. Metuchen, NJ: Scarecrow Press.
McHaney, Thomas L. 1976. *William Faulner: A Reference Guide*. Boston: G. K. Hall.
Sweeney, Patricia E. 1985. *William Faulkner's Women Characters: An Annotated Bibliography of Criticism*. Santa Barbara, CA: ABC-Clio Information Services.

It has been somewhat more difficult to trace the passing mentions and brief comparative references to stories. Five book-length studies have been published on the short stories: Hans Skei's *William Faulkner: The Short Story Career* (1981), Skei's *William Faulkner: The Novelist as Short Story Writer* (1985), James Carothers's *William Faulkner's Short Stories* (1985), James Ferguson's *Faulkner's Short Fiction* (1991), and the conference proceedings *Faulkner and the Short Story: Faulkner and Yoknapatawpha, 1990*, edited by Evans Harrington and Ann J. Abadie. Skei's monograph *Bold and Tragical and Austere: William Faulkner's* These 13: *A Study* (1977) is not readily accessible, but much of the information contained in it is available in Skei's subsequent works. The review of criticism attempts to be complete through 1990 although I have been able to include several book-length studies from 1991 and 1992.

Criticism of the short stories has not been so extensive as the interpretation of Faulkner's novels. The most important critical works center chiefly on the novels, and there has been limited integration of the short stories into the critical response. Although Faulkner's excellence in the genre is widely recognized, his short fiction has inspired little work utilizing contemporary theoretical applications. The body of criticism is uneven in breadth and quality. A particularly regrettable quality of the criticism for those stories most frequently anthologized is its repetitive nature. Although the dialogue between scholars can be energetic, the gains are often limited. By making available in summary the trends of critical thought for each story, perhaps this book can help future critics avoid adding new pages to older, hackneyed arguments. For example, "A Rose for Emily" has been extensively, and repetitiously, interpreted. Other less popular and admittedly less exceptional stories have been barely considered.

One area in which this lack is especially unfortunate is in studies of Faulkner's portrayal of women. Feminist readings of Faulkner will simply not be sufficient until such women as Minnie Cooper, Elly, Nancy, Emily, Mannie Hait, and numerous others are given place beside the likes of Eula Varner and Lena Grove. Although readings of these women in the short fiction do appear, they are as yet rudimentary. One might hope for a study that would examine both black and white female characters, and an especially fruitful beginning would be in James Watson's suggestions of similarities in the framing stories of "The Village"—"A Rose for Emily" and "That Evening Sun."

It would be remiss of me not to acknowledge my appreciation to two individuals who shared manuscripts with me. John Bassett most generously offered the manuscript of *Faulkner in the Eighties: An Annotated Critical Bibliography* for me to use well before the book was published. His work allowed me to direct my own research quickly and pointedly toward the short story criticism in the 1980s. Shortly after the 1990 Faulkner and Yoknapatawpha Conference on "Faulkner and the Short Story," Ann Abadie of the Center for the Study of Southern Culture forwarded to me copies of several of the conference papers. I am pleased to be able to include presentations from the conference in this volume.

I am especially grateful to four individuals who worked closely with me on the more limited form of this study that became my dissertation: Joseph Flora, Linda Wagner-Martin, Fred Hobson, and Mary Davis of the University of North Carolina at Chapel Hill. They generously shared their own expertise, abundant encouragement, patient instruction, and constant enthusiasm for an ever-lengthening project.

Recently, as I have worked to bring this project to conclusion, I have enjoyed the insights of Judy Jo Small, who has shared her experience in writing the Sherwood Anderson volume for this series.

To Everett Emerson I owe the deepest expression of appreciation. I feel a profound sense of good fortune for having had the opportunity to call him my teacher, mentor, and friend. From the inception of this project to its conclusion, I have benefited from his wise counsel and enthusiasm while he served both as the director of my dissertation and the general editor of the series. He has offered guidance, gently applied, rigorously perceptive.

Now the book is in the hands of Faulkner scholars; let the responsibility for errors of fact and judgment that become apparent fall to me alone.

# Abbreviations

The following abbreviations of titles are used in parenthetical citations:

| | |
|---|---|
| AILD | *As I Lay Dying* |
| BW | *Big Woods* |
| CS | *Collected Stories of William Faulkner* |
| DRM | *Doctor Martino and Other Stories* |
| FD | *Flags in the Dust* |
| FU | *Faulkner in the University* |
| GDM | *Go Down, Moses* |
| LG | *Lion in the Garden: Interviews with William Faulkner: 1926–1962* |
| S | *Sanctuary: The Corrected Text* |
| SAR | *Sartoris* |
| SF | *The Sound and the Fury* |
| SL | *Selected Letters of William Faulkner* |
| T | *The Town* |
| T13 | *These 13* |
| US | *Uncollected Stories of William Faulkner* |
| WFM 6 | *William Faulkner Manuscripts 6*: The Sound and the Fury. 2 vols. |
| WFM 9 | *William Faulkner Manuscripts 9*: These 13 |
| WFM 11 | *William Faulkner Manuscripts 11*: Doctor Martino and Other Stories |
| WFM 13 | *William Faulkner Manuscripts 13*: Absalom, Absalom! |
| WFM 15 | *William Faulkner Manuscripts 15*: The Hamlet. 2 vols. |
| WFM 21 | *William Faulkner Manuscripts 21*: The Town. 2 vols. |
| WFM 24 | *William Faulkner Manuscripts 24: Short Stories* |

*The Country*

# Barn Burning

## Publication History

"Barn Burning" was first published in June 1939 in *Harper's*. Faulkner's agent, Harold Ober, received the story on November 19, 1938, but he was able to place it only on the sixth submission when, in March 1939, *Harper's* purchased the story for $400. Before that the *Saturday Evening Post*, *Red Book*, *The American Magazine*, *Country Gentleman*, and *Cosmopolitan* had all rejected it.

In spite of its early rejections, "Barn Burning" won the first O. Henry Memorial Award for the best story published in an American magazine in the previous year, a prize that included a cash award of $300. It opens *Collected Stories* (1950), although Faulkner's working list for the collection indicates that he had initially omitted it, based on his erroneous recollection that the story was the opening of *The Hamlet*.

In 1945, Faulkner and Albert Bezzerides prepared a fifty-page treatment of the story for a film version, but it was never produced. More than a decade later, Gore Vidal adapted "Barn Burning" for a CBS telecast on August 17, 1954. The most recent television version, first broadcast March 17, 1980, was a forty-one-minute adaptation by Horton Foote for the *American Short Story* series on PBS (*SL* 274; Meriwether [1961] 1971, 162–63; Blotner 1974, 1005, 1031, 1185; Blotner 1984, 400–01; Skei 1981, 92–93; Phillips 1988, 176; see also Kawin 1977, 53–55, and Karl 1989).

## Circumstances of Composition, Sources, and Influences

The relationship between "Barn Burning" and *The Hamlet* draws most of the attention about the textual development of the story. Extant manuscripts available in the *William Faulkner Manuscripts 15* show the title of the longer work originally to have been "Barn Burning," with that title marked through and replaced with "Book One, Chapter I" of what was first named "The Peasants" and later changed to *The Hamlet*.

In a September 1938 letter to his daughter Jill, Faulkner wrote that he was working on a new story Joseph Blotner identifies as "Barn Burning." Faulkner continued to work on the text through October; then, it seems, on November 7, 1938, he dated the manuscript, deleted the title "Barn Burning," and added the book and chapter headings. Most subsequent discussions accept this chronology, but Blotner's 1984 biography casts some doubt on this dating of events. In the biography Blotner indicates that the November 7, 1938, date and titles were the first efforts at the story that was completed within the next ten days and forwarded to Ober as a short story (*SL* 275, n. 6; *WFM 15*: I: Introduction xi; Blotner 1974, 1001–002, Notes 142; Blotner 1984, 400–01; see also Minter 1980, 177).

It is not clear what relationship the manuscript and typescript tied to *The Hamlet* have to the copy that Ober was circulating among magazines. In his introduction to the manuscript volumes Thomas McHaney suggests that the manuscript might be the original of the story that Faulkner composed in September and October. Comparisons of manuscript, typescript, magazine text, and *Collected Stories* versions reveal numerous early modifications. The typescript contains extended passages about Sarty's sisters. Other alterations include the marginal addition in the manuscript that adds Ab's description of the sweat, from blacks and whites, required to construct de Spain's house. Also, at the conclusion of the story, Sarty's call to Ab appears in the manuscript without the initial call to "Pap." There are three starts of the final passage describing the "slow constellation" before Faulkner brings the story to conclusion. Frequent word revisions and paragraphing changes distinguish the typescript from the magazine version, but the magazine and collected versions differ only in one correction (*wher's* to *where's*), and capitalization of *Negro* in the collected text (*WFM 15* 1:Introduction xi, 216–63; "Barn Burning" 86–96; *CS* 3–25).

Critics have found both historical and biographical links to the fictional world of "Barn Burning." Richard Moreland reports that the work of Albert C. Smith documents barn burning as a method of choice for protesters who owned no property in the post–Civil War South (1989, 64; 1990, 17). The threat of fire touched Faulkner's ancestors in a personal way. According to the *Oxford Eagle*, December 10, 1904, damage to a storehouse owned by Faulkner's grandfather J. W. T. Falkner was repaired, and in the same paper, a separate note indicated that three "incendiaries" were tried. Blotner does not indicate whether the reports were linked (1974, Notes 41). Also, in April 1917, J. W. T. Falkner lost a building to fire; his loss, uninsured, was approximately $5,000 (Blotner 1974, 189).

Other studies offer psychological correspondences between Faulkner's life and the lives of Ab and his son Sarty. Warren Beck suggests that both Faulkner and Sarty were painfully confronted with a need to separate themselves from a "flawed heritage," Faulkner's being regional, Sarty's familial. Faulkner, unlike Sarty, could "repudiate what remained socially unamended" without loosing the ties completely (Beck 1976, 326). Michael Grimwood reads several elements of the text biographically: Ab's wound is not a legitimate war wound, recalling the fabrication of Faulkner's aviation injury; Sarty's "ne'er-do-well father" and the "heroic namesake" both reflect resemblances to Faulkner's life, and the fictional child was defended by his mother as was Faulkner (Grimwood 1987, 137–38).

Joan Hall traces a historical association to Ab in the narrator's remark that Ab went "to war as Malbrouck himself did: for booty" (*CS* 25). Hall recalls that in the 1930s Winston Churchill had written a six-volume biography about his ancestor, the first Duke of Marlborough. Marlborough's reputation brought him both praise as a military leader and criticism as a profiteer during war. One specific action for which he was remembered was his order to burn crops, an act that devastated Bavaria in 1704. Hall finds a more positive contextual reference to Marlborough in *A Fable*. Faulkner's source is uncertain, the Churchill volumes representing only one of numerous possibilities (Hall 1989, 65–68).

Literary influences ranging from classical mythology to Faulkner's twentieth-century contemporaries are typically believed to enhance the characterizations of Ab and Sarty Snopes. Mythological associations include Ab's likeness to Achilles (the wounded heel) and Prometheus (stealing fire) (Mitchell 1965, 183; see also Bradford 1981, 336). Gayle Wilson links Ab to the motif of the Fisher King who appears to be living but is dead and brings barrenness to the land (1970–71, 287). M. E. Bradford pinpoints additional likenesses to Ab: the character of Talus in Book V of Spenser's *Faerie Queene* and Satan in *Paradise Lost* (1981, 336, 337). For William Stein, Ab's "motiveless malignity" likens him to William Shakespeare's Iago (Stein 1961, 731–32). From a different perspective, Volpe likens Sarty's watching his sisters work over the boiling pot of lye soap to another Shakespearean reference, the opening scene of *Macbeth* (1980, 77–78). Richard Adams believes that the description of Ab Snopes "against the stars but without face or depth—a shape black, flat, and bloodless as though cut from tin" comes from Faulkner's reading of Conrad, specifically from *The Nigger of the "Narcissus"* in the opening of which the crew appears "very black, without relief, like figures cut out of sheet tin" (quoted in Adams 1962, 130). Adams interprets the image as indicating "more or less mechanistic alienation from humanity, or from life" in the work of both artists (1962, 130).

Ab has precursors in the American literary tradition as well. His portrait in black is "surely a historical extension of Hawthorne's ubiquitous 'Black Man'" (Stein 1961, 731–32). Or he could be a latter-day creation of Melville's Ahab (Mitchell 1965, 186; see also Bradford 1981, 336).

Huckleberry Finn seems to be the compelling literary predecessor of Sarty Snopes, but the discussions focus chiefly on differences between the two youths. Lionel Trilling distinguishes the simplicity of Huck's comprehension from the inchoate perception of Sarty (1967, 324; see also Gold 1966, 78). For Karl Zender, comparisons between Huck Finn and Sarty Snopes demonstrate a more optimistic vision in Twain's text than Faulkner's vision. Huck is not responsible for his father's death; also, he has a literal West into which he can move. Sarty has only the "dark wood," a "space, unlocatable on any map, [that] is the dark terrain of the self through which Sarty must journey if he is to become a mature adult" (Zender 1989, 55–56).

Kathy Cackett draws more contemporary comparisons between Ab Snopes and F. Scott Fitzgerald's Jay Gatsby. Both men are linked to images of errant timepieces; both are often portrayed standing alone against an expansive sky (1989, 10).

## Relationship to Other Faulkner Works

As Michael Millgate phrases it, "Barn Burning" is one of Faulkner's "narrative or emotional spin-offs from the creative surges which generated major novels" (1980, 103). Hans Skei notes that in the period from 1933 to 1941, many of Faulkner's stories bore some relationship to his novels but managed also to retain their identity as short stories (1981, 80). If the proliferation of critical response, both comparative and specific to the story, can be taken as a measure, "Barn Burning" demonstrates the appropriateness of Skei's observation. James Carothers sees "Barn Burning," like "Wash" and "The Hound," as self-contained and related only superficially to *The Hamlet* (1985, 127, 131).

Faulkner's own recollection regarding the initial merging and subsequent split of these two texts offers the most convincing accounting of the relationship between "Barn Burning" and *The Hamlet*. Writing to Malcolm Cowley in August 1945, Faulkner describes the construction of the Snopes saga, first reviewing several short stories focusing on the Snopeses, then continuing: ". . . one day I decided I had better start on the first volume or I'd never get any of it down. So I wrote an induction toward the spotted horse story, which included BARN BURNING, and WASH, which I discovered had no place in that book at all" (*SL* 197; Cowley 1966, 26). Faulkner's view implies that he initially saw "Barn Burning" as part of the novel even though the manuscript alterations suggest its existence first as story, then as novel. It is also possible that Faulkner planned dual uses from the beginning, but Blotner's suggestion that Faulkner might have thought to use it in the novel because he had been unable to sell the story does not fit the chronology of known rejections that occurred after Ober received the story on November 19, 1938 (*WFM 15* I:Introduction xi; Blotner 1974, Notes 142; Skei 1981, 92–93).

As *The Hamlet* evolved, "Barn Burning" was essentially eliminated from the narrative. Pagination clues indicate that the story remained the opening of the novel "until a fairly late stage," and when "Barn Burning" won the O. Henry Memorial Award, it was described as part of a forthcoming novel (Millgate [1966] 1989, 185; Blotner 1974, 1031). Faulkner's own remarks offer little help. Writing to Cowley in September 1945, Faulkner articulated his view that "Barn Burning," the story, was related to the beginning of *The Hamlet* in the same way that the stories "The Hound" and "Spotted Horses" were related to their novelistic renderings (*SL* 202; Cowley 1966, 31). But as Edwin Hunter notes, the year that lapsed between the publication of the two texts reflected substantial rewriting of the novel, and as Gary Stonum points out, the relationship between story and novel was apparently viewed as so tangential that the frontispiece of *The Hamlet* does not acknowledge the story even though credit is listed for "Spotted Horses," "Fool About a Horse," "The Hound," and "Lizards in Jamshyd's Courtyard" (Hunter 1973, 84; Stonum 1979, 176 n. 12).

Faulkner makes the distinction that stories offer "simple content" while novel versions are more suggestive though longer (*SL* 202; Cowley 1966, 31). In the case of "Barn Burning," the opposite is true. The version of "Barn Burning" that was finally included in the novel's first chapter was a greatly abbreviated retelling. In 1954, Peter Lisca identified three major differences between the texts: the novel version, reduced to about one-third its original length, relegates Sarty to a brief reference as an unnamed son, establishes the fear of barn burners as an enabling factor for Flem, and with the change to Ratliff as narrator, makes Ratliff the "indirect instrument of the Snopes' success" (1954, 8). A number of critics judge Colonel Sartoris Snopes's absence from the novel as necessary because he was an atypical Snopes. For Floyd Watkins and Thomas Young, the novel version eliminates Sarty, "perhaps because he would be incongruent with the Snopeses' greater ruthlessness in the novel" (1959–60, 328–29). For Millgate, the story might have served effectively as the opening, but it would have introduced Sarty, who does not appear elsewhere in the novel, and might have introduced the Snopes family too favorably ([1961] 1966, 66–67; [1966] 1989, 185).

As Beck views the making of the novel, the choice not to include "Barn Burning" reflects Faulkner's recognition of different imperatives for the novel, particularly reflected in its "deliberate tempo and indeterminate air." "Barn Burning," he writes, is a "miniature *bildungsroman*" in which Sarty, given his family line, may have been viewed as a "distractingly improbable Snopes" whose actions make him unsuitable for the novel. And the issue of Ab's death becomes a fact of Sarty's story, not necessarily inconsistent with the narrative of the novel (Beck 1976, 278–80). Daniel Hoffman follows Beck's argument that the rejection of Sarty's story as the opening of *The Hamlet*, an action that would have focused attention on an unlikely Snopes, shows Faulkner's mastery of his craft (1989, 80–81). Noel Polk offers a somewhat different explanation, arguing that Faulkner may have realized that Sarty was not necessary to hold the trilogy together because the confrontation between Mink and Flem "became the dramatic and thematic point of reference toward which all the trilogy drove" (1983, 113).

Because Sarty's perspective shapes the narrative focus of the short story, to eliminate him from the novel required a new narrative approach, and V. K. Ratliff now assumes the role of narrator. Millgate observes, "It is interesting to compare the two versions to see how a change in point of view has turned tragedy into comedy." It becomes in *The Hamlet* a tall tale lacking Sarty's agony (Millgate [1961] 1966, 66–67; [1966] 1989, 185; see also Moreland 1989, 48–70 and Moreland 1990, 134ff). James Meriwether suggests that the decision to omit Sarty's story may have been "made to tighten the novel," although he felt that its presence would not have disrupted the episodic structure. Further, the omission of Sarty reveals less a change of intention or design than a change in strategy (Meriwether [1961] 1971, 61–62; see also Blotner 1974, 1009; Skei 1981, 44–45).

Edward Holmes points out that the differences between the two versions relate to the need in *The Hamlet* to tell the story in Ratliff's colloquial manner and further to facilitate Ratliff's use of the story to disturb Jody Varner by dehumanizing Ab Snopes as dramatically as possible. It is, Holmes notes, the only one of Faulkner's retold stories that is transformed from an unmistakably tragic mood to a comic rendering (1966, 31–34, 44).

Olga Vickery observes similar distinctions between the short story version and the novel version, adding that in the novel Ab's "viciousness" becomes Mink's, but also noting that with Ratliff's altered barn burning story, Jody begins the accommodation of the Snopeses "that leads to his own dispossession" ([1959] 1964, 308–09). Lewis Leary describes the novel version as a story "of sly trickery," like "Spotted Horses," gathered as part of the "fragments of a comic history of Yoknapatawpha County" assembled for *The Hamlet* (Leary 1973, 150). For Creighton (whose use of *Joby* for Jody Varner is distracting), the "interior view" presented in "Barn Burning" conflicts with the novel's "external perspective," and the serious tone of the story is unworkable with the spirit of the Snopes chronicle (1977, 22–23; see also Pikoulis 1982, 155). Grimwood believes that the serious tone of "Barn Burning" anticipates the variously modulated tone of *The Hamlet*, but "Barn Burning" could appear only in synopsis because it violates the novel's vernacular idiom and focus on business (Grimwood 1987, 138, 141).

One significant change from short story to novel is the newly introduced confrontation between Ab Snopes and Major de Spain after the barn has been burned. Although Sarty believes at the story's end that his father has been shot, in the novel Ab survives to taunt de Spain. The altercation contributes to the shift from a tale of a tragic father-son relationship to a "battle of wits," ending with Ab's victory over de Spain (Kartiganer 1979, 116–17; see also Brooks 1983, 19).

Another difference between the texts concerns the circumstances of Ab's war wound. Melvin Backman identifies two versions of Ab's having been shot in the heel: the account from "Barn Burning" describes Ab as being shot by a provost's man, and the account from *The Hamlet* attributes the injury to Colonel Sartoris, who shoots when Ab tries to steal the Colonel's stallion (Backman 1966, 143 n. 8).

Still another revision occurs in the portrayal of the judge who sits for the trial of Ab. In the short story, the judge is more learned than he appears in the novel, suggesting that by the publication of the novel Faulkner had become quite critical of the legal system (Watkins and Young, 1959–60, 335).

There are screen adaptations of both "Barn Burning" and *The Hamlet*, and critics have questioned the fidelity of several of these versions. Merrill Skaggs argues that the PBS version of "Barn Burning" follows Faulkner's plot, but the need in the visual medium to externalize action shifts the emphasis to Ab's tale. In part, the shift has to do with the dominance of actor Tommy Lee Jones in the role of Ab Snopes. The way the story is told shows from the beginning Ab's control, and although voiceovers present Sarty's thoughts, explanations of the action are typically Ab's lines (Skaggs 1983, 5–15).

Gene Phillips finds the PBS remake of "Barn Burning" essentially "true to its literary source" though some plot differences exist. Significant portions of Faulkner's prose, especially the expressions of Sarty's thoughts, remain unaltered. The major changes from print to film include Sarty's learning from the conversation of other men the truth about his father's Civil War activities, Ab's tying Sarty up to prevent his warning de Spain, and in the final scene, Sarty's watching his family leave the area, thereby altering the story's implication that Sarty believes he is responsible for his father's death (Phillips 1988, 176–79). Phillips describes the impact of this film and that of Faulkner's "Tomorrow" as "stunning tributes to the remarkable capacity of human beings to survive dreadful tribulations and trials" (1988, 186). Perhaps to the dismay of those readers loyal to Sarty's goodness, Phillips shows how the adaptation of *The Hamlet* for film as *The Long Hot Summer* actually combines Sarty's admirable refusal to participate in barn burning with qualities of his less admirable brother, Flem, in the reconfiguration of Flem as Ben Quick (1988, 139).

Relational observations concerning "Barn Burning" include many other texts. Character comparisons comprise an important body of studies, especially as they look at Ab Snopes in other texts, and characters who seem to represent alternate versions of Ab and Sarty.

Beck reviews the various alterations in appearances of Ab Snopes, recalling, for example, that in *The Town*, Gavin Stevens suggests that Ab was hanged during the war, and that Ab is uncle, not father, to Flem (1963, 18–19). In Millgate's reading, the vivid characterization of Ab in "Barn Burning" is absent in all other texts; for example, "there seems no very close relationship . . . between the Ab Snopes of 'Barn Burning' and the Ab Snopes of *The Unvanquished*" (Millgate [1961] 1966, 67). The portrayal of Ab Snopes in "Barn Burning" is quite different from the way he is presented in the stories

"Riposte in Tertio" and "Vendée" in *The Unvanquished* and "Fool About a Horse" (Blotner 1974, 1001–002). Elizabeth Kerr likens the blood revenge that Mink Snopes exacts for insults from Flem and Houston in *The Mansion* to the same code of honor that motivates Ab's actions in "Barn Burning" (Kerr 1979, 214).

Noting that Faulkner often particularized distinguishing traits by which a character can be recognized, François Pitavy finds a similar use in the two-dimensional description of the characters Ab and Popeye of *Sanctuary* (1973, 62). Joseph Reed finds another image of the tin figure as character description in the portrait of Cash Bundren in *As I Lay Dying* (1973, 98).

Critics draw different conclusions about the relationship between Ab and Thomas Sutpen. For Leslie Fiedler, Ab Snopes is a "downgraded version" of Thomas Sutpen. In "Barn Burning," he has become not a war hero but a thief, and not a "builder of mansions in the wilderness but a barn burner, a dedicated destroyer" (Fiedler 1960, 446). Edmond Volpe likens Ab's crimes to others portrayed in Faulkner's fiction that find their source in "gradations of the inhumane ego-blindness." Ab is the "apotheosis" of this character; Thomas Sutpen is an inheritor. In both cases, the characters lack any recognition of individuality and rights separate from their own. Volpe adds that Yoknapatawpha's "many grotesques" are often victims of some sort of "psychological tyranny" or "victims of rigid religious and social concepts." These absolutes are countered by the empathy inherent in "Faulkner's code of the heart" (Volpe 1980, 81–82).

Carothers's work with Faulkner's veterans finds similarities in the World War I and Civil War veterans. They all bear physical or psychological scars that leave them "depressed and depressing, defeated and grotesque." A fellow among those men, Ab bears his physical limp (1987, 67–68).

Sarty, like Ab, has character parallels elsewhere in Faulkner's work, but his own character, unlike Ab's, remains undeveloped in further appearances. Faulkner once outlined what he conceived as Sarty's part in the Snopes trilogy: Flem's "youngest brother tries to keep his father from setting fire to his landlord's barn, believes he has caused the father to be shot, and runs away from home, goes west, has a son which the other Snopes know nothing about." The son, as the summary continues, is eventually reunited with other Snopeses, is married to a distant cousin Snopes, and produces a son who proves to be a Snopes of the worst kind. In fact, this story was not to appear in subsequent fiction (*SL* 108; see also Kerr 1983, 144; Grimwood 1987, 138–39).O. B. Emerson claims that Sarty is also the narrator of "Fool About a Horse" as published in 1936, but not as revised for *The Hamlet*; however, Blotner and Hoffman identify the unnamed narrator differently. For Blotner he is probably Quentin Compson; Hoffman thinks he is the son of a trader (Emerson 1984, 340; *US* 684–85; Hoffman 1989, 81). Ike McCaslin, like Sarty, renounces his heritage, but Ike ultimately repeats his father's sin by rejecting the black woman and her child (Volpe 1980, 81–82; see also Bradford 1981, 339).

One point of clarification ought to be made here regarding multiple appearances of another character, Reverend Whitfield. When asked about the apparent change in the character of Reverend Whitfield from *As I Lay Dying* to "Barn Burning," Faulkner indicated that the difference had to do with the public life a religious man had to live because of the "ignorant fanatic people of the isolated and rural South" (*FU* 114). The problem is of course that Whitfield does not appear in "Barn Burning." It is likely that the questioner meant to refer to "Shingles for the Lord," the story that follows "Barn Burning" in *Collected Stories*.

The pursuit of recurring thematic issues proves fruitful when applied to "Barn Burning." Not surprisingly, when Ab and Sarty are taken together, the father-son relationship provides rich ground for comparisons. Irving Malin, for example, studies the correspondence between the superego–ego and father–son relationships. He finds an especially close parallel between Sarty's inability to call his father evil and Bayard's unhappiness over his own refusal to avenge his father's death in *The Unvanquished* (Malin 1957, 81; see also Beck 1963, 18–19). Blotner sees a parallel between Sarty and Bayard from the standpoint of sons rejecting the ways of the fathers. Sarty rejects his father's retaliatory measures and Bayard rejects his father's gun (Blotner 1974, 1002). Applying his analysis of the tension created when Faulkner allows both fathers and sons to express points of view, Zender examines the dyad in "Barn Burning" as well as numerous other pairs including Mr. Compson and Quentin in various texts, Simon McEachern and Joe Christmas in *Light in August*, and the Old General and the Corporal in *A Fable*. Zender notes the difficulty created when Faulkner fails or is unable "to accommodate the demands of psychic growth to the realities of social existence" because time and again Faulkner's texts fail to acknowledge "that the symbolic father can be, and usually is, slain without irremediable damage being done to the social relation between father and son" (1989, 54–55).

Initiation experiences provide another basis for thematic comparison. Carothers lists as initiation stories *The Unvanquished*, *The Reivers*, "Barn Burning," and "That Evening Sun" (1981, 114; see also Carothers 1985, 10, 60). James Ferguson declares the period from 1932 to 1942 to be one in which Faulkner was almost obsessively concerned with initiation. Ferguson's list adds to those stories already named "Uncle Willy," "Lion," "Mr. Acarius," and *Go Down, Moses* (1991, 41, 62).

Howell compares Sarty's isolation brought about by his "making a moral decision" to Horace Benbow's isolation in *Sanctuary* because he defends Lee

Goodwin (Howell 1959, 16). Skei finds a pattern of isolated individuals in "Barn Burning," "The Hill," "That Evening Sun," "Red Leaves," and "A Justice." Comparable experiences of existential crisis exist in "Mountain Victory," "Barn Burning," and "Red Leaves" (Skei 1992, 68–69).

The theme of family loyalty appears in numerous variations in Faulkner's fiction. For Leary the compelling comparison is found in the number of young boys who are placed in the center of conflicting loyalties, both in a sentimental presentation in "Two Soldiers" and in the more serious "Barn Burning," and in the fatal consequences of "Mountain Victory" (Leary 1973, 136–37). Polk reminds us that in *Requiem for a Nun* Gavin Stevens's persecution of Temple Drake Stevens, wife of his nephew Gowan, is an abrogation of family loyalty, linking it thematically with "Barn Burning" (1981, 66, 258 n. 12). John Duvall adds "Tomorrow" to those texts concerned with the theme of blood pride (1990, 78). Ferguson praises the power generated when the tension in the story is between conflicting forms of justice, especially blood ties versus an "intuitive sense of simple decency and compassion and of the integrity of others." "Barn Burning," "An Odor of Verbena," and "Mountain Victory" all illustrate the "irreducible complexity of moral choice" (Ferguson 1991, 78).

Faulkner's concern with class difference generates significant comparisons between "Barn Burning" and other Faulkner texts. Kerr's sociologically oriented observations of Faulkner's work include an analysis of the characterization of the white sharecropper, of which Ab serves as the "best example." She adds that although Ab was an undesirable tenant, he, as a white man, could react in ways that were impossible for black tenants (1976, 152). Citing the butler at the de Spain mansion in "Barn Burning" and "Shall Not Perish," Elnora in "There Was a Queen," and the groom in "Mountain Victory," Charles Peavy shows Faulkner's depiction of the disdain black servants felt for poor whites, who as a group lacked "quality" (1971, 21). Skei identifies a parallel suggestion of "class hatred" in "Fool About a Horse," "Barn Burning," and *The Hamlet* (1985, 221). Furthermore, class stratification continues over time as evidenced by the similarities in the conflicts between Wash Jones and Thomas Sutpen in "Wash" and Ab Snopes and Major de Spain in "Barn Burning" (1985, 218). Wesley Morris compares the class violence portrayed in *Absalom, Absalom!* and "Barn Burning," noting that although Wash's anger has specific roots, Ab's fury is class hatred in a "purer, more unself-conscious version" linked neither to the Civil War nor to slavery. Ab's rage also links him to Popeye in *Sanctuary*, a "more extreme representation of southern violence" (1989, 48).

John Pikoulis believes the representation of a degenerating community in Yoknapatawpha manifests itself in a shift in personal dealings—from competition based on talent to the "dangerous differences of wealth, power and status" present in the conflicts between Ab Snopes and de Spain in "Barn

Burning," and de Spain and Varner, Mink and Houston, and Flem and Armistid in *The Hamlet*. Pikoulis also sees in *The Unvanquished* and "Barn Burning" a passing of community strength, with greater conflict between classes and within families, more reliance on law to settle conflict, and greater neglect of the land (1982, 156–57, 135).

In Kerr's view, the decay of aristocratic families in Faulkner's fiction is paralleled by impotence within Snopes families, despite their apparent vigor: Ab's family consists of a sterile son (Flem), a runaway (Sarty), and "two bovine daughters" (1983, 145).

Suzanne Hunter Brown reads "Barn Burning" as a criticism of "aristocratic agrarian paternalism," an attitude that she also sees in "A Rose for Emily" in the brief remark about Colonel Sartoris, black women, and aprons. The Colonel was largely responsible for a local ordinance that required Negro women to wear aprons in public (1989, 321).

Lyall Powers pursues the line of a "Saving Remnant" in even the worst families of Yoknapatawpha, the Gowries and Snopeses. That Nub Gowrie can feel grief or Flem Snopes can have a brother like Sarty and other relatives who defy their Snopesism implies an ultimately comic vision in the development of Yoknapatawpha (Powers 1980, 202, 246–47).

In studying Faulkner's repeated use of materials, Moreland found that the artist was employing a process of "revisionary repetition" that "repeats some structured event, in order somehow to alter that structure and its continuing power, especially by opening a critical space for what the subject might *learn* about that structure in the different context of a changing present or a more distant or different past" (1990, 4). "Barn Burning" employs what Moreland calls a "primal scene" in Faulkner's fiction, a life-determining incident wherein a young child is refused entrance at the front door of the grand house and thereafter patterns his life according to what he believes the experience teaches him about his society. In *Absalom, Absalom!* Sutpen and his son Henry repeat the scene, but in "Barn Burning" Ab appears at the door and attempts to write his difference at the front door with the horse manure on his boot. That is, Ab rejects the social dichotomy implied by the primal scene. Ab fails in "Barn Burning," but in the next retelling of Ab's visit—Ratliff's version in *The Hamlet*—humor controls the revision. Ab's escape from apparent tragedy now offers an "exemplary scene of critical escape from oppressive social categories and oppositions, a scene that points a way out for others without pretending to point the one new way" (Moreland 1989, 48–54; Moreland 1990, 3–9).

The popularity of "Barn Burning" has much to do with the high regard critics have for its formal qualities, particularly its complex narrative perspective. Emphasizing the child's perspective, Marvin Fisher compares Sarty's ability to escape "through knowledge and primitive insight" in "Barn Burning" with the limited vision of the children in "That Evening Sun," an ability that allows them only to reduce adult actions "to an absurd, meaningless size" (Fisher 1960, 18). In addition to "Barn Burning" and "That Evening Sun," Millgate includes "Shingles for the Lord" as another text that utilizes the "young and innocent witness" who relates the story ([1961] 1966, 66). The strategy of using child narrators (such boys as Benjy Compson and Sarty Snopes, and the boyhood presentations of Isaac McCaslin and Bayard Sartoris) is effective in revealing the influence of the past through traditions and beliefs passed on to subsequent generations. The youthful male narrator, more capable than adults of seeing an individual's worth unrelated to those traditions, can have greater sympathy, can demand truth, and consequently represents a "moral outlook to inspire the reader" (Gold 1966, 78–79). In "That Will Be Fine" restricting the narrative perspective to a child's limited vision results in a different impression than that achieved by the greater range of the narrative approach of "Barn Burning." We get the impression that Sarty learns and grows from the experience but that Georgie does not (Hadley 1980, 63, 67).

Reed's analysis of Faulkner's narrative achievement in "Barn Burning" looks more precisely at the third-person point of view in the story. He believes the technique achieves a depth that is absent in such stories as "Shall Not Perish," "Two Soldiers," "Uncle Willy," or even "That Evening Sun" because they portray the child's development only in the present time of the child, not as the reminiscence of the adult (Reed 1973, 43; see also Carothers 1981, 113–14). (Of course, "That Evening Sun" opens with Quentin's adult perspective before it assumes the child's viewpoint.)

Another feature of "Barn Burning" is the articulation of thought at a more sophisticated level of language than the character's speech. Reed identifies this narrative approach not only in "Barn Burning" but also in *Light in August* and again (but less effectively) in *Intruder in the Dust* (1973, 121). Leland Cox adds *As I Lay Dying*, and Grimwood adds "Old Man" to the stories that employ the poetic articulation of thought (Cox 1982, 280; Grimwood 1987, 138).

Stephen Ross's study of voice in Faulkner's fiction examines his use of a "hierarchy of imaged speech" wherein one character quoting another may employ a more extreme version of dialect than that heard from the original speaker in order to emphasize the quoting character's perception of superiority. Ross identifies this quality in "Barn Burning," *Light in August*, "The Liar," and *Go Down, Moses* (1989, 110, 256 n. 29). Disembodied voices are sometimes used when the speakers have not yet entered the awareness of the central consciousness, as when courtroom voices are unidentified until Sarty is specifically addressed in "Barn Burning" and in *The Sound and the Fury* when golfers' voices and the voices of blacks seem to be disembodied sounds (Ross 1989, 14, 260 n. 22).

Another Faulknerian strategy is the cluttering of sensual appeals that opens both "Barn Burning" and "Dry September." The former confusion affects "senses and consciousness"; the latter provides "aesthetic confusion" introducing tone and theme (Reed 1973, 50).

Faulkner not only employed successful narrative strategies in multiple works, but also returned time and again to particular events and images. Trials as retellings, re-creations of history, and also as tests of a character's mettle become important occasions in Faulkner's fiction including "Barn Burning," *Sanctuary*, *Requiem for a Nun*, *The Hamlet*, and *Knight's Gambit* (Friedman 1984, 104). In certain situations, the test is one's suitability as a witness. Duvall points to several contexts in which a person is not allowed to testify against a relative. Although the circumstances are very different, "The Fire and the Hearth" (originally "Point of Law") turns comically on this point. In "Barn Burning" a more accurate legal view, that Sarty *can* testify, is played against the plaintiff's hesitancy about putting the child in that situation (Duvall 1990, 77).

Carothers finds that Faulkner characteristically obscures the certainty of a character's death. In the list of questionable demises, Carothers includes Ab Snopes and his older son of "Barn Burning," Nancy in "That Evening Sun," Elly in "Elly," Jubal in "Mountain Victory," the protagonist of "Carcassonne," Gail Hightower in *Light in August*, Mink Snopes in *The Mansion*, and George in "The Leg" (Carothers 1984, 219–20).

Critics recognize a diverse range of images that appear in "Barn Burning" as important in other Faulkner texts as well. According to William Ruzicka, Faulkner frequently creates a cosmological space that is "ordered, guided, and telic." Sarty is pictured against a cosmic background, as are Gavin Stevens, V. K. Ratliff, and Mink Snopes in *The Mansion*. The tone may vary, but it is essentially affirmative. Sarty Snopes pictured beneath wheeling stars affirms the actions he has taken (Ruzicka 1987, 115–16). Ruzicka could add "Dry September" to those texts projecting events against a defined cosmological order.

The fictional dwellings Faulkner created are as diverse as the characters that live in them and are typically described in order to reflect the character of the person: the Grierson house reflects Emily; Sutpen's Hundred, Sutpen; the steamboat, Ikkemotubbe; and many others. The mansion–cabin contrast in "Barn Burning" and in "Wash" emphasizes that the "houses often embody their own sets of social rules and exemptions" (Watson 1980a, 137). For Polk, the tactic of relating mansion and courthouse, an impression Sarty has, appears in *Requiem for a Nun*, the three Snopes novels, and *Absalom, Absalom!* and "represents the fulfillment of a dream." As Polk puts it, "mansions invariably represent some quality of life, some ideal, toward which most men strive, but which few attain." This quality is seen in *The Mansion*, the

Compson house in *The Sound and the Fury*, the Old Frenchman's place in *Sanctuary*, Sutpen's Hundred in *Absalom, Absalom!*, and "Barn Burning." These large dwellings contrast with lesser houses such as Mink's shack, Flem's tent, and rented houses (Polk 1981, 29; 1983, 112–13). According to Cox, when Sarty sees the de Spain house, it "symbolizes for him a fusion of his youthful concepts of truth and beauty" (1982, 280). Ruzicka identifies the de Spain mansion of "Barn Burning" as the only great house in the Frenchman's Bend area other than the Old Frenchman Place, but it connects with Manfred's house in Jefferson and "other built forms of the trilogy." Further, it is the "most specifically influential house-as-image" in Faulkner's Yoknapatawpha fiction. If Sarty's surging blood concretizes his sense of family loyalty, so does the de Spain house concretize his sense of honor when he identifies the huge white mansion with the courthouse (Ruzicka 1987, 71–72).

Kenneth Johnston finds that images of clocks and watches in such contexts as "A Rose for Emily" and *The Sound and the Fury* imply "decline and change in the South." He uses a clue from *Intruder in the Dust* to explain the significance of the silent clock in "Barn Burning" that has "stopped at some fourteen minutes past two o'clock of a dead and forgotten day and time" (*CS* 6). In *Intruder*, a reference to Pickett's charge at Gettysburg in July 1863 is timed at approximately 2:00. For Johnston, the clock reference in the short story implies a new time of new men and a new social order that replaces a still slowly retreating Southern planter-aristocracy. Major de Spain is, as Johnston notes, shocked by the fact that he has been brought to court by one of his tenant farmers. Johnston adds the clocklike sound of Ab's foot on de Spain's porch and the closing image of constellations moving slowly as further confirmation of an old order giving way to a new, less admirable force (1974, 434–36).

Ferguson finds a recurrent interest in "lost, maimed, and injured limbs" in Faulkner's work, appearing in such diverse texts as *As I Lay Dying*, *A Fable*, "The Tall Men," "Barn Burning," "Mountain Victory," "Death Drag," "The Leg" and numerous others, that in a Freudian interpretation "suggests the fear of castration" (1991, 66, 203 n. 11).

In Grimwood's reading, Sarty associates horseback riding with honor and freedom, recalling "Carcassonne" (1987, 138).

Because "Barn Burning" appears as the first story in *Collected Stories*, its place and context are often seen to enhance and be enhanced by the total work and by the opening section, "The Country." Millgate suggests that "Barn Burning" provides for *Collected Stories* the induction that it once was meant to be for *The Hamlet*. The story introduces "patterns of conflict which echo throughout the volume," including racial tensions, economic stratification, and insider/outsider conflicts. Further, the story introduces thematic issues that reverberate through the other stories, the strain between family bonds and the need for individuation, father-son relationships, and the clash "between social values and those which are primarily moral or aesthetic" (Millgate [1966] 1989, 270–72; see also Bradford 1981, 332, 339; Ferguson 1991, 158).

"Barn Burning" possesses particular relevance to "The Country." Millgate applies the terms *indestructible* and *enduring*—by which the Reverend Whitfield is described in the second story, "Shingles for the Lord"—to Ab Snopes in "Barn Burning." Similarly, aspects of "Shall Not Perish," the last story in "The Country," repeat qualities of "Barn Burning." Both stories refer to the Civil War and to social stratification, with a close look at the "poor whites" who enter the de Spain mansion (Millgate [1966] 1989, 270–72). Arthur Kinney sees the overt link among the stories in "The Country," the Yoknapatawpha hill country people, as coexisting with a deeper thematic link: the young boy coming of age. There is also a distinct bridge between the first and second stories: bartering. By the final story of the section, "Shall Not Perish," the anger and envy Ab Snopes expresses toward de Spain moves in another direction, from de Spain (the Major's son) to Mrs. Grier (Kinney 1980, 63–65). James Watson sees a reconciliation between de Spain and Grier as the appropriate end to "The Country," which opens with the conflict between de Spain and Snopes. Further, the final story, though clearly not as strong as the first, shows the completion of initiation when the child "accepts his right relation to family, the South, and the nation" (1980b, 222).

Carothers believes the similarities between "Barn Burning" and "Shingles for the Lord"—fathers who set fires and their young sons—"indicate the deliberate counterpoint of *Collected Stories*" for the second story presents these issues in a comic rendering of actions and consequences (1985, 64, 67; see also Bungert 1986, 149). Ferguson adds a note about the alternating tonalities in the stories of "The Country." Furthermore, the scope of the section, from "Barn Burning" to the World War II topic of the final story, "suggests a kind of expansive movement out and away from the constraints of rural life, positive as the values embodied in that life may be, and thus serves to prepare us for what is to come in the rest of the volume" (Ferguson 1991, 158). The links from story to story in the first section extend to the beginning story of the next section, bridging the two. Like "Barn Burning," "A Rose for Emily" focuses on a child mistreated by a father, and Emily, like Ab Snopes, exacts a violent, exploitive vengeance (Kinney 1980, 66).

If all the criticism of "Barn Burning" related to its links to other fiction, one might conclude that this much-anthologized story is popular only because it demonstrates so much of the total Faulknerian formula in one convenient package. The diverse interpretations of this story, however, reveal that it is not so easily bound.

## Interpretation and Criticism

Millgate judges "Barn Burning" to possess "considerable structural sophistication" and "great moral and emotional complexity" presented "in strict chronological order and in a style of great clarity" ([1961] 1966, 65–66). Ferguson believes "Barn Burning" displays Faulkner's gift for beginnings and the strength of evocative endings (1991, 132–34). These accolades, from early and recent readings of "Barn Burning," reflect the critical acclaim in which the story is generally held. When moving beyond superlatives to pinpointing meaning, however, critics differ as to whether the story's significance inheres in the character of Sarty or of Ab, or more generally in the cultural milieu into which they are placed.

Several critics find that Sarty provides the center of meaning for the story, especially as it relates to a young man's passage into adulthood. For Irving Howe, Sarty is a rare example of a sympathetically treated Snopes. The story captures the sense of the child "trapped in the soiled and dishonest world of his elders." Faulkner, Howe adds, skillfully manages the conflict by implying an understanding of the father's behavior while invoking sympathy for the son ([1952] 1975, 266). In Malin's psychoanalytic reading of Faulkner's work, Ab Snopes and Sarty Snopes represent a father–son, superego–ego parallel discernible in much of Faulkner's fiction. Sarty demonstrates that he can lie for his father, but that this loyalty cannot survive his learning about truth and justice. His flight from the fire seems only to be a flight from "conscience," but it actually portrays the knowledge that "we . . . must discover the meaning of our relationship to parental influence before we can call ourselves free" (Malin 1957, 80–81). In Fisher's judgment, Sarty's insight seems to be beyond a child's capacity, but his belief that his father will change and that life will get better seems entirely childlike. Sarty is very much like his father but, significantly, lacks his father's rage. His conflict is part of the extended tension between his two worlds—the sensory world and his inner fears, the values of society and his father's values, the world of the child and the adult. At each level, he must sacrifice one to enter the other (Fisher 1960, 16). Phyllis Franklin charts Sarty's progress toward maturity including a growing recognition of himself as an individual while still one of the threesome of male Snopeses. When forced to confront conflicting loyalties, Franklin adds, the source of Sarty's ethics may be inherent, but they may also be a learned system of values taught however timidly by his mother (Franklin 1967–68, 189–93). As Cox defines Sarty's initiation, the boy learns that he "must be able to cope with conditions of isolation, grief, and despair." Sarty calls his father "hero" because, believing that he is dead, the child needs to invest his memory with admirable qualities (Cox 1982, 281).

Building on the work of philosopher Gabriel Marcel and others, James Bowen and James Hamby define Sarty's behavior as the emergence of existential selfhood, a process that includes a turning from fidelity (including constancy, consistency, and loyalty) to sincerity (including "receptivity and openness to the future"). Sarty's development requires that he recognize his conflicting loyalties to father and to honesty. Sarty cannot avoid the tension between fidelity and sincerity given his father's determination to burn the de Spain barn. His choice to expose his father, a choice that inevitably means facing painful consequences, represents his movement toward selfhood (Bowen and Hamby 1971, 101–07).

Volpe pursues much the same interpretation as Bowen and Hamby, arguing that social and moral implications do not frame the conflict. "Barn Burning" is a psychological story that expresses Sarty's emerging sense of individuality in the shadow of his father's egomania. The "dramatic scenes, the characters and situations are objectifications, as in a nightmare, of the boy's psychological and emotional tensions." Part of that vision includes Ab's wife, who has already succumbed to him. Ab demands absolute fidelity to his own will, blood loyalty related to his satanic imaging; these images are the constructions of Sarty's nightmare. Conflict arises from any "they," aristocratic or peasant, that is not a constituent of Ab's will. Sarty's eventual resistance leaves him with grief, but not guilt, over the presumed death of his father. As Volpe concludes, "Sarty, appropriately, falls into a dreamless sleep, from which he awakens whole and at peace, ready for the future" (1980, 75–82).

According to Brooks, "Barn Burning" is one of Faulkner's "finest treatments of honor." In this reading, Sarty's conflict between his sense of honor conflicts with his loyalty to his father. Sarty responds to the "desirable orderliness" of the de Spain household whereas his father is enraged by it. He chooses to act honorably even though that action presumably means danger for his father, perhaps even contributing to his death. Sarty's subsequent life is unknown. The story ends when Sarty adheres to his commitment, a "customary economy" on Faulkner's part (Brooks 1983, 16–19; see also Skei 1985 218–19). Carothers adds to the interpretation of Sarty's conflict the boy's growing recognition that his father is right: if he does not "stick" to family, he will not remain in the family circle. His final choice represents conflicting alternatives that "have positive theoretical bases and negative practical consequences." Judgments are explicit throughout the text, particularly Sarty's mistaken judgments that Harris is an enemy, that de Spain is safe from the vengeful fire of Ab, his father, and that Ab was a war hero. The correction of Sarty's views "invites our sympathetic approval of the boy" but also serves to "imply significant reservations about our *judgment* of Sarty" (Carothers 1985, 60–62, 64; see also Ferguson 95–96).

Jane Hiles offers a fresh challenge to readings of Sarty's rejection of his father's authority by contending that Sarty's behavior is in fact a repetition of his father's way of life, a fight with his bloodline (heredity) that he actually loses. To prove her reading, Hiles shows how the cycle of "alienation, aggression, and flight" marks Ab's life in the context of barn burning and in his earlier Civil War activities. Sarty's behavior follows precisely the same pattern. The final vision, read by most critics as an affirming suggestion of Sarty's new strength and self-determination, is more accurately understood as a repetition of his father's flight into the woods as a wartime hideaway. As Hiles notes, facing his willful betrayal of family, Sarty "does not seek shelter with de Spain." Another issue relative to Hiles's interpretation includes Faulkner's sense of family as clan that he identifies in the Southern character and in its Scottish progenitors. Hiles attributes to Sarty what critic James Wilson describes elsewhere as the worst possible characteristic of Snopesism: insensitivity to family (1985, 329–37).

It is obvious from critical commentary on the character Sarty that one can hardly define him without commenting also on the man against whom he is most often defined. Ab has generated a good deal of attention, from those who give reasons to explain why Sarty must reject him to those who argue that his actions are understandable if not commendable, although perhaps even commendable in spirit.

Howe describes Ab Snopes in "Barn Burning" "as a man of bitter, almost crazed, purposefulness, his taste for arson a result of social envy." By naming his son after Colonel Sartoris, Ab reveals a "vague, pathetic ambition" (Howe [1952] 1975, 85; see also Cox 1982, 280). For Fisher, Ab is animal-like, and his hatred is instinctive. The methodical application of retaliation contrasts with Sarty's guilt over it (Fisher 1960, 14–15).

Like Volpe, Stein in much greater detail likens the portrait of Ab Snopes to "traditional iconography" of Satan. Ab's love of fire is an obvious parallel as is his consuming hatred, but his physical characterization also lends to the comparison: his attire is black; his hand is clawlike; and his dimensionless form, like a pattern cut from tin, relates to Satan's "illusory materiality." His wounded heel, an injury incurred when he was stealing horses, gives him a stiff, limping gait that contributes to his association with the "Bestial, deformed *Diabolus* of the middle ages." Further, his tramping through manure "betrays an affinity with the fecal tastes of the Devil." Ab's antagonism toward light and order is marked ironically by his name, *Abner* from the Hebrew "Father [God] is light." Stein concludes that Ab's contempt for order and tradition, seen in the Satanic associations and in his rootlessness, is linked with a materialistic vision that disdains "human dignity, courage, honor, and love" (1961, 731–32).

According to Charles Mitchell, Ab's motive in burning barns relates to his being shot in the heel. Although he may not be conscious of the connection, the injury represents a "moment in the past when authority imposed limits on his will." The wounded heel serves as symbol of Abner's will. Will dominates the inner man; the foot dominates the physical description. Like Stein, Mitchell relates Ab's unsubmissiveness to Satan, and the barn becomes his place of destruction as it stores the "goodness of a plantation owner's garden" and hence represents the Garden of Eden. By tracing other symbols in the story, Mitchell explains the continuing need to destroy. Like his unrestrained hog, Ab has a ravening appetite. Past injury continues to haunt his present reality as signified by the stopped clock and the stained white rug that represents a smear against the absolute power of the Lord. Ab refuses any symbol of limits like fences and master–slave images. Fire appears consistently in its classic guise as representing will. The preponderance of images implies further that Sarty, unlike his father, accepts the limits imposed on will. He works his own Eden, willingly erecting fences to impose limits (Mitchell 1965, 185–89).

Trilling focuses his interest on the compelling strength of Ab Snopes despite his meanness. Ab appears "more morally serious" than Major de Spain, especially when Ab's rage at life is compared with Major de Spain's rage over a soiled rug. Ab is without question a "paternal force" in Sarty's life however lacking he may be in "paternal virtue" (Trilling 1967, 321–24).

Carothers interprets Ab Snopes as something other than a "complete villain." His behavior is consistent: his violence occurs only when he feels his integrity is threatened. Even if Sarty's facts are in error, his judgment about his father's bravery is not totally wrong, for, as Carothers sees it, "there is something admirable in his spirit" (1985, 62–63).

Cackett places her discussion of Abner's actions in the context of the Adamic myth of America as defined by R. W. B. Lewis in *The American Adam*. Arguing that Ab as Adam reveals the darker implications of the Adamic individual, Cackett sees the story as revealing Faulkner's sense that "isolation, individuality, stoicism, and detachment from tradition and law is nothing more than a monstrous license to perpetuate havoc and failure to face the reality that humanity is cast into an imperfect world and forced to assume responsibility to alter that world as best as possible." Pursuing images of weight and weightlessness in the story, Cackett shows how images of Sarty progressively emphasize a sense of physical weight, representing his growing sense of moral responsibility by story's end (1989, 1–17).

Zender offers a provocative challenge to readers of "Barn Burning." Placing the text within the modernist tradition of offering multiple narrative perspectives, Zender argues that readers should not be content to understand Sarty's passage to maturity by denying the father because the transition does not typically endanger the literal father. Zender then constructs a reading wherein he identifies three encounters between Ab and Sarty as teacher–student relationships: occasions when Ab tries to teach Sarty "versions of Ab against which his son need not rebel." Zender describes these attempts as socioeconomic (when Ab tells Sarty about the labor that supports de Spain's life), heroic (when Ab refuses to rush hurriedly from de Spain's mansion), and psychological (when Ab leaves Sarty restrained in his mother's embrace rather than tied to the bed). For Zender, "enclosing Sarty inside the embrace is the last, urgent expression of a fatherly need, even a love, never spoken in its own form." Including Ab's perspective as well as Sarty's leaves an unresolved tension in the conclusion of the story. Once Ab is known more fully than as the "symbolic father," the "story pulls against itself in a troubling way." In this sense "Barn Burning" is a pivotal text, as it marks a shift in Faulkner's work from identifying primarily with the pupil to also identifying with the adult teacher (Zender 1989, 48–58).

Moreland, like Zender, suggests a more tolerant reading of Ab. As discussed in the previous section, Moreland sees in "Barn Burning" a revision of Faulkner's "primal scene," of rejection at the front door of the grand house. At the entrance to the de Spain house, Ab attempts to write his difference with the horse manure on his boot. Sarty is unable to see his father's action as a gesture asserting self-worth because Sarty accepts the socioeconomic structure that reads "Ab's social difference as only so much social filth." Ab's relentless burning of barns is one measure of his refusal to accept his being pigeonholed by society. By his actions Ab exposes the oppressive nature of the landlord–tenant relationship. Ab's conflict with the structured society manifests itself in Sarty's ambivalent reactions and his longing for resolution in terms of his father's reformation, a change that would require Ab's accepting society's definition of the "plantation as trickle-down source of moral and even economic blessings to all its humble dependents." Although the justice system should recognize Ab equally with de Spain, the verdict in their legal battle actually recognizes and endorses the social hierarchy (Moreland 1989, 48–70; Moreland 1990, 12–20, 130–39).

For Moreland, Faulkner's repetitions that include revision constitute offering "attempts to inscribe marks of change and difference within a linguistic social, or psychological structure." In "Barn Burning" writing difference includes not only Ab's peculiar signature on the carpet at the front door but also the oppositional terms of the narrative, a stylistic tendency by Faulkner to employ oxymorons. These oppositions are used to unsettle the normative structures. As Moreland notes, "Sarty finally cannot appreciate Ab's unaccountable difference from his society's dominant dialectics of master and slave, planter and tenant, white and black, clean and filthy, legal and criminal; unable to read Ab's difference as a potential criticism of the exclusive terms of those dialectics, Sarty reads that difference more simply as a condemnation of Ab and perhaps of Sarty himself"(1989, 50, 60–70; Moreland 1990, 12–20, 158).

As Moreland's recent reading of Ab makes clear, it is difficult to discuss Ab without asserting some judgments about the social order in which he is placed. For numerous critics, implications about the society, not the particular individuals, bear the thematic import. Most early readings reach conclusions far different from those of Moreland. Howell believes that the central issue of "Barn Burning" is not specifically with the child, Sarty, "but with an order of life that has preserved in a chaotic world a vestige of law and dignity and worth." Howell writes, "Faulkner's faith in the efficacy of the right sort of aristocracy is implicit in all of the Mississippi saga, and in the short story 'Barn Burning' it becomes the central thesis." Although the traditional moral code in this story is chiefly aligned with an aristocratic class, this is not always the case, as evidenced by Sarty's affiliation. His exposure to the de Spain mansion results in his standing firm for the traditional order it represents, but he is not allowed to be associated with the aristocracy. In breaking with his father's code, Sarty indeed aligns himself with moral values, but this is an action that in Faulkner's fiction results in isolation (Howell 1959, 13–19).

Franklin takes issue with Howell's reading, arguing that Howell builds his reading around George Marion O'Donnell's interpretation of Faulkner's world as comprising moral Sartorises and immoral Snopeses. The story, Franklin asserts, does not support the reading, particularly as Sarty acts with courage before he becomes acquainted with the de Spain house. Also, Ab's description of the de Spain house, built by the labor of slaves, points to an ugliness beneath the surface beauty, a beauty insufficient to justify the means by which it was created and maintained (Franklin 1967–68, 189–91).

Using a heuristic defined by Ruth Benedict in *Patterns of Culture*, Wilson identifies the polarities of the story as those of the Paranoid versus the Apollonian way of life. The former, represented by Ab, is a lawless and individualistic life where loyalty comes from blood ties; the latter, represented by Colonel Sartoris Snopes and Major de Spain, affirms the collective wisdom of the community where loyalty resides in formal structure, the law. Ab, the Paranoid, is consistently associated with coldness and death, while the barns he destroys, those of Harris and de Spain, represent productivity. Order is further outlined in the Apollonian choice in Sarty's comparison of the de Spain house to the courthouse and in the order implied by the constant reference to the military ranks of men. (Ab served as a "private" in the sense of service for personal profit.) The Apollonian way of life is ultimately represented by the fact that Ab Snopes is protected by the law in the course of two trials. When forced to make a choice, Sarty chooses the Apollonian way. Eventually, Sarty's passionate, life-affirming nature overcomes the influence of his passionless, life-destroying father. Wilson explains the frequent appearance of the number twelve in "Barn Burning" arguing that it is linked to the use of the number twelve in the "mythic-Christian concept of renewal and rebirth" that marks the movement from chaos to cosmos, ending with the image of Sarty at midnight entering a new day and new pattern of living (Wilson 1970–71, 279–88).

Sylvia Cook also sees Faulkner's work as typically affirming a superior quality in the upper classes that has the "capacity to inspire superior behavior among the lower classes." Sarty experiences an epiphany in de Spain's mansion. He is torn between two worlds, neither of which is pristine. His final action repudiates his father's way of life. It is a "heroic" action by which Sarty enters the complexity of the adult world. He becomes a tool of de Spain's pursuit of his father, an act of "violence no less immoral" than his father's destructive activities. Nevertheless, de Spain's house represents an order that is desirable even if flawed (Cook 1976, 53–55).

Bradford reads "Barn Burning" as a story in which Sarty becomes a "supporter of that larger family that is community and protector of right order." Bradford's analysis distinguishes between Sarty's loyalty to paternal order and his recognition that the individual who is his father is not an appropriate model of that order. Thus, Sarty's rejection of his father is his affirmation of the social imperative. Sarty has models of order that contrast with and finally convince him to oppose his father. De Spain himself is not Sarty's model, but de Spain's wife and his house represent beauty, refinement, and manners to which Sarty responds. Also, Sarty's mother and aunt show generosity that is seen again in the action in the courtroom scenes. Bradford points out that these encounters do not make the child into a gentleman but draw "from him an awareness of his *already present inclination* to act that part." Nevertheless, Sarty's identity is chiefly as an opposer of the negative example of his father. Ab, Bradford argues, is motivated by an envious rage, envy not to own but to destroy (1981, 332–39).

Brenda Sartoris compares Ab's sharecropping arrangements with both Harris and de Spain to the feudal custom known as *cornbote* (rent paid to the manor in grain, services, or money, also conveying the sense of responsibility the landlord bore for the general wellfare of the peasants renting from him). Both the implied contractual arrangement between the two parties and the landlord's extended responsibility for the tenants' well-being are present in the relationships in "Barn Burning." Further, the sense of cornbote as punitive recompense for trespass is also seen in the penalties levied against Ab. These relationships affirm a defined societal order that Ab Snopes rejects (Sartoris 1983, 91–94).

The variant readings of "Barn Burning" and the difficulty one encounters when trying to separate a discussion of one character from the analysis of another reflects the complexity of the text. As Skei notes, the conflicts in "Barn Burning" are not reducible to a conflict between nature and culture because contradictory elements exist in both. If Sarty's goodness is inherent, then so is his father's evil. Similarly, de Spain's mansion represents the dual character of the cultured world (Skei 1985, 215). In like manner, to move into a discussion of formal qualities, specifically the narrative strategies employed, demonstrates how intricately the formal and thematic qualities are interwoven.

Faulkner's narrative strategies in "Barn Burning" combine Sarty's youthful interpretations with insights that reflect a retrospective and matured vision.

Sarty as narrator expands and enhances meaning and characterization. As Sarty presents his father, "Ab is a gigantic figure," an image that makes Sarty's reactions both "powerful" and "terrifying" (Millgate [1961] 1966, 65–66). Reed distinguishes a third-person omniscient narrator from the internal monologue and a reminiscent older self that convey Sarty's thoughts. Also, the stylistic rhythm of the narration follows the cycle of the family's action. Extended prose appears at moments of intense pressure; the cluttered prose opening reflects the tension of the moment, and the "incantatory, idyllic prose" represents the freedom of the conclusion. Dialogue interrupts narrative passages so methodically that Reed concludes, "The design of the telling is the design of the story" (1973, 43–46).

Charles Hadley's examination of "Barn Burning" utilizes the work of Gerard Genette and Mieke Bal. Hadley, like Reed, distinguishes a narrative voice (an anonymous narrator-focuser) who expands the vision of the child, Sarty, by focusing (seeing) with him and also by relating his thoughts and feelings, but revealing an existence beyond Sarty's consciousness through the less prevalent expression of the thoughts and feelings of other characters (Hadley 1980, 63–68).

Michael Hogan studies the frequent use of the progressive verb form by several twentieth-century writers. The form provides a means by which to make the narrative voice "self-conscious and dramatic and equivocal." The specific appearance of the progressive in "Barn Burning" creates the "dramatic present" in order to "immerse the reader in an ongoing experience" (1981, 13–19).

Baruch Hochman describes the "Faulknerian verbal surge" that extends beyond Sarty's knowledge but "serves to objectify his bewilderment." This observation is part of Hochman's larger study of the way in which characters, in this example Sarty, are both "utterly embedded in texts and absolutely detachable from them" (1985, 74).

Ross applies his taxonomy of four voices in Faulkner's work to "Barn Burning." The *phenomenal* voice that depicts speech or writing "as an event or object in the fiction's world" exists as part of the "phenomenal world experienced by Sarty," that is, part of the accrual of sensations in Sarty's environment. The second voice is *mimetic*, "imitative of talk." The act of speaking is "the fundamental form of rebellion" in the story: Sarty could refuse to lie, and Sarty tells de Spain of Ab's intentions. Silence is the act of loyalty. Sarty's private voice records his thoughts (a third, *psychic* voice). And a fourth, *authorial* voice "traversed by the 'institutional' discourse of history, or of literature" exists as an intertextual voice that is "identifiably Faulknerian yet necessarily in touch with other texts, other discourses, and other discursive practices in the world at large" (Ross 1989, 13–15).

Another strategy Faulkner utilizes that is closely tied to the flexibility of multiple voices is the manipulation of time, using reference to the stopped clock and references to Sarty twenty years later. The temporal structure enables Faulkner to express not only Sarty's adult perspective but also the maturing vision of the child as he begins to know what to ask and when not to question (Reed 1973, 43–46).

Ross's reference to accruing sensations accords with earlier observations that Faulkner employs synaesthesia to merge Sarty's diverse responses to the country store courtroom. He expresses his hunger, fear, loyalty, despair, and grief through his sense of smell, which serves both to show Sarty's attempt to divert his attention from the moment and to create an empathetic response in the reader (Reed 1973, 43; see also Volpe 1980, 77).

Despite the narrative and thematic complexities "Barn Burning" offers, critics have also found the presence of striking images that further enhance the text. Carothers recalls that a favorite tactic Faulkner employed for revealing character was the "metaphoric description of a character's eyes to imply his attitude towards the world." In "Barn Burning," Sarty's stormy grey eyes reflect his turmoil when he is called to testify against his father; his father's eyes are a cold grey, his brother's are muddy (Carothers 1985, 61–62).

Ferguson believes that one of Faulkner's strongest uses of a leitmotif is in the imaging of Ab Snopes's stiffness; it contributes to the characterization of a "person who is not only fiercely dedicated to the maintenance of what he considers to be his integrity but is also, as a moral being, profoundly *unnatural* because of his commitment to abstractions." It is especially important that the stiffness ascribed to Sarty will work itself out; nevertheless, it indicates a certain loyalty to Ab that Sarty will always possess (Ferguson 1991, 137–38).

Kinney notes that this story of innocence lost is filled with traditional images of death: "whippoorwills, dark trees, dark woods succeeding the sun, night" (1980, 64).

William Nicolet makes an interesting observation about Faulkner's use of product trademarks to reinforce themes. The scarlet devils and silver fish that Sarty observes in the store that serves as the courtroom are trademarks for deviled ham (confirmed by the Underwood Company) and sardines. But by emphasizing symbols rather than products, Faulkner implies the moral imperative of Sarty's choice, with Satan and Christ standing witness to his decision (Nicolet 1975, #25). (Skaggs points out that the deviled ham product is a 1930s anachronism in the pre–twentieth century general store [1983, 7]).

The depth and diversity of the critical response to "Barn Burning" demonstrate its important place in Faulkner's fiction. It is interesting that when pressed by the constraints of length for the *Portable Faulkner*, Cowley made the decision to omit "Barn Burning," noting in a letter to Faulkner that it "didn't seem as good to me as some of the other stories" and reasoning that "Spotted Horses" could satisfactorily "stand for the peasants" (Cowley 1966,

56). Cowley's observation notwithstanding, "Barn Burning" has long been recognized as one of Faulkner's best and most anthologized stories. The critical accolades for it appeared early and still continue. In 1959, Hyatt Waggoner commented that "Barn Burning" and "Wash" were "unsurpassed in their kind" (Waggoner 1959, 195). Recently Ferguson has praised the text for possessing "majestic solemnity" and "virtuosity . . . altogether dazzling" (Ferguson 1991, 21, 42). Among translations of the story are Russian and Chinese versions (Vashchenko 1984 196; Stoneback 1984, 240). Carothers sums up the impact of "Barn Burning," writing, "'Barn Burning' is, in part, an elaborate structure of visual metaphor and simile, some of which is expressed by the characters, some of which is overtly developed by the omniscient narrator, and all of which contributes to the developing conflict between father and son" (1985, 62).

## Works Cited

Adams, Richard P. 1962. "The Apprenticeship of William Faulkner." *Tulane Studies in English* 12:113–56.

Backman, Melvin. 1966. *Faulkner: The Major Years*. Bloomington: Indiana University Press.

Beck, Warren. 1961. *Man in Motion: Faulkner's Trilogy*. Madison: University of Wisconsin Press.

———. 1976. *Faulkner: Essays*. Madison: University of Wisconsin Press.

Blotner, Joseph. 1974. *Faulkner: A Biography*. 2 vols. New York: Random House.

———. 1984. *Faulkner: A Biography*. 1 vol. New York: Random House.

Bowen, James K., and James A. Hamby. 1971. "Colonel Sartoris Snopes and Gabriel Marcel: Allegiance and Commitment." *Notes on Mississippi Writers* 3:101–07.

Bradford, M. E. 1981. 'Family and Community in Faulkner's 'Barn Burning.'" *Southern Review* 17:332–39.

Brooks, Cleanth. 1983. *William Faulkner: First Encounters*. New Haven: Yale University Press.

Brown, Suzanne Hunter. 1989. "Appendix A: Reframing Stories." In *Short Story Theory at a Crossroads*. Ed. Susan Lohafer and Jo Ellyn Clarey. Baton Rouge: Louisiana State University Press, 311–27.

Bungert, Hans. 1986. "Faulkner's Humor: A European View." In *Faulkner and Humor: Faulkner and Yoknapatawpha, 1984*. Ed. Doreen Fowler and Ann J. Abadie. Jackson: University Press of Mississippi, 136–51.

Cackett, Kathy. 1989. "'Barn Burning': Debating the American Adam." *Notes on Mississippi Writers* 21:1–17.

Carothers, James B. 1981. "The Road to The Reivers." In *"A Cosmos of My Own": Faulkner and Yoknapatawpha 1980*. Ed. Doreen Fowler and Ann J. Abadie. Jackson: University Press of Mississippi, 95–124.

———. 1984. "Faulkner's Short Stories: 'And Now What's to Do.'" In *New Directions in Faulkner Studies: Faulkner and Yoknapatawpha, 1983*. Ed. Doreen Fowler and Ann J. Abadie. Jackson: University Press of Mississippi, 202–27.

———. 1985. *William Faulkner's Short Stories*. Ann Arbor, MI: UMI Research Press.

———. 1987. "'I Ain't a Soldier Now': Faulkner's World War II Veterans." *Faulkner Journal* 2:67–74.

Cook, Sylvia Jenkins. 1976. *From Tobacco Road to Route 66: The Southern Poor White in Fiction*. Chapel Hill: University of North Carolina Press.

Cowley, Malcolm. 1966. *The Faulkner-Cowley File: Letters and Memories, 1944–1962*. New York: Viking.

Cox, Leland H. 1982. *William Faulkner: Biographical and Reference Guide*. Detroit: Gale Research.

Creighton, Joanne V. 1977. *William Faulkner's Craft of Revision: The Snopes Trilogy, "The Unvanquished," and "Go Down, Moses."* Detroit: Wayne State University Press.

Duvall, John N. 1990. *Faulkner's Marginal Couple: Invisible, Outlaw, Unspeakable Communities*. Austin: University of Texas Press.

Emerson, O. B. 1984. *Faulkner's Early Literary Reputation in America*. Ann Arbor, MI: UMI Research Press.

Faulkner, William. 1939. "Barn Burning." *Harper's* 179 (June):86–96.

———. 1950. *Collected Stories of William Faulkner*. New York: Random House.

———. 1959. *Faulkner in the University: Class Conferences at the University of Virginia, 1957–1958*. Ed. Frederick Gwynn and Joseph L. Blotner. Charlottesville: University Press of Virginia.

———. 1977. *Selected Letters of William Faulkner*. Ed. Joseph Blotner. New York: Random House.

———. 1979. *Uncollected Stories of William Faulkner*. Ed. Joseph Blotner. New York: Random House.

———. 1987. *William Faulkner Manuscripts 15: The Hamlet*. 2 vols. Ed. Thomas L. McHaney. New York: Garland.

Ferguson, James. 1991. *Faulkner's Short Fiction*. Knoxville: University of Tennessee Press.

Fiedler, Leslie A. 1960. *Love and Death in the American Novel*. New York: Criterion.

Fisher, Marvin. 1960. "The World of Faulkner's Children." *University of Kansas City Review* 27:13–18.

Franklin, Phyllis. 1967–68. "Sarty Snopes and 'Barn Burning.'" *Mississippi Quarterly* 21:189–93.

Friedman, Alan Warren. 1984. *William Faulkner*. New York: Frederick Ungar.

Gold, Joseph. 1966. *William Faulkner: A Study in Humanism, from Metaphor to Discourse*. Norman: University of Oklahoma Press.

Grimwood, Michael. 1987. *Heart in Conflict: Faulkner's Struggles with Vocation*. Athens: University of Georgia Press.

Hadley, Charles. 1980. "Seeing and Telling: Narrational Functions in the Short Story." *Discourse and Style* 2:63–68.

Hall, Joan Wylie. 1989. "Faulkner's Barn Burners: Ab Snopes and the Duke of Marlborough." *Notes on Mississippi Writers* 21:65–68.

Hiles, Jane. 1985. "Kinship and Heredity in Faulkner's 'Barn Burning.'" *Mississippi Quarterly* 38:329–37.

Hochman, Baruch. 1985. *Character in Literature*. Ithaca, NY: Cornell University Press.

Hoffman, Daniel. 1989. *Faulkner's Country Matters: Folklore and Fable in Yoknapatawpha*. Baton Rouge: Louisiana State University Press.

Hogan, Michael. 1981. "Grammatical Tenuity in Fiction." *Language and Style* 14:13–19.

Holmes, Edward M. 1966. *Faulkner's Twice-Told Tales: His Re-Use of His Material*. The Hague: Mouton.

Howe, Irving. [1952] 1975. *William Faulkner: A Critical Study*. 3d ed. Chicago: University of Chicago Press.

Howell, Elmo. 1959. "Colonel Sartoris Snopes and Faulkner's Aristocrats." *Carolina Quarterly* 11.3:13–19.

Hunter, Edwin R. 1973. *William Faulkner: Narrative Practice and Prose Style*. Washington, DC: Windhover.

Johnston, Kenneth G. 1974. "Time of Decline: Pickett's Charge and the Broken Clock in Faulkner's 'Barn Burning.'" *Studies in Short Fiction* 11:434–36.

Karl, Frederick R. 1989. *William Faulkner: American Writer*. New York: Weidenfeld and Nicolson.

Kartiganer, Donald M. 1979. *The Fragile Thread: The Meaning of Form in Faulkner's Novels*. Amherst: University of Massachusetts Press.

Kawin, Bruce F. 1977. *Faulkner and Film*. New York: Frederick Ungar.

Kerr, Elizabeth M. [1969] 1976. *Yoknapatawpha: Faulkner's "Little Postage Stamp of Native Soil."* New York: Fordham University Press.

———. 1979. *William Faulkner's Gothic Domain*. Port Washington, NY: Kennikat.

———. 1983. *William Faulkner's Yoknapatawpha: "A Kind of Keystone in the Universe."* New York: Fordham University Press.

Kinney, Arthur F. 1980. "Faulkner's Narrative Poetics and Collected Stories." *Faulkner Studies* 1:58–79.

Leary, Lewis. 1973. *William Faulkner of Yoknapatawpha County*. New York: Thomas Y. Crowell.

Lisca, Peter. 1954. "The Hamlet: Genesis and Revisions." *Faulkner Studies* 3:5–13.

Malin, Irving. 1957. *William Faulkner: An Interpretation*. Stanford, CA: Stanford University Press.

Meriwether, James B. [1961] 1971. *The Literary Career of William Faulkner: A Bibliographical Study*. Princeton, NJ: Princeton University Library. Reprint. Columbia: University of South Carolina Press.

Millgate, Michael. [1961] 1966. *William Faulkner*. New York: Barnes & Noble.

———. [1966] 1989. *The Achievement of William Faulkner*. New York: Random House. Reprint. Athens: University of Georgia Press. Brown Thrasher Books.

———. 1980. "Faulkner's First Trilogy: Sartoris, Sanctuary, and Requiem for a Nun." In *Fifty Years of Yoknapatawpha: Faulkner and Yoknapatawpha 1979*. Ed. Doreen Fowler and Ann J. Abadie. Jackson: University Press of Mississippi, 90–109.

Minter, David. 1980. *William Faulkner: His Life and Work*. Baltimore: Johns Hopkins University Press.

Mitchell, Charles. 1965. "The Wounded Will of Faulkner's Barn Burner." *Modern Fiction Studies* 11:185–89.

Moreland, Richard C. 1989. "Compulsive and Revisionary Repetition: Faulkner's 'Barn Burning' and the Craft of Writing Difference." In *Faulkner and the Craft of Fiction: Faulkner and Yoknapatawpha, 1987*. Ed. Doreen Fowler and Ann J. Abadie. Jackson: University Press of Mississippi, 48–70.

———. 1990. *Faulkner and Modernism: Rereading and Rewriting*. Madison: University of Wisconsin Press.

Morris, Wesley, and Barbara Alverson Morris. 1989. *Reading Faulkner*. Madison: University of Wisconsin Press.

Nicolet, William P. 1975. "Faulkner's 'Barn Burning.'" *Explicator* 34:#25.

Peavy, Charles D. 1971. *Go Slow Now: Faulkner and the Race Question*. Eugene: University of Oregon Books.

Phillips, Gene D. 1988. *Fiction, Film, and Faulkner: The Art of Adaptation*. Knoxville: University of Tennessee Press.

Pikoulis, John. 1982. *The Art of William Faulkner*. Totowa, NJ: Barnes & Noble.

Pitavy, François. 1973. *Faulkner's* Light in August. Trans. Gillian E. Cook. Bloomington: Indiana University Press.

Polk, Noel. 1981. *Faulkner's* Requiem for a Nun: *A Critical Study*. Bloomington: Indiana University Press.

———. 1983. "Idealism in *The Mansion*." In *Faulkner and Idealism: Perspectives from Paris*. Ed. Michel Gresset and Patrick Samway, S.J. Jackson: University Press of Mississippi, 112–26.

Powers, Lyall H. 1980. *Faulkner's Yoknapatawpha Comedy*. Ann Arbor: University of Michigan Press.

Reed, Joseph W., Jr. 1973. *Faulkner's Narrative*. New Haven: Yale University Press.

Ross, Stephen M. 1989. *Fiction's Inexhaustible Voice: Speech and Writing in Faulkner*. Athens: University of Georgia Press.

Ruzicka, William T. 1987. *Faulkner's Fictive Architecture: The Meaning of Place in the Yoknapatawpha Novels*. Ann Arbor, MI: UMI Research Press.

Sartoris, Brenda Eve. 1983. "Cornbote: A Feudal Custom and Faulkner's 'Barn Burning.'" *Studies in American Fiction* 11:91–94.

Skaggs, Merrill Maguire. 1983. "Story and Film of 'Barn Burning': The Difference a Camera Makes." *Southern Quarterly* 21.2:5–15.

Skei, Hans H. 1981. *William Faulkner: The Short Story Career*. Oslo, Norway: Universitetsforlaget.

———. 1985. *William Faulkner: The Novelist as Short Story Writer*. Oslo, Norway: Universitetsforlaget.

———. 1992. "Beyond Genre? Existential Experience in Faulkner's Short Fiction." In *Faulkner and the Short Story: Faulkner and Yoknapatawpha, 1990*. Ed. Evans Harrington and Ann J. Abadie. Jackson: University Press of Mississippi, 62–77.

Stein, William Bysshe. 1961. "Faulkner's Devil." *Modern Language Notes* 76:731–32.

Stoneback, H. R. 1984. "The Hound and the Antelope: Faulkner in China." In *Faulkner: International Perspectives: Faulkner and Yoknapatawpha, 1982*. Ed. Doreen Fowler and Ann J. Abadie. Jackson: University Press of Mississippi, 236–56.

Stonum, Gary Lee. 1979. *Faulkner's Career: An Internal Literary History*. Ithaca, NY: Cornell University Press.

Trilling, Lionel. 1967. *The Experience of Literature: A Reader with Commentaries*. New York: Holt, Rinehart.

Vashchenko, Alexandre. 1984. "The Perception of William Faulkner in the USSR." In *Faulkner: International Perspectives: Faulkner and Yoknapatawpha, 1982*. Ed. Doreen Fowler and Ann J. Abadie. Jackson: University Press of Mississippi, 194–211.

Vickery, Olga W. [1959] 1964. *The Novels of William Faulkner*. Baton Rouge: Louisiana State University Press.

Volpe, Edmond L. 1980. "'Barn Burning': A Definition of Evil." In *Faulkner: the Unappeased Imagination: A Collection of Critical Essays*. Ed. Glenn O. Carey. Troy, NY: Whitston, 75–82.

Waggoner, Hyatt H. 1959. *William Faulkner: From Jefferson to the World*. Lexington: University of Kentucky Press.

Watkins, Floyd C., and Thomas Daniel Young. 1959–60. "Revisions of Style in Faulkner's 'The Hamlet.'" *Modern Fiction Studies* 5:327–36.

Watson, James G. 1980a. "Faulkner: The House of Fiction." In *Fifty Years of Yoknapatawpha: Faulkner and Yoknapatawpha 1979*. Ed. Doreen Fowler and Ann J. Abadie. Jackson: University Press of Mississippi, 134–58.

———. 1980b. "Faulkner's Short Stories and the Making of Yoknapatawpha County." In *Fifty Years of Yoknapatawpha: Faulkner and Yoknapatawpha 1979*. Ed. Doreen Fowler and Ann J. Abadie. Jackson: University Press of Mississippi, 202–25.

Wilson, Gayle Edward. 1970–71. "'*Being Pulled Two Ways*': The Nature of Sarty's Choice in 'Barn Burning.'" *Mississippi Quarterly* 24:279–88.

Zender, Karl F. 1989. "Character and Symbol in 'Barn Burning.'" *College Literature* 16.1:48–59.

# Shingles for the Lord

## Publication History

"Shingles for the Lord" first appeared in the February 13, 1943, issue of the *Saturday Evening Post*. Faulkner's agent Harold Ober received the story on July 17, 1942; he submitted it to the magazine on July 21, and on July 28, the *Post* purchased the story for $1,000. After its appearance, no Faulkner story was published in a major magazine for seven years. "Shingles for the Lord" appears as the second story in *Collected Stories* (Blotner 1974, 1109, 1120; Skei 1981, 101).

## Circumstances of Composition, Sources, and Influences

"Shingles for the Lord" was the seventh and probably the best story Faulkner wrote in a six-month creative flurry that lasted from January to July 1942 and was stimulated by his pressing need for money (Blotner 1974, 1107–08). Hans Skei rates the artistic quality of these seven stories as generally better than the response from editors would indicate; nevertheless, with the exception of the high price Faulkner received from the *Post* for "Shingles for the Lord" and one other story, the income generated was insufficient to meet Faulkner's financial needs (1981, 101–02).

Although the final version of "Shingles for the Lord" proves satisfying for most readers, its beginnings were inauspicious. Joseph Blotner reports that when composing the story, Faulkner had to dictate part of it to his stepdaughter's husband, Bill Fielden, because the author himself was too intoxicated to work at his desk. The story went through several versions; Faulkner typed one typescript on the verso of another (Blotner 1974, 1109).

Despite the *Post*'s quick acceptance of "Shingles for the Lord," comparisons of the published text with the twenty-one-page carbon typescript show numerous differences. Blotner speculates that *Post* editors, not Faulkner, made "considerable revision" to the story (*WFM 24* Introduction xv; see also Skei 1981, 101). Those changes include such grammatical regularization as punctuating contractions, adding commas in compound sentences, setting off nonrestrictive elements, and adding paragraph breaks, especially when speakers of dialogue changed. There are omissions of several types such as deletion of the word *nigger* that appears as part of the description of the cook and in other passages from the story. James Ferguson notes that the elimination of a conversation between Pap and Maw removed an unnecessary distraction since Maw is not an important character in the text (1991, 125).

Once the story was published, the description of Grier aiming the flying shingle at Quick's shin generated a response to the *Post* from reader Dean F. W. Bradley. He argued that Grier's blows would actually splinter the shingles. The editors forwarded the letter to Faulkner, who answered Bradley that the "minor liberty" in describing the use of the frow was taken "in order to tell the story," which he believed appropriate, but he added that he would be careful "to be explicit in facts" (*SL* 168).

When Faulkner selected "Shingles for the Lord" for *Collected Stories*, he indicated that he needed to make some changes in it (*SL* 274, 277). From magazine to *Collected Stories*, the changes primarily involved altering references to the borrowed *frow* to a more precise *froe and maul*. Further, *fice* is changed to *fyce*, and *modren* becomes *modern* in Solon's use of the word, but Pap continues to use *modren* ("Shingles" 14ff; *CS* 27–43).

Skei speculates that Faulkner's purchase of a farm in 1938 gave him the familiarity he needed to write the "country stories," produced in 1941 or 1942. Faulkner's major period of short fiction writing (1928–1932) produced no works set in this environment (Skei 1985, 267, 321 n. 5). When asked about the relation "Shingles" bore to "fact," Faulkner responded: "Well, these people that I know, they are my people and I love them. They might well have done this. I just got to it before they did" (*FU* 83). He may have also had the Quick family of Lafayette County in mind when writing this story, but its strongest antecedents are probably literary, in the traditions of Southwestern humor (Blotner 1974, Notes 153; Ferguson 1991, 127). Ferguson finds the dialect in this story, as in many others, to be indebted to the oral tradition (1991, 116). Charles Wilson believes Reverend Whitfield's name recalls the English minister George Whitefield, "who effectively introduced the revival to the South in the colonial era" (1991, 36).

## Relationship to Other Faulkner Works

"Shingles for the Lord," "Two Soldiers," and "Shall Not Perish," all written in 1942, focus on the Grier family of Frenchman's Bend. (References in the other Grier stories help locate "Shingles for the Lord" in Frenchman's Bend [Skei 1985, 271].) They are all narrated by one of the Grier sons, but critics differ in their identification of the child in "Shingles for the Lord." Blotner articulates the general opinion that the narrator is Res Grier's second son, Pete Grier's unnamed younger brother, but Skei suggests that if one assumes Res is the same as in other stories, it is more likely that the narrator here is Pete, rather than the younger brother, who narrates the other stories (Blotner 1974, 1108; Skei 1985, 271; see also Kinney 1980, 63–64).

Shared characters and locations in "Shingles for the Lord," "Two Soldiers," and "Shall Not Perish" invite search for further similarities. In Joseph Reed's view, the stories are alike in their respective efforts at the "suspension of remarkable events in the midst of commonplace routine" (1973, 35). "Shingles for the Lord," however, contrasts with the other Grier stories because it is written in a humorous vein (Skei 1985, 271). For Karl, the Griers are not "compelling" in any of the three contexts because they become "lost in the ideological points" that Faulkner is making (1989, 675).

"Shingles for the Lord" also bears relation to other of Faulkner's fiction through its characters and themes. Reverend Whitfield, for example, makes multiple appearances. Once asked to explain the change in Whitfield's character from *As I Lay Dying* to "Barn Burning," Faulkner seemed to suggest that Whitfield's behavior in the novel was a result of limited opportunities that come with living in an isolated, rural area (*FU* 114). It is likely that the reference in this exchange should have been to "Shingles for the Lord" and not to "Barn Burning" since Whitfield is not present in that story. The consensus is that Whitfield's most estimable appearance is in "Shingles for the Lord." Blotner deems Whitfield the "most impressive character" of the story, embodying in the short story, as he had not done in *As I Lay Dying*, the "best qualities of these hill people" (*WFM 24* Introduction xv). According to Cleanth Brooks, Whitfield shows himself in "Shingles" to be the "natural leader of his congregation," but he could certainly be the same Whitfield who in a weaker moment engages in an affair with Addie Bundren ([1963] 1990, 13–15). Elizabeth Kerr describes Whitfield in the short story as a "vigorous, self-reliant minister, firm in faith," whose demeanor differs from his illicit behavior in the novel, and André Bleikasten contrasts the unflattering descriptions of Whitfield in *As I Lay Dying* and *The Hamlet* with the more positive portrait of him as respectable leader in "Shingles for the Lord" (Kerr [1969] 1976; Bleikasten 1973, 152 n. 21; see also Everett 1969, 169; Blotner 1984, 439).

Res Grier reappears, too, if not as himself, at least in the type of character in Faulkner's work known as the yeoman farmer. Skei points out that a reference in "By the People" describes the action of "Shingles" but contains inconsistencies including the reference to Grier as Eck Snopes, a lapse, Skei suggests, in Faulkner's memory (1985, 271, 321 n. 9). Grier is similar to Anse Bundren in *As I Lay Dying* (Blotner 1974, 1109, Notes 153; 1984, 438). Karl sees this resemblance but feels that the Griers lack the Bundrens' intensity (1989, 675). Others of the local folk, Vernon Tull and Henry Armstid, appear in *As I Lay Dying*. Armstid is also in "Spotted Horses," "Lizards in Jamshyd's Courtyard," *The Hamlet*, and *Light in August*. Tull appears again in *Sanctuary* (Holmes 1966, 101, 112–113). Even Grier's fyce receives further attention by way of references in *The Mansion* and "By the People" (Blotner 1974, 1712, Notes 192; see also Stonum 1979, 192; Minter 1980, 243–44; Skei 1985, 279; 1987, 253).

M. E. Bradford contends that Faulkner's portraits of the yeomen farmers and their like, including Byron Bunch in *Light in August* and the convict in *The Wild Palms*, are "always affirmative and admiring." In "Shingles for the Lord," Grier momentarily trades his dignity for a new WPA way of thinking that results in his humiliation (Bradford 1965, 94, 99 n. 7). James Carothers believes that the ironic treatment of these characters in the novels is replaced by a more tolerant rendering in "Shingles for the Lord" (1985, 66). Brooks considers the portrait of poor white characters in "Shingles for the Lord" to provide "something of a balance for his more somber accounts" ([1963] 1990, 13–15).

In a survey of trickster figures prevalent in Faulkner's fiction, Carothers includes "Shingles for the Lord" in a lengthy list of both successful and foiled tricksters. Grier's effort to outwit Quick resembles the behavior of the early leaders of Jefferson in Yoknapatawpha County when they sought to avoid paying Alexander Holston for his lock that had been stolen in "A Name for the City" and *Requiem for a Nun*, and Flem Snopes's conniving in "Centaur in Brass" (Carothers 1984, 226; Carothers 1985, 48).

Thematic issues raised in "Shingles for the Lord" link it to a variety of other works in which the author voiced similar opinions. As Blotner notes, a decade after Faulkner wrote "Shingles for the Lord," at a Delta Council meeting on May 15, 1952, he reiterated the belief expressed in the story that people needed to stand on their own so that welfare could facilitate those who eventually would also regain their ability to be self-supporting. Res Grier, who assimilates "WPA terminology and benefits" into his own language and life, and Solon Quick are antithetical to the self-sufficiency represented by the McCallums of "The Tall Men" (Blotner 1974, 1417; Blotner 1984, 439).

Brooks sees religion portrayed here (though Methodist, not Baptist, as Brooks states) in a "genial light." It possesses, in the emblem of the baptizing shirt, the stability, power, and dignity that are antithetical to the portrait of religious tyranny described in *The Town* (Brooks [1963] 1990, 13–15).

Louis Brodsky makes an unexpected comparison of the story to Faulkner's work on "The De Gaulle Story." The film script, like "The Tall Men," "Shingles for the Lord," "Two Soldiers" and certain early segments of "Delta Autumn," reinforces the "countervailing motifs: compassion, equality, patriotism, and personal liberty" when they are placed in opposition to "oppression and violence and injustice" (Brodsky 1990, 101). Carothers argues that critics dismiss "Shingles for the Lord," "The Tall Men," "Race at Morning," and "Mule in the Yard" as sentimental tales that lack reality because the initiations portrayed in them are recognitions of "virtue and humor" rather than confrontations with "evil and horror" (1985, 11).

Some relational observations compare the formal qualities of "Shingles for the Lord" with the narrative strategies Faulkner uses elsewhere. The story is one of Faulkner's comic texts, though critics focus on different aspects of the humor of the story. John Longley likens "Shingles for the Lord" to "A Courtship" because both represent the "purest essence of social comedy," and Carothers emphasizes its "broad humor and colloquial style" that links it to "Spotted Horses," "Race at Morning," and "Fool About a Horse" (Longley [1957] 1963, 115; Carothers 1985, 116). Heide Ziegler counts "Shingles for the Lord" among the comic texts employing slapstick stage comedy, including "Uncle Willy," "Mule in the Yard," and some parts of *The Hamlet* and *Go Down, Moses*. The emphasis is on the "scenic element" limited essentially "to brief descriptions" (Ziegler 1989, 118). Ferguson adds that "Shingles for the Lord," "Love," "Was," "My Grandmother Millard," and "all the comic swindle stories" depend on "games, stratagems, tricks, reversals, puzzles, or surprises" in the resolution of the plot (1991, 136).

Another prevalent Faulknerian strategy found in this story is location of the narrative consciousness in the mind of a young male child. "Shingles for the Lord" follows this pattern, present in a variety of stories such as "Barn Burning" and "That Evening Sun" (Millgate [1961] 1966). Reed identifies the narrative approach of a "little boy who knew too much" in "That Will Be Fine," "Two Soldiers," and "Shingles for the Lord" (1984, 142). Hans Bungert argues that the narrative approach, "comedy of limited perception," becomes "one of the constituents of comedy" for numerous works including "Shingles for the Lord," "Uncle Willy," "Was," *The Reivers*, and much of *The Unvanquished* (1986, 146–47).

In his study of architectural structures in Faulkner's fiction, William Ruzicka examines the significance of the church in numerous works, among them "Shingles for the Lord," *Intruder in the Dust*, *The Unvanquished*, and *The Mansion*. Despite very different contexts, the common function of the church in all the stories is "for the implementation of grace, in whatever concrete form it may need to take." Churches are almost always portrayed "in difficult circumstances, with congregation or structure in near dissolution, in which the practice of faith becomes genuinely heroic and the working of grace particularly strenuous" (1987, 83–85).

In *Collected Stories*, "Shingles for the Lord" follows the powerful "Barn Burning" in the first section entitled "The Country." A common element of stories in "The Country" is that they are all set in Yoknapatawpha County but on the outskirts of Jefferson. Michael Millgate argues that "Barn Burning" sets up the poles of conflict that shape the volume, and "Shingles for the Lord" comes next, presenting alternate perspectives: arson is deliberate in the first story and accidental in the second; the relationships between fathers and sons are very different in the two stories. Both stories suggest similar traits of "poor whites." That these men, Whitfield specifically but the others also, are held indestructible and enduring echoes traits of Ab Snopes, who precedes them, and the McCallums in the next story, "The Tall Men." According to Millgate, the need for explicit portrayal of these characteristics in "Shingles for the Lord" "underlines its relative weakness as a story" (Millgate [1966] 1989, 271; see also Carothers 1985, 64, 66; Bungert 1986, 149).

The alternation of tonalities in the section balances the serious tone of the first and third stories with the comic tone of the second, "Shingles for the Lord," and fourth (Ferguson 1991, 158). Arthur Kinney adds that the narratives of the Grier boy (Kinney names Pete rather than the younger brother) are linked to Sarty Snopes's narrative in that these stories demonstrate an "unfolding awareness . . . by which coming of age vanquishes boyhood idealism and pride." The narrator sees, where his father does not, the "analogy between his deception of Solon and Solon's somewhat more prolonged attempt to get something for nothing." This effort to use the government program for personal gain is then inverted in the next story, "The Tall Men" (Kinney 1980, 63–64).

Although "Shingles for the Lord" has garnered a few fans who praise it, the story has not really generated either a wide readership or a deep body of critical response. The story is of interest mainly because of its relation to other Faulkner works.

## Interpretation and Criticism

Faulkner found the humor of "Shingles for the Lord" still to be fresh when he reread the story in preparation for *Collected Stories* (*SL* 304; Blotner 1974, 1323). The laughter has not been lost on critics. According to Longley, the atmosphere of the story "is one in which all real hostility and violence are kept carefully at arm's length and all comic denouements are obtained by the cross-currents of human self-assertion within a group of people who really do have a common, commendable, purpose—however much they may succeed in getting in each other's way." It is a comedy of manners that "creates every nuance of the cross-currents of rivalry and self-assertion that swirl against the ideals implied by the dedication to the task at hand," diminishing any need for acquaintance with the region ([1957] 1963, 120, 115). Blotner describes it as a "tart-tongued comedy" and one of Faulkner's "funniest" (1974, 1108; 1984, 438). Carothers joins those who praise the story, counting it among Faulkner's better comic stories. It includes "slapstick, broad farce, witty provincial horse-trading, and grim humor." Violence is present but subdued, and the destruction of the church is comic because no one is hurt and there is a promise of that it will be rebuilt immediately. There is a tolerance for the characters' foibles, including the rhetoric of Whitfield and Quick, the eccentricities of the Killigrews, and even the church attendance of a Snopes (Carothers 1985, 64–66). David Dowling describes "Shingles for the Lord" as a story that "weaves delicately between tall tale and social history" (1989, 155). Walter Everett offers a dissenting opinion when he judges the comedy of this story to "lack the vitality" typical of Faulkner's comic tales (1969, 169).

Independence, business, and religion are the thematic issues around which the story revolves. According to Dowling, the characters alternate "between a vertical or spiritual sense of events and their own importance, and an intense preoccupation with worldly calculation and barter." Whitfield's perception of man's endurance is weighed against the commercial element that "threatens, literally, to destroy the church" (Dowling 1989, 155).

Res Grier does not hold up well under scrutiny. For Longley, Grier's apparently greater need than most of his neighbors makes him overpossessive, defensive, and self-assertive ([1957] 1963, 120). W. V. Myres's early analysis of "Shingles for the Lord" includes his observation of the emphasis on the Griers' poverty but also on their "dignity which vacillates from the sublime to the ridiculous." The story becomes a parable of poetic justice in which Grier's prideful actions are punished. His initial failure is that he gets to the church to repair the roof late because he has waited until the morning he needed the froe and maul to try and borrow them from Mr. Killegrew. Whitfield's censure anticipates the poetic justice yet to come. Grier's need to outwit Solon in the dog trade increases in the context of Solon's waiting for, then blaming Grier for, the loss of "work-units." The consequences of Grier's prideful retaliation become more serious. Grier's effort to avoid shame, not work, must be punished in order that his pride be kept "ordinate and his view of himself realistic." Every effort of avoidance is met with a return upon himself of greater humiliation (Myres 1969, 224–30). Everett describes Grier as an overreacher whose own ineptitude undermines his dealing with Quick, and in Kerr's estimation, Grier is an example of an inefficient landowner because he cannot generate adequate income from his seventy acres (Everett 1969, 169; Kerr [1969] 1976, 152–53). Skei also sees Grier's "hard luck" as a consequence of his general lack of planning, discipline, and patience. He seeks to improve his condition with quick, substantial improvements rather than steady effort, with negative results compounding all the while (Skei 1985, 271–72). Carothers comes to Grier's defense when he points out that Grier's desire for revenge does not negate the virtues of "his wit, imagination, and sense of fair play" (1985, 68).

According to Reed the commentary on business in the story is "gentle," not "overt." The narrator understands the business deals and concepts of "work units" and "dog units" but does not have a "clear view of his father's excessive pride" (Reed 1973, 35). For the child, who had slept with the dog when it was a puppy, the barter is important.

Elmo Howell examines Faulkner's portrait of the country church as revealing his affection for, but limited experience with, the country people he sought to portray. His distrust of formal religion manifests itself in the negative portrayal of churchgoers in numerous texts; consequently, his efforts in "Shingles for the Lord" to convey the "salutary effect of religion in the rural community" is unsatisfactory. Whitfield's portrayal here as an authoritarian, paternalistic figure is artificial and does not complement the independence of the "yeoman element." Further, the church, designated Methodist in the story, is "obviously Baptist," and the baptizing gown implies baptism by immersion (Howell 1967–68, 205–210).

Both Myers and Ruzicka argue that the church is the center of the community portrayed. It records the births, marriages, and deaths of its members (Myres 1969, 227). Ruzicka argues that the meaning of the story is located in church building specifically: when the shingles break loose and the lantern falls into the church, Res and his son hang above the church fire in an "image of the threat of perdition." Whitfield's nightshirt, Ruzicka adds, "is the garment of the church's *genius loci*, which it wears in its ascension to the heavens as the dissolving church loses the substance which holds its character as a place." Despite the apparent destruction of the church, the "resilient *genius loci* of a meaningful place" cannot be extinguished; as both Whitfield and the narrator perceive, the church that encloses the "sacred space" will be rebuilt (Ruzicka 1987, 84). Skei also reads both church building and preacher as representatives of "permanence and indestructibility" that is made "possible only because the men in the community are willing to work to rebuild the church," an attitude that emphasizes Grier's lack of "permanence and indestructibility" and his son's awareness of his father's failing (1985, 272). Carothers softens the lesson Grier's son takes from his father's behavior. He learns of his father's fallibility but also durability as well as the "true significance of the church" as he confronts his feelings about its destruction (Carothers 1985, 67–68). Also citing the endurance of the church despite the loss of the structure, Wilson describes the story as a "marvelous evocation of the landscape and spirit of Southern rural folk religion." "Without describing any worship service," Wilson adds, "Faulkner conveys the spiritual significance of this small institution to its people" (1991, 36–37).

Critics express some skepticism concerning the child's presentation of thoughts and actions, but most are complimentary. Ferguson points out that the chronology of the story is straightforward (1991, 127–28), but the narrative voice is not quite as simply designed. Reed shows how Faulkner achieves the contrast between everyday life and the event of the fire through the excitement with which the child captures an event that is "different and exciting." Reed's estimation is that the child possesses adult understanding of the everyday business, yet retains the childlike enthusiasm for an unexpected event (1973, 35–37). Carothers contends that the young Grier boy narrating the story "employs metaphor appropriate to his background and experience." Elsewhere, however, Carothers discusses more fully problems he finds with the narrative voice in that through his metaphors, the narrator exhibits a "sensibility far more articulate than that which might be expected of him," especially in those passages in which he describes Whitfield and the burning of his baptizing shirt. Carothers concludes that this disparity constitutes the greatest weakness of the story, but does not, given its comic nature, undermine its overall effectiveness (1985, 21–22, 66–67). When Ferguson places this story within the oral tradition, he adds the qualifier that to some extent the substance is lost in the attention to telling and some stylistic inconsistencies (Ferguson 1991, 116).

Carothers employs the description of Grier's removing shingles to demonstrate Faulkner's signature techniques including the use of colloquial idiom by approximating the dialect and grammar, the contrast of long and short sentences, combining "negative qualification" with "positive assertion," and the overall effect of capturing a "single image, a frozen moment" (1985, 21–22).

"Shingles for the Lord" has been panned, applauded, and ignored. When considered at all, it has been compared primarily to other of Faulkner stories. "Shingles for the Lord" was included in *A Faulkner Reader*, and it has recently been translated into Chinese. H. R. Stoneback notes the "humor and pathos," the "sense of community among country people," and a "delight in shrewd trading" in "Shingles for the Lord" to which Chinese readers respond

(1984, 243–44). It has been held in good company, grouped with "Was" and "Mule in the Yard" as "notable stories" (Waggoner 1959, 199), and with "Barn Burning" and "Mule in the Yard" as products of a "later, riper period" (Putzel 1985, 275). "Shingles for the Lord" is also memorable, even if not remarkable, because it comes from Faulkner's last concerted effort to write independent short fiction (Skei 1981, 102; Skei 1985, 287).

## Works Cited

Bleikasten, André. 1973. *Faulkner's* As I Lay Dying. Trans. Roger Little with the collaboration of the author. Bloomington: Indiana University Press.

Blotner, Joseph. 1974. *Faulkner: A Biography*. 2 vols. New York: Random House.

———. 1984. *Faulkner: A Biography*. 1 vol. New York: Random House.

Bradford, M. E. 1965. "Faulkner and the Jeffersonian Dream: Nationalism in 'Two Soldiers' and 'Shall Not Perish.'" *Mississippi Quarterly* 18:94–100.

Brodsky, Louis Daniel. 1990. *William Faulkner, Life Glimpses*. Austin: University of Texas Press.

Brooks, Cleanth. [1963] 1990. *William Faulkner: The Yoknapatawpha Country*. New Haven: Yale University Press. Reprint. Baton Rouge: Louisiana State University Press.

Bungert, Hans. 1986. "Faulkner's Humor: A European View." In *Faulkner and Humor: Faulkner and Yoknapatawpha, 1984*. Ed. Doreen Fowler and Ann J. Abadie. Jackson: University Press of Mississippi, 136–51.

Carothers, James B. 1984. "Faulkner's Short Stories: 'And Now What's to Do.'" In *New Directions in Faulkner Studies: Faulkner and Yoknapatawpha, 1983*. Ed. Doreen Fowler and Ann J. Abadie. Jackson: University Press of Mississippi, 202–27.

———. 1985. *William Faulkner's Short Stories*. Ann Arbor, MI: UMI Research Press.

Dowling, David. 1989. *William Faulkner*. New York: St. Martin's.

Everett, Walter K. 1969. *Faulkner's Art and Character*. Woodbury, NY: Barron's Educational Series.

Faulkner, William. 1943. "Shingles for the Lord." *Saturday Evening Post* 215 (13 February):14–15, 68, 70–71.

———. 1950. *Collected Stories of William Faulkner*. New York: Random House.

———. 1959. *Faulkner in the University: Class Conferences at the University of Virginia, 1957–1958*. Ed. Frederick Gwynn and Joseph L. Blotner. Charlottesville: University Press of Virginia.

———. 1977. *Selected Letters of William Faulkner*. Ed. Joseph Blotner. New York: Random House.

———. 1987. *William Faulkner Manuscripts 24: Short Stories*. Ed. Joseph Blotner. New York: Garland.

Ferguson, James. 1991. *Faulkner's Short Fiction*. Knoxville: University of Tennessee Press.

Holmes, Edward M. 1966. *Faulkner's Twice-Told Tales: His Re-Use of His Material*. The Hague: Mouton.

Howell, Elmo. 1967–68. "Faulkner's Country Church: A Note on 'Shingles for the Lord.'" *Mississippi Quarterly* 21:205–10.

Karl, Frederick R. 1989. *William Faulkner: American Writer*. New York: Weidenfeld and Nicolson.

Kerr, Elizabeth M. [1969] 1976. *Yoknapatawpha: Faulkner's "Little Postage Stamp of Native Soil."* New York: Fordham University Press.

Kinney, Arthur F. 1980. "Faulkner's Narrative Poetics and *Collected Stories.*" *Faulkner Studies* 1:58–79.

Longley, John Lewis, Jr. [1957] 1963. *The Tragic Mask: A Study of Faulkner's Heroes*. Chapel Hill: University of North Carolina Press.

Millgate, Michael. [1961] 1966. *William Faulkner*. New York: Barnes & Noble.

———. [1966] 1989. *The Achievement of William Faulkner*. New York: Random House. Reprint. Athens: University of Georgia Press. Brown Thrasher Books.

Minter, David. 1980. *William Faulkner: His Life and Work*. Baltimore: Johns Hopkins University Press.

Myres, W. V. 1969. "Faulkner's Parable of Poetic Justice." *Louisiana Studies* 8:224–30.

Putzel, Max. 1985. *Genius of Place: William Faulkner's Triumphant Beginnings*. Baton Rouge: Louisiana State University Press.

Reed, Joseph W., Jr. 1973. *Faulkner's Narrative*. New Haven: Yale University Press.

———. 1984. *Three American Originals: John Ford, William Faulkner, and Charles Ives*. Middletown, CT: Wesleyan University Press.

Ruzicka, William T. 1987. *Faulkner's Fictive Architecture: The Meaning of Place in the Yoknapatawpha Novels*. Ann Arbor, MI: UMI Research Press.

Skei, Hans H. 1981. *William Faulkner: The Short Story Career*. Oslo, Norway: Universitetsforlaget.

———. 1985. *William Faulkner: The Novelist as Short Story Writer*. Oslo, Norway: Universitetsforlaget.

———. 1987. "William Faulkner's Late Career: Repetition, Variation, Renewal." In *Faulkner: After the Nobel Prize*. Ed. Michel Gresset and Kenzaburo Ohashi. Kyoto: Yamaguchi, 247–59.

Stoneback, H. R. 1984. "The Hound and the Antelope: Faulkner in China." In *Faulkner: International Perspectives: Faulkner and Yoknapatawpha*, 1982. Ed.

Doreen Fowler and Ann J. Abadie. Jackson: University Press of Mississippi, 236–56.

Stonum, Gary Lee. 1979. *Faulkner's Career: An Internal Literary History*. Ithaca, NY: Cornell University Press.

Waggoner, Hyatt H. 1959. *William Faulkner: From Jefferson to the World*. Lexington: University of Kentucky Press.

Wilson, Charles Reagan. 1991. "William Faulkner and the Southern Religious Culture." In *Faulkner and Religion: Faulkner and Yoknapatawpha*, 1989. Ed. Doreen Fowler and Ann J Abadie. Jackson: University Press of Mississippi, 21–43.

Ziegler, Heide. 1989. "Faulkner's Rhetoric of the Comic: The Reivers." In *Faulkner's Discourse: An International Symposium*. Ed. Lothar Hönnighausen. Tübingen: Max Niemeyer Verlag, 117–26.

# The Tall Men

## Publication History

"The Tall Men" appeared in the May 31, 1941, issue of the *Saturday Evening Post*. Harold Ober received the manuscript on March 19, 1941, and was able to make a sale in six days to the *Saturday Evening Post* for $1,000. "The Tall Men" appeared in "The Country" section of *Collected Stories* (1950) and was adapted for television (Blotner 1974, 1070–1071, Notes 148; Karl 1989, 858).

## Circumstances of Composition, Sources, and Influences

"The Tall Men" is the product of about two weeks' work, and according to Hans Skei, its quick success may relate to Faulkner's renewed commitment some months earlier "to serious and concentrated short story writing" (Skei 1981, 97). Although Joseph Blotner writes, "At a time when he needed money perhaps a bit more badly than usual, Faulkner had written not a potboiler but a story which embodied some of his deepest feelings and strongest convictions," Skei argues that Faulkner wrote the story "to make money" (Blotner 1974, 1070–1071; Skei 1981, 97). Faulkner's own comment, in a letter to

Robert Haas, is that he was writing stories during this period to pay off delinquent income tax debts. He indicates that the anticipated fee from the sale of "The Tall Men" would cancel that debt (*SL* 139). Nevertheless, Faulkner apparently did have some regard for the story: his proposed list for the *Collected Stories* shows the comment "Yes" beside the title (*SL* 274). Some differences exist between the extant carbon typescript and the published version of "The Tall Men." The typescript contains fewer paragraph breaks than the printed version, and some of its passages are missing from the published story. These changes may have been made by the *Post* editors, but Faulkner retained them when he used the story in *Collected Stories* (*WFM 24* Introduction xiv, 330–50).

"The Tall Men" has a few minor biographical associations. The location of the McCallums' farm relative to Jefferson is a near match to the location of Faulkner's Greenfield farm relative to Oxford (Kerr [1969] 1976, 60 n. 46). A match in the extended Falkner family includes a likeness between Buddy McCallum's wound received in France during World War I and the similar experience of Faulkner's brother Murry C. Falkner, Jr. (Blotner 1974, Notes 148).

The more compelling familial ties also entail literary relationships. Elmo Howell shows that Faulkner's brother John's novel *Men Working*, published in 1941, reflects the attitude that WPA and other federal aid programs were corruptive, and Michael Grimwood notes that the plot of "The Tall Men" "loosely resembles" John Faulkner's "Good Neighbors" (Howell 1964, 323; Grimwood 1987, 260). Additional literary links show the story as inheriting thematic concerns from Henry David Thoreau's *Civil Disobedience* and possibly from the poetry of Faulkner's contemporary Donald Davidson. Ward Miner associates the assertion of the individual over the law in this tale with Thoreau without his Transcendentalism (1952, 153). Howell does not make a claim for influence, but he observes a likeness between Faulkner's McCallums and the tall Tennesseans in Davidson's poetry whose tallness is not in their diet "but in the seed of man" (1962, 81–82).

## Relationship to Other Faulkner Works

The critical interest that "The Tall Men" generates frequently involves establishing its relationship to Faulkner's other works. According to Olga Vickery, "The Tall Men" is an adjunctive story because it provides supplementary information about the people and places of Yoknapatawpha ([1959] 1964, 300). James Ferguson views Faulkner's reuse here of characters created much earlier as nostalgic (1991, 41).

Faulkner returned to the McCallum family that he had characterized much earlier (as the *MacCallum* family) in *Sartoris/Flags in the Dust* (*WFM 24*

Introduction xiv). Howell calls the farm described in *Sartoris* "Faulkner's Utopia, a country of tall men with clean minds and pure hearts and nature still in a virginal state of innocence." The time of the short story is later than the time portrayed in the novel, and Buddy, the youngest of the McCallum sons, is now the middle-aged father of draft-aged twin sons (Howell 1962, 80–81; Howell 1964, 324–25). Another McCallum appearance involves Rafe McCallum's role in *Knight's Gambit*, and Gavin Stevens comes into "The Tall Men" by way of a reference to him made by another character (Blotner 1974, 1070; Holmes 1966, 113–14).

The McCallums represent a character type that prevails not only in "The Tall Men" but also in other Faulkner short stories and novels: the independent yeoman farmer or hill dweller. M. E. Bradford's catalog of yeoman characters begins with Faulkner's own list from *The Town* and includes such family names as Frazier, Muir, Turpin, Murray, Haley, and McCallum, with the McCallums representing the best or finest of these. In other fiction, Jackson Fentry, the Griers, Mr. Ernest, Byron Bunch, and the tall convict also belong to this group (Bradford 1962, 32, 36). McHaney also sees Jewel Bundren, Jack Houston, and Mink Snopes as yeoman types (1975, 154). Within that characterization, certain differences exist. Howell adds the fiercely independent Gowries to those to whom Faulkner would pay "grudging respect," but Elizabeth Kerr points out that the Gowries lack a "rustic gentility" possessed by others of the group (Howell 1964, 330–31; Kerr 1976, 137). Also, the McCallums represent a self-sufficiency that contrasts with the personalities of Res Grier and Solon Quick as portrayed in "Shingles for the Lord" (Blotner 1984, 438).

The qualities of character often admired in "The Tall Men" relate most explicitly to the independence of these men and sometimes to their overt patriotism. James Carothers, for example, contends that "The Tall Men," like "Race at Morning," "Shingles for the Lord," and "Mule in the Yard," is lightly regarded because it leads to a "discovery of goodness in men" instead of the presumed discovery of evil that is more typical in initiation stories (1985, 11).

Critics generally see the McCallums in a positive light, but some find a darker side of the family. Albert Devlin's reading of *Sartoris* and "The Tall Men" offers a view of them that is far from idyllic. He argues that the MacCallums of *Sartoris* "in no sense represent normality" (1971, 83). The sons are unfulfilled, poorly adjusted individuals dominated by their father, Virginius (Anse in "The Tall Men"); their lives "indicate pathology." In the womanless household, some sons assume roles and behavior described as feminine, and a close reading reveals that they are not happy. As Devlin points out, "A family in which nearly all the sons fail to marry, in which nearly all the sons fail to sever parent-child relations and establish sexual ones, is hardly the ideal fantasized by Faulkner critics"; they are more nearly a "paradigm of arrested development" (1971, 83–90).

Wesley Morris and Barbara Morris argue that the short story constitutes a revision of the McCallums from their original appearance in *Sartoris/Flags in the Dust*. Although the novel presents their lives and characters as an "alternative to that doomed pseudo-aristocratic heritage that is so much a part of young Bayard's self-destructive temperament," in the short story, it is the McCallums' way of life that is doomed. Morris and Morris add that this revision is paralleled in the revision of the Sartoris myth, particularly in the demythologizing of John Sartoris in *The Unvanquished* (1989, 53).

"The Tall Men" and a number of other texts beginning in the 1940s exhibit a different attitude toward war and patriotism from that expressed in "The Wasteland" stories related to World War I. Skei identifies "The Tall Men" as Faulkner's "first patriotic story," a quality that he and readers before and after him have associated with numerous late texts (Skei 1981, 80; Skei 1987, 255). Blotner links "The Tall Men" with "Two Soldiers" in its portrayal of the patriotism of the country's hill people; "The Bear," which was probably composed after "The Tall Men," expresses a similiar sentiment as do "Delta Autumn," "Shall Not Perish," and *A Fable* (Blotner 1974, 1097, Notes 150; Skei 1981, 80, 97; Skei 1987, 255; Karl 1989, 652).

Thomas Nordanberg draws specific correspondences between the attitudes various characters hold in "The Tall Men," "Two Soldiers," and "Shall Not Perish." Res Grier's attitude toward military service resembles the draft investigator's; the two Grier sons reflect the attitude of the McCallums; Mrs. Grier expresses the same hopeful vision for moral growth as Deputy Marshal Gombault (Nordanberg 1983, 116–118). Louis Brodsky includes with these patriotic stories the film project "The De Gaulle Story," which also examines the issues of patriotism and personal liberty, and compassion and equality (1990, 101). Skei adds that in "Snow," other World War II stories, and some World War I stories, individuals find themselves alienated from the larger community because they have retained integrity, pride, and self-esteem in a world in which these qualities seem to have degenerated. These character types, however, are usually less influential in the community than other characters, and in some respects their independence has meant absolving themselves of responsibility within the community (Skei 1985 265–67, 272; 1992, 69).

"My Grandmother Millard and General Bedford Forrest and the Battle of Harrykin Creek" is a Civil War story, but Nordanberg sees a similarity between it and "The Tall Men" in their positive handling of war. He explains this by noting that both stories were written at about the same time (1983, 107). Taking a different approach, Ferguson associates the "conflict between primitive, intuitional spontaneity and the corruptions of mechanization and civilization" (as portrayed in the McCallums and the federal agent) with Granny Millard's gradual corruption and also with Lucas Beauchamp's defeat of "city slickers" in "Race at Morning" (1991, 41, 55).

The amputation depicted in "The Tall Men" is part of a larger pattern in Faulkner's fiction. The amputation described resembles another situation with Doctor Peabody as told by Suratt in *Sartoris* (Holmes 1966, 113–14). Ferguson applies a Freudian interpretation of fear of castration to Faulkner's preoccupation with "lost, maimed, and injured limbs" apparent in "The Tall Men," "Barn Burning," "Mountain Victory," "Death Drag," *As I Lay Dying*, and *A Fable* (1991, 203 n. 11).

Comparisons of "The Tall Men" and "The Leg" elicit diverse responses. Arthur Kinney notes that "The Tall Men" is third from the beginning of the *Collected Stories* and "The Leg," another amputation story, is fourth from the end of the collection (1980, 64). For Grimwood, "The Tall Men" and "The Leg" reflect a "minor Faulknerian pattern" in which dismemberment becomes an occasion for the display of courage. Grimwood writes, "The five-foot-five author of 'The Tall Men' must have found consolation in an amputation that heightens stature and enhances virility" (1987, 314 n. 40). David Dowling sees "The Tall Men" as "Faulkner's attack on abstraction." Unlike "The Leg," "The Tall Men" depicts a leg buried in a family plot, an action that serves "as a clear-eyed affirmation of who and where the people are" that contrasts with the abstractions of "alphabets and rules and recipes" (Dowling 1989, 155; *CS* 59).

In a different context, Ferguson analyzes Faulkner's concern with the "danger of abstraction" imposed "on the complexities of human experience." "Legality" as an abstraction proves destructive in "The Tall Men," "By the People," "Point of Law," and "Lo!"; "community" as an abstraction is negatively weighed against the "individual" in "The Tall Men," "Uncle Willy," "Dry September," and "Red Leaves" (Ferguson 1991, 81, 82).

Stylistic features of "The Tall Men" reflect some techniques apparent in earlier works and some strategies unique to Faulkner's later fiction. Joseph Reed notes that the investigator fits the category of "faulty witness" whose assumptions are wrong, also utilized in "Hair," "Turnabout," and "Dr. Martino" (1973, 26). Ferguson distinguishes the federal investigator as a third-person limited "viewpoint character" who remains on the periphery as a "necessary but somewhat obvious narrative *device*" by which Faulkner emphasizes his themes. "Knight's Gambit" is another instance where the viewpoint character, in this case Chick Mallison, is essentially a device; Bogard in "Turnabout" represents a more skillful handling of this technique. Additionally, Ferguson relates Joseph Gold's argument that Faulkner moved from "metaphor" to "discourse" in his later work to stories of the 1940s like "The Tall Men"; and like "Race at Morning," "The Tall Men" employs a didactic tone (Ferguson 1991, 41, 42, 55, 100–01).

The arrangement of the stories in *Collected Stories* frequently adds a contextual emphasis unavailable when they are considered independently. Michael Millgate describes the tension in "Barn Burning," "Shingles for the

Lord," and "The Tall Men" as generated in the conflict "between social values and those which are primarily moral or aesthetic." In "The Tall Men," the contrast is enhanced by the presence of the government investigator (Millgate [1966] 1989, 271). Kinney finds that the juxtaposition of "Shingles for the Lord" and "The Tall Men" in "The Country" calls attention to the contrast between the effort to use federal regulations for individual aggrandizement in "Shall Not Perish" and the attempt to avoid the same in "The Tall Men." The sons are not punished but make their "escape to enlist in Memphis" while the marshal delays the agent. In this context, deception is linked to good intentions, the effort of self-protection (Kinney 1980, 64).

These relational observations, even though they are often only brief remarks, constitute a substantive portion of the critical corpus focusing on "The Tall Men" and follow the same paths as interpretations of the story.

## Interpretation and Criticism

Skei's summative remark that "The Tall Men" is a "strong, at times sentimental, story of patriotism and self-sufficiency" recognizes the predominant interpretive poles for the story (1981, 97). The independence of the McCallums is played against the issue of patriotism in times of war and against federal aid systems. However, discussions that examine flaws in the McCallum family impede a view of this story as a simple and affirming if too didactic tale.

Critics disagree on whether "The Tall Men" conveys the possibility of individuality in modern American society. Ray West places "The Tall Men" within a story type that juxtaposes the "forms of the past" and the "actions of the present" in order to examine those forms in the context of "present action"; such placement allows ambiguities to be discovered and perhaps resolved (1952, 95). Although West does not indicate the particular direction this story takes, others have been more explicit. Bradford aligns the McCallums with the "plain folk" described in F. L. Owsley's sociological study *Plain Folk of the Old South*. Owsley argues that the majority of the white population of the antebellum South fell into the group of small, independent farmers, and Bradford sees Faulkner's independent hill-country farmers as representative of the "oldest southern tradition, that of the frontier" (1962, 30–32). Yasuo Hashiguchi believes that Buddy's reaction to his injury implies much of the meaning about individual responsibility stressed in "The Tall Men" and that the marshal's retelling of the McCallum family history further enhances the display of courage. Individualism is not lost; it survives much as the old-fashioned ways, furnishings, and words survive in the text (Hashiguchi 1963, 9–10; see also Howell 1964, 323–332).

When seen as a story that affirms the strength of individual character in the modern world, it becomes an initiation text in which the investigator is the initiate. Bradford hopes the investigator learns from the marshal the metaphoric import of the "tall" stature of physically undistinguished men—the strength of backbone lost but not irrecoverable in modern man (1962, 33–36). Hashiguchi traces the investigator's "progress from innocence to knowledge, with the deputy marshal . . . as the mentor." The investigator's behavior when burying the leg, respectfully not putting it down until it is laid in the hole, implies the success of initiation (Hashiguchi 1963, 8–9). Nordanberg adds that "The Tall Men" is an explicit expression of the faith Faulkner bore in modern man's ability to overcome his shortcomings and rise to the needs of the looming crisis of war (1983, 112–15). Carothers defends the possibility of discovering good rather than evil in an initiation, but concludes that "The Tall Men" suffers from its overt didacticism (1985, 68–69).

Taking a darker view are those who believe the point of "The Tall Men" is that these men of character are no longer viable models. In the story line of "The Tall Men," "an old-fashioned patriotism which the Federal man cannot understand" inheres in the twins' independence (Howell 1962, 80–81). Edmond Volpe's reading of the McCallums is that they are the sole example of Faulkner's individualism, the "right of a man to live his own life," but they are "anachronisms." The McCallum's patriarchal structure recognizes the father's authority as the final mortal authority and the social unit as the family; therefore, the draft system, like crop allotments, "is to them a limitation of freedom and an insult to their sense of responsibility" (Volpe 1964, 21–22). And for Grimwood, Faulkner locates the decline of American moral fiber in the failure to transmit values from one generation to the next (1987, 260).

Like Volpe, Morris and Morris's reading suggests that the McCallums' way of life in its rejection of modernity is doomed despite the affirmation that they "espouse a more heroic, individualistic code of behavior." Their resistance to modernism has not been completely successful: they resisted price supports for cotton but eventually had to change from growing cotton to raising cattle. The tone of the story also implies a passing of this way of life, exhibited, for example, in how Buddy McCallum's attitude "occasionally slips from the heroic to passive acceptance" (Morris and Morris 1989, 51–53). Frederick Karl sees in the story a lost garden vision as the government usurps the ideal of the pastoral "as an integrative force in men's lives," and Ferguson reads the text as implying that the McCallum's Eden will be overcome by the modern world (Karl 1989, 652; Ferguson 1991, 55).

Two contexts for the McCallums' demonstration of their independence are their refusal to participate in federal aid programs and their determination not to be held accountable to draft regulations but to enlist for military duty when they deem their services are needed. As Nordanberg explains it, the McCallums view service in the war as an individual citizen's responsibility, not as an exchange of services (1983, 114–15, 151). The larger theme, according to Miner, "is the weakness of the law in forgetting that men are individuals and as individuals are greater than the law" (1952, 152–53; see also Everett 1969, 170–71). Howell identifies "The Tall Men" as Faulkner's "first deliberate attack on the social policies of the New Deal administration" (1964, 324, 326). Jean Weisgerber finds that in "The Tall Men" Faulkner rejects "economic liberalism of the industrial type," but "he praises nonetheless the patriarchal and agrarian variety" ([1968] 1974, 76). Kerr contends that while Faulkner uses federal aid systems in the story to demonstrate his opposition to governmental bureaucracy, the story presents only one form of assistance and does not include its positive effects (Kerr [1969] 1976, 154; Kerr 1983, 261). Blotner sees Faulkner's point to be the "way politics and war were affecting even the most remote residents of places such as Lafayette County." Faulkner disliked WPA programs that he saw impinging on the independent farmers of the region. The McCallums are in an ever-decreasing number of farmers who retained their independence. Faulkner exposes the "concomitant weakening he saw in the moral fiber of the descendants of once-independent Scotch-Irish settlers who had emigrated to find freedom as well as to make better lives for themselves" (Blotner 1974, 1070–71, 1082; see also Nordanberg 1983, 113).

In Sylvia Cook's reading, "The Tall Men" delivers a direct attack on the political theory that motivated welfare legislation and insists on the rights of the individual over the group. The effect is "to create a naïve and unrealistic dichotomy between the heroic McCallum supermen and the faceless, spineless, dehumanized machine-people created by federal bureaucracies." Cook adds that these characters are hardly the same as other poor whites, "those living on depleted soil without even the possibility of buying the most basic farm tools" (Cook 1976, 40, 59–62).

The McCallums of "The Tall Men" are admired by many—but not all—of the critics who have analyzed the family. Bradford is not critical when he observes that the McCallums "are a family of men; when one of them marries, his wife presents him with a few sons and then quietly dies." The paternalistic order is represented by the rustic dwelling that has housed several generations and the burial plot in which the McCallums rest together (Bradford 1962, 33, 35). (Buddy's wife is buried with her own people.) In fact, Bradford finds, "They are what is rare in Faulkner's fiction, a completely happy family, beholden to no man, asking no one's help or advice" (1962, 32).

The male-only family is not, however, universally respected. Kerr writes that "only in a male chauvinist society could this family be considered admirable and enviable." The reverse oedipal relationship, "strong attachment between father and son or between mother and daughter," exists between Virginius McCallum and his sons in *Sartoris* and later in "The Tall Men" between Buddy and his sons. It interferes with "normal family and individual patterns of life." Despite its stand for independence and individuality, the story reveals this particular family structure to represent a tight conformity. The twin sons leave to enlist, acting, Kerr observes, "like automatons, not as if they had made a significant choice, when they kissed their father and left." With the youngest generation, the twin sons, unmarried and heading for enlistment, the family's future seems questionable (Kerr 1983, 395–96, 141, 147–48; see also Devlin 1971, 83–90).

Very little has been written about the formal aspects of "The Tall Men" beyond some general observations about the narrative perspective and a few prevalent images. The action is presented in a straightforward manner through an omniscient narrator and Marshal Gombault, who corrects the investigator's assumptions (Everett 1969, 170; Blotner 1974, 1070; Bradford 1962, 34).

Morris and Morris find an imagistic purpose for the absence of women. The masculine image of the household provides a means by which Faulkner can contrast the "stoic heroism" of the McCallums "with those weak and effeminate people who are willing to accept government handouts," programs that are further "imagistically associated" with the modern, urban world (Morris and Morris 1989, 52). Similarly, William Brevda notes how in "The Tall Men" and elsewhere Faulkner associates neon lights with an obviously modern, diminished way of life in which the neon has become "artificial sun and moon to a modern world of around-the-clock commercialism and hedonism." In the story, neon operates as the "central image and metaphor" that differentiates the McCallum's life from "'the rest of the world'" (Brevda 1990, 224–25).

Hashiguchi builds on the all-too-obvious metaphoric meaning of *tall* by reaching back to archaic definitions of the word that relate it to one's character. Tracing additional word definitions, Hashiguchi points out that the marshal's use of the word *curious* to describe the McCallums is most accurately understood as not only "extraordinary or eccentric, odd" but also as "exhibiting care or nicety." Word meanings enhance the ambiguous texture of the story. Several words invoke continuity, including the word *Jackson*, as place, past leader, and son, and *Anse* as grandfather and grandson (Hashiguchi 1963, 10, 11 n. 21).

Faulkner scholars have not typically made a place for "The Tall Men" in their critical speculations. For those who have, the consensus is that it is a story that affirms individual independence, particularly as manifested in the model of the McCallums; however, most add that its "lesson" is entirely too obvious. Walter Everett concludes that "Faulkner expounds his sermon to the detriment of his narrative," and Carothers is convinced that the story becomes a wearying "refutation of one cliché by another." The story may indeed anticipate sentiments expressed in Faulkner's Nobel address, but it also confirms the sense that his fiction lost power when his themes were more explicitly expressed (Everett 1969, 171; Carothers 1985, 69). Karl ranks "The Tall Men" among Faulkner's stories as "close to being one of his worst" (1989, 652).

The alternate readings that Devlin and Kerr offer make it difficult to continue to affirm this family's values, and a nagging suspicion arises that the McCallums are finally unable to counter the impingement upon their lives precisely because they are uneducated, isolated, and more stubborn than stalwart. For these reasons, it is disconcerting to close with H. R. Stoneback's observation that "The Tall Men" has been well received in China. Stoneback explains that for the Chinese readers this "neglected Faulkner masterpiece" represents the essentials of Faulkner's vision; his affirmation of pride, honor, discipline, patriotism, and history are qualities important to the Chinese (1984, 241–42).

## Works Cited

Blotner, Joseph. 1974. *Faulkner: A Biography*. 2 vols. New York: Random House.

———. 1984. *Faulkner: A Biography*. 1 vol. New York: Random House.

Bradford, M. E. 1962. "Faulkner's 'Tall Men.'" *South Atlantic Quarterly* 61:29–39.

Brevda, William. 1990. "Neon Light in August: Electric Signs in Faulkner's Fiction." In *Faulkner and Popular Culture: Faulkner and Yoknapatawpha, 1988*. Ed. Doreen Fowler and Ann J. Abadie. Jackson: University Press of Mississippi, 214–241.

Brodsky, Louis Daniel. 1990. *William Faulkner, Life Glimpses*. Austin: University of Texas Press.

Carothers, James B. 1985. *William Faulkner's Short Stories*. Ann Arbor, MI: UMI Research Press.

Cook, Sylvia Jenkins. 1976. *From Tobacco Road to Route 66: The Southern Poor White in Fiction*. Chapel Hill: University of North Carolina Press.

Devlin, Albert J. 1971. "*Sartoris*: Rereading the MacCallum Episode." *Twentieth Century Literature* 17:83–90.

Dowling, David. 1989. *William Faulkner*. New York: St. Martin's.

Everett, Walter K. 1969. *Faulkner's Art and Character*. Woodbury, NY: Barron's Educational Series.

Faulkner, William. 1941. "The Tall Men." *Saturday Evening Post* 213 (31 May):14–15, 95, 96, 98–99.

———. 1950. *Collected Stories of William Faulkner*. New York: Random House.

———. 1977. *Selected Letters of William Faulkner*. Ed. Joseph Blotner. New York: Random House.

———. 1987. *William Faulkner Manuscripts 24: Short Stories*. Ed. Joseph Blotner. New York: Garland.

Ferguson, James. 1991. *Faulkner's Short Fiction*. Knoxville: University of Tennessee Press.

Grimwood, Michael. 1987. *Heart in Conflict: Faulkner's Struggles with Vocation*. Athens: University of Georgia Press.

Hashiguchi, Yasuo. 1963. "The 'Tall' in William Faulkner's 'The Tall Men.'" *Kyushu American Literature* 6:8–12.

Holmes, Edward M. 1966. *Faulkner's Twice-Told Tales: His Re-Use of His Material*. The Hague: Mouton.

Howell, Elmo. 1962. "William Faulkner and the Plain People of Yoknapatawpha County." *Journal of Mississippi History* 24:73–87.

———. 1964. "William Faulkner and the New Deal." *Midwest Quarterly* 5:323–32.

Karl, Frederick R. 1989. *William Faulkner: American Writer*. New York: Weidenfeld and Nicolson.

Kerr, Elizabeth M. [1969] 1976. *Yoknapatawpha: Faulkner's "Little Postage Stamp of Native Soil."* New York: Fordham University Press.

———. 1983. *William Faulkner's Yoknapatawpha: "A Kind of Keystone in the Universe."* New York: Fordham University Press.

Kinney, Arthur F. 1980. "Faulkner's Narrative Poetics and *Collected Stories.*" *Faulkner Studies* 1:58–79.

McHaney, Thomas L. 1975. *William Faulkner's* The Wild Palms: *A Study*. Jackson: University Press of Mississippi.

Millgate, Michael. [1966] 1989. *The Achievement of William Faulkner*. New York: Random House. Reprint. Athens: University of Georgia Press. Brown Thrasher Books.

Miner, Ward L. 1952. *The World of William Faulkner*. Durham, NC: Duke University Press.

Morris, Wesley, and Barbara Alverson Morris. 1989. *Reading Faulkner*. Madison: University of Wisconsin Press.

Nordanberg, Thomas. 1983. *Cataclysm as Catalyst: The Theme of War in William Faulkner's Fiction*. Acta Universitatis Upsaliensis. Studia Anglistica Upsaliensia #49. Stockholm: Almquist & Wiksell.

Reed, Joseph W., Jr. 1973. *Faulkner's Narrative*. New Haven: Yale University Press.

Skei, Hans H. 1981. *William Faulkner: The Short Story Career*. Oslo, Norway: Universitetsforlaget.

———. 1985. *William Faulkner: The Novelist as Short Story Writer*. *Oslo, Norway: Universitetsforlaget*.

———. 1987. "William Faulkner's Late Career: Repetition, Variation, Renewal." In *Faulkner: After the Nobel Prize*. Ed. Michel Gresset and Kenzaburo Ohashi. Kyoto: Yamaguchi, 247–59.

———. 1992. "Beyond Genre? Existential Experience in Faulkner's Short Fiction." In *Faulkner and the Short Story: Faulkner and Yoknapatawpha*, 1990. Ed. Evans Harrington and Ann J. Abadie. Jackson: University Press of Mississippi, 62–77.

Stoneback, H. R. 1984. "The Hound and the Antelope: Faulkner in China." *In Faulkner: International Perspectives: Faulkner and Yoknapatawpha*, 1982. Ed. Doreen Fowler and Ann J. Abadie. Jackson: University Press of Mississippi, 236–56.

Vickery, Olga W. [1959] 1964. *The Novels of William Faulkner*. Baton Rouge: Louisiana State University Press.

Volpe, Edmond L. [1964] 1989. *A Reader's Guide to William Faulkner*. New York: Noonday. Reprint. New York: Octagon Books.

Weisgerber, Jean. [1968] 1974. *Faulkner and Dostoevsky: Influence and Confluence*. Trans. Dean McWilliams. Athens: Ohio University Press.

West, Ray B., Jr. 1952. *The Short Story in America 1900–1950*. Chicago: Regnery.

# A Bear Hunt

## Publication History

"A Bear Hunt" first appeared in the February 10, 1934, issue of the *Saturday Evening Post* with illustrations by George Brehm; it was one of four Faulkner stories that appeared in magazines that month. The *Post*'s acceptance of this comic tale came swiftly. In a letter that Joseph Blotner dates from autumn 1933, Faulkner writes his agent, Morton Goldman, that he mailed the story directly to the *Post* in order to expedite matters. He says that he would like $1,000 for the story, but in a follow-up letter, probably from December 1933, he expresses his pleasure in receiving $900 and confesses that the amount is $200 more than he expected (*SL* 76; see also Blotner 1974, 822–25 and Skei 1981, 82).

Faulkner did not include "A Bear Hunt" in the *Doctor Martino* collection (1934) because he did not believe it was suitable (*SL* 76). The story was not used again until it appeared in *Collected Stories* (1950) and *Big Woods* (1955), each time with revisions (see Skei 1981, 82).

## Circumstances of Composition, Sources, and Influences

Blotner confidently dates the composition of this story between Thanksgiving and Christmas of 1933 based not only on correspondence between Faulkner and Goldman, but also on a Thanksgiving hunting trip experience that Faulkner incorporated into the tale (1974, 822–23; see also Skei 1981, 79, 129 n. 7).

Revisions in the three published versions of "A Bear Hunt" reflect a range of intentions from avoiding legal prosecution to maintaining thematic unity. When Faulkner was preparing the *Collected Stories*, he asked for a copy of the story in order to make "a correction of locale" (*SL* 274), but alterations of names rather than changes in locale are the most important differences among the three published versions of the story. The *Post* version identifies the sewing machine agent as V. K. Suratt. In *Collected Stories* and *Big Woods* his name is changed to the more familiar V. K. Ratliff. Blotner explains that this change had nothing to do with Faulkner's growing conception of Yoknapatawpha. Suratt had appeared in several stories and novels, but by the time Faulkner was working on *The Hamlet*, Hugh Miller Suratt of Lafayette County threatened to sue if the character Suratt appeared again (1974, 1010). The name Ratliff provided a satisfactory revision for subsequent appearances because it, too, was a local name (1974, 1010). Another name change, that of the hiccuping Lucius from *Collected Stories* to *Big Woods*, did relate to the growing complexity of Yoknapatawpha relationships. In 1934 and 1950, Lucius was a Provine. In 1955, he became a Hogganbeck, son of Boon. Lucius Hogganbeck is a friend and co-conspirator of two Provine brothers in the *Big Woods* revision. A third name change is less clear in purpose, though perhaps it was a movement closer to the living model. Originally, the black man who enjoys a long-awaited revenge on Lucius is Old Man Bush. In *Collected Stories* and *Big Woods* he is Old Man Ash. Blotner believes the real-life model is Uncle Ad, who used to cook at General Stone's hunting camp. In fact, as they relate the details of the story, both Blotner and Michael Grimwood use the name *Ad* rather than either *Bush* or *Ash* (Blotner 1974, 823; Grimwood 1987, 249–50).

Once Faulkner extracted the story from the *Post*, he replaced the sanitized expletive *son* with *sonabitch (Post* 74, 76; *CS* 72, 77).

The *Big Woods* text adds a genealogical observation that helps to establish Lucius Hogganbeck's appropriateness in the tale. Unable or unwilling to support his family, Lucius is supported by Major de Spain, son of the original Major de Spain, who supported Boon Hogganbeck (*BW* 146; Carothers 1985, 100). A paragraph about the members of the hunting club is also included. Uncle Ike is the only one of the previous generation of hunters present during the time of Lucius's hiccups and Ash's revenge (*BW* 145).

Source studies for "A Bear Hunt" trace more biographical than historical influences in the tale. In his early comparison of the settlement of Mississippi and Faulkner's creation of Yoknapatawpha, Ward Miner argues that Faulkner increases the importance of the Indians. As an example, Miner cites the extension of Indian inhabitants in the fictional region to the time of "A Bear Hunt," around 1900 according to his estimation. In the census records for Lafayette County for 1860 and after, no Indians were listed (Miner 1952, 91). The presence of the Indian mound in the story is supported by the existence of several around Oxford (Dabney 1974, 19). The omnipresence of the mounds in the minds of the characters, however, is an embellishment. Calvin S. Brown, an Oxford resident, shared with Lewis Dabney the following observation: "The Civil War was very much alive in local oral tradition, but not the Chickasaws. Our knowledge of them was essentially like our knowledge of the Incas and the Pharaohs, though perhaps a bit more real because of the arrowhead." Faulkner makes the link between the two pasts, Indians and Civil War, explicit in "A Bear Hunt" (1974, 20–21). Grimwood links a later depiction of the mounds to Faulkner's consciousness of time and of man's monuments, including his own fictional masterpieces, that withstand time's passing (1987, 262–63).

Personal hunting experiences enhance and perhaps add credibility to the details of the story. Thomas McHaney makes available a Ripley, Mississippi, man's recollection of his first deer hunt, a memoir that validates the world portrayed in Faulkner's fictional hunts (1970, 315–20). In addition to Faulkner's modeling Old Man Ash after Uncle Ad, Blotner points out that here, as in many of the hunting tales, the author has patterned Major de Spain's camp on the hunting camp about thirty miles west of Oxford that belonged to James Stone and at which Faulkner was a familiar guest. Even more important for the particular situation on which the comedy of this story turns was the prolonged episode of hiccups Faulkner experienced during his Thanksgiving 1933 trip to the camp. As Blotner recounts the events, the hiccups lasted so long that his friends took him into a nearby town, Batesville, for help. The hiccups ruined Faulkner's hunting trip but gave him material for the story he wrote almost immediately afterward (Blotner 1974, 822).

The literary inheritance of "A Bear Hunt" has received little attention. Joseph Reed questions whether Faulkner was acquainted with the tradition of captivity narratives but suggests that "A Bear Hunt" parallels them "albeit involving latter-day Indians" (1973, 63 n. 3). By general consensus, the story is in the tradition of Southwestern humor. Faulkner's real bout of hiccups is transformed into a tall tale in which Ratliff enjoys the engaged attention of a sympathetic audience.

## Relationship to Other Faulkner Stories

Critics of the tales frequently note the shared setting of "A Bear Hunt" and "Lion." "A Bear Hunt" was the first hunting tale, and it captured the first portrait of the "bottomland" (Early 1972, 5). Faulkner hoped to sell "Lion" based on his quick success in placing "A Bear Hunt" (*SL* 90; Blotner 1974, 885). Walter Taylor believes that "A Bear Hunt," like "Lion," was "brought into *Go Down, Moses*" (1983, 220 n. 8). James Carothers argues to the contrary that "A Bear Hunt" should not be understood as a source for *Go Down, Moses*. The stories that were revised for *Go Down, Moses*, including "Lion," were not incorporated into *Collected Stories* (Carothers 1985, 89). Although "A Bear Hunt" and "The Bear" are very different stories, some links exist between them. John Pikoulis compares the mystery of the Indian mounds described in "A Bear Hunt" to the power invested in Ben (1982, 208). Frederick Karl, on the other hand, sees "A Bear Hunt" as "a trying out for the later 'The Bear.'" Although it is clear that they share common settings and some common characters, Karl exaggerates the bond between the stories here and elsewhere, as when he equates "A Bear Hunt" and "The Bear" as Faulkner's "most famous hunting pieces" (Karl 1989, 503, 160). Richard Moreland describes both stories as criticizing the hunter myth of the regenerative powers of violence (1990, 177 n. 9).

Character repetitions in "A Bear Hunt" form a network of associations with other stories. Arthur Kinney includes "A Bear Hunt" among those works that contain Compsons (1982, 10; see also Kinney 1989, 93). Although Compsons can only be confirmed by name in the *Big Woods* version, two other important family associations, McCaslin and de Spain, are identified in all versions (see Holmes 1966, 101–02). This story introduces Ike McCaslin for the first time; he appears here as one of the older hunters. Given the circumstances for changing Suratt to Ratliff, the sewing machine agent serves as another character link when either Suratt or Ratliff appears. Gary Stonum comments that in this early appearance, Ratliff descends more directly from the tradition of Southwestern humor (1979, 175). Carothers believes that "the practical-joking Ratliff of 'A Bear Hunt' is a much different character from the mild, affable salesman of *The Hamlet*" (1985, 47). When Lucius Provine becomes Lucius Hogganbeck, the story becomes related to those tales that establish a Hogganbeck line including "A Courtship," "Lion," *Go Down, Moses*, and *The Reivers*. It is significant that this change heightens the irony of Lucius Hogganbeck's terror at the Indians' prank. He is after all part Indian himself. His great-grandmother was a Chickasaw, and his great-grandfather David

Hogganbeck was friend to Herman Basket, a likely ancestor to the moonshiner John Basket. Obviously, the presence of Indians, especially John Basket, links "A Bear Hunt" to the Indian stories, particularly "Red Leaves," "A Justice," and "A Courtship," stories in which either Three Basket or Herman Basket appears.

Samway compares Ash to Lucas Beauchamp in *Intruder in the Dust*. Each man exhibits a strong sense of identity and confidence that "will sustain him in a crisis," and both Ash and Lucas are talking about money at the conclusions of the respective texts. "Centaur in Brass" involves two other black characters, Tom-Tom and Turl, in money schemes, but in this case after overcoming their differences they work together to thwart Flem Snopes's money-making scheme (Samway 1980, 238–39). Ferguson makes similar observations, grouping Ash with various other black characters who outwit their white antagonists. In addition to Ash, Lucas in *Go Down, Moses*, Tom-Tom, and Turl, Ferguson cites Ringo from *The Unvanquished* as more active than Bayard in helping Granny Millard conspire against Union troops (1991, 61, 75, 78).

"A Bear Hunt" opens with an unnamed narrator establishing the context of Ratliff's tale. Reed compares the presence of the unnamed narrator to the narrative technique employed in "Hair." He calls both of these "gossip" stories in which an "our town" consciousness is developed. In "A Bear Hunt" the unnamed narrator "gently leads us as outlanders into the story." By doing so, Faulkner establishes the familiarity that allows Ratliff's "assumption that his hearers have a common background of information." Although the end results vary, Reed compares the development of camaraderie in "A Bear Hunt," "Hair," and *Light in August*. Reed contrasts the purpose of the unnamed narrator's reminiscence in this story, "historical exposition," with the more complex uses of the narrator's reminiscence in "A Justice" and "That Evening Sun" (1973, 24–26, 34, 135).

Several critics have tried to identify the unnamed narrator in "A Bear Hunt." Blotner likens him to the narrator of "A Rose for Emily" (1974, Notes 116), but most who seek to identify the speaker find closer associations with Quentin Compson. Everett made the early observation that in the material added to *Big Woods*, the frame narrator identifies himself as General Compson's grandson (1969, 133). John Hunt argues that Quentin narrates "A Bear Hunt" only in the *Big Woods* version (1982, 370). Hunt finds it curious that Faulkner revives Quentin this late, considering that after *Absalom, Absalom!* Faulkner retired Quentin as a narrator (1982, 375). Estella Schoenberg believes that although Quentin is not named as narrator in earlier versions, "details of one kind or another point to his identity." The speaker is an adult recalling an adolescent experience; he describes himself as a member of a "literate, town-bred family." Schoenberg finds the most compelling argument for Quentin as narrator in the speaker's attitudes that "echo or duplicate the attitude of Quentin as it has been established in other stories." She suggests that even though the internal story was written after the hunting trip of Thanksgiving 1933, the frame story "was not necessarily invented at the same time" (Schoenberg 1977, 18, 20; *CS* 63, 65). Skei finds the narrator of the introductory section "the chief interest" of the story (1985, 221). He, like Schoenberg, believes there is reasonable evidence to suggest that Quentin is the frame narrator in the versions that precede the *Big Woods* text (1985, 317 n. 13; see also Ragan 1987, 8).

Carothers's study of the trickster character distinguishes early tales with simple tricks from later tales that require "more sophisticated development and comic reversals," as when the trickster is tricked (1984, 225). "A Bear Hunt" falls quite comfortably into this second group. Ratliff's trick is turned on him when Ash adds to the plot (Carothers 1984, 225–26).

Even with the name changes that occur, Dorothy Tuck describes the published versions of "A Bear Hunt" as "essentially the same" (1964, 161). Nevertheless, the internal unity of *Collected Stories* and *Big Woods* expands the interpretive context possible for "A Bear Hunt." Michael Millgate observes the contrasting mood "A Bear Hunt" provides in its placement in *Collected Stories* between "The Tall Men" and "Two Soldiers," but he also adds that the protagonists Ratliff and Provine have backgrounds similar to those of the other characters in this section, "The Country" ([1966] 1989, 271; see also Ferguson 158). Kinney finds that "A Bear Hunt" enriches the context of "Two Soldiers" and "Shall Not Perish," two more somber stories that follow the comic tale. According to Kinney, the "exploitation of men for the restoration of one's pride or for a good laugh . . . turns to something more earnest and deadly" in the subsequent stories (1980, 65). Associations in *Big Woods* also enhance the meaning of the tale. The intensity of a black man's revenge, harbored for nearly twenty years, is increased by the juxtaposition of the hunting camp story with the steamboat episode of "A Justice."

Despite the numerous associations of "A Bear Hunt" with Faulkner's other stories, it is not necessary to read this story in the larger Yoknapatawpha context. As Skei has noted, "A Bear Hunt" is one of the "more autonomous" tales of the county (1985, 212–13).

## Interpretation and Criticism

Olga Vickery observes that hunting stories are usually treated seriously and places "A Bear Hunt" "on the periphery"; it degenerates, she claims, to the level of a "private joke" (1964, 303–04). Much more recently, Ferguson has described the story as "little more than a rather elaborate but crude joke" (1991, 39). Others, however, have found that the story suggests a broader dimension by which to interpret Ash's trick. Duane Gage believes that Faulkner consistently portrayed Indians as unjustly treated in order "to accentuate the relationships between the races in the South" (1974, 33). This attitude is clearly reflected in Faulkner's concern with the artist's renderings for *Big Woods*. When corresponding with editor Saxe Commins, Faulkner made a lengthy suggestion for illustrator Edward Shenton regarding the headpiece to "A Bear Hunt." He expressed his idea for the illustration as follows: "What about the Indians? . . . It could be something symbolical and allegorical . . . : the wilderness, the Indian of the now, dispossessed of heritage, and in the back ground [*sic*] the shadowy figure of what he once was, the wild man, the king? Say enough of the man to show him driving the handles of a plow maybe, a battered hat on his long hair, with maybe a single shabby wild flower or sprig of greenery in one of the holes in it, in the back ground the shadowy ancestor with a war club and his head-dress a regal affair of plumes as the Muskoghean wore?'" (*SL* 377). Shenton's drawing closely reflects Faulkner's suggestions.

Blotner notes that in this story several strains of the Yoknapatawpha population are pictured: Indians, blacks, and whites (1974, 823). When the three races are brought together in a tale, critics typically find the arrangement a rich source for discussion. Charles Nilon sees the black's character revealed as the story develops in "A Bear Hunt" (1965, 33). By the end of the story, Ash loses his image as one of the accoutrements of the hunting camp and becomes a man whose dignity has been injured and eventually restored at least partially. Like "Was" and "Centaur in Brass," this comic version of a chase is compounded with elements of the detective story. Further, evasion becomes a means of survival for the black character (1965, 47).

In a later study, Nilon adds that Faulkner combines violence and humor to create a "comic portrayal of black movement." Pictures of the black character initially "depend upon the mythology of the stereotype" but gradually move toward a revelation of the humanity of the individual. In "A Bear Hunt" Ash is portrayed through violence and humor to break the stereotype and reveal the man (Nilon 1981, 239–41). Everett observes that Ratliff is outspoken in his view of the injustices done to the Indians by whites (1969, 133). Gage interprets Ash's action as a serious, "subtle comment on race relations, with the Indians becoming an instrument for the black man's revenge" (1974, 31). In Skei's study of the short stories, he discusses the manner in which the "bargains, deceits and lies" of Faulkner's tall tales force the humor "to give way to seriousness when the bargains come to involve people and destinies" (1985, 212–13).

In the stories from 1933 to 1941, protagonists suffer an injustice that they either have carried with them over time or that they discover suddenly. In "A Bear Hunt" the injustice portrayed is racial (1985, 213). Skei explains further,

"Behind the farcical plot of 'A Bear Hunt' lies the problem of human interrelations and interdependence, and once more the failure to understand and communicate is demonstrated" (1985, 220).

John Longley interprets "A Bear Hunt" as a comedy of manners that "by definition will reflect the manners and mores of a given time and place." He contends that although Provine, Ratliff, and Ash do not appear to be suitable for "the delicate criteria of the comedy of manners," Ratliff's trickery is turned on him; Provine's gluttony, meanness, and cultural ignorance are punished; and Ash's old wrong is redressed. Longley concludes that Ash's confession that he acts in "memory of a celluloid collar" protects the comic atmosphere from "sentimental idealism" ([1957] 1963, 115–20). Skei concurs with Longley's judgment that "A Bear Hunt" can be interpreted as a social comedy (1985, 220). He adds that in the pressure to conform to the role of breadwinner, men are limited in much the same way females are restricted by rigid roles (1985, 220).

David Ragan discusses "A Bear Hunt" specifically within the context of *Big Woods*. In this context, the outer narrative emphasizes that the world Quentin Compson describes "is vastly different" from that of Isaac in the preceding stories and from that of the narrator of "Race at Morning," which comes later in the collection (1983, 312). Given the consistency of Ratliff's narrative, Ragan's comments about the nature of the hunt and hunters apply to the various versions of the text. The hunters are portrayed as rather self-absorbed and unsympathetic to Lucius's discomfort; camaraderie among them is lacking. Ragan points out that comparisons of people to machines emphasize "the modern economic forces which contribute to the disappearance of the wilderness and the resulting dehumanization of man" (1983, 312). Frederick Karl similarly views the comedy of "A Bear Hunt" as influenced in the introduction by an atmosphere of death (1989, 508). He cites "decline" as characteristic of the tale, especially as reflected in Lucius Provine and the members of the hunting camp. Karl concludes, "While the inner tale is mildly amusing, what sticks is the makeup of the camp and the figures of death living on memory" (1989, 509).

Carothers describes the narration in "A Bear Hunt" as "a hybrid first- and third-person" (1985, 20). The introductory narrator moves from third- to first-person narration as he moves toward his own recollection of a night on the Indian mound. Once Ratliff takes over, there is no return to this other narrator to add closure to the opening frame narration. Walter Everett sees the conclusion as sufficiently unifying the tale because the apparent digression about Provine's wildness suddenly has a point (1969, 133).

Stephen Ross describes Ratliff's voice in "A Bear Hunt" as *mimetic*, "voice imitative of talk." Ratliff tells the story to an implied audience. "Vocalization" of the story is strong because Ratliff establishes time and place of telling and employs present tense and a colloquial manner; thus, readers become listeners. "A Bear Hunt" provides diverse examples of characters' speech representing various socioeconomic groups—in this case, black, country white, and town colloquial. Differentiation among speakers seeks to establish the relative positions of the speakers in the text rather than to reflect the "region's sociolinguistic configurations." Furthermore, transcription by narrators of others' speech "can be less sophisticated than the discourse that contains it, but not more." In "A Bear Hunt," the town narrator introduces Ratliff and can mimic Ratliff's speech, but Ratliff does not tell this story or other stories in the discourse of a town narrator (Ross 1989, 15, 75–76, 101–03, 109–10, 256 n. 27)

The humor in "A Bear Hunt" includes the slapstick beating Ratliff receives and the more subtle humor of the revenge plot (Everett 1969, 133). Skei cautions that "to over-emphasize the serious elements" would "be a misinterpretation in itself" (1985, 222). Perhaps just for that reason, this tale does not share the stature of other stories set at the hunting camp.

## Works Cited

Blotner, Joseph. 1974. *Faulkner: A Biography*. 2 vols. New York: Random House.

Carothers, James B. 1984. "Faulkner's Short Stories: 'And Now What's to Do.'" In *New Directions in Faulkner Studies: Faulkner and Yoknapatawpha, 1983*. Ed. Doreen Fowler and Ann J. Abadie. Jackson: University Press of Mississippi, 202–27.

———. 1985. *William Faulkner's Short Stories*. Ann Arbor, MI: UMI Research Press.

Dabney, Lewis M. 1974. *The Indians of Yoknapatawpha: A Study in Literature and History*. Baton Rouge: Louisiana State University Press.

Early, James. 1972. *The Making of* Go Down, Moses. Dallas: Southern Methodist University Press.

Everett, Walter K. 1969. *Faulkner's Art and Character*. Woodbury, NY: Barron's Educational Series.

Faulkner, William. 1934. "A Bear Hunt." *Saturday Evening Post* 206 (10 February): 8–9, 74, 76.

———. 1950. *Collected Stories of William Faulkner*. New York: Random House.

———. 1955. *Big Woods*. New York: Random House.

———. 1977. *Selected Letters of William Faulkner*. Ed. Joseph Blotner. New York: Random House.

Ferguson, James. 1991. *Faulkner's Short Fiction*. Knoxville: University of Tennessee Press.

Gage, Duane. 1974. "William Faulkner's Indians." *American Indian Quarterly* 1:27–33.

Grimwood, Michael. 1987. *Heart in Conflict: Faulkner's Struggles with Vocation*. Athens: University of Georgia Press.

Holmes, Edward M. 1966. *Faulkner's Twice-Told Tales: His Re-Use of His Material*. The Hague: Mouton.

Hunt, John W. 1982. "The Disappearance of Quentin Compson." In *Critical Essays on William Faulkner: The Compson Family*. Ed. Arthur F. Kinney. Boston: G. K. Hall, 366–80.

Karl, Frederick R. 1989. *William Faulkner: American Writer*. New York: Weidenfeld and Nicolson.

Kinney, Arthur F. 1980. "Faulkner's Narrative Poetics and *Collected Stories.*" *Faulkner Studies* 1:58–79.

———. 1982. Introduction. In *Critical Essays on William Faulkner: The Compson Family*. Ed. Arthur F. Kinney. Boston: G. K. Hall, 1–41.

———. 1989. "The Family-Centered Nature of Faulkner's World." *College Literature* 16:83–101.

Longley, John Lewis, Jr. [1957] 1963. *The Tragic Mask: A Study of Faulkner's Heroes*. Chapel Hill: University of North Carolina Press.

McHaney, Thomas L. 1970. "A Deer Hunt in the Faulkner Country." *Mississippi Quarterly* 23:315–20.

Millgate, Michael. [1966] 1989. *The Achievement of William Faulkner*. New York: Random House. Reprint. Athens: University of Georgia Press. Brown Thrasher Books.

Miner, Ward L. 1952. *The World of William Faulkner*. Durham, NC: Duke University Press.

Moreland, Richard C. 1990. *Faulkner and Modernism: Rereading and Rewriting*. Madison: University of Wisconsin Press.

Nilon, Charles H. 1965. *Faulkner and the Negro*. New York: Citadel.

———. 1981. "Blacks in Motion." In "A Cosmos of My Own": *Faulkner and Yoknapatawpha* 1980. Ed. Doreen Fowler and Ann J. Abadie. Jackson: University Press of Mississippi, 227–51.

Pikoulis, John. 1982. *The Art of William Faulkner*. Totowa, NJ: Barnes & Noble.

Ragan, David Paul. 1983. "'Belonging to the Business of Mankind': The Achievement of Faulkner's Big Woods." *Mississippi Quarterly* 36:301–17.

———. 1987. *William Faulkner's Absalom, Absalom!: A Critical Study*. Ann Arbor, MI: UMI Research Press.

Reed, Joseph W., Jr. 1973. *Faulkner's Narrative*. New Haven: Yale University Press.

Ross, Stephen M. 1989. *Fiction's Inexhaustible Voice: Speech and Writing in Faulkner*. Athens: University of Georgia Press.

Samway, Patrick H., S.J. 1980. *Faulkner's Intruder in the Dust: A Critical Study of the Typescripts.* Troy, NY: Whitston.

Schoenberg, Estella. 1977. *Old Tales and Talking: Quentin Compson in William Faulkner's Absalom, Absalom! and Related Works.* Jackson: University Press of Mississippi.

Skei, Hans H. 1981. *William Faulkner: The Short Story Career.* Oslo, Norway: Universitetsforlaget.

———. 1985. *William Faulkner: The Novelist as Short Story Writer.* Oslo, Norway: Universitetsforlaget.

Stonum, Gary Lee. 1979. *Faulkner's Career: An Internal Literary History.* Ithaca, NY: Cornell University Press.

Taylor, Walter. 1983. *Faulkner's Search for a South.* Urbana: University of Illinois Press.

Tuck, Dorothy. 1964. *Crowell's Handbook of Faulkner.* New York: Thomas Y. Crowell.

Vickery, Olga W. [1959] 1964. *The Novels of William Faulkner.* Baton Rouge: Louisiana State University Press.

# Two Soldiers

## Publication History

"Two Soldiers" was an immediate and popular success in the 1940s. It first appeared in the March 28, 1942, issue of the *Saturday Evening Post*. Faulkner's agent, Harold Ober, had received the story only two months earlier, on January 30, 1942, and the *Post* made a quick purchase of it on February 5, 1942, for $1,000. The Columbia Broadcasting System paid Faulkner a modest $25 for permission to produce "Two Soldiers" as its first story for television; however, the broadcast was not done as scheduled because of machine failure. In 1945, Whit Burnett purchased "Two Soldiers" for a high school text for $50, a better price than his original offer of $25. Faulkner agreed to the deletion of the words *hell* and *nigger* from the text provided every alteration was marked by an asterisk to indicate that the passage had been changed. Commenting to Ober on this arrangement, Faulkner said, "This may be good for the children in fact; it will be teaching them at an early and tender age to be ever on guard to protect and shield their elders and teachers from certain of the simple facts of life." When the story appeared in Burnett's anthology, *Time to Be Young*, no alterations were made. In 1946 Cagney Productions, a film studio, purchased the story through agent John McCormick for $3,750. "Two Soldiers" was placed fifth in "The Country" section of *Collected Stories* (1950) (Blotner 1974, 1097–98, 1169, 1181, 1219; Skei 1981, 100; *SL* 191–92).

## Circumstances of Composition, Sources, Influences

"Two Soldiers" was the second of seven stories Ober received from Faulkner between January and July 1942, part of a six-month effort to turn stories into income (Skei 1981, 100–01). When Faulkner included the story in *Collected Stories*, he made no changes in the text.

Critics have expressed scant interest in examining biographical associations in the story; perhaps there is little evidence that they exist. A geographic association was found by only one critic, Elizabeth Kerr, who noted that references in "Two Soldiers" to the Sardis Reservoir ("that Government reservoy up at Oxford") help to locate Oxford as northwest of the fictional Jefferson (1976, 36 n. 16; *CS* 81).

## Relationship to Other Faulkner Works

The majority of responses that "Two Soldiers" generates are relational in their orientation. Olga Vickery, for example, classifies "Two Soldiers" as adjunctive because it functions to "add more information about certain characters, situations, or the history of Yoknapatawpha County" ([1959] 1964, 300).

"Two Soldiers" shares the Grier family with "Shingles for the Lord" and "Shall Not Perish." Bradford includes the Griers and the other families in the Grier stories in his list of yeoman farmers whom, Bradford believes, Faulkner always treats positively. Other yeomen include Byron Bunch in *Light in August*, the convict in *The Wild Palms*, and the MacCallums (spelled McCallums in "The Tall Men") in *Sartoris*. The Griers have been able to support themselves on their land because of their good stewardship. Pete Grier's motivation to enlist reflects neither a discontent with home nor a dream of gaining glory in war, because for him land literally represents country and when any parcel is attacked, it must be defended (Bradford 1965, 94–96; see also McHaney 1975, 154).

Kerr sees the Grier family as displaying a much broader set of rural characterizations. She contends that the type represented by the Griers runs the gamut from industrious to lazy, landowners and landless. Res Grier, as portrayed in "Shingles for the Lord" and "Two Soldiers," and Anse Bundren in *As I Lay Dying* represent landowners who fail to use land efficiently. Grier is "more energetic than Anse Bundren, but even more hapless." But both Grier and Bundren possess education and family backgrounds of both men are "superior" to those of either Mink or Ab Snopes (Kerr [1969] 1976, 152–53).

Another character who appears in "Two Soldiers" and extensively throughout Faulkner's fiction is the young, innocent male. Lewis Leary finds the "bravery or honesty or loyalty of boys" to be a recurrent preoccupation in stories such as "Two Soldiers," "Barn Burning," and "Mountain Victory" (1973, 136–37).

Characters on a journey constitute a general pattern with wide variations in Faulkner's fiction. The "naïve traveler" in "Two Soldiers" resembles Lena Grove and the Snopeses Virgil and Fonzo (Blotner 1974, Notes 151). James Carothers identifies the motif of the "perilous journey" in the numerous trips to Memphis made by a variety of Faulkner's characters. The journey typically begins for a limited, specialized purpose but includes unanticipated "discoveries" on the road or, in many cases, after the character's arrival in Memphis. "Two Soldiers," "There Was a Queen," *Sartoris/Flags in the Dust*, and *The Reivers* are some of the texts that exhibit this pattern (Carothers 1981, 116–18; see also Ferguson 1991, 62).

Related to the Grier child's journey in "Two Soldiers" is another recurring character trait Ferguson identifies in Faulkner's fiction: monomania. Typically, the obsessed character fails; but in comic or sentimental contexts, he or she may find qualified success, as in "Thrift," "My Grandmother Millard and General Bedford Forrest and the Battle of Harrykin Creek," "Go Down, Moses," "Dull Tale," and "Two Soldiers." In this last instance, the narrator in "Two Soldiers" finds Pete, but the narrator must return home (1991, 79–80).

Minor character notes mention that Mrs. Habersham in "Two Soldiers" also appears in *Intruder in the Dust*, and one line suggests the incident of the "Apache Snopes" children in *The Town* (Blotner 1974, Notes 151–52).

Critics identify strong thematic links between "Two Soldiers" and other Faulkner texts, both fictional and nonfictional. Patriotism dominates as a thematic concern here, but critics differ in their judgments of how well Faulkner presents the issue. "Two Soldiers" is especially close to "Shall Not Perish" because the latter story sets out the consequences of the choice Pete makes in "Two Soldiers." According to Elmo Howell, the patriotism of the two stories comes from the characters' being "schooled in the tradition of loyalty" within a tightly knit family. Res Grier, like his wife, is proud of Pete's decision even though he suggests that the young man should wait. Howell adds that Faulkner repudiates this attitude in *A Fable* (1966, 89–92). Floyd Watkins compares the "superficially and sentimentally patriotic" tone of Ike McCaslin in "Delta Autumn" to the tone of "Two Soldiers" and "Shall Not Perish," and Joseph Blotner notes a likeness between the focus "on the patriotism of the county's hill people" in "Two Soldiers" and "The Tall Men" (Watkins 1971, 252; Blotner 1974, 1097). In a later comment, Blotner remarks that "Two

Soldiers" and "Shall Not Perish" take a stand against further warfare (1976, 15). Ferguson criticizes "Two Soldiers" and "Shall Not Perish" for their "saccharine inanities," their "didactic and sententious" tone, and their "altogether offensive jingoism" (1991, 42).

Hans Skei, like Blotner, groups "Two Soldiers," "Shall Not Perish," and "The Tall Men" together "as strongly patriotic and rather sentimental reactions to the new war," World War II. The stories demonstrate Faulkner's belief "in America and in America's strength," and "Two Soldiers" and "Shall Not Perish" bring the consequences of the war into lives of the people of Frenchman's Bend (Skei 1985, 265, 267). Skei comments elsewhere that these late stories of war—"Two Soldiers" and "Shall Not Perish"—contrast "mood, setting, narrative technique, attitude (patriotism), and vision of what war is like" with the World War I stories such as those collected in *These 13* and "Turnabout" (Skei 1977, 17). Thomas Nordanberg contends that although they may reflect a need to capture the sentiments of more lucrative magazines, the three World War II stories also indicate a "radically changed approach to the theme of war" consistent with Faulkner's own feelings (1983, 119–20, 151–52; see also Carothers 1987, 67–74).

Michael Millgate finds another resemblance between "Two Soldiers" and "The Tall Men," specifically in the instructions Pete's mother gives him as he leaves in the first story, and Buddy McCallum's advice to his sons in "The Tall Men." Both parents stress the "necessity for a proper dignity and pride in one's name and for a right pattern of behaviour in relation to the superior authority of the State" (Millgate [1966] 1989, 271). According to Nordanberg, Pap Grier resembles the draft investigator in "The Tall Men": both consider participation in the war effort to be a legal obligation rather than the outgrowth of personal conviction (1983, 116).

Reed expands the group of stories about patriotism in his discussion of the way regionalism progresses toward nationalism in Faulkner's fiction, noting the overt nationalism in such stories as "Two Soldiers" and "Shall Not Perish" as well as in *The Hamlet*, *The Town*, and *The Mansion*, and "Lo!" The critic notes that the presence of patriotism may be "irritating," as in "Two Soldiers," but is "never there just to show the flag" (Reed 1984, 52–53).

The regional impact of war is not the only expression of a regional concern that critics believe this story shares with other texts. For Blotner, "Two Soldiers" shows Faulkner's dissatisfaction with growing federal assistance programs, a position the author reiterates a decade later at a Delta Council meeting, and both "Two Soldiers" and "Shall Not Perish" reflect his sentiments against social injustice (1974, 1417; Blotner 1976, 15). In the incident in "Two Soldiers" when the narrator seeks to exchange an egg for a bus ticket, he learns that he must pay his fare in cash. James Snead compares this episode with a concern expressed in *The Hamlet* that "notions of wholeness and community" erode when money becomes the basis of exchange (1986, 148).

Louis Brodsky likens the thematic focus of "The De Gaulle Story," a movie script Faulkner worked on in 1942, to the stories written in the early 1940s, including "The Tall Men," "Shingles for the Lord," "Two Soldiers," and some portions of "Delta Autumn." Although the film script and stories represented extremely different media, Faulkner developed in both types conflicting thematic concerns such as oppression, violence, and injustice versus "compassion, equality, patriotism, and personal liberty" (Brodsky 1990, 101).

James Ferguson identifies the initiation theme as the "most important archetype" in Faulkner's work during the decade from 1932 to 1942. "Two Soldiers," "Uncle Willy," "Lion," "Barn Burning," and sections of *The Unvanquished* and *Go Down, Moses* all relate to this theme (Ferguson 1991, 41).

Skei, like some other critics, faults "Two Soldiers" and "Shall Not Perish" for their "cheap sentimentalism"; consequently, he finds the significance of these stories in their narrative approaches and rural settings rather than their thematic concerns (Skei 1985, 268). Certainly, the use of a young male narrator repeats an important strategy in Faulkner's fiction. The younger Grier son tells this story; most believe he also narrates the other two Grier stories, although some critics of "Shingles for the Lord" suggest that it may be told by the older brother, Pete (see Blotner 1974, 1100, 1108; Skei 1985, 271; Kinney 1980, 63–64).

In the numerous Faulkner stories that employ the narrative perspective of a young male, the children's perceptiveness varies widely. Reed considers the narrator of "Two Soldiers" and "Shall Not Perish" to be somewhat more innocent of "adult complexities" than the narrator of "Shingles." Reed also sees the same "narrative shape" of the "little boy who knew too much" in the narrator of "Two Soldiers," "Shingles for the Lord," and "That Will Be Fine," but Carothers distinguishes the "innocently naïve" narrator of "Two Soldiers" from the "damnably naïve" narrator Georgie in "That Will Be Fine" (Reed 1973, 37; Reed 1984, 142; Carothers 1985, 20). Ferguson adds "Race at Morning" to this list of innocent boys telling tales (1991, 106).

"Two Soldiers" shares with other stories several formal Faulknerian strategies. Ferguson reminds us that despite Faulkner's talent for constructing complex plots, the author also wrote straightforward stories including the early New Orleans sketches, "Artist at Home," "Turnabout," "Shingles for the Lord," "Mr. Acarius," and "Two Soldiers" (1991, 126–28). For Reed, all three of the Grier stories seek the "suspension of remarkable events in the midst of commonplace routine"; he considers "Two Soldiers" and "Shall Not Perish" "gimmicky" and "Two Soldiers," "almost icky" (1973, 35).

Ostensibly, the logic of grouping the first six stories in *Collected Stories* involves their geographical location, but the interplay of these "country" tales suggests richer implications. Arthur Kinney believes that because the paired stories, "Two Soldiers" and "Shall Not Perish," follow two stories, "Shingles for the Lord" and "A Bear Hunt," in which persons are tricked and exploited in a humorous context, they show the deadly turn such trickery can take in the context of war (1980, 65). Skei notes that four of the stories of the first section were composed in the early forties. He speculates that their position in the early pages of the collection "may indeed reflect Faulkner's satisfaction with them and his own beliefs in what they show of lasting and valuable human qualities," though they are not given the critical esteem accorded his other works (Skei 1985, 267).

Ferguson notes the tonal shifts between comic and serious stories in "The Country," with the final two dominated by pathos. He also sees the section opening out—from the narrowly defined geography of "Barn Burning" to the World War II stories at the end of the section, and from a portrayal of rural life, its constraints and values, outward to the world. This broadening of perspective, he says, prepares us "for what is to come in the rest of the volume." But in describing the variations of quality in *Collected Stories*, Ferguson estimates that "to move within a space of about one hundred pages from the majestic solemnity of 'Barn Burning' to the bathos of 'Two Soldiers' or 'Shall Not Perish' is something of a shock" (1991, 158, 2).

Ferguson's disdain for "Two Soldiers" is not unique and may explain why the story has not benefited from any critical discussion devoted explicitly to its text. This lack of attention results in interpretive remarks that paint broad strokes and offer little substantive explication. To be sure, many respondents would add that the lapse reflects a weakness of the story, not a failure of the critical community.

## Interpretation and Criticism

The transition from relational studies to interpretation in this section takes an admittedly negative tone; Faulkner's own words serve to balance opinions about "Two Soldiers," for Faulkner liked his story very much. When asked to prepare a brief comment on his regard for "Two Soldiers," Faulkner replied, "I like it because it portrays a type which I admire—not only a little boy, and I think little boys are allright, but a true American: an independent creature with courage and bottom and heart—a creature which is not vanishing, even though every articulate medium we have—radio, moving pictures, magazines—is busy day and night telling us that it has vanished, has become a sentimental and bragging liar" (*SL* 184).

Two critical comments indicate the range of opinions "Two Soldiers" generates among readers. Walter Everett considers the story to be a "display of Faulkner's virtuosity" that "evokes laughter and tears" and remains sincere rather than "trite" or "mawkish" (1969, 176). Frederick Karl, however, describes it as a "piece of patriotic fluff" linked directly to the attack on Pearl

Harbor and virtually certain for acceptance by the *Post*, an act Karl asserts is a "form of literary prostitution" producing an "inferior" work specifically to meet the demands of the magazine. The resulting text is a "meretricious" story generating stereotypical characters and action and predictable responses (Karl 1989, 661–62).

A few judgments about character development offer some elaboration on the Griers. Millgate sees the narrator, who is the second soldier, as "the chief embodiment of those qualities of simple determination, endurance, and courage which Faulkner finds so admirable in these people" ([1966] 1989, 271). Bradford defends the Griers' effort to dissuade Pete from enlisting as no "attempt to deny the propriety of his decision" because the reference to the family's service in World War I affirms the sense of duty that has returned to them (Bradford 1965, 95). But Nordanberg believes Pete contrasts with his father by his patriotism and industry. Similarly his younger brother reflects a "self-sacrificing spirit," an attitude Faulkner represents as valuable (Nordanberg 1983, 116). As Skei observes, patriotism and family loyalty are tightly intertwined in this story (1985, 268).

Commenting on the skill with which "Two Soldiers" is told, Blotner describes the young Grier child as "not entirely naïve" (1974, 1097). Skei, however, argues that the narrator's violent behavior and patriotism work against his believability. He seems to exist for the thematic emphasis more than for delineating an authentic character. The point of view that should limit perspective to the child's knowledge lapses into the role of "author's mouthpiece" and comments on behavior of other characters. Skei understands the time between experience and narration "is not unusually wide" (1985, 268–69, 277).

Everett finds a comic element in the story. The humor arises from the narrator's singlemindedness when placed against adult understanding of his position, including examples such as his mother's early dismissal of him. Further, because the narrator even from his retrospective viewpoint fails to see how deeply he is affected by Pete's leaving, the story escapes excessive sentimentalism. Everett does, however, see a structural weakness in the McKellogg incident; he thinks it "lacks justification" and is thereby intrusive rather than well integrated (1969, 176–77).

In discussing the status of Faulkner studies in Japan, Kiyoyuki Ono notes that some Japanese readers have found the portrayal of the Japanese in "Two Soldiers" to be harsh (1985, 5).

"Two Soldiers" is not of the caliber of "That Evening Sun" or "Barn Burning," but it is not a failed story either. Despite its weaknesses, the story is "competent" and "mildly entertaining" (Skei 1985, 269). Faulkner's annotation beside its name in the list of those stories to be included in *Collected Stories* was simply "*YES*," the only *yes* to receive the added emphasis of capitalization (*SL* 274). We ought to return to "Two

Soldiers," interpretive tools in hand, to see if more thorough scrutiny reveals something as yet seen only by its creator.

## Works Cited

Blotner, Joseph. 1974. *Faulkner: A Biography*. 2 vols. New York: Random House.

———. 1976. "The Sole Owner and Proprietor." In *Faulkner: Fifty Years After The Marble Faun*. Ed. George H. Wolfe. University: University of Alabama Press, 1–20.

Bradford, M. E. 1965. "Faulkner and the Jeffersonian Dream: Nationalism in 'Two Soldiers' and 'Shall Not Perish.'" *Mississippi Quarterly* 18:94–100.

Brodsky, Louis Daniel. 1990. *William Faulkner, Life Glimpses*. Austin: University of Texas Press.

Carothers, James B. 1981. "The Road to *The Reivers*." In *"A Cosmos of My Own": Faulkner and Yoknapatawpha 1980*. Ed. Doreen Fowler and Ann J. Abadie. Jackson: University Press of Mississippi, 95–124.

———. 1985. *William Faulkner's Short Stories*. Ann Arbor, MI: UMI Research Press.

———. 1987. "'I Ain't a Soldier Now': Faulkner's World War II Veterans." *Faulkner Journal* 2:67–74.

Everett, Walter K. 1969. *Faulkner's Art and Character*. Woodbury, NY: Barron's Educational Series.

Faulkner, William. 1942. "Two Soldiers." *Saturday Evening Post* 214 (28 March):9–11, 35–36, 38, 40.

———. 1950. *Collected Stories of William Faulkner*. New York: Random House.

———. 1977. *Selected Letters of William Faulkner*. Ed. Joseph Blotner. New York: Random House.

Ferguson, James. 1991. *Faulkner's Short Fiction*. Knoxville: University of Tennessee Press.

Howell, Elmo. 1966. "William Faulkner and *Pro Patria Mori*." *Louisiana Studies* 5:89–96.

Karl, Frederick R. 1989. *William Faulkner: American Writer*. New York: Weidenfeld and Nicolson.

Kerr, Elizabeth M. [1969] 1976. *Yoknapatawpha: Faulkner's "Little Postage Stamp of Native Soil."* New York: Fordham University Press.

Kinney, Arthur F. 1980. "Faulkner's Narrative Poetics and Collected Stories." *Faulkner Studies* 1:58–79.

Leary, Lewis. 1973. *William Faulkner of Yoknapatawpha County*. New York: Thomas Y. Crowell.

McHaney, Thomas L. 1975. *William Faulkner's* The Wild Palms: *A Study*. Jackson: University Press of Mississippi.

Millgate, Michael. [1966] 1989. *The Achievement of William Faulkner*. New York: Random House. Reprint. Athens: University of Georgia Press. Brown Thrasher Books.

Nordanberg, Thomas. 1983. *Cataclysm as Catalyst: The Theme of War in William Faulkner's Fiction*. Acta Universitatis Upsaliensis. Studia Anglistica Upsaliensia, #49. Stockholm: Almquist & Wiksell.

Ono, Kiyoyuki. 1985. "Faulkner Studies in Japan: An Overview." In *Faulkner Studies in Japan*. Ed. Kenzaburo Ohashi and Kiyoyuki Ono. Athens: University of Georgia Press, 1–12.

Reed, Joseph W., Jr. 1973. *Faulkner's Narrative*. New Haven: Yale University Press.

———. 1984. *Three American Originals: John Ford, William Faulkner, and Charles Ives*. Middletown, CT: Wesleyan University Press.

Skei, Hans H. 1977. *Bold and Tragical and Austere: William Faulkner's* These 13: *A Study*. University of Oslo Department of Literature.

———. 1981. *William Faulkner: The Short Story Career*. Oslo, Norway: Universitetsforlaget.

———. 1985. *William Faulkner: The Novelist as Short Story Writer*. Oslo, Norway: Universitetsforlaget.

Snead, James A. 1986. *Figures of Division: William Faulkner's Major Novels*. New York: Methuen.

Vickery, Olga. [1959] 1964. *The Novels of William Faulkner*. Baton Rouge: Louisiana State University Press.

Watkins, Floyd C. 1971. *The Flesh and the Word: Eliot, Hemingway, Faulkner*. Nashville: Vanderbuilt University Press.

# Shall Not Perish

"Shall Not Perish" first appeared in the July–August 1943 issue of *Story*. Faulkner sent "Shall Not Perish" to his agent, Harold Ober, shortly after "Two Soldiers," a related story, had been published by the high-paying *Saturday Evening Post*. Ober received the typescript from Faulkner on April 24, 1942, had it retyped, and began a thirteen-month effort to sell the story. After eight magazines rejected "Shall Not Perish," *Story* purchased it in May 1943 for $25. Despite this difficult and modest beginning, "Shall Not Perish" eventually reached another audience as a television drama. On February 11, 1954, the CBS Lux Video Theatre telecast an adaptation by Faulkner with performances by Raymond Burr and Fay Bainter. Television critics were uniformly critical of the telecast, but Faulkner earned $1,500 for the television script. "Shall Not Perish" was placed sixth in *Collected Stories* (1950) (*WFM 24* Introduction xiv–xv; Meriwether [1961] 1971, 162; Blotner 1974, 1456, 1150, Notes 188; Skei 1981, 101).

## Circumstances of Composition, Sources, and Influences

"Shall Not Perish" was the fifth of seven stories Ober received between January and July 1942. Faulkner's creative surge in this period had an explicit financial motivation. After this burst of short fiction, he wrote new short stories irregularly, usually in relation to the production of novels (Skei 1981, 101–02).

Extant prepublication documents reveal a number of revisions in "Shall Not Perish." Joseph Blotner notes a significant alteration in the use of dialect. Originally, the narrator's dialect resembled that used for the same speaker in "Two Soldiers." Eventually, however, Faulkner adopted a more formal diction except in some passages of dialogue. The goal, Blotner suggests, was to reflect greater maturity in the narrator at the time of recounting this story and to achieve a greater sense of "tragic dignity." Other revisions were spurred by Faulkner's unsuccessful effort to sell the story to the *Post*, whose editors considered it overwritten and artificial. Faulkner simplified the elevated rhetoric, but his frustration was obvious. He wrote to Ober, "I think it's all right now. I should have written it this way at first; it never had tasted quite right to me. Goddamn it that's what having to write not because you want to write but because you are harassed to hell for money does." Facing yet another rejection from the *Post*, Ober suggested that Faulkner eliminate the ties between this story and "Two Soldiers." In revision, Faulkner did not change the names, but he did reduce specific references to the other story, and he shortened the manuscript by five pages. Some of the items lost in cutting include references to Dorsey Tull, who offers a picture of Pete to the family, and a brief account of the relationship between Mr. and Mrs. Grier, who have stopped touching. As if the patriotic impulse were not sufficiently affirmed, an early ending added, after noting the westward course of America, "And the young and the strong died to advance it." An interesting addition present in the later typescript and in the published versions is the addition of "and women" in the following passages: "and the names of the men and the women who did the deeds" and "the men and women still powerful seventy-five years and twice that and twice that again afterward" (*SL* 150–51; *WFM 24* Introduction xiv–xv, 413–65; *CS* 114; Blotner 1974, 1100–01, 1105).

"Shall Not Perish" is a text that bears marks from Faulkner's life and from regional and national events. The title of the story comes from the closing sentence of Abraham Lincoln's "Gettysburg Address": "and that government of the people, by the people, for the people, shall not perish from the earth" (Everett 1969).

John Cullen and Floyd Watkins identify several references particular to the Oxford, Mississippi, community. The Northern woman in the story who contributes money to build a museum resembles Mary Buie, an Oxford native who lived in Chicago and the North. The Confederate monument described in the story is not the one in front of the Oxford courthouse but the statue on the University of Mississippi campus, and the description of the jail fits the Lafayette County jail Faulkner saw in Oxford (Cullen and Watkins [1961] 1975, 64–65).

Cullen and Watkins also recall a family in Lafayette County named *Quick*. The fictional Quicks owned a sawmill, a characteristic that recalls the real Ad Quick, who was a farmer and a miller. A real-life Sulton Quick may be a source for Solon Quick, and Solon's insistence that his wife pay him for her rides into town can be traced to one of Faulkner's acquaintances (Cullen and Watkins [1961] 1975, 76).

A national event may have inspired the description of de Spain's son's death. Robert Harrison likens the fictional incident to the death of "America's first air hero of World War II," Captain Colin P. Kelly, Jr. Three days after the attack on Pearl Harbor, Kelly was killed when his plane crashed during an attack by Japanese fighters (Harrison 1985, 183).

These sources from the national and local scene add to the texture of the story, but the more substantial correspondences exist between "Shall Not Perish" and Faulkner's fictional milieu.

## Relationship to Other Faulkner Works

The most intimate relationship "Shall Not Perish" bears in the body of Faulkner's fiction is with "Two Soldiers," to which "Shall Not Perish" acts as a sequel. The young Grier child, Pete's brother, dominates the narrative consciousness in these stories and probably also in "Shingles for the Lord" (see Blotner 1974, 1100, 1108; Skei 1985, 271; Kinney 1980, 63–64).

The Grier family of Frenchman's Bend becomes part of a larger gallery of people from the hill country about whom Faulkner typically writes with affection. M. E. Bradford includes the families in the Grier stories in his list of yeoman farmers from the hill country and adds others with similar background such as Byron Bunch in *Light in August*, the convict in *The Wild Palms*, and the MacCallums in *Sartoris* (McCallums in "The Tall Men"). According to Bradford, Faulkner's treatment of these people is always positive. The Griers, he contends, have been able to support themselves on their land because of their good stewardship. In Pete's perspective, in "Two Soldiers," his stewardship to his land represents his duty to his country, and when the country is threatened, it must be defended (Bradford 1965, 94–96). In Elizabeth Kerr's less affirming view, Res Grier is one of the rural characters who, like Anse Bundren in *As I Lay Dying*, tends to be inefficient in his farming ([1969] 1976, 152–53). For Thomas McHaney, the "hill-country people" in this story, "The Tall Men," "Two Soldiers," *As I Lay Dying*, and *The Wild Palms* represent a "hardworking, literal minded, almost fanatically persevering set of individuals" (1975, 154).

Charles Peavy tracks through various stories a recurring disdain displayed by the fictional black household domestics toward poor or town-bred whites in several texts: the butlers in "Barn Burning" and "Shall Not Perish," Elnora toward Narcissa in "There Was a Queen," and the groom in "Mountain Victory" (1971, 21).

Other characters that appear in "Shall Not Perish" link it broadly to the spectrum of Faulkner's fiction. The appearance of Major de Spain and the mention of other characters including Colonel Sartoris and Rosa Millard spread the connections of this story to numerous additional fictional contexts in Yoknapatawpha (see Cantwell [1953] 1985, 149; Holmes 1966, 112).

Olga Vickery classes "Shall Not Perish" with other "adjunctive" stories that "simply add more information about certain characters, situations, or the history of Yoknapatawpha" (1964, 300). The patriotic urge in this story and others, however, demonstrates that broadening the fictional county is only one aspect of the story. In Blotner's opinion, "Shall Not Perish" and "Two Soldiers" represent precursors to the heightened responsibility Faulkner felt after receiving the Nobel Prize to address issues of national and international importance (1976, 15). Similarly, James Carothers places "Shall Not Perish" with the fiction that reflects a "rhetoric of advocacy" that Faulkner adopted after 1940, and for James Ferguson, the stories from 1941 and 1942, including these two texts, affirm the argument made by Joseph Gold that Faulkner's later work exchanged metaphor for discourse (Carothers 1985, 25; Ferguson 1991, 42).

For Elmo Howell, the patriotism in "Shall Not Perish" and "Two Soldiers" originates in a loyalty first learned as a "strong attachment to home." In "Shall Not Perish," the extension of family and regional loyalty "ends with the transfiguration of this love in the broader concept of nation and brotherhood." According to Howell, this fervent patriotism expressed in Pete's unquestioned need to join the war after the attack on Pearl Harbor contrasts with the pacifism in *A Fable*—for example, in the suggestion that the Corporal and his men refuse to fight (1966, 89–96). To the list of Faulkner's patriots, Watkins adds Ike McCaslin in "Delta Autumn" (1971, 252).

In Thomas Nordanberg's view, the stories written after 1941 show a marked change in the otherwise negative treatments of war that appear "intimately related to the state of world politics." "Shall Not Perish," "Two Soldiers," "The Tall Men," and "My Grandmother Millard and General Bedford Forrest and the Battle of Harrykin Creek" were all written around the same time and share a portrayal of war altered from that of Faulkner's earlier works. His later novel *The Mansion* also fits this pattern. Even *A Fable* in some ways suggests a similar vision (Nordanberg 1983, 107, 151–53; see also Carothers 1987, 67–74). "Overt national feeling" is, according to Joseph Reed, expressed as well in *The Hamlet, The Town, The Mansion*, and "Lo!" (1984, 52–53). Hans Skei describes the World War II stories as "written by a man who believes in America and in America's strength, and who is capable of giving fictional probability to his beliefs by showing some of his low and poor people reacting to the demands of their country." Among these folk Skei includes Jackson Fentry in "Tomorrow" and another World War II text, "Snow." Elsewhere, Skei argues that in stories concentrating on a "collective crisis" Faulkner's narrators stress a loss of values typically described as the "old verities of the heart." These works included war stories like "All the Dead Pilots" from the World War I stories and "Shall Not Perish" and "The Tall Men" from the World War II stories (Skei 1985, 265, 267, 272; Skei 1987, 255; Skei 1992, 69).

Faulkner's turn toward didacticism is not always perceived as mixing well with his imaginative contexts. Reed regards "Shall Not Perish" and "Two Soldiers" as "perhaps too gimicky for serious discussion" (1973, 35). Skei judges "Shall Not Perish" in some ways stronger than "Two Soldiers," but both suffer from being "overwritten" and varying between "cheap sentimentalism and dramatized grief and despair," too often the former; they are most interesting for scene and use of narrator (1985, 267–69). For Ferguson, the two stories are "didactic," "sententious," and filled with "saccharine inanities" and "altogether offensive jingoism" (1991, 42).

The strong ties between "Shall Not Perish," "Two Soldiers," and the third Grier story, "Shingles for the Lord," extend to strategies of form. Reed believes that these three stories all present the "suspension of remarkable events in the midst of commonplace routine." In the case of "Shall Not Perish," the narrative contrasts everyday simplicity with the "excess of the adults' wordy response to grief." The narrator here and in "Two Soldiers" "is just at the point of perceiving some adult complexities" whereas in "Shingles for the Lord" he manages a return to childhood excitement (Reed 1973, 35, 37, 181).

In making his selections for *Collected Stories*, Faulkner indicated to Robert Haas that "Shall Not Perish" was not to be included. His comment was "No. Topical, not too good" (*SL* 274). Again, about one month later, Faulkner sent Malcolm Cowley a version of the table of contents that did not include "Shall Not Perish," but this story and three others also missing from the listed contents were subsequently added (Cowley 1966, 116, 120).

Critics have noted that the positioning of "Shall Not Perish" as the concluding text of "The Country" section of the collection complements the much stronger opening text, "Barn Burning." Michael Millgate identifies many echoes from one to another: "references to the Civil War, close delineations of social differences, and descriptions of poor whites entering the De Spain mansion." The differences between the stories represent changes across time: the contrasting attitudes with which Ab Snopes and Mrs. Grier enter the mansion, the further removal of the Civil War into the past, and present concern with World War II. The effect, Millgate argues, is to show that the South has outgrown "old limited loyalties." Mrs. Grier and de Spain are separated by economic disparities much as Ab Snopes and de Spain were, but she sees the possibility of common ground in human values. Although the narrator's grandfather identifies with the Confederate cavalry, the narrator identifies "with the strength of the single nation which is the contemporary United States" (Millgate [1966] 1989, 271–72). James Watson sees the two stories as establishing "boundaries of a complete action." "Shall Not Perish" completes the "pattern of initiation" begun with Sarty in "Barn Burning." Although Sarty "flees family and society," the Grier child finds his place within his family, his region, and his nation. This conflict "between loyalty to self and responsibility to society" exists as conflict between Snopes and de Spain in "Barn Burning" but ends in reconciliation between Grier and de Spain in "Shall Not Perish" (Watson 1980, 222).

Arthur Kinney (who errs in naming Pete Grier as the narrator in all three Grier tales) supplements the interpretation of the cumulative contextual strength of "The Country." The stories of initiation show how gaining maturity (or simply majority) "vanquishes boyhood idealism and pride." The theme of "getting even" appears in variant serious and comic forms, "more earnest and deadly" in the context of a world war in the last two stories. Kinney, in contrast to Millgate and Watson, finds no reconciliation between Grier and de Spain (1980, 63–66).

Skei observes that the opening section contains four stories written in 1941 or 1942 and suggests that their placement in the first section of *Collected Stories* "may indeed reflect Faulkner's satisfaction with them and his own beliefs in what they show of lasting and valuable human qualities" (1985, 267). Ferguson acknowledges the parallels Millgate draws between "Barn Burning" and "Shall Not Perish," but adds that the latter story "somewhat mars the symmetry of the arrangement" of the section's tonalities, ranging back and forth between serious and comic (1991, 158).

## Interpretation and Criticism

Although "Shall Not Perish" has been able to fit comfortably in the context of "The Country," on its own it fails to garner much respect. Walter Everett catalogues his complaints: the "patriotic exhortation" does not meliorate the "weak dramatic narrative" or the "inappropriateness of language," the climax is undercut by sentimentality, the language used by the narrator is mature beyond his years, and the speech of de Spain and Mrs. Grier is equally artificial (1969, 167–68). Nordanberg concludes that the "propagandistic nature detracts something from the literary value" of the story; Carothers calls it a "lesser effort," and Frederick Karl describes it as "not narrative, but a sermon, a brief homily on what makes America great" (Nordanberg 1983, 119; Carothers 1985, 18; Karl 1989, 665).

Only H. R. Stoneback and Tao Jie offer positive readings. Stoneback recounts the unanticipated popularity of "Shall Not Perish" in China, favored for its presentation of "certain crucial Faulkner notions about place and community, about the dignity and pride of the country people." The approbation of the Chinese persuades Stoneback to rank the text as "one of the most neglected of all Faulkner stories" (1984, 240–42; Jie 1992, 190).

Extended critical responses are rare, but general comments typically follow the same analytical paths found in relational studies: issues of patriotism and community. One perspective this story offers that deserves some attention is the portrayal of the different economic backgrounds of the Griers and de Spains. Cleanth Brooks believes the disparate economic groups delineated are presented "with nicety and conviction," particularly in Mrs. Grier's lack of desire for the things of de Spain's house and in her insistence on taking the paid-for ride home with Quick rather than accepting de Spain's offer to be driven home by his chauffeur ([1963] 1990, 21). For Dorothy Tuck these rural characters possess endurance and understanding that are absent in the wealthier de Spains (1964, 176–77). And as Blotner observes, the story characterizes the hill people as exhibiting "dignity, patriotism, self-sacrifice, love, and compassion," reflecting Faulkner's own feelings (1974, 1100).

The portrait of de Spain is harsh, especially in comparison with Mrs. Grier as they both react to the loss of a son. Kinney argues that de Spain is envious of the poorer hill family because they have a second son representing the second chance that he lacks (1980, 63–66). Skei contends that the two deaths gain significance in the contrast between the parents' reactions. De Spain's ties to the past are "exaggerated and foolish," and they prohibit his adjustment to present realities—a condition apparently not passed on to his son, who goes to fight a present war (Skei 1985, 269–70).

Although the story portrays economic disparity and striking differences in the parents of the soldiers, it also emphasizes ubiquity in the impact of national crisis. In Bradford's view Mrs. Grier is really the protagonist of the story. Her role is to forward a "Jeffersonian ideal of a Republic of 'independent' men" that is by its extension in her son's commentary affirmed, elucidated, and extended in the next generation. Her words provide justification and consolation for the deaths of the two young men. De Spain's bitterness over the course of the nation after the Civil War is absolved in Mrs. Grier's argument that the independence and courage of individuals remain in the present generation (Bradford 1965, 96–98).

For Everett, the conspicuous association between the story and the Gettysburg Address points to the author's intention "to encourage Americans to be resolute in defending freedom and to console those mourning for dead sons" (1969, 167–68). Nordanberg believes the goal of "Shall Not Perish" is to establish the meaningfulness of Pete's death even though the circumstances seem futile. Mrs. Grier reflects an affirmation of the present that de Spain criticizes (Nordanberg 1983, 116–20). Skei asserts that the death of young men from different classes equalizes the tragedy across the county. Further, the brevity of grieving for the Griers contrasts the temporary conditions of war and heroism with the eternal nature of the land that "demands dedicated work in ever-lasting repetitions of the changing seasons" (Skei 1985, 270).

The structure of the tale, especially in the events that occur after Mrs. Grier and her son visit de Spain's mansion, confirms the thematic press toward continuity of the national spirit across community and generation. This text uses the movies in a manner that is not explicitly critical, unlike a good deal of Faulkner's fiction, although it may be too obvious that the movie playing is a Western serial (*CS* 112). Bradford defines the rest of the story as a thematically related digression from the focus on the deaths of the two young men. The museum reinforces the sense of generational ties, and the young narrator continues his mother's line of thinking, implying that the "old verities" have been successfully passed down to the youngest Grier (Bradford 1965, 98–100; see also Everett 168). Nordanberg understands the museum scene to affirm a sense of the American community as stronger and more significant than any regional loyalty just as the narrator's recollection of the grandfather's behavior exhibits a patriotism unattached to region or generation (1983, 116–20). Although Blotner sees no humor in the story, in Skei's opinion the museum scene provides comic relief in the recollections of Grandpap. It also demonstrates the education of young Grier: he has learned that he and his family are part of a larger, national community (Blotner 1974, 1100; Skei 1985, 270–71).

Another element of the text that supports the sense of continuity in the story is the image of the wheel and hub as the wheel of life. Kerr explains that the movement of the characters is toward the hub, Jefferson, that "reinforces the unifying function of this image." Further, each spoke comprises multiple additional hubs ([1969] 1976, 34–35).

Not everyone finds the sense of continuity and community in "Shall Not Perish" to be an optimistic vision. Kinney sees a "potential horror" not understood by the narrator in his final vision of America, for it implies that the pettiness and corruption present in Frenchman's Bend is not self-contained but is a condition of the larger world (1980, 63–66). Charles Nilon examines the minstrel stereotypes used to portray de Spain's servant. As Nilon notes, the stereotypes reflect the young narrator's conception of blacks and therefore cast some doubt on him as the positive hope others have made him (Nilon 1981, 236).

Certainly, the observations of Kinney and Nilon open issues that question the palliative nature of a mediocre story. The racial epithets by which the narrator refers to de Spain's butler are copied from his father, Res Grier (*CS* 104, 106). And de Spain does not seem to realize that his criticisms of the national condition could justly apply to his relationship with his household staff (*CS* 108). Finally, it is disconcerting that Mrs. Grier accepts so readily and patiently the role of women not to understand but only to respect men's need to respond to national crises, a quality that she indicates has passed through the female line for several generations (*CS* 109).

Finally, "Shall Not Perish" does not seem to have overcome in time the original objections raised by editors of the *Post*. In its contemporary moment, the story did not inspire, and for most readers, it has never overcome that failing.

## Works Cited

Blotner, Joseph. 1974. *Faulkner: A Biography*. 2 vols. New York: Random House.

———. 1976. "The Sole Owner and Proprietor." In *Faulkner: Fifty Years after The Marble Faun*. Ed. George H. Wolfe. University: University of Alabama Press, 1–20.

Bradford, M. E. 1965. "Faulkner and the Jeffersonian Dream: Nationalism in 'Two Soldiers' and 'Shall Not Perish.'" *Mississippi Quarterly* 18:94–100.

Brooks, Cleanth. [1963] 1990. *William Faulkner: The Yoknapatawpha Country*. New Haven: Yale University Press. Reprint. Baton Rouge: Louisiana State University Press.

Cantwell, Robert. [1953] 1985. "Introduction to *Sartoris*." In *Critical Essays on William Faulkner: The Sartoris Family*. Ed. Arthur F. Kinney. Boston: G. K. Hall, 146–60.

Carothers, James B. 1985. *William Faulkner's Short Stories*. Ann Arbor, MI: UMI Research Press.

———. 1987. "'I Ain't a Soldier Now': Faulkner's World War II Veterans." *Faulkner Journal* 2:67–74.

Cowley, Malcolm. 1966. *The Faulkner-Cowley File: Letters and Memories, 1944–1962*. New York: Viking.

Cullen, John B., and Floyd C. Watkins. [1961] 1975. *Old Times in the Faulkner Country*. Chapel Hill: University of North Carolina Press. Reprint. Baton Rouge: Louisiana State University Press.

Everett, Walter K. 1969. *Faulkner's Art and Character*. Woodbury, NY: Barron's Educational Series.

Faulkner, William. 1943. "Shall Not Perish." *Story* 23 (July–August): 40–47.

———. 1950. *Collected Stories of William Faulkner*. New York: Random House.

———. 1977. *Selected Letters of William Faulkner*. Ed. Joseph Blotner. New York: Random House.

———. 1987. *William Faulkner Manuscripts 24: Short Stories*. Ed. Joseph Blotner. New York: Garland.

Ferguson, James. 1991. *Faulkner's Short Fiction*. Knoxville: University of Tennessee Press.

Harrison, Robert. 1985. *Aviation Lore in Faulkner*. Amsterdam and Philadelphia: John Benjamins.

Holmes, Edward M. 1966. *Faulkner's Twice-Told Tales: His Re-Use of His Material*. The Hague: Mouton.

Howell, Elmo. 1966. "William Faulkner and *Pro Patria Mori*." *Louisiana Studies* 5:89–96.

Jie, Tao. 1992. "Faulkner's Short Stories and Novels in China." In *Faulkner and the Short Story: Faulkner and Yoknapatawpha, 1990*. Ed. Evans Harrington and Ann J. Abadie. Jackson: University Press of Mississippi, 174–205.

Karl, Frederick R. 1989. *William Faulkner: American Writer*. New York: Weidenfeld and Nicolson.

Kerr, Elizabeth M. [1969] 1976. *Yoknapatawpha: Faulkner's "Little Postage Stamp of Native Soil."* New York: Fordham University Press.

Kinney, Arthur F. 1980. "Faulkner's Narrative Poetics and *Collected Stories*." *Faulkner Studies* 1:58–79.

McHaney, Thomas L. 1975. *William Faulkner's* The Wild Palms: *A Study*. Jackson: University Press of Mississippi.

Meriwether, James B. [1961] 1971. *The Literary Career of William Faulkner: A Bibliographical Study*. Princeton, NJ: Princeton University Library. Reprint. Columbia: University of South Carolina Press.

Millgate, Michael. [1966] 1989. *The Achievement of William Faulkner*. New York: Random House. Reprint. Athens: University of Georgia Press. Brown Thrasher Books.

Nilon, Charles H. 1981. "Black in Motion." In *"A Cosmos of My Own": Faulkner and Yoknapatawpha 1980*. Ed. Doreen Fowler and Ann J. Abadie. Jackson: University Press of Mississippi, 227–51.

Nordanberg, Thomas. 1983. *Cataclysm as Catalyst: The Theme of War in William Faulkner's Fiction*. Acta Universitatis Upsaliensis. Studia Anglistica Upsaliensia, #49. Stockholm: Almquist & Wiksell.

Peavy, Charles D. 1971. *Go Slow Now: Faulkner and the Race Question*. Eugene: University of Oregon Books.

Reed, Joseph W., Jr. 1973. *Faulkner's Narrative*. New Haven: Yale University Press.

———. 1984. *Three American Originals: John Ford, William Faulkner, and Charles Ives*. Middletown, CT: Wesleyan University Press.

Skei, Hans H. 1981. *William Faulkner: The Short Story Career*. Oslo, Norway: Universitetsforlaget.

———. 1985. *William Faulkner: The Novelist as Short Story Writer*. Oslo, Norway: Universitetsforlaget.

———. 1987. "William Faulkner's Late Career: Repetition, Variation, Renewal." In *Faulkner After the Nobel Prize*. Ed. Michel Gresset and Kenzaburo Ohashi. Kyoto: Yamaguchi, 247–59.

———. 1992. "Beyond Genre? Existential Experience in Faulkner's Short Fiction." In *Faulkner and the Short Story: Faulkner and Yoknapatawpha, 1990*. Ed. Evans Harrington and Ann J. Abadie. Jackson: University Press of Mississippi, 62–77.

Stoneback, H. R. 1984. "The Hound and the Antelope: Faulkner in China." In *Faulkner: International Perspectives: Faulkner and Yoknapatawpha, 1982*. Ed. Doreen Fowler and Ann J. Abadie. Jackson: University Press of Mississippi, 236–56.

Tuck, Dorothy. 1964. *Crowell's Handbook of Faulkner*. New York: Thomas Y. Crowell.

Vickery, Olga. [1959] 1964. *The Novels of William Faulkner*. Baton Rouge: Louisiana State University Press.

Watkins, Floyd C. 1971. *The Flesh and the Word: Eliot, Hemingway, Faulkner*. Nashville: Vanderbilt University Press.

Watson, James G. 1980. "Faulkner's Short Stories and the Making of Yoknapatawpha County." In *Fifty Years of Yoknapatawpha: Faulkner and Yoknapatawpha 1979*. Ed. Doreen Fowler and Ann J. Abadie. Jackson: University Press of Mississippi, 202–25.

*The Village*

# A Rose for Emily

## Publication History

"A Rose for Emily" first appeared in the April 1930 issue of *Forum* magazine, marking Faulkner's initial publication of a short story in a national magazine. Although Faulkner was already a published poet and novelist, his work in short fiction to this time included only the New Orleans sketches and two stories that had appeared in a student newspaper, "Landing in Luck" and "The Hill." A note in Faulkner's handwriting on a carbon typescript indicates that he sold the story to *Forum* on January 20, 1930. Like so many of his stories it underwent rejection before it was accepted for publication. The story-sending schedule notes a submission to *Scribner's*. Alfred Dashiell returned the story to Faulkner with a letter dated October 7, 1929, in which Dashiell complimented its "good characterization and unusual situation" but explained that it did not meet *Scribner's* immediate needs.

"A Rose for Emily" was collected in *These 13* (1931), which was tentatively titled *"A Rose for Emily" and Other Stories*, and appeared in "The Village" section of *Collected Stories* (1950). Malcolm Cowley included "A Rose for Emily" in the *Portable Faulkner*. Unlike several other Faulkner stories, this one was not dramatized. Faulkner turned down an opportunity to sell the television rights to the story for $4,000 (Meriwether [1961] 1971, 20–21, 85, 174, 176–80; Meriwether 1973, 260; Blotner 1974, 632, 692; Skei 1981, 51–52, 117 n. 2; Karl 1989, 953).

## Circumstances of Composition, Sources, and Influences

The earliest verifiable date for the existence of "A Rose for Emily" is October 7, 1929, but it might have been written as early as 1926 or 1927, that is, sometime before February 1927 when Faulkner proposed to write a collection of stories about his hometown people (Skei 1981, 36, 26). Because "A Rose for Emily" is in most characteristics better than the somewhat similar "Miss Zilphia Gant," François Pitavy suggests that "A Rose for Emily" was written after a 1929 redrafting of "Miss Zilphia Gant" (1972, 133–34). Although Joseph Blotner confirms that "Miss Zilphia Gant" was submitted to *Scribner's* in December 1928, Pitavy's argument regarding order of composition, based on the quality of the two stories, may still apply (*US* 700). Recently, James

Ferguson has suggested that Faulkner revised "Miss Zilphia Gant" after he wrote "A Rose for Emily" (1991, 29).

Extant documents for "A Rose for Emily" provide opportunities to evaluate Faulkner's sharpening of a narrative. The Alderman Library at the University of Virginia holds a five-page incomplete holograph manuscript and a seventeen-page complete carbon typescript that track significant improvements made in the story (*WFM 9* Introduction xiii–xiv, 188–214). Dating the revisions, like dating the original composition, is speculative. Both Blotner and Hans Skei indicate that the revisions were made between *Scribner*'s rejection and *Forum*'s acceptance of the story (Blotner 1974, 632, 646; Skei 1981, 14). Max Putzel, however, asserts that the text sent to *Forum* was probably the same version that *Scribner*'s rejected (1985, 229). Although the carbon typescript bears the handwritten note dating the sale to *Forum*, it is obviously an earlier version than the one that appeared in that magazine. In addition to the significant differences in the story, the typescript does not contain the sectional divisions present in the published text.

Michael Millgate's analysis of the extant manuscript and typescript focuses on two major improvements, both of which constitute deletions: the removal of "otiose abstract formulations" and the removal of an extended conversation between Emily and Tobe. From manuscript to typescript, the conversation between the two is expanded. Emily, nearing death, and Tobe discuss the effect the discovery will have on the town. Tobe knows what is in the room, and they discuss their respective plans depending on which one predeceases the other. Tobe is the beneficiary in Emily's will.

In the typescript the description of the corpse is "more explicitly ghoulish" than in the published versions because the typescript includes a description of "a substance like hardened sealing-wax" that glues the grin to the pillow. Millgate finds the omission of this material beneficial because it preserves the "fruitful ambiguities" and the "central theme of withdrawal into unreality and illusion." The final choices Faulkner made in the published versions demonstrate his growing awareness that the narrative is better if it is allowed "to make its own points, to establish its own ambiguities and implications, without elaborate underscoring" (Millgate [1966] 1989, 263–64; *WFM 9* 210–14). Ferguson concludes that the scene between Emily and Tobe, if retained, "would have virtually destroyed the story because of its explicitness and its egregious violation of point of view" (1991, 34).

Like Millgate, most critics praise the craftsmanship evidenced by the revisions. Linda Wagner sees "A Rose for Emily" as an example of Faulkner's more mature use of "conventional description" for ironic purposes; he fills the text with details even while omitting crucial information "the reader really needs to know" (1975, 153). Skei believes the changes in the story "increased its dramatic tension and density" and demonstrated Faulkner's "acute understanding of narrative handling and an awareness of detail and effect that Poe would have been proud of" (1981, 14). He considers Faulkner's "artistic 'growth,'" demonstrated within that particular story, to be "remarkable," but qualifies his support of Millgate's judgment by noting that Faulkner's artistic development is evident in "A Rose for Emily" only if his revisions to the story were made at a time "much later" than the original writing (Skei 1981, 51–52; see also Skei 1977, 64–65).

Other changes are relatively minor when compared to the improvements discussed by Millgate and others, but they do have some relevance to the critical response to the story. In the early, holograph text, Miss Emily bears the surname Wyatt rather than Grierson (Blotner 1974, 632). The chronology of the story, kept rather obscure in the published text, is more specifically delineated in the earliest prepublication version. In the holograph text, Colonel Sartoris remits Emily's taxes in 1904 "from the death of her father 16 years back, on into perpetuity" (*WFM 9* 188). That date is changed to 1894 in the typescript and the reference to the time of Mr. Grierson's death is omitted (*WFM 9* 198–99). Also in the holograph text, Faulkner describes Emily's relationship to the town as "a tradition, a duty and a care"; he tries twice, then abandons the effort to include "tribulation" (*WFM 9* 188).

From the *Forum* to *These 13,* changes in the story are minimal and minor. They include omitting a comma between "squarish, frame," spacing the previously compounded "abovestairs," and omitting "Negro" from the early description of Tobe (*Forum* 233, 238; *T13* 167, 181). The text of *Collected Stories* shows no changes from the version in *These 13.*

Faulkner asserted that "A Rose for Emily" was "all fiction," a story that originated with an image "of a strand of hair on the pillow in the abandoned house" (*FU* 199, 26). His comments, however, have not deterred speculations about historical and literary precursors. John Cullen and Floyd Watkins suggest that a model for Emily and her relationship with Homer Barron existed in the courting of Mary Louise Neilson, a young Oxford woman, by Captain Jack Hume, a New Englander who worked with the W. G. Lassiter Paving Company, hired to pave the streets in Oxford. Neilson and Hume married despite her family's objections. "Miss Mary," like "Miss Emily," was raised primarily by her father. Captain Jack, like Homer, was quick with a joke and accomplished with "cuss words." Cullen and Watkins propose that Faulkner wrote about the "'events that were expected but never actually happened'" ([1961] 1975, 70–71). (Blotner's 1974 biography includes Cullen's recollection but misstates Jack Hume's name as "Jack Barron." The 1984 biography corrects Jack Hume's name [Blotner 1974, 631–32; 1984, 247].)

In his work on Yoknapatawpha names, James Hinkle has discovered three additional anecdotes that may have served as sources for the story. In tracing the name *Grierson*, Hinkle found that it was not a Lafayette County name but that the similar name *Frierson* was. A family of Friersons of College Hill included a number of sisters, two of whom were Sally Wyatt Frierson and Em

Frierson. Em Frierson was incorporated into Lafayette legend when she was forced, by order of a Yankee officer, to play all the Southern songs she knew. The name *Wyatt* is used for Emily's aunt and in the original story was Emily's surname. Hinkle suggests that based on the pronunciations of *Frierson* (FRY-er-son, or the Southern FRY-uh-son) that Grierson should probably be pronounced (GRY-er-son or GRY-uh-son).

He also links "A Rose for Emily" with the account of "Emily and the Baron" by popular historian Harnett T. Kane. Kane recounts the tale of the elopement of a young woman from Mobile and a supposed baron from France. Emily Blount had two suitors, Henry Maury and Baron Henry Arnous de Riviere. Her mother supported the marriage to the Baron; her father supported neither. Emily eloped with the Baron, and they fled to Europe where they were the subject of much newspaper gossip. Eventually Emily returned alone to Mobile, reopened a few rooms in the family home, and lived reclusively until her death in 1917. Hinkle makes another nominal association that he has followed from his viewing of photographs in the Cofield collection. A house known as the Homer Duke house in Oxford during Faulkner's lifetime resembles Emily's house, including the encroachment of gasoline pumps. He states that the house and name Homer might be borrowed, but that the Duke family did not contribute to the action of the narrative (Hinkle 1984, 191–95).

Peter Hays suggests that "A Rose for Emily" is a tribute of sorts from a poet-turned-fiction-writer to the poet Emily Dickinson. He traces the growth in Dickinson's popularity through the 1920s by the attention given to both her poetry and a widely read biography. Many of Emily Grierson's characteristics resemble legendary aspects of Dickinson: dressing in white, being reclusive, having a close if oppressive relationship with her father, being devastated by her father's death, and exhibiting a fascination with death. Hays adds that suggestions of necrophilia appear in Dickinson's poems 577, 1209, and 1344. He speculates that Faulkner could hardly have failed to know of the work and life of Emily Dickinson at the time he composed "A Rose for Emily" (Hays 1988, 105–10).

Another body of criticism looks for fictional rather than historical analogues. Most of these comparisons reside in the tradition of Gothic fiction, specifically Southern Gothic, and the characterization of either the unmarried woman or the murderous lover. John Hagopian notes that an important aspect of Faulkner's Gothic strain is his application of Gothic elements to the psychological condition of a character, in this case Emily (1962, 48). The technique is similar to that of the novels of Charles Brockden Brown.

Edward Stone includes Hawthorne's Hepzibah Pyncheon in *The House of Seven Gables* and the "impeccable spinsters" of Sarah Orne Jewett among the literary antecedents of Emily (Stone 1960, 433–43; 1969, 5–15, 85–100). Terry Heller likens Emily's giving local children china painting lessons to the kindness of Hepzibah Pyncheon (1972, 314). Making another Faulkner–Hawthorne connection, Daniel Barnes finds "A Rose for Emily" to be strongly influenced by Hawthorne's "The White Old Maid." He compares the image in Hawthorne's text of Edith, a young, grief-stricken woman, resting her head on the pillow beside the body of her suitor, to Emily's similar action as revealed by the discovery of the strand of hair. Edith also gives a lock of hair to another young woman who is somehow responsible for the man's death. As part of a pact for Edith's silence about the woman's role in the suitor's death, the two agree to return to the mansion many years later. In the meantime, the community regards the house as a place of mystery, and it becomes an outdated relic. Edith remains unmarried, assumes the habit of wearing a white, shroudlike garment, is identified by the townspeople with her insanity, and is isolated by her eccentricity. In Hawthorne's tale, as in Faulkner's, there is suspense and then resolution attached to the act of bursting into a mysterious upstairs room in the mansion. Another similarity is that Edith, like Emily, is tended over the years by a black male servant. Barnes concludes that "A Rose for Emily" and Faulkner's place in the Gothic tradition is more heavily indebted to Hawthorne than to Poe (1972, 373–77).

Cleanth Brooks and Robert Penn Warren offer an early comparison of Faulkner and Poe, specifically calling attention to the manner in which the houses in "A Rose for Emily" and "The Fall of the House of Usher" manifest characteristics of their respective inhabitants (Brooks and Warren 1946, 409–10). George Snell makes a more general comparison of the two writers, calling Faulkner's story a "logical development" from Poe but one that has been "brought to a higher degree of force" in the localization of detail in a familiar context (1947, 99). James Stronks attributes the idol-like image of Emily at the window to the influence of Edgar Allan Poe's "To Helen," comparing three descriptions of Emily that recall the image or particular words from the lines "Lo! in yon brilliant window-niche / How statue-like I see thee stand" (Stronks 1968, 11). Aretta Stevens endorses Stronks's argument. She believes that a similar description in *The Hamlet* of Eula at a window along with specific associations of Eula with the Trojan Helen, who was not posed at a window, increases the likelihood that Faulkner was influenced by the image of Helen in Poe's poem (Stevens 1968, 3; see also Edwards 1974, 21–25).

Stone also pursues the tradition of Southern Gothic in "A Rose for Emily" by way of Poe. He finds that the moral depravity of the protagonist and the effect of "total horror, rather than a climax of horror" recall "The Cask of Amontillado" more strongly than "The Fall of the House of Usher" (Stone 1960, 439). Walter Allen distinguishes Faulkner's Gothic elements from Poe's in that Faulkner makes the horror metaphoric: necrophilia represents the "lost, bewildered, ruined, post-war South" (1981, 184).

In another comparison within the consideration of "A Rose for Emily" as a Gothic tale, Stone develops a suggestion by Randall Stewart that George Washington Cable's "Jean-ah Poquelin" is closely related to "A Rose for Emily." Both stories picture somewhat mysterious and archaic aristocrats entrenched with their respective secrets in old homes against an encroaching and curious community. Both Cable's and Faulkner's stories establish a concrete time and place that Poe's tale lacks. But Stone argues that Faulkner adds a modern touch to the tradition of Gothic horror, rendering the story impassive by treating both Emily and the community with sympathy and reproach. Further, the scrutiny Faulkner gives to Emily's attitudes, behavior, and family history offers a pathological examination not present in Cable. This constant development of Emily's mental state dispels suspense so that it is not the major movement of the story as it is in Poe's "Usher" or Cable's "Poquelin." When the narrator offers the final view of Emily's bridal room, the reader's sense of Emily's mysteriousness increases; however, in Poe's "Usher" and Cable's "Poquelin," the conclusion resolves the mystery, and the reader completes these stories with an increased understanding of the respective protagonists.

Stone marks the work of Freud as a critical divider between early portraits of "odd" women and Faulkner's "abnormal" characters (1960, 433–43; 1969, 5–15, 85–100). James Mellard criticizes Stone's argument, particularly his claim that the story distinguishes its use of Gothic by placing it in a particular, familiar setting. Mellard argues that the distinguishing mark of Faulkner's use of Gothic is the way in which he makes it a "*retrospective* Gothic," revealing itself as a Gothic tale after the end in a reconsideration of the text (1986, 39–41).

The literary ancestors to "A Rose for Emily" also include Charles Dickens's Miss Havisham in *Great Expectations* and Robert Browning's Porphyria in "Porphyria's Lover." James Stewart notes that both Emily Grierson and Miss Havisham are jilted by their suitors; he contrasts Compeyson's note to Miss Havisham with Homer Barron's visit to Emily's house (but it should be noted that no scene in the story explicitly portrays Barron's breaking an engagement with Emily). Both women react by trying to freeze time, setting aside a room in which the memory is preserved. Whereas Miss Havisham's response is known, Homer Barron's murder (and corpse) is necessarily kept secret. Stewart comments that the murder repeats a pattern already established in which Emily refuses to acknowledge anything that displeases her. Unlike Miss Havisham, Emily is the main character of the story. She assumes an almost allegorical significance as "the South" (Stewart [1958] 1970, 56–57; see also Stone 1960, 433–43; 1969, 5–15, 85–100).

Joseph Gold draws similar comparisons between Miss Havisham and Emily in a much broader investigation of the influence of Dickens on Faulkner. He expands the comparisons beyond the two female characters to add that in addition to Satis House in *Great Expectations*, the Clennam house in *Little Dorrit* can also be compared to the Grierson house. Mrs. Clennam's frigidity may be likened to Emily's, and Dickens's Rosa Dartle in *David Copperfield* is a similarly "neurotic, frustrated and consequently dangerous woman" (Gold 1969, 69–79; see also Blotner 1974, 632; Edwards 1974, 21–25).

Walter Allen believes the comparison of Emily to Miss Havisham comes not only from the similarity in the use of preserved rooms in the two stories, but also because in each case there is a sense of "authority with which the scene is executed, the acclimatization as it were of the horrific to the normal world" (1981, 183–84).

Baruch Hochman sees both "A Rose for Emily" and *Great Expectations* as examples of how presenting events out of the chronological order in which they occurred "generates deep time perspective and serves as a vehicle for the time themes of the texts." He notes a contrast, however, in that the cause of Miss Havisham's behavior is revealed while the "history and development" of Emily is obscured. He expands his comparison to liken Emily to Moll Flanders and Shakespeare's protagonists because in these texts the reader is "challenged to seek an ordering of motives that might bestow coherence upon the traits and motives the character presents to our consciousness." Emily is distinctly modern, however, in the manner of conveying the complexities of her motivations "through very deliberate, self-conscious manipulations of time sequence, voice, and focalization" (Hochman 1985, 149–52).

The parallels between "A Rose for Emily" and "Porphyria's Lover" are also strong although not as explicit as those of Emily's and Miss Havisham's tales. Hines Edwards points out that apparently neither Porphyria nor Homer Barron suspected the dangerous insanity of their lovers (1974, 21–25). Another study of correspondences between the poem and the story likens their "similar prototypes of the imaginative will gone berserk." Their respective attempts to eternalize a moment of time are instances of "romantic madness" much like Keats's frozen moment on the Grecian urn: "Forever wilt thou love, and she be fair!" These are, Mark Winchell points out, acts of love, however perverted, rather than hate. The murderers are similarly distanced from their lovers by social class. Both seek to prevent abandonment by their lover. (Not all critics find evidence for this assumption in "A Rose for Emily.") Another point of comparison is that neither story incorporates a sense of omnipotent judgment of the murders. Also both stories are narrated from a limited point of view. And finally, both texts rely on images of hair in their narratives (Winchell 1983, 57–63).

According to Mellard, another possible analogue is William Blake's "The Sick Rose." Mellard has not successfully located evidence to show that Faulkner knew Blake's poem, but he bases his argument on internal similarities in the works. In this reading the rose represents Homer. The worm that destroys the rose is Emily, or more abstractly it is her murderous love. After

Homer disappears, Emily's hair grays, and she assumes a "masculine vitality" and becomes obese. The increasing repulsiveness of her physical changes reflects her status as the detested "worm of destruction" (Mellard 1986, 37–39).

Brooks traces the influence of Sherwood Anderson on Faulkner's early works, particularly the New Orleans sketches and stories from the early 1930s. He recalls that Anderson's first section of *Winesburg, Ohio* is entitled "The Book of the Grotesque" (1973, 382–83). Brooks finds Emily to bear a kinship with Anderson's Alice in "Adventure," and that both these characters resemble the woman in Eliot's *The Waste Land* who is bored and hysterical. Emily is a grotesque in Anderson's sense that she takes a "partial truth to be her whole truth" (1973, 387; see also Brooks [1978] 1990, 107, 156; Brooks 1987, 51–52).

In 1973, Marion Barber and Paul Levitt published articles that examined the striking similarities between "A Rose for Emily" and John Crowe Ransom's poem "Emily Hardcastle, Spinster," first published in 1923. Correspondences include humor to emphasize the grotesque, the symbolic possibility of seeing the female character as a metaphor for the South, an evocation of sympathy for both Emilys, name similarities, and narrative technique. Both texts open with the death of the respective Emily, then retrace her life. The narrator in each text is a member of the community who has been witness to at least some of the events recounted. Ransom's "pepper-and-salt," male narrator was one of the unsuitable suitors. This narrator's hair color recalls Emily Grierson's hair color, changed with age. The two Emilys are both aristocrats in their small communities. Ransom's Emily Hardcastle refuses to change with a changing community and finds no suitor equal to her position. She finally accepts a "grizzled Baron," death. The choice of a baron is a play on Emily's barrenness, and in combination with the name Hardcastle, invokes chivalric tradition in the courtship. Emily Grierson's Homer Barron also suggests her barrenness and her marriage to death (Barber 1973, 103–05; Levitt 1973, 91–94). Skei believes that Ransom's poem is the only text that can accurately be described as a source for Faulkner's story. He considers the others, including those of Poe, Dickens, Browning, and Hawthorne, to be "literary parallels" (Skei 1977, 64).

Ricardo Landeira spans the nineteenth and twentieth centuries when he develops a lengthy comparison of Carlos Fuentes's *Aura* (1962), Faulkner's "A Rose for Emily," and Henry James's *The Aspern Papers* (1888). Although Landeira concedes that there is no direct line of influence between "A Rose for Emily" and the later *Aura* or the earlier *The Aspern Papers*, he highlights such correspondences as a heightened consciousness of the past, a female protagonist who is either literally or figuratively widowed, older houses that reflect the mistress's character, and rejection of these women by their social peers. Typically, Landeira's comparisons between the James and Fuentes works are stronger than either text's resemblances to "A Rose for Emily." The specifics, such as a matching of Emily's letter written on aged stationery with a letter dictated by Juliana, seem to be forced comparisons and add little understanding to Emily's story (Landeira 1975, 125–43).

Matters pertaining to Emily are not the only bases for literary comparisons. Brooks suspects that Faulkner was influenced by the popular writer Irvin S. Cobb. Although his emphasis is on stories other than "A Rose for Emily" as bearing Cobb's imprint, Brooks believes the narrator in Faulkner's story may have been inspired by Cobb's first-person narrator, a "well-informed member of the community" not directly involved in the plot but a good observer and storyteller (1973, 384–85; see also Brooks 1987, 47–49).

The character Tobe has also generated some comparisons. Catherine Starke describes him as representative of the liberated former slave whose legal freedom does not dissolve his attachment to a white family. According to Starke, Tobe is a later-day version of the type she finds in such writers as Joel Chandler Harris, John Trowbridge, Frank Stockton, Charles Waddell Chesnutt, Sarah Orne Jewett, Thomas Dixon, and O. Henry (1971, 49–61). Landeira associates Tobe with the biblical figure Tobias. Tobe's faithfulness matches that of his namesake, who had similar care of a woman who would not leave her home (Landeira 1975, 139).

Danforth Ross believes the language of the story is influenced by Mark Twain and more generally the Southern oratorical style ([1961] 1970, 61). Recently John Rabbetts has associated the strong individualists in Faulkner's fiction with the influence of Southwestern humorists. Rabbetts interprets Emily Grierson's behavior as an "individualistic will turned rank by years of introspection" (1989, 50).

## Relationship to Other Faulkner Works

If Emily recalls Miss Havisham, Miss Pyncheon, and other fictional women, the character and the story also have close ties with other parts of the Faulkner canon. Skei calls "A Rose for Emily" the "first story about Faulkner's townspeople in any real sense" (1981, 51). In a survey of the fiction, one notices quickly that a number of the fictional residents are dissatisfied women. Emily Grierson is counted in that number, and her character generates most of the comparative observations that measure "A Rose for Emily" against other texts in Faulkner's work.

Three stories, "A Rose for Emily," "Dry September," and "Miss Zilphia Gant," have been closely linked by a number of critics, and recently have been described by Frederick Karl as a "spinster group" in which sexual repression has violent repercussions and shows "Faulkner's view of four women who are trapped and/or consumed by the male world" (1989, 408n).

In a much earlier critical observation, O'Connor finds the parallel of repressive rules that eventually manifest violence, "each in its own specialized Freudian milieu," in both "A Rose for Emily" and "Miss Zilphia Gant." Most critics endorse O'Connor's opinion that "A Rose for Emily" is the more masterfully drawn of the two stories (1954, 162, 70–71). Millgate contends that frustration and isolation drive both Emily and Minnie Cooper of "Dry September" to madness ([1961] 1966, 65). In judging the responses of all three women, Emily, Minnie, and Zilphia, to their respective abandonments, Edward Holmes considers Zilphia the most successful of the three, although Emily and Minnie are treated more compassionately. He speculates that Zilphia was the first of the three characters created, but sees Emily as the most effectively drawn (Holmes 1966, 80–83).

Pitavy finds a distinct difference between "Miss Zilphia Gant" and the other two stories in that "A Rose for Emily" and "Dry September" reveal information about the major female character through a public perspective. Information about the community creates a frame of reference for the "private tragedies" of Emily and Minnie (Pitavy 1972, 134–35). Sally Page joins in evaluating "A Rose for Emily" as a more masterful story than "Miss Zilphia Gant." Like Pitavy, Page sees the influence of the community in both "A Rose for Emily" and "Dry September" as a significant factor in the frustrated lives of Emily and Minnie. In both cases these women are excluded from normal interaction: Emily is separated because of her higher social class, which is perpetuated by a smug community. Given her treatment by her father and the community, Emily is described by Page as "forced to become engaged in a defiance of time and reality." Like Minnie Cooper, deprived of the normal fulfillment of her sexuality, Emily lives a death-in-life existence, and the severity of her repression manifests itself in criminal acts. In both cases, the women's physical appearance reflects the decay of their lives (Page 1972, 97, 99–100, 102).

Brooks finds the situations of Emily and Minnie "generally analogous" but the women are very different. He also links Emily to Mrs. Gant (Zilphia's mother) in that both are considered "crazy" by their neighbors. Zilphia, her mother, and Emily all exhibit obsessive behavior and iron wills. Emily and Zilphia are victims of overbearing parents, and as they grow older, they assume the characteristics of their parents. Both stories demonstrate Faulkner's interest in "feminine psychology," but the characters are very different from Cecily Saunders in *Soldiers' Pay*, the females in *Mayday*, or Patricia Robyn in *Mosquitoes*. Brooks adds that much of the effectiveness that "A Rose for Emily" possesses but that "Miss Zilphia Gant" lacks is achieved by the use of a narrator in "A Rose for Emily." The narrator of Emily's history succeeds in bringing the community to life (Brooks [1978] 1990, 110, 152–55, 164; Brooks 1987, 51). Skei believes that the stories of Minnie and Emily offer easy comparisons but that Emily, unlike Minnie, achieves a more complete withdrawal (1985, 112–13, 124).

As indicated in Brooks's comments that extend beyond the three stories, Emily has been perceived within a broader range of female characters in both the short fiction and novels. Irving Malin finds a pattern in Faulkner's fiction in the portrayal of daughters who, under the influence of an authoritative father, sublimate their sexuality in other activities and become "masculine." He includes Emily Grierson, Louise King (under Dr. Martino's influence), Rosa Coldfield, and Drusilla Hawk as examples (Malin 1957, 81).

Elizabeth Kerr looks at larger cultural patterns in her study of Faulkner's attitude toward the Southern ideal of womanhood. She concludes that he rejects the model and responds sympathetically to those female characters who have been limited by the Southern ideal even when they behave in reprehensible ways. Kerr likens Emily Grierson to Rosa Coldfield and Minnie Cooper in their similar failure to obtain husbands even though they have assumed marriage as the appropriate role for women. They are contrasted to Narcissa Benbow, who gains a husband but reveals herself to be more concerned with maintaining the appearance of propriety than with her integrity. These characters join company with a host of others in the fiction to demonstrate in numerous variations that whether the woman adheres to or rebels against the ideal, her life offers her little satisfaction and much frustration. Women like Granny Millard and Jenny Du Pre, whose lives reflect a measure of satisfaction and useful membership in society, are typically older women for whom conditions during the war allowed possibilities beyond normally prescribed roles. Kerr sees in Temple Drake, Emily Grierson, and Elly examples of women who rebel against the Southern code of conduct. Both Emily and Elly commit murder in their efforts. Kerr adds that Mr. Grierson's behavior toward Emily resembles Ruby's father's actions in *Sanctuary*, although he uses a gun rather than a horsewhip to eliminate suitors (Kerr 1961–62, 1–16; Kerr [1969] 1976, 159, 214; Kerr 1983, 148).

Emily and Joanna Burden of *Light in August* also share interesting parallels. Elmo Howell finds in Joanna a means by which to understand Emily's murdering Homer in the earlier story. After an extended sexual relationship with Joe Christmas, Joanna tries to reform both herself and Joe. Even though she is reluctant to do it, she determines to kill Joe when he refuses to repent. Howell believes that Emily is similarly motivated. Both women believe killing their lover is a moral act (Howell 1966, 15). Stone sees that for both Emily and Joanna Burden, becoming fat, especially noticeable in their faces, is associated with their sexual activity (1969, 12; see also Mortimer 1983, 31–32). Pitavy believes the description of Joanna's body as dead during intercourse with Joe Christmas recalls the necrophilia in "A Rose for Emily" (1973, 142).

Page analyzes the female characters in Faulkner's fiction who, because of the perversion of their sexuality, are portrayed in images of decay and death. The list is lengthy, including, along with Emily, Mrs. Compson, the adult Caddy, Temple Drake, Elly, Zilphia, Minnie Cooper, Rosa Coldfield, Charlotte

Rittenmeyer, and others. Page notes that although Faulkner believed such perversion was a "destructive force in human life," he treated the women "more with sympathy than with judgment" (1972, 93–95, 102, 108–09, 134, 178).

Ilse Lind's study of Faulkner's women focuses on his use, in advance of his contemporaries, of physical or biological motivations for their behavior, especially stressing the influence of the sex drive. This emphasis, Lind argues, contributes to the sense of determinism prevalent in Faulkner. For example, Emily Grierson, Minnie Cooper, and Zilphia Gant, among numerous other female characters, behave compulsively because of their repressed sex drive. These women become mentally distorted and lose any rational understanding of their actions. There is an inevitable clash between their internally motivated impulses and "socially determined impulses" that occurs with a "tragic relentlessness" (Lind 1978, 89–101; see also Carothers 1992, 49).

Victor Strandberg contends that because Faulkner's females must define themselves according to the acquisition of lover or husband and children, the unmarried women must resort to fantasy but do so by projecting the fantasy onto some real object or event. Judith Sutpen has her wedding dress, Rosa Coldfield has Sutpen's proposal, and Emily Grierson has the bridal chamber including the "skeletal bridegroom" (Strandberg 1981, 46–47).

Both Kinney and Kerr find further parallels between Emily and other female characters in the novels. Kinney finds different facets of Emily Grierson's personality reflected in two female characters in *Absalom, Absalom!* Judith Sutpen repeats the imperiousness with which Emily treated other people whereas Rosa maintains "desperately frozen memories" as Emily did (Kinney 1978, 691). Kerr considers Emily comparable to Miss Habersham in *Intruder in the Dust* "in age, background, and circumstance," except that Miss Habersham rejects the myth of Southern womanhood and creates her own unique identity (1979, 170).

Noel Polk finds "A Rose for Emily" to be the "classic study" of the character who sees in an oppressive elder both what she fears she will become and that part of her own consciousness, her conscience, that disapproves of her and generates self-hatred. The oppressive presence in Emily's life, her father, resembles Temple Drake's father, Zilphia Gant's mother, and Elly's grandmother. Polk notes that the ebony cane Emily uses resembles the one used by Temple Drake's father. Her black attire and thin watch chain recall Popeye and various other characters, Simon McEachern among them. Polk also finds the "gray-haired old woman, repressing or repressed, or both" who is commonly framed in a window or among pillows especially prevalent in Faulkner's work between the two versions of *Sanctuary* (1929 and 1930). Emily Grierson is obviously a major representative of this group that Polk enlarges to others such as Elly, Minnie Cooper, and somewhat more surprisingly, Miss Jenny in "There Was a Queen." The stories of "repression and frustration" especially prevalent in the years from 1927 to 1931 include "A Rose for Emily" and such others as "Elly." They give way to "less sexually intense, more open, more spacious, more external" stories such as "Lizards in Jamshyd's Courtyard," "Red Leaves," and "Mountain Victory" at the later end of the period (Polk 1984, 84–85; Polk 1985, 31–33; see also Ferguson 1991, 37, 74).

Like Polk, Skei observes that in a number of stories composed before 1930, Faulkner presents conflicts between a young girl or woman and an overbearing parental authority. He includes among these "Miss Zilphia Gant," "Elly," "Dry September," and "A Rose for Emily." This conflict is also apparent in an earlier story, "Adolescence," and in the novel *Soldiers' Pay*. It is, Skei believes, "one of the most central oppositions in the satires of the major period" (1928–1932). Skei also pursues the manner in which Emily, Elly, Zilphia, and Minnie suffer the "fate of being women in what is definitely a man's world" as well as a highly class-conscious, small town setting. They are all disappointed by the men with whom they form close relationships, and they feel the strains of restrictions on their lives because they are female. Emily does not react as swiftly as Elly to the constraints she meets, but she lives through several crises during her long life. The consequences of the two women's actions are, nevertheless, comparable. Skei shows the different ways these women demonstrate "how social position can be used with devastating effect." Emily manipulates the limited power and privacy she has to conceal her crime, but the consequences far outweigh the gains from misused power (Skei 1985, 104, 114–15, 123, 127, 178–79).

James Carothers, James Watson, and Frederick Karl expand the number of women who share traits with Emily. Carothers adds to the list of "frustrated women" previously identified in "A Rose for Emily," "Elly," "The Brooch," and "Miss Zilphia Gant," the characters of Mrs. Compson of *The Sound and the Fury* and Ike McCaslin's wife in *Go Down, Moses* (1985, 20). Emily, Elly, and Zilphia all "feel the debilitating consequences of sexual frustration, and all three are betrayed by men" (Carothers 1985, 104). Watson adds *Flags in the Dust*, *Sanctuary*, "There Was a Queen," and "The Leg" to the numerous novels and stories that like "A Rose for Emily," focus on sexual repression (1987, 101). Karl finds correspondences between Emily's bridal/funeral chamber and Judith's vigil over the body of Charles Bon in "Evangeline" (1989, 441).

Stephen Ross finds the unifying characteristic of Emily Grierson, Rosa Coldfield, Jenny Du Pre, and Rosa Millard, in the authority they possess, "disproportionate to any social position except that of 'Southern ladies' or 'old undefeated spinster aunts,'" as Faulkner once referred to them (1989, 223, 264 n. 27).

Minrose Gwin discusses Emily, Drusilla Hawk, Caddy Compson, Temple Drake, and Rosa Coldfield as objectified female characters. They reflect images created by a patriarchal world that "Faulkner both reproduces and challenges." Quoting Myriam Díaz-Diocaretz, Gwin explains how, once the image is created, woman becomes whatever that image names her to be. When the analysis is turned to perceive of "woman as the process of disruption," another reading of these women is possible. Of Emily, Minnie Cooper, and Joanna Burden, Gwin writes that although readers tend to perceive "Faulkner's world in terms of moral oppositions," some female characters demonstrate a "creative process of mind" that "seems in itself to be morally ambiguous." Although in conventional terms their behavior may "have morally negative results," the creative process provides a "powerful freeing force for their own psyches, which have been squeezed, compartmentalized, and devalued because of gender." Gwin describes the creative "play" of Emily as follows:

> Emily Grierson "plays" creatively by breaking down paternal and societal restraint. She subverts the Law of the Father. Within her own physical space, the bedroom, she subverts the culturally defined signifiers of marital love—the rose-shaded lights, the tarnished hairbrush, the discarded clothing. She thereby creates a play of signifiers which undermine their own referentiality, even within the repressive margins of patriarchal order—inside the Father's House. (Gwin 1990, 14, 26)

The parallels between Emily and other Faulkner characters are not limited to female figures. Harry Campbell and Ruel Foster consider Emily to be one of Faulkner's "moderns." These are weak or evil characters who are "victims of their internal failures to conform to the external world" and whose aberrations manifest themselves in a variety of forms (Campbell and Foster 1951, 48–49). Ross compares Emily to Quentin Compson in their similar though losing efforts against naturalistic forces hostile to the individual. Despite their inevitable failure, they are treated with compassion (Ross [1961] 1970, 61–62).

In his study of Faulkner's place in the Calvinist tradition, Robert Barth lists one manifestation of human depravity in Faulkner's fiction as sexual perversion. He assumes that Emily practices necrophilia and includes her perversion with Benjy's and Popeye's assaults on females, partner sharing in *Pylon*, the incestuous inclinations of Quentin, Charles Bon, and Carothers McCaslin, and Ike Snopes's bestiality (1964, 114–15; Barth 1972, 26).

Melvin Backman draws a comparison between Emily and Gail Hightower of *Light in August*. Both are characterized as "death-in-life" figures, flabby and associated with foul odors. Each one "clutches so deludedly at a dead past that life itself is denied." They are linked to dying light, both being "eastern idols" who watch the sun set from windows (Backman 1966, 81; see also Mortimer 1983, 31–32). Another of these decaying, obese characters Backman might have included is Moketubbe of "Red Leaves."

Jack Scherting compares Emily's longing for her father to Quentin's incestuous desires for his sister, Caddy. Both situations involve an effort "to subvert the reality of time and change." Scherting points out that the incest theme also appears in Lucius McCaslin's begetting a child from his own child (1980, 405).

Yasuhiro Yoshizaki compares the pathological personalities of Emily Grierson and Popeye in *Sanctuary*. He notes that Popeye feels no guilt when he kills animals or people. These two characters are perhaps more murderous than others, but they join company with a variety of characters who demonstrate "psychologically abnormal reactions" in Faulkner's fiction (Yoshizaki 1982, 119–20).

Carothers finds additional grounds for comparison in the negative portrayals of characters found in stories and novels. Emily Grierson's withdrawal is like Minnie Cooper's, but they both also resemble the stagnant lives of such different characters as Moketubbe in "Red Leaves," Old Man Meadowfill in "Hog Pawn," Jason Compson in *The Sound and the Fury*, Gail Hightower in *Light in August*, and Otis in *The Reivers* (Carothers 1981, 118–19).

Brooks finds striking the number of male and female characters whose mothers died or effectively abandoned them when they were relatively young. In the novels *Light in August*, *Go Down, Moses*, *Flags in the Dust*, *Soldiers' Pay*, *The Unvanquished*, *The Wild Palms*, nearly so in *Requiem for a Nun*, and in "A Rose for Emily," the mother's absence serves a variety of artistic needs. In "A Rose for Emily" the absence facilitates Faulkner's desire "to isolate Miss Emily Grierson almost completely and to throw her back on her own resources" (Brooks 1987, 66–70).

Emily is not the only subject in the story that can be compared to characters in other Faulkner works. Holmes compares the three errant suitors, Homer Barron in "A Rose for Emily," the banker in "Dry September," and the painter in "Miss Zilphia Gant." Although the painter does marry Zilphia, he proves no match for the influence of Mrs. Gant and absents himself from the scene as the banker does and as Homer apparently intended to do (Holmes 1966, 82). Pitavy also finds these resemblances and adds Lucas Burch to the list of errant suitors. In terms of their order of creation, Pitavy ranks Zilphia's beau as the earliest model for the suitors that follow (Pitavy 1972, 137–38). T. J. Stafford compares the faithful endurance of Tobe to the constancy of Dilsey in *The Sound and the Fury*. Like Dilsey, he serves and protects his white employer and finally survives her (Stafford [1968–69] 1970, 88–89).

The narrator of "A Rose for Emily" rivals Emily for attention, and in the view of some critics, is the most important character in the story. His presence lends itself to character comparisons with other storytellers in the canon and also moves into comparisons of other formal strategies. Millgate proposes that although the narrator is not named as such, Faulkner may have originally thought of him as Quentin Compson (1980, 29). Brooks also compares the effective use of a narrator in "A Rose for Emily" with the less successful narration in "Idyll in the Desert." The "Idyll" narrator knows the protagonists, but he is not so fully immersed in the community as is the

"Emily" narrator. Further, the strategy does not elicit in the reader the same degree of acceptance of the woman's fidelity to her long departed lover as that developed in "A Rose for Emily" and even in "Miss Zilphia Gant" (Brooks [1978] 1990, 164). Ferguson describes the narrators of "A Rose for Emily" and "Death Drag" as having "no real substance as human beings," but similarly serving to underscore the "contrast between the values of the community and of the outsiders who are the subjects of these stories" (1991, 110).

Joseph Reed uses "A Rose for Emily" as a touchstone in his analysis of Faulkner's narrative technique. He compares the narrator's role in this text with such diverse stories as "Hair" and "A Bear Hunt" as well as the novels *As I Lay Dying* and *Light in August*. The narrator in "A Rose for Emily" initiates the reader into Emily's history with a meticulousness absent in "Hair." Although "Hair" seems at first to work like "A Rose for Emily," even with subgroups in the community expressing different opinions, there is less need to relate the history of the characters since they are "outlanders" rather than members of the community. Reed compares "Hawkshaw-watching" with "Emily-watching," but he notes that the narrator of "Hair" is revealed to be wrong in his assumptions about the conclusion of the Henry Stribling (Hawkshaw)-Susan Reed courtship.

"A Bear Hunt" is another text that uses the "our town" consciousness although in an abbreviated form. It achieves the "benefits which are to be had from collaboration and joint discovery." In "A Rose for Emily" there is an "appeal for our empathetic participation in the town"; this overture to the reader is not apparent in the more "dispassionate but not really neutral" town and narrator of "Dry September." The narrative complexity of *As I Lay Dying* necessitates a stretch in our allegiance not required in "A Rose for Emily." The reader of the novel is more easily led to empathize with the various isolates in the Bundren family, but this association is alleviated by the interspersing of the community's views. Reed also compares the telling of Hightower's career to the narrative pattern in "A Rose for Emily" (1973, 24-26, 51-52, 87-89, 134).

Hugh Ruppersburg calls the narrator in "A Rose for Emily" a "character-symbol," that is, by collecting the bits of information the town knows, he "becomes an encompassing symbol of community reaction." The narrator shares this quality with several characters in *Light in August*—Byron, Stevens, and Sheriff Kennedy (Ruppersburg 1983, 15, 46). Louis Brodsky finds a forerunner of the narrator in the early Faulkner poem "Elder Watson in Heaven." This narrator employs a "collective, communal 'we'" similar to that found in "A Rose for Emily" (Brodsky 1990, 47).

The web of intertextual relationships between this story and other Faulkner works increases considerably with the appearance of Colonel Sartoris. The Griersons "accept or represent the Sartoris standard." In terms of chronology, Colonel Sartoris in the novel *Sartoris* dies in 1876, but he is living in 1894 in the short story, the year in which he remits Emily's taxes (Cantwell [1953] 1985, 149, 159 n. 1).

Critics have also found particular settings, themes, and images present in "A Rose for Emily" that recur in other fictions. "A Rose for Emily" and "Miss Zilphia Gant" share with "That Evening Sun" a similar setting and period of time. Further, all three encompass but do not reveal an act of violence (Millgate [1961] 1966, 64).

Brooks classifies "A Rose for Emily" as an extreme depiction of courtly love. Especially relevant to this interpretation is the view that the courtly lover's real love is death, and an ambivalent mix of love and hate actually attaches to the object of the lover's passion. Brooks includes among Faulkner's courtly lovers Gavin Stevens and Labove in *The Hamlet*, Bayard Sartoris in *The Unvanquished*, and Quentin Compson in *The Sound and the Fury*. Unlike the other examples, "A Rose for Emily" presents a literal fulfillment of the lover's desire (Brooks [1963] 1990, 192–205). André Bleikasten likens the disturbing presence of a corpse in *As I Lay Dying* to the similar situation in "A Rose for Emily." In both cases, the "time separating the corpse's first appearance and its burial is prolonged to excess, beyond tolerable bounds" (Bleikasten 1973, 116).

Béatrice Lang contends that the "intagliated, prismatic technique" of "Dr. Martino" resembles the same approach in "A Rose for Emily" and other stories in which the true nature of the central character is obscured (1976, 23).

Watson studies houses in Faulkner's fiction, noting how diverse they are in embodying "their own sets of social rules and exemptions." Emily's house is one example. Homer Barron's name contributes to the characterization of the barrenness of the home (Watson 1980a, 137–38). Watson also compares the coverage of lengthy periods of time in "Victory" and "A Rose for Emily." Both texts eschew dates for events and employ episodic structure and broken chronology (Watson 1987, 98).

Carothers notes the diverse development of violence that results in murder in "The Hound," "Wash," "A Rose for Emily," "Dry September," "Mountain Victory," *The Unvanquished*, and *Knight's Gambit* (1985, 20–21).

Skei shows how Faulkner repeatedly emphasizes the importance of the historical dimension. "A Rose for Emily" shares this concern with such diverse stories as the Indian tales, "Mountain Victory," and "There Was a Queen." The point is repeated that although man tries to deny change and its concomitant uncertainty and unpredictability, change is inevitable. Skei generalizes from the work of Ray West, concluding that the story says "man must cope with his time, past and present, and that he cannot ignore the present and make time stand still or otherwise yield to his demands" (Skei 1985, 204, 310 n. 27).

In his extended work on Faulkner's short stories, Ferguson identifies a wide range of relationships among them. He finds Faulkner's "awareness of the dangers of abstraction" prevalent in the short stories. "A Rose for Emily," "Mountain Victory," "Victory," and "Wash" present the danger in adhering to the abstraction of social class. Ferguson also groups "A Rose for Emily" with such diverse stories as "Lizards in Jamshyd's Courtyard," "Tomorrow," and "Honor," and the sketch "Sunset." All of these stories share the characteristic of beginning at "virtually the ends of their *fabulae*." One of Faulkner's techniques of opening is a "quiet," distanced introduction, appearing in such stories as "A Rose for Emily," "That Evening Sun," and "A Courtship." Faulkner used sexually charged imagery in obvious fashion in a number of stories, but the imagery is much more subtle in "such mature stories as 'A Rose for Emily,' 'Fox Hunt,' 'Mountain Victory,' and 'The Brooch'" (Ferguson 1991, 81, 129, 133, 142–43).

Several studies have examined the means by which Faulkner imposes unity on his story collections. In many respects, the issues dealt with in the collections reiterate those observations already made about relationships between "A Rose for Emily" and other stories in *These 13* and *Collected Stories*. Millgate observes that in planning *These 13* Faulkner separated "A Rose for Emily" and "Dry September" despite, or possibly because of, the similar characterizations of Emily and Minnie. By avoiding the more obvious links, he prevented a presentation of fragmented clusters and gained a contrapuntal effect within the sections (Millgate [1966] 1989, 261–62). Putzel finds the middle section of *These 13* that includes "A Rose for Emily" to be unified by a "single moral theme." Putzel does not articulate the precise nature of that theme, but emphasizes that all of the stories possess a vitality that comes from their being stories written when Faulkner was a young adult (1985, 291).

In his study of *These 13*, Watson finds a recurrence of symbolic death-by-water images. He traces these images in "Red Leaves," "A Justice," "Dry September" (somewhat less convincingly), and "A Rose for Emily" (Watson 1980b, 213). As an older, obese woman, Emily looks "bloated, like a body long submerged in motionless water, and of that pallid hue" (*CS* 121). In further links between the stories in the collection, Watson points out how the protagonists and narrators of "A Rose for Emily" and "Hair" "emerge as counterparts of one another." He compares Hawkshaw's loss of his fiancée, Sophie Starnes, to Emily's loss of Homer, as Hawkshaw's subsequent life while living out his obligation to Sophie is barren. He, however, eventually enjoys the reward of fidelity. The lives of both Hawkshaw and Emily serve as a "lesson to the narrator, who acquires understanding of himself and his own frailties thereby." These narrators "fail to credit the humanity of their subjects and are forcefully reminded of it in the end" (Watson 1980b, 216–17).

Ferguson emphasizes "variations in tonality" in the separate sections of *These 13*. In the second part, the horror of "Red Leaves" and "A Rose for

Emily" is relieved by comedy in "A Justice" and "Hair," followed in turn by the despair of "That Evening Sun" and "Dry September." He agrees with Watson (see below) that the ritual murders of the opening and closing stories provide further unity. Similarly, the "alienated female protagonists" in "A Rose for Emily" and "That Evening Sun" link the second and penultimate stories (Ferguson 1991, 150–51).

In *Collected Stories* "Dry September" and "A Rose for Emily" remain separated by several intervening stories; however, the juxtaposition of "A Rose for Emily" and "Hair" exploits the obvious. The third story in "The Village" section, "Centaur in Brass," employs a first-person narrator who speaks for Jefferson in much the same way the narrator recounts Emily's story. By contrast, the narrator of "Hair" is more specifically characterized by including details of his life (Millgate [1966] 1989, 272).

Philip Momberger defines "The Village" as the nightmarish portrayal of disintegrating moral and social structures of the community. The collapsing families in "Elly," "That Evening Sun," and "A Rose for Emily" all reside in dark houses. Further in the larger human family, the outcasts who are suffering—Emily, the aviators in "Death Drag," Will Mayes in "Dry September," and Nancy in "That Evening Sun"—are all abandoned (Momberger 1978, 20–31).

Kinney looks for unity in the narrative design of *Collected Stories*. He likens the sympathetic treatment of Emily to the presentation of Susan Reed of "Hair" in her "slow decline" rather than to the portrayal of Hawkshaw. Kinney also points to thematic threads that link "A Rose for Emily" to "Barn Burning." Both Emily and Sarty Snopes are mistreated by their fathers. They are both alienated, and they both "save themselves by turning on their own people." As a result they are made human and therefore proper subjects for a sympathetic response. Kinney adds that Emily, like Ab Snopes, exacts an exploitive vengeance: she kills Homer; Ab burns the barn. These common threads serve as links between the two stories, each of which opens a new section in *Collected Stories*. In a cumulative building of impressions within the collection, the deaths of Emily and the body servant in "Red Leaves" become "outward realizations" of spiritual deaths in such other characters as Sarty Snopes, Elly, Uncle Willy, Moketubbe, John Sartoris, and Alexander Gray (Kinney 1980, 66–67, 71).

Watson believes that "A Rose for Emily" and "That Evening Sun" serve as framing stories for "The Village." As Watson explains, "The white spinster and the black washerwoman share the same destiny for the same human reasons; in addition they represent two extremes of the isolated life between which other characters in 'The Village' work out their own destinies with varying degrees of failure or success" (1980b, 221).

Ferguson emphasizes that many of the linking characteristics of *These 13* appear again in "The Village" section of *Collected Stories*. In this instance, "A

Rose for Emily" and "That Evening Sun" respectively open and close the section. The tone of the stories fluctuates through "heavy" and "light" variations (Ferguson 1991, 158–59).

Given the extensive use of "A Rose for Emily" as a comparative text within the Faulkner canon, it is somewhat surprising that Faulkner himself made no further use of Emily's tale. In contrast to the stories told and retold in the Yoknapatawpha fiction, her story is not recaptured in other texts and does not become legendary in Jefferson (Kerr 1983, 281–82).

## Interpretation and Criticism

Examinations of "A Rose for Emily" span more than a half-century and analyze the story from many different critical perspectives. Formal considerations of Faulkner's story-making technique accompany psychological interpretations that seek to explain the pathological mentality of a murderer or interpret Emily's behavior as a consequence of the culture's narrowly prescribed role for women. Other readings enlarge the significance of the text to represent a symbolic clash of post–Civil War North and South or antebellum South and modern South. These symbolic overlays are closely related to and typically develop from the readings in which Emily is seen in the human effort of seeking to control time but inevitably failing. A recent interpretation suggests that the clash is not between North and South but is rather an ideological struggle between aristocracy and democracy. Most efforts at interpretation attempt to find meaning beyond Lionel Trilling's early, dismissive evaluation of the story as "essentially trivial in its horror because it has no implications, because it is pure event without implication" (1931, 492).

Many critics seek to understand Emily's story by understanding her individual psyche. Viewed chronologically, these criticisms reveal a more recent willingness to make explicit use of the terms of psychoanalysis and also to suggest more feminist renderings of the text. O'Connor aligns himself with those who see the story as the effects of repressed desires, showing how the "denial of normal emotions invites retreat into a marginal world, into fantasy." He disagrees with the interpretation of the story as revolving around Old South–New South issues because although it may add to the tone of the work, such a reading does not represent the "poles of conflict" in the story (O'Connor 1954, 68–69; see also O'Connor [1952] 1970, 44–45).

Faulkner himself described Emily as repressed and restricted by a father who wanted a housekeeper. He added that the repression of desire inevitably manifests itself in some other form. Emily, Faulkner said, "was a young girl that just wanted to be loved and to love and to have a husband and a family" (*FU* 184–85). Although that image of a repressed female has been endorsed by a great many respondents to the text, few have described the conflict in the story in the religious terms Faulkner used when he called it a conflict between God and Satan within Emily: having defied her traditional upbringing, she breaks the law of God by committing murder. Faulkner explained her continued allegiance to the corpse as her expiation for the crime. He did not believe, however, that pity for Emily was unwarranted (*FU* 58–59).

Brooks and Warren describe Emily as a "conscious aristocrat" who "insists on meeting the world on her own terms," an attitude in which both the admirable and the horrible reside. She demonstrates "pride, isolation, and independence," typical characteristics of the hero (1946, 409–14; see also Brooks 1973, 387–88, and Brooks [1978] 1990, 157).

Malin links Emily's behavior to her relationship with her father. He argues that Emily's attachment to her father interferes with her normal development. Immediately after Mr. Grierson's death, she attempts to deny that he is dead, but in subsequent years she assumes his role. Despite the unresolved attachment to her now-deceased father, Emily enters into a sexual relationship with Homer Barron. Her allegiance to her father drives her to murder Homer "so that he will resemble the dead father she can never forget." For Malin, Emily is the kind of character Faulkner distrusts because her identification with male roles "not only perverts the woman's desire for natural affection and motherhood—it creates social tensions" (1957, 37–38). Charles Allen sees Emily's sleeping with Barron's corpse as her means of lying also with her father, but he draws quite a different conclusion from the text. Despite its psychotic character, Emily's behavior represents a "fierce exercise of her human will" and a "laudable sense of traditional social and moral values." Faulkner satirizes the "bland conformity" that the community would press upon her (Allen 1960, 59–60).

Howell believes Emily kills Homer "because her finer nature reasserts itself" with the realization that "she has violated the laws of God and man." The Grierson cousins are effective in their censure of the relationship between Emily and Homer, and Emily decides to "annihilate the source of evil that has brought a corruption into her life." Her method of removal, although influenced by her insanity, is conducted with "calm deliberation" and planning. According to Howell, Emily achieves a victory over her inappropriate desires. She "retrieves her dignity by reasserting the values in which she was trained." Howell takes issue with the assumption that Homer intended to leave Emily. He argues that textual evidence indicates otherwise. Homer describes himself as a bachelor, he stays after the paving project is completed, and when he enters the kitchen, there is no indication that his intention is to terminate the relationship (Howell 1966, 14–15).

Gil Muller examines Emily as the "artist as outsider and as visionary." He traces images of art in each section of the story as well as Emily's short-term profession as a teacher of china painting. He argues that Emily's career as artist culminates in the "three-dimensional tableau" that the townspeople discover in the upstairs bedroom. In that creation, Homer Barron's petrified corpse assumes the status of art object. Emily's creation fuses the bridal and funereal, the "emotions of a lifetime," the "sublime and perverse." The townspeople who originally thought of Emily and her father as tableau, that is, a set-piece of upper-class Jefferson society, are confronted with another tableau that reveals the "interior life of the artist" Emily (Muller 1975, Item 79).

Norman Holland offers an extended interpretation implementing a psychoanalytic approach, but he insists that his own analysis is unique to his individual reading. He does not dismiss other interpretations, including the historical focus as a South–North conflict and the mythic reading of Emily as the goddess Persephone, creator and destroyer (here the monument is in conflict with progress); however, he believes the story is predominantly a study of the individual who defends against change with incorporation and denial. Holland links Emily's defensive strategies to a childhood developmental stage of learning to control body functions such as moving one's bowels (the anal stage). Emily's story is one of retention, that is, "about the difficulty one has in giving up prized things from a certain house (or body)." Emily, in defiance, retains in her house her father and Homer. She also becomes obese. The movements in and out of house, or room, or body also relate to her deprived sexuality. (On the level of a North–South conflict, Emily is also the model of the South's effort to stall change. Holland calls this condition a state of "social constipation.") Emily's wish to *have* her father becomes a wish to *be* her father; hence, as she ages she assumes a masculine appearance and character. The inappropriateness of taking a Yankee lover corresponds with her forbidden desire for her father. Homer becomes a portion of the "dirt, dust, and smell" that Holland sees pervade the story. By murdering Homer, Emily acts as her father did to protect her, but she also has the forbidden lover she desires (1975, 20–38; see also Holland 1972, 1–35).

Holland also considers the role of the community in Emily's behavior. He uses Erik Erikson's explanation of shame as visual exposure as an important way to understand the community's constant watching of Emily. When shame becomes a significant means of control, it results in defiantly shameless behavior (Emily's consorting with a Northern man) and secretiveness (Emily's concealing a corpse). From the beginning, the roles of women and men are differentiated, but Emily and the narrator are throughout the development of the story "curiously androgynous." The town's distinction between roles mirrors the external control in Emily's life as long as her father lived and before she "incorporated his masculinity into herself." Emily's voice reinforces the image of her retentiveness. Whereas Homer is loquacious and merry, a quality that represents his potency, when Emily speaks, her voice is cold—yet another form of retention. The story reflects the process of denial and incorporation, both in Emily's behavior and in the narrator's control over telling the story. The impetus for action resides in the statement "with nothing left, she would have to cling to that which had robbed her, as people will" (*CS* 124). According to Holland, the story is about "perceiving change as robbery and resisting that robbery by taking into oneself the outer being that seeks to force you to change" (1975, 20–38; see also Holland 1972, 1–35).

Wayne Tefs takes issue with Holland's undue neglect of the concluding revelation of the corpse and hair at the end of the story and contends that Holland has anesthetized the "terror and horror" that come from the incest motif. He is particularly critical of associating the adult Emily's personality with infantile origins, as if the fictional character were an appropriate subject for "depth analysis." Tefs draws on Holland's argument that in using psychoanalytic techniques in literary study the most important minds are the reader's and the author's and the least important is the character's. Tefs argues that a fictional character lacks sufficient context to be a subject for psychoanalytic explanation. In the specific case of "A Rose for Emily," the interpretation loses the "sense of relatedness between the work and the reader" (Tefs 1974, 50–57).

Judith Fetterley interprets "A Rose for Emily" from a feminist perspective as the "story of a *lady* and of her revenge for that grotesque identity." In Fetterley's reading, grotesqueness "results when stereotypes are imposed upon reality," with the subsequent implication that the "real grotesque is the stereotype itself." Fetterley underscores the importance of the tableau of Emily and her father. Emily's "identity is determined by the constructs of her father's mind" from which she cannot escape. This identity extends to a community that insists, unlike Faulkner, in defining her as "Miss Emily." (Faulkner's titular tribute omits the label "Miss.") Being defined as a "lady" makes her a community monument, forces her to assume a code of noblesse oblige, and makes her the object of community gossip when she rejects that role. The remission of taxes by Colonel Sartoris is as oppressive as his edict that Negro women should wear aprons. His action denies Emily economic independence. As Fetterley observes, "a lady, if she is to survive, must have either husband or father, and . . . , because Emily has neither, the town must assume responsibility for her." The narrator, like Mr. Grierson, Judge Stevens, and Colonel Sartoris, adapts a patriarchal attitude by taking it upon himself to define Emily's life. His asides reveal a contempt for women's opinions, but he exempts Emily from that group because she is a "real lady." She becomes in his definition more and more objectified and less human. The violence acted upon Emily's life has consequences for the community. She gets away with murder because the community refuses to see her as anything but a lady. Thus, she does not have to be a reasonable or responsible taxpaying member of the community, nor does she have to declare her purpose in buying the poison. A lady might kill herself, but she would not kill a man. She is protected from the odor emanating from her house (as if she cannot smell it herself) because the other women assume that it is the fault of a man's ineptitude in matters of housekeeping. Thus, the violence is reciprocal, though Emily's power is only to react, not to act. Fetterley concludes that the story is a "supreme analysis of what men do to women by making them ladies; it is also an exposure of how this act in turn defines and recoils upon men" (1978, 34–45).

Brooks rejects as simplistic the analogies drawn between Emily and the Old South as well as the argument that her necrophilia extends to society's necrophilic "living with a dead but unburied past." He dispenses with the notion that the narrative is peculiarly Southern by citing instances of corpses discovered long after death in London, in Massachusetts, and in Portland, Oregon, and Albuquerque, New Mexico. Brooks believes Emily's mental state reflects the "malaise of the age." She exhibits her defiant nature when she entertains Homer despite the community's disapproval. Brooks accepts the interpretation that Homer Barron is about to desert Emily. When she reacts to Homer's leaving, she crosses the line from "harmless obsession" to "homicidal mania" (Brooks [1978] 1990, 384–88, 153–54, 157).

Barbara Lupack also finds the tableau representations of Emily with her father and Emily with Homer to reinforce the similarities between the two men. The picture of Emily with her father clearly reflects his domination of her; his back is turned to her, indicating his lack of concern for her own personhood. Lupack argues that as Emily is very nearly imprisoned in her house, she does not intend to let the second man part from her or her house (1981, 6–7).

Scherting offers another psychoanalytic interpretation that investigates the motive for murder, an issue he believes has been inappropriately neglected. He does not find sufficient evidence for the often argued view that Emily acts because Homer has jilted her. Scherting claims that Faulkner consciously exploited the literary possibilities of Freudian psychology in a story of a female's oedipal fixation on her father. Homer Barron serves, after Mr. Grierson's death, as surrogate. Because of her father's oppressive watchfulness over her, Emily has been prevented from forming an attachment to a person other than her father. When he dies, she denies his death in a retreat from reality and a regression into childhood. (Her shortened hair makes her look girlish.) Nevertheless, she clings to her father's image. Scherting finds evidence to suggest the association between Homer and Mr. Grierson. Both are pictured holding a horsewhip, and both are strong willed. Poisoning Homer is a murder/marriage that allows her to retain the present object of "her unresolved Oedipal desires" as she was unable to do when her father died. The final description of the corpse also contains enough ambiguous language to allow interpretation of either Homer or Mr. Grierson as the person referred to. Both the corpse and the crayon portrait of Mr. Grierson are described as "profound." Homer's individual visage has been obliterated by decay, but her father's image remains sharp in the portrait. Additionally, the phrase "The long sleep that outlasts love, that conquers even the grimace of love, had cuckolded him" may refer either to Emily's death or to Homer's having been cuckolded by the remembrance of the father. Scherting places the blame squarely on Mr. Grierson "for Emily's distorted sexuality." He extends the interpretation to the historical context by arguing that the South, like the Griersons, "attempted to protect itself through isolation and to perpetuate its values through relationships which were fundamentally incestuous and inevitably debilitating" (Scherting 1980, 397–405; see also Polk 1984, 85–86).

Strandberg supplies a list of correlations between Freud and Faulkner by which Emily might be understood. The "rich brew" includes oedipal fixation, trauma, regression, narcissism, and sexual perversion (Strandberg 1981, 77).

For Skei, Emily is motivated by a refusal to accept change, a tendency toward madness in the family, an overprotected childhood, and a failure to maintain contact with reality. Her life teaches her that change brings loss. She fails to "adjust to a world almost completely transformed during her lifetime." Emily lives her life "acting out what she has reason to believe is her alleged role as a woman, no matter how misunderstood it is. She only does 'as people will,'" but she succeeds only by seclusion. Her solution is ultimately unworkable because isolation and withdrawal offer no life. Emily is a "living dead person" and a fallen monument. Skei suggests that the community may feel some grudging admiration for Emily's independence. When she dies and is buried among the Civil War veterans, she returns to the age in which she had ensconced her life for perhaps fifty or sixty years (Skei 1985, 112, 123–24; see also Skei 1977 72–78; *CS* 119).

Hochman notes how the altered sequence of events presents an initially fixed picture of Emily then interposes images of her in past experiences. Although a cluster of possibilities exists to explain what happened and why it happened, no certain explanation is validated as the cause. The resulting picture of Emily is "multiply ambiguous." The final image of her is fixed, but how she progressed to that point is fluid. Hochman's observations are pertinent to the text though they are somewhat diminished by apparently inaccurate descriptions of particular incidents of the story. He describes the tableau of Emily and Mr. Grierson as the father's horsewhipping a suitor. Perhaps Hochman agrees with those critics who read the "strand" of gray hair as a "lock," for he describes the hair on the pillow as a "pigtail" (1985, 149–52).

Mellard explains that Emily seeks the "plenitude of power and knowledge associated with the father . . . and symbolized in the Phallus." Foiled in her effort to keep her father (either living or dead), Emily substitutes Homer Barron as "her symbol of phallic power in life and in death." She takes his power through contiguity, either "by physical proximity or even ingestion," hence her obesity and her association with Blake's worm destroying the rose (Mellard 1986, 37–45).

In his study of letters in Faulkner's fiction, James Watson shows that Emily's letter to the town is "expressive of her life alone in the old house." Her writing is on archaic paper, in an old-fashioned hand, in faded ink. Emily's refusal to accept postal delivery or the necessary house numbers and mail box places her "beyond the appeal of all letters, and so beyond the need to respond" (Watson 1987, 95–96).

Hal Blythe suggests that Emily's motive for murder is to avenge Homer's "pseudo-courtship" that he has been using to cover his homosexuality. Blythe sees in Homer's name, his preference for the company of young men, and in the sterile image of dust that covers his corpse, evidence of Homer's homosexuality. When Emily discovers his deception, she murders him and arranges the body and bedroom in the image of the chivalric ideal. The story becomes, in this reading, another of Faulkner's stories of sexual deviation that reflects the "decay of an Old South tradition" (Blythe 1989, 49–50).

John Duvall suggests that the female subject's position as sexual being in the patriarchal world delineated by Faulkner includes the role of spinster as providing only an illusory independence from male authority. Like Fetterley, Duvall sees the narrator's attitude as confirming spinsterhood to be a negative role for females. He notes the juxtaposition of the narrator's explanation of Emily's unmarried state with the comment about her aunt's insanity, the point being "that a woman would be insane if she refused marriage." The story makes a strong critique of a system that denies a woman's unmarried status but accords privileges to male bachelorhood. Emily's action forces the community to think about its gender assumptions, but Duvall adds that the behavior of the Jefferson community in "Dry September"—that is, its disregard for Will Mayes's guilt or innocence—represents its failure do so (1990, 119–29).

As these analyses reveal, numerous critics judge Emily mad. The ultimate discovery of the "long strand of iron-gray hair" on the pillow beside the decomposed corpse has raised among the critics some discussion as to whether Emily was necrophilic (*CS* 130). Many critics assume that the hair is sufficient evidence of necrophilia and incorporate that assumption into their interpretations. Maurice Coindreau, whose French translation of the story greatly pleased Faulkner, assumes necrophilia when he describes Emily as "an old maid who for many years spends each night beside the skeleton of her lover" (1971, 65). A few critics, however, question the certainty of the issue. Howell reads the evidence of the dust-coated room to mean that it has been undisturbed for the forty years. He contends that the evidence of the story suggests that Emily's hair turned gray and grew long after her father's death and her own subsequent illness during which her hair was cut. Howell adds that reading necrophilia into the text is inconsistent with the sympathy and admiration for Emily that prevails in the titular tribute to her. If she is necrophilic, she is not tragic (Howell [1961] 1970, 59–60; Howell 1966, 13–14).

Sister Mary Bride agrees with Howell that the reading of necrophilia in the story is "artistically untenable." She adds, however, that Howell misinterprets the hint as an exploitation of its horror value. She argues that the implication is too obvious and commonly read to be lightly dismissed and sees it as part of Faulkner's ambivalence toward the South. For Bride, Emily and the Old South are analogous. The paradoxical ending implies both respect (a rose) and contempt for her and the South. It is a "revolting spectacle of an aging and impotent culture couching with a corrupt materialism which its nobler components had rejected" (Bride [1962] 1970, 66–67).

Hagopian contributes another reading that denies the presence of necrophilia in the story. He dismisses Howell's reading as inconsistent with the textual evidence and explains the presence of the hair in a different manner altogether. In the classical tradition of ancient Greece, the offering of a lock of hair was a gesture of grief, farewell, or remembrance over the grave or corpse. Emily's upbringing would likely have included reading Homer, thus her acquaintance with the tradition. Accordingly, "strand" must be read as "lock." Hagopian further connects this argument with the fact that Barron's first name is Homer and that it would be another confirmation of Emily's rootedness in tradition (Hagopian 1962, 44–46; see also Hagopian and Dolch 1964, Item 68).

Ruth Sullivan believes that arguments against necrophilia in the text deny "clear signs Faulkner leaves that Miss Emily slept for years next to the decaying body of the man she murdered" (1971, 164). Arthur Clements responds to Howell's reading with a middle-of-the-road argument holding that Emily must have lain with the corpse at some distant time after the murder, but not for many years before her death. Like Howell, Clements focuses on the length and color of Emily's hair. He reads the evidence as suggesting that only after Homer's murder is it stated that her hair became iron-gray in color like the strand on the pillow. Clements suggests that Emily might have discontinued lying with the corpse during the period of time she gave painting lessons because after this she is noticed only in the downstairs windows (Clements [1962] 1970, 64–65). Scherting counts at least two occasions on which Emily lies with Homer's body. He believes one time must have involved positioning the body in an embrace because the suffering involved in arsenic poisoning would have left it contorted. At a later time, when her hair had assumed its salt-and-pepper appearance, she visited the chamber again (Scherting 1980, 403 n. 8).

Emily lives in seclusion that is at least partially self-imposed, but she does not live in a vacuum. Brooks and Warren discuss the story's extension beyond a case study of abnormal psychology. They contend that the story obtains significance in the interplay between Emily and the community for which she serves the function of "idol and scapegoat" (Brooks and Warren 1946, 409–14). The community admires her as a representative of its past, but it feels superior to her because of her failure to establish normalcy within her contemporary world. All of Emily's actions are measured "against the counterforce of tradition, convention, decreed usage, and received moral law." The community itself responds variously with curiosity, pity, outrage, envy, admiration—a full mix of emotions that reinforce its own humanity. Brooks suggests that the community would ultimately recognize Emily as a victim, one who "had not willed the great warping of her life," and that her effort to meet life on her own terms was somehow "heroic" (Brooks 1978, 5, 14–15; Brooks [1978] 1990, 158–63; Brooks 1987, 40–41). Related to this notion of Emily as heroic is the "warrior metaphor" by which she defeats the community. The narrator describes her actions with such words as *vanquished*, *invincible*, *rout*, and *invasions*. Thus, as a "romantic heroine," Emily receives a tributary rose (Strandberg 1981, 4, 7, 20–21).

Hagopian explains Emily's murder of Homer as necessary because the community no longer lives by the code mandating that a gentleman should avenge her honor. Because she was reared in and was part of an older aristocratic tradition "and [was] at heart a sentimentalist," Emily must do what others have failed to do for her. Mr. Grierson is a representative of the "sterile courtesy and gentility" of the past; unlike Judge Stevens and Colonel Sartoris he has been unable to make "practical adjustments to necessity." The model he offers his daughter lacks vitality, but so does her relationship with Homer because he does not have sufficient character to help her adopt a new life. Consequently, Emily is completely thwarted and falls victim to the insanity present in her family. Emily is insane, perhaps necrophilic, but also tragic. Hagopian believes it is erroneous to emphasize the larger thematic implications of time to the exclusion of considering the madness of Emily. He does not deny, however, the importance of time in the story in terms of cultural history, personal experience, and aesthetic technique (Hagopian 1962, 46–47).

Page, Skei, and Carothers all observe the ways in which the community's concern for Emily turns attention back to its self-involvement. Page discusses the community's need to ostracize Emily for its own benefit, noting that in this attitude the townspeople seek to release their hostility and to enhance their sense of self-righteousness (Page 1972, 100). Skei adds that the description of Emily as "tradition, a duty, and a care" describes the attitudes of three successive generations toward her (*CS* 119; Skei 1985, 109; see also Skei 1977, 66). From a slightly different perspective, Carothers shows how the community becomes the focus of Faulkner's criticism. He describes "A Rose for Emily" as no mere Gothic tale but, "among other things, an expression of moral outrage, an indictment those conventions and customs which drive Miss Emily to murder Homer Barron" (Carothers 1985, 22).

The extent to which Colonel Sartoris's remission of Emily's taxes is seen as a benevolent act varies. Holland places it in the context of divergent male and female roles emphasized in the text. The idea could only be a man's, and only a woman would believe it (Holland 1975, 28). Walter Sullivan, however, contrasts it as an example of the "best of ways" of community as opposed to its "worst of ways" such as the murder of Joe Christmas (1976, 40).

Whether Colonel Sartoris helps or hurts Emily, he is not the most important representative of the Jefferson community relating to her. That honor goes to the narrator. Despite how little is actually known about the storyteller, a significant amount of effort has been expended to characterize this individual. Nikolaus Happel examines the narrator's role in an attempt to define the "we" to which the narrator belongs. The narrator offers objective reporting of some facts, but also identifies himself as a participant in the action. He is never an "I," and the "we" occurs in various references throughout the story that include suggestions of "people," "ladies," and "older people." Eventually "we" comes to represent the collective community. Happel notes that although the aldermen at first are not "we," they are eventually gathered into the collective "we" that taxes Emily. The narrator distinguishes as "they" those who wait until after Emily's funeral before "they" open up the room; however, "we" look at the corpse. Happel concludes that although the "we" is obscure, it is certain that the "depicted reality and the world of the narrator coalesce." In one respect, however, the narrator distances himself from the community's attitude. Happel comments that although a rose is never mentioned in the story, "bought flowers" are. These purchased flowers fail to express a sincere sympathy for Emily, and if linked to the flower of the title "must be construed as irony . . . directed against the lovelessness of the townsfolk." The narrator's recognition of their lack of sympathy helps to demonstrate the genuineness of his own sympathy for Emily (Happel [1962] 1970, 68–70).

Helen Nebeker, like Happel, follows closely the pronoun usage and references to try to characterize the narrator. Nebeker defines several groups within the text including the "Old Aristocracy," "Post–War Generation," "Newer Rising Generation," "Newer Second Generation," and a "Composite Product." The composite is a subculture "we" linked with all other groups and responds both to civic duty and to Southern honor. The "narrative we" is a member of the Post–War Generation and is chronologically and perhaps socially Emily's peer. This "narrative we" reveals knowledge of Emily's trip to the pharmacy and the instructions on the arsenic, the fact of the sealed room unentered for forty years, and, by implication, long-held knowledge of the murder and perhaps even participation in sealing the room. By keeping the murder hidden and protected all those years, "we" preserve the "honor and myth of the South," but when the murder is revealed, it offers "frightening comment on the moral fabric of the Southern social structure" (Nebeker 1970, 3–13).

Ruth Sullivan sees the narrator as a major character of the story, finding it erroneous to assume the teller's impartiality. The narrator is plural, of indeterminate age, name, gender, and occupation. What is known is that the narrator-group watches Emily for fifty or sixty years, demonstrating a consistent curiosity but an ambivalent mix of affection and revulsion for her. Sullivan applies a psychoanalytic interpretation to the somewhat "unsavory qualities" of the narrator (to whom she refers as "he" for convenience). The teller is pre-oedipal, expressing the voyeuristic, aggressive, and sadistic conflicts typical of that phase of human life and of the infantile mind. The voyeuristic watching and after-death invasion of Emily's bridal chamber are a symbolic rape of Emily in which the community, like Emily, participates in necrophilia. The narrator's aggressive response to Emily comes from his frustration with her failure to satisfy his sexual curiosity. He perceives of her as mother figure, and he both idealizes and degrades her. Emily is portrayed as above the reach of the community and its laws—the unapproachable parent. An attempt to "masculinize" her image is an effort to protect the image of "mother as virgin," but this image eventually succumbs to the image of "mother as whore" when she becomes the object of gossip concerning her relationship with Homer Barron. The narrator also experiences "anxiety over loss of the loved object" expressed particularly in his relentless watching of Emily. Sullivan associates the combined images of eyes, eating, and killing with both the narrator's and Emily's use of eyes. By portraying Emily as a "black widow spider" or possessor of the "Evil Eye," the narrator enacts his condemnation of Emily as a bad mother. But in doing so, he assumes a similar role toward her. Sullivan concludes that "A Rose for Emily" focuses on "types of perversion—Miss Emily's necrophilia and the narrator's voyeurism—that are motivated by frustrated sexual needs and by fears about loss of the loved object" (Sullivan 1971, 159–78).

Heller suggests that the narrator is distinguished from the rest of the community as the story unfolds because he treats Emily with a sympathy that is absent from the community at large. Heller stresses that the order of retelling is the narrator's rearrangement, even though he has already participated in finding the corpse in the bedroom. Heller's examination of the details leads to the conclusion that neither the past nor the present generation has treated Emily as an individual but rather relegated her to various stereotypes. Their labels and treatment reflect their different perceptions of Emily although both are reactions to an "idea of Emily." The communities of both generations are constantly disproved in their judgments, and they are repeatedly being circumvented by Emily. Actually, the images of the text emphasize the mystery of Emily and encourage the reader not to judge her. Heller mentions the staircase in her house and the watch chain she wears as images that lead to incompleteness—darkness at the top of the stairs and no watch at the end of the chain. As this critic points out, at the end, the reader still knows little about Emily but has developed sympathy for her because of her victimization by a close-minded community. At the same time, the community is criticized for its presumption of knowledge and lack of sympathy (Heller 1972, 301–18). For John Gerlach, Heller's observation that at the story's end the reader is left with more rather than less mystery runs counter to the effect of revelation in most surprise endings (1985, 173 n. 11).

Brooks sees the narrator, estimated to be in his fifties or sixties when Emily dies, as fully aligned with the conscience of the community, although he adds that there are identifiable subgroups within the community and across generations. The narrator does not impose his own judgments. He is fully enmeshed in the Jefferson community, possesses a sense of history, and is a good observer and storyteller. His intention extends beyond the story to "deeper meanings," and he maintains Emily's humanity (Brooks [1978] 1990, 158; Brooks 1987, 32).

Scherting contends that the narrator is most likely male. When he distinguishes between male and female opinion, he associates himself with the male view. Scherting also believes that the narrator is a naïve raconteur in his failure to explain Emily's derangement or motive for murder (1980, 397). Walter Allen goes further and sees Faulkner in the unnamed storyteller, acting as spokesman of the community (1981, 183). Very recently, Michael Burduck has argued that the narrator is a woman who with other women of the community makes up the "we" that press the men of the community into action as Emily's behavior runs counter to local norms (1990, 209–11).

Emily's association with male characters includes her relationship to Tobe, who passes from youth to old age in her employment. Charles Nilon opens a new interpretive arena with the examination of Tobe's significance in the story. He describes Tobe's exit after Emily's death as "an act of consideration" from "one of Faulkner's faithful servants" (Nilon 1965, 32). In his later analysis of the journey (or escape) motif of black characters in Faulkner's fiction, Nilon describes Tobe's movement as "quiet." Nonetheless, it is a movement that reveals "his need to control his life by living it on his own terms." Tobe's life reflects such a movement, particularly in his leaving after Emily's death (Nilon 1981, 227–29).

Stafford sees Emily's movement toward decay as countered by Tobe's movement toward purposeful activity. Although Tobe is not talkative, he is busy gardening, marketing, and cooking to sustain Emily. The townspeople's speculation that Tobe has killed an animal underscores his protective role and altruism. Stafford points out that in the section in which Emily does act—riding around town with Homer and buying arsenic—Tobe is absent. Although he is Emily's potential source of contact with the outside world and her model of a purposeful, healthy individual, she does not benefit from his example. Emily's failure "to avail herself of his humanity" helps to explain the perversion of her relationship with Homer and her general failure in relationships. In this reading, her pride is constrictive and unadmirable, especially as contrasted with Tobe's more effective, purposeful character. The name

"Tobe" ("to be") reflects the liberation he will enjoy once Emily dies (Stafford [1968–69] 1970, 87–89).

Mikio Shiroma seeks to redress the general absence of concern for Tobe. Shiroma believes that given Tobe's concealment of and perhaps participation in Homer's murder, he must be given the same admiration that critics hold for Emily. Over the years, Tobe becomes one of three men with whom Emily forms an "intimate" relationship, the others being her father and Homer Barron. Colonel Sartoris also has a limited relationship with her. In fact, his decree regarding black females serves to diminish Tobe, who himself assumes the duties normally ascribed to women. Unfortunately, Shiroma's evidence linking Tobe to Mr. Grierson and Homer Barron is flimsy; nevertheless, the point that the Jefferson community and the critical community ignore his individual being in the text is accurate (1986, 21–27).

The efforts to counter Trilling's remarks about "A Rose for Emily" include interpretations that reach beyond understanding individual motives or interactive failures within the specific community. C. W. M. Johnson charges Brooks and Warren with stopping short of seeing Emily's failure to accept change, which is what he believes to be the theme of the story: resistance to change necessitates that one "love and live with death." Johnson ascribes to this message an "implied criticism of the South" ([1948] 1970, Item 45).

West contends that the story is preoccupied with change as it is played against an established social structure of the past. He endorses the comments of C. W. M. Johnson, but argues that Johnson does not press his discussion far enough beyond the issue of resistance to change. For West, the meaning of the story resides in the presentation of the two images of time: the meadow untouched by winter and the mechanical progression along which the past becomes a diminishing road (*CS* 129). Emily's tragedy extends to those Southerners who worship the past and deny present realities. He adds that by extension it is also the tragedy of the North in Homer Barron's abandonment of "traditional obligations of social decorum." West sees both positions as ineffective but views Emily's effort as heroic although she is flawed, like many heroes, by excessive hubris. By further implication the story suggests that mankind is generally "confronted by the necessity to select and honor that of the past which is applicable and helpful, to recognize and accept that of the present which is beneficial or which cannot be escaped" (West [1948] 1970 36–37; 1952, 92–94).

West examines the means by which Faulkner develops the conflict between present time and past time. Present time is represented by Homer Barron, the new aldermen who tax Emily, the new generation, and the narrator. Past time is represented by Colonel Sartoris, Tobe, and the board of aldermen who rescinded Emily's taxes. The conflict is also manifested in the changes in Emily's appearance and behavior. Emily did not always resist, but she was constantly thwarted, first by her father, then by Homer Barron, so that she finally denied time. The confused mix of past and present creates a distorted atmosphere of unreality. Both Emily and her house are fallen monuments. In the roseate room upstairs, Emily creates the timeless meadow. Of course, death overtakes her as an ultimate comment on her inability to stop time. West adds, however, that Barron's rejection of the past is equally untenable because in his unreflective pragmatism he fails to consider defeat in the form of either tradition or death. The unnatural atmosphere acts as a preparation for the concluding revelation (West [1948] 1970, 36–37; [1949] 1973, 192–98).

For Lewis Leary, Emily's behavior "speaks symbolically of every person who allows love to die or who murders love, yet clings to the sham, the unreal semblance, the dead body of love" (1973, 136).

John Jacobs studies the ironic allusions present in the name Homer Barron that contribute to the story's eulogy to the "metaphoric death of a nation." *Homer* recalls Homer of classical legend in that his life provides subject matter for rumor and speculation. Jacobs also compares the way attention to the person of the epic poet or Homer Barron is secondary to the function they serve in the movement of the narrative and their similar preference for the company of men rather than women. *Barron* also presents ironic allusions. The suggestion of the nobility is ironically offset by Homer's status as a laborer who lacks a chivalric demeanor. That Emily takes such a man as a lover is a backlash against her father's aristocratic airs. Further, since in the tableau of Emily and her father Mr. Grierson guards the back-flung front door, Homer is seen entering through the kitchen door. His continued presence in the house, albeit as a corpse, continues to "affront his [Mr. Grierson's] internal power." Finally, Jacobs adds, the surname reflects the barrenness of the relationship. This quality is significant in emphasizing "the impossibility of the old, aristocratic South's conjoining with the industrialized North to procreate an integral culture." The ambivalence of the townspeople toward Emily can be understood in their recognition that the aristocratic way of life she represents is no longer viable (Jacobs 1982, 77–79).

When asked if Homer represented the North and Emily the South in a revised ending of the Civil War, Faulkner responded that if that were so it was only incidental to his effort "to create flesh-and-blood people." He did not disregard the possibility of that reading but added that it was not a part of the conscious development of the story (*FU* 47–48; 58–59). Some critics who follow the argument of regional criticism in the story interpret it not as a national North–South dichotomy, but as a temporal Old South–Modern South conflict. Irving Howe does not believe the interpretation of the story in terms of North–South conflicts is defensible. He does see in the story a "caustic parable of Southern experience," relating to "the decay of human sensibility from false gentility to genteel perversion" (Howe [1952] 1975, 70, 265).

Walter Slatoff believes the antithetical relationship between the past and present South is "dramatically asserted" in "A Rose for Emily" (1960, 91, 103). Ross understands Faulkner's contextual milieu to be the "disintegrating South," in transition from a culture antagonistic to naturalistic forces to one in support of them. Emily is shown to be combating the realities of the present world at the price of her own distorted personality. Although Ross believes Faulkner's fiction endorses older, more traditional societies "favorable to the dignity of man," he identifies one source of Emily's "tortured life" as her father's protective domination. She can only assert herself after his death, but her involvement with a "'naturalistic' man" necessitates his death to ensure his fidelity (Ross [1961] 1970, 61–62).

Marvin Magalaner and Edmond Volpe believe that Emily's necrophilia is emblematic of an entire society that "lived with a dead but unburied past" in such continued forms as the law that required black females to wear aprons on the street. The South, like Emily, seeks to hold on to a way of life "even when it is dead" (Magalaner and Volpe [1961] 1970, 63). Gold describes Homer as a symbol of the New South and by extension, the present. The story makes a "forthright statement about the effect of past on present and the responsibility that follows the discovery of this effect" (Gold 1966, 24–25). The regional line of argument enjoyed little further development in the 1970s, generally being dismissed in criticism of the 1980s.

Frank Littler follows those who emphasize the interplay of past and present in the story. He observes how the organization of the work (the narrator's associative memories generating new bits of the story) keeps the "interpenetration of past and present" before the reader. In linear time, Emily changes, as does the town's attitude toward her. The town gives tribute to a woman who attempts, though she inevitably fails to achieve, the thing that others desire: "to dominate time." Littler does not extend the implications of his interpretation to a regional meaning (Littler 1982, 80–85). Skei comments that Homer Barron's northern background "is not the single most important fact about this story" and holds that a tale such as "Fox Hunt" makes more of a South–North contrast (1985, 313 n. 9). Putzel specifically dismisses the view he once held that this story focuses concern on "caste and class in the South" (1985, 221).

Still another critic removes the regional but retains an interpretive stance based on oppositional ideologies. Dennis Allen understands the story as a playing out of aristocratic versus democratic perspectives. He shows how the law that required black women to wear aprons on the town streets, "fathered" by Colonel Sartoris, established a separation of classes based on physical distinction—race and gender. "At its most basic," Allen writes, "the aristocratic perspective assumes a set of codified social distinctions that define people and rank them by degree." To maintain a distinct aristocratic class, such physical realities as sexuality (a merging) and death (an inevitable leveling) must be denied. Mr. Grierson, for example, guards his daughter from exogamy, not incest. The relationship between the father and daughter, however, is not physical. The association of the aristocratic with the godlike or angelic implies creation without intercourse. Allen observes how little is known of Emily's mother. When Emily's father dies, Emily assumes a masculine demeanor; she recreates her father in herself. Allen observes that the only procreative activity in the Grierson house is painting, an activity that involves copying an already extant image. When Emily kills Homer and preserves him, she denies both sexuality and death. Allen notes, however, the ambiguous movement in Emily between aristocratic and democratic impulses. She possesses a "copresence of opposites" that are not merged: she is fat but thin, living but dead, female but male. Similarly, the townspeople reveal their own ambivalence toward her. They want to see her as representing an aristocratic element in their life. Hence, she can vanquish a board of aldermen, intimidate a druggist, and compel them to spread lime around her house under cover of darkness. On the other hand, the town wants her to pay taxes like other people. Increasingly, the divergent voices within the community merge through greater use of first-person plural pronouns, becoming one voice. The conflict between the ideologies is thus shown to be more an internal than an "external battle between different ideological camps." Allen concludes that "A Rose for Emily" demonstrates both the "impulse to identify differences and to erect taxonomies and the contrary desire to deny distinctions" (Allen 1984, 685–96).

In addition to the analyses of characters and meaning, there have been numerous studies of style in "A Rose for Emily." Snell describes the story as technically flawless. The gradual revelation of information does not reveal but prepares for the ending (Snell 1947, 96–99). Leonard Doran believes that "A Rose for Emily" represents Faulkner's most effective use of suspense. It is retrogressive suspense, growing from an incident that has already occurred but that has not yet been revealed (Doran 1951, 40). Howe, like Snell, recognizes the technical skill of the story but criticizes the way in which it calls attention to this technical skill ([1952] 1975, 265). Campbell and Foster find a surrealistic quality in "A Rose for Emily" in the juxtaposition of the conventions of "romantic love, the bridal night, and Southern womanhood" with murder and the image of the lover sleeping with the loved one as a corpse. The strand of hair on the pillow operates as an objective correlative for the reader's ambivalent response—attraction and repulsion (Campbell and Foster 1951, 99–100). Millgate notes that the "shock ending" of "A Rose for Emily" is somewhat uncharacteristic of Faulkner's stories ([1961] 1966, 64).

Some critics have noted a comic strain in the text. Charles Allen classifies "A Rose for Emily" as "comical in intent and execution," by which he means that "comical man . . . survives with a measure of dignity." He concedes that Emily is not a typical comic protagonist; nevertheless, the tone of the story includes "gently satiric" criticism of the rigid community that would intimidate her and admiration for her resistance. She possesses a "laudable sense of traditional social and moral values," which is characteristic of Faulkner's comics (Allen 1960, 59–60). According to Happel, tension between the macabre and the comic resides in the numerous oddities of the story. The smell, for example, is treated (literally) in a most delicate, odd, and somewhat comic manner because a lady cannot be accused of smelling bad. Similarly, Emily's intimidation of the druggist results in his labeling the arsenic as intended for use against rats, an apt description of the unmarriageable Homer. Emily's restrictive view of life is not without its comic element, particularly in the way she nonplusses the aldermen (Happel [1962] 1970, 70–71). Dorothy Tuck finds irony in the townspeople's envy of Emily although hers is truly a miserable life. Tuck believes the town reacts only with horror at the concluding revelation (1964, 175).

One popular point of inquiry over the years has been the relationship of the title "A Rose for Emily" to the text. Faulkner minimized the significance of the title when he indicated that it simply reflected Emily's lack of a fulfilling life (*FU* 87–88). Other respondents have had more to say about the nature of that reflection. Going notes that the noun *rose* is not used in the story, but that the upstairs bedroom has a rose hue. The title may suggest the rose as a tribute to Emily's effort to triumph over time. The "we" of the story amends Homer's failure to present a rose to Emily as a part of the courtship ritual. Perhaps, Going adds, Emily is the rose herself, a treasured memory. The title could also recall the line from *Romeo and Juliet*, "That which we call a rose by any other name would smell as sweet," but with a gruesome twist. Going finds most interesting the relationship between the title and a line in a Faulkner poem that referred to the rose as a symbol for lovers (Going [1958b] 1970, 54–55).

Hagopian suggests that the rose in the title may be an ironic reference to the corpse, playing off the community's distress over the horrible smell that emanates from the house as the corpse rots (Hagopian 1962, 48). J. F. Kobler shifts from investigating the meaning of the rose to discussing the effect of referring to Emily Grierson as "Miss" or "Poor" throughout the text but only as "Emily" in the title. "Miss" is typically used in references that acknowledge her status as a Grierson, but the use of her first name undercuts that respect with its implication that she is a child. She becomes "Poor Emily," Kobler notes, during the courtship with Homer Barron because by consorting with a Yankee laborer she has forfeited the town's respect. Finally, Faulkner's omission of a title attached to Emily's name in the story title affirms her humanity. She becomes "just plain Emily," finally released from the obligations conferred by titles (Kobler 1974, Item 65).

Scherting finds the title of the story a perfect enhancement of the oedipal theme he develops to explain Emily's motives for murder. He recalls that in ancient Rome, a rose suspended in a room indicated that confidential activities were occurring there: they were sub rosa. Neither Emily nor the town recognizes the oedipal nature of her actions hence the appropriateness of the rose suspended above the story text (Scherting 1980, 404).

In a contrary interpretation, Mary Louise Weaks believes the rose stands for Homer Barron and the bedroom. Homer is a rose in that he "brought hope back into her [Emily's] lonely existence," and he was preserved just as a rose is often preserved as a memento. The significance extends also to the rose-colored room. In it, Emily "unconsciously strove to reaffirm her femininity," and Homer eventually becomes an inextricable part of the room. The rose represents the fantasy world in which Emily enjoys both love and control (Weaks 1981, 11–12). Elizabeth Kurtz also sees Homer as the rose that has been preserved as a memento of a former time. She argues that Emily's "fragile emotional equilibrium" is destroyed when she realizes that Homer is not interested in marriage, so she acts to keep the memento of him as "proof that love once flourished" (Kurtz 1986, 40).

Littler finds that the quality of the rose as a traditional representation of "youth, beauty, and love" that is also "ephemeral and fades quickly" reflects both phases of Emily's life—the hopefulness of youth, and the decay of the later years. These are of course most specifically reflected in the rose tints in the bridal chamber, once fresh, eventually dust covered (Littler 1982, 80–81).

The most substantive studies of Faulkner's craftsmanship in "A Rose for Emily" concern point of view and structure. The importance of the narrator leads to curiosity about this person (or persons) and about the way the narration influences the story. Kenneth Kempton thinks the author gives the narrator an objective, reportorial stance. He remarks that the narrator "stands at the furthest possible position from the heart of the story and still is within it." References to the narrator, who is either male or female, increase as the story progresses, but his or her recounting remains dispassionate and keen (Kempton [1947] 1970, 30–31). Stone describes the narrative point of view as omniscient, an opinion that subsequent discussions disprove (1960, 433–43). In his brief summary of "A Rose for Emily," Walter Everett states that in the revelation of the strand of hair on the pillow the reader and the narrator reach the deeper implications of Emily's life "simultaneously" (1969, 166).

For Reed, "A Rose for Emily" demonstrates the "central concerns of narrative strategy." He believes that dismissing the work as a "ghost story" is a disservice to the text and to the genre of the ghost story. The ghost story requires a collaboration between teller and hearer. Suspense, created by controlling revelations, is the core of the story. The use of the first person provides believability and elicits an empathetic response. The story must provide sufficient evidence for the reader to be able to anticipate the outcome. In "A Rose for Emily," Faulkner provides the requisites of the genre. Reed argues that the narrator provides the alternate points of view of the various subgroups of the townspeople, but that the reader continues to identify with him because he seems to offer a more objective perspective. The time sequences serve to create a memory that both the narrator and reader come to share. Similarly the reader feels some resentment at the high-handedness of the Griersons. We, as readers, Reed says, "surrounded Emily with attitudes which isolated her and perhaps forced her desperate love and its extreme end." As the story progresses, Emily is increasingly objectified and distanced by the descriptions of her that further align the reader with the narrator and alienate Emily. In the final revelation, the reader shares a sense of guilt for the horrible effect of the alienation. Additionally, "classic reversal" occurs in which "empathy with 'our town' is instantly converted to empathy with the hitherto distanced individual" (Reed 1973, 12–20).

Joseph Garrison believes that "A Rose for Emily" presents a "critique of that kind of narrative art that naïvely assumes the possibility of an omniscient presentation of the truth and, in that naïvete, fails to see the encroaching contours of its own biases." Garrison observes that the narrator, while identifying at the beginning the limits of perception of the contemporaries, seems to hold himself immune to those biases, revealing his own judgmental nature by calling fixtures of the past and present "eyesores." He also seems more concerned with placing the events in time, and relative to one another, than in developing Emily's complexity or sensitivity. The effect is to reveal that the narrator's perception is as limited and provincial as that of the other townspeople. His is but one version that might have been told, an omniscient view being impossible (Garrison 1979, 341–44).

Putzel continues Reed's praise of the "our town" narrator. He itemizes the diversity of voices revealed, showing a "collection of attitudes" rather than a tight consensus. Among the contrasts, Putzel lists "generation offset by generation, officials by plain citizens, ladies by a 'cabal' of menfolk, blacks by 'people,' Baptist strangers by 'Episcopal' kinsmen," and even Homer Barron as compared with the old Confederate soldiers. This diversity expands the particular Jefferson community to portray a "universe in flux" with Emily remaining the only constant through several generations. Putzel believes the "triumph" of the story is "its disdain for our sympathy." Readers participate in watching, with some enjoyment, Emily's life and crime. Faulkner's pity, then, turns toward the readers for "our unwitting cruelty. For it convicts us as accomplices after the fact" (Putzel 1985, 221–23).

Skei is not quite as enthusiastic about the accomplishments of the narrative point of view as are Reed and Putzel. The occasion of Emily's death initiates the narrative, and the subsequent episodes are added, not in chronological sequence, but "by way of association, implication, or closeness to the narrator." Skei questions the motive of the narrator for perpetuating an interest in Emily when the general interest has shifted to another life-style and newer interests. Skei also finds the very nature of the narrative voice somewhat confusing. The sense of the voice as that of the community at large can only partially apply. In fact, Skei contends that Faulkner may not have attended to narrative problems with absolute accuracy. Distinctions between "we" and "they" separate the narrator from other members of the community. It is difficult to explain how the narrator would know the business of the aldermen's meeting, see Emily's archaic paper on which she wrote the mayor, see her open the poison and read the label, but not know the details of the Baptist minister's meeting with Emily. The generational changes one narrator would have to assume are multiple. These circumstances suggest the appearance of an omniscient narrator in company with the presentation of a more limited view. Olga Vickery holds that the authorial presence occurs as an additional but not subsuming perspective, a view that Skei applies to "A Rose for Emily" (Skei 1985, 109–11, 123; Vickery [1959] 1964, 299; see also Skei 1977, 66–72).

Another important area of analysis is the story's structure. Happel contends that the nonchronological rendering of certain details and sequences enhances the tension. At the conclusion of the story, the tension is resolved, but the reader is compelled to reconsider the events and character of Emily (Happel [1962] 1970, 70–71). This nonlinear rendering of events has prompted a flurry of efforts to establish their chronology. The following summation does not present the various chronologies, but emphasizes the points at which the critics diverge in dating the events of the story. Although passing time is an important issue in the story, the only specific date in the text is the 1894 remission of taxes by Colonel Sartoris. A more general reference indicates that the Grierson house was built in the 1870s (*CS* 119). These dates, along with references to Emily's age and the passage of a certain number of years between events, suggest a vague chronology in the story. As the revisions of the manuscript suggest, Faulkner progressively deemphasized specific time frames.

Despite the lack of specificity, a number of critics have sought to establish a precise chronology. Going suggests that attempting to set a time line for events in the story shows how the imprecise dating, based on internal references and others established in the *Portable Faulkner*, reinforces the "elusive, illusive quality of time that lies at the heart of the story." He builds his chronology from the 1924 date suggested in the *Portable Faulkner* as the time of Emily's death (Going [1958a] 1970, 50–53). Hagopian devises an alternative chronology that varies from Going's by several years at each point (1962, 49–50). Robert Woodward offers yet another version, again slightly different. Unlike Going, he does not hesitate to date Emily's death after the actual year of publication of the story (Woodward [1966] 1970, 84–6).

Paul McGlynn establishes the story's chronology based on the importance of time as an "unseen character that battles, defeats, and mocks everyone." His actual chronology varies from those of other critics but, like Woodward's, places Emily's death after 1930. He estimates that Emily visited the room with the corpse for approximately two years before she closed it off. In the ensuing forty years, she suffers for the two-year attempt to thwart time (McGlynn [1969] 1970, 90–2).

Responding specifically to McGlynn, Nebeker devises another chronology that resolves the discomforting, though possible, projection of Emily's death after the publication date of the story. In her chronology, Nebeker also circumvents an apparent conflict in earlier assignments of dates between Emily's estimated age when she gives painting lessons and the general time frame. If 1894, the year Colonel Sartoris remitted her taxes, is also the year in which he arranges for his daughters and granddaughters to take lessons from Emily, it places her father's death some ten years earlier and her death in 1928, making the story's time contemporary with its publication. Nebeker makes the convincing point that Sartoris would likely arrange both schemes—the tax payment and the painting lessons—so as to preserve the dignity of an impoverished aristocrat of the community. Nebeker also speculates that the room must have been sealed immediately upon the complaints of odor and lime treatment around the house. Since the narrator records no further complaints even though the lime did not reach the source of the odor, the room must have been sealed at that time. Perhaps, Nebeker adds, once the corpse mummified, Emily entered the room again (1971, 471–73; see also Nebeker 1970, 11–12).

G. R. Wilson, Jr., takes up the argument, responding to both McGlynn and Nebeker, although his suggested chronology is closer to McGlynn's. Wilson rejects Nebeker's contention that Mr. Grierson dies ten years before Colonel Sartoris remits Emily's taxes in 1894. He also dismisses her claim that Emily might have visited the room in later years, after the smell diminished. Wilson, like McGlynn, dates Emily's death after 1930, specifically 1936. He argues that given the importance of time in the story this projective dating was a subtle means of emphasizing the timelessness of the story's concerns (Wilson 1972, 56, 44, 58–62).

Brooks suggests his own version of a chronology heavily influenced, he acknowledges, by the prior chronologies of Going and Hagopian. He estimates that Emily lived from 1852 to 1926. He holds that critics placing her death as late as 1938 fail to consider the attendance at her funeral by a few Confederate veterans. Brooks calculates a fifteen-year-old soldier in 1865 would be eighty-eight in 1938 and that in fact by 1938 an extremely small number of Confederate veterans were still living (Brooks [1978] 1990, 382–84).

William Hunter establishes a chronology that accommodates Cowley's dating the story, presumably with Faulkner's agreement, at 1924, the date of Emily's funeral; however, he finds another possibility more satisfactory—that Emily lived from 1846 to 1920. Like other critics who have puzzled over the time span, he finds that Emily could not have been forty when she gave china-painting lessons. She was more likely fifty (Hunter 1980, Item 18).

Apart from trying to recreate a datable sequence of events, studies of structure reveal the existence of order other than linear. They often consider how Faulkner's ordering of the story affects the reader's reaction to it. William Davis finds that the description of Emily in section four, "Thus she passed from generation to generation—dear, inescapable, impervious, tranquil, and perverse" (*CS* 128), is representative of the community's relationship to Emily in each section of the story. In section one, the community is paying its respects at the funeral of its "dear" citizen. As the story unfolds, the several senses of the word "dear" apply to Emily. In section two, the narrator recounts the experience of the inescapable smell, and section three demonstrates Emily's imperviousness to public opinion. Section four encapsulates her apparent abandonment by Homer and the passage of her middle and elder years. Davis adds that the idol images that refer to Emily show her fixed nature in time. But by the final section her resistance to change and passing time is impossible, and "time ultimately fixes her in a rather perverse manner." In actuality, it is time that is shown to be dear, inescapable, impervious, and tranquil. Emily's failing has been "to covet life too highly," consequently making "something 'dear' a perversity" (Davis 1974, 34–38; see also Petry 1986, 52–54).

According to Watkins, the sectional divisions of the text are based on incidents of intrusion and isolation. Each intrusion by a member or members of the community constitutes a particular crisis, a forward movement of the plot, and an enhancement of the story's suspense. He compares the resultant symmetry with that achieved by Hawthorne in *The Scarlet Letter*. A symmetrical pattern developed through the five sections consists of one intrusion, two intrusions, isolation, two intrusions, and one intrusion (by the whole community). Watkins concludes that the central section represents the "indomitableness of the decadent Southern aristocrat; the enclosing parts reveal the invasion of the aristocracy by the changing order" ([1954] 1970, 46–47). Hagopian finds Watkins's structural analysis particularly enlightening. He adds that another feature of each section involving intrusion is the presence of death. Part I refers to Colonel Sartoris's death; Part II concerns Mr. Grierson's death; Part IV involves Emily's death; and Part V reveals Homer's death. The recurring concern over death enhances the sense of horror in the story (Hagopian 1962, 46). Ferguson makes a tentative link between Watkins's structural analysis of the story and a musical pattern of "theme and variation" (1991, 140–41).

Employing a structuralist methodology, William Hendricks presents a descriptive analysis of the plot's construction. His basic unit of analysis is the "'narrative proposition', consisting of a plot 'action' and the dramatis personae who participate in that act." He offers sufficient theoretical basis for his procedure, the detailed nature of which inhibits summary. Nevertheless, some of the more general conclusions regarding plot structure may be extracted. After identifying the narrative propositions in the story, Hendricks groups these into episodes and concludes that two interrelated subplots exist in the text. One subplot involves the remission of Emily's taxes, and the other concerns her relationship with Homer Barron. Although Hendricks expresses some reluctance with the terms, he describes Emily as passive in the tax subplot and active in the Barron subplot. In the Barron subplot, Hendricks observes how the purchase of the arsenic is embedded between public appearances of Emily and Barron and how his three-day disappearance paves the way for his permanent disappearance to occur without arousing the suspicion of the townspeople. Emily, not Homer, dominates in the relationship. She succeeds in obtaining another corpse to replace the body of her father, which was taken from the house for burial only after Emily's attempt to prevent it. In the tax subplot, Emily is a more passive element. The active agents are the older social order represented by Stevens and Sartoris, and the new order represented by aldermen who would tax Emily and tell her that her house smells. On both issues, the new order is defeated. Its goal is to devalue the older order, but it succeeds in doing so only by exposing Emily's necrophilia at the end of the story. As Hendricks observes, if the matter were simply the taxes, the community's relationship with Emily would be completed at her death. It continues, however, until it exposes and devalues her. Thus, the necrophilia provides a "global cohesion of the story as a whole," not the culmination of either subplot (Hendricks 1977, 257–95).

Menakhem Perry offers an analysis of "A Rose for Emily" within a larger discussion on the effect of order in a literary text. His discussion opens with a theoretical discussion of literary dynamics, explaining how "ordering and distribution of the elements in a text may exercise considerable influence on the nature, not only of the reading process, but of the resultant whole as well." Hypotheses of meaning constructed during the reading process are either confirmed, contradicted, or modified. Even when hypotheses prove insufficient, they continue to exert influence in the text. Perry faults the numerous critics who have read the story as a conflict of values, either past–present, South–North, or Old South–New South, without examining the bases for giving these interpretations precedence over understanding Emily's actions based on psychopathological motivation. He concludes that the story "does not make statements about the nature of the past, nor does it advance any thesis on the place of the past within the present; likewise, it is not just a portrait of an impressive woman of principle, nor, alternatively, a pathological case-history."

Perry arrives at this conclusion after extensive and detailed analysis of the order of information presented and the way the reader seeks to impose meaning while reading. Initially the past–present conflict seems plausible, especially given the reader's ignorance about Homer's murder. Clues that might indicate murder, such as the purchase of rat poison, are so contextualized that they seem to substantiate the values conflict rather than Emily's madness. Information about Emily is further diffused by being filtered through the narrator's limited perspective. The narrator reflects the community's ambivalence toward Emily. Its view corresponds to the reader's mixed response but also encourages the reader to be more favorable toward the story. Looking at the text continuum of "A Rose for Emily," Perry shows the order of information as implying a conflict of values and demonstrates how difficult it is to abandon such a frame for meaning once the full disclosure of murder is made. "A Rose for Emily," Perry argues, "seeks the borderline between the wish to live free from any limitation and utter madness" (1979, 35–64, 311–61).

Holland uses "A Rose for Emily" as a subject text in his development of a theory of transactive criticism (reader-response criticism). Such criticism is based on the belief that we as individual readers "re-create literature for ourselves" (1975, 248). Thus, the subject matter, rather than being an objective text, represents the "transaction between reader and a text" (1975, 248). Holland argues that each "reader responds to a literary work by assimilating it to his own psychological processes, that is, to his search for successful solutions within his identity theme to the multiple demands, both inner and outer, on his ego" (1975, 128). Holland proceeds in his study by analyzing the interpretations of "A Rose for Emily" by five undergraduate readers whose own identity themes are reinforced in their interpretations of the story. Although Holland offers a full discussion of his own interpretation of the story, he eschews any assertion of objective truth achieved by being a professional critic and limits his understanding to a claim only of his individual rendering (1975, 130).

Many critics have challenged Holland's work. Tefs responds to Holland's psychoanalytic interpretation of the text by questioning the validity of psychoanalyzing a fictional character who lacks a fully constructed biography. Elizabeth Long and Brooks counter Holland's emphasis on readers as creators of a text's meaning. Long contends that although Holland denies an "ontological status" to the text, he portrays his readers' personalities as "unified and coherent." She adds that even though Holland disavows the ability of the story "to constrain response," the responses of the students whose interpretations of the story Holland analyzed show categorical similarities in their mutual focuses on social structure, regional issues, familial relationships, sexuality, and authority (Long 1985, 56). Brooks concludes that the "principal merit" of Holland's reader-response oriented treatment of "A Rose for Emily" is the "light it throws on the stereotypes of the South and Southern culture that still flourish in the minds of our college students and others in the 1970s" ([1978] 1990, 388).

John Skinner praises the "formal subtlety" of "A Rose for Emily," believing that it has been underestimated in the proliferation of subjective interpretations. The structure of the story results from the associative logic of the narrator. After establishing the death of Emily at the opening of the story, he (Skinner believes the narrator's attitudes reveal him to be male) leaves the linear account to recall two important earlier events in each section of the story only to return to the linear account in the final section. Skinner analyzes the relationship of these events closely to demonstrate the structural complexity, including the extensive use of analepses (looking back at a past event) and anachronies ("the discrepancy between story-order and text-order"). He concludes that the "web of anachronies, each with its temporal/spacial variants, seems like a series of subtle musical variations, whilst the return to the first narrative suggests the recapitulation of a long awaited theme." In this reading, Skinner sees the narrator as the "chief character," who presents "the ugly banality of Emily's existence," the *fabula*, "in all the allure of colorful *suzhet*" (1985, 42–51).

Mellard links his view of "A Rose for Emily" as retrospective Gothic to the psychoanalytic phenomenon called *Nachträglichkeit*, a "deferred action." Deferred action occurs as "the reinterpretation of an earlier event or scene in light of a later one and within certain structures emanating from culture or language or the . . . Symbolic." Applying the process to "A Rose for Emily," Mellard rephrases it as the reader's "deferred interpretation." The "primal scene," not actually viewed but imagined, is the seduction of Homer Barron by Emily in the upstairs bedroom. Only in the light of the final scene of the corpse and the gray hair is the first scene reinterpreted in association with arsenic and odor. The reader's response at the conclusion is "chill or thrill at the recognition of the sexual and thanatic significance of the earlier scene." In fact, it is the combination of sex and death that makes Faulkner's story effective as Gothic fiction (Mellard 1986, 37–45).

Grounding their study in the view that a text is like a psyche, Mary Arensberg and Sara Schyfter read "A Rose for Emily" as "one text which seems to seek a cure for its obsession with origins." The text attempts a return to the primal chamber (the bedroom where the text ends) but at the same time avoids reaching that point with the intermediate narrative placed between recounting the death and viewing the bedroom scene. When the community views the bridal/funeral chamber, it hopes to "unravel Miss Emily's sexual history" but finds that the "phantom landscape . . . fails to reveal the imagined encounter." Rather, it poses several unresolvable possibilities including the lover's attainment of "ecstatic perfection" preserved (repetition of fantasy), the preservation of Emily's virginity by her killing Homer before he could either leave her or triumph over her (violation of the origin), Homer's homosexuality that would align him with other protective males in her life (androcracy of the text), and Emily's ability to approach the male only when he is dead (writing as necrophilia). A final possibility represents coitus interruptus, that is, the intrusion of the community as a "scene of transgression that interrupts the parental embrace." Thus, the text begins where it ends in the "primal chamber." Arensberg and Schyfter point out that "textuality is analogous to the psychoanalytic process in that it re-imagines but never re-creates the first idea. The tension between the invisible, always inaccessible past and its representations ultimately lead to the exhaustion of all fantasies and the fiction of closure." Arensberg and Schyfter argue that the Faulkner narrative is an inversion of Freud's "theme of three caskets" wherein the choice of the third woman (Mother Earth—death) becomes "the theme of the three fathers" (1986/1987, 123–34).

Austin Wright includes "A Rose for Emily" as an example of final recalcitrance in the modern short story. Recalcitrance occurs when some force of the story resists its shaping form. The ending of "A Rose for Emily" employs a mimetic resistance, one form of final recalcitrance, in which the end fails to explain what has happened; consequently, the reader must "reconstruct not merely motivation but a cause-and-effect chronology" (Wright 1989, 124).

Suzanne Brown suggests that Faulkner was exploring the limitations of the short story in "A Rose for Emily" by playing with the tension between sequential and configurational organization. The story offers two organizational patterns, a "linear, sequential organization" and a "configurational, spatial patterning." The townspeople, including the narrator, repress time and sequence in their attitudes toward Emily. For them, she is a symbol, a monument outside of time. The narrator's rose, the story, is also outside of time in that it will not fade and die. Despite their efforts to keep Emily apart from time and thereby maintain the social taxonomy of the town, they are also aware of Emily's story in its sequential form. For example, they know that in her youth her father kept suitors from her, then abandoned her when he died. When they perceive of Emily in these terms, she elicits their pity. The younger generation is more inclined to see her as person rather than as a symbol, and they would prefer that view in order that she be required, like other citizens, to pay her taxes. Yet even though they have abandoned the past, they need some symbol of continuity with their past, that is, Emily. The consequence is "that embracing the present while sentimentalizing the past as a dead symbol falsifies and perverts both" (Brown 1989, 317–27).

If, according to Brown, Emily is caught in the ambivalent responses of the community, she is similarly caught in her own ambivalences. Ultimately, Homer's murder denies sequence and temporality by representing for her the joining of her oedipal attachment to her father with the later passion for her lover; it "preserves Homer from death and change"; it "negates her sexual 'fall,'" and it reinstates her status as icon. After the murder, she accepts the town's perception of her as beyond time, as seen in her desexing herself. Nevertheless, Emily also tries to live in time. She courts Homer, she wears a gold watch, and she decorates the bedroom in shades of rose "suggestive of her 'woman's life' which exists in time and can decay." At another level, critics tend, even when they have studied sequential patterns in the story, to apply configurational interpretations to the text. The evidence of the text itself, in the narrator's inability to confront the story sequentially, criticizes this method of making meaning. When, on the other hand, Emily is viewed in the sequential movement of her life, she is better understood as changing her status from victim to victimizer. This movement reflects "her conversion from acceptance of a role as symbol to performance of a role as sign maker and manipulator. Her affair with Homer is her attempt to liberate her physical life from the configurational reading assigned to it by her neighbors and accepted by herself; when this attempt fails, she decides that she will at least design and control the configuration by which the sequential nature of her existence is denied" (Brown 1989, 317–27).

Eric Montenyohl draws a number of parallels between "A Rose for Emily" and folk legend based on the "style, form, narrative order, structure, and language" of the story. A number of legend motifs appear in the story, such as a victim being lured into a house and killed, a girl killing a man sleeping with her, murder by poisoning, and necrophilism, all of which relate it to a "local horror legend." It also includes the test for a suitor and inspection of suitor motifs. Stylistic elements also link the story to qualities of the folk legend. The treatment of time, the depth of characterization of the protagonist (her aging, internal motivations, and madness), the hometown setting, the use of a townsperson as narrator, and even the predominant colors have correspondences in legend. The story is presented "as it travels along the legend conduit." The diversity of critical interpretations of "A Rose for Emily" does not make the story different from legend; rather it complements the "dialectics of the legend." While acknowledging other characteristics that distinguish the literary text from folklore, Montenyohl also shows that the associative movement from one incident to another and the resistance Emily shows to converting from orality to a written society fall within the qualities of legend (1989, 1, 4–6).

Ferguson believes that "A Rose for Emily" represents the most complex handling of time in the short stories. The text opens in present time with Emily's funeral, then alludes to the year her taxes were remitted, then returns to near present time. Then the movement goes backward in the *fabula* to the time of Mr. Grierson's death. From that point, the story moves in a "roughly chronological order" until it returns to present time in the fifth section. The "narrative manipulation of time calls attention *to* time," the effect of which is to force the reader to participate actively in recreating the *fabula*. Ferguson adds that Faulkner's management of a panoramic approach in "A Rose for Emily" is superior to its use elsewhere. In this story, it is "not only effective but essential" (Ferguson 1991, 129–31).

The critical canon of "A Rose for Emily" has become as bloated as the character herself, although this surfeit of attention does not necessarily mean that the story has been overvalued. Skei judges "A Rose for Emily" as significant because apparently it provided the impetus for Faulkner to begin a regular schedule of submitting stories to magazines for publication; it is the best-known, most frequently anthologized, and most critically discussed story; and it serves as the introduction to Faulkner for many readers (1981, 52, 33). Additionally, with "Dry September" it is one of the early stories translated into French by Coindreau (Blotner 1974, 766).

Some critics, like Brooks, have faulted their colleagues for blatant misreadings (see Brooks [1978] 1990, 384–88). A number, as the interpretations summarized in this chapter demonstrate, have found the text amenable to applications of new theoretical approaches that have themselves been quite diverse. The story even earned attention in a Richard Armour satire of Faulkner (1964, 154–58). The needless repetition in the critical canon, however, proves frustrating. Often the most interesting part of the criticism is its dialogic nature, a quality that is partially obscured in this review. There is little evidence to suggest a tapering off of published responses to the text, and if the readings prove as challenging as some of the more recent re-visionings, they may be welcome enhancements to a currently very uneven critical canon.

## Works Cited

Allen, Charles A. 1960. "William Faulkner: Comedy and the Purpose of Humor." *Arizona Quarterly* 16:59–69.

Allen, Dennis W. 1984. "Horror and Perverse Delight: Faulkner's 'A Rose for Emily.'" *Modern Fiction Studies* 30:685–96.

Allen, Walter. 1981. *The Short Story in English*. New York: Oxford University Press.

Arensberg, Mary, and Sara E. Schyfter. 1986/1987. "Hairoglyphics in Faulkner's 'A Rose for Emily'/Reading the Primal Trace." *Boundary 2* 15 (Fall/Winter):123–34.

Armour, Richard. [1964] 1970. "William Faulkner." In *A Rose for Emily*. Ed. M. Thomas Inge. Columbus, OH: Charles E. Merrill, 73–75.

Backman, Melvin. 1966. *Faulkner: The Major Years*. Bloomington: Indiana University Press.

Barber, Marion. 1973. "The Two Emilys: A Ransom Suggestion to Faulkner?" *Notes on Mississippi Writers* 5:103–05.

Barnes, Daniel R. 1972. "Faulkner's Miss Emily and Hawthorne's Old Maid." *Studies in Short Fiction* 9:373–77.

Barth, J. Robert. 1964. "Faulkner and the Calvinist Tradition." *Thought* 39:100–20.

———. 1972. *Religious Perspectives in Faulkner's Fiction: Yoknapatawpha and Beyond*. Notre Dame, IN: University of Notre Dame Press.

Bleikasten, André. 1973. *Faulkner's* As I Lay Dying. Trans. Roger Little with the collaboration of the author. Bloomington: Indiana University Press.

Blotner, Joseph. 1974. *Faulkner: A Biography*. 2 vols. New York: Random House.

———. 1984. *Faulkner: A Biography*. 1 vol. New York: Random House.

Blythe, Hal. 1989. "Faulkner's 'A Rose for Emily.'" *Explicator* 47.2:49–50.

Bride, Sister Mary. [1962] 1970. "Faulkner's 'A Rose for Emily.'" In *A Rose for Emily*. Ed. M. Thomas Inge. Columbus, OH: Charles E. Merrill, 66–67.

Brodsky, Louis Daniel. 1990. *William Faulkner, Life Glimpses*. Austin: University of Texas Press.

Brooks, Cleanth. [1963] 1990. *William Faulkner: The Yoknapatawpha Country*. New Haven: Yale University Press. Reprint. Baton Rouge: Louisiana State University Press.

———. 1973. "A Note on Faulkner's Early Attempts at the Short Story." *Studies in Short Fiction* 10:381–88.

———. 1978. "The Sense of Community in Yoknapatawpha Fiction." *The University of Mississippi Studies in English* 15:3–18.

———. [1978] 1990. *William Faulkner: Toward Yoknapatawpha and Beyond*. New Haven: Yale University Press. Reprint. Baton Rouge: Louisiana State University Press.

———. 1987. *On the Prejudices, Predilections, and Firm Beliefs of William Faulkner*. Baton Rouge: Louisiana State University Press.

Brooks, Cleanth, and Robert Penn Warren. 1946. *Understanding Fiction*. New York: Crofts.

Brown, Suzanne Hunter. 1989. "Appendix A: Reframing Stories." In *Short Story Theory at a Crossroads*. Ed. Susan Lohafer and Jo Ellyn Clarey. Baton Rouge: Louisiana State University Press, 311–27.

Burduck, Michael L. 1990. "Another View of Faulkner's Narrator in 'A Rose for Emily.'" *University of Mississippi Studies in English*, n.s., 8:209–11.

Campbell, Harry Modean, and Ruel E. Foster. 1951. *William Faulkner: A Critical Appraisal*. Norman: University of Oklahoma Press.

Cantwell, Robert. [1953] 1985. "Introduction [to *Sartoris*]." In *Critical Essays on William Faulkner: The Sartoris Family*. Ed. Arthur F. Kinney. Boston: G. K. Hall, 146–60.

Carothers, James B. 1981. "The Road to The Reivers." In *"A Cosmos of My Own": Faulkner and Yoknapatawpha 1980*. Ed. Doreen Fowler and Ann J. Abadie. Jackson: University Press of Mississippi, 95–124.

———. 1985. *William Faulkner's Short Stories*. Ann Arbor, MI: UMI Research Press.

———. 1992. "Faulkner's Short Story Writing and the Oldest Profession." In *Faulkner and the Short Story: Faulkner and Yoknapatawpha*, 1990. Ed. Evans Harrington and Ann J. Abadie. Jackson: University Press of Mississippi, 38–61.

Clements, Arthur L. [1962] 1970. "Faulkner's 'A Rose for Emily.'" In *A Rose for Emily*. Ed. M. Thomas Inge. Columbus, OH: Charles E. Merrill, 64–65.

Coindreau, Maurice Edgar. 1971. *The Time of William Faulkner*. Ed. and trans. George McMillan Reeves. Columbia: University of South Carolina Press.

Cullen, John B., and Floyd C. Watkins. [1961] 1975. *Old Times in the Faulkner Country*. Chapel Hill: University of North Carolina Press. Reprint. Baton Rouge: Louisiana State University Press.

Davis, William V. 1974 "Another Flower for Faulkner's Bouquet: Theme and Structure in 'A Rose for Emily.'" *Notes on Mississippi Writers* 7:34–38.

Doran, Leonard. 1951. "Form and the Story Teller." *Harvard Advocate* 135:12, 38–41.

Duvall, John N. 1990. *Faulkner's Marginal Couple: Invisible, Outlaw, Unspeakable Communities*. Austin: University of Texas Press.

Edwards, C. Hines, Jr. 1974. "Three Literary Parallels to Faulkner's 'A Rose for Emily.'" *Notes on Mississippi Writers* 7:21–25.

Everett, Walter K. 1969. *Faulkner's Art and Character*. Woodbury, NY: Barron's Educational Series.

Faulkner, William. 1930. "A Rose for Emily." *Forum* 83 (April):233–38.

———. 1931. *These 13*. New York: Jonathan Cape and Harrison Smith.

———. 1950. *Collected Stories of William Faulkner*. New York: Random House.

———. 1959. *Faulkner in the University: Class Conferences at the University of Virginia, 1957–1958*. Ed. Frederick Gwynn and Joseph L. Blotner. Charlottesville: University Press of Virginia.

———. 1977. *Selected Letters of William Faulkner*. Ed. Joseph Blotner. New York: Random House.

———. 1979. *Uncollected Stories of William Faulkner*. Ed. Joseph Blotner. New York: Random House.

———. 1987. *William Faulkner Manuscripts 9*: These 13. Ed. Noel Polk. New York: Garland.

Ferguson, James. 1991. *Faulkner's Short Fiction*. Knoxville: University of Tennessee Press.

Fetterley, Judith. 1978. *The Resisting Reader: A Feminist Approach to American Fiction*. Bloomington: Indiana University Press.

Garrison, Joseph M., Jr. 1979. "'Bought Flowers' in 'A Rose for Emily.'" *Studies in Short Fiction* 16:341–44.

Gerlach, John. 1985. *Toward the End: Closure and Structure in the American Short Story*. University: University of Alabama Press.

Going, William T. [1958a] 1970. "Chronology in Teaching 'A Rose for Emily.'" In *A Rose for Emily*. Ed. M. Thomas Inge. Columbus, OH: Charles E. Merrill, 50–53.

———. [1958b] 1970. "Faulkner's 'A Rose for Emily.'" In *A Rose for Emily*. Ed. M. Thomas Inge. Columbus, OH: Charles E. Merrill, 54–55.

Gold, Joseph. 1966. *William Faulkner: A Study in Humanism, From Metaphor to Discourse*. Norman: University of Oklahoma Press.

———. 1969. "Dickens and Faulkner: The Uses of Influence." *Dalhousie Review* 49:69–79.

Gwin, Minrose C. 1990. *The Feminine and Faulkner: Reading (Beyond) Sexual Difference*. Knoxville: University of Tennessee Press.

Hagopian, John V. 1962. "'A Rose for Emily.'" In *Insight I: Analyses of American Literature*. Ed. John V. Hagopian and Martin Dolch. Frankfurt am Main: Hirschgraben-Verlag, 42–50.

Hagopian, John V., and Martin Dolch. 1964. "Faulkner's 'A Rose for Emily.'" *Explicator* 22:Item 68.

Happel, Nikolaus. [1962] 1970. "William Faulkner's 'A Rose for Emily.'" In *A Rose for Emily*. Ed. M. Thomas Inge. Trans. Alfred Kolb. Columbus, OH: Charles E. Merrill, 68–72.

Hays, Peter L. 1988. "Who Is Faulkner's Emily?" *Studies in American Fiction* 1:105–10.

Heller, Terry. 1972. "The Telltale Hair: A Critical Study of William Faulkner's 'A Rose for Emily.'" *Arizona Quarterly* 28:301–18.

Hendricks, William O. 1977. "'A Rose for Emily': A Syntagmatic Analysis." *PTL: A Journal for Descriptive Poetics and Theory of Literature* 2:257–95.

Hinkle, James. 1984. "Some Yoknapatawpha Names." In *New Directions in Faulkner Studies: Faulkner and Yoknapatawpha, 1983*. Ed. Doreen Fowler and Ann J. Abadie. Jackson: University Press of Mississippi, 172–201.

Hochman, Baruch. 1985. *Character in Literature*. Ithaca, NY: Cornell University Press.

Holland, Norman N. 1972. "Fantasy and Defense in Faulkner's 'A Rose for Emily.'" *Hartford Studies in Literature* 4:1–35.

———. 1975. *5 Readers Reading*. New Haven: Yale University Press.

Holmes, Edward M. 1966. *Faulkner's Twice-Told Tales: His Re-Use of His Material*. The Hague: Mouton.

Howe, Irving. [1952] 1975. *William Faulkner: A Critical Study*. 3d ed. Chicago: University of Chicago Press.

Howell, Elmo. [1961] 1970. "Faulkner's 'A Rose for Emily.'" In *A Rose for Emily*. Ed. M. Thomas Inge. Columbus, OH: Charles E. Merrill, 59–60.

———. 1966. "A Note on Faulkner's Emily as a Tragic Heroine." *Serif* 3.3:13–15.

Hunter, William B., Jr. 1980. "A Chronology for Emily." *Notes on Modern American Literature* 4:Item 18.

Jacobs, John T. 1982. "Ironic Allusions in 'A Rose for Emily.'" *Notes on Mississippi Writers* 14:77–79.

Johnson, C. W. M. [1948] 1970. "Faulkner's 'A Rose for Emily.'" In *A Rose for Emily*. Ed. M. Thomas Inge. Columbus, OH: Charles E. Merrill, 35.

Karl, Frederick R. 1989. *William Faulkner: American Writer*. New York: Weidenfeld and Nicolson.

Kempton, Kenneth Payson. [1947] 1970. "From *The Short Story*." In *A Rose for Emily*. Ed. M. Thomas Inge. Columbus, OH: Charles E. Merrill, 30–31.

Kerr, Elizabeth M. 1961–1962. "William Faulkner and the Southern Concept of Woman." *Mississippi Quarterly* 15:1–16.

———. [1969] 1976. *Yoknapatawpha: Faulkner's "Little Postage Stamp of Native Soil."* New York: Fordham University Press.

———. 1979. *William Faulkner's Gothic Domain*. Port Washington, NY: Kennikat.

———. 1983. *William Faulkner's Yoknapatawpha: "A Kind of Keystone in the Universe."* New York: Fordham University Press.

Kinney, Arthur F. 1978. "Form and Function in Absalom, Absalom!" *Southern Review* 14:677–91.

———. 1980. "Faulkner's Narrative Poetics and Collected Stories." *Faulkner Studies* 1:58–79.

Kobler, J. F. 1974. "Faulkner's 'A Rose for Emily.'" *Explicator* 32:Item 65.

Kurtz, Elizabeth Carney. 1986. "Faulkner's 'A Rose for Emily.'" *Explicator* 44.2:40.

Landeira, Ricardo López. 1975. "'Aura,' 'The Aspern Papers,' 'A Rose for Emily': A Literary Relationship." *Journal of Spanish Studies: Twentieth Century* 3:125–43.

Lang, Béatrice. 1976. "'Dr. Martino': The Conflict of Life and Death." *Delta* 3(November):23–33.

Leary, Lewis. 1973. *William Faulkner of Yoknapatawpha County*. New York: Thomas Y. Crowell.

Levitt, Paul. 1973. "An Analogue for Faulkner's 'A Rose for Emily.'" *Papers on Language and Literature* 9:91–94.

Lind, Ilse Dusoir. 1978. "Faulkner's Women." In *The Maker and the Myth: Faulkner and Yoknapatawpha*, 1977. Ed. Evans Harrington and Ann J. Abadie. Jackson: University Press of Mississippi, 89–104.

Littler, Frank A. 1982. "The Tangled Thread of Time: Faulkner's 'A Rose for Emily.'" *Notes on Mississippi Writers* 14:80–86.

Long, Elizabeth. 1985. *The American Dream and the Popular Novel*. Boston: Routledge & Kegan Paul.

Lupack, Barbara Tepa. 1981. "The Two Tableaux in Faulkner's 'A Rose for Emily.'" *Notes on Contemporary Literature* 11.3:6–7.

McGlynn, Paul D. [1969] 1970. "The Chronology of 'A Rose for Emily.'" In *A Rose for Emily*. Ed. M. Thomas Inge. Columbus, OH: Charles E. Merrill, 90–92.

Magalaner, Marvin, and Edmond L. Volpe. [1961] 1970. "Society in 'A Rose for Emily.'" In *A Rose for Emily*. Ed. M. Thomas Inge. Columbus, OH: Charles E. Merrill, 63.

Malin, Irving. 1957. *William Faulkner: An Interpretation*. Stanford, CA: Stanford University Press.

Mellard, James M. 1986. "Faulkner's Miss Emily and Blake's 'Sick Rose': 'Invisible Worm,' *Nachträglichkeit, and Retrospective Gothic*." Faulkner Journal 2:37–45.

Meriwether, James B. [1961] 1971. *The Literary Career of William Faulkner: A Bibliographical Study*. Princeton, NJ: Princeton University Library. Reprint. Columbia: University of South Carolina Press.

———. 1973. "Faulkner's Correspondence with Scribner's Magazine." *Proof* 3:253–82.

Millgate, Michael. [1961] 1966. *William Faulkner*. New York: Barnes & Noble.

———. [1966] 1989. *The Achievement of William Faulkner*. New York: Random House. Reprint. Athens: University of Georgia Press. Brown Thrasher Books.

———. 1980. "'A Cosmos of My Own': The Evolution of Yoknapatawpha." In *Fifty Years of Yoknapatawpha: Faulkner and Yoknapatawpha 1979*. Ed. Doreen Fowler and Ann J. Abadie. Jackson: University Press of Mississippi, 23–43.

Momberger, Philip. 1978. "Faulkner's 'The Village' and 'That Evening Sun': The Tale in Context." *Southern Literary Journal* 11.1:20–31.

Montenyohl, Eric L. 1989. "Folklore and Faulkner: Toward an Expansion of the Relations of Folklore and Literature." *Motif: International Newsletter of Research in Folklore and Literature* 7 (February):1, 4–6.

Mortimer, Gail L. 1983. *Faulkner's Rhetoric of Loss: A Study in Perception and Meaning*. Austin: University of Texas Press.

Muller, Gil. 1975. "Faulkner's 'A Rose for Emily.'" *Explicator* 33:Item 79.

Nebeker, Helen E. 1970. "Emily's Rose of Love: Thematic Implications of Point of View in Faulkner's 'A Rose for Emily.'" *Bulletin of the Rocky Mountain Modern Language Association* 24:3–13.

———. 1971. "Chronology Revised." *Studies in Short Fiction* 8:471–73.

Nilon, Charles H. 1965. *Faulkner and the Negro*. New York: Citadel.

———. 1981. "Blacks in Motion." In "A Cosmos of My Own": *Faulkner and Yoknapatawpha 1980*. Ed. Doreen Fowler and Ann J. Abadie. Jackson: University Press of Mississippi, 227–51.

O'Connor, William Van. [1952] 1970. "The State of Faulkner Criticism." In *A Rose for Emily*. Ed. M. Thomas Inge. Columbus, OH: Charles E. Merrill, 44–45.

———. 1954. *The Tangled Fire of William Faulkner*. Minneapolis: University of Minnesota Press.

Page, Sally R. 1972. *Faulkner's Women: Characterization and Meaning*. Deland, FL: Everett/Edwards.

Perry, Menakhem. 1979. "Literary Dynamics: How the Order of a Text Creates Its Meanings [With an Analysis of Faulkner's 'A Rose for Emily']." *Poetics Today* 1:35–64, 311–61.

Petry, Alice Hall. 1986. "Faulkner's 'A Rose for Emily.'" *Explicator* 44.3:52–54.

Pitavy, François. 1972. "A Forgotten Faulkner Story: 'Miss Zilphia Gant.'" *Studies in Short Fiction* 9:131–42.

———. 1973. *Faulkner's Light in August*. Trans. Gillian E. Cook. Bloomington: Indiana University Press.

Polk, Noel. 1984. "'The Dungeon was Mother Herself': William Faulkner: 1927–1931." In *New Directions in Faulkner Studies: Faulkner and Yoknapatawpha, 1983*. Ed. Doreen Fowler and Ann J. Abadie. Jackson: University Press of Mississippi, 61–93.

———. 1985. "The Space between Sanctuary." In *Intertextuality in Faulkner*. Ed. Michel Gresset and Noel Polk. Jackson: University Press of Mississippi, 16–35.

Putzel, Max. 1985. *Genius of Place: William Faulkner's Triumphant Beginnings*. Baton Rouge: Louisiana State University Press.

Rabbetts, John. 1989. *From Hardy to Faulkner: Wessex to Yoknapatawpha*. New York: St. Martin's.

Reed, Joseph W., Jr. 1973. *Faulkner's Narrative*. New Haven: Yale University Press.

Ross, Danforth. [1961] 1970. "From The American Short Story." In *A Rose for Emily*. Ed. M. Thomas Inge. Columbus, OH: Charles E. Merrill, 61–62.

Ross, Stephen M. 1989. *Fiction's Inexhaustible Voice: Speech and Writing in Faulkner*. Athens: University of Georgia Press.

Ruppersburg, Hugh M. 1983. *Voice and Eye in Faulkner's Fiction*. Athens: University of Georgia Press.

Scherting, Jack. 1980. "Emily Grierson's Oedipus Complex: Motif, Motive, and Meaning in Faulkner's 'A Rose for Emily.'" *Studies in Short Fiction* 17:397–405.

Shiroma, Mikio. 1986. "A Rose for Tobe: A New View of Faulkner's First Short Story." *Kyushu American Literature* 27:21–27.

Skei, Hans H. 1977. *Bold and Tragical and Austere: William Faulkner's These 13*: A Study. University of Oslo Department of Literature.

———. 1981. *William Faulkner: The Short Story Career*. Oslo, Norway: Universitetsforlaget.

———. 1985. *William Faulkner: The Novelist as Short Story Writer*. Oslo, Norway: Universitetsforlaget.

Skinner, John L. 1985. "'A Rose for Emily': Against Interpretation." *Journal of Narrative Technique* 15:42–51.

Slatoff, Walter. 1960. *Quest for Failure: A Study of William Faulkner*. Ithaca, NY: Cornell University Press.

Snell, George. 1947. *The Shapers of American Fiction*. New York: Dutton.

Stafford, T. J. [1968–1969] 1970. "Tobe's Significance in 'A Rose for Emily.'" In *A Rose for Emily*. Ed. M. Thomas Inge. Columbus, OH: Charles E. Merrill, 87–89.

Starke, Catherine Juanita. 1971. *Black Portraiture in American Fiction: Stock Characters, Archetypes, and Individuals*. New York: Basic Books.

Stevens, Aretta J. 1968. "Faulkner and 'Helen'—A Further Note." *Poe Newsletter* 1:31.

Stewart, James T. [1958] 1970. "Miss Havisham and Miss Grierson." In *A Rose for Emily*. Ed. M. Thomas Inge. Columbus, OH: Charles E. Merrill, 56–57.

Stone, Edward. 1960. "Usher, Poquelin, and Miss Emily: The Progress of Southern Gothic." *Georgia Review* 14:433–43.

———. 1969. *A Certain Morbidness: A View of American Literature*. Carbondale: Southern Illinois University Press.

Strandberg, Victor. 1981. *A Faulkner Overview: Six Perspectives*. Port Washington, NY: Kennikat.

Stronks, James. 1968. "A Poe Source for Faulkner? 'To Helen' and 'A Rose for Emily.'" *Poe Newsletter* 1:11.

Sullivan, Ruth. 1971. "The Narrator in 'A Rose for Emily.'" *Journal of Narrative Technique* 1:159–78.

Sullivan, Walter. 1976. *A Requiem for the Renascence: The State of Fiction in the Modern South*. Mercer University Lamar Memorial Lectures, No. 18. Athens: University of Georgia Press.

Tefs, Wayne A. 1974. "Norman N. Holland and 'A Rose for Emily'—Some Questions Concerning Psychoanalytic Criticism." *Sphinx* 1.2:50–57.

Trilling, Lionel. 1931. "Mr. Faulkner's World." Nation 133 (4 November ):491–92

Tuck, Dorothy. 1964. *Crowell's Handbook of Faulkner*. New York: Thomas Y. Crowell.

Vickery, Olga W. [1959] 1964. *The Novels of William Faulkner*. Baton Rouge: Louisiana State University Press.

Wagner, Linda Welshimer. 1975. *Hemingway and Faulkner: Inventors/Masters*. Metuchen, NJ: Scarecrow Press.

Watkins, Floyd C. [1954] 1970. "The Structure of 'A Rose for Emily.'" In *A Rose for Emily*. Ed. M. Thomas Inge. Columbus, OH: Charles E. Merrill, 46–47.

Watson, James G. 1980a. "Faulkner: The House of Fiction." In *Fifty Years of*

*Yoknapatawpha: Faulkner and Yoknapatawpha* 1979. Ed. Doreen Fowler and Ann J. Abadie. Jackson: University Press of Mississippi, 134–58.

———. 1980b. "Faulkner's Short Stories and the Making of Yoknapatawpha County." In *Fifty Years of Yoknapatawpha: Faulkner and Yoknapatawpha* 1979. Ed. Doreen Fowler and Ann J. Abadie. Jackson: University Press of Mississippi, 202–25.

———. 1987. *William Faulkner: Letters and Fictions*. Austin: University of Texas Press.

Weaks, Mary Louise. 1981. "The Meaning of Miss Emily's Rose." *Notes on Contemporary Literature* 11.5:11–12.

West, Ray B., Jr. [1948] 1970. "Faulkner's 'A Rose for Emily.'" In *A Rose for Emily*. Ed. M. Thomas Inge. Columbus, OH: Charles E. Merrill, 36–37.

———. [1949] 1973. "Atmosphere and Theme in Faulkner's 'A Rose for Emily.'" In *William Faulkner: Four Decades of Criticism*. Ed. Linda Welshimer Wagner. East Lansing: Michigan State University Press, 192–98.

———. 1952. *The Short Story in America 1900–1950*. Chicago: Regnery.

Wilson, G. R., Jr. 1972. "The Chronology of Faulkner's 'A Rose for Emily' Again." *Notes on Mississippi Writers* 5:56, 44, 58–62.

Winchell, Mark Royden. 1983. "For All the Heart's Endeavor: Romantic Pathology in Brow[n]ing and Faulkner." *Notes on Mississippi Writers* 15:57–63.

Woodward, Robert H. [1966] 1970. "The Chronology of 'A Rose for Emily.'" In *A Rose for Emily*. Ed. M. Thomas Inge. Columbus, OH: Charles E. Merrill, 84–86.

Wright, Austin M. 1989. "Recalcitrance in the Short Story." In *Short Story Theory at a Crossroads*. Ed. Susan Lohafer and Jo Ellyn Clarey. Baton Rouge: Louisiana State University Press, 115–29.

Yoshizaki, Yasuhiro. 1982. *Faulkner's Theme of Nature*. Kyoto: Yamaguchi Shoten.

# Hair

## Publication History

According to Faulkner's schedule for submitting stories to publishers, after five unsuccessful attempts, the sixth submission landed "Hair" in the *American Mercury* for May 1931. Faulkner records sending the story to the *American Mercury* on March 20, 1930 (an early rejection); the *Saturday Evening Post*, April 3, 1930; back to the *Saturday Evening Post*, January 1, 1931; *Woman's Home Companion*, January 10, 1931; *Scribner's*, January 29, 1931; and again to the *American Mercury*, February 27, 1931 (Meriwether [1961] 1971, 172–73). What payment Faulkner received for the story is uncertain. Faulkner included "Hair" in *These 13* (1931) and *Collected Stories* (1950).

## Circumstances of Composition, Sources, and Influences

The twenty-one-page typescript of "Hair" held in the William B. Wisdom Collection of the Tulane University Library does not aid in establishing a specific composition date for the story (Bonner 1980, 32; *WFM 9* Introduction xii). The first evidence of "Hair" appears on the story-sending schedule as the earliest noted submission date, March 20, 1930; but as Hans Skei cautions, the first dated appearance on the sending schedule does not necessarily approximate a composition date. "Hair" may have existed in partial or complete form for some time prior to March 20, 1930 (Skei 1981, 57, 61).

Composition histories of two stories that have close character associations with "Hair" tend only to obscure further that story's composition date. Skei conjectures that "Hair" was probably composed after "Smoke," a story that first appears on the sending schedule February 5, 1930, but there is no evidence of when Faulkner actually wrote "Smoke." Consequently, it cannot be determined whether the character Gavin Stevens, who appears in both stories, was created first in "Smoke" or in "Hair" (Skei 1981, 57). James Carothers believes that Stevens most likely appeared in "Smoke" first because it is less specific in the details of Steven's appearance and character (1985, 95).

Another character, Susan Reed, appears in a 1928 revision of "Moonlight," which Faulkner told James Meriwether was originally composed somewhere between 1919 and 1921 (Watson 1987, 93; Meriwether 1971, 315). The young woman was originally named Cecily Binford. Whether Cecily Binford was renamed Susan Reed before or after her appearance in a manuscript version of "Hair" is unknown.

Although no manuscript evidence exists to confirm their claims, Skei and Noel Polk make the reasonable suggestion that Faulkner revised "Hair" before he resubmitted it to the *Post* (Skei 1981, 61; *WFM 9* Introduction x).

The compositional developments of "Hair" after its first appearance in the *American Mercury* are obviously more accessible. When Faulkner collected "Hair" for *These 13*, he made some revisions, mostly related to copyediting, that Skei describes as "unimportant" (1981, 125 n. 203). These include deleting apostrophes in most contractions and removing the period after *Mr* and *Mrs*. Other revisions include minor changes in phrasing that clarify but do not significantly alter the story. The text from *These 13* was used in *Collected Stories* with one alteration: *courthouse* in *These 13* is changed to *clubhouse* in *Collected Stories* (*T13* 221; *CS* 141). This change is a movement away from the sense of the passage in which it occurs. The image of Jefferson is much stronger if the boys are pictured in the courthouse yard, close to the post office and soda fountain as described in the passage.

Biographical and literary associations have received only cursory review. Joseph Blotner offers two links. A minor biographical coincidence involves Hawkshaw's faithful payment of the mortgage. At about the time this story first appears on the story-sending schedule, Faulkner was contemplating purchasing the Shegog property. He did, of course, make that purchase and renamed the place Rowan Oak. Blotner also compares the conversational narrator who directly addresses the reader to Sherwood Anderson's narrators (1974, 650).

The names *Henry Stribling* and *Hawkshaw* have generated some literary associations. According to the narrator of "Hair," the children named the newcomer Stribling "Hawkshaw" because, as they reasoned, "he was a detective, maybe because that was the last thing in the world anybody would suspect him to be" (*CS* 141). William Bache records the connection made by Robert Gorham Davis that the nickname is also the detective's name in Tom Taylor's melodrama *The Ticket of Leave Man* (1954, 55). In a study of the influence of comic strips on Faulkner, M. Thomas Inge suggests that Faulkner may have derived some characters' names from the funny papers. Henry Stribling's nickname, "Hawkshaw," was very likely inspired by Gus Mager's *Hawkshaw the Detective*, a strip that began in 1913 (Inge 1986, 188). Henry's surname, Stribling, recalls T. S. Stribling, who enjoyed recognition and profit from his short and long fiction in the 1920s and 1930s.

The unexpected marriage announcement that Stevens makes at the end of the story follows the surprise ending formula of O. Henry (Ferguson 1991, 133). Nevertheless, it is in Faulkner's own works where the most interesting precursors and inheritors are located.

## Relationship to Other Faulkner Works

Faulkner frequently re-uses individual characters and character types to link the stories of Yoknapatawpha. Although Susan Reed does not appear outside of "Hair" and "Moonlight," her characterization provides a base for comparison. Sally Page likens Reed to a "number of young women characters whose physical beauty represents the elusive but powerful dream of an idealized and perfect beauty"; Reed is a "fragile but compelling girlish" version (1972, 176). Blotner believes that Reed, like Corinthia Bowman in "Selvage" (renamed Elly in "Elly") and Amy in "The Brooch," is "harassed into profligacy by circumstances and an inflexible malevolent older woman." He also compares Reed to Candace Compson's daughter, Quentin Compson (Blotner 1974, 683, Notes 93; Blotner refers here to Susan's guardian as Mrs. Murchett; she is Mrs. Burchett). Peggy Flynn categorizes Reed as one of Faulkner's sister figures. These females, because they literally bear the future (the legitimate children), are protected by a brother or brother figure. Dominant models of this type appear in *Mosquitoes*, *The Sound and the Fury*, and *Sanctuary*, but there are numerous others throughout the fiction (Flynn 1976, 99–117). Arthur Kinney believes that Reed is "more sympathetically defined" than either Emily of "A Rose for Emily" or Minnie of "Dry September" because the character Stribling has the "ability to see through the decline of Susan" (1980, 67). Skei adds that the trapped female, whose confinement is both biological and social, appears in "Mistral," "Black Music," and "Honor" as well as "Hair" (1985, 101). Carothers lengthens this list of women who are "driven to perverse or violent rebellion against the prevailing community standard" to include Caddy Compson, Charlotte Rittenmeyer, Eula Varner, Minnie Cooper, Elly, and Zilphia Gant (1992, 49).

Stribling's other love, his fiancée, Sophie Starnes, may have at one time suggested further family ties in the fiction. The name "Starnes" appears in "The Liar" and in the manuscript of *As I Lay Dying*. Another minor character, the barber Maxey, reappears in *As I Lay Dying* (Blotner 1974, Notes 93–94, 108).

Gavin Stevens also becomes a linking device between "Hair" and numerous other short and long works including *Requiem for a Nun*, *Knight's Gambit*, and the Snopes trilogy (see Holmes 1966, 103). "Hair" marks Stevens's second appearance according to the sending-schedule dates, but his first appearance in publication. Skei attributes little importance to the character of Stevens in either "Hair" or "Smoke" (Skei 1981, 124 n. 167); however, Carothers sees these early roles as somewhat more important than Skei does. He compares the unfavorable portrait of Stevens in "Smoke" to the more favorable characterization in "Hair," where he is described as "a smart man: not like the usual pedagogue lawyer and office holder" (Carothers 1985,

96; *CS* 144). In "Hair" Stevens does not immediately tell the narrator that Hawkshaw and Reed have married, but this information saves the story from an unhappy ending. This role, according to Carothers, makes Stevens "significant" to the story (1985, 96). Judson Watson argues that the two texts "should be read together as consciously paired stories." In "Hair," Stevens demonstrates his skill at storytelling, and in "Smoke," he displays his courtroom skills. Together these stories "represent a deliberate intertextual response" to prior models of inadequate attorneys (J. D. Watson 1990, 349).

Another character type important in Faulkner's fiction that is presented in "Hair" is the salesman–narrator, described as a "drummer" in the story. Everett recognizes the similarity between this narrator and Ratliff (1969, 144). Page, Joseph Reed, and James Tuttleton wrongly call the narrator "Ratliff" (Page 1972, 176; Reed 1973, 25–26; Tuttleton 1977, 288). Skei makes the point that this narrator is not Ratliff, as the narrator of "Hair" is married and has a daughter. As Skei notes, "This piece of information is important in the greater design of the story: the narrator's misunderstanding and faulty judgment is partly a result of his fear that his daughter might one day act and behave like Susan Reed" (1985, 175–76). For Blotner, the drummers in "Hair" and in "Dry September" are very different. The narrator of "Hair" is a "much more humane one than Plunkett's accessory in the murder of Will Mayes" (1974, 650). The difference in degree and significance of their actions is undeniable, but in terms of their willingness to participate in the community consciousness, the drummers are very much alike. François Pitavy believes the "remarkable effectiveness" of "Hair," "A Rose for Emily," and "That Evening Sun" is to some extent related to the use of a limited narrator and the absence of the omniscient author (1972, 134).

Henry Stribling (Hawkshaw) makes a second appearance in "Hair." He had been introduced in another short story, "Dry September," published in *Scribner's* in January 1931. Blotner places the events of "Dry September" ("Drouth") before "Hair" (1974, 650), but it is more precise to see these stories as concurrent rather than contiguous in time. Stribling is new to Jefferson when he first meets Reed, yet his acquaintance with and faith in Will Mayes imply that he has known Mayes for some years (*CS* 169–70). John Crane dates the action of "Dry September" as seven or eight months prior to Hawkshaw's marriage and leave-taking in "Hair" (1985, 412).

Despite Stribling's prior appearance in "Dry September," and perhaps because of his less central role in that story, William Van O'Connor counts "Hair" as "the first [story] in which his [Faulkner's] subject is a 'countryman.'" Stribling, like the later Byron Bunch, "is gentle, almost ascetic, hard working, and dedicated"; he possesses "dignity and stature" and ultimately lives a "successful life" (O'Connor 1954, 68; see also Backman 1966, 84). Pitavy adds that Hawkshaw and Bunch share physical similarities and that the words describing their relationship to love are very nearly the same (1973, 166 n. 19). Carothers compares the devotion of Stribling to both Sophie Starnes and Susan Reed to the devotion displayed by Jackson Fentry in "Tomorrow" and Byron Bunch to Lena Grove in *Light in August*. He comments that in "Tomorrow" Stevens presents this capacity for devotion as a positive value that his nephew Chick should always remember (Carothers 1985, 98). John Duvall adds to the comparisons with his observation that both Stribling and Bunch work in traditionally male environments, a barbershop and a mill, respectively. In the view of their co-workers, both men are somewhat mysterious because they are so private. Noting the similarities of wording in the two texts, Duvall comments that in the communal opinion these men "have lived past the time when they could be capable of any passion," and the community, in both instances, is wrong. They both challenge the presumption that they should marry virgins. Both men "step outside the realm of what communal voices say is permissible," and in the end, both couples leave Jefferson. Roger Schumann in *Pylon* is another male character who "subverts partriarchal values by accepting a woman whose sexuality breaches cultural limits" (Duvall 1990, 1–3, 83; see also Carothers 1992, 48–51).

Taking a more general view, Olga Vickery sees Stribling's patient waiting for Reed to grow up as one variation in the pattern of "Reluctant Lover stories" ([1959] 1964, 304). Blotner considers Stribling an early example of a Faulkner character type: the "good, decent, frugal, self-effacing man who is almost a victim but who is finally rewarded" (1974, 650). Skei observes that despite the narrator's misunderstanding of Stribling and Reed, he is sympathetic to Stribling. Stribling is representative of a Faulkner type who "goes quietly about his work, adjusting his life in accordance with some kind of established design or plan which is worthy of sacrifice and painful endurance" and who is inevitably misjudged (Skei 1985, 177). Ferguson recognizes a multiplicity of father figures somehow involved in a sexual triangle. Although comparable mother figures typically thwart relationships, the father figures may be involved. Stribling is, and so are Sutpen in "Wash," Weddel in "Mountain Victory," Dr. Martino in "Dr. Martino," and numerous others (1991, 70–71).

Additional parallels between "Hair" and other Faulkner works can be found. In 1934 Aubrey Starke offered a perceptive analysis of Faulkner's fiction in which he aligned the attitudes of the close-knit group of white men with the values of Snopesism. He asserted that these men seen in "Hair" and "Dry September" might not be named elsewhere but were probably participants in the lynching of Lee Goodwin in *Sanctuary* (Emerson 1984, 59). Reed compares the comradery of the groups in "Hair" to that in "A Bear Hunt" and *Light in August* (1973, 135). He might add that the narrators of both short stories are caught by a limited understanding of the relationships between other characters in the stories. In "Hair" the narrator is not beaten, but he is exposed.

James Watson, studying letters in Faulkner's fiction, examines the busy period of short story work between December 1927 and January 1932 and counts twenty-four out of thirty-eight stories that use letters directly or indirectly. "Hair" "relies on letters to tie together aspects of plot, provide background information, and span geographical distances between characters." Watson includes with "Hair" such stories as "Smoke," "Divorce in Naples," "Black Music," and "Ad Astra" (Watson 1987, 94).

Ferguson suggests that Faulkner's return to Stribling came out of his strong interest in selflessness. In fact, that quality appears time and again in the stories. Among the other selfless characters are Rogers in "Honor," Howes in "Artist at Home," Brix in "Snow," and the woman who cares for her ill lover in *Idyll in the Desert* (1991, 36, 80–81). "Hair" also utilizes a tactic common to Faulkner's fiction, that is, identifying the "controlling symbol" in the title (Ferguson 1991, 141).

Michael Millgate observed that Faulkner avoided making a link between "Hair" and "Dry September," the two stories with Henry Stribling, by not juxtaposing them in *These 13*, opting for a more complex, contrapuntal organization ([1966] 1989, 261–62). In *Collected Stories*, however, Millgate believes Faulkner uses "opportunistic connections" in placing "A Rose for Emily" and "Hair" as adjacent texts. But then rather than following "Hair" with "Dry September," he again ignores the character link and uses "Centaur in Brass." The effect of this order, Millgate argues, is to emphasize "the sense of Jefferson itself as a place, a social entity" ([1966] 1989, 272).

Philip Momberger's evaluation of the "The Village" as a community in disintegration includes conflict between males and females. In "Hair" familial tensions cut across gender and age to add to the sense of moral and social decay. Momberger adds that "Susan Reed's near-death from a self-induced abortion" is one of "The Village" images that subverts the idea of female as "vehicle of life." Furthermore, both Susan and Hawkshaw are victimized by being outsiders in the minds of the Jefferson citizens (Momberger 1978, 21, 24–25, 30–31).

James Watson sees the juxtaposition of "A Rose for Emily" and "Hair" as emphasizing the oppositional natures of the protagonists and the narrators in the two stories. Stribling, unlike Emily, moves from a barren life to one that begins anew with Susan Reed. Similarly, the narrator of "Hair," unlike the narrator of "A Rose for Emily," "acquires understanding of himself and his own frailties" through observing the unexpected marriage of Stribling and Reed (Watson 1980, 216).

Ferguson points out an alternating pattern of tonalities within the sectional divisions in *These 13* and *Collected Stories*. In the former collection, the humor of "A Justice" and "Hair" relieve the horror of "Red Leaves" and "A Rose for Emily," and they intercede as love stories between the corruption of these opening stories and racial conflict of the last two, "That Evening Sun" and "Dry September" (Ferguson 1991, 151, 158).

Exploring the relationship of "Hair" to other Yoknapatawpha stories is generally the approach critics take in examining this story. However, it is certainly deserving of analysis as an individual work of fiction.

## Interpretation and Criticism

Sorting out "who knows what" is a point of entry into the critical response to "Hair." The community is an important "who." According to Everett, the community's knowledge and Stribling's assumed ignorance about Susan Reed's character create the tension of the story. Hawkshaw's disillusionment seems inevitable (1969, 144). Joseph Reed notes that Faulkner often uses a group as a reference point against which to define the individual; in "Hair," the whole town is the group. It is a story of an "our town" consciousness being occupied by "outlander" characters. In the conclusion of the story, the narrator, the town, and the reader are wrong in their expectations that Stribling's devotion will prove wasted (Reed 1973, 20, 25–26). Ferguson contends, however, that this narrator offers personal information about himself in a way that distinguishes him from the disembodied voice of the community and gives him more substance than as a mere device (Ferguson 1991, 109–10).

Skei calls "Hair" the "most typical gossip story in Faulkner's career" (1985, 175). The sense of the community's need to define its members, especially those outsiders who come into the community, infiltrates the children. They, like the adults, watch Stribling. According to Maxey, the people watch him "for two days about the square" (*CS* 140). When the children fail to learn anything about him, they create his identity in the nickname "Hawkshaw." It apparently suited everyone because "Hawkshaw he remained for the twelve years he stayed in Jefferson" (*CS* 141).

What the narrator knows and does not know is crucial to the text. Dorothy Tuck's summary of "Hair" incorrectly emphasizes what the barbers know about Stribling without calling attention to the narrator's considerable efforts to make his own discoveries (1964, 167). Olga Vickery emphasizes Faulkner's use of a fallible narrator who is concerned with correcting his misperceptions or limited understanding ([1959] 1964, 297). Everett sees the "contrast between a verbose person [the narrator] and a laconic person [Stribling]" as a "secondary" theme (1969, 144).

Skei is less convinced than Vickery that the narrator improves his perception as the story progresses. Although the narrator tries to give specific time references to record the Starnes's deaths and Stribling's moves and mortgage payments, he is inconsistent in establishing reliable time frames for his own movements. His trip to Division was "last week," but then it is "three months" before his next trip to Jefferson. Skei points out that the telling could be done at different times, or, more likely, the vague reference is an error made by the author. Whatever the reason, the result is to undermine further the credibility of the narrator. In fact, as Skei interprets the story, the narrator is culpable for participating in gossip about matters for which he does not have full knowledge or understanding. The choice of this narrator is decisive in the way the character of Susan Reed is presented. Throughout his telling the story, the narrator "accumulates information but does not increase his understanding." The narrator's failure to comprehend the significance of his own story reinforces the story's theme and underscores his comment that a "talking man hasn't got time to learn much about anything except words" (*CS* 133). Faulkner's choice of this particular narrative strategy for "Hair" shows how first-person narration can contradict seeming closeness to the story's subject and character. It also shows Faulkner's "attempts to solve the problem of the limitations of point of view inherent in this kind of narrator." Skei also sees some distance between what the narrator understands and what the reader understands. On this point Skei differs from Joseph Reed, who sees the reader as becoming involved in the community mind-set. Skei believes that the reader is less surprised than the narrator at the conclusion. Borrowing Wayne C. Booth's term, Skei describes Faulkner's use of communication between reader and author as "secret communion." Skei sees this device repeated more effectively in Jason's section of *The Sound and the Fury* (1977, 92–93; 1985, 311 n. 30, 175–76).

Judson Watson believes that skillful storytelling is a major concern of "Hair." Gavin Stevens enters the story relatively late but for the reason of establishing "his credentials as a storyteller." His presentation conveys his generosity and his skill as a listener. A subtle competition between the narrator and Stevens develops in which Stevens extracts details from the salesman before Stevens contributes the information that Stribling and Reed have married. Watson concludes: "Thus love conquers all, but the theme of the framing tale asserts itself too: storytelling conquers all, and, make no mistake, in the few lines he speaks here, Gavin Stevens *is* a storyteller. He privileges speech, generously calculates rhetorical effects, makes an emphatic moral point, and rarely takes his eye (or ear) from his interlocutor" (Watson 1990, 349–54).

"Hair" has gained some critical attention because of the narrator's rather blunt, though not unambiguous, evaluation of female sexuality. He states: "There's not any such thing as a woman born bad, because they are all born bad, born with the badness in them. The thing is, to get them married before the badness comes to a natural head. But we try to make them conform to a system that says a woman can't be married until she reaches a certain age.

And nature don't pay any attention to systems, let alone women paying any attention to them, or to anything" (*CS* 133). Critics attempt to place this assessment within Faulkner's portrayal of women characters generally and to understand whether or how much the narrator's words iterate Faulkner's thoughts. According to Everett, "the innate badness of women" is a secondary theme (1969, 144). Page believes that the narrator's remark reflects Faulkner's recognition "that the sexual allure of the beautiful virgin gives her a power which is potentially destructive" (1972, 176).

Tuttleton believes the appraisal turns on itself and destroys its own credibility. He comments on the way the perceived ruin of Susan Reed, caused by her sexual activity, is undercut by the narrator's explanation of her behavior. Tuttleton argues that when the narrator says "There's not any such thing as a woman born bad, because they are all born bad, born with the badness in them" (*CS* 133), he is not voicing Faulkner's opinion. Faulkner's point is the opposite: "Sex is a great natural procreant urge," not evil, but a natural, "irrepressible energy" (Tuttleton 1977, 288).

Skei, like Tuttleton, is more positive than some other critics in his reading of Faulkner's understanding of women's roles. He comments that the alternate portrayals of women in Yoknapatawpha "as either something to exhibit and admire and worship or something to use and discard, may account for some of the problems that the female characters face." Skei observes that those who maintain most harshly the traditional codes of behavior are older women, but he asserts that Faulkner's attitude toward female characters is one of understanding. The author is "unexpectedly critical in his descriptions of the lives women are allowed to live" because "he is very clearly aware that there are forces outside these women that condition them" (Skei 1985, 101).

Duvall reads the narrator's attitude as expressing a "male fear of female sexuality" that he would like to subsume in male control by legitimizing her sexuality in marriage. He establishes the paradigm of conflict as "woman-chaos-nature/man-order-culture." Duvall cautions that critics who adopt the language of the fictional characters to analyze the text enter into the limited perspectives of the characters. In this instance, Duvall is specifically critical of Everett's use of the narrator's language to express the theme of the story (1986, 42–43; Duvall 1990, 10, 60, 119–20). Carothers also pursues the means by which Stribling subverts the norms of the community. In the eyes of the townspeople, Susan is condemned for her presumed sexual activity while Stribling is assumed normal for his presumed sexual activity; but he counters the norms that circumscribe him just as he ignores those that define Susan (1992, 48–51).

Everett is correct in his appraisal that the plot is "well constructed" (1969, 145). The narrator's job puts him in the various towns, and it is reasonable that he would notice the seasonal changes in the empty house in Division. The detail of Susan Reed's hair resembling that of Sophie Starnes is also an effective means by which to link Stribling's past with his intended future. But when Everett concludes that the "characters generally lack the realism typical in Faulkner's work" (1969, 145), he misses the point of the obliqueness of the characters. As the narrator, the children, and the barbers demonstrate, what is not known is likely sketched in with details that may or may not reflect a true understanding of the individual. Susan Reed is known only by her reputation as distilled in the barber shop. That the accuracy of those impressions is not measurable is crucial to the conclusion and the point of the story.

Most critics pause to glance at "Hair" on their way to other Faulkner works, but few offer extended discussions of this story. O'Connor made an early assessment of "Hair" as "not, for Faulkner, a very good story" (1954, 68). Most critics deal with pieces of the story and do not offer summative remarks. Faulkner himself neglected to include a remark about "Hair" in his early planning list for *Collected Stories*, but Bonner claims that Faulkner counted it among his favorite three in *These 13* (1980, 32). In short, Faulkner fleshes out some interesting characters and tackles some difficult narrative options in this story; nevertheless, the achievements of "Hair" are outperformed in other texts.

## Works Cited

Bache, William B. 1954. "Moral Awareness in 'Dry September.'" *Faulkner Studies* 3:53–59.

Backman, Melvin. 1966. *Faulkner: The Major Years*. Bloomington: Indiana University Press.

Blotner, Joseph. 1974. *Faulkner: A Biography*. 2 vols. New York: Random House.

Bonner, Thomas, Jr., comp. 1980. *William Faulkner: The William B. Wisdom Collection: A Descriptive Catalogue*. New Orleans: Tulane University Libraries.

Carothers, James B. 1985. *William Faulkner's Short Stories*. Ann Arbor, MI: UMI Research Press.

———. 1992. "Faulkner's Short Story Writing and the Oldest Profession." In *Faulkner and the Short Story: Faulkner and Yoknapatawpha, 1990*. Ed. Evans Harrington and Ann J. Abadie. Jackson: University Press of Mississippi, 38–61.

Crane, John K. 1985. "But the Days Grow Short: A Reinterpretation of Faulkner's 'Dry September.'" *Twentieth Century Literature* 31:410–20.

Duvall, John N. 1986. "Faulkner's Critics and Women: The Voice of the Community." In *Faulkner and Women: Faulkner and Yoknapatawpha, 1985*. Ed. Doreen Fowler and Ann J. Abadie. Jackson: University Press of Mississippi, 41–57.

———. 1990. *Faulkner's Marginal Couple: Invisible, Outlaw, Unspeakable Communities*. Austin: University of Texas Press.

Emerson, O. B. 1984. *Faulkner's Early Literary Reputation in America*. Ann Arbor, MI: UMI Research Press.

Everett, Walter K. 1969. *Faulkner's Art and Character*. Woodbury, NY: Barron's Educational Series.

Faulkner, William. 1931. "Hair." *American Mercury* 23 (May):53–61.

———. 1931. *These 13*. New York: Jonathan Cape and Harrison Smith.

———. 1950. *Collected Stories of William Faulkner*. New York: Random House.

———. 1979. *Uncollected Stories of William Faulkner*. Ed. Joseph Blotner. New York: Random House.

———. 1987. *William Faulkner Manuscripts 9:* These 13. Ed. Noel Polk. New York: Garland.

Ferguson, James. 1991. *Faulkner's Short Fiction*. Knoxville: University of Tennessee Press.

Flynn, Peggy. 1976. "The Sister Figure and 'Little Sister Death' in the Fiction of William Faulkner." *University of Mississippi Studies in English* 14:99–117.

Holmes, Edward M. 1966. *Faulkner's Twice-Told Tales: His Re-Use of His Material*. The Hague: Mouton.

Inge, M. Thomas. 1986. "Faulkner Reads the Funny Papers." In *Faulkner and Humor: Faulkner and Yoknapatawpha, 1984*. Ed. Doreen Fowler and Ann J. Abadie. Jackson: University Press of Mississippi, 153–90.

Kinney, Arthur F. 1980. "Faulkner's Narrative Poetics and *Collected Stories*." *Faulkner Studies* 1:58–79.

Meriwether, James B. [1961] 1971. *The Literary Career of William Faulkner: A Bibliographical Study*. Princeton, NJ: Princeton University Library. Reprint. Columbia: University of South Carolina Press.

———. 1971. "The Short Fiction of William Faulkner: A Bibliography." *Proof* 1:293–329.

Millgate, Michael. [1966] 1989. *The Achievement of William Faulkner*. New York: Random. Reprint. Athens: University of Georgia Press. Brown Thrasher Books.

Momberger, Philip. 1978. "Faulkner's 'The Village' and 'That Evening Sun': The Tale in Context." *Southern Literary Journal* 11.1:20–31.

O'Connor, William Van. 1954. *The Tangled Fire of William Faulkner*. Minneapolis: University of Minnesota Press.

Page, Sally R. 1972. *Faulkner's Women: Characterization and Meaning*. DeLand, FL: Everett/Edwards.

Pitavy, François L. 1972. "A Forgotten Faulkner Story: 'Miss Zilphia Gant.'" *Studies in Short Fiction* 9:131–42.

———. 1973. *Faulkner's Light in August*. Trans. Gillian E. Cook. Bloomington: Indiana University Press.

Reed, Joseph W., Jr. 1973. *Faulkner's Narrative*. New Haven: Yale University Press.

Skei, Hans H. 1977. *Bold and Tragical and Austere: William Faulkner's These 13: A Study*. University of Oslo Department of Literature.

———. 1981. *William Faulkner: The Short Story Career*. Oslo, Norway: Universitetsforlaget.

———. 1985. *William Faulkner: The Novelist as Short Story Writer*. Oslo, Norway: Universitetsforlaget.

Tuck, Dorothy. 1964. *Crowell's Handbook of Faulkner*. New York: Thomas Y. Crowell.

Tuttleton, James W. 1977. "'Combat in the Erogenous Zone'": Women in the American Novel between the Two World Wars." In *What Manner of Woman: Essays on English and American Life and Literature*. Ed. Marlene Springer. New York: New York University Press, 271–96.

Vickery, Olga W. [1959] 1964. *The Novels of William Faulkner*. Baton Rouge: Louisiana State University Press.

Watson, James G. 1980. "Faulkner's Short Stories and the Making of Yoknapatawpha County." In *Fifty Years of Yoknapatawpha: Faulkner and Yoknapatawpha 1979*. Ed. Doreen Fowler and Ann J. Abadie. Jackson: University Press of Mississippi, 202–25.

———. 1987. *William Faulkner: Letters & Fictions*. Austin: University of Texas Press.

Watson, Judson D., III. 1990. "'Hair,' 'Smoke,' and the Development of the Faulknerian Lawyer Character." *Mississippi Quarterly* 43:349–66.

# Centaur in Brass

## Publication History

"Centaur in Brass" first appeared in the February 1932 issue of the *American Mercury*. In this same month, the *Saturday Evening Post* published another story about Flem Snopes, "Lizards in Jamshyd's Courtyard." According to the story-sending schedule, in August 1931 Faulkner submitted "Centaur in Brass" to *Scribner's* (August 11), and after its rejection there, to *Harper's* (August 23) where it was also rejected. He offered the story to *Scribner's* first because in June 1931 the magazine had published the first Snopes story ("Spotted Horses") and its editor had subsequently requested more stories about Flem Snopes, maintaining that *Scribner's* should have first refusal of all Flem Snopes stories. When Faulkner explained that he would not give up the opportunity to submit Snopes stories to the higher paying *Saturday Evening Post*, assistant editor Kyle Crichton understood. There is no evidence, however, that Faulkner submitted "Centaur in Brass" to the *Post*. Once *Scribner's* received "Centaur in Brass," Crichton rejected it because it concluded with Flem's defeat. The *American Mercury* editor felt better about the text. The entry for submission to the *American Mercury*, dated October 5, 1931, is circled on the schedule, Faulkner's way of indicating an acceptance. "Centaur in Brass" was not collected until it appeared in *Collected Stories* (1950). Still later Faulkner revised and incorporated "Centaur in Brass" into the opening chapter of *The Town* (1957) (Meriwether [1961] 1971, 41, 45, 171, 176–80; Meriwether 1973, 268–71; Blotner 1974, 699; Skei 1981, 72).

## Circumstances of Composition, Sources, and Influences

The range of dates proposed for the composition of "Centaur in Brass" is relatively narrow. James Meriwether suggests that "Centaur in Brass" may have existed for some time prior to its appearance on the sending schedule in August 1931. Faulkner's earliest work on the Snopes material (*Father Abraham*) was done in late 1926 or early 1927 and included the spotted horses episode. According to Faulkner, he set this work aside for about two years. Michael Millgate suggests that in summer 1930 Faulkner returned to the Snopes material for short stories and produced, among others, "Centaur in Brass" (Millgate [1966] 1989, 180–82). Hans Skei, however, dates the origin of "Centaur in Brass" in 1931 (Skei 1981, 72).

The revisions tracked in the story's development are primarily the changes that occurred in the transition from short story to novel chapter. (These are discussed in detail in the following section.) A twenty-four-page original typescript with some corrections is in the William B. Wisdom Collection at Tulane University (Bonner 1980, 32). Faulkner made limited changes to the text for *Collected Stories*. One transposition of words is corrected (*American Mercury* 201; *CS* 150). The figures in the *American Mercury* text that record Flem's payments for the brass against the balance fall about $100 short. The amount is corrected in *Collected Stories*. It increases from a second payment of $125 to a more painful $220 (*American Mercury* 210; *CS* 167). More interesting in terms of the story's maintaining an identity distinct from *The Town* is that Faulkner never revised his use of the name *Suratt* to *Ratliff* in the short story.

Biographical commentary on "Centaur in Brass" is relatively scarce. Joseph Blotner suggests that the image of Tom-Tom and Turl's fall into the ravine borrows from a similar fall Faulkner took years earlier on a possum hunt. Blotner also observes that the unnamed, first-person narrator "used the kind of technical terminology about boilers and gauges which Faulkner had doubtless learned at the Oxford power plant" (Blotner 1974, Notes 101, 699–700).

"Centaur in Brass" follows in the tradition of Southwestern humor. James Carothers describes it as a "self-contained comic tale worthy of comparison with the best of Mark Twain's efforts in the same genre." He draws particular comparisons between Flem Snopes and Jim Smiley, both characterized initially as humorous characters. They are also both tricksters who are ultimately tricked by the people they target as their victims. "Both stories," Carothers adds, "are brilliant object lessons in the frustration of the comic overreacher" (Carothers 1985, 121; see also Carothers 1984, 224–26; Putzel 1985, 275).

## Relation to Other Faulkner Works

Faulkner had a specific long-range plan for "Centaur in Brass." In 1945, he wrote to Malcolm Cowley that "Centaur in Brass" and "Mule in the Yard" would be incorporated into the second Snopes volume he planned—*The Town* (Blotner 1974, 1187; *SL* 197; Cowley 1966, 26). By 1948, when Faulkner was planning the *Collected Stories*, he indicated that "Centaur in Brass" would be part of the Snopes saga "when and if I get the other two volumes done" (*SL* 274). Thus, "Centaur in Brass" shares close ties with the other Snopes stories and novels. One must include in this list "Spotted Horses," "Lizards in Jamshyd's Courtyard," *The Hamlet*, *The Town*, and *The Mansion* for Flem Snopes. "Barn Burning," "Mule in the Yard," "My Grandmother

Millard and General Bedford Forrest and the Battle of Harrykin Creek," "There Was a Queen," *The Unvanquished*, and *Sanctuary* are among those texts in which the Snopes line is presented. In fact, Flem Snopes's position at the power plant is even mentioned in *Sartoris* (Cantwell [1953] 1985, 148; Emerson 1984, 60).

It is the use of Flem Snopes in particular in "Centaur in Brass" that provides the basis for most comparative readings within the body of Faulkner's fiction. The links are especially close between "Centaur," "Mule in the Yard," which in revision includes Flem, and "Lizards in Jamshyd's Courtyard." "Centaur in Brass" is set after the action of "Lizards." It is the first story to focus on Flem while he lives in Jefferson, a period of Flem's life not used again until *The Town* (Holmes 1966, 41; Blotner 1974, 699; Carothers 1985, 121). According to Blotner, it differs from previous stories about Flem because it is "basically humorous" (Blotner 1974, 700). It is particularly close to "Mule in the Yard" because both stories use humorous episodes to show how the "too-clever mercenary machinations of a Snopes result in frustration and financial loss" (Creighton 1977, 56). Further, both "Centaur in Brass" and "Mule in the Yard" present the possibility of overcoming the Snopeses "by their own petty overreaching and by the native wits of those who dare to oppose them." This attitude reappears in *The Town* and *The Mansion* (Carothers 1985, 123).

The extent of the changes made in "Centaur in Brass" when Faulkner incorporated it into *The Town* is the focus of most of the commentary about the story. Edwin Hunter calculates that the twenty-five-year gap between the short story's first appearance and its becoming a part of the novel is the longest stretch for any story subsequently worked into a novel (1973, 82, 85). Dorothy Tuck describes the story as "relatively unchanged" in *The Town* (1964, 163). Millgate believes that "Centaur in Brass," like "Mule in the Yard" and "The Waifs," is incorporated into *The Town* in such a way that it maintains its identity as a "discrete, static" episode; it is "set off against the flow of the narrative" but also reinforces the meaning of "Snopesism" and acts as a counterpoint to the "irrelevance and ineffectuality of Gavin Stevens's anti-Snopes crusade" (Millgate [1966] 1989, 236–37).

Speaking generally about the process, Carothers finds that short story material is often moved into the novels with "relatively few changes" even though the "novelistic context always alters the significance and emphasis of the elements of the original story." "Centaur in Brass," like "Mule in the Yard," "Wash," and the Al Jackson stories, follows this pattern. Speaking specifically, however, Carothers describes "Centaur in Brass" as "substantially reworked" when incorporated into *The Town* (1985, 26, 121). James Ferguson believes that "Centaur in Brass" is somewhat weak as a short story, though less so than "Lizards in Jamshyd's Courtyard" or "Spotted Horses," because of the need to supply background information about Snopes. These stories, he believes, are enhanced by incorporation into the novels because of the fuller context the larger works provide (Ferguson 1991, 132).

Important differences can be found between "Centaur in Brass" and its retelling in *The Town*. The presentation of Flem's defeat is the most significant alteration; in *The Town*, this event is softened and made only "momentary" (Blotner 1974, 699; Skei 1981, 72–73). Joanne Creighton also finds the presentation of Flem an important change that shifts thematic emphasis. Flem becomes "more dominant and more formidable" in *The Town*. He makes only one payment for the brass, and the amount is considerably reduced. The tainted water tower, noted in the story as Snopes's "monument," is redefined as his "footprint" (*T* 3). Rather than a monument to failure, it now represents the footprint that marks the spot, according to Snopes, "*where I was when I moved again*" (*T* 29). Snopes's monument is his wife's affair, now with Manfred de Spain not Major Hoxey, because it remains an exploitable opportunity. The town responds to the affair, no longer with outrage at Flem's inaction but with silent consent. When, later, the affair is forced into the public arena, it then serves to expose the town's "moral hypocrisy." As Creighton concludes, turning a story of Flem's defeat into an example of his gaining strength in the defeat "turns a casual egg-stealing tramp into a frighteningly incorrigible opportunist." Suratt in the short story admits reluctantly that Snopes is the superior trader. In the novel Ratliff is less willing to make any such admission or admit admiration for the other's skill (Creighton 1977, 50–55, 164 n. 38, 165 n. 40; see also Hunter 1973, 86).

Skei believes that, in revision, Flem's experience becomes a "kind of lesson to him, making him rely even more heavily and exclusively on himself in the future" (1981, 72–73). Carothers adds that the Snopes watching by Charles's family, especially Gavin Stevens, and also by V. K. Ratliff, is an important alteration. However, for Carothers, "Centaur in Brass" portrays the "chicanery of the Snopeses . . . with considerably more tolerance" than in *The Town*. Carothers also lists further changes in the information about Flem's wife, who is not named in the short story. The wife's presumed adultery with Major Hoxey is a variation on the adultery of Eula and Colonel Winword in *Father Abraham* (Carothers 1985, 133, 20, 119).

Another important alteration in the transition between short story and novel is the change in point of view. Charles Mallison is the narrator of the section of *The Town* in which this story reappears. He recounts the story he has heard from Gowan Stevens's, who worked at the plant, and from Harker. In this account, Harker actually goes out to Turl's house and witnesses the conflict between Turl and Tom-Tom. He also aids in the deception of Flem by his two co-workers (Holmes 1966, 42–43). Creighton describes the narration of the short story as "fuzzy" because it intermingles first-person singular, first-person plural, and omniscient points of view. The narrator speaks collectively when relating the town's "knowledge, opinions, and prejudices" about Flem's activities and his wife's purported affair with Major Hoxey. But the narrator also uses "I" in his narration, relates incidents he did not witness, and has information known only by a few people. Although it is presumed that the narrator relies on accounts of Harker and Turl, "blurring of focus results from the inconsistent point of view." The narration in the novel is more carefully credited to "additional perceivers" but maintains the flexibility that the first-person singular, first-person plural, and omniscient perspectives offered in the short story. In the longer work the account is narrated in the Charles Mallison section; Mallison learns of the matter from Gowan Stevens, who is added in the novel as an employee of the plant, and from his uncle Gavin and Ratliff, who indoctrinate him into Snopes's activities. In this account, Harker gets a fuller account from Gavin, who learns it from Tom-Tom. Charles's narration differentiates between eye-witness accounts and what he "had to imagine" when he had no specific source of information. In the novel, Harker witnesses firsthand the centaur-like figure the antagonists Tom-Tom and Turl make. He has gone to Tom-Tom's house to prevent the fight between the two men (Creighton 1977, 51–52).

The combined effects of increasing Flem's dominance and filtering the story through several consciousnesses diminishes the roles of Tom-Tom, his wife, and Turl. In its position in the chronicle of Flem Snopes's progress, the role of the three black characters "is minor and tangential and appropriately condensed" (Creighton 1977, 52). It should also be noted that Turl of "Centaur in Brass" is identified as Tomey's Turl Beauchamp. Even though this identification links Turl to *Go Down, Moses*, it is another instance of Faulkner's ignoring chronology. Tomey's Turl would be a septuagenarian in the time frame of *The Town* (see Brooks [1963] 1990, 448). Stephen Ross observes that the representations of dialect are much heavier in the short story than in the novel. This reduction of dialect in the novel is typical of Faulkner's movement "toward more subtle" representations of speech during his career (1989, 104). One minor difference is that the number of Tom-Tom's marriages increases from three to four (*CS* 152; *T* 16).

John Bassett sees Faulkner's use of "Centaur in Brass" at the beginning of *The Town* as a means of demythologizing the world portrayed in *The Hamlet*. "Centaur" presents a "real and vulnerable" Snopes who can be defeated. Within the context of the novel, the episodes described in "Centaur in Brass," "Mule in the Yard," and "The Waifs" convey different meanings from those they present as isolated stories. Contextualized, they "epitomize the thrust of the novel." They reflect the novel's concern with the "turning of fact into fiction, the demands of the conventions of both narrative form and audience, the use of oral fictions for personal or social reasons" ([1988] 1989, 215, 218).

George Anderson believes that alterations in the story reflect the novel's concern with respectability. In the novel, both "Centaur in Brass" and "Mule in the Yard" seem to contrast an "essentially healthy, though oppressed, black society" with "the corrupt white world." In this effort, Anderson sees an elimination of racial stereotyping in the characterizations of both Tom-Tom and Turl as they appear in *The Town* (1990, 377–85).

"Centaur in Brass" has received attention beyond its relationship to the Snopes fiction. Patrick Samway likens Tom-Tom's surviving the "potentially dangerous situation" set in motion by Snopes to Lucas Beauchamp's experience in *Intruder in the Dust*. Both men, incidentally, are in their sixties (Samway 1980, 239). Millgate observes that Buck Conners, who is ready with a warrant to arrest Tom-Tom and Turl in "Centaur in Brass," reappears in *Light in August* with the slightly revised name *Connors* (1987, 48).

Most observations relate to recurring thematic issues in Faulkner's fiction. Olga Vickery groups "Centaur in Brass" with Faulkner's stories that employ a contest formula including sexual rivalry such as a romantic triangle. On this basis, "Centaur in Brass" can be compared to such other works as "A Courtship," "Wild Palms," *Pylon*, "The Fire and the Hearth," and "The Bear." Vickery adds that these triangles can include complicating issues such as adultery (as in "Centaur in Brass"), racial prejudice, and incest. The tone ranges from comedy to "unrelieved horror." The various depictions of a romantic triangle exhibited in "Centaur in Brass," "A Courtship," and "Artist at Home" all culminate in a reconciliation of husband and lover, emphasizing the "perception of the recurrence of a relatively limited number of patterns of human action"; in this way they introduce "into the Faulknerian design the perdurable limiting conditions of human existence" and a recognition of "our common humanity." This recognition emphasizes both the repetition of human activity and its embodiment of "eternal verities." Human freedom in Faulkner's view is located not in "limitless opportunities" but in the "infinite variety of responses to those actions which man either can or must perform" (Vickery [1959] 1964, 303–05).

Charles Nilon's examination of black characters in Faulkner's stories identifies them as "simple, lowly, uneducated people." They are typically victims, but they "are usually morally superior to their oppressors." "Centaur in Brass," "A Bear Hunt," "A Justice," and "Was" mix violence with grotesque humor in a satiric approach different from those stories in which the black character dies (Nilon 1965, 33).

Nilon finds that black characters in Faulkner's fiction move on two levels: individuals move in day-to-day activity, and individual movements cohere in general movement that is emblematic of the survival of the black person. The movement is presented as "pictures that define the black journey as 'going to cross Jordan.'" The crossing "means becoming persons and being free to confront freedom." Nilon pursues this image in "Centaur in Brass" and "Pantaloon in Black" particularly, but it is also developed in such scenes as the literal portrayal of a river crossing in *The Unvanquished*, in Tobe's exit in "A Rose for Emily," and in Will Mayes's murder in "Dry September" (Nilon 1981, 227–29).

Skei studies the portrayal of corruption and misuse of power within comic narratives. These humorous stories involve "unbelievable bargains, incredible shrewdness and unlimited greed." The Snopes stories, including "Centaur in Brass," fall into this category as do "Death Drag" and the World War I story "Thrift" (Skei 1985, 160). Similarly, Carothers compares the efforts of the founding fathers of Jefferson to avoid paying Alexander Holston for his lock in "A Name for the City" and *Requiem for a Nun* with Flem's action in "Centaur in Brass" and Res Grier's in "Shingles for the Lord" (1985, 48).

Ferguson places "Centaur in Brass" in a group of stories that use a pattern "in which children or childlike characters, in spite of their confrontations with the world of evil, ugliness, and corruption, continue to maintain their fundamental innocence—because they are not yet ready to understand that world, because they can never understand it, or because they simply refuse to do so." In a variation, "an innocent (or often only an apparent innocent) confronts the world of corruption head-on and achieves a kind of victory over it, a kind of triumph." When race is added as another element to the pattern, typically, a member of a "supposedly inferior race" will gain advantage over a white character. Among these stories, Ferguson groups "Centaur in Brass," "Lo!," "Yo Ho and Two Bottles of Rum," and "A Bear Hunt." Additionally, the activities of Lucas Beauchamp in *Go Down, Moses* and Ringo in *The Unvanquished* are a part of this pattern. Ferguson also fits "Centaur in Brass" into a group of stories involving a "quest for justice." These have a happy ending with regard to the black characters as they attain some retribution for the way a white character has exploited them. "Centaur in Brass," "A Bear Hunt," and "Gold Is Not Always" fit this pattern (Ferguson 1991, 57, 60–61, 74–75, 78).

John Matthews examines Faulkner's short fiction to see how it "internalizes the conditions of the literary marketplace, and how several of his early short stories represent the circumstances of their own production." Focusing on "Red Leaves," "There Was a Queen," "Spotted Horses," "Lizards in Jamshyd's Courtyard," "Dry September," "Centaur in Brass," and "Mule in the Yard," Matthews seeks to locate within the short stories the sense of curtailment, aesthetic commodification, mass cultural consumption, and resistance to the demands of the market (1992, 3–37).

Blotner offers a brief formal comparison in his observation that the impressionistic title recalls the imagery present in the title of one of Faulkner's poetry collections, *The Marble Faun* (Blotner 1974, 699). Joan Serafin includes the titular reference and image of the centaur in her listing of classical references in Faulkner's work. As Serafin's work demonstrates, the image of the centaur reappears frequently in such works as "Fox Hunt," *Soldiers' Pay*, "Wash," and *Absalom, Absalom!* (1983, 32, 15; see also Mortimer 1983, 35–36).

In examining the group perspective in Faulkner's fiction, Peter Nicolaisen observes that the events the groups "watch and comment on are nearly always connected with a breach of law." The catalogue of crimes includes "murder, rape, arson, theft, bootlegging, a mutiny, or . . . litigations of various sorts." Nicolaisen's list of specific incidents includes the workers at the power plant watching Snopes steal the brass fitting from the power plant in "Centaur in Brass" (1989, 92).

Skei has tried to find a controlling logic for the decisions Faulkner made concerning which Snopes stories would be included in collection. "Barn Burning," "Centaur in Brass," and "Mule in the Yard" appear in *Collected Stories*. Faulkner did not include two other stories about Flem Snopes, "Spotted Horses" and "Lizards in Jamshyd's Courtyard." Once "The Hound" was used in the Snopes saga, it was not collected although it had appeared in *Doctor Martino*. To some extent the choice seems to rest on whether the particular story had already appeared in a Snopes novel, but Skei's conclusion is that no consistent pattern governed Faulkner's use of the Snopes stories as separate texts (1981, 44).

Because of the numerous thematic similarities between this story and other Faulkner works, it should not be surprising that critics find "Centaur in Brass" an appropriate addition to "The Village" section of *Collected Stories*. Millgate suggests that as the third story in the section it builds on and adds to the delineation of Jefferson "as a place, a social entity." Like "A Rose for Emily" it employs a first person narrator who speaks as a "generalised voice of Jefferson" (Millgate [1966] 1989, 272).

Philip Momberger sees "The Village" as a picture of "social and moral disintegration." "Centaur in Brass" includes one of the portraits of estranged spouses that appear in the tales. Like Nancy and Jesus and Mr. and Mrs. Compson in "That Evening Sun," the husbands and wives of both races experience conflict (Momberger 1978, 20–25).

James Watson believes that "The Village," opening with "A Rose for Emily" and concluding with "That Evening Sun," examines the individual in society. When a story such as "Centaur in Brass" is read in the context of other stories in which characters "work out their own destinies with varying degrees of failure or success," its meaning is enhanced by the larger context (Watson 1980, 221–22).

Arthur Kinney traces a pattern of exploitation that links the stories within "The Village" and also makes connections between "The Country" and "The Village." Kinney compares Res Grier's tricking Solon Quick and Vernon Tull in "Shingles for the Lord" with Flem Snopes's manipulations of Tom-Tom and

Turl. The exploitation theme appears again in "Death Drag." By association, Flem's tactics are equated with the "paltriness of the con artist" (Kinney 1980, 66–67).

Ferguson sees "Centaur in Brass" comfortably situated in "The Village" section of *Collected Stories*, a section he believes bears an "impressive unity." All the stories revolve around the "relationship between individual and communal values." In the series of stories "Centaur in Brass" follows "Hair"; together they offer some relief from the preceding horror of "A Rose for Emily" and the intense seriousness of the subsequent four stories (Ferguson 1991, 158).

## Interpretation and Criticism

*Scribner's* associate editor Kyle Crichton was one of the earliest advocates for and interpreters of the character of Flem Snopes. After having asked for more Snopes stories, his explanation for rejecting "Centaur in Brass" came in two letters to Faulkner. Crichton believed that Snopes was a "monumental figure." He was "mean" and "cagy" and far too interesting to receive the premature "come-uppance" that would end his adventures much too soon. Crichton suggested that Faulkner save "Centaur in Brass" to "come as the end of a line of other stories about Flem." He hoped that Flem would be "triumphant to the point where everybody in America will hate him in unison. Then it will be time for his downfall" (Meriwether 1973, 270–71). Carothers suggests that Faulkner took Crichton's concern for the demise of Flem Snopes seriously because the author did not return to Flem Snopes as a central character until he wrote *The Hamlet* (Carothers 1985, 121–22).

In *The Town*, Faulkner redefined Flem Snopes's downfall of "Centaur in Brass" as an initiating experience that marked the rise of his prominence in Jefferson. For Irving Howe, "Centaur in Brass" shows the early Flem as a "petty conniver" before he attains the status of "banker scrupulously obeying the letter of the law and thereby invulnerable to obvious moral attack or legal prosecution" ([1952] 1975, 108). Blotner contends that "Centaur in Brass" establishes the lines of Flem's rise in his movement from enterprise to enterprise, his poisoning the town, and his willingness to use his wife, Eula, for his own career advancement (1974, 700).

The matter of the romantic triangle involving Snopes, his wife, and Major Hoxey, discussed earlier within the context of recurring patterns in Faulkner's fiction, receives additional analysis regarding its importance within "Centaur in Brass." Blotner identifies two love triangles: a triangle of "normal sexuality" including Tom-Tom, his wife, and Turl, which is contrasted with the "unnatural triangle" of Flem, Eula, and Major Hoxey (Blotner 1974, 700). Carothers sees the relationship between Tom-Tom and Turl paralleling the one between Flem and Major Hoxey, the difference appearing in the reactions of the deceived husbands. Flem does not foresee Tom-Tom's wrath, the "natural consequences" of his discovery of Turl's relationship with his wife, and it is Flem's failure that precipitates his downfall (Carothers 1985, 121).

Just as Snopes could not relate to the possibility of spousal jealousy, he could not anticipate that the enmity he had forged between Tom-Tom and Turl could be healed. Given their personalities and the circumstances, the two men should never have been friends. The relationship between Snopes and Major Hoxey is unnatural, like a centaur, and promotes evil designs. By contrast, the friendship between Tom-Tom and Turl, which is unnatural in that they are rivals for Tom-Tom's wife, results in their ability to defeat Snopes. When they realize they have been "touched and forced to act by evil," they become friends. Their friendship may be understood, according to Nilon, in the comments of the omniscient narrator who proposes a point of view different from that expressed by Harker, the night engineer, when describing the new alliance between the two black men. The reconciliation is either the "sanctuary beyond despair" or "nigger nature." For Nilon, the omniscient narrator's perspective, sanctuary, is the correct interpretation. The second is Harker's opinion, which needs to be articulated in order to underscore the fact that Tom-Tom and Turl's actions deny the validity of such diminishing characterizations. In the end, Tom-Tom and Turl are the victors, employing Flem's early explanation of needing the brass for the water tank as their reason for putting the collected brass in the tank (Nilon 1965, 48, 53–54).

Skei argues that the "interpretive problem" of the story is to determine whether Flem is defeated because of coincidence, because "there is a limit to exploitation," or because people working cooperatively can defeat him even if he cannot be avoided. Skei, like Nilon, believes that the key to Flem's defeat is Tom-Tom and Turl's alliance, their acting together. Skei points out that given "their place in the social hierarchy of Jefferson" and the presumptions about their "nature," the black characters cannot be manipulated by the pressure of social convention and the desire for respectability, as Flem seems to assume they can (Skei 1985, 187–89).

Several critics have studied the racial themes that emerge when Tom-Tom and Turl behave in a way that is contrary to the expectations of the white onlookers. Although he does not find "Centaur in Brass" a "notable" story, Howe says it "provides insight into the Faulkner who is something more than a traditional Southerner" in its scenario in which a "Snopes is defeated by two Negro laborers" (Howe [1952] 1975, 263).

Nilon traces the story's exposure of the evil in racial stereotyping and the presumed etiquette of relations between races. Evasion is one survival technique the blacks use. Neither black man completely disregards Snopes's instructions to him because, as Nilon notes, deliberate disobedience would have severe consequences. Harker's report of the chase scene incorporates the characteristics of blackface comedy. In fact, the humorous element of the story depends upon comic stereotypes of blacks: "razors, whiskey, watermelon, confessions induced by fear of death, unfaithful wives, butcher knives, a man whose sexual proclivities are unusually great, and the idea that Negro women are unchaste." Another stereotype of black character is the presumption that blacks steal. Snopes builds his entire plan on the knowledge that the missing brass will be attributed to theft by the black workers. Similarly, the etiquette of race relations is also carefully developed. Snopes is able to manipulate the black men by threatening that they could lose their jobs. Harker, as a white man, may address blacks about marriage and extramarital relationships "to indicate goodwill and kindly interest," but a reciprocal comment from a black to a white man would be unacceptable. Another aspect of Harker's behavior is to use "Mr." in references to Flem Snopes when he is talking to the black men. This story is in short the "kind of story that a white man might tell white men." Harker recognizes the story as one of a white man who is bested by a black man, but because the white man "is so despicable," Harker betrays no convention by telling the story. But he fails to grasp the full importance of the event he is describing, according to Nilon. Harker recognizes the meaning of particular events, but he does not realize that in its broad implications the story serves as an "example of the Negro's moral superiority" (Nilon 1965, 48, 51–52).

Nilon explains the deconstruction of stereotype further in a later study. Faulkner's portrayal of black characters within a journey motif sometimes includes a transformation of journey into flight. In "Centaur in Brass" the personal journeys of the two black men coalesce into an "escape and pursuit" pattern designed by Flem Snopes. They "move in opposition to each other until they are able to join forces and move against Flem Snopes." Movement is an "insistence of Faulkner's black characters on their right to be human even when their movement . . . does not meet the approval of the narrator or of the white participants in the scene." The movement constitues creating pictures of behavior that often involves revising or breaking the pictured behavior of stereotype. Turl, for example, fits the stereotype of the very sexually active black male. However, in seeking the cause of Turl's behavior, the stereotype is exposed. Turl's behavior has given him an identity in the community. Tom-Tom has defined himself quite differently by his years of dependable job performance and by establishing a home.

Another picture-breaking movement occurs in the use of the chase scene that is typically a comic portrayal of the black man running. When Tom-Tom rises from the cot and clings to Turl, the running scene that begins as slapstick comedy ends in surrealism. The introduction of the centaur image implies a relationship not of antagonism but of mutual dependence—both men are hurt when Turl tries to free himself by bumping into trees; Tom-Tom tries to change Turl's direction when he sees the impending fall into the ditch. The culminating image of moonlight, ditch, and Turl's legs running in the air departs from the comic tradition. Then the men are in conversation together; the knife and their battle are no longer at issue. Harker as narrator portrays these men within stereotypical conventions, but the patterns are subverted, and the narrator's ambivalence toward these accepted images is revealed. When compared to Flem Snopes, Tom-Tom and Turl are shown to possess a moral superiority and an impressive ability to outwit a shrewd opportunist (Nilon 1981, 228–30, 238–51). Max Putzel also admires Tom-Tom and Turl, describing them as underdogs who also possess humor "that endows these two clowns with singular grace" (Putzel 1985, 279).

According to Matthews, the "treatment of female subjectivity" is "crucial to the manipulation of desire in the mass market." Faulkner's short stories, to a greater degree than his novels, "demonstrate the objectification and silencing of women in the theatre of male desire." In "Centaur in Brass," Mrs. Snopes functions as the "commodification of eros." In the romantic triangle she "mediates the business and personal relations between the present and would-be male powers of Jefferson." Similarly, in the second triangle, Tom-Tom's wife has the status of property. She is equated with the gold watch and chain that are part of Tom-Tom's Sunday adornments, and Tom-Tom locks her in the bedroom when he plots to confront Turl. After the men resolve their conflict, she prepares a meal for them, remaining in the background, "shadowy and covert and unspeaking" (*CS* 165). Both wives "stand in for the financial objects that drive men" in a culture in which the "erotic turns out to be a pronounced sublimation of the economic" (Matthews 1992, 26–29).

Evaluations of the formal characteristics of the story have generally been complimentary, but the praise is not unqualified. Millgate praises the tale's "narrative intricacy and its splendidly ironic reversals" ([1966] 1989, 236). Blotner notes the combination of farce and tall tale elements in the tone and an "element of fabliau" in the seduction of Tom-Tom's wife (Blotner 1974, 700). Putzel calls "Centaur in Brass" "lighthearted and cheerful." It exhibits a "virtuosity" built on "concealment from each observer of what the others (and the reader) know is happening." The humor derives from the satisfaction of watching the two abused black men best the white man. "It is a kind of bravura piece in the all-American repertory, a gem of southern humor" (Putzel 1985, 278–79).

Countering those critics who admire the story's narrative achievements are those who identify some confusion in the telling. The careful development of narrators and eye witnesses in *The Town* alters a somewhat problematic handling of narrative point of view in the short story. Edward Holmes's description of the varied perspectives indicates the source of criticism. He traces a "communal first person plural" in the opening of the story that is only later identified as the character Harker. Harker shares narrative responsibilities with an omniscient narrator. At one point, Harker drops the plural "we" for "I" (Holmes 1966, 42). Ferguson speaks most pointedly about the problems of narrative perspective, arguing that "Centaur in Brass" is an "egregious example of carelessness in the handling of point of view." Following Creighton's analysis that the narrator cannot have had knowledge of some of the activities he tells about, Ferguson concludes that the "handling of point of view in 'Centaur in Brass' is rather thoroughly botched" (1991, 114).

Most critics do not consider "Centaur in Brass" an autonomous text. They almost always consider it in the context of the novel despite the differences between story and novel episode, and it is regularly omitted in considerations of Faulkner's short stories. In his appendix on re-used material, Holmes does not include "Centaur in Brass" separately but treats it in his extended discussion of *The Town* (Holmes 1966, 99–115, 41–43). Critical works that provide story synopses such as Walter Everett's and Robert Kirk and Marvin Klotz's tend not to offer a summary of the story except as an episode in the novel. Kirk and Klotz's listing of the *Collected Stories* notes that stories incorporated into novels are treated with those novels (1963, 256). Everett identifies the short story, but also offers commentary only as part of *The Town* (1969, 137, 118–19). More recently, Thomas Connolly has offered a summary of characters and action that treats the story and novel separately (1988, 282–86, 343–62).

Sufficient differences between the texts warrant treatment of the short story as an independent writing. Nilon's work establishes a particular strength in the scenario of the trickster tricked in the subversion of stereotype specifically as it appears in "Centaur in Brass." As Flem Snopes's defeat is diminished in the retelling in *The Town*, so too is this perspective diminished. It is best studied, therefore, in the short story. Faulkner himself seemed to do two things to establish the story's autonomy: first, he collected the story even though he anticipated its eventual use elsewhere; second, he did not revise the name *Suratt* to *Ratliff* in this story even though he made exactly that revision in "A Bear Hunt" for *Collected Stories*. Matthews also treats the work specifically as a magazine piece. "Centaur in Brass" is not completely assimilated by the context of the novel, and the critical commentary should not, as it so often does, assume this to be the case. The story, like Flem Snopes within it, is "not impregnable: impervious" (*CS* 151).

## Works Cited

Anderson, George. 1990. "Toward a Reading of *The Town* as a Chronicle: Respectability and Race in Three Episodes." *Mississippi Quarterly* 43:377–85.

Bassett, John E. [1988] 1989. "Yoknapatawpha Revised: Demystifying Snopes." In *Visions and Revisions: Essays on Faulkner*. Ed. Bassett. Locust Hill Literary Studies No. 4. West Cornwall, CT: Locust Hill, 213-31.

Blotner, Joseph. 1974. *Faulkner: A Biography*. 2 vols. New York: Random House.

Bonner, Thomas, Jr., comp. 1980. *William Faulkner: The William B. Wisdom Collection: A Descriptive Catalogue*. New Orleans: Tulane University Libraries.

Brooks, Cleanth. [1963] 1990. *William Faulkner: The Yoknapatawpha Country*. New Haven: Yale University Press. Reprint. Baton Rouge: Louisiana State University Press.

Cantwell, Robert. [1953] 1985. "Introduction [to *Sartoris*]." In *Critical Essays on William Faulkner: The Sartoris Family*. Ed. Arthur F. Kinney. Boston: G. K. Hall, 146–60.

Carothers, James B. 1984. "Faulkner's Short Stories: 'And Now What's to Do.'" In *New Directions in Faulkner Studies: Faulkner and Yoknapatawpha, 1983*. Ed. Doreen Fowler and Ann J. Abadie. Jackson: University Press of Mississippi, 202–27.

———. 1985. *William Faulkner's Short Stories*. Ann Arbor, MI: UMI Research Press.

Connolly, Thomas E. 1988. *Faulkner's World: A Directory of His People and Synopses of Actions in His Published Works*. Lanham, MD.: University Press of America.

Cowley, Malcolm. 1966. *The Faulkner-Cowley File: Letters and Memories, 1944–1962*. New York: Viking.

Creighton, Joanne V. 1977. *William Faulkner's Craft of Revision: The Snopes Trilogy, "The Unvanquished," and "Go Down, Moses."* Detroit: Wayne State University Press.

Emerson, O. B. 1984. *Faulkner's Early Literary Reputation in America*. Ann Arbor, MI: UMI Research Press.

Everett, Walter K. 1969. *Faulkner's Art and Character*. Woodbury, NY: Barron's Educational Series.

Faulkner, William. 1932. "Centaur in Brass." *American Mercury* 25 (February):200–10.

———. 1950. *Collected Stories of William Faulkner*. New York: Random House.

———. 1957. *The Town*. New York: Random House.

———. 1977. *Selected Letters of William Faulkner*. Ed. Joseph Blotner. New York: Random House.

Ferguson, James. 1991. *Faulkner's Short Fiction*. Knoxville: University of Tennessee Press.

Holmes, Edward M. 1966. *Faulkner's Twice-Told Tales: His Re-Use of His Material*. The Hague: Mouton.

Howe, Irving. [1952] 1975 *William Faulkner: A Critical Study*. 3d ed. Chicago: University of Chicago Press.

Hunter, Edwin R. 1973. *William Faulkner: Narrative Practice and Prose Style*. Washington, DC: Windhover.

Kinney, Arthur F. 1980. "Faulkner's Narrative Poetics and *Collected Stories*." *Faulkner Studies* 1:58–79.

Kirk, Robert W., and Marvin Klotz. 1963. *Faulkner's People: A Complete Guide and Index to Characters in the Fiction of William Faulkner*. Berkeley and Los Angeles: University of California Press.

Matthews, John T. 1992. "Shortened Stories: Faulkner and the Market." In *Faulkner and the Short Story: Faulkner and Yoknapatawpha, 1990*. Ed. Evans Harrington and Ann J. Abadie. Jackson: University Press of Mississippi, 3–37.

Meriwether, James B. [1961] 1971. *The Literary Career of William Faulkner: A Bibliographical Study*. Princeton, NJ: Princeton University Library. Reprint. Columbia: University of South Carolina Press.

———. 1973. "Faulkner's Correspondence with Scribner's Magazine." *Proof* 3:253–82.

Millgate, Michael. [1966] 1989. *The Achievement of William Faulkner*. New York: Random House. Reprint. Athens: University of Georgia Press. Brown Thrasher Books.

———. 1987. "'A Novel: Not an Anecdote': Faulkner's Light in August." In *New Essays on Light in August*. Ed. Michael Millgate. Cambridge: Cambridge University Press, 31–53.

Momberger, Philip. 1978. "Faulkner's 'The Village' and 'That Evening Sun': The Tale in Context." *Southern Literary Journal* 11.1:20–31.

Mortimer, Gail L. 1983. *Faulkner's Rhetoric of Loss: A Study in Perception and Meaning*. Austin: University of Texas Press.

Nicolaisen, Peter. 1989. "Group Perspective and Group Behavior: Notes on Faulkner's 'Forensic Imagination.'" In *Faulkner's Discourse: An International Symposium*. Ed. Lothar Hönnighausen. Tübingen: Max Niemeyer Verlag, 90–98.

Nilon, Charles H. 1965. *Faulkner and the Negro*. New York: Citadel.

———. 1981. "Blacks in Motion." In "A Cosmos of My Own": *Faulkner and Yoknapatawpha 1980*. Ed. Doreen Fowler and Ann J. Abadie. Jackson: University Press of Mississippi, 227–51.

Putzel, Max. 1985. *Genius of Place: William Faulkner's Triumphant Beginnings*. Baton Rouge: Louisiana State University Press.

Ross, Stephen M. 1989. *Fiction's Inexhaustible Voice: Speech and Writing in Faulkner*. Athens: University of Georgia Press.

Samway, Patrick H., S. J. 1980. *Faulkner's Intruder in the Dust: A Critical Study of the Typescripts*. Troy, NY: Whitston.

Serafin, Joan M. 1983. *Faulkner's Uses of the Classics*. Ann Arbor, MI: UMI Research Press.

Skei, Hans H. 1981. *William Faulkner: The Short Story Career*. Oslo, Norway: Universitetsforlaget.

———. 1985. *William Faulkner: The Novelist as Short Story Writer*. Oslo, Norway: Universitetsforlaget.

Tuck, Dorothy. 1964. *Crowell's Handbook of Faulkner*. New York: Thomas Y. Crowell.

Vickery, Olga W. [1959] 1964. *The Novels of William Faulkner*. Baton Rouge: Louisiana State University.

Watson, James G. 1980. "Faulkner's Short Stories and the Making of Yoknapatawpha County." In *Fifty Years of Yoknapatawpha: Faulkner and Yoknapatawpha 1979*. Ed. Doreen Fowler and Ann J. Abadie. Jackson: University Press of Mississippi, 202–25.

# Dry September

## Publication History

"Dry September" was first published in the January 1931 issue of *Scribner's*. Faulkner's schedule for submission of works for publication shows that it was sent under the title "Drouth" to the *American Mercury* on February 8, 1930, and to *Forum* on March 7, 1930. After substantial revision, Faulkner submitted the story to *Scribner's* on April 21, 1930, only to have it promptly returned. He learned in a letter from *Scribner's*, dated April 28, that the manuscript had been returned mistakenly without having been read. Faulkner resubmitted the story, which *Scribner's* then purchased for $200 (Meriwether [1961] 1971, 172, 176–79; Blotner 1974, 654; Meriwether 1973, 260; Skei 1981, 59). "Dry September" was revised for inclusion in *These 13* (1931); the *Collected Stories* (1950) text is the same one revised for *These 13*. "Dry September" and "A Rose for Emily" are distinguished as the earliest Faulkner texts to be translated into French by Maurice Coindreau (Blotner 1974, 766).

## Circumstances of Composition, Sources, and Influences

Although the first record of this story is the February 1930 date on the sending schedule, "Dry September" may have been written as early as 1926 or

170  *Dry September*

1927. In February 1927 Faulkner indicated that he was writing some stories about his townspeople (*SL* 34–35). Hans Skei suggests that "Dry September" may have been a part of that effort (1981, 26).

The University of Virginia holds the extant manuscript and carbon typescript of "Drouth." One typescript page about "Plunkett and three others" is in the inventory of the Rowan Oak papers. These documents establish "Drouth" as the story published as "Dry September." References in correspondence with *Scribner's* are also to "Drouth" (*WFM 9* Introduction x; Meriwether 1973, 260). Although there is no conclusive evidence of who authorized the title or why it was changed, Skei argues that even if the suggestion to retitle the story originated with the magazine, the change was probably Faulkner's (Skei 1981, 60). When Faulkner collected the story he retained the title "Dry September."

The study of these prepublication texts reveals a great deal about this story, one generally included among Faulkner's best short fiction. Skei believes the carbon typescript may be the one *Scribner's* purchased and used as the setting copy of the magazine. Noel Polk, however, describes the carbon typescript as consisting of two different kinds of onionskin paper, suggesting that it "is a composite of two different typings" (Skei 1981, 59–60; Kinney and Fowler 1983, 330; *WFM 9* Introduction xiv). Sectional divisions appear in the early eight-page manuscript even though in later drafts Faulkner usually divided his works. This uncharacteristic feature may indicate that Faulkner felt confident either with his material or its direction or both, but the symbolic elements, positioning, and balanced movement of the narrative make it doubtful that the story "was written in one burst of sudden inspiration" (Skei 1981, 59).

Critics generally agree that by switching the opening to the barbershop rather than beginning with Minnie Cooper's portrait, Faulkner made a revision that strengthens the story. Michael Millgate praises the effect gained by establishing the mood of violence among the men before introducing Minnie ([1966] 1989, 263). Believing this switch to be the most important alteration of the story, Joseph Blotner judges the revised opening to be "much more powerful and ominous" than the original one (1974, 653, Notes 94). Skei describes the effect as a shift in point of view, narrative pace, and time that creates a greater sense of immediacy, speed, and action. It further allows Faulkner to exploit the climate as representing the feelings of the people in the community. As a result, Skei contends that "Dry September" begins with "one of the strongest, most concentrated and symbolic pictures in Faulkner's whole career" (Skei 1981, 60; see also Ferguson 1991, 122–23, 133).

Millgate sees the deletion of certain material to be even more important than the revised opening. In the manuscript opening of section three, two paragraphs describe the "terrible" life choices available to women. Millgate believes that the more powerful and concrete demonstration of that view through describing the lives of Minnie and Mrs. McLendon makes the abstract discussion unnecessary ([1966] 1989, 262–63; see also Putzel 1985, 224–25; Ferguson 1991, 122–23).

One other change Faulkner made before publication involves naming the town in which the lynching occurs. Originally unidentified, in "Dry September" the town becomes Jefferson. Blotner suggests this was Faulkner's effort to work his stories as well as his novels into the overall design for his body of fiction (Blotner 1974, 654).

Changes made in the text after its appearance in *Scribner's* involved numerous alterations of punctuation in the *These 13* version. Most important, Plunkett is renamed McLendon in *These 13* and thereafter. William Bache considers this revision the only significant change from the magazine to the collected version. He contends that the change to an *M* initial in the surname reinforces the interrelationship of McLendon with Mayes, Minnie, moon, and moving picture (1954, 56). John Crane errs when he includes this revision with those made before the story's first publication (1985, 411). From *These 13* to *Collected Stories* two changes, *o* to *of* and *clinched* to *clenched*, are corrective but of minor consequence (*T13* 264, 277; *CS* 171, 190).

"Dry September" touches Faulkner's life in the way it reflects regional events and as a harbinger of Faulkner's own behavior years later. Though it occurred too late to inspire the story, a drought was reported in the *Oxford Eagle* in 1930 under the headline "Record-breaking Drought Enters Eighty-Seventh Day and Still No Rain in Sight" (Blotner 1974, Notes 94). Speculating about Faulkner's exposure to racially motivated violence and its effect on his fictional portrayals, John Pilkington suggests that the author probably recalled the mutilation and lynching of Nelse Patton in 1908 (Pilkington 1981, 119). If "Dry September" does have this precedent in Faulkner's childhood experience, it also finds echoes later in his life. In March 1951, Faulkner took a stand that recalled Hawkshaw's attitude in "Dry September" as well as Lucas Beauchamp's in *Intruder in the Dust*. Faulkner stated publicly that he did not believe trial evidence warranted the execution of Willie McGee, a black man convicted of raping a white woman. Like Hawkshaw, Faulkner received harsh criticism for his public stand (Blotner 1974, 1377–78).

The only character association that has been studied is a model for Minnie Cooper. Blotner parallels Minnie Cooper with Mrs. Minnie Porter, Faulkner's sixth-grade teacher for a short time in 1909, prior to her suffering a nervous breakdown. A photograph of Mrs. Porter taken many years later shows a woman with short gray hair, round spectacles, darkly circled eyes, a mouth tilting toward the right, and a "cheek creased as though in a permanent tic" (1974, Notes 93).

Analyses of "Dry September" have included claims of literary influence, but in the balance of other approaches this kind of attention has been relatively limited. Several critics have placed Faulkner's use of the lynching experience in the context of the archetypal pattern of sacrificing a scapegoat. These studies typically link Faulkner's text with *The Golden Bough* by Sir James Frazer. The early work of John Vickery and Daniel Weiss are discussed more fully below (Vickery 1962, 5–14; Weiss 1963, 71–79; see also Johnson 1972, 269–78). Because Faulkner omits any description of Mayes's murder in the story, Charles Nilon believes that Faulkner, like Hawthorne in *The Scarlet Letter*, is interested in examining causes and effects of an action rather than the act itself (1965, 44). Jack Stewart likens the "spiritual desiccation" of "Dry September" to that of T. S. Eliot's *The Waste Land* or Dante's *Inferno* (1979, 238).

Lawrence Dessner looks at the mix of realistic descriptions and symbolist imagery in the story and speculates about the influence of French symbolists and English romantic poets. Dessner cites Blotner's argument that Faulkner felt their influence as early as 1922. Dessner includes the work of Mallarmé, Baudelaire, and Verlaine among the French, and Keats among the English poets whose work might have influenced "Dry September." The *lacrimae rerum* ("the lament over the tears of things") that appears in their works also compares with the story's attempt at "high seriousness of a comprehensive and tragic view of the human condition." The yoking of beauty with terror ("colored lithographs of life caught in its terrible and beautiful mutations" [*CS* 181]) is preceded by such English decadents as Beardsley, Swinburne, and Wilde. Dessner also finds certain Old Testament echoes in strings of "and-clauses" that appear when Hawkshaw strikes Will, and again when McLendon strikes his wife. The vats recall biblical "bottomless pits" that continue to reappear in Western literature (Dessner 1984, 151–61).

Comparisons of narrative strategies include several arguments that focus on a Hemingway–Faulkner similarity. Bache finds Faulkner's inclusion of movies as commentary on the story to be like Hemingway's use of movies in "The Killers" (1954, 54). Joseph Flora also sees Hemingway's influence on Faulkner in the violent episode when Hawkshaw strikes Will Mayes. Flora suggests that the brief lapse into violence is likely influenced by Hemingway's scene in "Indian Camp" when Uncle George, representative of "ordinary wisdom," curses the woman who bites him while he is assisting in an unanesthetized Caesarean operation on her. In both situations the unexpected behavior of Hawkshaw and Uncle George provides a shock (Flora 1982, 44 n. 9). Frederick Karl sees McLendon as similar to Hemingway's characters who are dissatisfied with domestic life. McLendon needs to repeat the exhilaration of war by repeated violence (1989, 408).

Ira Johnson compares "Dry September" to Erskine Caldwell's treatment of a lynching in his 1930 story "Saturday Afternoon." Johnson makes no claim for influence of one on the other, but he argues that Faulkner is the more successful in creating the texture of a community with variant responses to the lynching and with a greater sense of complicity in the actions that lead to lynching, including Minnie Cooper's desperate grasp for attention (1972, 269–78). Annamária Széky examines both of these stories in a study of the lynching story as an identifiable sub-genre of the short story; in this sub-genre, "presentation goes together with a certain set of techniques, as the plot, the characters, the motives and the conflicts are more or less fixed and the central event is always the same" (1978, 185).

Bache follows Robert Gorham Davis in linking Hawkshaw's name to the detective named Hawkshaw in Tom Taylor's *The Ticket of Leave Man* (Bache 1954, 55). M. Thomas Inge believes that the name may have been inspired by Gus Mager's *Hawkshaw the Detective*, a comic strip begun in 1913 (1986, 188). According to the explanation in "Hair," the young boys of Jefferson gave the newcomer Stribling the nickname "Hawkshaw" because they imagined him to be a detective—since "that was the last thing in the world anybody would suspect him to be" (*CS* 141).

## Relationship to Other Faulkner Works

Olga Vickery defines "Dry September" as an adjunctive story in Faulkner's Yoknapatawpha fiction. That is, it supplements the information about the county, its history, and its various citizens (Vickery [1959]1964, 300). The setting, themes, and characters that "Dry September" shares with other stories and novels have generated numerous and fruitful comparisons of this story with other specific texts.

Faulkner himself was apparently reluctant to make easy and obvious connections in his short stories when he organized his first collection, *These 13*. As Millgate observes, "Dry September" was paired with neither "A Rose for Emily" nor "Hair." Either possibility could have exploited obvious parallels of particular characters or character types in the respective texts (Millgate [1966] 1989, 261, 272–73).

Henry Stribling's appearance in "Dry September" and "Hair" generates a variety of comments, particularly those emphasizing how information in one story explains action in the other. When Blotner places the events of "Dry September" before the events of "Hair," he refers to the concluding action in "Hair" when Stribling (Hawkshaw) leaves Jefferson (1974, 650). It is more accurate to say that events of "Dry September" occur during the span of time covered in "Hair." According to information in "Hair," Hawkshaw arrives in Jefferson in 1919 and lives there twelve years before he leaves with Susan Reed. When the events of "Dry September" occur, he has obviously been in town long enough to know Will Mayes and Minnie Cooper. Széky believes that Hawkshaw's characterization in "Hair" illuminates his behavior in "Dry

September" (1978, 191–92). For Skei, the presentation of Hawkshaw in "Hair as an "almost ascetic, next to mute" character contrasts strongly with his more talkative presentation in "Dry September." His demonstrations of "tolerance and faith and fidelity" toward Susan Reed in "Hair" "are placed in a more correct perspective in 'Dry September,'" but when the reader knows his quiet manner in "Hair," his outspoken courage in "Dry September" becomes remarkable (1977, 113–14, 154).

Crane speculates beyond the evidence of either text, however, to establish the time of certain events. By using information from the payment schedule and other information offered in "Hair," he dates the lynching episode in "Dry September" in September 1929, eight months before Hawkshaw leaves Jefferson as recounted in "Hair" (1985, 418). Crane's argument, however, lacks a sufficiently thorough explanation for how he arrives at the specific year in which to set the lynching. Crane believes that Hawkshaw's marriage to Susan Reed as reported in "Hair" was influenced by the lynching experience in "Dry September." He contends further that Hawkshaw abandons Susan for a period in "Hair" and that this loss of faith indicates a mid-life weariness in Hawkshaw similar to the crises experienced by John McLendon and Minnie Cooper (1985, 410–20).

Unlike Hawkshaw, Minnie Cooper does not reappear as a character in other fiction, but numerous critics have outlined a recurring type into which Minnie's character fits neatly. Polk points out that a cluster of "repressing or repressed" gray-haired old women appeared in the fiction composed from 1927 to 1931 (1985, 31–32). Karl calls "Dry September," "A Rose for Emily," and "Miss Zilphia Gant" a "spinster group" in which the four major female characters, "trapped and/or consumed by the male world," reveal how sexual repression can lead to explosive behaviors (1989, 408 note).

Specific correspondences between Minnie and Emily abound though the language of comparison and the degrees of sympathy vary considerably. Irving Malin labels Minnie Cooper, like Emily Grierson, the stereotyped "old maid looking under her bed at night" (Malin 1957, 38). Millgate suggests that Minnie and Emily are driven mad "by frustration and isolation" ([1961] 1966, 65). Edward Holmes, however, sees the portrayal of both women as compassionate (1966, 80–83). François Pitavy points out that in "A Rose for Emily" and "Dry September," information about the female character is set in the context of the community's attitude toward her: what the reader knows about her is what the public knows (Pitavy 1972, 131–39).

According to Sally Page, Minnie and Emily are decaying women because they resist the role of motherhood, which, in Faulkner's view, sustains moral order. Though they are presented sympathetically, they are shown to lack a sense of individual well-being and an acceptable place in the community. Further, in Page's interpretation, when sexuality is misused, it is equated with death, an association that both Minnie and Emily bear. Page adds that Minnie suffers from an abnormal home life. In this characteristic, Minnie is like Emily and a long list of suffering daughters. In Minnie's case, she lives with her invalid mother and her aunt, who assumes the household responsibilities that Minnie should bear (Page 1972, 94, 97, 100, 108–09, 134). Széky parallels Emily's "progression to perverted craziness" with Minnie's "growing more and more bitter and hysterical" (1978, 192).

Arthur Kinney finds the picture of Minnie alone in the porch swing to be like the image of the single gray hair in "A Rose for Emily" in that both reflect empty dreams (1980, 67). John Duvall shows how Faulkner's spinsters have no life options but maintain a "critically destructive power." The two stories exhibit different standards for unmarried middle-aged women and unmarried middle-aged men. Neither Homer Barron nor Minnie's banker friend is criticized for his bachelor ways. In fact, Duvall points out that the bachelors' party referred to in "Dry September" recalls numerous positively portrayed bachelor subgroups within the communities in Faulkner's fiction. These congenial groups provide a striking contrast to the isolated female spinsters. Duvall interprets Minnie's social standing as an impediment to marriage. When she forces the town to "realign its perception of her" by the alleged rape, the cost is "staggering"—madness. Duvall points out that neither Emily nor Minnie is able to force the community to recognize its repressive system or to make significant social change (Duvall 1990, 127–29).

Many of the comparisons of the women in "Dry September" and "A Rose for Emily" can also be applied to "Miss Zilphia Gant." As Holmes notes, both Minnie and Zilphia experience brief courtships. He adds that Zilphia's dreams about black men correspond to Minnie's claim of a sexual attack by Mayes (1966, 80–83). Pitavy identifies the "frustrated, sex-starved, and child-starved woman" as characterized by Minnie, Zilphia, and Emily. Zilphia and Minnie have observed their friends marry and establish homes while they remain alone (Pitavy 1972, 131–39). Like Holmes, Polk associates Minnie's and Zilphia's fantasies about black men, but he goes further to claim that the other women in the community, given their interest in the details of the alleged attack, reveal the similarity of their fantasies to Minnie's own (Polk 1984, 81–82).

Page's discussion of Minnie's and Emily's association with death and decay is applicable to a number of characters in a variety of ways. Among these "images of death" that Page adds are Rosa Coldfield in *Absalom, Absalom!*, Margaret Powers and Cecily Saunders in *Soldier's Pay*, Addie Bundren in *As I Lay Dying*, Temple Drake in *Sanctuary*, and Charlotte Rittenmeyer in *The Wild Palms* (Page 1972, 94, 97, 100, 108–09, 134).

Continuing the examination of the broad spectrum of female characters, Elizabeth Kerr analyzes the concept of Southern womanhood as portrayed in Faulkner's fiction. Kerr notes that Minnie Cooper is an example of the unmarried woman who is allowed little freedom or possibility of personal fulfillment.

Her retreat into vicarious fulfillment and fantasy demonstrates the danger inherent in such a restrictive code. Kerr's list includes Minnie and Emily along with such others as Elly, Ellen Sutpen, and Narcissa Benbow, who manifest a variety of responses to Southern gyneolatry (Kerr 1961–62, 1–16; see also Kerr [1969] 1976, 159). Mimi Gladstein adds that the myth of Southern womanhood was used as a rallying cry to stir white male courage. In the action of "Dry September," McLendon purportedly acts to protect Minnie, but his failure to refer to her by name underscores his perception of her as an object rather than as an individual and reveals the falsity of his justifying the violence as an act of virtue (Gladstein 1986, 17–18; see also James Snead 1986, 4–5).

The brief view of Mrs. McLendon in "Dry September" adds to the information about Faulkner's female characters. Walter Everett diminishes the domestic violence that is part of Mrs. McLendon's situation when he describes her as being snarled at by her husband (1969, 141). Blotner is more accurate in his perception of her as another portrayal of the trapped woman, an image vividly captured in "Fox Hunt" (Blotner 1984, 256). Skei adds that a common feature of many of these characters is the presence of a "stifling parental authority" (1985, 104). For Minnie, victimization has come at the hands of her invalid mother (Polk 1985, 31–32). Ferguson notes that Minnie joins company with those female characters who fit a pattern of the "wronged woman striking back." In this case Minnie is not reacting to rape but to a lack of recognition (Ferguson 1991, 74). Most recently, James Carothers has identified these numerous females as "driven to perverse or violent rebellion against the prevailing community standard" (1992, 49).

Comparisons of "Dry September" with other short stories reflect a broad spectrum of critical concerns encompassing thematic and formal considerations as well as those of character. Millgate notes, for example, that "That Evening Sun" and "A Rose for Emily" share a common setting with "Dry September" in both place—Jefferson—and time of action. The stories are also alike in being "on the very edge of scenes of violence and horror which we do not actually witness" (Millgate [1961] 1966, 64).

"Dry September" and "Red Leaves" resemble one another in several ways. For Nilon, the presence of Will Mayes generates a "study of attitudes toward the Negro rather than a study of Negro character" in much the same way that the body servant of "Red Leaves" does (1965, 43–44). Lewis Dabney believes that "Red Leaves" allows for "more complex characterization" of the black man than does "Dry September." The body servant, unlike Will Mayes, is not the stereotyped "cringing 'good nigger'" (Dabney 1974, 91–92). Marjorie Pryse finds in both "Dry September" and "Red Leaves" the act of "marking" characters, a social symbolism that identifies outcasts in a particular community. The body servant of "Red Leaves" is marked but attains a definition of self within his social role. Like the servant, Minnie, Will, Hawkshaw, and

McLendon are all marked so that the larger community may define itself against them. These characters are visible in a society that values invisibility. They reveal ambiguity within a society that wishes to define itself in unconfused roles of "white" and "black." The process of removing the deviant restores the "homogeneity" of the community (Pryse 1979, 92–107). Pryse places her examination within a recurring pattern of "marking" that she identifies in the American novel, specifically in the works of Hawthorne, Melville, Faulkner, and Ellison (1979, 92–107). Kerr reminds us that both "Red Leaves" and "Dry September" are given autumnal settings (1983, 15).

Patrick Samway identifies in "Dry September," "Red Leaves," and one additional story, "The Hound," a common impression that "nature can assimilate the various forms of violence . . . and not be thwarted in the process." The body servant is inevitably to be buried, and in "Dry September" and "The Hound" images of dust cover both scenes. The image reappears in the novel *Intruder in the Dust* (Samway 1980, 248–49).

Ferguson groups together "Dry September," "Red Leaves," and "That Evening Sun" as stories in which characters achieve justice from a personal perspective but in so doing reveal their failure "to understand the dignity and integrity of those whom they destroy": McLendon and his group's killing Will Mayes, the Indians' intention to bury the body servant with their chief, and Jesus's presumed intention to kill Nancy (Ferguson 1991, 78–79). Related to the self-serving retributive justice in Faulkner's short fiction is characters' propensity toward abstraction that Faulkner consistently portrays as destructive. "Race" as an abstraction leads to fatal consequences in both "Dry September" and "Pantaloon in Black." "Community" as an abstraction is no better, given the examples of the conflict between community and the individual as already seen not only in "Dry September" and "Red Leaves" but also in "Uncle Willy" and "The Tall Men" (Ferguson 1991, 81–82).

The contrasting issues of community and isolation initiate a varied range of story connections. For Joseph Reed, the community of "Dry September" is noted for the way it sours both events and people, propelling them to violence. It lacks the sense of closeness and familiarity expressed positively in some of Faulkner's other stories with the small-town setting (Reed 1973, 50–55). Cleanth Brooks also pursues the characterization of community in the very early sketch "Sunset." Brooks argues that the understatement of "Dry September" reveals more about the forces that destroy Will Mayes than does the more obvious presentation of the black man's death in "Sunset." Faulkner is also able to develop subtly the social context that precipitates the Jefferson lynching more fully than he could have in the newspaper sketch "Sunset" (Brooks [1978] 1990, 109–113). Skei likens the men gathered at the square in "Dry September" to a similar group in "Spotted Horses." In neither case does the group attempt to interfere with the exploitation, if not murder, of others (1985, 184).

The intense imagery of "Dry September" provides another basis for comparison and contrast with imagery in other short stories and even the early poetry. Page describes the "cold moon and the lidless stars" as an image of cosmic death that she likens to the "cold world of reality faced by Faulkner's marble faun" (1972, 101; *CS* 101). Skei contrasts the image of a friendly, companionate moon over the closing scene in "Divorce in Naples" with the remote moon of "Dry September" (Skei 1977, 134, 202 n. 257). He compares the evocation of feeling in the descriptions of moonlight, heat, and mockingbirds in "Moonlight" and the later use of the moon and climate in "Dry September" but notes that "Moonlight" is not as successful as "Dry September" in achieving the synthesis of environment and action (Skei 1985, 36).

Watson finds parallels to "Dry September" in ritual deaths, especially the image of death-by-water, pictured in such other stories as "Red Leaves," "A Justice," and "A Rose for Emily." He cites specifically Minnie's breathing "deeply, something like a swimmer preparing to dive" (*CS* 180) and McLendon driving away from street lamps "nimbused as in water" (*CS* 176). Watson claims that these images of wetness provide a "pointed contrast to the desiccated setting," but the brevity of the explanation makes it difficult to accept his view that Minnie and McLendon are "described in terms of water" (1980, 213–14). Ferguson sees Faulkner's use of the leitmotif as a means of achieving coherence. Examples Ferguson cites include the phrase "tolled away" in "Uncle Willy" and eye images in "Gold Is Not Always," "Was," and "Tomorrow." Of "Dry September" Ferguson says that the "hammerlike repetition of the word *dust*" is a "brilliant instance" of the device (1991, 137–38).

Bruce Kawin points out that in Faulkner's work film does not receive flattering portrayals. In "Dry September," film is escapist, and in *Pylon* and in *The Wild Palms*, film is described as if it were germ ridden and contagious (Kawin 1977, 156; Kawin 1979, 116–17).

Ferguson contrasts a problematic use of "selective omniscience" as the narrative stance in "Dr. Martino" with its more successful adaptation in "Red Leaves" and "Dry September." "Knight's Gambit" achieves effects similar to the selective omniscience in "Dry September" and "Red Leaves" (1991, 90–91, 102).

"Dry September" also excels, in Ferguson's view, in the way it achieves closure. The final scene, McLendon's returning home, provides "in encapsulated form the basic tensions of the work." This technique also appears in "Red Leaves," "Ad Astra," and "Lizards in Jamshyd's Courtyard" (1991, 134).

John Matthews examines Faulkner's consciousness of the demands of the literary marketplace as these affect his short fiction. Stories as diverse as "Dry September," "Mule in the Yard," "Centaur in Brass," "Red Leaves," "Spotted Horses," "There Was a Queen," and "Lizards in Jamshyd's Courtyard" reflect a sense of curtailment and aesthetic commodification to satisfy mass cultural consumption. But even while Faulkner accomodates the need for brevity, these texts also possess a sense of resistance to the demands of the market (Matthews 1992, 3–37).

Many of the thematic parallels in the short fiction are intensified in collection. In the arrangement of *These 13*, Skei finds that placing "That Evening Sun" next to "Dry September" creates a less obvious contrast than might have occurred if "Dry September" and "A Rose for Emily" had been paired, but the selected two are reasonable in their shared mood of "horror, despair, [and] loneliness" (1977, 48). James Watson asserts that within the context of *These 13*, "Red Leaves" and "Dry September," the first and last stories of Part II, represent "extremes rather than normative conditions of the community" (1980, 216; see also Ferguson 1991, 151).

Millgate notes that the isolated individuals—McLendon, Minnie, and Hawkshaw—of "Dry September" become part of a larger pattern of isolation within "The Village" section of *Collected Stories* (Millgate [1966] 1989, 261, 272–73). The condemnation of vices in the community link "Dry September" to such stories as "That Will Be Fine" and "Uncle Willy" (Blotner 1974, 883). Philip Momberger aligns "Dry September" with those tales from "The Village" section that focus on racism and ostracism as signs of the disintegrating community. Like "That Evening Sun" and "Elly," "Dry September" shows the consequences of racism in violent eruptions, and in both "Dry September" and "That Evening Sun" civil authority provides no remedy. The outsiders, including those in "Dry September," "A Rose for Emily," "Death Drag," and "That Evening Sun," are "finally abandoned to suffer alone (Momberger 1978, 21, 25–27). Ferguson notes that "Dry September" is integrated into the central section of an alternating series of serious and light stories in "The Village" (1991, 158).

Skei emphasizes that "Dry September," like many of Faulkner's best stories, is basically independent of his novels (Skei 1985, 290). Nevertheless, some of the most insightful relational studies discover parallels between "Dry September" and the novels. Joseph Reed, for example, includes a number of novels in his observation that Minnie Cooper is isolated by her own group as are Eula Varner, Quentin and Caddy Compson, and Darl Bundren (1973, 20).

The appearance of *Sanctuary* just one month after the publication of "Dry September" stimulates interest in their respective portrayals of violence and the murder of a supposed rapist (Carothers 1985, 45–46; Pilkington 1981, 119). When Alfred Dashiell of *Scribner's* published "Dry September," he seemed sensitive to the shock that the story's focus on rape and lynching would give some readers. In fact, the small number of objections elicited by the story provided a contrast to the response to *Sanctuary* the next month (Blotner 1974, 684). Hyatt Waggoner finds the kindness of both Hawkshaw and Horace Benbow ineffectual, a comparison Carothers reaffirms much later (Waggoner 1959, 198; Carothers 1985, 27, 45–46). In her analysis of the double standards that existed for whites and blacks in the fictional community of Yoknapatawpha, Kerr points out that the white man (albeit the wrong one) accused of the sexual assault of Temple Drake receives a trial, but Will Mayes is immediately lynched for the alleged, though highly doubtful, rape of Minnie Cooper ([1969] 1976, 204–05). Duvall finds in both *Sanctuary* and "Dry September" an ideology "that women are not safe from violence and rape unless 'good' men decide it is worth their while to protect them from 'bad' men." He expands this idea to show that these men may be good publicly and bad privately, as seen in the example of McLendon. Duvall contends that in both *Sanctuary* and "Dry September" "men idealize woman in the abstract, while hating individual women for being so desirable" (Duvall 1990, 71).

Although *Light in August* is closer in time of publication to *Sanctuary* than to "Dry September," critics typically find more points of comparison between *Light in August* and "Dry September" than between the two more contemporary texts. Within a discussion of the interplay of Faulkner's works, Millgate suggests that "Dry September" may perhaps have close ties with *Light in August* in the same way that "Barn Burning" relates to *The Hamlet* or "That Evening Sun" to *The Sound and the Fury* (Millgate 1980, 103; 1987, 49). The bond is affirmed by the reappearance of McLendon and Maxey in the novel. McLendon actually reappears not just in *Light in August*, but also in *The Town* and *The Mansion* (Blotner 1974, Notes 108, 207; Carothers 1985, 18). Ann Hayes makes one of a number of comparisons between McLendon and Percy Grimm. To her, they are both exploiters of other people (1961, 65). Both Dorothy Tuck and François Pitavy compare McLendon to Grimm, with Pitavy referring to McLendon as a "brutal prefiguration of Percy Grimm" (Pitavy 1973, 166–67 n. 19; Tuck 1964, 165–66). Carothers itemizes the particulars of the McLendon–Grimm bond as their self-appointment as vigilantes, their assumption of the correctness of their motives, their disregard for the process of law, and their application of "excessive and vicious punishment" (Carothers 1985, 44–46; Carey 1964, 28; Bleikasten 1990, 312). Polk finds that Faulkner generally presents his law enforcement officers as "competent, honorable, sensible and even courageous men who take their jobs seriously" and that the lynchings in "Dry September" and *Light in August* are performed outside the law by self-appointed vigilantes (1980b, 174). According to Széky, a sheriff in conflict with the lynchers is part of the pattern of the lynching story. "Dry September" represents a departure from that characteristic although Széky sees Hawkshaw's figure as filling the law enforcement role "to a certain extent" (1978, 189, 194).

Critics also find numerous characteristics shared by Minnie and Joanna Burden. Malin describes Joanna in the same terms he uses for Minnie and Emily, the stereotyped "old maid looking under her bed at night" (Malin 1957, 38). Lee Jenkins believes that Minnie and Joanna both exhibit characteristics of "pent-up sexual tension" as a result of "sexual repression in the face of the imagined black threat" (1981, 92). Carothers adds that both white women who precipitate the manhunts are "of questionable reliability or character," but he also adds that Minnie does not have the same sense of Will Mayes's "reality" that Joanna has of Christmas as an individual (Carothers 1985, 44–46). Eric Sundquist observes an important difference between Joanna Burden in *Light in August* and Minnie Cooper: Minnie's rape by Mayes is imagined, but Joanna's relationship with Christmas actually occurs. As Sundquist sees it, Joanna's abolitionist sentiments must be established before her intimacy with Joe Christmas can be portrayed. He suggests that otherwise their intimacy might have been "too dangerous to elaborate." He notes, however, that once Joanna has been murdered, she, like Minnie, "becomes as white and respectable and Southern as the communal hysteria requires" (Sundquist 1983, 84).

Comparisons of Hawkshaw and Byron Bunch extend the associations between "Dry September" and *Light in August*. Backman sees in both an "unassuming Christianity" that seeks to awaken conscience (1966, 84). Pitavy adds another element to the character comparisons when he likens the attempts by the light-skinned Hawkshaw and the light-skinned Bunch to save, respectively, Will Mayes, who is black, and Joe Christmas, who is suspected of having black blood (Pitavy 1973, 166–67 n. 19). Carothers sees both Will and Joe as pursued for their "alleged breaches of the color line." He points out, however, that Mayes is innocent, but Christmas is not. Mayes is black; Christmas's race is a matter of uncertainty. Mayes does not have a reputation for violence. Christmas does. Mayes is caught and killed quickly; Christmas is the subject of an extended search. In short, Mayes is "pathetic" while Christmas is "tragic" (Carothers 1985, 44–46).

Millgate shows that in both texts a public definition of an individual evokes a response from the reader that must subsequently be revised when the private individual is more fully revealed. Minnie Cooper's story is "plausible until the reader is given a glimpse of her psychological condition." In much the same way, Joe Christmas "appears simply hateful until the reader begins to understand what lies behind and beneath his public self" (Millgate 1987, 32–33). There are additional minor comparisons: Lena's unreliable beau, Lucas Burch, recalls Minnie's banker (Pitavy 1972, 137–38); the women's musings about Joanna Burden's murderer can be linked to their curiosity over Minnie's alleged rapist (Millgate [1966] 1989, 128, 318 n. 5; see also Polk 1980a, 110–13; Peters 1983, 89).

Broadening still further the associations between "Dry September" and the novels, Kinney discerns a pattern of "secret sharers" in Faulkner's fiction in which a dialectic must be resolved. Minnie and McLendon in "Dry September" are one such pair "linked sardonically by the glow of the silver screen and the glare of headlights on the blank wall." Among the numerous other secret sharers are Lena Grove and Joe Christmas in *Light in August*, and Charles Mallison and Lucas Beauchamp in *Intruder in the Dust* (Kinney 1978, 74–75).

Not surprisingly, comparisons of "Dry September" and *Intruder in the Dust* have been fruitful; frequently they revolve around character comparisons. Nilon sees repeated in *Intruder in the Dust* the tendency noted in both "Dry September" and "Red Leaves" to use a black character to examine racial attitudes generally rather than to develop a detailed portrait of a particular black character (1965, 43–44). Kerr contrasts the self-sustaining life Miss Habersham leads in *Intruder in the Dust* and the "horrifying case" of Minnie. Kerr does not discuss the differences in their ages, but she does suggest that even Miss Habersham probably had an unfulfilling social life (1983, 169).

Carothers argues that Hawkshaw serves as an analogue for Charles Mallison in *Intruder in the Dust*, yet the differences between their effectiveness in the particular situations marks in *Intruder in the Dust* a new stage in Faulkner's writing "in which his central character attempts to act positively, and achieves some significant results." Mallison's effort to save Lucas Beauchamp and the order of the community is successful but the tentative effort Hawkshaw makes on behalf of Will Mayes fails (Carothers 1981, 274–75; 1985, 27).

Blotner also interprets the fact of Beauchamp's survival, "no matter how thin the thread by which his life hangs suspended," as a contrast to the ugliness of "Dry September." Even though the Gowries and the people of Beat Four behave like the lynch mob in "Dry September," Beauchamp's survival "presages a day when lynching and the threat of lynching" will disappear from Yoknapatawpha (Blotner 1983, 19–20; see also Peters 1983, 84). Walter Taylor comes to the opposite conclusion when he argues that the failures of Hawkshaw in "Dry September" and Gail Hightower in *Light in August* underscore the "miraculous," hence unlikely, saving of Beauchamp by a teenager and an elderly woman (1983, 163). John Bassett comments that in contrast to more conventional lynching stories like "Dry September," *Intruder in the Dust* deflects emphasis from the lynchers, victims, and atmosphere, focusing more on Chick Mallison ([1986] 1989, 167).

Viewed in the pattern of Faulkner's chase stories in which the object is a human being, "Dry September" resembles not only *Light in August* but also "Pantaloon in Black" in *Go Down, Moses* (Vickery 1964, 304). Nilon finds Rider comparable to Will Mayes. Again, the black character generates an examination of attitudes toward him rather than an examination of his character (1965, 43–44). Taylor draws a slightly different conclusion when he observes that in contrast to "Dry September," "Pantaloon in Black" develops a more fully realized black man who becomes the lynch victim (1983 139; see also Taylor [1972] 1989, 62).

Also building on similarities between "Dry September" and *Go Down, Moses*, Weiss parallels the events of "Was" and "Dry September." Superficially, the stories seem contrasting in their respective comic and tragic representations. Actually both can be interpreted within the myth that the black man is extremely potent sexually and the concomitant view "that his potency renders him incapable of higher functions and drives him to illicit acts of lust, accompanied, if necessary, by violence." Weiss places his argument within the mythological interpretation of the Saturnalia. "Was" and "Dry September" are "fertility rites described at two widely separated historical moments." One story seeks prevention of and one punishment of a sexual transgression. Sophonsiba resembles Minnie in that both are threatened by spinsterhood. "Uncle Buck and Plunkett [McLendon] are both solitaries, misogynists for whom the chase holds all the pleasures their natures know." Buck puts on a necktie; McLendon makes a "necktie" of another sort for his victim. Will Mayes and Tomey's Turl are both treated like objects, or animals, and they are both believed to possess great sexual potency. Sophonsiba gains Uncle Buck by way of Tomey's Turl, and Minnie regains recognition of her sexuality by way of Will (Weiss 1963, 71–79).

Two more novels have been compared to "Dry September" though in less concrete ways than matching characters and narrative patterns. The use of weather to set the tone of the short story recalls a similar use of nature in *As I Lay Dying*. Cleanth Brooks examines Addie Bundren's use of the weather to mirror her feelings, while Doc Peabody's comments about weather relate to its effects on humans. Brooks compares the suggested link between weather and behavior in these two passages with the implications that the weather provokes action in "Dry September" (Brooks [1963] 1990, 30; see also Kerr [1969] 1976, 207–08; Blotner 1974, 653). Arthur Ford finds a sense of doom shadowing the lives of the people in "Dry September" in much the same way that the lives in *The Sound and the Fury* inevitably succumb to a "senseless world" (1962, 220). Blotner compares the death of Will Mayes with the castration and institutionalization of Benjy. Both represent a "crucifixion of the innocent" (Blotner 1974, 654).

The extensive effort to examine the relationships between "Dry September" and other works demonstrates both the importance of the story within the Faulkner canon and way in which it individually captures many of the thematic and technical concerns important to the author. Once removed from a comparative context, "Dry September" withstands close scrutiny from a number of different theoretical approaches and survives on its own with its reputation for excellence solidly in place.

## Interpretation and Criticism

The many interpreters of "Dry September" vary in the degree of culpability for the lynching they assign to the individual participants and the community. Those whose critical analyses are psychologically oriented focus on sexual fulfillment, frequently placing responsibility individually on McLendon,

Butch, and the other mob members who act to fill vacuous, sexually repressed lives. Hawkshaw is held accountable with varying degrees of severity for his failure to save Mayes. The analyses of Minnie's psychological state demonstrate the close intertwining of the psychological and sociological interpretations of the story.

The absence of any indication that Minnie Cooper was in fact attacked by Will Mayes spurs critics to explain her accusation, an act that had such violent repercussions. Malin interprets Minnie based on his understanding of "Faulkner's disgust with women who tighten their feelings so much that they become men." The effect, in Malin's view, is that it "perverts the woman's desire for natural affection and motherhood—it creates social tensions." He sees Minnie's failed relationship with the banker resulting in a distrust of men and a refusal to pursue further relationships. Her accusation of rape is a part of her "sex wish-fulfillment" (Malin 1957, 38).

Ralph Wolfe and Edgar Daniels also attribute Minnie's acts to the desperate recognition that "she has reached the autumn years and faces the horrifying knowledge that she has come to the end of a consistently unsatisfactory sexual trail" (1964, 158–59; see also Crane 1985, 410–20). Page notes Faulkner's use of physical characteristics to mirror Minnie's fragile mental health. The boudoir cap, the sheer lingerie, the voile dresses all reflect Minnie's denial of the reality of her middle-aged life. Page errs in placing Minnie at forty (Hawkshaw's estimate) rather than thirty-eight or thirty-nine (the narrator's statement) and relegating her to a "social class slightly below the norm" rather than placing her with the "comfortable people—not the best in Jefferson"; although these errors are bothersome, they do not significantly alter Page's argument (Page 1972, 100–01; *CS 173*).

Ellen Douglas observes that in life and literature women have typically had little means other than sexuality by which "to reward and punish men and to control the behavior of men." One consequence has been that on occasion women have made "hysterical accusations" like Minnie's in "Dry September" (Douglas 1981, 162; see also Széky 1978, 184, 192). Taylor believes that Minnie projected her repressed sexuality onto Mayes, then "borrowed it back" (1983, 55). Skei calls Minnie a "parasite" on her community, but he acknowledges that the descriptions of the lives of the "ladies" indicate that little meaningful activity is available to them. In Faulkner's texts, women who try to break loose from their rigid societal roles generally fail. Minnie uses the "power of her social prestige and of racial prejudice" in her effort to regain social recognition. She knows that as a woman she can exploit the prejudice of her community.

Skei believes that Faulkner's female characters misuse "female power" because they misunderstand it. The consequences are disproportionate and frequently horrible: the female manipulators become manipulated, and any gain they make is countered by some form of loss. Skei believes the pattern of behavior indicates that if the women had been "less selfish and more considerate, much suffering and pain could have been avoided" (1985, 113, 127, 178–79). Max Putzel's description of Minnie is that she has only her self-centeredness as an explanation for her frustration. Her final hysteria involves her own self-pity rather than any sense of remorse or self-knowledge (Putzel 1985, 226–28).

The final images of Minnie and McLendon are nearly matched. According to Howard Faulkner, neither Minnie nor McLendon is able to escape her or his own complicity in Mayes's murder. They are both eventually left exposed, literally unclothed, as a symbol of their lost humanity. They have both forfeited their humanness, as shown in the insane laughter of one and the animal-like panting of the other (Faulkner 1973, 47–50). In the view of several critics, McLendon's motivations to action are very much like Minnie's.

Kinney's comparison of the narrative movement, "the heated rise, powerful climax, and abrupt fall" to orgasm vividly describes the emphasis of much of the psychological criticism. He adds that the orgasm is McLendon's, not Minnie's, though the "object of passion" remains Will Mayes (1980, 67). Kinney's image obviates such early observations as William Van O'Connor's description; in O'Connor's admittedly brief synopsis of "Dry September" he speaks of McLendon's "sadism" and "shame" (1954, 68). Wolfe and Daniels (responding to Ford's analysis discussed below) contend that "Dry September" is best understood by means of a sexually oriented interpretation. They find that "the degree of emotional involvement in the affair of the supposed rape is in direct proportion to the degree of the characters' own sexual maladjustment." The leaders of the lynching are the estranged husband McLendon and the teenager Butch, who, unlike other teenage boys in the story, is coupled with no one. Wolfe and Daniels distinguish these sexually frustrated males from the rest of the community (1964, 158–59).

Donna Gerstenberger and Frederick Garber suggest that McLendon has lost his "outlet in approved violence" that his war service allowed him. His identity exists in his pistol and is shed when it is removed. His failure in marriage "suggests a sexual basis for his violent actions" (Gerstenberger and Garber 1969, 406–07). Taylor calls McLendon and his lynching companions Puritans whose lives reflect repressed guilt and repressed sexuality. These "male defenders of light" serve vicarious punishments on the blacks and women upon whom the white males' repressed desires have been projected. Taylor concludes that to a certain extent the tragedy of those men exceeds that of Mayes because they have murdered a "man instead of Christ" and therefore enjoy "no relief from the pervading spiritual drought" (Taylor 1983, 55).

Putzel pictures this story as shaped by impotence. He places McLendon in the pattern of the soldier who survived World War I but was left spiritually dead. He is a man who acts violently toward his wife and then shows "contrasting solicitude" for the pistol he places on the table beside his bed (1985,

226–28; see also Carothers 1987, 67). Crane ascribes McLendon's motivation to his frustration with the dullness of middle age that holds no promise of the excitement he recalls from his young adult years (Crane 1985, 410–20). David Dowling believes McLendon acts "out of suppressed lust for Minnie," not to protect Southern womanhood (1989, 146).

Hawkshaw is interpreted from positions of praise and blame for his efforts to help or his failure to save Will Mayes. In a 1931 review of *These 13*, Robert Cantwell suggested that the story is not about conflict between the active McLendon and the weak Hawkshaw; that tension dissolves into a "lack of conflict, for the barber's effort dies in an attack of nausea" (Emerson 1984, 23). Wolfe and Daniels count Hawkshaw as "one of the three major antagonists of the Negro." They interpret his behavior as an "insidious" encouragement of the lynching because he is the first person to name Will Mayes, and his protests fuel the others' outrage. Only when Mayes strikes Hawkshaw and Hawkshaw strikes back does Hawkshaw realize his participation in the murder (Wolfe and Daniels 1964, 158–59).

Taking a contrasting stand, Gerstenberger and Garber understand Hawkshaw's character as a foil for the other two white characters (1969, 406–07). Howard Faulkner also counters that a misreading of the moon's rise away from Jefferson results in the indictment of Hawkshaw by Wolfe and Daniels. Hawkshaw's failure increases the sense of despair that characterizes the town but does not include him in the guilt of the others. As the moon rises away from the dust, so Hawkshaw brushes the dust from himself (H. Faulkner 1973, 47–50). Carothers points out that "merely to attempt decisive action" as Hawkshaw does evokes no heroism (1981, 262). According to Crane, Hawkshaw, like Minnie and McLendon, is facing a mid-life crisis, but unlike the others, he is able to "salvage" his life as well as Susan Reed's, as demonstrated by their marriage in "Hair" (1985, 410–20; Carothers 1992, 50).

Polk's study of respectability in Faulkner's fiction shows the means by which the benefits and harms of respectability are injected in various degrees into the writer's fictional communities. Sexual repression is one of the most pernicious ways in which respectability becomes repression. As an example, Polk cites the vicarious release Minnie's friends seek when they press her for details about her alleged attack (1980a, 110–13). Polk's study demonstrates how the critical focus of "Dry September" shifts easily from the motives of the individual to the manipulations of the community.

Sociological interpretations of "Dry September" constitute a large and important portion of critical discussions of the text. The issue of race relations in the South is obviously a major concern. Kerr and Pryse both include in their discussions of the fictional text references to sociological studies of actual lynchings (Kerr [1969] 1976, 221–22; Pryse 1979, 93). As for the fictional depiction of events in "Dry September," Kerr calls it the "most terrible such episode in Faulkner" (Kerr [1969] 1976, 221). Everett assigns the story similar value when he defines it as a "devastating anti-lynching polemic" (1969, 140). Carothers contextualizes the effort a bit more mildly when he includes "Dry September" among those works of Faulkner that explore contemporary racial attitudes (Carothers 1985, 20). Most but not all critics define the exploration positively. Irving Howe, for example, sees "Dry September" as powerful but very nearly stereotyped "in its acceptance of the view that Southern ladies are likely to accuse black men when they have prolonged difficulty in finding white ones" ([1952] 1975, 70).

Glenn Carey argues that Faulkner presents a study of racial intolerance, including the elements of bigotry, hatred, irresolution, apathy, and self-preservation. Jefferson represents an "intolerant society," and its citizens demonstrate the various attitudes present in the community. Minnie is a "sexually frustrated psychoneurotic" who is able to damage the community. (Carey misstates her age as in the forties.) McLendon is the white supremacist; Butch is the illogical, irresponsible conformist. Hawkshaw is "conscientious but irresolute." When he escapes from the car just as Mayes calls to him, he flees his responsibility to stand firm for his fellow man. His subsequent limp represents the crippling effect of his failure on himself and his community (Carey 1964, 27–30). Széky interprets the dryness of the title and town as an indication of the social climate and racial attitudes. The more reluctant lynchers are motivated by social pressure to participate. They are all, including Minnie and McLendon, influenced by the past, and they are incapable of escaping the "tangle of circumstances in which they live and suffer" (Széky 1978, 195–96).

Nilon hints that the possibility for change inheres in the closing image of McLendon. Nilon traces the journeys of black characters in Faulkner's fiction, symbolically crossing Jordan, as an effort to define themselves individually. Whether the journey is controlled by the black character or some pursuer, as in the case of "Dry September," the movement during the journey and the effect it has on the white narrator or observer is important. In "Dry September" McLendon's behavior at home indicates that the rationalizations that have previously justified his treatment of blacks are no longer satisfactory (Nilon 1981, 227–33). Karl believes this story is an early development of the racial theme in which "in the face of injustice, the good man is silenced by intimidation. The worst may lack all conviction, but the good go along or leave" (1989, 408–09).

Another community issue involves the degree to which the town itself is accountable for the lynching. Wolfe and Daniels argue that the men act as individuals, separate from the community at large. Gerstenberger and Garber interpret "Dry September" as a "study in group violence" into which Hawkshaw becomes temporarily drawn, to his surprise and consequent revulsion (Gerstenberger and Garber 1969, 406–07). Howard Faulkner shows how the burden of guilt is extended to the community that gathers around Minnie and McLendon. The women are continuously described as false in their concern for Minnie. They bear the same "repudiation of truth" that she does. The men who join with McLendon lose their individuality: their actions are anonymous, and their guilt is collective. The depth of self-destruction is manifest in the bottomless pit into which the body of Mayes is cast. Although Faulkner is not harshly critical of Hawkshaw, he concludes that Hawkshaw's resistance in the context of this community is a "puny" effort. The story "is preeminently one of terror" (H. Faulkner 1973, 47–50; *CS* 174).

In Széky's view, the people's "snobbery and wish for revenge" especially as seen in sections two and four, "make such events [as the lynching] possible" (1978, 193). Erskine Peters points out that both the lynchers and Hawkshaw exhibit some fear of public opinion. The group of men fear that their plans have been overheard, yet Hawkshaw does not appeal for public assistance to save Mayes. Peters concludes that the community at large does not perceive the heinous nature of lynching (1983, 91). Interpreting the chain of events somewhat differently, Carothers absolves the community from responsibility with his assertion that the murder occurs "almost before the community has been informed of the 'crime'" (1985, 45). Karl believes the hot, bored town awaits some excitement just as Minnie does. Karl is somewhat misleading when he counterpoises the "cool" of the barber shop and Hawkshaw to the dry heat of the town. It is true that Hawkshaw tries to inject a "cool" head, but the barber shop is described as stifling (1989, 408–09).

In "Dry September," film provides one medium for teaching social roles, especially gender-determined behaviors. Obeisance to those roles, however, demands a much greater price than the cost of an admission ticket. In Bache's analysis of "Dry September," Minnie Cooper and John McLendon act out their lives in a parodic version of the Hollywood romance script. The progression of the scenes details the handsome hero avenging the honor of the beautiful young girl. The theater scene in which Minnie goes into hysterics reveals the falseness and hollowness of their behavior. Minnie and McLendon are inextricably linked by the reciprocal nature of their roles. The images of Minnie's brightness relate to McLendon's hotness. At the story's conclusion, their respective attitudes are reversed. Minnie moves from lonely to hysterical; McLendon moves from hysterical to lonely. Mayes serves as an opposing image. The heat of Minnie and McLendon contrasts with the "cool, wet job" of Will Mayes at the ice plant. Mayes is a crucified Christ figure. The rising moon after his death "represents the moral ascendancy of Mayes over his betrayers and murderers." Ironically, at the story's end, the ladies try to soothe Minnie with ice, which only provides a momentary relief (Bache 1954, 53–57; see also Gerstenberger and Garber 1969, 406–07). Paul Rogalus believes that the movie serves as contrast to the behavior of Minnie and McLendon. The "beautiful unreal" of the theater "is oblivious to the world of the real and suffering" including these two people, who "are desperate and very dangerous individuals" (Rogalus 1990, 211–12).

Page and Pryse both examine the main characters in their roles as outsiders. Page sees Minnie as a possession rather than a member of the Jefferson community. The other women can measure their own success by Minnie's failure (Page 1972, 100–01). Pryse's study of socially stigmatized characters considers Minnie, McLendon, and Mayes all "marked," that is, identified as an unsatisfactory other, by their community. Pryse demonstrates how the problematic nature of Hawkshaw's behavior reestablishes the ambiguity that McLendon's actions try to erase. Pryse qualifies the marked quality of McLendon; it is obvious to the reader but not to the community. The character achieves a visibility acceptable in the community because it strives to eliminate social deviance. However, his failure to enjoy peaceful calm at the end reveals to the reader the continued presence of "inner ambiguities" within him. Pryse misstates Hawkshaw's identity by attaching the accusation of "Northerner" made by one of the speakers in the barbershop to him (it is directed to another speaker [*CS* 170–71]) and by describing him initially as an "impartial observer" (from his first words Hawkshaw defends Mayes) (Pryse 1979, 92–107).

Skei's sympathy for Minnie is clear. He believes she is trying "to make life bearable." She acts "arbitrarily" because what she misses is what she sees idealized in movies. Her sense of failure comes from her age and because she is single, an unacceptable state in a society where couples are the norm. She is confronted with these ideals in every context including film (1977, 115, 198 n. 225; 1985, 124–25).

Edmond Volpe sees "Dry September" as a "haunting vision of the human being stretched to the breaking point, the pitiable victim of rigid sterile social traditions and of the moral sterility of an indifferent universe." He notes that the word *insane* was omitted from the published text though it had originally been part of the phrase "and the insane and lidless stars." Minnie and McLendon are treated with compassion even though they are not absolved of the horror of their actions. Volpe associates the sixty-two days without rain with the approximately sixty years that had elapsed between the end of the Civil War and the time of the story. Both Minnie and McLendon engage in fantasy lives "rooted in the sexual roles ordained for them by the codes and traditions of their society," roles they have been unable to fill. Minnie's self-concept exists in the "pre-marital stage" wherein her attractiveness and sexuality are of primary importance. Her society prevents her from finding meaningful alternatives; she cannot perceive herself in any other role. Similarly, McLendon defines himself within a narrow concept of "masculinity" into which racial codes have been enmeshed: he must protect women and children from black males—and as they present a physical danger to this group, these free blacks represent an economic threat to poor whites.

Volpe notes an interesting deletion from the manuscript concerning the makeup of the lynch mob. In the manuscript of "Drouth" Faulkner identified the kind of men who carried out lynchings as "mechanics, clerks, laborers, loafers." Hawkshaw, according to Volpe, does oppose the traditions of the community, but he acts as he does because he knows the particular individuals involved. Volpe adds that when Hawkshaw strikes Will, he demonstrates the strength of tradition even as it determines his behavior. He recognizes the futility of his effort and extracts himself from the scene (Volpe 1989, 60–65). (Volpe's observations about the lynchers match Széky's view that in typical lynching stories, the white lynchers are frequently "just as poor and miserable as black men," and they act to assert their superiority over another group [1978, 188].)

Gerstenberger and Garber, along with other critics, note that the story's scope and implications are raised beyond the specific community, with the moon contributing a cosmic sense and the repetition of "Jees Christ" recalling another scapegoat slaying. The effect implies "that the world repeats itself infinitely." "Dry September" represents one turn of that repetitive cycle (Gerstenberger and Garber 1969, 406–07).

John Vickery's use of myth in his criticism adds a dimension to the understanding of "Dry September" that subsequent critics have accepted at least in general outline if not in all details. He interprets the story through the ritual of the scapegoat in primitive and classical patterns. He sees it as an ironic rendering of the scapegoat ritual in which the white society that holds itself up as a superior race is shown clinging to rituals "most commonly found in those of a low level of intellectual and social culture." He cites the work of Sir James Frazer and Jane Harrison in his comparison of Faulkner's text to the ritual of the scapegoat. In its original intent, the scapegoat ritual served to protect the community from disaster or drought. Expulsion of the scapegoat usually occurred in September. The participants in the Jefferson ritual maintain the roles of the ancient pattern. As the scapegoat, Mayes is regarded as a criminal, beaten in ritualistic manner, taken out of town, slain, cast into a body of water (the bottomless vat), and not returned to the community. McLendon takes the role of "warrior priest whose task it was to expel the evils threatening the community." By beating the scapegoat, he accomplishes his task which is "to prevent or dispel vegetative infertility such as drought." Minnie Cooper parallels Will Mayes as a minor scapegoat whose punishment is enacted over time. She is chosen on social rather than racial terms, and she faces verbal rather than physical punishment and expulsion. Vickery notes that the doubling of the scapegoats is consistent with the primitive ritual in which two outcasts, a male adorned with a black emblem and a female adorned with a white emblem, were sacrificed. Hawkshaw represents the only major figure "not intrinsically a part of the ritual." He is supposed to inject truth and rationality and to expose the scapegoat pattern as "fallacious, outmoded, and conducive only to increased frustration and anguish" because it has lost any element of the solemnity or significance of the ancient observance. Hawkshaw's protestations are not the only means by which the irony of ritual is exposed. Minnie herself becomes an instrument of revenge on the community. She returns, even if only temporarily, by duping the community into another enactment of the ritual and another sacrifice of an innocent victim. Vickery interprets her laughter as "her secret knowledge of the revenge she has inflicted on the community."

Another irony of the lynching is that the scapegoat ceremony was associated with the Saturnalia, a festival in which sexual union was celebrated and in which "total freedom for the whole of mankind" was symbolized. Vickery incorporates Faulkner's belief that the survival or damnation of the South depended on whether white Southerners reformed their attitudes toward blacks. In killing Will Mayes, the community does not avoid disaster but instead extinguishes its hope of salvation (Vickery 1962, 5–14).

Like John Vickery, Weiss associates the ritualized treatment of Will Mayes with the Saturnalia. In the degradation of the ritual, however, the comic Saturnalia is replaced by the tragic sacrifice of the Crucifixion. Weiss traces the decline of the ancient cult of the priest-assassin to the point that killing a god and executing a criminal have become undifferentiated. In "Dry September" the ritual lynching is reduced to a travesty. Weiss makes many points similar to Vickery's regarding the roles of the participants in the ritual. He adds that in ancient practice, in an effort to bring rain, a slave or black animal was thrown into water. But the movement of the "rain-giving" moon away from rather than toward the community reveals the futility of enacting the now distorted, destructive ritual (Weiss 1963, 71–79).

Various critics have engaged in the mythic interpretation either to supplement or, on occasion, to refute its applicability to "Dry September." Gerstenberger and Garber emphasize that the choice of the scapegoat is influenced by the geographical region in which the story is set. From the beginning of the story, it is clear that the choice will be racially motivated (Gerstenberger and Garber 1969, 406). Page supports John Vickery's interpretation of Minnie as a scapegoat (1972, 100).

Peters analyzes the lynching as an effort "to affirm and reinstitute the racial myths of the culture." He sees Mayes, as representative of the black community, becoming the scapegoat of a psychology that gives greater credence to what it wishes to be true than to what is true. In this psychology, white equals humanity and black equals bestiality; consequently, the presumed rape is seen as an assault on humanity. Even if Hawkshaw could protect Mayes, the community would demand the sacrifice of some other black in order to "appease the gods of the social order and the rage within themselves" (Peters 1983, 88–91).

Skei does not support those interpretations that he believes reduce the "burden of the lynching episode" by understanding it as ritual or individual sexual frustrations. He emphasizes that only within a "rather peculiar social system" that clearly elevates one class of people over another class considered inferior would justice and truth be so immediately dismissed. As Skei points out, the town cannot be absolved from responsibility for Mayes's death since it fails to act to prevent it (1977, 109–110, 117–18; 1985, 124).

Waggoner interprets the violence of "Dry September" as an assertion of an individual's existence against the threat of insecurity and isolation. In his view, the story's comment on "modern man" supersedes the social exploration of race relationships and mob violence. He sees Minnie and McLendon as victims, although they, unlike Mayes, do not evoke sympathy. Their need for self-assertion is played against recurring images of death. Minnie is threatened by aging, which obscures any concern for the consequences of her accusations, and she strives to regain her sexual allure. McLendon is consistently portrayed in life–death (stillness–violence) contrasts such as being both "furious" and "rigid" or "posed" and "roving." According to Waggoner, McLendon can combat the threat of death only by imposing death. In Waggoner's reading of the story, Hawkshaw is the only character whose sense of self does not require affirmation in violence (1959, 196–99).

John McDermott interprets "Dry September" as a pleading "for a healing measure, a spiritual reconciliation with the source of love and truth," Jesus Christ. McDermott sees the poles of the story as thoughtful inaction, represented by Hawkshaw, and thoughtless action, represented by McLendon, who is himself a representative of evil. Hawkshaw's "I can't" originally suggests a promise of action but reveals itself to be a failure of action. His denial of Mayes's pleadings recalls Peter's denial of Jesus. Hawkshaw reveals the absence in the community of "Dry September" of a "man whose basic roots lie in the soil of clear thought and courageous action." The consequence is that he limps, retches, and chokes in the dusty atmosphere of his evil world (McDermott 1976, 31–34; *CS* 173).

Stewart's comparison of "Dry September" to Eliot's *The Waste Land* and Dante's *Inferno* proceeds from his view of the story as a "symbol of the human condition and the dusty hole at the center of the story a symbol of unfathomable evil." The Southern community's fixation on its past inhibits a "spiritual regeneration" and results in a "maelstrom of futile and degenerate passions." Mayes's death is an outward manifestation of the murderers' "spiritual darkness." The climate is hellish in its physical, psychological, social, and spiritual dimensions. Stewart traces the images that lend to the depiction of Jefferson in September as hell. The cars are demonic; the dust and street lights create an atmosphere of "dead air and glare." The sound of "serpentine hissing" links in evil all the women and men grouped around the main characters. Minnie's cohort is made up of "harpies, subtle tormentors, exploiters, devils." The evil touches everyone, even Hawkshaw. "The unregenerate human condition" Stewart sees presented here "is a maze with no exit, a series of vicious circles like those of Dante's Inferno" (1979, 238–43).

Dessner's understanding of "Dry September" is that the story "presents, and mourns, a world irretrievably corrupt and fallen." His interest in the symbolic exceeds his concern with social, political, or personal turmoil. The images include both "recognizably literary" images and "Mississippi things" that "become expressive of ideas and feelings." Sometimes the two merge. The overwhelming sense is of matters beyond control. For example, the rumor is like an unstoppable fire sweeping through dry grass. Within the barbershop, a place for cosmetic improvement, the pleasant fragrances do little to abate the odor of stale breath and perspiration. The images of intractable bodily processes continue: McLendon's sweating, the feel of Mayes's breath and his odor, Minnie's uncontrollable trembling and laughter, Hawkshaw's automatic striking of Will, and Hawkshaw's subsequent retching. Dessner shows how the early reference to a man in the barbershop as a "desert rat in the moving pictures" (*CS* 170) prepares the later association in the theater with the posters of "terrible and beautiful mutations" (*CS* 181), and finally together imply that life, just like film, presents "grotesque and random deviations from an ideal norm" (Dessner 1984, 155–62).

Dessner's discussion of the unredeemable world of "Dry September" reveals how difficult it is to consider any critical approach to the text without reference to its formal aspects. An assessment by C. B. Palmer in 1931 set a negative tone that few adopted. Palmer thought the conclusion of the story was a "disappointment, making too neat a finish of the whole bloody business" (Emerson 1984, 22). Joseph Reed uses several superlatives in his judgment of the technical achievement of "Dry September": the story reflects Faulkner's "highest reach of the confident use of third person"; it is "one of Faulkner's most rigidly controlled stories," and it "is the most claustrophobic of Faulkner's fiction." Reed finds a movement of circularity within and between the sections so that "atmosphere, metaphor, theme, character, structure, merge in frustration, compulsion, entrapment, and isolation." The disciplined selection of narrative patterns includes the dramatic rendering of the first section that is rarely interrupted by the narrative presence, and the objective, remote introduction of Minnie in the second section that seems to be the voice of the "anatomist or the abnormal psychologist" (Reed 1973, 50–55). Ferguson describes the organization as a symmetrical pattern alternating focus on McLendon and Minnie in a "kind of ABABA form" suggestive of musical structure (1991, 140–41).

Dessner faults the narrator's presentation of characters as "stock roles" because it casts doubt on his "lesson in the psychosocial manifestations of bigotry." Dessner views the narrator's voice as sometimes distinct from the "local manner." He, like the astronomical viewers, sees the world from beyond the human perspective, but his view, especially as understood in his description of the theater, is of "life as an endless dream, without progress or point, mere accumulation, a freak show, 'beautiful and terrible' at once, with nothing to choose between the two words" (1984, 152–62).

Skei describes the narrative point of view as third person omniscient that shifts frequently to pursue unfolding action in the different domains of the story. This strategy permits Faulkner to omit the actual murder of Mayes in order to follow Hawkshaw once he leaps from the car. Further, it controls the merger of imagistic language and action, and the distribution of sympathy. Skei agrees with Reed that the control is so deftly handled that it does not reveal itself (Skei 1985, 114). Putzel joins in praising the "balance and design" that characterize this very disciplined story, and Ferguson adds that it "reveals about as well as any of Faulkner's short stories what can be achieved by letting dialogue and objective description carry the burden of the narrative" (Putzel 1985, 228; Ferguson 1991, 93–94).

Not all critics have been as positive, particularly with regard to characterization. Howe sees a tendency toward abstraction in Faulkner's characterization of blacks. He describes "Dry September" as a "paradigm of all lynching stories" that is "populated not with men but with Murderer and Victim" ([1952] 1975, 127). In another early study, Bache stretches the interpretive depths of Will Mayes's name if not his character, finding implications in *maize*, the product reaped in the dry season, and *maze*, the complex problem of race relations in the South. Bache further asserts that *Will*, his first name, represents the lost consciousness of the white man, pointed to by the common initials of Will Mayes and white man (1954, 55). William Griffin exposes the superficial nature of Bache's speculation on Mayes's name with a few of his own trivialized homonym studies; nevertheless, Griffin's complaint about Bache's interpretation by "infinite expansion" does not completely diminish Bache's argument (Griffin 1956, 27–31). Millgate describes the characters as fully realized whereas Everett criticizes their lack of depth in their personification of particular positions and in their understanding of their actions (Millgate [1961] 1966, 65; Everett 1969, 140–41). Watson asserts that the symbolic enrichment of the text gives the characters of "Dry September" a depth beyond superficial stereotypes. Watson explains, "By drawing upon the psychology of sexual identity, on the mythology of seasonal renewal, and on regional legends of black virility, he [Faulkner] roots his characters in a particularized place redolent of universal as well as regional realities" (1980, 213–14).

Walter Allen compliments Faulkner's management of a great deal of information in the limited space of the story by successfully letting the presentation of action "carry its own comment." He also praises the use of colloquial speech and the means by which the author introduces the weighty presence of the community behind the major character (1981, 184–86).

Howard Faulkner believes that through its symbolism the story avoids the mere restatement of a "nearly-clichéd situation." He is especially interested in Faulkner's use of the moon; it is different from the traditional associations with fertility and hope. Combined with the presentation of the landscape it "intensifies the confinement in which the people of Jefferson live" (Faulkner 1973, 47–50; *CS* 174). Page makes the related observation that "no image of feminine fertility" in "Dry September" redeems the community from a sense of a wasteland and death (1972, 101).

Millgate thinks that the evocation of heat and drought are not only "atmosphere" but also "active agents" because "they offer a natural provocation to violence." Further, the symbolic import of the natural elements relates "to the acts of passionate unreason and the lives of sterile unreality with which the story deals" (Millgate [1961] 1966, 65). Everett considers the weather to be the "most potent force in the story" (1969, 140). The weather provides "symbolic reinforcement of the emotional climate which bred the storm of violence" (Blotner 1974, 654). Brooks, like Blotner, sees the weather and the blood in the twilight and the moon as reflections rather than causes of human actions ([1978] 1990, 112). Skei dismisses suggestions of a causal relationship between the "climate, landscape and social conditions" and the murder of Mayes (1985, 124).

Ford counts the use of the word *dust* fifteen times in the third section of "Dry September." The repetition of the image links the first, third, and final sections of the story. He suggests that the ever-present dust may refer to the "guilt of the town or the crime itself which none of the people can escape" but that it more likely "stands for the whole perverted attitude of the Southern town." As he points out, even Hawkshaw, who was moved to strike Mayes, is covered in dust when he leaps from the car. At the close of section three, the implication is that the ever-present dust will absorb the dust raised by the actions of the murderers whose "guilt will be assumed and excused by their society." Dreams provide the recurring image that holds sections two and four together in their focus on Minnie Cooper. She rejects reality and nurtures the illusion of her youth even to the point of claiming rape in order to regain the attention of the town. In the concluding section dreams are merged with dust to give an overall unity to the story. The hot, dry walk to the theater leads to the confrontation between reality and unreality. As Ford concludes, neither dust nor dreams can conceal the reality of the events nor the doomed lives of the people (1962, 219–20; see also Ferguson 1991, 138–39).

Bache hears in hissing sounds in the story the serpent in the Garden of Eden, but the prevailing impression is that the setting is hellish (1954, 55). Janice Moore also find the hissing an important image, defining the people of the community as serpents. She adds that even the young people entering the theater are associated by the "hissing alliteration" present in the sentence that introduces them. She believes that Faulkner's imagistic pairing of dust and snakes may have its basis in Isaiah 65:25, "and dust shall be the serpent's food." The images eventually include the whole community that is condemned for its racial prejudice (Moore 1983, 47).

For Crane, the title "Dry September" reflects the stage of life of the major characters rather than a causal link between the weather and the violence. They are all in middle-aged crises with little prospect of achieving the attention that was theirs in earlier years. Crane, however, undermines his argument with errors. He should have included detailed textual citations to support his chronology of events, as some of his suggestions seem to provide more information than the story itself reveals. He refers to Minnie as "about forty" though he could use the narrator's, rather than Hawkshaw's, information and state her age as thirty-eight or thirty-nine. This type of inaccuracy is repeated in his reference to McLendon as "Jackson" McLendon when in the story his first name is given as "John" (Crane 1985, 410–20).

Joan Winslow slightly alters the course of critical response when she examines language as subject in "Dry September." She contends that the story presents the extreme ends that misused language may attain. Winslow is especially interesting in her analysis of language use by the four major characters. Minnie and McLendon effectively manipulate the community by their use of abstract language. Both depend on stereotype to rouse people to action. Minnie, herself a victim of "linguistic oppression," redefines herself as "cousin" rather than "aunt" and eventually relies on the abstractions of racism and Southern chivalry to motivate action. Demonstrating the power of language, Minnie does not have to speak but can count on the chain of rumor to reveal her story. Hawkshaw tries without success to inject particularized concrete language about the named individuals involved in the barber shop discussion, but he is constantly opposed by the abstract threats and accusations of his opponents. Winslow does recognize that in Hawkshaw's doubts of Minnie Cooper's accusation, he too falls into a dependence on his own stereotyped understanding of unmarried women. Like Hawkshaw, Will Mayes tries to engage the lynchers in concrete dialogue that will individualize them and break the anonymity of mob action. By his appeals such as "Mr. John" and "Mr. Henry" he "tries to force the others into their normal social role of paternalistic superior." While the abstractions are exposed in their ineptness, such as when the assumed Southerner–Northerner attitudes are exploded, the overall sense is that misused language exerts itself over language properly used. Clearly, however, neither McLendon nor Minnie enjoys a victory beneficial to their community or themselves as a result of their successful manipulations of language. They are left literally exposed (Winslow 1977, 380–86).

Olga Vickery argues that the author's refusal "to dramatize the conclusive action" effectively intensifies the emotional impact and implies a continuation of events beyond the particular text (Vickery 1964, 301). Flora presents a fuller discussion of this characteristic in his examination of "conspicuous silence" in "Dry September." Conspicuous silence serves to define the characters' emotions and involve the reader in the moral issues of the story. According to Flora, conspicuous silence occurs in the story when there is a retreat from the action, particularly the actual murder of Mayes. There is silence also on the matter of the rape. This does not mean the reader is unaware that the rape is imagined and the murder is real, but omission of the explicit articulation forces the reader to experience "the horror of the events more deeply," and tension is increased. The rapid pace of the narrative contributes to a sense of nervousness and interruption, implying that the narrator wants to move quickly through the story. The withdrawals from heightened moments of action lend a further sense of avoidance. The description of the barbershop adds to the tension with its short, clipped speeches by speakers who are easily confused and, for the most part, only vaguely identified. When, however, the choice between McLendon's plan and Hawkshaw's plan to resolve the rumor must be made, the moment is frozen. It is a "vital silence" emphasizing that the men must choose between the alternatives. The moment stresses the responsibility the men in the mob bear for their actions. When Hawkshaw leaps from the car, the reader remains with him rather than experiencing the murder. The reader is faced with the question of what his or her own response would have been. While Hawkshaw does not reappear in the last two sections of the story, the narrator points to the community's guilt in the murder as he acknowledges the townspeople's satisfaction that the square is empty of Negroes and remarks on their prying curiosity as they comfort Minnie. Flora notes the contrast between the last view of Hawkshaw moving down the road and McLendon's stillness in a silent world. McLendon is "an isolated and spiritually dead man," revealed by a "telling silence" that closes the story (Flora 1982, 34–36, 44–45).

In a study of Faulkner's rhetoric, Gail Mortimer examines the way his narratives disclose the tension between "constant awareness of change" and the inevitably futile effort "to make things cohere and stay the same." The tension manifests itself in part in the obfuscation of boundaries that seek to define and retain permanence. "Dry September" sets "vocabulary asserting the violence of the transition from life to death" against vocabulary presenting the "illusion of merely apparent life" in the opposition of Will Mayes's death and Minnie Cooper's life. The scenes involving Will Mayes are characterized by "confusion of personal boundaries" in which surfaces are covered with sweat or dust (implying the sense of returning to dust, death) and are consequently blurred boundaries. Life-affirming air seems scarce, and lifelike motion is projected onto inanimate objects (the moon). These images contrast with the descriptions of Minnie's life, filled with "illusion and falsity." To further blur the boundaries, the motivating action, the rape, is an oxymoron, an absent action, because it did not occur at all (Mortimer 1983, 54–57).

In his study of the modern short story, Austin Wright examines ways in which resistance to the form that shapes the short story occurs, a condition he calls "recalcitrance." Sometimes that recalcitrance occurs at the conclusion "by cutting off our expectations for clarification." In "Dry September," Wright describes recalcitrance as an "unexplained juxtaposition . . . in which a lynching episode is presented from several points of view and in which the center of the story is found within a compound protagonist" (1989, 124–26).

"Dry September," in the estimation of Matthews, offers "one of Faulkner's most penetrating studies of cultural consumption." The vigilantes' disregard for the truth of Minnie's accusation relates to the way the "mass media produce a reality suited to the desires of its consumers and also produce audience desires suited to its reality": in this case "society . . . has eroticized the commodity as it has commodified eros." Minnie's sexual desires are turned to the purchase of erotic lingerie, and her reestablished allure is presented in the context of her walking in the square where children eat ice cream and the young men whose eyes follow her lounge in the doorway of the drugstore. The marketplace, like film and magazines, is able "to stimulate sexual desire and then simulate gratification." The story's resistance to the power of the marketplace is in the final portraits of Minnie and Mrs. McLendon. McLendon beats his wife when she, by waiting up, challenges the definition of women "as objects of desire or obstacles to its fulfillment," and Minnie's breakdown at the movie reveals the consequences of becoming, as woman, "object of screened dramas of white male desires, desires played out vicariously in the products of the culture industry" (Matthews 1992, 23–26).

Despite the quantity of interpretive attention given to "Dry September," one symbol that has not been explored is the bleeding moon image, present in both the short story and *The Unvanquished*. In her study of the phrase "no bloody moon" in *The Unvanquished*, Winifred Frazer interprets it to mean "no bloody women" (1986, 162–79). Although Frazer's analysis does not generalize beyond *The Unvanquished*, her discussion might produce interesting corollaries in "Dry September." Similarly a comparison of "Dry September" with "Blood-Burning Moon" in Jean Toomer's *Cane* seems a compelling topic as yet not investigated. A frequent note voiced in the critical reaction to "Dry September" is praise for complex interweaving of the various aspects of the text. Skei's remarks about the strength of the story's opening reflect in many respects the quality of the entire work. The high regard in which "Dry September" is held is not unwarranted.

## Works Cited

Allen, Walter. 1981. *The Short Story in English*. New York: Oxford University Press.

Bache, William B. 1954. "Moral Awareness in 'Dry September.'" *Faulkner Studies* 3:53–59.

Backman, Melvin. 1966. *Faulkner: The Major Years*. Bloomington: Indiana University Press.

Bassett, John E. [1986] 1989. "Gradual Progress and *Intruder in the Dust*." In *Vision and Revisions: Essays on Faulkner*. Ed. Bassett. Locust Hill Literary Studies No. 4. West Cornwall, CT: Locust Hill, 167–79.

Bleikasten, André. 1990. *The Ink of Melancholy: Faulkner's Novels from* The Sound and the Fury *to* Light in August. Bloomington: Indiana University Press.

Blotner, Joseph. 1974. *Faulkner: A Biography*. 2 vols. New York: Random House.

———. 1983. "Continuity and Change in Faulkner's Life and Art." In *Faulkner and Idealism: Perspectives from Paris*. Ed. Michel Gresset and Patrick Samway, S.J. Jackson: University Press of Mississippi, 15–26.

———. 1984. *Faulkner: A Biography*. 1 vol. New York: Random House.

Brooks, Cleanth. [1963] 1990. *William Faulkner: The Yoknapatawpha Country*. New Haven: Yale University Press. Reprint. Baton Rouge: Louisiana State University Press.

———. [1978] 1990. *William Faulkner: Toward Yoknapatawpha and Beyond*. New Haven: Yale University Press. Reprint. Baton Rouge: Louisiana State University Press.

Carey, Glenn O. 1964. "Social Criticism in Faulkner's 'Dry September.'" *English Record* 15.2:27–30.

Carothers, James B. 1981. "The Myriad Heart: The Evolution of the Faulkner Hero." In "A Cosmos of My Own": *Faulkner and Yoknapatawpha 1980*. Ed. Doreen Fowler and Ann J. Abadie. Jackson: University Press of Mississippi, 252–83.

———. 1985. *William Faulkner's Short Stories*. Ann Arbor, MI: UMI Research Press.

———. 1987. "'I Ain't a Soldier Now': *Faulkner's World War II Veterans*. Faulkner Journal 2:67–74.

———. 1992. "Faulkner's Short Story Writing and the Oldest Profession." In *Faulkner and the Short Story: Faulkner and Yoknapatawpha, 1990*. Ed. Evans Harrington and Ann J. Abadie. Jackson: University Press of Mississippi, 38–61.

Crane, John K. 1985. "But the Days Grow Short: A Reinterpretation of Faulkner's 'Dry September.'" *Twentieth Century Literature* 31:410–20.

Dabney, Lewis M. 1974. *The Indians of Yoknapatawpha: A Study in Literature and History*. Baton Rouge: Louisiana State University Press.

Dessner, Lawrence Jay. 1984. "William Faulkner's 'Dry September': Decadence Domesticated." *College Literature* 11:151–62.

Douglas, Ellen. 1981. "Faulkner's Women." In *"A Cosmos of My Own": Faulkner and Yoknapatawpha 1980*. Ed. Doreen Fowler and Ann J. Abadie. Jackson: University Press of Mississippi, 149–67.

Dowling, David. 1989. *William Faulkner*. New York: St. Martin's.

Duvall, John N. 1990. *Faulkner's Marginal Couple: Invisible, Outlaw, Unspeakable Communities*. Austin: University of Texas Press.

Emerson, O. B. 1984. *Faulkner's Early Literary Reputation in America*. Ann Arbor, MI: UMI Research Press.

Everett, Walter K. 1969. *Faulkner's Art and Character*. Woodbury, NY: Barron's Educational Series.

Faulkner, Howard. 1973. "The Stricken World of 'Dry September.'" *Studies in Short Fiction* 10:47–50.

Faulkner, William. 1931. "Dry September." *Scribner's* 89 (January):49–56.

———. 1931. *These 13*. New York: Jonathan Cape and Harrison Smith.

———. 1950. *Collected Stories of William Faulkner*. New York: Random House.

———. 1977. *Selected Letters of William Faulkner*. Ed. Joseph Blotner. New York: Random House.

———. 1987. *William Faulkner Manuscripts 9*: These 13. Ed. Noel Polk. New York: Garland.

Ferguson, James. 1991. *Faulkner's Short Fiction*. Knoxville: University of Tennessee Press.

Flora, Joseph M. 1982. "The Device of Conspicuous Silence in the Modern Short Story." In *The Teller and the Tale: Aspects of the Short Story*. Ed. Wendell M. Aycock. Vol. 13 of the Proceedings Comparative Literature Symposium Texas Tech University. Lubbock: Texas Tech Press, 27–45.

Ford, Arthur L. 1962. "Dust and Dreams: A Study of Faulkner's 'Dry September.'" *College English* 24:219–20.

Frazer, Winifred L. 1986. "Faulkner and Womankind—'No Bloody Moon.'" In *Faulkner and Women: Faulkner and Yoknapatawpha, 1985*. Ed. Doreen Fowler and Ann J. Abadie. Jackson: University Press of Mississippi, 162–79.

Gerstenberger, Donna, and Frederick Garber. 1969. "William Faulkner, 'Dry September.'" In *Microcosm: An Anthology of the Short Story*. Ed. Donna Gerstenberger and Frederick Garber. San Francisco: Chandler, 406–07.

Gladstein, Mimi Reisel. 1986. *The Indestructible Woman in Faulkner, Hemingway, and Steinbeck*. Ann Arbor, MI: UMI Research Press.

Griffin, William J. 1956. "How to Misread Faulkner: A Powerful Plea for Ignorance." Tennessee Studies in Literature 1:27–34.

Hayes, Ann L. 1961. "The World of The Hamlet." In *Studies in Faulkner*. Ed. Ann L. Hayes et al. Carnegie Series in English 6. Pittsburgh: Department of English Carnegie Institute of Technology, 3–16.

Holmes, Edward M. 1966. *Faulkner's Twice-Told Tales: His Re-Use of His Material*. The Hague: Mouton.

Howe, Irving. [1952] 1975. *William Faulkner: A Critical Study*. 3d ed. Chicago: University of Chicago Press.

Inge, M. Thomas. 1986. "Faulkner Reads the Funny Papers." In *Faulkner and Humor: Faulkner and Yoknapatawpha, 1984*. Jackson: University Press of Mississippi, 153–90.

Jenkins, Lee Clinton. 1981. *Faulkner and Black-White Relations: A Psychoanalytic Approach*. New York: Columbia University Press.

Johnson, Ira. 1972. "Faulkner's 'Dry September' and Caldwell's 'Saturday Afternoon': An Exercise in Practical Criticism." *Tradition et Innovation. littérature et paralittérature*: Actes du Congrès de Nancy, 269–78.

Karl, Frederick R. 1989. *William Faulkner: American Writer*. New York: Weidenfeld and Nicolson.

Kawin, Bruce F. 1977. *Faulkner and Film*. New York: Frederick Ungar.

———. 1979. "The Montage Element in Faulkner's Fiction." In *Faulkner, Modernism, and Film: Faulkner and Yoknapatawpha, 1978*. Ed. Evans Harrington and Ann J. Abadie. Jackson: University Press of Mississippi, 103–26.

Kerr, Elizabeth M. 1961–62. "William Faulkner and the Southern Concept of Woman." *Mississippi Quarterly* 15:1–16.

———. [1969] 1976. *Yoknapatawpha: Faulkner's "Little Postage Stamp of Native Soil."* New York: Fordham University Press.

———. 1983. *William Faulkner's Yoknapatawpha: "A Kind of Keystone in the Universe."* New York: Fordham University Press.

Kinney, Arthur F. 1978. *Faulkner's Narrative Poetics: Style as Vision*. Amherst: University of Massachusetts Press.

———. 1980. "Faulkner's Narrative Poetics and Collected Stories." *Faulkner Studies* 1:58–79.

Kinney, Arthur F., and Doreen Fowler. 1983. "For the Record: Faulkner's Rowan Oak Papers: A Census." *Journal of Modern Literature* 10:327–34.

McDermott, John V. 1976. "Faulkner's Cry for a Healing Measure: 'Dry September.'" *Arizona Quarterly* 32:31–34.

Malin, Irving. 1957. *William Faulkner: An Interpretation*. Stanford: Stanford University Press.

Matthews, John T. 1992. "Shortened Stories: Faulkner and the Market." In *Faulkner and the Short Story: Faulkner and Yoknapatawpha, 1990*. Ed. Evans Harrington and Ann J. Abadie. Jackson: University Press of Mississippi, 3–37.

Meriwether, James B. [1961] 1971. *The Literary Career of William Faulkner: A Bibliographical Study*. Princeton, NJ: Princeton University Library. Reprint. Columbia: University of South Carolina Press.

———. 1973. "Faulkner's Correspondence with Scribner's Magazine." *Proof* 3:253–82.

Millgate, Michael. [1961] 1966. *William Faulkner*. New York: Barnes & Noble.

———. [1966] 1989. *The Achievement of William Faulkner*. New York: Random House. Reprint. Athens: University of Georgia Press. Brown Thrasher Books.

———. 1980. "Faulkner's First Trilogy: *Sartoris, Sanctuary*, and *Requiem for a Nun*."

*In Fifty Years of Yoknapatawpha: Faulkner and Yoknapatawpha 1979*. Ed. Doreen Fowler and Ann J. Abadie. Jackson: University Press of Mississippi, 90–109.

———. 1987. "'A Novel: Not an Anecdote': Faulkner's Light in August." In *New Essays on Light in August*. Ed. Michael Millgate. Cambridge: Cambridge University Press, 31–53.

Momberger, Philip. 1978. "Faulkner's 'The Village' and 'That Evening Sun': The Tale in Context." *Southern Literary Journal* 11.1:20–31.

Moore, Janice Townley. 1983. "Faulkner's 'Dry September.'" *Explicator* 41:47–48.

Mortimer, Gail L. 1983. *Faulkner's Rhetoric of Loss: A Study in Perception and Meaning*. Austin: University of Texas Press.

Nilon, Charles H. 1965. *Faulkner and the Negro*. New York: Citadel.

———. 1981. "Blacks in Motion." In *"A Cosmos of My Own": Faulkner and Yoknapatawpha 1980*. Ed. Doreen Fowler and Ann J. Abadie. Jackson: University Press of Mississippi, 227–51.

O'Connor, William Van. 1954. *The Tangled Fire of William Faulkner*. Minneapolis: University of Minnesota Press.

Page, Sally R. 1972. *Faulkner's Women: Characterization and Meaning*. Deland, FL: Everett/Edwards.

Peters, Erskine. 1983. *William Faulkner: The Yoknapatawpha World and Black Being*. Darby, PA.: Norwood.

Pilkington, John. 1981. *The Heart of Yoknapatawpha*. Jackson: University Press of Mississippi.

Pitavy, François. 1972. "A Forgotten Faulkner Story: 'Miss Zilphia Gant.'" *Studies in Short Fiction* 9:131–42.

———. 1973. *Faulkner's Light in August*. Trans. Gillian E. Cook. Bloomington: Indiana University Press.

Polk, Noel. 1980a. "Faulkner and Respectability." In *Fifty Years of Yoknapatawpha: Faulkner and Yoknapatawpha 1979*. Ed. Doreen Fowler and Ann J. Abadie. Jackson: University Press of Mississippi, 110–33.

———. 1980b. "'I Taken an Oath of Office Too': Faulkner and the Law." In *Fifty Years of Yoknapatawpha: Faulkner and Yoknapatawpha 1979*. Ed. Doreen Fowler and Ann J. Abadie. Jackson: University Press of Mississippi, 159–78.

———. 1984. "'The Dungeon was Mother Herself': William Faulkner: 1927–1931." In *New Directions in Faulkner Studies: Faulkner and Yoknapatawpha, 1983*. Ed. Doreen Fowler and Ann J. Abadie. Jackson: University Press of Mississippi, 61–93.

———. 1985. "The Space between Sanctuary." In *Intertextuality in Faulkner*. Ed. Michel Gresset and Noel Polk. Jackson: University Press of Mississippi, 16–35.

Pryse, Marjorie. 1979. *The Mark and the Knowledge: Social Stigma in Classic American Fiction*. Columbus: Ohio State University Press.

Putzel, Max. 1985. Genius of Place: *William Faulkner's Triumphant Beginnings*. Baton Rouge: Louisiana State University Press.

Reed, Joseph W., Jr. 1973. *Faulkner's Narrative*. New Haven: Yale University Press.

Rogalus, Paul. 1990. "Faulkner's 'Dry September.'" *Explicator* 48:211–12.

Samway, Patrick H., S.J. 1980. *Faulkner's* Intruder in the Dust: *A Critical Study of the Typescripts.* Troy, NY: Whitston.

Skei, Hans H. 1977. *Bold and Tragical and Austere: William Faulkner's* These 13: *A Study.* University of Oslo Department of Literature.

———. 1981. *William Faulkner: The Short Story Career.* Oslo, Norway: Universitetsforlaget.

———. 1985. *William Faulkner: The Novelist as Short Story Writer.* Oslo, Norway: Universitetsforlaget.

Snead, James. 1986. *Figures of Division: William Faulkner's Major Novels.* New York: Methuen.

Stewart, Jack F. 1979. "The Infernal Climate of Faulkner's 'Dry September.'" *Research Studies* 47:238–43.

Sundquist, Eric J. 1983. *Faulkner: The House Divided.* Baltimore: Johns Hopkins University Press.

Széky, Annamária R. 1978. "The Lynching Story." *Studies in English and American [Budapest]* 4:181–99.

Taylor, Walter. [1972] 1989. "'Pantaloon': The Negro Anomaly at the Heart of *Go Down, Moses.*" In *On Faulkner: The Best from American Literature.* Ed. Louis J. Budd and Edwin H. Cady. Durham, NC: Duke University Press, 58–72.

———. 1983. *Faulkner's Search for a South.* Urbana: University of Illinois Press.

Tuck, Dorothy. 1964. *Crowell's Handbook of Faulkner.* New York: Thomas Y. Crowell.

Vickery, John B. 1962. "Ritual and Theme in Faulkner's 'Dry September.'" *Arizona Quarterly* 18:5–14.

Vickery, Olga W. [1959] 1964. *The Novels of William Faulkner.* Baton Rouge: Louisiana State University Press.

Volpe, Edmond L. 1989. "'Dry September': Metaphor for Despair." *College Literature* 16:60–65.

Waggoner, Hyatt H. 1959. *William Faulkner: From Jefferson to the World.* Lexington: University of Kentucky Press.

Watson, James G. 1980. "Faulkner's Short Stories and the Making of Yoknapatawpha County." In *Fifty Years of Yoknapatawpha: Faulkner and Yoknapatawpha 1979.* Ed. Doreen Fowler and Ann J. Abadie. Jackson: University Press of Mississippi, 202–25.

Weiss, Daniel. 1963. "William Faulkner and the Runaway Slave." *Northwest Review* 6.3:71–79.

Winslow, Joan D. 1977. "Language and Destruction in Faulkner's 'Dry September.'" *CLA Journal* 20:380–86.

Wolfe, Ralph Haven, and Edgar F. Daniels. 1964. "Beneath the Dust of 'Dry September.'" *Studies in Short Fiction* 1:158–59. Also printed in *Itinerary: Criticism* 3 (1977):159–60.

Wright, Austin M. 1989. "Recalcitrance in the Short Story." In *Short Story Theory at a Crossroads.* Ed. Susan Lohafer and Jo Ellyn Clarey. Baton Rouge: Louisiana State University Press, 115–29.

# Death Drag

## Publication History

"Death Drag" was first published in January 1932 in *Scribner's* under the hyphenated title "Death-Drag." The short-story-sending schedule indicates that publication came only after a number of rejections, the first of which was from *Scribner's*. On its initial submission to *Scribner's*, December 16, 1930, Alfred Dashiell rejected the work because he felt the Jewish characterization was "too nearly a caricature" and the story did "not seem to have enough significance to carry its length." From Faulkner's sending schedule, the subsequent submissions can be tracked from month to month. On January 5, 1931, Faulkner forwarded the story to the *Saturday Evening Post*, which rejected it; on February 1, 1931, Faulkner sent it to the *American Mercury*, where it was also refused. April 5, 1931, was the date of the next submission, this time to *Collier's*. James Meriwether explains that the listing on the sending schedule under *Woman's Home Companion* has the added notation of *Collier's* beside the story title because both magazines were owned by the same company and received submissions at the same address. A letter from Faulkner to Ben Wasson confirms that the magazine targeted was *Collier's*, which also returned the story. On June 5, 1931, Faulkner forwarded "Death Drag" to his agent, Ben Wasson, to let him pursue publication efforts. Several months later, in a letter to Faulkner dated September 28, 1931, Alfred Dashiell requested another reading of "Death Drag." On Faulkner's instruction, Wasson sent the story back to *Scribner's*, and on October 8, 1931, Dashiell wrote to Faulkner that he would buy the story for $250. In the ten months that had elapsed, "Death Drag" accrued an "average" submission-rejection score (Meriwether [1961] 1971, 25, 82, 171, 176–80; 1973, 263, 271–72; Blotner 1974, 683, 708; Putzel 1977, 103; Skei 1981, 68; *SL* 50–51; *WFM 9* 1–2).

"Death Drag" was collected in *Doctor Martino* (1934), Malcolm Cowley's *Portable Faulkner* (1946), and *Collected Stories* (1950). RKO purchased the movie rights to this story and "Honor," for which Faulkner received a total of $6,600 (Blotner 1974, 1219).

## Circumstances of Composition, Sources, and Influences

Critics have not speculated on the original date of composition of "Death Drag." References about its origin typically begin with the December 1930 date on the sending schedule. Joseph Blotner describes the story sent as a "new" one (1974, 676). Ilse Lind claims the story was written between December 1 and 16. She associates the Ginsfarb character in "Death Drag" with a community production of *Corporal Eagen*, performed in September 1930. In this play Faulkner had the role of Izzy Goldstein, a character who spoke in Yiddish–English dialect and whose costume included a wax nose. Lind adds that the dialogue of the play included stereotyped ethnic images (1989, 127–29). The similarity of characters in the play and the short story leads her to claim that the story was written sometime after the September production.

Two prepublication versions of "Death Drag" exist: a holograph manuscript entitled "A Death Drag" and a carbon typescript entitled "A Death-Drag" (*WFM 11* 67–104). Thomas McHaney does not believe these versions establish authoritatively the revisions made between *Scribner's* first rejection and its eventual purchase of the story. The documents are close to the published text although there are some revisions from manuscript to typescript (*WFM 11* Introduction ix).

Among the more interesting features of the manuscript are Ginsfarb's heavy dialect and the explicit reference to his having been in the clothing business. Subsequent versions do not mention the type of business he was in. The distinctiveness of the manuscript is in what it lacks. As the manuscript ends, the plane flies away. The final conversation about the car is not present. Also, several remarks that emphasize Ginsfarb's concern with money are missing. When the driver offers to carry the fliers to town, the manuscript does not indicate that he offers the service free of charge. Ginsfarb's comment that he "won't take less," made while he was riding in the car, does not appear. James Ferguson observes that often the exposition in stories is reduced between prepublication and published versions. A long conversation between Captain Warren and Jock becomes a much briefer report by Warren about the conversation in the later version (Ferguson 1991, 124; *WFM 11* 67–77).

There are fewer differences between the carbon typescript and the published story. Most significant, the stereotype of the Jewish characters, reflected in their dialect, is moderated. McHaney suggests that these alterations may have been made on the lost ribbon copy (*WFM 11* Introduction ix). Blotner suggests that Faulkner answered Dashiell's charge of caricature by emphasizing rather than diminishing the likeness of character and caricature: the author added the line by the narrator that Ginsfarb spoke "in the diction of Weber and Fields in vaudeville" (1974, Notes 103; *CS* 103). Although that line is added, the published version also shows that the spelling in Ginsfarb's speeches has been normalized. The carbon typescript employs dialectal spelling whereas the magazine does not (*WFM 11* 78–104; *Scribner's* 34–42). Other revisions include substituting *England* for *Toronto*, giving Warren the rank of "Captain," and a change from Warren as an ex-R.A.F. pilot to a member of the Royal Flying Corps, a more prestigious organization that preceded the R.A.F. (Blotner 1974, Notes 98).

From magazine to collection in *Doctor Martino* one spelling in a Ginsfarb speech is corrected from *Wot* to *What*, Jock's reference to Ginsfarb as an anesthetized _____ is rephrased to *bastard*, and a quotation mark is dropped (*Scribner's* 40–42; *DRM* 92, 96, 97). Only one correction of *When* to *Then* distinguishes the *Collected Stories* text from the *Doctor Martino* version (*CS* 203; *DRM* 94).

Searches for biographical parallels have been fruitful although Faulkner himself minimized ties between the story and his life. When asked if the story was based on his own life, he responded "Not too much." He went on to say that he had done a little barnstorming just after World War I but that he could not recall any experiences like the episode described in the story. He remembered the time as one when airplanes were still unusual and people were willing to pay high prices for a ride (*FU* 68).

Unlike Faulkner, critics have tended to stress biographical similarities. Aubrey Starke made an early identification of Warren, an "ex-R.A.F. pilot" who walked with a limp, as a projection of Faulkner (Emerson 1984, 60; see also Blotner 1974, 676). James Watson links Faulkner's creation of an "aviator persona" in letters about himself to his "practice of writing himself into his texts in guises of concealment." Watson locates this persona in "Death Drag," "Honor," "Turnabout," *Flags in the Dust*, *Pylon*, and film scripts like *War Birds* (Watson 1987, 4).

Lind makes compelling observations that liken Faulkner not to Warren but to Ginsfarb. Both are short, need money, and are "public entertainers"—one a stuntman, one a writer for popular magazines. As a "metaphoric projection" of Faulkner, Ginsfarb "can be construed to represent Faulkner's deeply felt frustration at this time in relation to his being a patrician without money and a genius who is forced to withhold the full exercise of his powers in order to attend to the grubby work" of short story production for income. Associating himself with a Jewish character in a tradition that links Jews with money involves scapegoating on Faulkner's part, but the association also includes representing the "creative spirit of the artist" with a "figure that flies freely in the air as an aerial stuntsman." Lind concludes that the story "is a remarkable literary study of the intra-psychic processes involved in the use of stereotype" wherein negative feelings are projected onto a "socially rejected Other" while simultaneously binding self to that "Other through psychic identification with it" (1989, 130–31).

The aviation topic was related to the flights Faulkner had taken to the Memphis and Oxford-Lafayette County airports in the two years prior to writing "Death Drag," according to Blotner. The story's fictional airport is very similar to the Oxford-Lafayette County airport, and its characters may owe something to Faulkner's conversations with the "tramp aviators" he met at the Memphis airport (Blotner 1974, 676; Blotner 1984, 270; see also Harrison 1985, 147). More generally, Hans Skei notes that the story recreates the scene of the air circuses of the late 1920s and early 1930s (Skei 1985, 140). Lind records a particular barnstormer's appearance in Oxford soon after the opening of the local airport. The man's name was Irvin, and he may have been Jewish (Lind 1989, 128).

Murry Falkner recalls an incident when a baloonist ran into trouble in a flight over Oxford. Crashing in the Falkners' backyard, the balloon draped the barn and the basket hit the roof of the chicken house. The baloonist was thrown out of the basket onto the roof from which he slid down into a pile of hay. He was confronted there by the astonished Maude Falkner and Mammie Callie, and he ran away. The recollection is complete with the scurrying Falkner boys racing to follow the balloon's flight to their own yard (Falkner 1967, 41–43). Although Falkner does not make a specific association between this event and the story, the parallels between it and Ginsfarb's landing are strong.

Frederick Karl finds another link in Faulkner's "grim and unrelenting" tale: the author's ever-threatening financial woes during the Depression (1989, 426). In addition to Faulkner's own expanding financial obligations, Lind believes that monetary burdens confronting the extended Falkner family contribute to the "wasteland mood" of "Death Drag." The bank to which the Falkners had turned as a result of earlier money problems failed. Also, William's father lost his job with the university (Lind 1989, 127–28).

Finding literary antecedents is a bit more difficult than detecting either biographical or relational ones. John Hagopian believes "Death Drag" draws from the traditions of the tall tale and the Yiddish joke. Ginsfarb's reaction to his rescue, "Will you ruin me yet?" follows like the punchline of a Yiddish joke, and the fantastic leap to the barn is a tall-tale action. Ginsfarb fits the picaresque comic hero in the line of Don Quixote, acting as Jock's Sancho Panza. Ginsfarb is also a clown, a "Jewish Pagliacco." The subject matter is "Kafkaesque" (Hagopian 1962, 56–58). Robert Harrison speculates that the extreme caricature of Ginsfarb may owe something to the cartoon character Andy Gump (1985, 147). Neither Hagopian nor Harrison develops these literary inheritances in detail. Overall, as an ethnic stereotype, Ginsfarb's character has richer implications for interpretations of the particular text and its relation to Faulkner's other fictions.

## Relationship to Other Faulkner Works

In a letter to Cowley about the *Portable Faulkner*, Faulkner writes of "Death Drag": "What about dropping DEATH DRAG, if something must be eliminated?

That was just a tale, could have happened anywhere, could have been printed as happening anywhere by simply changing the word Jefferson where it occurs, once only I think." In a subsequent letter, Faulkner clarified that he wanted "Death Drag" eliminated only if a choice had to be made in order to make room for the Compson Appendix (*SL* 205, 207).

Actually, the town is not named in the story, but anyone familiar with Faulkner's Jefferson is likely to assume a Jefferson setting just as Faulkner did. The familiar landmarks are there (Watson locates the post office) as well as a character or two who appear in other Jefferson stories (Watson 1987, 94). And even if "Death Drag" is not absolutely identified as a Jefferson tale, it is without question enmeshed in the intricacies of plot, theme, and style that are Faulkner if not Yoknapatawpha.

It is a critical commonplace to say of "Death Drag" that it resembles "Honor" and anticipates *Pylon* (O'Connor 1954, 89; Volpe 1964, 174n; Holmes 1966, 102; Wittenberg 1979, 134; Minter 1980, 146–47; Skei 1985, 312; Karl 1989, 409, 427). Michael Millgate describes Faulkner's attitude toward the aviators as "incredulous amazement, compounded equally of admiration and horror" ([1966] 1989, 138).

Skei finds that dreams and dreamers are an important motif in Faulkner's fiction, especially as represented by the veterans (particularly the pilots) of World War I. In "Death Drag" and "Honor," a brief flashback reveals the characters' service in the war and shows it to be a decisive experience in their lives. Both stories also use the barnstorming way of life to show the inability of many of these men to return to "normal life." The aviators in "Death Drag" may retain some of their dreams but they are otherwise losers, and they are not representative of the men who will modernize the small towns. The dreams reflected in the air shows of these stories affect participants and audience. The show represents the "dream of the easy, free life which the fliers are anxious to keep alive, and the dream of progress and prosperity shared by all inhabitants of the small town." Along with its promise, however, the arrival of modern air travel brings with it "lies, deceit, illegalities, human misery, and death" (Skei 1985, 102–03, 140–41; see also Carothers 1987, 67).

Numerous resemblances can be found between "Death Drag" and *Pylon*. When Irving Howe compares the story to the novel, he judges "Death Drag" to be more successful because the experience of stunt pilots is examined with a "terseness and fluency *Pylon* lacks" ([1952] 1975, 219–20). Duane MacMillan develops the most specific comparisons of the two texts, suggesting that the action in "Death Drag" provides an outline of the action in *Pylon*. The impact of the story "is largely the result of the physical existence of a group of stunt fliers and the danger inherent in such a life." Both texts involve three-member stunt crews performing similarly described, life-threatening stunts played before an audience that is thrilled by the risks the fliers are taking. The size of the crowd and the number of stunts differ, but the pattern is essentially the same (MacMillan 1973, 200).

The portrayal of the aviator's life-style is quite similar in "Death Drag" and *Pylon*. In both works the aviators are bonded together in a way that makes them somehow different from normal people. The airmen are portrayed as more "vitally alive" than the townspeople (Hagopian 1962, 55, 59). MacMillan adds that the aviators in both works are constantly moving, living without financial security, usually trying to stay ahead of the law, and daily facing physical danger and imminent death. The two crews have clearly defined responsibilities; both meticulously keep account of their debts; both subordinate legality and safety to profits and crowd-pleasing. They are all outsiders, lacking a desire for respectability, security, or routine; they have no tradition and foresee no future toward which to direct their actions. Their own group is closed to outsiders; they manipulate and exploit one another in both texts, and they have little concern for personal comfort or social attachments (MacMillan 1973, 200–202, 206–08).

Not surprisingly, the similarities between the two aviator groups generate some particular comparisons of specific characters. Jiggs and Ginsfarb bear strong physical resemblances, but Feinman is Ginsfarb's psychological match. Like Ginsfarb, Feinman is avaricious. "Death Drag" explicitly captures Ginsfarb's hatred for his stunt flying. In *Pylon*, although there is less a sense of hatred, there is no sense of fulfillment or pleasure (MacMillan 1973, 200–202, 206–08). According to Millgate, *Pylon* does not develop the experience of individuals like Captain Warren (Millgate [1966] 1989, 148). MacMillan, on the other hand, believes that the Reporter reacts to the stunts much as Jock does (1973, 201).

In addition to "Honor" and *Pylon* a significant number of other aviator stories bear resemblances to "Death Drag." Edmond Volpe mentions "Landing in Luck" (Volpe 1964, 174n). Cleanth Brooks groups "Death Drag" with a number of stories including those about fighter pilots of World War I. He includes "Ad Astra," "All the Dead Pilots," "Turnabout," Faulkner's review of *Test Pilot* by Jimmy Collins, *Soldiers' Pay*, and *Flags in the Dust*. "Reckless courage" is a common theme in these stories. "Death Drag" differs from the others in working out the theme "in comic terms—albeit comedy filled with absurdity and black humor" (Brooks [1978] 1990, 403–05).

Blotner notices the shift from a young wounded hero in a story like "The Leg" to an older veteran, Captain Warren, in "Death Drag" (Blotner 1976, 12). Like Monaghan and Bayard Sartoris, he is a "drifter and war casualty" (1974, 678; 1984, 270; see also Harrison 1985, 147). Michel Gresset shifts the poles of comparison from Warren and Sartoris to the town and Sartoris. According to Gresset, the community is fascinated by the aviators in much the same way that Bayard Sartoris is fascinated by glamor. Whereas Sartoris "is doomed to repeat military gestures in a civilian setting," in the short story Warren can act as interpreter for the community to decipher the airmen's "incomprehensible prestige" into human activity. He sees the destructive effects the life has had on Jock, and he can spare the community from the immobilizing effects of glamor (Gresset 1989a, 140).

Nancy Sederberg considers "With Caution and Dispatch" to be a "fascinating culmination" of the themes, characters, and motifs of Faulkner's World War I and flying stories. "With Caution and Dispatch" resembles "Death Drag," "Honor," and "Turnabout" in its character types. "Death Drag" and "Honor" use the machines as means of earning money and as entertainment; similarly, "With Caution and Dispatch" suggests the "serious and antic aspects of war." The forty-seven-page typescript that appears in condensed form as the first section of the story includes airplane descriptions that recall those in "Death Drag" and "All the Dead Pilots." Also, the sense of stasis in the later story repeats images in "Death Drag" and "Turnabout" (Sederberg 1985, 190, 198, 200 n. 21, 203 n. 58).

Relational studies of "Death Drag" have not been restricted merely to other aviator stories. Characters, themes, and formal considerations invite a broad range of associations.

The portrayal of Ginsfarb as a Jewish character generates substantial discussion. Generally, as an "ethnic caricature" Ginsfarb is like Mac-Wyrglinchbeath the Scot, Comyn the Irishman, Ploeckner the Prussian, and numerous others (Harrison 1985, 147). Several critics examine the Jewish stereotype in its numerous manifestations in Faulkner's work. Alfred Kutzik points out that the heavily caricatured Ginsfarb and the handsome Jake are described by the narrator as racially different from the townspeople. In fact, a large number of works, including *Soldiers' Pay*, *Mosquitoes*, *The Sound and the Fury*, *Sanctuary*, "There Was a Queen," "Death Drag," "Honor," *Pylon*, *The Wild Palms*, "The Bear," *Intruder in the Dust*, and *Requiem for a Nun*, contain strong anti-Semitic sentiments conveyed in ideology or characterizations of Jews that are "entirely and unequivocally negative." Kutzik locates a shift in anti-Semitic portrayals to a "veritable philo-Semitism" in Faulkner's work. With the appearance of *A Fable* in 1954, Faulkner's texts undergo a revision of Jewish characters. In this novel in the positive characterization of Lieutenant Levine and in the later novel *The Town* (1957), the negative stereotype, especially as it is delineated in "Death Drag," is most radically revised (Kutzik 1965, 216, 220; see also Dobkowski 1979, 103). Lind adds *The Mansion* and *Knight's Gambit* to texts with references to Jews and suggests that the list is likely longer because the references often constitute single words or phrases. She departs from the analyses of Kutzik and Michael Dobkowski because she believes that Faulkner's attitude toward Jewish people is more complex and more sympathetic than either of the earlier critics indicates (Lind 1984, 119–42).

Blotner finds similarities between Warren and Gavin Stevens. Each man "knew the world but chose to live out his life in Jefferson." Warren actually reappears in a Stevens story, the novella *Knight's Gambit* (Blotner 1974, 1286; Blotner 1976, 12; Blotner 1984, 270).

An interesting range of thematic concerns links "Death Drag" to a diverse group of Faulkner's works. "Death Drag," according to Skei, shows Faulkner's portrayal of misused and corrupt power set in a comic context filled with outrageous examples of bargains, shrewdness, and greed. This story is a less significant demonstration than "Thrift" or "Spotted Horses" (Skei 1985, 160). Harrison also associates "Death Drag" and "Thrift"; the "flaw of venality" is present in both (1985, 147).

The aerial stuntman as artist figure in "Death Drag" found in Lind's study appears in a comparable image of the poet in "Carcassonne" on a flying horse and the flying image of Bayard Sartoris as a World War I pilot (1989, 131).

Gresset finds that in Faulkner's fiction voice, the "evocation, both literally and metaphorically, of this quintessential human characteristic," is aligned with the individual. Part of Gresset's argument involves an examination of the word *puny* in various contexts, usually used by the narrator. The word appears early in "Death Drag" when a groundling points out in a "puny" voice the beginning of Ginsfarb's stunt; it is used with regularity in various other texts. The word, Gresset contends, serves "as an objective correlative of 'a passion for unfact,'" that is, the "existence of puny" relates to the "essence of idealism" or the "potency of impotence" (1989b, 184–88).

Wolf Kindermann describes the juxtaposition of "erratic, frantic, or automaton-like movements" to images of "steady progress or motion" in Faulkner's fiction. Ginsfarb's leap joins a lengthy list of erratic movements, such as Bayard Sartoris's automobile accident in *Sartoris* and the Bundrens' efforts to save Addie's coffin from the river in *As I Lay Dying*. Kindermann adds that Faulkner employs a modern, "secularized version of the Christian vanity motif" in an "Icarian image of a man's fall from height." These falls, like Ginsfarb's, or John Sartoris's leap in *Sartoris*, or Donald Mahon's plane crash in *Soldier's Pay*, contrast with the earthbound, steady motion of those characters who "keep in touch with the seasons and the cycle of life" (Kindermann 1989, 48–49).

Ferguson believes that solipsism accounts for many of the problems of Faulkner's characters. Solipsists insist on a justice that balances with their vision. Ginsfarb is one of many examples, perhaps one of the more extreme ones, that reflects a "gap between the desires and aspirations of the individual and the larger realities of human existence." Ginsfarb, unlike many of these characters, achieves his own form of justice because he receives the balance of his fee from Captain Warren (Ferguson 1991, 74–75).

Ferguson also argues that a key theme in Faulkner's stories is the danger of abstraction. "Death Drag," like "Honor," "There Was a Queen," "An Odor of Verbena," "Wash," and others, examines the consequences of the "most abused of all abstractions—honor" (1991, 81).

Another similarity that Ferguson notes is the extent to which Faulkner exhibits a fascination with "lost, maimed, and injured limbs." A partial list of stories in which this concern appears includes *As I Lay Dying*, *A Fable*, "The Tall Men," "Barn Burning," "Mountain Victory," and "Death Drag." Ferguson comments, "In Freudian terms, this preoccupation suggests the fear of castration" (1991, 203 n. 11).

The pervading formal comparison of "Death Drag" to other Faulkner fiction is concerned with the narrative stance of the story. The narrator assumes a communal "we" much as in "A Rose for Emily." In both stories, the events are characterized "through the town's speculation about their nature and meaning." Blotner likens this voice to Charles Mallison's "we" in *The Town* (Blotner 1974, 676, 894, 1606). Linda Wagner adds "Hair," "Idyll in the Desert," and possibly the fourth section of *The Sound and the Fury* as other works that use a townsperson as narrator. These speakers, Wagner adds, are forerunners of Ratliff (1975, 172, 199). Millgate speculates that the early voice of the townspeople as in "Death Drag" and other stories may have belonged to Quentin Compson even though he is not named (1980, 29). Skei claims that the "Death Drag" narrator is more careful than some others about acknowledging when he does not know certain information firsthand—more so, for example, than the speaker in "A Rose for Emily" (1985, 155). Although the narrators of "Death Drag" and "A Rose for Emily" lack "real substance as human beings," they function thematically because they contrast the community values with those of the outsiders who are the focus of the story (Ferguson 1991, 110).

Walter Slatoff places "Death Drag" with the wide range of Faulkner's fiction that Slatoff sees as portraying "potential or imminent activity." In "Death Drag," the tension in Ginsfarb's face is described as though he were, by choice, carrying a bomb that might possibly explode, and the airplane suggests "potential activity" because it possesses a "quality immobile and poised and dynamic" (Slatoff 1960, 55; *CS* 189).

Pursuing still another quality of the story, Ferguson points out that "Death Drag" shares structural similarity with "Mountain Victory," "Divorce in Naples," and "Dull Tale": all these stories begin rather conventionally with a scene that indicates the basic plot tensions and also includes substantial "panoramic background information." The ending is also conventional in that it is a leave-taking, just as it is in such stories as "Mistral," "Snow," and "Divorce in Naples" (Ferguson 1991, 129, 136).

A distinctive feature of Faulkner's short stories is that when one is gathered in a collection, its characterization and theme is enhanced by the surrounding stories. According to Blotner, "Death Drag" contains a character, Jock, "pushed by circumstances beyond the normal boundaries of feeling." In this regard he resembles Monaghan in "Honor," Weddel in "Mountain Victory," and Louise King in "Dr. Martino" (Blotner 1974, 688). Although Blotner does not limit his observation specifically to the *Doctor Martino* context, all his examples come from that collection. Béatrice Lang, however, does direct her observation to that particular grouping. She identifies death as the unifying theme of the *Doctor Martino* collection. "Dr. Martino," "Mountain Victory," "Honor," "Black Music," and "Death Drag" all have characters who reflect the "waste world of the living dead" (Lang 1976, 31). Viewing the collection a bit more broadly, Ferguson shows how the theme of justice, prevalent in Faulkner's work overall, may be seen in various manifestations of the quid pro quo in some of the *Doctor Martino* stories, including "The Hound," "Death Drag," "There Was a Queen," "Smoke," and "Turnabout" (Ferguson 1991, 153–54).

When "Death Drag" is seen within the framework of "The Village" tales of *Collected Stories*, the emphasis shifts. According to Millgate, the cumulative effect of "The Village" is to emphasize the theme of isolation that "becomes the more apparent and the more appalling in the context of the continuing cohesive life of the small town." With this strategy Faulkner links such disparate stories as "Death Drag" and "That Evening Sun" (Millgate [1966] 1989, 273). Philip Momberger's view of "The Village" is that it "typifies the rending of the human community." In "Death Drag," as in "A Rose for Emily" and "That Evening Sun," the outcast characters are "finally abandoned to suffer alone" (Momberger 1978, 21, 27). For Arthur Kinney, "Death Drag" serves in "The Village" to combine the sense of death from "A Rose for Emily," "Dry September," and "Hair" with the theme of exploitation in "Centaur in Brass." Kinney sees Ginsfarb as a tawdry con artist whose "crass greed" betrays the dreams of the townspeople. The story reveals the need for heroes among a dispirited people, a theme that serves to link "Death Drag" to the next two stories, "Elly" and "Uncle Willy" (1980, 67–68). Ferguson sees "The Village" stories as a series of investigations examining "the theme of the relationship between individual and communal values." "Death Drag" is located in the central group of "intensely serious stories" that includes "Dry September," "Elly," and "Uncle Willy" (1991, 158).

## Interpretation and Criticism

Faulkner described "Death Drag" as a story about a "human being in conflict with his environment and his time. This man who hated flying, but that was what he had to do, simply because he wanted to make a little money" (*FU* 68). Faulkner's reference here to Ginsfarb is matched by a similarly dark vision of Jock. Faulkner was asked whether Jock's reason for refusing Warren's offer to stay in town and then to take his coat was his pride.

Faulkner responded that it was. Then he continued, "The—it's—'course is probably true of all flying people out of that war, most of them would have been better off if they had died on the eleventh of November, that few of them were any good to try to take up the burden of peace, and this man was lost and doomed. Of course, Warren was different. He had managed to cope with 1919, but this other man would never cope with 1919. He was hopeless, he was doomed" (*FU* 48).

Critical responses to the text, like Faulkner's comments, seem also to revolve around characterizations in the story. Olga Vickery places "Death Drag" among those Faulkner stories whose main quality is to reveal character ([1959] 1964, 305).

Some critics look to the aviators to get an accurate representation of the contemporary scene. One interpretation sees the aviators as part of a "vanished period of American life—an aspect of the Jazz Age that worshipped noise, speed, and dare-devil stunts." Despite its links to jokes and tall tales, the story is not comic; the aviators "are too grotesque to be simply laughable." These men are incapable of joining in a community relationship with ordinary people. The story reiterates their separateness: they are recognized as different from the townspeople, and the town, unnamed, is specifically described as interchangeable with any other small American town (Hagopian 1962, 55–57).

The story, Karl asserts, reflects America's frame of mind in late 1930, in its "taking something as glamorous as aviation and stunt flying and transforming it into a death wish." The vision is of America as wasteland. Everything is flawed in the story—the barely adequate landing strip, each phase of the stunt, the stuntman's limp, the fliers' general lack of money, and their worn and torn clothing (Karl 1989, 426).

According to Harrison's study, social distinctions that exist in aviation are blurred in the story by the common poverty of the three fliers. Difference in rank appears only in the description of the goggles that Jock and Ginsfarb wear. Faulkner's perspective is the pilot's (Harrison 1985, 147).

More explicit analysis of individual characters focuses almost exclusively on Ginsfarb. The responses are for the most part sympathetic. Howe describes the characterization of a Jewish merchant now stunt jumper as a "savage incongruity." He is a "large aching figure of modern loneliness" who is "alien by birth and need" (Howe [1952] 1975, 220). William Van O'Connor describes Ginsfarb as so intensely determined "that the very solidity of the earth and the laws of physics seem to give way before him." O'Connor interprets Ginsfarb as a man who is "frustrated almost beyond endurance" but who is able "to win a thin margin of victory" (O'Connor 1954, 89).

For Hagopian, the stunt flying provides background for an "unusual, tragi-comic treatment of the Wandering Jew." The stereotype is made personal in the distinct figure of Ginsfarb, who rises above stereotype because of his superiority over the townspeople. He possesses the "vitality, daring, and bravado" that they lack; he is "scrupulously honest in his financial transactions," and "he has inspired the devotion of Jock the pilot." He is a man who, in Captain Warren's words, "deserved justice" (Hagopian 1962, 55–56, 58).

MacMillan's estimation of Ginsfarb is the most critical. Because Ginsfarb, unlike most of the other aviator characters, really risks his life in order to earn money, the reader's estimation of him may be softened, but he remains a corrupt character. There is a clash between the glamorous appearance of the daredevil and Ginsfarb's cynical and mean nature (MacMillan 1973, 206–07).

According to Blotner, Faulkner walked an "exceedingly narrow line . . . mixing the tragic and the farcical." Ginsfarb's physical appearance, his large head and nose and a sharklike jaw, make him a grotesque (Blotner 1974, 678). Brooks characterizes Ginsfarb as a "desperate man" whose rage at being reduced to stunt flying makes him seem inattentive to the danger of the stunts. He is, in Brooks's judgment, neither a "gay cavalier nor a self-conscious hero" ([1978] 1990, 404–05).

Karl and Lind deal more explicitly with the use of stereotype in the Jewish characters. Karl notes that every stereotype of Jewish character appears in the two stuntmen, Ginsfarb and Jake. In his reading, for Faulkner the Jew represents "that part of the world which made everything part of the cash nexus" and consequently "commercializes all heroical potentialities in life" (Karl 1989, 427).

Lind's analysis of Ginsfarb as stereotype has much to do with her argument of similarities between author and character as discussed above. She believes that Howe and O'Connor offer insufficient interpretations of Ginsfarb as a survivor and that the fullest understanding may be reached through biographical parallels. Lind shows how the stereotype is constructed and then subverted. Typical of this comic image, Ginsfarb has only a surname, and he possesses the expected physical attributes—a large nose and a loud, patterned jacket and vaudevillian "Weber and Fields" pronunciations (*CS* 187). The comic attributes of the stereotype, however, give way to its darker aspects, those of the "criminal Jew." Ginsfarb violates aviation law and is dirty. The effect, Lind contends, is "to convey the idea that Ginsfarb's operation, as a money-making enterprise, is a dirty business." Further, Ginsfarb is portrayed as unpatriotic when he expresses disdain over the idea of serving in the war, and cowardly when the aviators perceive the need to advertise his exploits under the name "Demon Duncan" instead of "Ginsfarb." Ginsfarb is not wholly a stereotype; his motivation is "grim necessity," rather than greed. His fearlessness contradicts any presumption of cowardice and actually seems a magical power. His face is tragic, not comic. Lind concludes that the stereotype is deconstructed but is also transformed by having been put "to service in relation to a worthy artistic aim" (Lind 1989, 129–31).

In Harrison's view, Ginsfarb's death drag is not portrayed as heroic, but the life-saving efforts of the pilot, who himself is a "washout and technically even a criminal," demonstrate skill and courage (Harrison 1985, 147).

Faulkner's comments about Warren have received little critical supplement. Blotner notes that Warren has sympathy for Jock that the other townspeople lack, and as discussed earlier, Gresset sees him as having escaped the immobilizing trap that compels Bayard Sartoris to try to repeat the glories of past actions (Blotner 1974, 677–78; Gresset 1989a, 140).

The formal characteristics of "Death Drag" have generated analysis chiefly following the same concerns seen in the relational comments. According to Howe, "'Death Drag' is one of the few Faulkner stories that creates a dramatic fable with a distinct beginning and a firm end, and creates it in terms of the emotional urgency that the story form requires. . . . the central idea or *donnée* of the story is so conclusive there is no need for him to do anything but allow it to move, uncluttered, toward its end." The swift movement into and out of the narration of one event mimics the manner of the fliers themselves. Faulkner succeeds in maintaining a "firm point of view through harsh economy and ironic qualification" (Howe [1952] 1975, 264, 219–20).

Francis Connolly traces the various threads the narrator weaves together—what he experienced himself and what he has been told so that he develops a composite impression. Exposition comes after rather than before action and therefore complicates the chronology. Connolly stresses Faulkner's attempts to portray the emotional tone and focus of the stuntmen, the bystanders, and Captain Warren. The "lyric, comic, and melodramatic sides of his story" are all considered (Connolly 1955, 705).

Hagopian describes the narrator as an older male "with a certain poetic sensibility." He observes that in the second section, when the narrator conveys the information Captain Warren has shared, the diction reflects a more straightforward style. He contends that the time of Warren's recollection is several months after the flight and the implication is "that Ginsfarb may have died in the course of his dare-devil act." Part III further reinforces the possibility of Ginsfarb's death as it returns to the time of the stunt, because the language implies death in its descriptions of "groans" and "dead voices." The final section, returning to Warren's account, inverts the expectation of death and reveals the "comic reversal of Ginsfarb's dogged persistence" (Hagopian 1962, 58).

Few comments relate to the imagery of the story, but those that have dealt with the repetition of images have done so profitably. Part of Hagopian's argument about Ginsfarb's survival is the association of the words *death* and *groan* with descriptions of the fall. The pervasiveness of terms related to death, he also points out, is applied to aviators and community. While the paint on the plane is "dead black" and all three aviators speak in a "dead voice," the town is one of thousands of "dead clottings." The effect is to portray the townspeople as even less alive than the aviators (Hagopian 1962, 58–59; *CS* 185, 189, 197). Lind traces the "dark coloration of its imagery" particularly in the recurring use of *black* and *death* as part of the "essential somberness of this comic tale." It is part of Faulkner's probing into "'the dark . . . heart of things'" (Lind 1989, 131).

Harrison praises Faulkner's technical accuracy in describing aviation. Among his numerous observations of Faulkner's attention to actual conditions of flight, Harrison notes that barnstormers did "buzz" small towns and watch for signs of interest before landing and setting up a show, and in Ginsfarb's defense, one hundred dollars was a low price for performing the stunt. The scant loop, however, would have required no less fuel than a well-executed loop (Harrison 1985, 147–51).

"Death Drag" has been both dismissed and praised by critics. Walter Everett refers to "Death Drag" as a "sketch" weakened by the unexplained bond among the threesome (1969, 138). Max Putzel ranks "Death Drag" as the "slightest" of Faulkner's stories on the war and its aftermath (1985, 125). Yet in an early review, William Rose Benét describes the story as one in which Faulkner "deals in grim humor that is most effective"; Howe considers it a "small masterpiece"; Hagopian includes it with "A Rose for Emily" and "That Evening Sun" in his analyses of selected Faulkner stories (Benét 1934, 645; Howe [1952] 1975, 220; Hagopian 1962, 41–59). Skei remarks that the story presented the contemporary scene "with poignancy and understanding," and Ferguson groups "Death Drag" with stories of "considerable merit" (Skei 1981, 68; Ferguson 1991, 36). The stereotyping of Ginsfarb and Jake initially seems superficial, but as Lind's work makes clear, studying Faulkner's use of stereotype yields provocative interpretation. Additional critical inquiry into "Death Drag" might include further examination of narrative perspective. The narrator admits retelling a composite portrait and adds that the retelling "is hard" because except for Warren, the witnesses "had so little in experience to postulate it with" (*CS* 200). What might this limitation imply about the village, Jefferson (that Faulkner saw in this tale even if he did not state it), but that is also a "small town interchangeable with and duplicate of ten thousand little dead clottings of human life about the land" (*CS* 198)? Perhaps with further effort, the critical community too may come to a clearer, composite understanding of the text. Faulkner, like Warren, has provided enabling clues.

## Works Cited

Benét, William Rose. 1934. "Fourteen Faulkner Stories." *Saturday Review of Literature* 21 April, 645.

Blotner, Joseph. 1974. *Faulkner: A Biography*. 2 vols. New York: Random House.

———. 1976. "The Sole Owner and Proprietor." In *Faulkner: Fifty Years After* The Marble Faun. Ed. George H. Wolfe. University: University of Alabama Press, 1–20.

———. 1984. *Faulkner: A Biography*. 1 vol. New York: Random House.

Brooks, Cleanth. [1978] 1990. *William Faulkner: Toward Yoknapatawpha and Beyond*. New Haven: Yale University Press. Reprint. Baton Rouge: Louisiana State University Press.

Carothers, James B. 1987. "'I Ain't a Soldier Now': Faulkner's World War II Veterans." *Faulkner Journal* 2:67–74.

Connolly, Francis. 1955. *The Types of Literature*. New York: Harcourt, Brace.

Dobkowski, Michael N. 1979. *The Tarnished Dream: The Basis of American Anti-Semitism*. Westport, CT: Greenwood.

Emerson, O. B. 1984. *Faulkner's Early Literary Reputation in America*. Ann Arbor, MI: UMI Research Press.

Everett, Walter K. 1969. *Faulkner's Art and Character*. Woodbury, NY: Barron's Educational Series.

Falkner, Murry C. 1967. *The Falkners of Mississippi*. Baton Rouge: Louisiana State University.

Faulkner, William. 1932. "Death-Drag." *Scribner's* 91 (January): 34–42.

———. 1934. *Doctor Martino and Other Stories*. New York: Harrison Smith and Robert Haas.

———. [1946] 1977. *The Portable Faulkner*. Rev. ed. Ed. Malcolm Cowley. London: Penguin.

———. 1950. *Collected Stories of William Faulkner*. New York: Random House.

———. 1959. *Faulkner in the University: Class Conferences at the University of Virginia, 1957–1958*. Ed. Frederick Gwynn and Joseph L. Blotner. Charlottesville: University Press of Virginia.

———. 1977. *Selected Letters of William Faulkner*. Ed. Joseph Blotner. New York: Random House.

———. 1987. *William Faulkner Manuscripts 9*: These 13 Ed. Noel Polk. New York: Garland.

———. 1987. *William Faulkner Manuscripts 11:* Doctor Martino and Other Stories. Ed. Thomas L. McHaney. New York: Garland.

Ferguson, James. 1991. *Faulkner's Short Fiction*. Knoxville: University of Tennessee Press.

Gresset, Michel. 1989a. *Fascination: Faulkner's Fiction, 1919–1936*. Trans. Thomas West. Durham, NC: Duke University Press.

———. 1989b. "Faulkner's Voice." In *Faulkner's Discourse: An International*

*Symposium*. Ed. Lothar Hönnighausen. Tübingen: Max Niemeyer Verlag, 184–94.

Hagopian, John V. 1962. "'Death Drag.'" In *Insight I: Analyses of American Literature*. Ed. John V. Hagopian and Martin Dolch. Frankfurt am Main: Hirschgraben-Verlag, 55–59.

Harrison, Robert. 1985. *Aviation Lore in Faulkner*. Amsterdam and Philadelphia: John Benjamins.

Holmes, Edward M. 1966. *Faulkner's Twice-Told Tales: His Re-Use of His Material*. The Hague: Mouton.

Howe, Irving. [1952] 1975. *William Faulkner: A Critical Study*. 3d ed. Chicago: University of Chicago Press.

Karl, Frederick R. 1989. *William Faulkner: American Writer*. New York: Weidenfeld and Nicolson.

Kindermann, Wolf. 1989. "Visual Motion in Faulkner's Narrative Art." In *Faulkner's Discourse: An International Symposium*. Ed. Lothar Hönnighausen. Tübingen: Max Niemeyer Verlag, 46–52.

Kinney, Arthur F. 1980. "Faulkner's Narrative Poetics and *Collected Stories*." *Faulkner Studies* 1:58–79.

Kutzik, Alfred J. 1965. "Faulkner and the Jews." *Yivo Annual of Jewish Social Science* 13:213–26.

Lang, Béatrice. 1976. "'Dr. Martino': The Conflict of Life and Death." *Delta* 3 (November): 23–33.

Lind, Ilse Dusoir. 1984. "Faulkner's Relationship to Jews: A Beginning." In *New Direction in Faulkner Studies: Faulkner and Yoknapatawpha, 1983*. Ed. Doreen Fowler and Ann J. Abadie. Jackson: University Press of Mississippi, 119–42.

———. 1989. "The Language of Stereotype in 'Death Drag.'" In *Faulkner's Discourse: An International Symposium*. Ed. Lothar Hönnighausen. Tübingen: Max Niemeyer Verlag, 127–31.

MacMillan, Duane. 1973. "*Pylon*: From Short Stories to Major Work." *Mosaic* 7:185–212.

Meriwether, James B. [1961] 1971. *The Literary Career of William Faulkner: A Bibliographical Study*. Princeton, NJ: Princeton University Library. Reprint. Columbia: University of South Carolina Press.

———. 1973. "Faulkner's Correspondence with *Scribner's Magazine*." *Proof* 3:253–82.

Millgate, Michael. [1966] 1989. *The Achievement of William Faulkner*. New York: Random House. Reprint. Athens: University of Georgia Press. Brown Thrasher Books.

———. 1980. "'A Cosmos of My Own': The Evolution of Yoknapatawpha." In *Fifty Years of Yoknapatawpha: Faulkner and Yoknapatawpha 1979*. Ed. Doreen Fowler and Ann J. Abadie. Jackson: University Press of Mississippi, 23–43.

Minter, David. 1980. *William Faulkner: His Life and Work*. Baltimore: Johns Hopkins University Press.

Momberger, Philip. 1978. "Faulkner's 'The Village' and 'That Evening Sun': The Tale in Context." *Southern Literary Journal* 11.1:20–31.

O'Connor, William Van. 1954. *The Tangled Fire of William Faulkner*. Minneapolis: University of Minnesota Press.

Putzel, Max. 1977. "Faulkner's Short Story Sending Schedule." *Papers of the Bibliographical Society of America* 71:98–105.

———. 1985. *Genius of Place: William Faulkner's Triumphant Beginnings*. Baton Rouge: Louisiana State University Press.

Sederberg, Nancy Belcher. 1985. "'With Caution and Dispatch': 'Deliberate speed, majestic instancy.'" In *Critical Essays on William Faulkner: The Sartoris Family*. Ed. Arthur F. Kinney. Boston: G. K. Hall, 190–203.

Skei, Hans H. 1981. *William Faulkner: The Short Story Career*. Oslo, Norway: Universitetsforlaget.

———. 1985. *William Faulkner: The Novelist as Short Story Writer*. Oslo, Norway: Universitetsforlaget.

Slatoff, Walter J. 1960. *Quest for Failure: A Study of William Faulkner*. Ithaca, NY: Cornell University Press.

Vickery, Olga W. [1959] 1964. *The Novels of William Faulkner*. Baton Rouge: Louisiana State University Press.

Volpe, Edmond L. [1964] 1989. *A Reader's Guide to William Faulkner*. New York: Noonday. Reprint. New York: Octagon Books.

Wagner, Linda Welshimer. 1975. *Hemingway and Faulkner: Inventors/Masters*. Metuchen, NJ: Scarecrow Press.

Watson, James G. 1987. *William Faulkner: Letters and Fictions*. Austin: University of Texas Press.

Wittenberg, Judith Bryant. 1979. *Faulkner: The Transfiguration of Biography*. Lincoln: University of Nebraska Press.

# Elly

## Publication History

"Elly" first appeared in *Story* magazine in February 1934, a month in which three other Faulkner stories were published in three different magazines. From records in the story-sending schedule, the earliest publication effort can be dated sometime before March 25, 1930, with submission to *Scribner's* under the title "Salvage." December 1928 is a likely date for the submission. Faulkner wrote an undated letter to Alfred Dashiell of *Scribner's* as a cover to a carbon copy of "Salvage." He assumed that the original, sent in December, had been lost because he had received no response (*SL* 42; see also Blotner 1974, 604). The reply to Faulkner's follow-up was a rejection letter from *Scribner's* dated February 23, 1929. The *Scribner's* editor thought the story "too febrile" to be of use to the magazine (Meriwether 1973, 259). Faulkner tried again with *Forum*, dating his submission April 16, 1930, and *Liberty*, May 2, 1930. Both of these submissions carried the title "Selvage" not "Salvage." It is unclear whether or not these different titles reflect changes in the story as well as in the title. The title "Elly" was used on a substantially revised text when submission efforts resumed some years later (Meriwether [1961] 1971, 175, 177–79; Skei 1981, 49–50).

Apparently, Faulkner let Ben Wasson handle publication attempts for "Elly." On July 21, 1933, Wasson forwarded it to Alfred Dashiell at *Scribner's* with a glowing comment: "This story called ELLY . . . seems to me to be one of the most brilliant stories he has ever written. I know that you will be inclined to agree with me." But a letter from Dashiell that almost certainly refers to "Elly" records his disappointment; he thought the story seemed "to verge too closely on the pathological" (Meriwether 1973, 275–76). Earlier "febrile" and now "pathological," "Elly" would not appear in *Scribner's*. It is uncertain what if any submissions Faulkner or Wasson may have attempted between the *Scribner's* rejection and the *Story* acceptance. In all likelihood "Elly" did not bring the author much money. *Story* paid low rates for its acquisitions, usually not more than $25 (Skei 1981, 113 n. 5). "Elly" was included in two collections: *Doctor Martino and Other Stories* (1934) and *Collected Stories* (1950).

## Circumstances of Composition, Sources, and Influences

The composition history of "Elly" includes an uncommon instance of collaboration between Faulkner and another author. The 1929 rejection letter from *Scribner's* refers to a joint authorship with "E. Oldham" (Meriwether 1973, 259). Estelle Oldham Franklin had been back in Oxford for some time awaiting her divorce from Cornell Franklin and her marriage to Faulkner. According to Blotner, the joint composition was a "sequential rather than a simultaneous collaboration." Estelle had the original idea but was dissatisfied when she wrote the story. When she showed the story to Faulkner, he wanted to work with her on a revision. Although Estelle was not interested, she was willing for Faulkner to do what he could with the draft. According to Estelle's later recollections, Faulkner's manuscript retained essentially the same plot, but the "texture thickened and darkened" (Blotner 1974, 604).

The earliest extant manuscript is entirely in Faulkner's handwriting. No "Salvage" texts are known to exist, although the extant manuscripts and typescripts of "Selvage" and "Elly" are available in *William Faulkner Manuscripts 11*. They include a manuscript and typescript of "Selvage" and a manuscript of "Elly." Hans Skei suggests that these documents represent intermediate versions of the story. It is possible that "Salvage" and "Selvage" may refer to the same story by way of "a slip of the pen or of memory," but Skei believes that the manuscript of "Selvage" is probably "a totally new manuscript based on the refused carbon typescript from *Scribner's*." The "Elly" manuscript is substantially revised from the "Selvage" version. It shows some differences from the published story; nevertheless, even if additional revisions and the making of a typescript intervened between it and the *Story* text, the "Elly" manuscript is probably a very late version (1981, 49–50). From his study of the story's development in the available "Selvage" and "Elly" manuscripts and typescripts, Edmond Volpe concludes that although the revisions substantially retain the original plot, they significantly improve by means of expansion the "connections between the external and internal dramas." In "Selvage" the reader must work much harder to infer from meager suggestions the underlying causes for the actions of the young woman (named Corinthia Bowman). The addition of the flashback, approximately eight pages in *Collected Stories*, conveys Elly's mental state more explicitly (Volpe 1989, 273–74).

The flashback constitutes the most substantial and important development in the text, but deletions also serve to emphasize Elly's mental state. Volpe describes several emotionally charged passages that are deleted. Eliminating some of the Elly–Paul conversations (or arguments) heightens concentration on the conflict within Elly herself (Volpe 1989, 275).

Volpe suggests that "'Adolescence' may have been 'Elly' in embryo" although Blotner's note in *Uncollected Stories* makes no similar claim (Volpe

1989, 278 n. 10; *US* 704). The story resembles "Elly" in that both stories include situations of conflict between a young female and her grandmother, but "Adolescence" maintains its identity as an autonomous story.

Once "Elly" appeared in print, Faulkner made no further revisions in the subsequent collections. The only difference is the correction of a typographical error that appeared in the magazine text.

Just as the story originated with Estelle Oldham Franklin, the biographical correspondences begin with her life. As a young woman, she accepted a marriage proposal from a student at the University of Mississippi—Ole Miss. Blotner suggests that her acceptance was probably as lighthearted as the acceptance she had already given to Cornell Franklin. She probably had no real intention of marrying either man. Her father, however, was furious and declared that she could not marry the student. In his revised biography, Blotner adds that the young man "had Negro blood" (1974, 193; 1984, 233).

Frederick Karl also detects the presence of Estelle in Elly's story but in a much different way. He argues that for Faulkner Estelle became the "standard by which other women could be measured," and that his fiction usually contained an Estelle figure. Karl compares Elly's relationships with Paul and Philip to the actual Estelle–Faulkner–Franklin triangle. Paul's unacceptability represents Faulkner's lack of equivalent social standing with Estelle. The Falkners were "socially beneath" the Oldhams. The comparison also extends to Elly's reflection of Estelle's own rebellious streak (1989, 380–81). Another story that began with Estelle's ideas was "Idyll in the Desert" (Blotner 1974, 643). Karl believes that it, too, recalls Faulkner's relationship to Estelle but in a more subtle manner (1989, 406).

Suggestions of literary influence also affect the development of characters, their conflicts, and how they are portrayed. Norman Nicholson contends that "Elly" exhibits "a search through the Negro blood for the 'dark consciousness' of pure sensation and for contact with the primitive." He likens this quality to D. H. Lawrence's portrayals of women who give themselves to Mexican Indians or gypsies ([1943] 1945, 137). (Nicholson incorrectly states that Elly is pregnant. She only suggests the possibility to press Paul into marriage and to irritate her grandmother [[1943] 1945, 137].) M. E. Bradford calls "Elly" an "ironic dissection" that recalls the work of Sherwood Anderson but is less compassionate than Anderson's work (1968, 181).

Alice Petry finds numerous literary analogues for particular characteristics in "Elly," for example, George Washington Cable's "Madame Delicieuse," which employs blood-related characters to represent generational conflicts in the South. She maintains that Faulkner's use of doubles could have been inspired by models in the work of Joseph Conrad, Charles Dickens, Fyodor Dostoevsky, Samuel Clemens, and Henry James, all writers Faulkner admired. Petry notes that if Elly is interpreted in the tradition of the flapper, she should be seen as a failed flapper because she is guilt-ridden. Petry points out that like Elly, F. Scott Fitzgerald's Nicole Diver also tries to commit vehicular homicide and suicide in *Tender Is the Night* (1986, 226, 229, 232–33 nn. 4, 8, 21). Joan Serafin reaches back to classic literature in her analogy between the story of Pyramus and Thisbe and Elly's whispering to Paul through the angle in the wall (1983, 32–33).

Critics examining literary associations between "Elly" and other works typically find few in the works of other authors. By comparison, the most significant literary influences on the short story are the recurring characters, themes, and techniques in Faulkner's own *oeuvre*.

## Relationship to Other Faulkner Works

Dorothy Tuck finds Elly "a unique female character in Faulkner's fiction" (1964, 166). It is true that few Faulkner women are quite so determined. Within Faulkner's short fiction, Skei find Elly's opposition to her guardians more extreme than that of other females (1979, 15). Nevertheless, as Skei and numerous other critics have agreed, Elly particularly and the story generally are characteristically Faulkner as the particular comparison that follow will demonstrate.

In his study of Faulkner's work from 1927 to 1931, Noel Polk identifies several predominant concerns that bear particular relevance to "Elly." The earliest stories from this period are frequently "intense, internalized stories of repression and frustration," often pairing a domineering authority figure with a child or young adult (Polk 1985, 33).

Elly's grandmother resembles a number of Faulkner matriarchs in both appearance and attitude. Bradford likens Elly's grandmother to the matriarchs Virginia DuPre in "There Was a Queen" and Samantha Ewing in "Golden Land." These women possess "totemic significance" in "their agency as value transmitters" (1968, 182 n. 4). Frequently, the response to these women is more specifically critical than Bradford's interpretation. Blotner compares the familial pattern established in "Elly"—a young person opposed by "a harsh and tyrannical parent-figure"—to that in "Miss Zilphia Gant" and "Adolescence" (1974, 604). Polk extends the list of gray-haired authority figures, particularly mothers or grandmothers, to include—with Elly's grandmother—Jenny DuPre in "There was a Queen," Caroline Compson, Caddy Compson, and Mrs. Bland in *The Sound and the Fury*, Addie Bundren in *As I Lay Dying*, Narcissa Benbow and Belle Mitchell in *Flags in the Dust* and other works, and Mrs. Boyd in "The Brooch" (1985, 31–32; Polk 1984, 65–67). James Carothers adds Rosa Coldfield in *Absalom, Absalom!* to comparisons with Elly's grandmother (1985, 27).

Paired with the domineering mother figure is the child who is the recipient of her attention. Not surprisingly, some of the bad mothers that critics compare to Elly's grandmother compare also with Elly because when these women were younger, they, too, felt the weight of a repressive hand. The list of characters and stories with Elly-like characters is long and often repeated from critic to critic. The grounds of comparison are often different, however, and sometimes contradictory, demonstrating that even when certain types are discernible in the fiction, the individual characters can be quite different.

Irving Malin presents one of the earliest examinations of Elly, defining her as one of Faulkner's "willful flappers." These are women intent on enjoyment, particularly sexual freedom. He includes Elly with Temple Drake of *Sanctuary*, Cecily Saunders of *Soldiers' Pay*, and Patricia Robyn and Jenny Steinbauer of *Mosquitoes*. Elly and Temple are especially similar in that they become corrupt and destructive. Malin argues that Faulkner "does not suggest adequately the abuses which are responsible, in part, for a Temple or an Elly," fails to incorporate an "investigation of male influences," and is (excluding Temple) "unfair and sensational" in his portrayal of willful women (1957, 31–35).

Elizabeth Kerr examines a wide range of Faulkner's females in the novels and short fiction. She finds in Elly and Narcissa Benbow, who appears in *Sartoris* and several other stories, evidence "that strange turmoil may exist beneath the appearance of virtue and that the 'pure young girl' may actually be a skillful hypocrite [*sic*]" (1961–62, 6). Kerr adds that Faulkner fashions various responses to the "cult of pure Southern womanhood." Elly's extreme behavior compares to the rash actions of Narcissa, Emily Grierson, and Drusilla in *The Unvanquished*, Minnie Cooper in "Dry September," and Caddy Compson. Both Elly and Emily "resort to murder to escape from the role society offers them." Their selfish motives for murder contrast with Nancy's unselfish and therefore more excusable murder in *Requiem for a Nun* (Kerr [1969] 1976, 159, 214–15). Bradford finds parallels in the characterizations of Elly, Temple Drake, and Charlotte Rittenmeyer of *The Wild Palms*. These three females all refuse to accept limitations on their freedom and reject "the duties which come with [their] sex"; by these actions, they injure themselves and people around them (1968, 186).

Sally Page finds similarities in Elly, Zilphia Gant, Temple Drake, and Cecily Saunders based on their "perversion of physical love." Characters who misuse sexuality are associated with violent, painful, and horrifying portrayals of death. They are found in "Elly," "Miss Zilphia Gant," "Dry September," "A Rose for Emily," "Idyll in the Desert," *As I Lay Dying*, *Absalom, Absalom!*, and *The Wild Palms* (1972, 94, 134). Peggy Flynn, like Page, believes these women are related to death, an association between the sister figure and "Little Sister Death," a figure from St. Francis of Assisi. Flynn explains that Faulkner alters the figure of Little Sister Death, which originally represents the dying saint, "welcoming death with abiding faith, as a beloved sister." Flynn continues, "Conversely, Faulkner began with the pleasant and familiar figure of the little sister, transforming her, by means of a dark and perverted love, into a symbol of pain and death" (Flynn 1976, 105–17). Elly's rejection of authority, manifested by her promiscuity, is also seen in "Hair" and "The Brooch" (Blotner 1974, 683). Béatrice Lang adds "Dr. Martino" to those stories in which the female character's deviance from the norm constitutes pathological behavior (1976, 23). Elly, like Temple, "reacts with shallow pettiness" when faced with tragedy (Flynn 1976, 115–16). Ilse Lind also comments that for female protagonists such as Marietta in *The Marionettes*, Caddy, Temple, and Elly, Faulkner depicts the loss of virginity as leading to death (1986, 31).

Based on an extensive study of story composition, Skei, like Polk, concludes that the young girl in conflict with authority figures is most prevalent in Faulkner's early stories, especially those written before 1930; this theme appears in a number of the works in *Doctor Martino and Other Stories*. Skei adds "Adolescence," "Nympholepsy," Mrs. Blair in "Fox Hunt," and Louise King in "Dr. Martino" to the stories and characters that fit the list. These conflicts involve "an incessant fight for power" especially in "Elly," "Fox Hunt," "Dr. Martino," and "The Brooch." Typically, according to Skei, the women reconcile themselves in some form of "silent acquiescence." Elly, however, distinguishes herself by rebelling early in her life. She also differs from some of the other female characters by being one of the few sexually active women from an upper-class background. She contrasts with Zilphia Gant because Elly, unlike Zilphia, lives in a two-parent home with seemingly decent, well-adjusted people (Skei 1979, 15–16, 18, 22 n. 1–2; Skei 1985, 38, 107, 114, 120–121, 125, 127, 160).

Carothers adds Ike McCaslin's wife in *Go Down, Moses* to the extensive catalogue of "frustrated women" comparable to Elly in Faulkner's fiction (1985, 20). Elsewhere, Carothers identifies a group of women who come into conflict with the negative attitude toward female sexuality that constitutes the "prevailing community standard": Elly, Caddy Compson, Charlotte Rittenmeyer, Eula Varner, Emily Grierson, Minnie Cooper, and Zilphia Gant (1992, 49). James Ferguson notes three points of similarity in these stories: the trapped woman's revenge, the "Terrible Mother," and the romance with an outsider. Ferguson includes "Frankie and Johnny," "Adolescence," "The Leg," "Mistral," and "Mountain Victory" among the stories portraying "women in difficult or impossible situations" (Ferguson 1991, 34, 70, 74, 80).

The domination of the young woman sometimes results in a forced marriage. Elly becomes engaged to Philip. The narrator of "Hair" argues that Susan Reed's problem was that she was ready for marriage before she was old enough (*CS* 133). The idea of a forced marriage also appears in "Fox Hunt" (Blotner 1974, 645; see also Skei 1985, 104). "Elly" compares with stories that take a slightly different twist on the marriage theme. Estella Schoenberg traces the "theme of the murdered bridegroom" in several long and short works:

Paul de Montigny in "Elly," Charles Bon in "Evangeline," and *Absalom, Absalom!*, Dalton Ames and Herbert Head (Quentin's wish to kill them) in *The Sound and the Fury*, the fiancé in "Mistral," and Brix in "Snow." Not all of these, Paul for instance, technically become husbands, but they follow a similar pattern. Schoenberg adds that Thomas Sutpen resembles Paul because he too is killed for refusing to be a bridegroom (1977, 50–58; see also Pilkington 1981, 165–66). "A Rose for Emily" easily fits into this topical grouping.

"Elly" reflects other Faulknerian concerns in addition to the battling guardians and children. The matter of Paul's heritage relates to Faulkner's attention to racial issues in the South. In his review of *Doctor Martino*, William Rose Benét observes that characters in both "Mountain Victory" and "Elly" are "suspected of being negroes" (1934, 645). Charles Nilon analyzes the connotative value of the label "Negro." He shows how in *Light in August* and "Elly" social behavior is affected by the label. In "Elly," the conflict between the social code and Elly's individual desires compels her to try to kill her lover and herself (Nilon 1965, 74–75). Nilon omits the death of Elly's grandmother, but once her grandmother threatens to expose Elly's relationship with Paul, Elly considers her grandmother's death to be necessary (*CS* 221). The prejudice has passed from one generation to the next. It reveals itself in Elly's friend's comments and in Elly's grandmother's recoil "violently backward as a snake does to strike" (*CS* 209, 211). In an earlier study Kerr argues that Faulkner makes a "startling departure from convention" in his portrayal of miscegenation in "Elly." Elly pursues a man of color even though mixed-race sexual relations usually involved white men and women of color ([1969] 1976, 165 n. 44). Carothers emphasizes that "Elly," like "Dry September," "That Evening Sun," and "There Was a Queen," scrutinizes more contemporary racial attitudes than the investigations in such other works as *Go Down, Moses* (1985, 20). Erskine Peters believes that in "Elly," *Light in August*, *Absalom, Absalom!*, and *Go Down, Moses*, Faulkner is trying "to deracinate" the "myth of miscegenation" (1983, 116). Other specific correlations between "Elly" and *Absalom, Absalom!* include the image in both texts of the older women, the grandmother and Rosa Coldfield, recoiling at contact with black flesh (Peters 1983, 117). Paul and Charles are both from Louisiana with French origins and both are killed. Charles's death constitues the death of a kinsman, as does the death of the grandmother (Hall 1986, 108 n. 7). In both texts, the racial issue is complicated by a sense of mixed motives in people's reactions to one another. In both works a desire for revenge serves as a motive for the romantic relationships (Peters 1983, 117; Hall 1986, 65).

Carothers associates "Elly" with those stories in which discovery of evil is basic to the plot. In "Elly," "Pennsylvania Station," and "That Will Be Fine," the respective protagonists fail to recognize the evil that touches their lives. He contends that in Elly's case she "refuses to understand her own willfulness" (Carothers 1985, 10).

Tracing recurring patterns in Faulkner's short fiction, Olga Vickery characterizes several varieties of the hunt. She places "Elly" (not "Miss Elly," as she titles the story) in a subclassification of hunt stories in which human game is the object of the hunter's sexual desires. Vickery traces this pattern in a wide range of the stories, some of which include "My Grandmother Millard," "Hair," "A Rose for Emily," and "Elly." The same pattern appears in Ike's love for the cow in *The Hamlet* and Joanna Burden's pursuit of Joe Christmas through her garden in *Light in August*. Elly, Emily, and Joanna Burden demonstrate how, when a woman is the Obsessed Lover, "humor is replaced by an intensity bordering on hysteria" (Vickery [1959] 1964, 304).

Skei links "Elly" to "The Leg" through the first name used for Elly, Corinthia. It reappears in the name Everbe Corinthia, a character in "The Leg." Everbe Corinthia is a beautiful female "who casts a spell over the young boys." Skei does not use the name as a means by which to link "Elly" with *The Reivers* in which another Everbe Corinthia appears (Skei 1979, 21).

Skei credits Karen Endres with pointing out in an unpublished paper that the name Ailanthia, which is shared by Elly and her grandmother, appears in *Sanctuary* in the form "Ailanthus," the genus name of the heaven-tree planted in the corner of the jailyard (Skei 1979, 24 n. 13). Petry adds that although the tree is a lovely shade tree, it has a foul smell and is known locally as "stinkweed." Like the Ailanthias in the story, it is both attractive and repulsive. Faulkner's use of shared names across generations appears elsewhere, such as the Quentins in *The Sound and the Fury* and the Bayard Sartorises in *Sartoris* (Petry 1986, 231, 222).

Carothers finds that Faulkner frequently presents death ambiguously. Death is suggested through imagery and the details of a situation but the actual death is left unconfirmed. "Elly" has this characteristic as do "The Leg," "That Evening Sun," "Barn Burning," "Mountain Victory," and "Carcassonne," *Light in August* and *The Mansion* (Carothers 1984, 219).

In his investigation of letters in Faulkner's fiction, James Watson groups the notes in "Elly" with correspondence in "Idyll in the Desert," "A Rose for Emily," and "Miss Zilphia Gant" based on their common use of letters to "convey the themes of separation and betrayal." Using old dance cards as the means of communication might suggest "the dark, back side of acceptable courtships." Like the letters in "There Was a Queen," "The Leg," "Miss Zilphia Gant," and "A Rose for Emily," the notes in "Elly" contribute to the "language and the psychology of sexual repression" (Watson 1987, 95, 101). Unlike the other correspondence, the dance card notes are woman-to-woman and may also imply a desperate, unsuccessful effort by women to find a mutual voice within their circumscribed context.

Faulkner attempts in "Elly" as he does in so many of his works, *Absalom, Absalom!* and "Carcassonne," for example, to find a way to express thought as Stephen Ross describes it, "more powerfully than speech can." In "Elly," the effort to capture "loud thinking" appears in the image of Elly's blood talking to her (Ross 1989, 142–44; *CS* 211).

According to Ferguson, the use of a flashback so that the story may begin *in medias res* appears in "Elly" and "The Brooch." Other stories, including the highly regarded "Dry September," "Red Leaves," and "Mule in the Yard," adopt the technique of beginning at a moment of crisis in the story. (Ferguson adds, however, that the unfolding action in "Elly" is barely credible.) Use of the third-person limited narrative in "Elly," "The Brooch," and "The Hound," because of the constraints it imposes on perspective, emphasizes the solipsism of these stories (Ferguson 1991, 98, 128–29, 144).

Within the fourteen stories in *Doctor Martino*, "Elly" is one of a number about people in revolt, including the protagonists of "Beyond," "Wash," "Black Music," and "The Leg" (Ferguson 1991, 154). "Elly" makes an appropriate fit in "The Village" section of *Collected Stories*. In Philip Momberger's estimation, these ten stories build a picture of a disintegrating community. He compares Elly's boredom with the town with the wasteland attitude present in Quentin Compson's need to look to other times in "That Evening Sun" and with the description of the town in "Death Drag." "Elly" also reflects the racial and familial conflicts in the other stories and the oppressive need to keep up appearances (Momberger 1978, 21–25, 29–31). Arthur Kinney views the ten stories as various portrayals of a dispirited community. Elly's need for love and recognition is ignored until she causes the wreck, an action that must be given attention. (Kinney incorrectly identifies Elly's mother, not her grandmother, as one of the victims.) Elly, Sarty Snopes, Uncle Willy, Alec Gray, and Moketubbe (not Motubbe) are characters from different sections of the collection who have experienced the death of the spirit (Kinney 1980, 68, 71). The position of "Elly," preceding "Uncle Willy," informs the text of that story regarding the potential danger of individuals who clash with the community. The consequences of Elly's behavior imply that Uncle Willy's protégé is lucky to have survived Willy's westward escape. Ferguson identifies a tonal pattern in the "impressive unity" of "The Village" that opens with a "heavy" story followed by two "light" stories, locates four "heavy" stories in the center of the group, returns with two additional "light" stories, and closes with another "heavy" story to complement the opening text, "A Rose for Emily" (1991, 158).

## Interpretation and Criticism

In the transition from considering "Elly" in the context of Faulkner's other fiction to focusing on its individual characteristics, Judith Wittenberg's cautionary guide for judging Faulkner's women seems especially relevant: "The extraordinary multivalence of Faulkner's oeuvre as a whole and of each individual work within itself . . . makes broad-based assessments hazardous and demands that they be somewhat tentative. One can nevertheless discern some general tendencies in Faulkner's portrayal of women and women-related issues that show him, on the whole, to be neither pro- nor anti-female, but rather an absorbed student of the endlessly variegated human scene" ([1982] 1986, 235). "Elly," even though aspects of it echo in other Faulkner works, is neither rigidly patterned nor open to easy, complementary interpretations.

A significant divergence in the critical response to "Elly" occurs around the issue of whether Faulkner treats Elly sympathetically. Malin believes that Faulkner "cannot tolerate" Elly's destructive self-indulgence. He adds, however, that her "maladjustment was produced by her social environment" (Malin 1957, 34).

Considering the idealized Southern woman in Faulkner's work, Kerr concludes that the author portrays most negatively, even though sometimes with sympathy, those women who cling to the ideals of that convention. Elly is ruthless but pitiable because she is trapped by a narrow range of choices. Kerr notes that "Elly's brief plea to be allowed to get a job . . . is Faulkner's closest approach to the problem of the career girl in the South" (1961–62, 1–6).

Of all the critics, Bradford presents the most unsympathetic interpretation of the story. He challenges the readings of Malin, Kerr, and Nilon and asserts that they offer an "unmistakable illustration of what foolishness may proceed from a determination to make everything in Faulkner into a buttress for received sociological dogmas." Bradford's own rendering of the story is that it is "an exposé" of a female who rejects the traditional role assigned to her in Southern society. He understands Faulkner to be decidedly "old fashioned" in this regard and totally unsympathetic, uncharacteristically so, in his portrait of "Elly" (1968, 179–87). Bradford's reading is the most severely critical of Elly's character and has received little confirmation in subsequent analyses.

According to Walter Everett, the motivation for Elly's behavior comes from her guilt about her "sexual exploits" and her hatred of her grandmother. Elly's guilt is linked to her grandmother's disapproval of her flirtations, but Everett believes the story is weakened by Faulkner's failure to provide sufficient motive to explain the intensity of Elly's hatred (1969, 141).

Page argues for a sympathetic view of Elly, noting that Faulkner has been able to arouse sympathy for an unadmirable character. For Faulkner, as Page interprets him, the "only source of moral order and endurance is woman's ability to fulfill the creative and sustaining role of motherhood." When a woman does not submit herself to her "natural role," she "becomes the image of death." Elly has been thwarted by the repressive force of her grandmother, who, like numerous other mother/grandmother figures in Faulkner, "reject[s] the normal reproductive process of life." The ironic effect is that sexuality "becomes the single driving force" of her life. Contrary to Everett,

Page believes that frequently directing attention to the grandmother establishes the "direct relationship between cause and effect." When the story opens, Elly is already perverted. At the end, she remains essentially a whimpering child. Faulkner's care to display the causes as well as the consequences of Elly's perversion enable a sympathetic response in the reader (Page 1972, 93–96, 108–09, 134, 178).

Skei criticizes Malin's simplistic classification of Faulkner's women as "sexual" or "asexual" and Bradford's unsympathetic reading of "Elly." Skei contends that Elly "does not act out of some natural badness." In "Elly," as in most of Faulkner's stories, the author uses conditions in the social environment rather than personal traits as the motivational force behind the character's behavior. Based on his examination of manuscripts, Skei concludes that when Faulkner revised stories he tended to eliminate generalized statements about the nature of women (1979, 16, 22, 24 n. 17; Skei 1985, 107–08).

Skei does not, however, see Elly as totally a product of her environment. The actions she takes are her means of escaping the trap she senses she is in. She even acquiesces temporarily and plans her marriage to the reliable beau Philip. Finally, however, her actions are violent and disastrous. The story suggests no solution. In her individual battle with the social system she is doomed to fail (Skei 1979, 19–20; Skei 1985, 122).

Skei considers Elly's hatred of her grandmother a displaced anger at a restrictive community; but the direct social criticism is somewhat obscured because it is so pointedly at the older generation represented by Elly's grandmother. While the grandmother does represent the tradition and authority that Elly opposes, part of Elly's rage stems from fear of her parents and a society that offers her very few options. Elly wants more than Jefferson can give her. Even though she resents her, Elly believes that her grandmother is the only person really alive in their household (Skei 1979, 15–19; Skei 1985, 107–08).

Polk argues that Elly's sense of a wasted life exceeds her rage. Her decision to have sexual intercourse with Paul serves the effect of a "doubly intense sin." Not only does she give up her virginity but she does so to a racially mixed partner. Polk sees Elly's rebellion as momentary, "a chance to store up some excitement, some quality of living" for her lifeless future. She fails, however, to escape the guilt represented by the intrusive presence and intimate bond she shares with her grandmother. The bond between the two women is established by their shared name "Ailanthia," the cards, the "queer umbilical cord" they use for communication, and the grandmother's position between Elly and Paul on the ride home. Elly's close association with her grandmother represents not only what Elly is afraid to become but also her own disapproving consciousness (Polk 1984, 67, 84).

Petry offers a psychoanalytic analysis of "Elly" according to which Faulkner builds upon a complexity of doublings in the relationship between Elly and her grandmother. Elly (Ailanthia II) represents the id and the grandmother (Ailanthia I), the superego. The women also stand for the conflicting mores of New South and Old South, respectively. As doubles of one another, Elly and her grandmother share the same name, the same home, and the same commanding stare. Elly even begins to walk like an old woman when she is upstairs, where both she and her grandmother have their rooms. The role of the double operates in "Elly" to depict an opposing side of the self: the grandmother and Elly have an antagonistic relationship, but the grandmother acts in some measure as Elly's "guardian angel." She appears when Elly, hidden in the shrubbery with Paul, thinks of her. The danger of Elly's murdering her double is that the action is also suicidal. Elly's self-destructive actions build toward her death. Despite her stated intention to do so, she does not take the train home. After the crash, Elly whimpers in a childlike manner waiting to be rescued. Even if she has not lost her life, she has killed the "stronger, sexual side" of herself (Petry 1986, 222–24, 229–30).

Petry does not see revenge as a motive in Elly's behavior. The conflict is the struggle between the id and the superego. The absence of the parents as significant characters emphasizes the intensity of the conflict between Elly and her grandmother. Petry explains: "Elly's crisis is this: How (if at all) can the nationwide call for sexual freedom accommodate the persistent myth of the virginal Southern belle—let alone the personal situation of one Elly, age eighteen, of Jefferson?" Elly tries, in her engagement to Philip, to accept the older standard of behavior, but her failure to maintain that stance indicates its "limited relevance." Elly is "trapped between the meaningless, suffocating strictures of the Old and the equally meaningless chaos of the New," and her behavior is unmistakably out of control. She alternately displays "catatonic lethargy and manic motion." The destructiveness of the ending, Petry claims, argues by way of a "'worst case' scenario" a sign of hope and "encourages honesty by demonstrating the damaging effects of falsehood" (1986, 221–32).

Volpe sees Elly "torn by irreconcilable forces unravelling into madness." Like Petry, he finds the text to reflect the conflict within Elly, but for him the conflicting social forces act symbolically to reveal her psychological trauma rather than vice versa. And he goes further than Petry in his contention that Elly actually goes mad. For him, the flashbacks reveal the causes of her mental state, and the forward-moving parts of the story—including dialogue, action, description, and characterization—show her inner turmoil. Adjectives such as "implacable" and "irrevocable" reinforce the irreconcilable inner tension. Her grandmother "is a projection of part of her own personality." During the period of Elly's engagement—a relatively peaceful although dull time—her grandmother is not in the house. The community standards she rebels against are so completely internalized that by rejecting them, she also rejects part of herself. The equally strong needs of defiance and conformity cannot be reconciled, and as a result Elly goes insane. Her actions on the night preceding the wreck are "truly insane," totally self-involved, and signal her mental collapse (Volpe 1989, 273–80).

The third character in the triangle is Paul de Montigny. Carothers claims that he betrays Elly much in the fashion of the men who betray Emily Grierson and Zilphia Gant (1985, 104). Yet Paul maintains from the beginning of the relationship that he has no intention of marrying Elly (*CS* 212). Petry emphasizes that Faulkner did not develop Paul's character fully because his role in the story is as an agent. He is "obligingly amoral." The absence of development of both Paul and Philip keeps the focus on Elly and her relationship with her grandmother (Petry 1986, 221). Volpe adds that Paul "becomes a symbol of ultimate, irrevocable defiance" (1989, 279).

Bradford would probably find critical support for his observation that every element of the story is presented as it relates to Elly. Both narrative technique and development of imagery contribute to the effect of making this Elly's story exclusively. He notices imagery in the opening and closing of the story—for example, the opening description of the inadequate guard rail that separates Elly from the precipice works as a metaphor for her condition. The story maintains a clinical, objective, and detached tone. It is a "portrait etched in acid" (Bradford 1968, 181, 185–86; see also Volpe 1989, 275). Skei describes the closing scene as a "deadly tableau" of arrested motion (1979, 18). Volpe adds that the car plunging over the precipice represents Elly's plunge "into the abyss of madness" (1989, 280). Polk finds that images in "Elly" include the pattern of authority figures framed by windows or doors used in other Faulkner fiction. The grandmother's room is seen as "a single square of light" at the top of the stairs. Polk acknowledges that windows are also for looking out. As Elly, like other Faulkner characters, looks out her mother's window, she is both attracted and repelled by the world beyond. The house is consistently portrayed as dark, including the "screening vines" at the veranda (Polk 1984, 82–83; Polk 1985, 31; *CS* 208).

Petry discusses the use of mirrors as an important image in doubling narratives. Appropriately, Elly experiences moments of awareness in front of a mirror (1986, 224). In the closing image, Elly digs shattered glass, "clearly the symbol of a shattered looking glass," out of the palm of her hand (1986, 230). Another final image is the "blatantly sexual image" of blood staining Elly's skirt (Petry 1986, 230).

Skei makes the point that even though "Elly" is partially set in Jefferson, Faulkner does not use a narrator who speaks for the consciousness of the community. The omniscient narrator primarily restricts the view to what Elly sees. This approach works to the disadvantage of Elly's grandmother, who is the object of Elly's rage (Skei 1979, 16–17; Skei 1985, 108). The approach, "an atypically cold and objective narrative style," adheres to the "case study" approach followed by literary naturalists. The simple title "Elly" reinforces the focus of the study (Petry 1986, 220–21).

Kiyoyuki Ono argues that the sound of dripping water in the bathroom scene is an important image because it reveals Elly's motivation for action. The sound of the steady drip "makes Elly realize her intense hatred of her grandmother" (Ono 1985, 34).

Polk, Skei, Petry, and Volpe offer insightful readings of the thematic complexity and technical sophistication of "Elly." Nevertheless, the story is not among those ranked as Faulkner's best even though, with rare exception, those who have offered extended analysis of the text have found much to compliment. In his dissenting opinion Karl finds some matters of interest in the text. He states that "as personal revelation, the story is compelling; as fiction, dismal" (1989, 381). Quite to the contrary, Bradford values "Elly" as a "masterful piece of craftsmanship" (1968, 181). Volpe renders a different interpretation from Bradford's, but in terms of style he agrees that the story is "brilliantly wrought" (1989, 273). Skei insists on the value of "Elly" as one among the *Doctor Martino* stories that would provide a "good starting point" for a study of the women in Faulkner's short fiction (1979, 22). Petry would seem to guarantee contemporary attention to the text when she judges Elly as "one of the most confused women ever depicted in literature" (1986, 225). Studies of female characters in Faulkner's fiction can hardly be complete without considering Elly's portrait. "Elly" deserves both continued attention and an elevated status in the Faulkner canon.

## Works Cited

Benét, William Rose. 1934. "Fourteen Faulkner Stories." *Saturday Review of Literature*, 21 April, 645.

Blotner, Joseph. 1974. *Faulkner: A Biography*. 2 vols. New York: Random House.

———. 1984. *Faulkner: A Biography*. 1 vol. New York: Random House.

Bradford, M. E. 1968. "Faulkner's 'Elly': An Exposé." *Mississippi Quarterly* 21:179–87.

Carothers, James B. 1984. "Faulkner's Short Stories: 'And Now What's to Do.'" In *New Directions in Faulkner Studies: Faulkner and Yoknapatawpha, 1983*. Ed. Doreen Fowler and Ann J. Abadie. Jackson: University Press of Mississippi, 202–27.

———. 1985. *William Faulkner's Short Stories*. Ann Arbor, MI: UMI Research Press.

———. 1992. "Faulkner's Short Story Writing and the Oldest Profession." In *Faulkner and the Short Story: Faulkner and Yoknapatawpha, 1990*. Ed. Evans Harrington and Ann J. Abadie. Jackson: University Press of Mississippi, 38–61.

Everett, Walter K. 1969. *Faulkner's Art and Character*. Woodbury, NY: Barron's Educational Series.

Faulkner, William. 1934. "Elly." *Story* 4 (February):3–15.

———. 1934. *Doctor Martino and Other Stories*. New York: Harrison Smith and Robert Haas.

———. 1950. *Collected Stories of William Faulkner*. New York: Random House.

———. 1977. *Selected Letters of William Faulkner*. Ed. Joseph Blotner. New York: Random House.

———. 1979. *Uncollected Stories William Faulkner*. Ed. Joseph Blotner. New York: Random House.

———. 1987. *William Faulkner Manuscripts 11:* Doctor Martino and Other Stories. Ed. Thomas L. McHaney. New York: Garland.

Ferguson, James. 1991. *Faulkner's Short Fiction*. Knoxville: University of Tennessee Press.

Flynn, Peggy. 1976. "The Sister Figure and 'Little Sister Death' in the Fiction of William Faulkner." *University of Mississippi Studies in English* 14:99–117.

Hall, Constance Hill. 1986. *Incest in Faulkner: A Metaphor for the Fall*. Ann Arbor, MI: UMI Research Press.

Karl, Frederick R. 1989. *William Faulkner: American Writer*. New York: Weidenfeld and Nicolson.

Kerr, Elizabeth M. 1961–62. "William Faulkner and the Southern Concept of Woman." *Mississippi Quarterly* 15:1–16.

———. [1969] 1976. *Yoknapatawpha: Faulkner's "Little Postage Stamp of Native Soil."* New York: Fordham University Press.

Kinney, Arthur F. 1980. "Faulkner's Narrative Poetics and *Collected Stories*." *Faulkner Studies* 1:58–79.

Lang, Béatrice. 1976. "'Dr. Martino': The Conflict of Life and Death." *Delta* 3 (November):23–33.

Lind, Ilse Dusoir. 1986. "The Mutual Relevance of Faulkner Studies and Women's Studies: An Interdisciplinary Inquiry." In *Faulkner and Women: Faulkner and Yoknapatawpha, 1985*. Ed. Doreen Fowler and Ann J. Abadie. Jackson: University Press of Mississippi, 21–40.

Malin, Irving. 1957. *William Faulkner: An Interpretation*. Stanford, CA: Stanford University Press.

Meriwether, James B. [1961] 1971. *The Literary Career of William Faulkner: A Bibliographical Study*. Princeton, NJ: Princeton University Library. Reprint. Columbia: University of South Carolina Press.

———. 1973. "Faulkner's Correspondence with *Scribner's Magazine*." *Proof* 1:253–82.

Momberger, Philip. 1978. "Faulkner's 'The Village' and 'That Evening Sun': The Tale in Context." *Southern Literary Journal* 11.1:20–31.

Nicholson, Norman. [1943] 1945. *Man & Literature*. London: S.C.M. Press.

Nilon, Charles H. 1965. *Faulkner and the Negro*. New York: Citadel.

Ono, Kiyoyuki. 1985. "Life is Motion: An Aspect of William Faulkner's Style." In *Faulkner Studies in Japan*. Ed. Thomas L. McHaney. Kenzaburo Ohashi and Kiyoyuki Ono, comps. Athens: University of Georgia Press, 28–44.

Page, Sally R. 1972. *Faulkner's Women: Characterization and Meaning*. Deland, FL: Everett/Edwards.

Peters, Erskine. 1983. *William Faulkner: The Yoknapatawpha World and Black Being*. Darby, PA: Norwood.

Petry, Alice Hall. 1986. "Double Murder: The Women of Faulkner's 'Elly.'" In *Faulkner and Women: Faulkner and Yoknapatawpha, 1985*. Ed. Doreen Fowler and Ann J. Abadie. Jackson: University Press of Mississippi, 220–34.

Pilkington, John. 1981. *The Heart of Yoknapatawpha*. Jackson: University Press of Mississippi.

Polk, Noel. 1984. "'The Dungeon Was Mother Herself': William Faulkner: 1927–1931. In *New Directions in Faulkner Studies: Faulkner and Yoknapatawpha, 1983*. Ed. Doreen Fowler and Ann J. Abadie. Jackson: University Press of Mississippi, 61–93.

———. 1985. "The Space between *Sanctuary*." In *Intertextuality in Faulkner*. Ed. Michel Gresset and Noel Polk. Jackson: University Press of Mississippi, 16–35.

Ross, Stephen M. 1989. *Fiction's Inexhaustible Voice: Speech and Writing in Faulkner*. Athens: University of Georgia Press.

Schoenberg, Estella. 1977. *Old Tales and Talking: Quentin Compson in William Faulkner's* Absalom, Absalom! *and Related Works*. Jackson: University Press of Mississippi.

Serafin, Joan M. 1983. *Faulkner's Uses of the Classics*. Ann Arbor, MI: UMI Research Press.

Skei, Hans H. 1979. "The Trapped Female Breaking Loose: William Faulkner's 'Elly.'" *American Studies in Scandinavia* 11:15–24.

———. 1981. *William Faulkner: The Short Story Career*. Oslo, Norway: Universitetsforlaget.

———. 1985. *William Faulkner: The Novelist as Short Story Writer*. Oslo, Norway: Universitetsforlaget.

Tuck, Dorothy. 1964. *Crowell's Handbook of Faulkner*. New York: Thomas Y. Crowell.

Vickery, Olga W. [1959] 1964. *The Novels of William Faulkner*. Baton Rouge: Louisiana State University Press.

Volpe, Edmond L. 1989. "'Elly': Like Gunpowder in a Flimsy Vault." *Mississippi Quarterly* 42:273–80.

Watson, James G. 1987. *William Faulkner: Letters and Fictions*. Austin: University of Texas Press.

Wittenberg, Judith Bryant. [1982] 1986. "William Faulkner: A Feminist Consideration." *Modern Critical Views: William Faulkner*. Ed. Harold Bloom. New York: Chelsea House, 233–45.

# Uncle Willy

## Publication History

"Uncle Willy" appeared in the October 1935 issue of *American Mercury*. It is not certain what magazines may have rejected "Uncle Willy" before it was accepted by the *American Mercury*. It is also unclear what fee Faulkner received for the story; however, he was paid $250 by the same magazine for "That Will Be Fine," which had appeared in the magazine in July of the same year (Blotner 1974, 886–87; *SL* 91). In 1950, "Uncle Willy" became part of "The Village" section in *Collected Stories*.

## Circumstances of Composition, Sources, and Influences

The composition of "Uncle Willy" can be confidently dated in early 1935, though Hans Skei speculates that it may have been written after March 25, the completion date of *Pylon*. The short story was written as part of an urgent effort during the first part of 1935 to produce stories for magazine sale. Faulkner estimated his pace at about two stories per week (Skei 1981, 79–80, 87; *SL* 91).

A partial manuscript and partial typescript of "Uncle Willy" are located in the Rowan Oak Papers at the University of Mississippi, and a twenty-seven-page typescript is in the William B. Wisdom Collection at Tulane University. The extant texts contain some corrections and revisions, but Kinney and Fowler describe the Rowan Oak versions as "substantially as published in *Collected Stories*" (Bonner 1980, 33; Kinney and Fowler 1983, 328–29). The presence of revisions suggests that even if the generative impulse of the story was financial, the artist maintained a concern for his craft. At any rate, when the story was used in *Collected Stories*, it differed from the *American Mercury* version only in the capitalization of "Jamaica."

As several scholars and biographers have noted, a real-life parallel antedates Faulkner's protagonist. When he wrote this story, Faulkner apparently drew upon an incident that had occurred in Oxford the preceding fall: Bob Chilton was killed in an automobile accident. Local children were frequent patrons of the drugstore that Bob had operated with his brother, Top Chilton, and Ad Bush. During his sixties, Bob's drinking and associating with disreputable women in Oxford and Memphis caught the attention of the Oxford citizens (Blotner 1974, 882–83; see also Cullen and Watkins[1961] 1975, 111–13; Brown 1978, 13). Uncle Willy reflects these characteristics, although with some slight embellishment.

Faulkner's own need for privacy may also be reflected in Uncle Willy. Robert Harrison likens Faulkner's use of flying as an escape to Uncle Willy's plans. Harrison identifies many of the details related to flying with Faulkner's knowledge of aviation, and he adds that the "fact that it was enough to make both men stop drinking temporarily testifies to its force" (1985, 173–75). At the Faulkner and Yoknapatawpha Conference in 1984, Barry Hannah read a condensed version of "Uncle Willy." In Hannah's comments that enclosed the text, he compared, in fact called, Faulkner "Uncle Willy" (1986, 191–94).

Mrs. Christian is one of relatively few prostitutes in Faulkner's short stories. James Carothers parallels their portraits and the various reasons they became prostitutes with Faulkner's image of himself as a short story writer. Mrs. Christian challenges the "forces of moral order" in the community, who quickly inform her that she has gained neither respectability nor financial security in marriage. She makes an expedient settlement and leaves town. Mrs. Christian's contempt for the citizens of Jefferson "perhaps represents Faulkner's contempt for his own community" (1992, 42–44, 58–60).

The character Secretary recalls airman George MacEwen, "the Black Eagle," an acquaintance of Faulkner, and Job behaves in ways that resemble Ned Barnett, who worked for several generations of Faulkners (Blotner 1974, Notes 123; see also Harrison 1985, 173). Faulkner may also be incorporating political criticism into the text. According to Joseph Blotner, the author expressed his "anti-NRA [National Recovery Administration] feelings" in the tale through Uncle Willy's frustration over needing a doctor's permit to take flying lessons (1974, Notes 123).

"Uncle Willy" does not lack a literary inheritance. Leslie Fiedler believes Rip Van Winkle is an early model for Uncle Willy. Although Rip escapes his wife's tyranny by sleeping through the remainder of her life, Uncle Willy and his young followers "in their war against the mothers" fail in their efforts (Fiedler 1960, 332–33). Blotner identifies flight in this tale as a "Huck Finn" motif (1974, Notes 123; see also Volpe 1978, 177–81). Noel Polk and James Ferguson compare "Uncle Willy" to Sherwood Anderson's stories, and Polk also likens "Uncle Willy" to Eudora Welty's "Lily Daw and the Three Ladies"; all "illustrate the ways in which the claims of the community and those of the individual continually rasp against each other" (Polk 1980, 114–15; Ferguson 1991, 41). Welty's story appeared two years after "Uncle Willy" in the *Prairie Schooner*, Winter 1937.

## Relationship to Other Faulkner Works

"Uncle Willy" is a part of the Yoknapatawpha milieu due to its is setting in Jefferson. As Skei notes, there is an advantage for Faulkner in using a previously established setting as it requires less development, which might otherwise interrupt and slow the narrative (1985, 229). In spite of its locale, "Uncle Willy" is an independent story, meaning that it was not "reused in any form" (Skei 1985, 212–13). Nevertheless, there are reciprocal references between this and other Faulkner works. "Uncle Willy" contains a specific allusion to the earlier novel *As I Lay Dying*. The narrator recalls the time Darl Bundren is taken to the asylum in Jackson, Mississippi. Carothers calls this a *"functional allusion"* that "serves to dramatize the pathetic situation of Uncle Willy, but is not employed primarily to refer the reader back to" the novel (1985, 27; see also Holmes 1966, 115). Gary Stonum observes that *The Mansion* offers "a last retelling of stories from the whole span of his fiction" including references to "relatively obscure short stories," among them "Uncle Willy" (1979, 192).

Faulkner's use of familiar character types provides a point of comparison with other works. The child narrator is a familiar type. Blotner likens the unnamed narrator to Georgie of "That Will Be Fine." Like Georgie, this narrator "displayed only sympathy, loyalty, and love for the older man with whom he was juxtaposed" (1974, 883). Hugh Ruppersburg also compares these two narrators, adding *The Reivers* as still another narrative in which humor results from the use of a juvenile perspective that contrasts with the "mature vantage point" of the narrator as an adult (1983, 22). Hans Bungert identifies a variety of stories and novels that use a child or adolescent as narrator, including "Uncle Willy." The child narrator becomes a source of the comedy of the story, a pattern Bungert calls the "comedy of limited perception" (1986, 146–47). Skei points out that although the use of the child narrator is not unusual, this narrator's perspective is "radically different" from the view of the rest of the community, distinguishing him from other narrators (1989, 237).

The character Uncle Willy draws comparisons with fictional people as well as with Oxford resident Bob Chilton. In her analysis of the social structure of Yoknapatawpha, Elizabeth Kerr observes that numerous "extras" appear and reappear to "fill in the social class structure of the white caste." Among these, she lists Uncle Willy Christian ([1969] 1976, 129). Several critics trace the reappearance of Willy Christian in *The Town*, *The Mansion*, and *The Reivers* (Kerr [1969] 1976, 129; Gregory 1974, 116, 118; Carothers 1985, 18; Connolly 1988, 487). In a brief remark, Yasuhiro Yoshizaki ranks Uncle Willy among Faulkner's characters "who show psychologically abnormal reactions," meaning in Willy's case, his addiction to heroin (1982, 119–20).

Mrs. Merridew, the "good woman" of "Uncle Willy," is one among "women who are excessively devoted to preserving the structures of community stability and propriety at the expense of the well-being of life" (Page 1972, 184). She joins company with such women in *Soldier's Pay*, *Sanctuary*, and *Light in August* (Page 1972, 184; see also Volpe 1978, 178–79).

Certain thematic patterns also recur in "Uncle Willy." Edward Holmes compares "Uncle Willy" to *Sanctuary* and *Light in August* in its portrayal of the "evil of rigidity" (1966, 13). Joseph Gold makes the ironic comparison of the jail as a "place of refuge" in *Requiem for a Nun* to the restrictiveness of the church in "Uncle Willy" (1966, 105). Like "Dry September" and "That Will Be Fine," the standards of the community are portrayed negatively—self-righteous and stifling (Blotner, 1974, 883). Ferguson sees this same thematic pattern in such conflicts between individual and community in "The Tall Men," "Dry September," and "Red Leaves" (1991, 81–82).

Blotner observes that this is another text in which "Faulkner had again yoked comedy and violent death." He further links the narrative focus on experiences that meld a boy into a man in "Uncle Willy" to similar situations in the novels *Pylon* and *The Reivers*, and the screenplay *Mythical Latin-American Kingdom Story* (Blotner 1974, 883, 1795). In Ferguson's study, "Uncle Willy" is grouped with a large number of works concerned with initiation, a concern that is Faulkner's "most important archetype" in the decade from 1932 to 1942 (1991, 41).

Joseph Reed compares the narrative strategy in "Uncle Willy" to that of "The Fire and the Hearth" in *Go Down, Moses* and of *Absalom, Absalom!* The ending of each story "casts such a light on such issues that we are forced to change our mind about the story's premises" (1973, 190, 262). Ferguson judges the narrative voice to be much less effective than Faulkner's use of Quentin as adult and child narrator in "That Evening Sun" and "A Justice." In "Uncle Willy" the shifts in the narrative voice from adolescent to adult are not adequately contextualized as reflecting the passage of time and varied levels of mature understanding (Ferguson 1991, 113–14).

Skei places the stories written from 1933 to 1941 "along an axis of greed, corruption, and conformity" by which Faulkner demonstrates "that it is not very far, after all, from Jefferson to L.A." Skei sees "Uncle Willy," "Mule in the Yard," "That Will Be Fine," and "Golden Land" related by their common interest in these themes. "Uncle Willy," like "That Will Be Fine," shows the loss of "positive traditional values" in the diminishing agrarian character of

Yoknapatawpha County (Skei 1985, 216, 223). "Uncle Willy" is also linked to "Golden Land" and "There Was a Queen" as "stories in which 'mainstream America' and middle class values, rules, and regulations are presented and scrutinized through the fate of an outsider." The result is that the "loneliest figures in Faulkner's short fiction are lonely in the company of men" (Skei 1992, 69).

Heide Ziegler groups "Uncle Willy" with comic stories such as "Mule in the Yard" and "Shingles for the Lord" and parts of *The Hamlet* and *Go Down, Moses* because their humor often resembles stage comedy, sometimes approaching slapstick. The focus is on the "scenic element of the comic, with the comic always being confined to brief descriptions" (Ziegler 1989, 118).

Intertextual associations develop from the organization of *Collected Stories*. Philip Momberger believes that the cumulative impact of "The Village" section includes the impression that "institutional Christianity has ceased to be a unifying force for compassion and love." Just as Mrs. Merridew and her churchgoing friends try to reform Willy Christian (the "most innocent, loving, and charitable man in the Village"), so too does the Baptist minister try to alter Emily Grierson's behavior in "A Rose for Emily," and Mrs. Church express her disapproval of another woman's demeanor in "That Will Be Fine" (Momberger 1978, 28–29).

James Watson also looks at the story within the framework of "The Village." He argues that the particular excellence of the opening story, "A Rose for Emily," and the closing story, "That Evening Sun," enhances and enlarges the context in which the victories and defeats of intermediate stories such as "Uncle Willy" can be interpreted (Watson 1980, 221).

Kinney interprets the "The Village" section as portraying the "dispiritedness characterizing Jefferson." "Uncle Willy" and "Elly" contribute to this point by emphasizing an "increasing need for heroes" (Kinney 1980, 68). Ferguson sees the place of "Uncle Willy" in "The Village" as being one of the "four intensely serious stories" at the center of the section that pursues with "impressive unity" the "relationship between individual and communal values" (1991, 158).

Frederick Karl says "Uncle Willy," "That Will Be Fine," and "The Brooch" can best be described as "journeyman work." All were efforts by Faulkner in the spring of 1935 when he was desperate for money. Like "That Will Be Fine," "Uncle Willy" is a "country corn" story, an undistinguished class of stories "something below a tall tale" (Karl 1989, 542, 544). When in his "farmer" frame of mind, Faulkner would probably not object to producing something either "country" or "corn" as Karl uses the terms. What Faulkner has created in "Uncle Willy" is a story that reflects in another variant the thematic and artistic concerns that run through his fiction.

## Interpretation and Criticism

The obvious clash between Uncle Willy's behavior and the standards of the community is the object of most of the interpretive efforts pertaining to the story. Holmes believes that "Uncle Willy" primarily reflects Faulkner's criticism of "Southern Protestant rigidity" (1966, 13). Walter Everett's statement of theme, "an individual's struggle to get fun out of life," is too simplistic for this story (1969, 177); however, he does offer some explanation. Everett says the comic tone resides in the "satire directed against the religious figures who appear more interested in Uncle Willy's material assets than in the needs of his soul" whereas the story's "poignancy . . . resides in the inconsistency between the attitudes of the adults toward Uncle Willy and the attitude of the narrator toward him." The "do-gooders" bent on Uncle Willy's reform compare unfavorably with the Memphis prostitute who is honest about her motives (Everett 1969, 178–79).

Kerr's analysis focuses less on the comic tone than on the destructive effect (Willy's suicide) of the "meddling of 'respectable' church-goers." Kerr concludes, "[T]he self-righteousness of the women, their blindness to the human virtues as well as the vices of Uncle Willy, remains appalling, even when one discounts the admiration of the narrator" ([1969] 1976, 177). According to Kerr, the underlying causes of the church's attempt to compel Willy to reform reveal Faulkner's belief that organized religion often acts from motives "other than Christian sentiments" and that each individual must "work out his own religion" (1983, 261).

Edmond Volpe, like Kerr and Everett, concentrates on the obvious conflict between the individual and the community. He writes that Faulkner employs the form of a fable with a "simple traditional plot" in "chronological episodes" and with "stylized, familiar types" to tell another version of "Huck Finn's story: the struggle of natural innocence for survival." As Volpe observes, "In the great American tradition, Uncle Willy goes west to find the freedom to live as he wants." His love of fun is like that of a child. But in Faulkner's world, as Volpe reads it, "The child is not father to the man; the child is destroyed to make the man." He further views Uncle Willy Christian as the "true christian who lets the little children come unto him" (Volpe 1978, 177–81).

Polk also finds an ironic twist to Willy's surname "Christian," but he does not find Uncle Willy to be the harmless, "beloved fun-loving old drunk" that Volpe does (Volpe 1978, 180). In Polk's view, the conflict between Uncle Willy Christian's behavior and the community standards is complicated by a mixed sense of where sympathies should lie. Although the lines of battle are clearly drawn between Mrs. Merridew's faction and Uncle Willy, and although the narrator's sympathies are clearly with Willy, Willy is not by any means a positive influence on the children. In fact, the narrator's inability to see that indicates the degree to which Willy has manipulated him. Polk points out that Willy exposes the children to his addictive habits. They eat their ice cream while they watch him inject his heroin, and they help him obtain whiskey. The narrator writes Willy's dishonest letter to help him get an automobile; he also abets Willy's suicide. The humor "gets less and less funny as we realize how pernicious an influence Uncle Willy is on the children." Unfortunately, the alternative represented in Mrs. Merridew is also repellent, perhaps an "even more pernicious influence." Neither alternative is acceptable, but as Polk points out, "Faulkner does nothing to resolve the tension established by the conflict between these two polar extremes" (1980, 114–19).

According to Kinney, the town's extended neglect of Willy contrasts with its sudden urge to save him. The narrator recognizes that a "suicide of the spirit" has shown in Willy's eyes long before he kills himself in the plane. Willy's last effort has been "to bring excitement and the possibility of death back into his misspent, agonizing life." The narrator fails to make the community understand this (Kinney 1980, 68).

Skei argues that the conflict in "Uncle Willy" is between a "natural life where freedom and love of one's fellow man are important elements" and a "well-regulated, civilized 'normal' life where non-conformity is a deadly sin" (1985, 215). In this reading, Uncle Willy has become surrogate father because he has been willing to meet the boys "on their level" and has not exhibited rigid, socially restricted behavior. Although Willy's behavior is not portrayed as exemplary, Skei argues that until the meddling began, "he harmed nobody but himself and demanded nothing save to be left alone." By contrast, in Mrs. Merridew and her contingent, "Faulkner hardly ever painted Jefferson in so bleak colours as in this story." These meddling citizens replace Uncle Willy with a new clerk in the store who is apparently dishonest and criminal (1985, 223–24).

The narrator's role in the story generates a mixed response as critics debate whether he acted willfully or was simply "tolled away" (kidnapped), (*CS* 225). Dorothy Tuck thinks the narrator believes he has behaved properly (morally) "but knows with sorrow that he can never make the grownups understand" (1964, 181). Gold notes a repeated point in Faulkner's work: age is not synonymous with wisdom. The young narrator of the story "is the only person therein who is able to recognize a saint when one appears" (Gold 1966, 77–78).

Reed examines the complexity of the narrative in some detail, noting how the reader's sympathy changes as the story progresses. The opening paragraph indicates that the narrator "has already passed from innocence to experience," but it also conveys the adults' condescension to the child, a "condescension which talks down to the child's assumed innocence." The reader's early reaction to the story is a "stock Huck Finn response" against the reforming women. Yet when the narrator reveals that Uncle Willy is a drug addict, the reader becomes less strongly aligned with and more distanced from him. Although the child can accommodate a casual mix of ball games, ice cream, and drug injections, the reader cannot. The dissonance is eased somewhat when Uncle Willy "reforms," replacing heroin with alcohol in the last part of the story. By the end of the story, the narrator reveals his realization that he was used by Uncle Willy; he admits that "the one betrayed was me." As Reed explains, "[T]he boy assumed that Willy saw him and prized him for what he was—a peculiar mixture of youthful eagerness and mature disregard for public mores; but the final paragraph reverses this. Willy had used him and assumed too much on his innocence." For the reader, the story turns in this paragraph into something different from what it seemed to be along the way (Reed 1973, 38–4; *CS* 247; see also Polk 1980, 118). Reed's argument is basically sound, but it is somewhat clouded by the fact that the paragraph he quotes and from which he seems to draw his evidence is the third-from-last rather than the final paragraph. In the last paragraph, the narrator does not express a shared adult understanding that he was used by Willy, but a pressing need to make "Papa" and "them" understand that he willingly left with Willy (*CS* 247; see also Ferguson 1991, 59).

Skei's interpretation offers a better analysis of the last two paragraphs than does Reed's assessment. Skei believes that the narrator represents the implied author. But he adds that as a fourteen-year-old, the narrator, even if he is less influenced by preconceptions of "good" and "bad," tells his story with childlike emotion. Skei observes that in certain portions, especially the first paragraphs, the narrator seems to be grown and recalling the experience from an earlier time. Still, Skei concludes, like Tuck, that the undemanding, reciprocal friendship between the narrator and Willy is "difficult to understand or to accept." In this "story about a friendship lasting beyond death" the boy knows that Willy finally does not escape Jefferson, but in telling the story, the narrator understands that meaningful living reaches beyond arbitrary social codes toward 'love and understanding and human commitment" (Skei 1985, 215–16, 224–25, 318 n. 17).

Skei suggests that with the narrator's effort to evoke a sympathetic response, the story employs opposition. The narrator presents the opinions of the community then negates them with more positive defenses of Willy's or the boys' actions. In both opening and closing, the narrator orders the explanation of what "they" said about his being "tolled away," his own denial of that, and his estimation of Willy as the "finest man" he ever knew. Along with employing an argumentative rhetoric characterized by opposition and refutation, the narrator must convince the reader that Uncle Willy has value. The repeated use of "because" indicates his desire to explain. As Skei contends, "Everything is done to assure us that the deepest motivation for the boy's actions can be found in unspoilt love and compassion and commitment to people in need" (1989, 237–39).

Ferguson finds that the phrase "tolled away" (kidnapped) operates as a leitmotif in the story, lending it coherence (1991, 137).

The critical response to "Uncle Willy" has not been sufficient to explore the story thoroughly. Taken together, Reed, Polk, and Skei address the story's complexity most completely, but further analysis could include attention to the narrator's relationship to his father and to Old Job. The narrator's father, although not involved at the level of Mrs. Merridew, does participate in the legal transactions in the story, including the payoff to Mrs. Christian (*CS* 238). In one respect, his participation helps explain why the narrator has detailed knowledge of the adults' efforts on Willy's behalf. The father and Uncle Willy also offer very different role models for the impressionable young narrator. Another older male, Old Job, is as faithful to Willy as the narrator is. But in the final escapade, the narrator and Old Job view the responsibility of loyalty in very different ways. The young boy sees value in dying for individual independence; the old man sees value in living. And on still another level, an argument can be made that the narrator and his friends, who spend some time hiding and listening in the hedges, are as meddlesome as the adults. They take pains to help Uncle Willy learn their names again and put names and faces together. Their concern, especially the narrator's, seems genuine. But they may be protecting their interest—ice cream and prizes. They, like the adults, may be most interested in maintaining their community, too.

Faulkner's recorded comments on "Uncle Willy" do not help resolve the interpretive differences. When selecting the stories to be included in *Collected Stories*, Faulkner noted, "Yes. I like this one" (*SL* 274). Skei has been a faithful advocate of the value of this work. "Uncle Willy" demonstrates that Faulkner could have maintained the quality of the stories he wrote in the late 1920s and early 1930s. He did not continue, Skei notes, because Hollywood offered a more lucrative way to free his time for novels and ease his financial concerns (1981, 34). Skei writes elsewhere, "'Uncle Willy' is a superb story, and critics seem to have virtually overlooked it. Faulkner's British publisher, Chatto & Windus, may have felt some of the strength of the story, since they, when publishing Faulkner's collected stories in three volumes, used *Uncle Willy and Other Stories* as the title for the third volume, accompanying *These Thirteen* and *Dr. Martino and Other Stories* [*sic*]. The three volumes correspond to *Collected Stories*" (Skei 1981, 131 n. 70).

Karl, on the other hand, rates "Uncle Willy" as an "undistinguished" effort Faulkner was "fortunate to have accepted by the *American Mercury*." Although the idea of the loyal young man being affected by the nonconforming older man "is a sound one," Karl largely dismisses the story as representing the need to fill twenty pages (Karl 1989, 544). Karl's assessment of the story seems undeservedly harsh. Even if "Uncle Willy" falls short of Faulkner's best short fiction, the story offers a compelling if not complimentary view of the Jefferson community in "The Village" section of *Collected Stories*.

## Works Cited

Blotner, Joseph. 1974. *Faulkner: A Biography*. 2 vols. New York: Random House.

Bonner, Thomas, Jr., comp. 1980. *William Faulkner: The William B. Wisdom Collection: A Descriptive Catalogue*. New Orleans: Tulane University Libraries.

Brown, Calvin S. 1978. "Faulkner's Localism." In *The Maker and the Myth: Faulkner and Yoknapatawpha, 1977*. Ed. Evans Harrington and Ann J. Abadie. Jackson: University Press of Mississippi, 3–24.

Bungert, Hans. 1986. "Faulkner's Humor: A European View." In *Faulkner and Humor: Faulkner and Yoknapatawpha, 1984*. Ed. Doreen Fowler and Ann J. Abadie. Jackson: University Press of Mississippi, 136–51.

Carothers, James B. 1985. *William Faulkner's Short Stories*. Ann Arbor, MI: UMI Research Press.

———. 1992. "Faulkner's Short Story Writing and the Oldest Profession." In *Faulkner and the Short Story: Faulkner and Yoknapatawpha, 1990*. Ed. Evans Harrington and Ann J. Abadie. Jackson: University Press of Mississippi, 38–61.

Connolly, Thomas E. 1988. *Faulkner's World: A Directory of His People and Synopses of Actions in His Published Works*. Lanham, MD: University Press of America.

Cullen, John B., and Floyd C. Watkins. [1961] 1975. *Old Times in the Faulkner Country*. Chapel Hill: University of North Carolina Press. Reprint. Baton Rouge: Louisiana State University Press.

Everett, Walter K. 1969. *Faulkner's Art and Character*. Woodbury, NY: Barron's Educational Series.

Faulkner, William. 1935. "Uncle Willy." *American Mercury* 36 (October):156–68.

———. 1950. *Collected Stories of William Faulkner*. New York: Random House.

———. 1977. *Selected Letters of William Faulkner*. Ed. Joseph Blotner. New York: Random House.

———. 1979. *Uncollected Stories of William Faulkner*. Ed. Joseph Blotner. New York: Random House.

Ferguson, James. 1991. *Faulkner's Short Fiction*. Knoxville: University of Tennessee Press.

Fiedler, Leslie A. 1960. *Love and Death in the American Novel*. New York: Criterion Books.

Gold, Joseph. 1966. *William Faulkner: A Study in Humanism, from Metaphor to Discourse*. Norman: University of Oklahoma Press.

Gregory, Eileen. 1974. "Faulkner's Typescripts of *The Town*." In *A Faulkner Miscellany*. Ed. James B. Meriwether. Jackson: University Press of Mississippi, 113–38.

Hannah, Barry. "Faulkner and the Small Man." In *Faulkner and Humor: Faulkner and Yoknapatawpha, 1984*. Ed. Doreen Fowler and Ann J. Abadie. Jackson: University Press of Mississippi, 191–94.

Harrison, Robert. 1985. *Aviation Lore in Faulkner*. Amsterdam: John Benjamins.

Holmes, Edward M. 1966. *Faulkner's Twice-Told Tales: His Re-Use of His Material*. The Hague: Mouton.

Karl, Frederick R. 1989. *William Faulkner: American Writer*. New York: Weidenfeld and Nicolson.

Kerr, Elizabeth M. [1969] 1976. *Yoknapatawpha: Faulkner's "Little Postage Stamp of Native Soil."* New York: Fordham University Press.

———. 1983. *William Faulkner's Yoknapatawpha: "A Kind of Keystone in the Universe."* New York: Fordham University Press.

Kinney, Arthur F. 1980. "Faulkner's Narrative Poetics and *Collected Stories*." *Faulkner Studies* 1:58–79.

Kinney, Arthur F., and Doreen Fowler. 1983. "For the Record: Faulkner's Rowan Oak Papers: A Census." *Journal of Modern Literature* 10:327–34.

Momberger, Philip. 1978. "Faulkner's 'The Village' and 'That Evening Sun': The Tale in Context." *Southern Literary Journal* 11.1:20–31.

Page, Sally R. 1972. *Faulkner's Women: Characterization and Meaning*. Deland, FL: Everett/Edwards.

Polk, Noel. 1980. "Faulkner and Respectability." In *Fifty Years of Yoknapatawpha: Faulkner and Yoknapatawpha 1979*. Ed. Doreen Fowler and Ann J. Abadie. Jackson: University Press of Mississippi, 110–33.

Reed, Joseph W., Jr. 1973. *Faulkner's Narrative*. New Haven: Yale University Press.

Ruppersburg, Hugh M. 1983. *Voice and Eye in Faulkner's Fiction*. Athens: University of Georgia Press.

Skei, Hans H. 1981. *William Faulkner: The Short Story Career*. Oslo, Norway: Universitetsforlaget.

———. 1985. *William Faulkner: The Novelist as Short Story Writer*. Oslo, Norway: Universitetsforlaget.

———. 1989. "Inadequacies of Style in Some of William Faulkner's Short Stories." In *Faulkner's Discourse: An International Symposium*. Ed. Lothar Hönnighausen. Tübingen: Max Niemeyer Verlag, 234–41.

———. 1992. "Beyond Genre? Existential Experience in Faulkner's Short Fiction." In

248  *Mule in the Yard*

> *Faulkner and the Short Story: Faulkner and Yoknapatawpha, 1990*. Ed. Evans Harrington and Ann J. Abadie. Jackson: University Press of Mississippi, 62–77.

Stonum, Gary Lee. 1979. *Faulkner's Career: An Internal Literary History*. Ithaca, NY: Cornell University Press.

Tuck, Dorothy. 1964. *Crowell's Handbook of Faulkner*. New York: Thomas Y. Crowell.

Volpe, Edmond L. 1978. "Faulkner's 'Uncle Willy': A Childhood Fable." *Mosaic* 12.1:177–81.

Watson, James G. 1980. "Faulkner's Short Stories and the Making of Yoknapatawpha County." In *Fifty Years of Yoknapatawpha: Faulkner and Yoknapatawpha 1979*. Ed. Doreen Fowler and Ann J. Abadie. Jackson: University Press of Mississippi, 202–25.

Yoshizaki, Yasuhiro. 1982. *Faulkner's Theme of Nature*. Kyoto: Yamaguchi Shoten.

Ziegler, Heide. 1989. "Faulkner's Rhetoric of the Comic: The Reivers." In *Faulkner's Discourse: An International Symposium*. Ed. Lothar Hönnighausen. Tübingen: Max Niemeyer Verlag, 117–26.

# Mule in the Yard

## Publication History

"Mule in the Yard" was published as the lead story in the August 1934 issue of *Scribner's*. Since Faulkner was no longer keeping his short-story-sending schedule, the record of submission efforts is uncertain. Joseph Blotner and Hans Skei construct differing accounts. Based on his study of Faulkner's letters, Blotner contends that in late winter or early spring of 1934 Faulkner sent "Mule in the Yard" to his agent, Morton Goldman, for *Cosmopolitan*. The letter to Goldman on which Blotner bases his argument, however, does not name the manuscript.

Skei cites later comments by Faulkner to argue that the story sent to *Cosmopolitan* was not "Mule in the Yard" but "The Brooch." He references an earlier letter to Goldman in which Faulkner instructs him to show an enclosed manuscript to Alfred Dashiell at *Scribner's* but also to try it on the *Post*. Skei believes that the manuscript mentioned here is most likely "Mule in the Yard." A February 14, 1934, letter from Goldman to Dashiell specifically states that Goldman is sending "Mule in the Yard" to the magazine on Faulkner's instruction. *Scribner's* editors' fondness for the Snopes stories began with its publication of "Spotted Horses" in 1931. Kyle Crichton, an assistant editor at *Scribner's*, and Faulkner had once discussed the magazine editor's belief that *Scribner's* should have first chance at the Snopes stories. Faulkner's position was that he would not forfeit the opportunity to sell Snopes material to higher-paying magazines. Nevertheless, the order of submission in Faulkner's letter to Goldman suggests a sensitivity on Faulkner's part to honor *Scribner's* wish for more Snopes stories. Regardless of how long it took *Scribner's* to receive the story, the magazine accepted it quickly, offering to pay $300 if Faulkner cut the length by 1,000 words. Faulkner did so in a few days. Years later, "Mule in the Yard" appeared in *Collected Stories* (1950) and as a part of *The Town* (1957) (Meriwether 1973, 268–69, 27–79; Blotner 1974, 839–40; Skei 1981, 56, 82–83; *SL 79, 77*).

## Circumstances of Composition, Sources, and Influences

Though the actual composition time is vague, Blotner dates the composition of "Mule in the Yard" early in 1934; Skei dates it from late 1933 or early 1934 (Blotner 1974, 827, Notes 118; Skei 1981, 79).

Prepublication versions of "Mule in the Yard" include a ten-page manuscript, an incomplete typescript based on that manuscript, and a one-page fragment entitled "Alteration for Scribner's [sic]. Mule in the Yard." The holograph and typescript versions are reproduced in *William Faulkner Manuscripts 21:* The Town (Skei 1981, 83; Kinney and Fowler 1983, 328; *WFM 21* 1:346–65).

The manuscript and typescript give some indication of Faulkner's revision for *Scribner's*. Dashiell thought the story needed a faster pace, a goal that could be achieved if "some of the more philosophical passages" were deleted and if the "undue emphasis" given Old Het were reduced (Meriwether 1973, 279; Blotner 1974, Notes 118).

Joanne Creighton's study of the various texts shows that although Old Het's character remains the same in all versions, her development is more abbreviated in the short story than in either typescript or *The Town*. Condensing Het's portrait gives the story "dramatic immediacy" at the cost of the "delightful characterization of old Het." Het's poverty is more seriously described in the typescript than in either the short story or the novel. Apparent to those who would look beyond her cheerfulness was "that terror and dread of hunger which not even the security of a poorhouse can efface from the eyes of old negroes." This serious note was probably omitted because it was "at odds with the essentially cheerful and comic characterization," a quality even further enhanced in the novel (Creighton 1977, 58–59). Other of the philosophical asides present in the typescript but not in the published versions include comments about the death of Mr. Hait and the life of I. O. Snopes. Hait's death is reduced to a momentary whim of fate equated with the death of the mules, including literally their mixed and mangled corpses: "the risible and momentarily idle fates had decreed a brief and fatal comedy as though for a weekend's diversion" (*WFM 21* 1:360). I. O.'s harried, despairing life also receives fuller attention in the typescript than in published versions. The tone and inflated style of passages dealing with I. O. are similar to those employed in the description of Hait's death. Also, Gavin Stevens is mentioned as the witness who estimates the mule chases as a "logical part of what had been termed the selling price of her husband" (*WFM 21* 1:365).

From magazine to *Collected Stories* Faulkner changed only the reference to "Miss Mannie" in the magazine version to "Miz Mannie" in collection.

One would hardly expect to find any factual correspondence between Faulkner's life in Oxford and the raucous action of "Mule in the Yard," but there is one link. According to Calvin Brown, who finds numerous associations between Faulkner's fiction and life in Oxford during the 1920s and 1930s, the plot to collect damages from the railroad by having mules killed on the tracks did occur in Oxford and resulted in a lawsuit (1978, 13).

Much more obvious is the literary precedent of the Southwestern humor tradition that influences the story. James Carothers locates "Mule in the Yard" among the numerous stories of the trickster, more specifically, the trickster tricked. Faulkner's tricksters follow in the tradition of "Mark Twain and the Southwestern humorists, Shakespeare, Cervantes, and the Greek drama" (Carothers 1984, 224–26). John Rabbetts finds the "fiercely independent characters" in Faulkner's fiction to be influenced by Southwestern humor. Mannie Hait's "watchful, stoical resourcefulness" is one manifestation of this strong individualism (Rabbetts 1989, 50).

## Relationship to Other Faulkner Works

"Mule in the Yard" receives the most attention as an integral part of Faulkner's fiction. According to Robert Cantwell and later Carothers, "Mule in the Yard" has its origin in actions described in *Sartoris*. The particular reference in the novel is to an unnamed horse trader who frequently loses stock at the railroad track. When MacCallum suggests that the stock be given timetables, the trader pleads innocence and begins but does not complete the tale. The characterization of the horse trader would fit either Mr. Hait or I. O. Snopes. In the development into "Mule in the Yard," I. O. and Mrs. Hait become the focal characters (Cantwell [1953] 1985, 148–49; Carothers 1985, 44, 122, 150 n. 20; *SAR* 130–31; *FD* 138).

The story's closest links are with the short stories and novels that include members of the Snopes clan. The story is a "further exploration of the ingenuity and rapacity of the Snopeses in their incursions into the life of Yoknapatawpha County" (Blotner 1974, 827). In the case of "Mule in the Yard," I. O. is the Snopes of the moment.

Years before Faulkner wrote *The Town* he envisioned "Mule in the Yard" as one of the short stories that would eventually be included in the second volume in the Snopes trilogy (Blotner 1974, 1187; *SL* 197). Edwin Hunter erroneously indicates that only in writing the story into the novel, some twenty-three years after its publication, did Faulkner insert a Snopes character. Although Flem Snopes and Gavin Stevens are added later, I. O. Snopes appears in the story prior to its publication (Hunter 1973, 85, 88, 90, 96).

Creighton speculates that Faulkner used the prepublication typescript for his source text in writing *The Town* (1977, 165 n. 42); its changes include revisions of "characterization, plot, and descriptive detail" (Creighton 1977, 57). The ending rewritten for the novel incorporates Flem Snopes and Gavin Stevens's involvement in resolving the conflict. Despite some revision, the short story and novel text follow closely in narrative action for about ten pages. Then, the novel is expanded to add Snopes and Stevens (Holmes 1966, 40–41; see also Blotner 1974, 1614). By adding Flem's role, Faulkner makes the episode a further revelation of Snopes's own exploitation of people and his drive to obtain respectability (Creighton 1977, 61, 151–52).

Old Het and I. O. Snopes undergo some expansion in *The Town*; they are more like their original portraits in the manuscript than in the short story. In the novel, Old Het's presence is more strongly felt through the use of her eyewitness accounts to record action. I. O. remains consistently a "harried, petty opportunist" in every text, but the published story portrays him as "weaker and less vindictive." The typescript relies more on conjecture as to whether Snopes's mules get into Mrs. Hait's yard by accident or by Snopes's design. In the short story, the mules get there by accident, and Snopes apologizes for the intrusion. In the novel, he endures his fear of the animals in order to release the mules so that he might antagonize Mrs. Hait. From typescript to novel, I. O. Snopes's motivation becomes more specifically "his own distorted sense of justice and retribution." One of his prominent characteristics elsewhere is his manner of speaking with a confusing mix of pieced together proverbs and clichés, a Southwestern malaprop. This quality of speech is absent in the short story and in this particular episode in the novel. Although, as Creighton notes, it might not adequately justify the inconsistent diction, a comment Ratcliff makes later in the novel accounts for the difference in I. O.'s speech as a lack of time in the frantic efforts to catch the mule (Creighton 1977, 57–59; see also Holmes 1966, 40–41).

One of the major changes to the episode in the transition from short story to novel is revision in the point of view used—from the story's omniscient perspective to the novel's subjective recounting. As the episode opens, Charles Mallison introduces the narration as a recounting of "what Ratliff said happened" (Holmes 1966, 40–41). Richard Adams finds the revised narrative voice "no improvement on the earlier anonymous narrator's" (1968, 108). For Creighton, however, the subjective perspective strengthens the narrative. The specificity of Old Het's accounts as captured by Charles are superior to the "descriptive flourishes of the short story." V. K. Ratliff and Gavin Stevens are also added to the novel as "secondary perceivers" (Creighton 1977, 59–61).

From story to novel, the total effect of revisions is an "enrichment" of the story, according to Edward Holmes (1966, 40–41). Creighton also finds the version in the novel to be more skillfully rendered than in the short story (1977, 56). Carothers evaluates the changes in the novel to be consistent with the changes in Faulkner's "altered conception of the Snopes dilemma": "The comic force of 'Mule in the Yard' is undercut in *The Town* by the complexities of Charles Mallison's narration, and by the framing of the story within the context of Flem's activities in Jefferson" (Carothers 1985, 133–34).

George Anderson believes the revisions made in this story and "Centaur in Brass" "function to represent the essentially healthy, though oppressed, black society juxtaposed against the corrupt white world." Het's language is revised from "de" and "dem" to "the" and "they"; her childlike portrait becomes "more the adult *conscious* of playing the child," and a description of her as animal-like is deleted (1990, 383–84).

"Mule in the Yard" corresponds to several other Snopes stories. With "Centaur in Brass," another story incorporated into *The Town*, it focuses on the besting of a Snopes. I. O. and Flem are outwitted when their respective plans for profit turn to financial loss (Creighton 1977, 56). Carothers believes that the Snopeses' "chicanery" receives a more tolerant rendering in the two short stories than in *The Town*; both stories show that the "Snopeses, for all their cunning, can be overcome both by their own petty overreaching and by the native wits of those who dare to oppose them." According to Carothers, the possibility of defeating the Snopeses presented in these early stories weakens the argument that Faulkner was "soft" in the last two Snopes novels (Carothers 1985, 20, 123).

Additional minor similarities between "Mule in the Yard" and other Snopes fiction include resemblances between Mannie Hait and Maud Littlejohn in "Spotted Horses." Mannie curses the mule with the same words Maud Littlejohn uses against the horses. Mannie, however, is able to defeat I. O. Snopes (Blotner 1974, 827).

Although comparisons to other Snopes fiction predominate in the limited response to "Mule in the Yard," critics have also made thematic and formal comparisons between it and other Faulkner short stories. Hyatt Waggoner likens the comic mood of "Mule in the Yard" to "Was" and "Shingles for the Lord." Nevertheless, the humor and the element of the tall tale in these stories remain connected to the more serious themes in Faulkner, concerns Waggoner sees in Faulkner's comedy as essentially religious. A similar "awareness of man's situation as precarious" is integrated into the comedies of "Mule in the Yard," "Was," and "Spotted Horses" (Waggoner 1959, 199, 211). Heide Ziegler judges the comedy of "Mule in the Yard," "Uncle Willy," "Shingles for the Lord," and a number of other stories prior to Faulkner's final work in *The Reivers* to rely on brief description that sometimes comes close to slapstick (1989, 118).

Joan Serafin counts eighteen works in which Faulkner employs the "concept of apotheosis, the Roman idea of the soul's sharing the companionship of the gods after death." Usually the suggestion is "simply 'deification,'" as in the image of the bear in *Go Down, Moses*. In "Mule in the Yard," the mule takes on the "appearance and trappings of an apotheosis: hell-born and hell-returning" when it runs into the fog and out of sight (Serafin 1983, 14, 33; *CS* 251).

Mannie Hait's masculine characterization follows a pattern typical of Faulkner's masculinized female characters. Ilse Lind cites Sally Page's observation of masculine traits in Faulkner's women, especially those who have been forced into typically male roles. Within the context of *The Town*, however, Page believes that the imagery and theme of the episode convey a male–female conflict: the feminine (Mannie Hait and the cow) is attacked by the masculine (Snopes and the mule), but the feminine triumphs (Lind 1978, 102; Page 1972, 178–79, 165 n. 1).

Pursuing further the animal images, one might consider Gail Mortimer's discussion of mules as it relates to the story (1983, 120–21). Or one could, as Carothers does, establish a list of stories in which unsuspecting cows receive unwanted attention. The list would include "Mule in the Yard," "Afternoon of a Cow," and *The Hamlet* (Carothers 1985, 128).

Skei's study of short stories Faulkner wrote between 1933 and 1941 reveals a number of similarities. One is that many of these stories eventually were revised for novels. Over half were humorous. "Mule in the Yard" fits both these categories. "Mule in the Yard," "A Bear Hunt," "Fool About a Horse," "Lo!," and "Afternoon of a Cow" "excel in comic effects" that should not be overshadowed by their more serious concerns with injustice, revenge, and preservation of dignity. Skei also believes that these stories can be placed on a continuum of "growing greed, rapacity and corruption from old Yoknapatawpha via modern Yoknapatawpha to Californian life as depicted in 'Golden Land.'" "Mule in the Yard" falls at the end representing the least corruption. Mannie Hait's victory over I. O. Snopes demonstrates the possibility of justice "if no attention is paid to the losses involved in the fight for it." Old Het represents another feature of the stories of this period: the presence of a "stoic, often elderly person, who shows endurance and who by the community at large is forced to live on the fringes of society." She, like others of this pattern, "is the real hero," and she appropriately concludes the story (Skei 1985, 212–13, 216, 219, 220, 222).

Carothers considers "Mule in the Yard" to be one of Faulkner's "excellent but lesser-known stories." He believes that like "The Tall Men," "Race at Morning," and "Shingles for the Lord," it is mistakenly dismissed because its treatment of "virtue and humor" is perceived as "sentimental" and "untrue to life" (Carothers 1985, 18, 11).

James Ferguson identifies a number of variations of the pattern of an "innocent's" confrontation and victory over corruption. Although the pattern often involves children or minority characters, "Mule in the Yard," "Hand Upon the Waters," and "By the People" follow the pattern without incorporating elements of youth or race. Like Skei and Carothers, Ferguson also traces the theme of justice in the short fiction. He judges "Mule in the Yard" as possibly the "most completely satisfactory treatment of the motif of triumphant justice" (Ferguson 1991, 60, 75).

According to John Matthews, Faulkner's short fiction reflects an awareness of the literary marketplace. The stories exhibit a certain curtailment, aesthetic commodification, and mass cultural consumption along with a sense of resistance to the demands of the market. Matthews bases his conclusion on analyses of "Mule in the Yard," "Red Leaves," "There Was a Queen," "Spotted Horses," "Lizards in Jamshyd's Courtyard," "Dry September," and "Centaur in Brass" (1992, 3–37).

Joseph Reed and Ferguson, in admiring though brief treatments, compare stylistic achievements of "Mule in the Yard" with other Faulkner short stories. Reed likens the visual quality of "Mule in the Yard" to that of the highly regarded "Dry September" because, in both, atmosphere motivates action (Reed 1973, 52). Ferguson judges "Mule in the Yard" to be "technically virtually flawless," an estimation he extends to "Red Leaves," "That Evening Sun," "A Justice," "Dry September," and "Barn Burning." He points out that by opening "Mule in the Yard" with Old Het's cry, "Miss Mannie! Mule in de yard!" (*CS* 249), Faulkner opens the story "rather late in the *fabula* at a moment of maximum tension." The effect, present in such diverse stories as "That Evening Sun," "Dry September," "Red Leaves," some of the New Orleans sketches, and "Pantaloon in Black," is to gain intensity and to dramatize the influence of time in the characters' lives (Ferguson 1991, 147, 128–29).

In *Collected Stories*, "Mule in the Yard" enjoys a companionable fit in "The Village" section. Philip Momberger sees "The Village" as a rather dark vision of a disintegrating community. "Mule in the Yard," like most of the ten stories in the section, focuses on conflict between sexes that moves outside the home and into the public arena and also incorporates the image of the "frustration and gross distortion" of the woman as "perpetuator of the human community" in Mannie's masculine dress and mannerisms (Momberger 1978, 213–25, 31).

Arthur Kinney defines the characters of "The Village" as misfits. The comedy of "Mule in the Yard" and "That Will Be Fine" serves as a counterpoint to the "dispiritedness" of the other stories. The two stories also share a "tension between exposed comedy and concealed irony." The tension is reversed in the subsequent story "That Evening Sun" (Kinney 1980, 68).

James Watson understands "The Village" to be an examination of the "limits that a closed society imposes on the identity of the individual." The section is strengthened by its masterful opening with "A Rose for Emily" and closing with "That Evening Sun." Within this context, the "victories and defeats of stories such as 'Centaur in Brass,' 'Uncle Willy' and 'Mule in the Yard,'" are elevated "above their immediate contexts" (Watson 1980, 221).

## Interpretation and Criticism

Because of its inclusion in *The Town*, the short story "Mule in the Yard," like "Centaur in Brass," has been overlooked. Critical interpretation typically focuses on the novel episode. Robert Kirk and Marvin Klotz, Edward Holmes, and Walter Everett discuss the story in the context of *The Town* (Kirk and Klotz 1963, 256; Holmes 1966, 107; Everett 1969, 118–19, 155). Everett considers this portion the one place in *The Town* "distinguished by especially brilliant writing" (1969, 119). A more recent directory by Thomas Connolly does list the story separately (1988, 287).

To be analyzed thoroughly, the story needs to be considered alone, apart from the novel. Carothers emphasizes that whether the subject is "Mule in the Yard" or another incorporated text, the context of the novel "always alters the significance and emphasis of the elements of the original story," even if it undergoes "relatively few changes" (Carothers 1985, 26). John Bassett emphasizes the importance of the context of "Mule in the Yard" and other interpolated tales in *The Town*. He identifies their function within the novel as specific to their role as "contextualized discourses." Bassett's further point, that "as isolated magazine stories they would have different meanings," is important not only for understanding the episodes in the novel but also for recognizing the autonomy of the narratives as individual short stories ([1988] 1989, 218).

The critical response that focuses specifically on "Mule in the Yard" the short story proves scarce, and with the exception of Matthews's work, thin.

Most critics praise the work. Michael Millgate, when talking about the stories incorporated into *The Town*, describes "Mule in the Yard" as "one of Faulkner's greatest comic *tours de force*," possessing "furious crescendoes of farcical activity." In a separate comment specifically about the short story,

Millgate calls it a "comic masterpiece" ([1966] 1989, 236, 270). Carothers agrees, as does Skei, who considers the story "extravagantly humorous" (Carothers 1985, 123; Skei 1985, 219). Frederick Karl calls "Mule in the Yard" "something out of a pastoral idyll," and Ferguson labels it "ferociously funny" (Karl 1989, 514; Ferguson 1991, 185). When preparing the *Collected Stories*, Faulkner himself reread "Mule in the Yard" and enjoyed a good laugh (Blotner 1974, 1323; *SL* 304).

The female characters, victorious in the story without Flem Snopes and Gavin Stevens's intervention, have justly received attention. According to Skei, Old Het provides a good portion of the humor, and her "childish nonsense puts the other characters' stupidity and rapacity in relief." She offers an enduring will and "zest for life" that contrast with the grim, macabre humor (Skei 1985, 219–20).

Kinney is less flattering in his analysis. He considers Snopesism as it relates to the behavior of Mrs. Hait. He judges the humor of "Mule in the Yard" to be superficial. In its scenario of the trickster tricked, "Mrs. Hait is guilty of the same extortion and deception that characterize Snopes" (Kinney 1980, 68).

Matthews offers a more thorough analysis of the women, contending that the treatment of female subjectivity is "crucial to the manipulation of desire in the mass market." "Mule in the Yard" focuses on a woman who gains strength at least in part because "she defines a position for herself in the marketplace." The money she gains when her husband dies serves to prepare her for the future and gives her the ability to resist domination by men: "the money represents phallic empowerment in her society." Her bargaining over the mule proves her to be "resistant to mere sentimental or other 'feminized' gratifications." Mannie's accomplice in the story is Old Het. She, too, is indicative of the "awakening of female subjectivity" in the story. Her shopping bags represent a woman's power and the "capacity of economic enfranchisement to solidify female emancipation." As Matthews observes, Old Het's concluding observation contains both promise and threat: "Gentlemen, hush! Ain't we had a day!" (Matthews 1992, 29–33; *CS* 264).

Most additional observations have to do with the formal aspects of the text. Adams finds the strength of "Mule in the Yard" in its ability to overwhelm on the "sheer power of speed, noise, and confusion" (Adams 1968, 108). The story is technically "simple and straightforward, told in orderly chronology," but it is also unconventional in its use of the macabre (Blotner 1974, 827). The omniscient narrator, eliminated in the novel, facilitates the need to supply background information. The pace is brisk except when extended explanations are needed. (Skei 1985, 219–20; Ferguson 1991, 95).

According to Reed, Faulkner achieves a dramatic effect by skillful employment of the third person narrative perspective. He describes "Mule in the Yard" as largely "dramatic in the sense that it is the stage-directions and the setting, the performance and the atmosphere" that infuse the action with life.

The "immobile fog" provides contrast with the "frantic action—and the frantic conniving." It is a visual story; the women and the mule move surrealistically, developing a "metaphor for the strange machinations of Snopes and the strange death of Hait." Actions and reactions are foregrounded whereas motives and strategies are obscured (Reed 1973, 49–50).

The assessment of "Mule in the Yard" as a successful comic text should stimulate more extensive critical analysis of the story. Comedy is also not the only means of entry into the text, however, and on many levels, the story represents Faulkner's continuing exegesis of the relation between individual and community. Old Het relies on the community. Mannie benefits from the railroad company's sense of civic responsibility, but a brief aside implies a change in the railroad's sense of obligation to the community, and Mannie rejects the banking institution. Matthews's study links the economics of the text to gender issues. Building on his work or the earlier work of Page and Lind, other critics could give the short story further consideration in the broad context of Faulkner's portrayal of women. The title itself is suggestive of interpretation. The sterile hybrid arguably represents aspects of I. O., Mannie, and even Old Het. The literary challenge of "Mule in the Yard" is as yet insufficiently answered.

## Works Cited

Adams, Richard P. 1968. *Faulkner: Myth and Motion*. Princeton, NJ: Princeton University Press.

Anderson, George. 1990. "Toward a Reading of *The Town* as a Chronicle: Respectability and Race in Three Episodes." *Mississippi Quarterly* 43:377–85.

Bassett, John E. [1988] 1989. "Yoknapatawpha Revised: Demystifying Snopes." In *Vision and Revisions: Essays on Faulkner*. Ed. Bassett. Locust Hill Literary Studies No. 4. West Cornwall, CT: Locust Hill, 213–31.

Blotner, Joseph. 1974. *Faulkner: A Biography*. 2 vols. New York: Random House.

Brown, Calvin S. 1978. "Faulkner's Localism." In *The Maker and the Myth: Faulkner and Yoknapatawpha, 1977*. Ed. Evans Harrington and Ann J. Abadie. Jackson: University Press of Mississippi, 3–24.

Cantwell, Robert. [1953] 1985. "Introduction [to *Sartoris*]." In *Critical Essays on William Faulkner: The Sartoris Family*. Ed. Arthur F. Kinney. Boston: G. K. Hall, 146–60.

Carothers, James B. 1984. "Faulkner's Short Stories: 'And Now What's to Do.'" In *New Directions in Faulkner Studies: Faulkner and Yoknapatawpha, 1983*. Ed. Doreen Fowler and Ann J. Abadie. Jackson: University Press of Mississippi, 202–27.

———. 1985. *William Faulkner's Short Stories*. Ann Arbor, MI: UMI Research Press.

Connolly, Thomas E. 1988. *Faulkner's World: A Directory of His People and Synopses of Actions in His Published Works.* Lanham, MD: University Press of America.

Cowley, Malcolm. 1966. *The Faulkner-Cowley File: Letters and Memories, 1944–1962.* New York: Viking.

Creighton, Joanne V. 1977. *William Faulkner's Craft of Revision: The Snopes Trilogy, "The Unvanquished," and "Go Down, Moses."* Detroit: Wayne State University Press.

Everett, Walter K. 1969. *Faulkner's Art and Character.* Woodbury, NY: Barron's Educational Series.

Faulkner, William. [1929] 1961. *Sartoris.* New York: Random House.

———. 1934. "Mule in the Yard." *Scribner's Magazine* 96 (August): 65–70.

———. 1950. *Collected Stories of William Faulkner.* New York: Random House.

———. 1957. *The Town.* New York: Random House, Vintage Books.

———. [1973] 1974. *Flags in the Dust.* Ed. Douglas Day. New York: Vintage.

———. 1977. *Selected Letters of William Faulkner.* Ed. Joseph Blotner. New York: Random House.

———. 1986. *William Faulkner Manuscripts 21*: The Town. Ed. Michael Millgate. 2 vols. New York: Garland.

Ferguson, James. 1991. *Faulkner's Short Fiction.* Knoxville: University of Tennessee Press.

Holmes, Edward M. 1966. *Faulkner's Twice-Told Tales: His Re-Use of His Material.* The Hague: Mouton.

Hunter, Edwin R. 1973. *William Faulkner: Narrative Practice and Prose Style.* Washington, DC: Windhover.

Karl, Frederick R. 1989. *William Faulkner: American Writer.* New York: Weidenfeld and Nicolson.

Kinney, Arthur F. 1980. "Faulkner's Narrative Poetics and Collected Stories." *Faulkner Studies* 1:58–79.

Kinney, Arthur F., and Doreen Fowler. 1983. "For the Record: Faulkner's Rowan Oak Papers: A Census." *Journal of Modern Literature* 10:327–34.

Kirk, Robert W., and Marvin Klotz. 1963. *Faulkner's People: A Complete Guide and Index to Characters in the Fiction of William Faulkner.* Berkeley and Los Angeles: University of California Press.

Lind, Ilse Dusoir. 1978. "Faulkner's Women." In *The Maker and the Myth: Faulkner and Yoknapatawpha, 1977.* Ed. Evans Harrington and Ann J. Abadie. Jackson: University Press of Mississippi, 89–104.

Matthews, John T. 1992. "Shortened Stories: Faulkner and the Market." In *Faulkner and the Short Story: Faulkner and Yoknapatawpha, 1990*. Ed. Evans Harrington and Ann J. Abadie. Jackson: University Press of Mississippi, 3–37.

Meriwether, James B. 1973. "Faulkner's Correspondence with Scribner's Magazine." *Proof* 3:253–82.

Millgate, Michael. [1966] 1989. *The Achievement of William Faulkner*. New York: Random House. Reprint. Athens: University of Georgia Press. Brown Thrasher Books.

Momberger, Philip. 1978. "Faukner's 'The Village' and 'That Evening Sun': The Tale in Context." *Southern Literary Journal* 11.1:20–31.

Mortimer, Gail L. 1983. *Faulkner's Rhetoric of Loss: A Study in Perception and Meaning*. Austin: University of Texas Press.

Page, Sally R. 1972. *Faulkner's Women: Characterization and Meaning*. Deland, FL: Everett/Edwards.

Rabbetts, John. 1989. *From Hardy to Faulkner: Wessex to Yoknapatawpha*. New York: St. Martin's.

Reed, Joseph W., Jr. 1973. *Faulkner's Narrative*. New Haven: Yale University Press.

Serafin, Joan M. 1983. *Faulkner's Uses of the Classics*. Ann Arbor, MI: UMI Research Press.

Skei, Hans H. 1981. *William Faulkner: The Short Story Career*. Oslo, Norway: Universitetsforlaget.

———. 1985. *William Faulkner: The Novelist as Short Story Writer*. Oslo, Norway: Universitetsforlaget.

Waggoner, Hyatt H. 1959. *William Faulkner: From Jefferson to the World*. Lexington: University of Kentucky Press.

Watson, James G. 1980. "Faulkner's Short Stories and the Making of Yoknapatawpha County." In *Fifty Years of Yoknapatawpha: Faulkner and Yoknapatawpha 1979*. Ed. Doreen Fowler and Ann J. Abadie. Jackson: University Press of Mississippi, 202–25.

Ziegler, Heide. 1989. "Faulkner's Rhetoric of the Comic: The Reivers." In *Faulkner's Discourse: An International Symposium*. Ed. Lothar Hönnighausen. Tübingen: Max Niemeyer Verlag, 117–26.

# That Will Be Fine

## Publication History

"That Will Be Fine" was first published in the *American Mercury* in July 1935. In 1936 it was included in *The Best Stories of 1936* and the *Yearbook of the American Short Story*. When Faulkner's agent, Morton Goldman, asked Faulkner about accepting the *American Mercury* offer of $250 for the story, Faulkner responded that the amount would not be enough to help his difficult financial situation. By the time Goldman understood that this was a complaint and not a refusal of the offer, Faulkner was desperate. Faulkner told Goldman, "Good God yes, let them have the story and do anything they want with it, just so I get the money as soon as possible" (Blotner 1974, 886–87; see also *SL* 91). "That Will Be Fine" is in "The Village" section of *Collected Stories* (1950).

## Circumstances of Composition, Sources, and Influences

Joseph Blotner suggests that Faulkner began this story in March 1935 (1974, 882). As Hans Skei notes, it was produced as one of a particular flurry of stories written for money; Faulkner calculated that he was turning out two stories per week in this period (1981, 79–80; see also *SL* 91). A twenty-nine-page original typescript of "That Will Be Fine" is held in the William B. Wisdom Collection at Tulane University, and a complete manuscript and an incomplete typescript are a part of the Rowan Oak Papers at the University of Mississippi Library (Bonner 1980, 33; Skei 1981, 87–88; Kinney and Fowler 1983, 327–34). Bonner indicates that the complete typescript shows some corrections and deletions, and Kinney and Fowler describe "fairly heavy revisions" on the manuscript, but the partial typescript is "substantially as published in the *American Mercury*" (Bonner 1980, 33; Kinney and Fowler 1983, 328–29). From magazine text to *Collected Stories*, the story underwent no revisions.

Biographical elements in this story include the traditional Falkner family gatherings at the Big Place with Colonel and Sallie Murry Falkner and visits to Columbus and the Ripley home of Grandpa and Grandma Murry. Uncle Rodney in the story probably owes something to William Henry Falkner (son of William Clark Falkner), who, it was told, was killed by a vengeful husband (Blotner 1974, 882; 1984 343). Georgie's father's livery stable business may recall the livery stable that Murry Falkner managed for a time.

Little work has been done on literary influences on this tale. Noting that the comic tone is sustained despite Rodney's death, Skei ranks this story as "one of the Faulkner texts most clearly in the tradition of dark Southwestern humour" (1985, 226).

## Relationship to Other Faulkner Works

Even though it lies just within in the circle of Yoknapatawpha fiction, Skei counts "That Will Be Fine" among the half-dozen autonomous stories written between 1933 and 1941 (1981, 34; 1985, 212–13). "That Will Be Fine" is set in Jefferson and Mottstown, another small town some twenty miles south. Elizabeth Kerr compares Faulkner's Mottstown to Water Valley in Yalobusha County, Mississippi, about twenty miles from Oxford. She believes Mottstown and Memphis are locations that "tie Yoknapatawpha County into the non-fictitious South" (Kerr [1969] 1976, 67). Mottstown, like Memphis, is a part of the larger setting that reappears in various stories and novels.

The major Jefferson family units are not present in this tale, but certain character types recur. Joseph Gold sees "distinct resemblances" between Georgie's family and the Compsons (1966, 23). Blotner also points out several similarities between characters in "That Will Be Fine" and those in *The Sound and the Fury* and other stories of the Compson children. Dorothy Tuck, Blotner, and Skei particularly emphasize that Georgie and Jason Compson are both driven by their greed (Tuck 1964, 178; Blotner 1984, 343; Skei 1985, 226). Ferguson identifies point of view and the "use of Christian symbolism as a kind of ironic backdrop" as additional points of comparison between "That Will Be Fine" and *The Sound and the Fury* (1991, 41, 141–42). Blotner also likens Georgie to the "youthful extortioner," Virgil Beard, in *Sartoris* (1974, 882). John Rabbetts estimates the time of the story to be around 1900, the same general time setting of many of Faulkner's stories with confused children or young men (1989, 119, 238 n. 115).

Uncle Rodney has parallels in fiction as well as the biography. He resembles Uncle Maury Bascomb of *The Sound and the Fury* and is probably the same character as Uncle Rodney of "Sepulture South: Gaslight" (Blotner 1974, 882; 1984, 343, 593; and Skei 1985, 279; Ferguson 1991, 49). This last comparison would be limited to the character himself, however, because his family ties are drawn differently in the two stories. The two Uncle Rodneys may also be different characters. As James Carothers observes, Faulkner was known to give distinctly different characters in different texts identical names (1985, 27). Edward Holmes compares the description of Uncle Rodney with that of Turl in "Centaur in Brass." Both stories portray a man unfit for marriage and better suited for back-window escapades (Holmes 1966, 114).

Ferguson includes Rodney's death in the pattern of the quid pro quo present in Faulkner's short fiction. He comments, however, that death is far more extreme than the reader expects his punishment to be. Also, the laughter evoked when Georgie thinks Rodney's body is a side of beef is "very black comedy." Ferguson concludes that the "underrated" story generates complex responses (1991, 76-77).

"That Will Be Fine" also shares common thematic concerns with other stories. Blotner finds a parallel in the combination of comedy and violent death here and in "Uncle Willy." The community's "smugness, religiosity, and meddling" are critically portrayed here as they are in "Uncle Willy" and "Dry September" (1974, 883). Skei thinks "That Will Be Fine" is closely related to "Uncle Willy" because they both "demonstrate how the half-way agrarian county of Yoknapatawpha loses most of the positive traditional values [in] its pursuit of happiness and some elusive American dream." He ranks "Golden Land" as the only story that does a better job of displaying "injustice, revenge, lack of understanding, corruption, greed, conformity, and, in short, a perversion of all values" (1985, 223). Carothers interprets "That Will Be Fine" as a Faulknerian variation, one of many, on the theme of initiation. In this story, as in "Pennsylvania Station," the protagonist fails to perceive the evil in another character. That discovery is left to the reader (1985, 10).

Among the short stories, Joseph Reed discerns the repeated narrative advantage that Faulkner gains by using a child as storyteller because the child recounts the story without intrusive adult biases. Faulkner enjoys a variety of possibilities in this approach depending on how close the child moves toward experience and away from innocence. Similar narrative strategies in "That Will Be Fine" and *The Unvanquished* involve creating children's expectations that will not materialize quite as they are envisioned. As Reed explains, the portrayal of Georgie's anticipation of an exciting Christmas vacation parallels Bayard and Ringo's anxious anticipation of the stories Bayard's father will tell (1973, 37-38, 181).

For Charles Hadley, the presence of the child narrator in "That Will Be Fine" and "Barn Burning" invites comparison. The narrative strategies reveal that Colonel Sartoris Snopes has grown from the experience, but Georgie has not (Hadley 1980, 63-68).

Kinney likens the humor at the surface of the story with a similar characteristic in *The Wild Palms*. He contrasts the "tension between exposed comedy and concealed irony" with "That Evening Sun," the story that follows "That Will Be Fine" in "The Village" section of the *Collected Stories* (1980, 68).

Frederick Karl compares "That Will Be Fine" with several other stories as they bear on Faulkner's career. He ranks "That Will Be Fine" with "Uncle Willy" and "The Brooch" as "journeyman work." Like "Uncle Willy," "That Will

Be Fine" is "country corn, something below a tall tale." Karl suggests that these nostalgic stories chiefly reflect Faulkner's need to generate income and that "he was running out of material." Karl continues, "The imaginative component in the stories is small, the invention flaccid, and the development busy rather than trenchant. . . . There is no density, and no sense of a story welling up; only a sense of fictions growing out of a professional writer's need of production" (1989, 544–45).

In the context of the *Collected Stories*, "That Will Be Fine" echoes the themes and techniques of adjacent texts. The sense of a community's disintegration that Philip Momberger believes is the controlling image of "The Village" appears in the struggle within the family units and in the inflated importance of reputation in "That Will Be Fine" (1978, 21–24, 29). Ferguson labels "That Will Be Fine" a "light" variation in the tonal symmetry of the ten stories in "The Village." The balance Ferguson identifies is striking: one "heavy" story, two "light" stories, four "heavy" stories, two "light" stories, and one "heavy" story (1991, 158).

## Interpretation and Criticism

No article-length discussions devoted specifically to "That Will Be Fine" have been published. The limited interpretations available focus primarily on the story's criticism of the community and the use of dramatic irony. Reed has studied the "battery of narrative tools" child narrators provide Faulkner. In "That Will Be Fine" Faulkner avoids undue sentiment and nostalgia by creating a child narrator with whom the reader does not feel instant identification. Georgie "is a money-grubbing monster, with scarcely a hint of dawning consciousness." Reed makes the interesting suggestion that Rodney might be maimed rather than dead. The report of five shots, the discussion of the covered object, and the explanation that "now it belonged to Grandpa" strongly suggest that Rodney is dead (1973, 34–35). The conclusive statement is not available, however, because of the narrator's limited and sheltered awareness. As Reed himself observes, Georgie "is brought just to the point of revelation but left there, uninformed, because Faulkner's strategy of narration finds more profit from the unknowing opposition of innocence and experience" (1973, 37).

According to Blotner, Faulkner gains some narrative advantage by telling this story through a naïve seven-year-old. Georgie understands far less than the reader the significance of his observations. This comic dramatic irony turns suddenly more somber when Georgie describes the "side of beef" being carried into the house for Grandpa (1974, 882).

Discussing the narrative focus of the story at somewhat greater length, Hadley points out that Georgie is both narrative voice (recounting the story) and focusing agent (perceiving the story). The effect is that the events reported are given different valuation from what might be expected. For example, Georgie's interest in money makes him accentuate those actions that might earn him money and minimize other parts of the story, including the far more serious embezzlement and finally the shooting. Hadley concludes that Georgie's "mind acts as a sort of filter, distorting events and their significance. The reader must re-establish the hierarchy of importance of events and characters in the short story in order to understand the story" (Hadley 1980, 66–67).

Carothers calls Georgie "damnably naive" (1985, 20). He suggests further that, like "Honor," this story relies "on the implicit rejection of the storyteller's cynicism" to achieve its effects (1985, 107). Skei adds that Georgie seems to be recounting the story immediately after the events have occurred (1985, 225).

In his examination of Faulkner's use of mimetic voice ("represented speech in fiction"), Stephen Ross analyzes the effect of Georgie's narration as it utilizes a "fluid variety of direct, mingled, and indirect modes." When the narrator recounts the speech of other people, within a given paragraph, the movement is typically from indirect to direct quotation "that comes as a climax to the accumulated mingled speech modes in Georgie's narration." Ross adds that the voices we hear in Georgie's telling of the events allows us as readers to know more than he does yet remain within his telling of the tale (1989, 88–90).

As most critics interpret the story, the greed of seven-year-old Georgie derives from adult models. Gold's remarks focus on the failure of the adults to take responsibility for Georgie's development. The child is taught deception by Rodney and also by his mother and aunt. Their primary concern focuses on cover-up, protecting the family honor that is in fact lacking in Rodney's character. Gold argues that the "story clearly demonstrates that each generation is responsible for the values of the next," and that "the adults in the story are directly responsible for the material values that are at the heart of this child's world" (1966, 23–24). Walter Everett shows how the themes of "desire for money and sexual lust," as portrayed in the exploits of Georgie and Uncle Rodney, are neatly joined in Rosie's idea of a Christmas present for Grandpa. He believes that the dramatic irony provides the comedy of this story (1969, 172–73). Skei compares Georgie's obsession with Rodney's. He is as single-minded in his desire for money as his Uncle Rodney is single-minded in his pursuit of women. Georgie is the product of adult lessons, the final one of which he does not quite understand. Rodney's vice proves fatal. The critique of social values is important in this tale. The characters seem primarily concerned with "money and prestige and respectability." Only by inference can another set of values be detected, and that comes through the dramatic irony of the text (Skei 1985, 226, 215). Ferguson believes the story "suggests the figurative reality of Original Sin." Georgie is, in his estimation, "utterly corrupt, one of the most loathsome children in all of fiction" (Ferguson 1991, 59).

The final section of the story deserves some comment. Faulkner might have ended with the image of Rodney's body being carried toward his father's home. This ending would retain the thematic unity Everett perceives and the dramatic irony of Georgie's continued misunderstanding. Instead, the final section shows the men of the community, then the family, hustling to protect Georgie from the scene. There is a sense that they are establishing a pattern with him that parallels the protection of the family provides Rodney until his death. As Skei has noted, the parallels between Rodney and Georgie are undeniable.

The closing remark indicating Georgie's unreformed greed bodes ill. Matters will probably not go well for him. From this perspective, it is also possible to contrast Georgie with Quentin. In "A Justice" and "That Evening Sun," Quentin does not understand the implications of the events he has heard about or witnessed, but he does have a sense that they are important, and he will eventually reach a more adequate understanding of them. Of course, Quentin will also commit suicide. Georgie, on the other hand, remains happily oblivious. He has a fleeting sense of his own personal danger when Rodney picks up the stick, and he runs. But at the conclusion of the story, only a little later in time, Georgie is eager to catch a possum and earn another quarter.

The limited response to "That Will Be Fine" implies that most critics rank this story below Faulkner's finest. Carothers places it among Faulkner's "lesser efforts," and Karl considers it an "undistinguished story of childhood memories" (Carothers 1985, 18; Karl 1989, 575n.). Skei, however, lists "That Will Be Fine" with stories written after 1932 that "indicate that Faulkner might have sustained his short story efforts on the high level of quality and variety of his major period [1928–1932], if Hollywood had not intervened" (1981, 34). Hugh Ruppersburg describes the story as "hilarious and neglected" (1983, 9). It is not one of Faulkner's most remarkable efforts, but it has consistency of attitude, subtlety of detail, and brisk pacing—and it was ranked one of the best stories of 1936.

## Works Cited

Blotner, Joseph. 1974. *Faulkner: A Biography*. 2 vols. New York: Random House.

———. 1984. *Faulkner: A Biography*. 1 vol. New York: Random House.

Bonner, Thomas, Jr., comp. 1980. *William Faulkner: The William B. Wisdom Collection: A Descriptive Catalogue*. New Orleans: Tulane University Libraries.

Carothers, James B. 1985. *William Faulkner's Short Stories*. Ann Arbor, MI: UMI Research Press.

Everett, Walter K. 1969. *Faulkner's Art and Character*. Woodbury, NY: Barron's Educational Series.

Faulkner, William. 1935. "That Will Be Fine." *American Mercury* 35 (July):264–76.

———. 1950. *Collected Stories of William Faulkner*. New York: Random House.

———. 1977. *Selected Letters of William Faulkner*. Ed. Joseph Blotner. New York: Random House.

———. 1979. *Uncollected Stories of William Faulkner*. Ed. Joseph Blotner. New York: Random House.

Ferguson, James. 1991. *Faulkner's Short Fiction*. Knoxville: University of Tennessee Press.

Gold, Joseph. 1966. *William Faulkner: A Study in Humanism From Metaphor to Discourse*. Norman: University of Oklahoma Press.

Hadley, Charles. 1980. "Seeing and Telling: Narrational Functions in the Short Story." *Discourse and Style* 2:63–68.

Holmes, Edward M. 1966. *Faulkner's Twice-Told Tales: His Re-Use of His Material*. The Hague: Mouton.

Karl, Frederick R. 1989. *William Faulkner: American Writer*. New York: Weidenfeld and Nicolson.

Kerr, Elizabeth M. [1969] 1976. *Yoknapatawpha: Faulkner's "Little Postage Stamp of Native Soil."* New York: Fordham University Press.

Kinney, Arthur F. 1980. "Faulkner's Narrative Poetics and *Collected Stories*." *Faulkner Studies* 1:58–79.

Kinney, Arthur F., and Doreen Fowler. 1983. "For the Record: Faulkner's Rowan Oak Papers: A Census." *Journal of Modern Literature* 10:327–34.

Momberger, Philip. 1978. "Faulkner's 'The Village' and 'That Evening Sun': The Tale in Context." *Southern Literary Journal* 11.1:20–31.

Rabbetts, John. 1989. *From Hardy to Faulkner: Wessex to Yoknapatawpha*. New York: St. Martin's.

Reed, Joseph W., Jr. 1973. *Faulkner's Narrative*. New Haven: Yale University Press.

Ross, Stephen M. 1989. *Fiction's Inexhaustible Voice: Speech and Writing in Faulkner*. Athens: University of Georgia Press.

Ruppersburg, Hugh M. 1983. *Voice and Eye in Faulkner's Fiction*. Athens: University of Georgia Press.

Skei, Hans H. 1981. *William Faulkner: The Short Story Career*. Oslo, Norway: Universitetsforlaget.

———. 1985. *William Faulkner: The Novelist as Short Story Writer*. Oslo, Norway: Universitetsforlaget.

Tuck, Dorothy. 1964. *Crowell's Handbook of Faulkner*. New York: Thomas Y. Crowell.

# That Evening Sun

## Publication History

"That Evening Sun" was first published as "That Evening Sun Go Down" in the *American Mercury*, March 1931. Although the story became popular in subsequent years, its initial reception was inauspicious. Faulkner submitted it to *Scribner's* on October 6, 1930, but it was returned before the month ended. About two months later, K. S. Crichton, assistant editor at *Scribner's*, asked if Faulkner might resubmit a shorter version of a story he remembered under the title "That Evening Sun Go Down" but which from his description was undoubtedly "Spotted Horses" (Meriwether 1973, 262–63). At any rate, Crichton's request with its misremembered title was irrelevant. The story-sending schedule shows that by October 28, 1930, Faulkner had submitted the story to *American Mercury*, where it was accepted on the condition that it be revised. When published in March, it was the magazine's lead story and received cover treatment (Meriwether [1961] 1971, 175–80; Meriwether 1971, 308–09; *SL* 48–49; *WFM 9* Introduction x, Blotner 1974, 669, 670; Skei 1981, 65). Faulkner revised the story for collection in *These 13* (1931), and he used that version with minor alterations in *Collected Stories* (1950).

## Circumstances of Composition, Sources, and Influences

The earliest reference to "That Evening Sun" is October 1930. Consequently, discussions of its origin frequently assume a 1930 composition date. It is possible, however, that Faulkner wrote this story and "A Justice" nearer to the time he began *The Sound and the Fury*—in the first half of 1928, possibly even before he began the novel. David Minter observes that although the evidence for this conclusion is circumstantial, it is compelling (1980, 283 n. 6).

Many arguments placing "That Evening Sun" before *The Sound and the Fury* in chronological order focus on the characterizations of the children. Although Blotner does not claim proof of a pre-novel date for the story, he does say that "That Evening Sun" "is the kind of story of the experiences of the Compson children which WF [William Faulkner] said *S & F* [*The Sound and the Fury*] developed from" (1974, 566, Notes 82). In "That Evening Sun," Quentin lives to be older than he does in the novel (Leon Howard in Blotner 1974, Notes 82). Further, the adult Quentin of "That Evening Sun" does not reflect his preoccupation with Caddy's virginity, his incessant suicidal thoughts, or his "obsessive inner voices" (Samway 1985, 181). If composition of the three related texts followed in the order of "That Evening Sun," "A Justice," and *The Sound and the Fury*, then Quentin first appeared as a narrator in "That Evening Sun" (Hunt 1982, 369). Benjy does not appear in the story (Howard in Blotner 1974, Notes 82; Ferguson 1991, 201–202 n. 21). Ferguson adds that the Dilsey character in the short story is perhaps "so passive and ineffectual" because she had not yet assumed the stronger role she has in *The Sound and the Fury* (1991, 201–02 n. 21).

Other similarities also suggest that story and novel might have been written at about the same time. The story's description of the town in present time, including details of telephone poles and laundry trucks, seems more like the present time of *The Sound and the Fury*. The narrative of "seemingly detached episodes" is like the episodic narrative of Benjy's section of the novel (Slabey 1964, 176–77; see also Kinney 1982, 8). According to Ferguson, the earliest version of "That Evening Sun" ("Never Done No Weeping When You Wanted to Laugh") shares "striking similarities in style, dialogue, and point of view" with Benjy's section of the novel, and Blotner finds resemblances between the handwriting of "Never Done No Weeping When You Wanted to Laugh" and the manuscript of *The Sound and the Fury* (Ferguson 1991, 33; Blotner 1974, Notes 82). Minter finds a connection in the image of twilight that appears in both of these texts and "A Justice" (Minter 1980, 93).

Not all critics agree that the short stories came before *The Sound and the Fury*. Although Blotner places the discussion of "That Evening Sun" in the chapter entitled "June, 1927–September, 1928" in his 1974 biography of Faulkner, in the revised 1984 edition he puts the story in the "April 1930–January 1931" chapter, at which time records of the story do exist (1974, 565–67; 1984, 266). Irving Howe believes the story is an "offshoot" of *The Sound and the Fury*, and Stephen Whicher finds that it "bears all the earmarks of an afterthought, whose conclusion the earlier novel could hardly have anticipated" (Howe [1952] 1975, 70; Whicher 1954, 255). Gail Morrison dates the story from the fall of 1928, after *The Sound and the Fury* was completed, and Max Putzel places it in 1930 (Morrison 1983, 461; Putzel 1985, 229). John Matthews writes of Quentin's older voice in "That Evening Sun" as the "ghostly Quentin who survives through several textual avatars into *Absalom, Absalom!*," a statement that presumes Faulkner's intentional use of an already dead Quentin after *The Sound and the Fury* (1989, 71–72). The arguments on both sides are interesting for what they suggest about the writer's craft during a seminal period. However, Blotner's point in 1974 remains true: there simply is "no sending schedule, agent's record, or conclusive manuscript evidence which would permit accurate dating of the inception and writing of this story" (1974, Notes 82).

Noel Polk describes the textual history of "That Evening Sun" as the "most complicated of any in *These 13*." Nevertheless, critics have been able to make more verifiable observations about the development of the text than about the date of composition. "That Evening Sun" exists in several versions, both prepublication and published. The earliest known, undated, holograph manuscript is entitled "Never Done No Weeping When You Wanted to Laugh." Another version, a twenty-six-page, complete ribbon typescript gives the title "—That Evening Sun Go Down," but the carbon of that typescript shows the revision in Faulkner's hand to "That Evening Sun" (Morrison 1983, 461–74; *WFM 9* Introduction x).

When H. L. Mencken accepted the story for the *American Mercury*, he described it as "capital," but he balked at naming Nancy's husband "Jesus" and at referring to her pregnancy so explicitly. Mencken seemed unconcerned that the name change would affect both dialogue and imagery. He wrote, "I see no reason why he should be called Jesus—it is, in fact, a very rare name among Negroes, and I fear using it would make most readers believe we were trying to be naughty in a somewhat strained manner." Jesus's name became *Jubah* to eliminate Mencken's concern. (In a note to Mencken about the requested changes, Faulkner refers to the character as *Judah* although the magazine version uses *Jubah*.) Faulkner returned to the name *Jesus* in *These 13*. Norman Holmes Pearson correctly observes that the return to "Jesus" restores the "paradoxical tension which was otherwise lost" (Pearson 1954, 65; Manglaviti 1972, 649–52; Blotner 1974, Notes 99; *SL* 48–49; *WFM 9* Introduction x).

Faulkner did not incorporate all of Mencken's requests for revision. Mencken wrote, "It seems to me that the dialogue about Nancy's pregnancy, on pages four and five, is somewhat loud for a general magazine? [*sic*] I believe it could be modified without doing the slightest damage to the story." Faulkner wrote back that some reference to Nancy's pregnancy needed to be retained in order to maintain her husband "as a potential factor of the tragedy." He did concede to a more subdued reference to Nancy's pregnancy and submitted a revised version of those two pages. The *American Mercury* text explains Nancy's swelling apron as follows:

"He [Jubah] said it was a watermelon that Nancy had under her dress. And it was Winter, too.
 'Where did you get a watermelon in the Winter?' Caddy said.
 'I didn't,' Jubah said. 'It wasn't me that give it to her. But I can cut it down, same as if it was.'"

*These 13* reinstates the original imagery:

"He [Jesus] said it was a watermelon that Nancy had under her dress.
 'It never come off of your vine, though,' Nancy said.
 'Off of what vine?' Caddy said.
 'I can cut down the vine it did come off of,' Jesus said."

Faulkner remarked of his anesthetized revision of Nancy's pregnancy: "I did remove the 'vine' business. I reckon that's what would outrage Boston." (Manglaviti 1972, 651–53; Blotner 1974, 670–71; *"That Evening Sun Go Down"* 258; *T13* 236)

Mencken defended his suggestions to Faulkner as "his best editorial judgment." He made additional changes once Faulkner had returned the revised typescript. The revised typescript page shows the following description of Nancy's belly when she was found hanging struck through: ". . . her belly swelling a little, paling a little as it swelled, like a colored balloon pales with distension." The magazine version reads: ". . . found Nancy hanging from the window, stark naked" and *Collected Stories* text reads: ". . . found Nancy hanging from the window, stark naked, her belly already swelling out a little, like a little balloon" (Manglaviti 1972, 653; Blotner 1974, 670–71; "That Evening Sun Go Down" 258; *CS* 291–92; *SL* 48–49). Additional revisions are evident on the ribbon typescript used as setting copy. Some are in Mencken's hand and some are the work of another proofreader. They concern such matters as additional paragraph breaks and section divisions (Manglaviti 1972, 653–54; Blotner 1974, Notes 96).

When he revised the story for collection, Faulkner restored many of the deletions, but he retained paragraph and section divisions inserted by Mencken, even embellishing the division of the last section by further dividing it into two sections. Leo Manglaviti believes that Faulkner worked on his revisions for *These 13* from the manuscript titled "Never Done No Weeping When You Wanted to Laugh" and the *American Mercury* text. A line present in the typescript describes one of the actions Nancy threatened if Jesus were to take another wife. Among her threats the typescript adds, "Ara hand that touched her, I'd cut it off." This line does not appear in "Never Done No Weeping When You Wanted to Laugh," the magazine version, or the collected version (Skei 1977, 98–100; 192 n. 183; Morrison 1983, 467; Manglaviti 1972, 654; *WFM 9* 239). It was not unusual for Faulkner to agree to revisions to facilitate publication; James Carothers notes that stories such as "Spotted

Horses," "Snow," "Knight's Gambit," and "Shall Not Perish" were altered for publication (Carothers 1984, 207).

Although the preceding discussion focuses on the alterations that the story underwent specifically in relation to magazine publication, the extant manuscripts and published versions allow for ample study of the development of the text from the early holograph version to the version in *These 13*. The changes are significant. Pearson's early comparative study of the story at three stages—"Never Done No Weeping When You Wanted to Laugh," the *American Mercury* version, and the *These 13* version—identified the major areas of change. Pearson regards as particularly significant the substitution of the word *cabin* for *house* when the Compsons describe Nancy's dwelling because it contrasts the Compsons' perspective with that of Nancy and Jesus, who both refer to the dwelling as the "house," and represents Nancy and Jesus's "sense of the personal dignity of what had been invaded." Faulkner's deletion of material from the *Mercury* version to the *These 13* text demonstrates his awareness that direct presentation of action eliminated the need for explanation. Quentin's analysis of the Compsons' leaving Nancy's cabin is omitted; only the dramatic presentation of their exit remains. The primary alteration from the first manuscript version to the final text is the change in the "angle of reference." The point of view shifts from being "essentially Nancy's" to becoming Quentin's; as narrator, he shows the personal growth he experiences.

The Compson family presence increases throughout: the story begins and ends with them. (Pearson justifies Benjy's absence pointing out that Benjy's indifference to time makes him an inappropriate character in this particular story.) Quentin's reaction is crucial and is measured by the other children's lack of understanding: they cannot differentiate between Hallowe'en fright and Nancy's terror. The story becomes Quentin's "story of himself, as he had learned from it." The attempt to forestall the setting sun and inevitable death echo in his suicide (Pearson 1954, 61–70). According to Blotner, the early manuscript focuses on Nancy although it employs Quentin as an adult to narrate the story. The "clear implication" is that Nancy returns to her cabin and death. The version entitled "That Evening Sun Go Down" is increased in length with additional description, dialogue, and background information on Nancy. Subsequently, without altering the emphasis on Nancy's story, Faulkner developed the contrast of Quentin's adult perspective with that of his childhood, particularly showing his and Caddy's sensitivity (Blotner 1974, 565–66; see also Skei 1981, 65–67). Ferguson adds that the story is improved by the revised ending, done between magazine publication and inclusion in the collections. The deletion of Quentin's closing observation—"the white people going on, dividing the impinged lives of us and Nancy"—removes a too obvious statement of what the action demonstrates; it also eliminates a breach in the voice of the child narrator found in the inflated style of the phrase "dividing the impinged lives of us and Nancy" (Ferguson 1991, 33; "That Evening Sun Go Down" 267).

Skei claims that the version in *These 13*, subsequently used again in *Collected Stories*, is the "final, authoritative one" (1977, 97; 1981, 65). There are a few differences between the two collected versions, but these involve alterations of spelling, capitalization, and paragraphing. In the critical response to "That Evening Sun," the choice of source text has been irregular. In 1935, Edward O'Brien offered an extended close reading of the story in the *Short Story Case Book* series that depended on the particularities of the text. He used the magazine version, "That Evening Sun Go Down," but cited *These 13* (1935, 325–61). Similarly, Sterling Brown and George Snell cite the *These 13* text, but their references to specifics, such as to Jubah rather than Jesus, indicate their use of the magazine version (Brown 1931, 347, 350; Snell 1947, 99–101). Frederick Karl uses "That Evening Sun Go Down" as the operative title for his references to the story unless he is specifically referring to the title in collection (Karl 1989, 314ff).

The popularity of "That Evening Sun" has led to a search for analogues to the story in life and literature. The escapades of the Compson children in this story and other texts are typically linked to the activities of the Falkner boys—Billy, Johncy, and Jack—along with their cousin Sallie Murry (Blotner 1974, 566). Jackson Benson specifically likens Quentin Compson of "That Evening Sun" and *The Sound and the Fury* to Faulkner as a boy: a "quiet, observant, serious, somewhat introverted, and thoughtful child who had no really close friends outside the family" (Benson [1971] 1982, 217). John Faulkner's remembrances include a woman in the community who he believes served as a model for Nancy. Nancy Snowball, a woman who once cooked and washed for the Falkners, caught the children's interest with her ability to crawl through a barbed wire fence without having to touch the load of laundry balanced on her head (Faulkner 1963, 46). The threat Jesus posed to Nancy may be traced to the murder of a woman by her husband, Dave Bowdry, that took place near the Falkner home. A nearby ditch may have added to the fictional scene that is enhanced by the danger the ditch seems to convey—either by providing Jesus a place to hide or as dividing the safety of the Compson house and the danger of the cabin (Blotner 1974, 566; see also Cullen and Watkins 1975, 72–73).

Parallels found in literature and music relate less to characters and action than to the development of dialogue and imagery in the story. "That Evening Sun" is significantly enriched by the influence of blues music on the text. The title comes from the words to "St. Louis Blues." John Hagopian believes the relationship to the song is ironic, citing as an example the song's line "I'll love my baby till the day I die" (Hagopian 1962, 54; see also Utley 1964, 244; Nilon 1965, 45; Davis 1987, 77). Ken Bennett traces the story's rich associations with both blues music and black religious music; his work shows that the story's indebtedness goes much deeper than the mere borrowing of its title from Handy's "St. Louis Blues." The image of the evening sun appears in black religious music, sometimes to represent coming death and judgment. In the blues tradition, the setting sun is linked to despair and also to the "time when the black male proved his masculinity" and the prostitute's time to "shine." The character Jesus is much like the rambler character in the blues tradition who may be a criminal, a misfit, or a promiscuous lover. The language of the story is reminiscent of the double entendre prevalent in blues language, such as the reference to the vine and fruit to mean sexual promiscuity. Also, in blues language sexual acts and organs are referred to through common metaphors. Kitchen images are especially prevalent; frequently the kitchen represents the woman's body. Jesus's complaint ("I can't hang around white man's kitchen") becomes richer in that context. Voodoo also appears in blues lyrics, just as it does in the story. Nancy's discovery of the hog bone, a curse and also a phallic symbol, terrifies her. It implies "that Nancy's 'curse' is her promiscuity" (Bennett 1985, 339–42).

Comparisons with Hemingway, especially his short story "The Killers," have predominated in the list of important literary antecedents. O'Brien sees resemblances to Ernest Hemingway's style in the "laconic reporting" in the story of Nancy's confinement and attempted suicide in jail and patterns of dialogue in the story (1935, 329, 339). Ray West compares the use of initiation in Hemingway's "The Killers" to Quentin's awakening adult sensibilities in "That Eveing Sun"; he also finds similarities between Caddy's and Nick Adams's interest in the nature of evil (West 1952, 98; see also Pearson 1954, 61). Leonard Frey judges Faulkner's story to be "superior" to Hemingway's "The Killers" in that Nancy, the victim of the inevitable violence, remains the dominant character whereas in "The Killers" Nick Adams is the central figure rather than Ole Andreson (Frey 1953, 39–40; see also Slabey 1964, 180; Skei 1981, 66; Flora 1982, 41; Gerlach 1985, 131). Austin Wright makes the point that in both stories a "conflict with a range of possible outcomes" is initiated, but in each, the narrative ends without reaching any of the possible outcomes. The reader then must revise his or her sense of what constitutes the focus of the story. In both these cases, the "issue is precisely the failure of resolution" (Wright 1989, 126).

A number of other studies have made brief observations of literary links between "That Evening Sun" and a wide variety of texts. Collectively, the list demonstrates more the rich texture of the story than a single dominating influence on the story. O'Brien suggests that a comparison could be made of Balzac's and Faulkner's use of chiaroscuro in the development of atmosphere (1935, 351). Frey likens the irony in the story to ironic presentation in ballads such as "The Twa Corbies" and "The Wife of Usher's Well": in all these, although an objective presentation of the material is offered, the reader understands more than the narrator does (Frey 1953, 40). Frey regards the counterpoint in the mingled conversations of Caddy and Jason with Mr. Compson and Nancy as similar to the remarks of Edgar, Lear, and the Fool in Shakespeare's *King Lear* because in both texts the impact of their comments stems from their "varying degrees of awareness of their positions" (Frey 1953, 35). Richard Adams finds the phrase "a long diminishing noise of rubber and asphalt like tearing silk" to be "possibly derived from Flaubert." The image appears not only in "That Evening Sun," but also in such works as *Mosquitoes, The Wild Palms*, and *Intruder in the Dust*. (Adams's page reference to *These 13* is incorrect [1968, 47–48 n. 19; *T13* 232; *CS* 289]). Edward Richardson compares Nancy's terror with the "driving intensity" of scenes in *The White Rose of Memphis* by William Clark Falkner, William's great-grandfather (1969, 15). Mark Coburn considers Tom in Harriet Beecher Stowe's *Uncle Tom's Cabin* a literary analogue to the suffering Nancy (1974, 207–08).

John Rosenman traces the archetypal pattern of heaven and hell in Faulkner's story and in Ray Bradbury's much later *Dandelion Wine* (1957). Rosenman finds the resemblances striking but does not establish a direct line of influence from Faulkner to Bradbury. Rosenman credits the work of Maud Bodkin in *Archetypal Patterns in Poetry, Psychological Studies of Imagination* as his source for archetypal study (1978, 12–16).

As other scholars have, Robert Hamb[l]in links the title to "St. Louis Blues," but he suggests another possible parallel in William Blake's "Nurse's Song" from *Songs of Innocence and Experience*. In the poem, the setting sun is used as an emblem marking the inevitable passage out of childhood. He does not claim with certainty that Faulkner knew this poem, but he confirms the similar use of the image, just as both "recognized the archetypal initiation pattern in the exposure of children to the realities of time and experience" (Hamb[l]in 1979, 92–93). According to John Gerlach, the story bears an inverted relationship to Ephesians. The biblical letter establishes social codes of behavior including the admonition not to let the sun set on one's anger. In "That Evening Sun" the children manipulate parents, wives are prostitutes, and the character Jesus remains angry. The story's world is akin to that portrayed in Amos (Gerlach 1985, 140–41).

## Relationship to Other Faulkner Works

"That Evening Sun" has generated a number of comparisons within the body of Faulkner's fiction. As a story involving the Compson family, it joins *The Sound and the Fury, Absalom, Absalom!, The Unvanquished, Go Down, Moses, Requiem for a Nun, The Town, The Mansion*, "A Justice," "Lion," "Skirmish at Sartoris," "My Grandmother Millard," "Vendée," "Retreat," "Raid," "A Bear Hunt," "The Old People," "The Bear," "Delta Autumn," and the 1946 "Appendix: The Compsons" (Kinney 1982, 10; 1984, 156; 1989, 93; see also Carothers 1985, 27). Similarities with these texts focus especially on *The Sound and the Fury*, *Absalom, Absalom!*, "A Justice," and *Requiem for a Nun* (Slabey 1964, 176–80; see also Holmes 1966, 114). They typically involve considerations of characterization, theme, and narrative perspectives. Indeed, most criticism arises, either directly or indirectly, from a context that includes knowledge of the Compsons' lives beyond the short story. Dorothy Tuck considers "That Evening Sun" less accessible without its specific Yoknapatawpha context than the other frequently anthologized stories "A Rose for Emily" and "Barn Burning." Tuck argues that the story depends on *The Sound and the Fury* for the subtlety of characterization and tension present in the Compson family (1964, 159).

When emphasizing the intertextual relationships "That Evening Sun" shares with other Faulkner works, critics generally attach little significance to differences in family history and chronological inconsistencies. One obvious difficulty with relating "That Evening Sun" to other "Quentin" texts is that Quentin tells Nancy's story at the age of twenty-four even though, as recounted in *The Sound and the Fury*, he dies at twenty. Faulkner's reaction to Malcolm Cowley's concern over the problem was simply "Dont worry" (*SL* 208). Critics who attempt to date the events of the story do so based on extra-textual information. Hagopian believes the story is set in 1902, based on "information about the Compson children given in several other works of Faulkner" (1962, 50). Cleanth Brooks dates the action in 1898 ([1963] 1990, 334). Slabey recognizes temporal discrepancies in the Compson texts, but he dates the narration in 1910, the year Quentin commits suicide (1964, 173). Placing Quentin's narration of this story and perhaps "A Justice" just before his suicide represents his "vicarious return to the state of lost innocence" (Slabey 1964, 176–80; see also Brown 1976, 353–55). Skei dates the action of the story as generally around 1910 to 1915, although he does not believe establishing the chronology is particularly important (1977, 106, 103).

A number of critics have compared the personalities of the Compsons in the short story with their appearances in *The Sound and the Fury* and elsewhere. Leon Edel considers the story a "retrospective" text in relation to *The Sound and the Fury* in that the personalities of the Compson children already exhibit the characteristics more fully articulated in the novel. The story relates to the novel in the portrayal of the children's associations of the ditch because in both texts the children link the ditch with death or danger, the name *Nancy*, death, and decay, for in the novel, again, the children's response to a death—their grandmother's—provides the center of the action. In both texts, the innocence of the children is juxtaposed to the adult "world of suffering and death, bigotry and hatred and atrophy" that they will come to know in time (Edel 1962, 254–55; see also Brooks [1963] 1990, 335; Brooks 1983, 30–32). A number of critics have tried to account for Benjy's absence from the story. Brooks finds it curious, but others stress that Benjy simply has no place in the story (Brooks [1963] 1990, 447; see also Brooks 1983, 43); Pearson 1954, 67; Slabey 1964, 176–80; Brown 1976, 353–55; Beck 1976, 290ff; Momberger 1978, 25).

The Compson parents have also undergone scrutiny. Mrs. Compson is generally regarded as the same self-centered individual in both texts. Michael Millgate judges Jason Compson, Sr., as he appears in both "That Evening Sun" and *The Sound and the Fury* to be one of Faulkner's "well-meaning failures." He is the "intellectual of generous impulses but inadequate courage or will to action, tending always to dissipate his energies in talk." He shares this trait with Horace Benbow, Ike McCaslin, and Gavin Stevens (Millgate [1966], 1989, 117–18). Although there is some debate about the degree of Mr. Compson's culpability, Arthur Kinney sees Compson's "willed ignorance" of the danger Nancy faces presaging his later refusal to believe that Quentin will commit suicide and his inability to see how the Sutpen story "parodies" the Compsons and suggests their own decline (1982, 8–9).

Samway observes in a study not of Quentin, but of his father, that Mr. Compson appears as a "palpable, overwhelming presence" in "That Evening Sun," *The Sound and the Fury*, and *Absalom, Absalom!* He is always near Quentin; he is known through Quentin, and Quentin includes his father as one of the figures in his narration for the first time in "That Evening Sun." Samway believes that Mr. Compson of the short story is much like Mr. Compson as described in the Benjy section of *The Sound and the Fury*, and in *Absalom, Absalom!* Mr. Compson's final dismissal of Nancy's fear in his recommendation that she lock the door, extinguish the lamp, and go to bed resembles his words to both Benjy and Quentin in the closing of their respective sections of *The Sound and the Fury*. The image of Mr. Compson as a two-headed figure (by carrying young Jason on his back) is "an undeveloped image foreshadowing a dichotomy found later in *Absalom, Absalom!*"—that is, the sense of Quentin as two people (Samway 1985, 180–82, 184, 204).

Not only do "That Evening Sun" and *The Sound and the Fury* share characters, they also share motifs: pregnancy (Nancy and Caddy), suicide (Nancy, Quentin, and Mrs. Lovelady), "sun/shadow/time" images (Nancy, Quentin, Sutpen), issues of race and gyneolatry, and miscegenation (Slabey 1964, 176–80; see also Brown 1976, 353–55). Millgate observes that the title on the first page of *The Sound and the Fury* is "Twilight," a reference either to the section or to the work as a whole. "Twilight" bears an obvious likeness to the title "That Evening Sun Go Down" ([1966] 1989, 86). Ferguson likens Quentin's initiation in "That Evening Sun" to the initiation surrounding the death of Damuddy in *The Sound and the Fury* (1991, 57).

Not all critics have so easily accepted the interweavings of "That Evening Sun" with *The Sound and the Fury* and *Absalom, Absalom!* Carothers, for example, doubts that some of these relationships exist. He concedes that "That Evening Sun" relates to other Faulkner texts in this manner: the story "invites comparison with Faulkner's other first-person stories, with his other treatments of the relations between whites and blacks in Yoknapatawpha, and with his other renderings of Nancy, Dilsey, and the Compsons." However, in discussing the intertextual relationships among "That Evening Sun," *The Sound and the Fury*, and *Absalom, Absalom!*, Carothers states that people sometimes read the story "in search of help in dealing with the two novels," which he considers to be misguided. He specifically takes issue with the idea that the Compsons are consistently drawn with the same personalities. The problem, Carothers claims, is that it may not be appropriate to assume a "sameness" of the character as he or she appears in various contexts. He states that with respect to *The Sound and the Fury*, "the novel simply does not count in a reading of the story; they are two different texts, operating according to two different histories." Nor is the "past-haunted" Quentin of *Absalom, Absalom!* like the short story narrator. Carothers concludes that the "narrator of the story projects a calm, dispassionate, mature voice, a voice very different from that of the two Harvard Quentins." Carothers faults Tuck for assuming that the children have taken on personalities prior to the onset of action. Nancy's fear of reprisal from Jesus affects the children, especially Caddy and Jason. Her heightened state of emotion keeps them on edge as well. They quarrel, and they do not want to go to Nancy's cabin because it will not be fun. Quentin's remembrance of his question, "Who will do our washing now, Father?," reveals the child's recognition of an altered relationship and the adult's recognition of "its ironic inadequacy" (Carothers 1985, 11–13, 25, 47; see also Tuck 1964, 177–78; *CS* 309).

"That Evening Sun" and "A Justice" are related through the reappearance of the Compsons (again without Benjy) and more particularly in the use of Quentin's memories of his childhood. In both stories, the children react to the events of the internal narrative (Blotner 1974, 566). "That Evening Sun" differs from "A Justice," however, in that the children appear in both the story and the frame narrative of the older Quentin introducing a childhood recollection (Ferguson 1991, 57–58). Lewis Dabney believes that in the absence of contention between Caddy and Jason, "A Justice" possesses the "innocence hungered for in 'That Evening Sun' and *The Sound and the Fury*," but Ferguson argues that "A Justice" mutes the "contrast between innocence and corruption" more than "That Evening Sun" does (Dabney 1974, 73; Ferguson 1991, 57–58). In Putzel's analysis, Quentin does not experience in these two stories either the "varying distaste" of his brothers or the "unvarying compassion" of Caddy. The children are younger in "That Evening Sun" than they are in "A Justice," but "That Evening Sun" "depicts a later stage in the Compson family's moral decay" (Putzel 1985, 230, 238).

"That Evening Sun" and "A Justice" raise similar concerns about race, father-quest, adultery, miscegenation, and illegitimacy (Slabey 1964, 174–75).

The contrast comes in the degrees of protection offered by ostensibly empowered men—the chief protects his slave, but Jason Compson cannot protect Nancy (Dabney 1974, 89). According to Slabey, both stories convey the adult status of Quentin with a greater complexity of narration—"complex sentences, mature diction, figurative language." Slabey believes the point of view in "A Justice" is more subtle (1964, 174–75). "A Justice" reverses the narrative order by opening with the child's voice and closing with the adult Quentin (Ferguson 1991, 112). Millgate notes that Faulkner does not exploit the presence of the narrator by juxtaposing the stories in the first collection in which they both appeared, *These 13* ([1966] 1989, 261). Matthews examines "That Evening Sun," "A Justice," and "Lion" as framed stories narrated by Quentin. They share the common characteristic of having an older Quentin tell an event from his childhood that "points to the significance of the remembered incident in Quentin's later understanding of his culture." Each story establishes a "break or shift between the present narrator's backdropping and the episode's occurrence," and "in each, the frame narrator identifies a moment of *in*comprehension as the product of the story." "That Evening Sun" and "A Justice" specifically explore issues of racial and economic injustice. They examine the "destruction of communal cohesiveness and tradition" that has occurred in Quentin's world "for populations marginal to the Compsons" and probe the effects of this destruction in ways the novel *The Sound and the Fury*, which lacks a framing structure, does not (Matthews 1989, 71–75).

One of the consequences of leaving Nancy's anticipated murder outside the text has been the development of arguments about her fate based on evidence in other texts in which she is thought to be named or actually to be present. In *The Portable Faulkner*, Cowley suggested that the reference to Nancy in the ditch in *The Sound and the Fury* was confirmation of her murder. The passage appears in Benjy's narrative as follows, "T.P. lay down in the ditch and I sat down, watching the bones where the buzzards ate Nancy, flapping black and slow and heavy out of the ditch" (*SF* 40). Cowley's revised edition of *The Portable Faulkner* maintains that stance with no correction suggested in the Afterword (Cowley [1967] 1977, xiv, xxx–xxxiii). Since Cowley's first association of the passage in the novel with the story, a number of critics have adopted the interpretation. Harry Campbell and Ruel Foster suggest that the reference in the novel is a "flash forward" to the short story and provides confirmation of the implied murder in the story (1951, 92; see also Magny 1966, 70). William Van O'Connor also accepts this reading, even though he argues that Nancy reappears in *Requiem for a Nun* (1954, 68n.). Whicher argues convincingly that the conversation in *The Sound and the Fury* from which Cowley and others draw evidence of Nancy's death is more likely to be about an animal, probably a horse or pony. Whicher points out that the numerous animals, dogs, horses, cows, and pigs, of the Compsons and the fact that this Nancy was shot by Roskus implies that the Nancy whose bones are in the ditch is an animal only coincidentally named like the black woman in "That Evening Sun." His point is to emphasize the tenuousness of relationships between the two texts (Whicher 1954, 253–55; see also Slabey 1964, 178).

Estella Schoenberg also believes that the bones are those of another Nancy. Schoenberg finds it unrealistic to believe that even accepting the time of the story, a black woman's body would have been left unburied. She suggests that "Fancy," the name of the pony, is so similar to the name "Nancy" that possibly a typesetter misread one, resulting in a "seeming misprint" (1977, 17). The holograph manuscript and carbon typescript unmistakably say *Nancy*, but *Fancy* is a pony named in the story (*WFM 6* I:15, *WFM 6* II:87; *SF* 40).

Numerous critics believe that Nancy Mannigoe in *Requiem for a Nun* is the same character as Nancy in "That Evening Sun." Their history and experiences bear a close resemblance. Some critics argue that her reappearance in the later novel indicates that Nancy was not murdered by Jesus. Faulkner himself said that Nancy of "That Evening Sun" is the same Nancy who appears in *Requiem for a Nun*: "She is the same person actually. These people I figure belong to me and I have the right to move them about in time when I need them" (Blotner 1974, 1309; *FU* 79).

The matter of Nancy's reappearance has not been treated so offhandedly by all readers, however. Some critics have been concerned not only with chronological details but with consistency (or lack thereof) in Nancy's character from text to text. Slabey estimates that Nancy's age, counting from story to novel, would be over fifty-five (Slabey 1964, 178; see also Holmes 1966, 114). Tuck emphasizes the ironic contrasts between Nancy's situation in the two texts. In the story, the white family refuses to protect her and bears some responsibility for her assumed death, but in the novel, she sacrifices her life so that her white employer might gain "some kind of moral salvation" (Tuck 1964, 177–78).

William Brown argues that chronological discrepancies between the works are less significant than the inconsistencies in her character; he understands Nancy Mannigoe as a sacrificial character in *Requiem for a Nun*. She is a "nigger dopefiend whore" in both texts; in the short story and the novel "she is made to suffer for the sins of respectable citizens." As such, Brown likens her role to that of Joe Christmas in *Light in August* and Popeye in *Sanctuary* (Brown 1967, 445–49). Jessie Coffee describes Nancy as surviving the terror of the short story "only to be later hanged for strangling a baby" in the novel (1983, 33). Polk contends that the incident with Stovall is retold in Act II of *Requiem for a Nun* as an attempt to demonstrate Nancy's madness so that she might be saved by a plea of insanity (Polk 1981, 86).

Carothers argues, contrary to the preceding opinions, that the Nancy of the story is unlike the Nancy of *Requiem for a Nun*. The character in the novel is "neither a continuation of the story nor a resurrection of a character" (1985, 13). John Bassett points out that on the basis of "temporal consistency" the Nancy in *Requiem for a Nun* could not be the Nancy of "That Evening Sun" because she would be in her sixties in the novel. Bassett adds, however, that Faulkner concerned himself very little with such matters when he reused characters (Bassett [1988] 1989, 184). Ferguson believes that critics who take Nancy's reappearance in *Requiem for a Nun* as confirmation that her fears in "That Evening Sun" were unfounded "misread the story in a very fundamental way" (1991, 6).

Yet another text, *Sanctuary*, offers a graphic record of what may be Nancy's murder. When Goodwin is escorted to jail, one inmate already there is a man who has killed his wife. The description of that murder very nearly matches what Nancy had predicted as her fate. The unnamed inmate killed his unnamed wife when he "slashed her throat with a razor so that, her whole head tossing further and further backward from the bloody regurgitation of her bubbling throat, she ran out the cabin door and for six or seven steps up the quiet moonlit lane" (*S* 118; Blotner 1974, 609).

A footnote reference in Keen Butterworth's study of *A Fable* suggests that Nancy and Jesus are recalled in that novel in the episode about the lawyer's driver (1983, 111 n. 13).

Given the contradictory suggestions in apparently related texts, it is impossible to conclude with certainty whether Jesus killed Nancy. Nancy's reappearance in *Requiem for a Nun* is more specific than other references, but Faulkner did state matter-of-factly that this was the same Nancy. However, his sense of literary license does not make it impossible that he would resuscitate a character—whether Nancy after her murder, or Quentin (if one adopts a post–*The Sound and the Fury* composition date) after his suicide.

Dilsey's appearance in "That Evening Sun" compares most obviously to her role in *The Sound and the Fury*, but Ferguson suggests that she also resembles Alice in Faulkner's children's story *The Wishing Tree* (1991, 27).

Character links have provided the impetus for most relational studies; however, the recurrence of familiar Yoknapatawpha settings and similar thematic and narrative approaches have also been discussed. Typically these comments are brief. Millgate, for example, groups "That Evening Sun," "A Rose for Emily," and "Dry September" because their settings are similar in time and place ([1961] 1966, 64). Blotner parallels the description of the jail and surrounding area described in "That Evening Sun" with the jailhouse description in *Sanctuary* and *As I Lay Dying* (Blotner 1974, 826). Skei compares the image of present-day Jefferson in the introduction that frames the hunting tale description in "A Bear Hunt" to that in the opening of "That Evening Sun." Quentin is the narrator of the version of "A Bear Hunt" in *Big Woods* and may also be in the other published versions (Skei 1985, 317 n. 13).

Thematic parallels include a number of comparisons made on the basis of gender and race. Carol Harter likens Nancy to Ruby Goodwin (Ruby Lamar) and Madame Reba in *Sanctuary* as illustrations of her view that Faulkner's prostitutes are often his "most 'moral'" characters (Harter 1970, 218). Walter Taylor observes that Nancy is one of Faulkner's few sexually passionate black women (Taylor 1983, 55). In "That Evening Sun," like the early "Frankie and Johnny" and "Adolescence" or "The Leg," "Mistral," "Mountain Victory," "Dr. Martino," and numerous other stories, Ferguson believes that Faulkner develops "compassionate characterizations of women in difficult or impossible situations." "That Evening Sun," "A Rose for Emily," "Dry September," and "Fox Hunt" offer more objective, detached presentations of sexual themes than the earlier short fiction in which these appeared as a "sometimes excessive concern" (1991, 74, 36–37).

According to Skei, Mrs. Compson's complaining relates to the examples of misused power of social rank in "Dry September" and in "A Rose for Emily." The women in all three texts (Mrs. Compson, Emily Grierson, and Minnie Cooper) use their positions to assert themselves. Mrs. Compson gets Nancy out of her house regardless of what that may mean for Nancy. Here and elsewhere, the "consequences of misused power are in shocking disproportion to the gain" (Skei 1985, 178–79).

Issues involving race relations link "That Evening Sun" to a number of Faulkner's works. Robert Penn Warren's analysis of Faulkner's portrayal of the social definition of "nigger" created by a white society identified it as a search to discover the "reality behind the mask of such a definition." Among the characters confronting the falsity of the mask are those black women who attempt suicide. Eunice in "The Bear" is successful, Nancy in "That Evening Sun" is not, but in both cases, the white response is disbelief rather than sympathy (Warren 1966, 261; see also Kerr [1969] 1976, 213; Broughton 1974, 128; Peters 1983, 108). Charles Nilon makes an association between Nancy's victimization as a consequence of white selfishness in "That Evening Sun" and the lynch victims—Rider in "Pantaloon in Black" and Will Mayes in "Dry September." In these and other stories in which the lynch or crucifixion symbol is employed, including "Red Leaves," "Go Down, Moses," and "Mountain Victory," the symbol provides the means of the black character's victory. Nilon points out further that Nancy is particularly like the body servant in "Red Leaves" because both lose the ability to swallow when they are confronting death (Nilon 1965, 44, 46, 33). Brooks similarly compares Nancy's "helpless terror" to that of the body servant in "Red Leaves" (1983, 32). Erskine Peters names Jesus and Lucas Beauchamp in *Go Down, Moses* as characters who exemplify the system of "black American peonage." In another comparison, Peters compares Mrs. Compson's disgust over having blacks sleeping in her house with the reactions of the grandmother in "Elly" when Paul is brought into her son's home (1983, 103, 117).

Taking a different approach but also specifically comparing "That Evening Sun" and "Red Leaves," Skei observes Faulkner's recurring tendency to portray in black characters an irrational fear of nature, an apparent belief that it contains "some hidden force" that "may strike and hurt" them (Skei 1985, 198). Taylor interprets Nancy's actions as the "obverse of McClendon's [McLendon] and Minnie Cooper's behavior" in "Dry September." These white characters use a black character as scapegoat, and Nancy's definition of herself as "just a nigger" reflects the consequences of accepting that role (Taylor 1983, 55–57).

Like Nilon and Brooks, Robert Barth compares Nancy to the body servant in "Red Leaves." She waits for an inevitable "fate she cannot escape," much as he does. Barth's observations are grounded not in the consequences of racial discrimination but in his study of Faulkner's roots in the Calvinist Protestant tradition and the fatalism present in many of Faulkner's novels and short stories that Barth associates with that background (1964, 113).

Joseph Reed groups "That Evening Sun" with those stories in which Faulkner directs the narrative so that the reader develops sympathy for the isolated individual (1973, 20). Skei's list of stories that contain outsiders includes "That Evening Sun," "The Hill," "Barn Burning," "Red Leaves," and "A Justice" (1992, 69).

Ferguson associates "That Evening Sun" with stories in which achieving justice becomes a motivating force for action. Jesus's revenge in "That Evening Sun," the lynching of Will Mayes in "Dry September," and the death of the body servant in "Red Leaves" all constitute enactments of justice "*from someone's perspective.*" Yet in these stories apparent achievement of justice is undercut; "the reader is always achingly aware that some terrible wrongs have been—or will be—perpetrated" because those who administer justice, Jesus, McLendon, and the Indians, fail "to understand the dignity and integrity of those whom they destroy" (1991, 78–79).

Craig Werner points out that Faulkner used black folklore not only in "That Evening Sun" but also in *Sartoris* and "Pantaloon in Black." In doing so, Faulkner acknowledges the power within the black culture (Werner 1987, 40). But with a different effect, the author also repeatedly used black razor murders in his fiction. Hoke Perkins examines this recurring pattern, including in his study "That Evening Sun," *Sanctuary*, *Light in August*, and *Go Down, Moses* (1987, 223).

A number of critics have compared the point of view in "That Evening Sun" and other short stories to examine Faulkner's use of the child narrator, or the narrator who reflects both a child's and an adult's perspective. There is disagreement among them over how much the child Quentin understands of what he witnesses or whether this is an initiation story. Looking at the narrative contexts of "That Evening Sun" and "Barn Burning," Marvin Fisher finds that neither presents a typical initiation story because the Compson children remain uninitiated and Sarty Snopes has confronted his father's retaliation techniques before the action in "Barn Burning" (Fisher 1960, 14). Millgate extends the list of innocent witnesses as narrators to include "Shingles for the Lord" ([1961] 1966, 66). Quentin as a first-person narrator also resembles the later Lucius Priest in *The Reivers* (Millgate [1966] 1989, 257). Reed observes that in both "Barn Burning" and "That Evening Sun" a narrative voice offers mature judgment of the meaning of actions that "sharpens and objectifies the conflict" (1973, 45–46; see also Ruppersburg 1983, 22).

Beck ranks Quentin as the youngest narrator, nine in this text, who begins to perceive the effects of "an inequitable biracial society." Chick Mallison and Isaac McCaslin are both adolescent when they begin to acknowledge the realities of their social milieux (Beck 1976, 301). James Watson contrasts Quentin's recognition of the humanity of Nancy and Sam Fathers in "That Evening Sun" and "A Justice" with the narrators' failure to do so in "A Rose for Emily" and "Hair," a failure with which they are eventually confronted (1980, 216–17). According to Ferguson, the unnamed boy who narrates "Fox Hunt" is, like Quentin, an "observer-auditor who learns some ugly truths about life in the course of the narrative." Ferguson finds other comparable child narrators in *The Wishing Tree* and "Uncle Willy." The narrator of "Uncle Willy" assumes "even greater importance" in his story than Quentin does in either "That Evening Sun" or "A Justice," but the voice is not so effectively managed because it slips inconsistently between youth and adulthood (Ferguson 1991, 67–68; 27–28, 113). Yet another comparison might be made between Quentin and Georgie, the narrator of "That Will Be Fine." Although Georgie's greed spurs him to participate in his Uncle Rodney's intrigues, Georgie clearly has no understanding of the consequences of his uncle's behavior, nor does he realize that the height of the action involves his uncle's death. The story precedes "That Evening Sun" in *Collected Stories*, and its proximity heightens the narrative parallels with and differences from "That Evening Sun."

The absence of the specific action to which the whole movement of "That Evening Sun" seems headed, Jesus's murdering Nancy, is another quality of the story that is paralleled in other Faulkner texts. Millgate groups "That Evening Sun," "A Rose for Emily," and "Dry September" together on the basis that all three occur "on the very edge of scenes of violence and horror which we do not actually witness" (Millgate [1961] 1966). Olga Vickery contends that "That Evening Sun," "Dry September," and "Wash" develop narratives that "focus on a single effect and a single impression." In the case of "That Evening Sun," the assumption by readers that Nancy is murdered, when the story bears numerous references to the unfounded nature of her fear, reflects the capacity of "Faulkner's refusal to dramatize the conclusive action . . . to intensify the dominant emotion and to project it beyond the story itself." Faulkner places the reader in the position of accepting "continuation of the narrative" and recognizing "that his characters' lives extend beyond the formal confines of individual works" (Vickery [1959] 1964, 301). Claude-Edmonde Magny describes this narrative absence as a characteristic of Faulkner in which the reader "never sees what happens while it is in the process of happening, but only when it is past." Nancy, Magny says, waits "passively" for Jesus to come kill her. She is like Quentin, Caddy, Joe Christmas, and Thomas Sutpen, all of whom "wait for the unpredictable and necessary catastrophe which is to seize them" (Magny 1966, 68–69). Ferguson believes Faulkner achieves closure in "That Evening Sun" with a technique of returning to and stressing a controlling symbol, the arguing of the children, a technique prevalent in numerous stories (Ferguson 1991, 134).

Given the abundance of criticism responding to "That Evening Sun," surprisingly little examines patterns of imagery in this story and in other Faulkner texts. Blotner compares the "ominousness" of "That Evening Sun" to a similar feeling evoked in "Pantaloon in Black" (1974, 1038). Momberger contrasts the light-dark images in "That Evening Sun" with Faulkner's use of those images in the early New Orleans sketches. The darkness of "That Evening Sun" represents the absence of love and concern, but Nancy's association with the sun implies her "status as life-bearer." In the sketches, "human love is the only force that can transform darkness into light, chaos into community, living death into social and personal vitality" (Momberger 1978, 28, 31 n. 10). Peters believes that in "That Evening Sun" the image of darkness "conveys a strong sense of portentousness" unlike its use in Faulkner's other fictions (1983, 28). Carothers finds the irony of "That Evening Sun," as in such other works as "Dry September," *The Sound and the Fury*, and *Sanctuary*, to be "so pervasive" that some readers have seen these stories as evidence that "Faulkner approves of villainy and torture" (1985, 108). In an observation comparing "That Evening Sun" to *The Wishing Tree*, Ferguson adds that the styles of both are characterized by similar "simplicity, clarity, and objectivity." Both stories also examine fear and are alike in a child's accusing another character of being afraid (1991, 27–28).

In collection, "That Evening Sun" is grouped with several of the same stories. In both *These 13* and *Collected Stories*, however, Faulkner deemphasized some obvious parallels, and in so doing created other relationships that enhance the meaning of the text. Watson believes that the second section of *These 13*, of which "That Evening Sun" is the penultimate story, is characterized not only by a complementary enrichment of the stories but also by chronological progression. The first story, "Red Leaves," is set in the past; the final story, "Dry September," has a present-time setting. The intermediate stories intermingle past and present. They give the effect "of a past unfolding by steady stages into the present in a progression that approximates the cyclical motion of life" (Watson 1980, 217–19). Additional parallels between specific stories in the section are the similarities in the mood of "horror, despair, loneliness" and in the theme of racial conflict found in "That Evening Sun" and "Dry September," which appear side by side in this section (Skei 1977, 48; Ferguson 1991, 151). A different relation, the "obvious similarities between the alienated female protagonists," is emphasized in the grouping of "A Rose For Emily and "That Evening Sun" (Ferguson 1991, 151).

In *Collected Stories*, Faulkner placed "That Evening Sun" with a larger number of stories than he had in *These 13*. Millgate sees the thematic tie of isolation operating in such stories as "That Evening Sun," "Dry September," and "Death Drag." As in "Dry September," the victim in "That Evening Sun" is a black character (Millgate [1966] 1989, 272–73). Momberger also studies "That Evening Sun" specifically in the context of "The Village" section of *Collected Stories*. He argues that beyond the fact that these are all set in Jefferson, the total impact of the section is to convey a "nightmare vision of a community's social and moral disintegration" that "culminates in the chaotic violence of 'That Evening Sun.'" Consequently, the particular story transcends the concerns of Nancy and the Compsons and becomes a concluding comment on the "death of the communal spirit and the resulting deracination of the individual in Jefferson and, by extension, in the greater family of man." Quentin's present-time dissatisfaction with Jefferson parallels similar reactions by Elly in "Elly," the people of "Dry September," and the narrator of "Death Drag." Like "Centaur in Brass," "That Evening Sun" shows black and white families disintegrating, but the estrangement of spouses, parents and children, and siblings pervades all the stories, especially "Elly," "Centaur in Brass," and "That Will Be Fine" (Momberger 1978, 20–31).

The hostilities extend from private to public arenas in gender conflicts and age conflicts. As Momberger puts it, the "Villagers have neither the will not [sic] the capacity to establish fruitful relations with persons outside their domestic circles in the larger human family." The outcasts in these stories—Nancy in "That Evening Sun," and others in "Death Drag," "A Rose for Emily," and "Dry September"— are "finally abandoned to suffer alone." The need to keep up appearances also runs through several stories, including "Elly," "A Rose for Emily," "That Will Be Fine," and "That Evening Sun" (as when the jailer beats Nancy for trying to commit suicide in his jail). Racism pervades a number of the stories, resulting in violence in "Elly," "Dry September," and "That Evening Sun"; it is akin to other dehumanizing treatment of the individual in "Hair," "A Rose for Emily," "Uncle Willy," and other stories (Momberger 1978, 20–31).

Another pattern discernible in "The Village" is the recurring portrayal of "misfortunes visited upon the female principle," that is, woman's role as life-giver and "perpetuator of human community" is constantly thwarted and distorted in such permutations as necrophilia, erotic frustration, fantasized rape, near-death from abortion, promiscuity, and the adoption of masculine dress and manner. The community receives the promise of Nancy's pregnancy with indifference. "Custom, morality, and religion lose their integrative power and erode into sterile and divisive formalism" (Momberger 1978, 20–31; see also Ferguson 1991, 158).

Watson finds that the sections of *Collected Stories* are framed with stories that define both the "boundaries of a complete action" and the theme of the section. As frame stories for "The Village," "A Rose for Emily" and "That Evening Sun" set the thematic focus as the "limits that a closed society imposes on the identity of the individual"; in these stories, the individuals are two women—one white, one black. Watson points out that these two "stories involve betrayals of love ending in murder or the threat of murder." Also, "the aberrations in each proceed from the women's isolation in society." This reading, Watson contends, negates interpretations of Emily Grierson as a symbol of the South and of "Nancy's self-imposed agonies [as] an allegory of southern racial guilt." For Watson, these women "represent two extremes of the isolated life between which other characters in The Village work out their own destinies with varying degrees of failure or success" (1980, 221). Kinney describes the characters of "The Village" as "misfits." Nancy's fears and superstitions are dismissed, by Ms. Compson specifically and the white community by extension, as "meaningless racial characteristics." The story reverses the movement in the preceding "That Will Be Fine" in which the story's tension is generated from "exposed comedy and concealed irony" (Kinney 1980, 68).

Examining "That Evening Sun" in isolation is impossible for anyone familiar with Faulkner's writing. Critics will almost invariably bring to their readings of the text knowledge of the Compsons—Quentin's suicide or Caddy's later sexual activities, facts not referred to in this story. This prior knowledge leads to an inevitable association of "That Evening Sun" with other works in which the Compsons appear. Also, the thematic and formal issues that are prominent in this story are also important in much of Faulkner's other fiction.

## Interpretation and Criticism

From the earliest analyses of "That Evening Sun" critics saw it as a story about fear. For Robert Cantwell, the nervousness and tension were the story (Emerson 1984, 23). Sterling Brown described it as a "masterpiece of suspense and terror" (1931, 347). In his early review of *These 13*, Lionel Trilling complimented Faulkner's setting "That Evening Sun" in the children's minds "as they come into contact with primitive fear" but recorded his displeasure with Faulkner's incorporation of "social implications" in his fiction. According to Trilling, Faulkner is best in those texts in which he "can exploit emotion in some strange and hitherto unexplored setting of mind or place" (1931, 491).

Snell analyzed the story as an "exigent study of terror" (Snell 1947, 99). The impression comes through a "gradual unfolding" without the employment of a climactic action or denouement (Snell 1947, 101). Howe, too, described the story as an evocation of "primitive terror—the image of a human being waiting to be killed by another" (Howe [1952] 1975, 266–67).

Another early respondent identified two of the important formal characteristics of the story as the effect of the narrative point of view and the absence of climactic scene and denouement (O'Brien 1935, 325–61). In 1964, Slabey described the story as constructed around a double plot—Nancy's "physical behavior" and Quentin's "subjective response." The dualities multiply into a complex web of themes and symbols including social and psychological worlds, masters and servants, physical actions and consciousness, different levels of fear, darkness and light, all of which revolve around relationships between races, parents and children, "good and evil, love and hate, reality and imagination, past and present, ignorance and knowledge, freedom and fate, fastness and slowness of time, aloneness and solidarity" (Slabey 1964, 181–83). Slabey's catalogue represented then, and continues to represent, the focal points of criticism.

The greatest diversity in criticism has centered around the degree to which Nancy imagines Jesus's threat and the degree to which she is responsible for her trouble. Some misstatements about Nancy in the body of criticism should be dismissed. Edel describes her as a rape victim, a circumstance not borne out by the text (1962, 254–55). Nancy is not the daughter of Dilsey as claimed in Francis Utley's analysis (1964, 244). Margaret Alexander identifies Nancy as one of Faulkner's characters whose names are symbolic, claiming that Nancy "Mannigoe" (in *Requiem for a Nun*) suggests that "she goes with many men" (1978, 108). This surname does not appear in the text of "That Evening Sun."

Several readings emphasize Nancy's deterioration as the story progresses. Heilman describes her as experiencing a "terrified hallucination" (1950, 80). Other critics mark her decline from the early description of her "grace and balance" as she carried the laundry to her "mental and emotional collapse." To close the story with the children's bickering is appropriate, "for the disordered world of the children always poised on the edge of infantile violence is exactly the kind of world in which Nancy suffers. All the good will in the world cannot mitigate the fear of violence aroused by a betrayal and corruption of love." Nancy will, without question, be killed because "all the lines of force in the story move powerfully in that direction" (Hagopian 1962, 51–54).

Jim Lee also suggests that the story is a portrait of Nancy's moral and mental demise. He develops his reading around the lack of evidence of Jesus's presence: no one other than Nancy senses or sees Jesus; none of the children sees the bone she claims he left as a sign to her, and Jesus's recorded threats were aimed at Stovall rather than Nancy. Jason Compson, Sr., is most likely correct when he says that Jesus has left town. Nancy's obsession with a sense of his presence reflects her deteriorating mental condition caused by guilt over her prostitution, a behavior she tries unsuccessfully to justify. In the absence of the character Jesus, her being at his mercy comes more pointedly to mean that she is left to the damnation or forgiveness of the "other Jesus" (Lee 1961, 49–50; *CS* 297).

Brooks believes the issue of Nancy's guilt is obscured by criticism that focuses on the appropriateness of Mr. Compson's behavior. Nancy feels such intense guilt and strong attachment to Jesus that she believes "she deserves to suffer at his hands." Her possessiveness is emphatic when Compson suggests he probably has another woman, and her own sense that he "belongs to her whether or not she belongs to him" nurtures her obsession. Brooks adds that regardless of the accuracy of Nancy's fear, the point of the story is to capture the fear, which "is transmitted with utter conviction" (Brooks 1971, 235–37).

Leland Cox believes Nancy's fear "has no rational foundation" but is nevertheless very real to this woman who is a "prostitute addicted to alcohol and cocaine" (Cox 1982, 277–79). Skei compares Nancy's "irrational fear of what the darkness may have in store for her" to the Compsons' unconcern. Her terror has roots in superstition, gossip, and in her knowledge that in a predominantly white community when black individuals "disappear" in the dark of night, they are not looked for in the light of day. Skei believes that Faulkner "places inexperienced and immature people in untouched nature" in order to show that fear is easily evoked and does not necessarily "have logical explanations." They tend to expose the "thin layer of culture and civilized manners" that prove useless when confronted by that nature (Skei 1985, 198–99, 200).

Sympathetic responses to Nancy define her as a victim. Frey sees her as the central figure of the story and its victim (1953, 33). She believes in "measure for measure" (a judgment by which Frey implies culpability), but "she also manifests an inherent fear of death" (1953, 33–34). Nilon describes Nancy as "one of Faulkner's good people," based on her acceptance of suffering. Nilon's view of the story as another lynching tale locates the cause of Nancy's suffering with Stovall, her unborn child's father. Jesus may speak boldly, but he must turn his anger on Nancy rather than on the white man who fathered the child, and in so doing, he becomes the agent of the white community (Nilon 1965, 44–47). Coffee accepts the portrayal of Nancy as being drunk when she challenges Stovall; nevertheless, she is being abused by both blacks and whites (1983, 33). Reed observes that whether or not Nancy's fear of Jesus is real, she suffers also from the quarrelsome demands the Compson children make on her (1973, 33–34).

Sally Bethea answers Scottie Davis's argument that Nancy's character generates her suffering. Bethea addresses each of Davis's charges of vindictiveness, masochism, and irresponsibility and challenges his use of source materials. To the charge of masochism, Bethea points out that Nancy clings to the window despite her attempted suicide. Bethea adds that Jason's references to who is a "nigger" explicitly link the story to the issue of race relations (Bethea 1974, 87–92).

Slabey believes Nancy possesses "more moral dignity than her white employers." She comes to their assistance when Dilsey is ill, but they do not respond in kind. She achieves a self-knowledge that Quentin lacks in adulthood. Her fate includes the burden of being black in the South as reflected in her own assessment: "I ain't nothing but a nigger. . . . It ain't none of my fault" (Slabey 1964, 176, 182; *CS* 293).

Mimi Gladstein examines the cultural and sexual stereotyping that adheres in Nancy's characterization. As a black woman, she is perceived as less human than white characters and as a "repository for the white man's lust." In her relationship with Stovall, Nancy illustrates the abuse of the black woman used by the white man. Nevertheless, she is "damned for her enforced 'usability'" (Gladstein 1986, 20). Carothers's examination of images of prostitution includes a sympathetic description of Nancy as a "doomed victim of the racial, sexual, and economic matrices by which she is defined" (1992, 41–42).

A fair portion of criticism through the 1970s displayed little sympathy for Nancy. She is, in Snell's words, "not a good Negress" (1947, 100–01). West contends that Nancy's "wanton living midway between the worlds of whites and blacks has left her unprotected by the code of either, susceptible both to the lawful fury of Mr. Stovall and to the animal-like fury of her Negro lover" (1952, 98). West does not explain sufficiently why Stovall's fury is "lawful" while Jesus's is "animal-like" or even why Quentin's knowledge of how the world works is more significant than Nancy's. Nancy Hale describes Nancy's behavior at the conclusion of the story as "paralyzed by fatalism," unable to act further to prptect herself. Hale describes the Compsons as believing the threat of Jesus's presence and credits them for being "willing to let her sleep in their house for safety," an offer Nancy refuses ([1962] 1977, 141).

Mel Bradford takes issue with readings that lay blame for Nancy's situation on the community. He specifically discounts Nilon's reading. Bradford believes that Nancy's reference to herself as a "nigger" involves a depreciative value judgment also used by Dilsey and other black characters. Nancy's self-definition "means by this that her difficulties are, at least in some measure, a consequence of the weakness of her character, her mortality or human frailty." The children each respond to Nancy's frailty in ways appropriate to their individual characterizations; Jason offers an ironic syllogism, with the unstated conclusion: Dilsey is a nigger, Jesus is a nigger, I am not a nigger. As Jason's behavior demonstrates later, he rejects "his share in human finitude in whose name Nancy cries out for mercy." Quentin and Caddy show a greater ability to empathize with Nancy's frailties, too much so, as their later actions reveal. Their self-condemnation and response make "the potential for tragedy in the human condition" the thematic issue rather than "the tragedy of being Negro" (Bradford 1966, 1, 3).

Patrick Hogan also dismisses readings that hold the community and more particularly the Compsons accountable for Nancy's tragedy. Hogan itemizes the events that have diminished the fairly clearly demarcated obligations that the Compsons might have felt toward a woman who cooked and did laundry for the family: the former warning to Jesus to stay away from the Compsons' house, Nancy's arrest record, her relationship with white men, and her suicide attempt. Given these conditions, Hogan argues that little could be done for Nancy by the Compsons or the community. Nancy, even more than the reader, "seems to be more clearly reconciled to the possible justice of her fate" (Hogan 1966, 3).

Walter Everett sees Nancy's "moral cowardice" and culpability, and Jesus's anger, as contrasted to and refuted by the example of Dilsey. Additionally, the children's innocence as to what they are witnessing "accentuates Nancy's guilt" (Everett 1969, 172). Scottie Davis joins those critics who dismiss the community's responsibility in Nancy's situation; for Davis, the source of trouble is within Nancy, a "pathetic and weak" woman who is a "vindictive, masochistic, irresponsible martyr." Nancy is vindictive when she suggests in anger that she would cut Jesus just as she fears he will cut her, masochistic in her attempted suicide and her refusal of proffered protection from the black community, and irresponsible in neglecting her work duties because of her prostitution and when she decides to sit in her cabin and wait for Jesus. Like Everett, Davis believes Dilsey's presence in the story offers a contrast against which Nancy's behavior may be judged (1972, 30–32).

E. W. Pitcher offers an alternate reading of "That Evening Sun." His suggestion that "what chiefly happens on all levels of the story is that people lose things, or fear losing them," does not differ from other readings; however, one of the main points of his argument is that Nancy's fear and guilt stem from an abortion. Pitcher claims, without citing the text, that Nancy says the child she is carrying is Jesus's, and that no evidence suggests Jesus would kill her for bearing another man's child. Since Jesus did not react violently to Nancy on first learning of her pregnancy, it seems unreasonable to suggest that he would come back into town to kill her. Thus, Nancy's fear must have another source. Pitcher believes her reaction to Caddy's question about why Jesus is mad when she drops the cup but her hands retain the shape of the cup is "symbolic confirmation of an abortion." Furthermore, after the kitchen scene, no additional references to pregnancy appear. Nancy's fear then is for the "loss of her immortal soul." Pitcher also believes that the chronology of events is altered so that some of the incidents Quentin recalls occur after the night of terror, thus proving that Nancy survived that night (1981, 131–35).

When Faulkner created the narrative frame for Nancy's story the orientation shifted, some critics contend, from Nancy's experience to the

Compsons' responses. Howe asserts that the story belongs to the Compsons because it brings them into "distinct being" by conveying their various reactions to death when they are placed in proximity to it, and by acting as a test for their "moral stamina" (Howe [1952] 1975, 266–67). Skei believes the addition of the historical introduction shifts the focus from Nancy's story to Quentin's and the Compsons' (Skei 1977, 98–99). Ferguson believes the story belongs to both Nancy and Quentin; the frame was a late addition. It adds complexity in the contrast between the young and adult Quentins. The thematic concerns—youth versus maturity, innocence versus corruption—are enhanced by the narrative point of view. The technique further reveals the artist's interest in the process of storytelling, that is, as it affords a "means of reliving the past, revenging oneself on time, trying to come to terms with temporal realities through narration" (Ferguson 1991, 112). Most especially, the concern has been to discover what Quentin understood as a child, how that understanding contrasts with his adult perceptions, and how his childhood understandings did or did not differ from the perceptions of Caddy and Jason.

West interprets "That Evening Sun" as an initiation story in which the initiation into knowledge is the "whole action" of the plot. Quentin recognizes that the "knowledge of evil is a permanent condition of human life." Jason distances himself from Nancy's terror just as he distances himself from her race, and Caddy "is intrigued by the nature of evil itself" (West 1952, 97–100). Pearson believes that Quentin's query about the laundry separates him from Caddy and Jason as it reveals his "recognition of the finality of Nancy's fate," an understanding that marks his initiation into the knowledge of evil (1954, 66). Leslie Fiedler also describes the experience of the story as Quentin's "ocular initiation." He argues that Quentin relives the experience in both *The Sound and the Fury* and *Absalom, Absalom!* and commits suicide "on the verge of manhood" (Fiedler 1960, 340).

In his argument that Faulkner's use of limited point of view "controls the meaning of the action," Fisher interprets the innocence and childish fears of Quentin, Caddy, and Jason as forming an ironic counterpoint to the real, adult terror of Nancy. His reading argues for Quentin's continued innocence and uses the question about laundry as only an awareness of leaving rather than death (Fisher 1960, 13–18). Tuck describes Quentin's level of awareness at the conclusion as that of one who "placidly accepts Nancy's expected death" (1964, 178). Slabey does not see Quentin's query about laundry as a recognition of evil but merely an awareness of leave-taking (Slabey 1964, 181). Beck believes the contrast between Quentin's response and that of Caddy and Jason distinguishes his "acuteness of intuition," even in his youth, "that finally was to make a hypersensitive life insufferable." Already he seems to understand generally the gossip about Nancy; he observes that his mother considers his father to be intentionally antagonistic, and he already shares an understanding with his father. Quentin initially shows concern when he asks

Nancy, as she sits in the cold kitchen, "What is it?" Additionally, his closing question fixes his concern on a specific event. Beck suggests that the order of closing observations—first Quentin's, then Caddy and Jason's—serves to distinguish Quentin's perceptiveness from the others' childishness. In reverse order, Quentin's query might have appeared limited and indifferent (Beck 1976, 291–96). Momberger believes that Quentin acts like a passive observer and shows little more understanding than Caddy and Jason, neither of whom grasps the import of the events (1978, 26).

Hamb[l]in believes the innocence of the children serves more than the functional role of counterpoint to Nancy's terror. The children illustrate the "state of childhood innocence poised on the threshold of the fall into awareness of the reality of evil"; for them, ignorance as well as innocence is juxtaposed to matters of an adult world. Through Quentin the two stages intersect briefly: the story describes an epiphany in which the onset of mature perceptions and understanding overtakes Quentin's innocence. Nancy's effort to explain her behavior to Quentin confirms his dawning maturity, and he is the child who understands when Nancy is referring to the biblical Jesus and her mortal mate. His closing question strikes a balance between his dawning adult vision and his "egocentric view of childhood." The adult world contains evil, some imagined and some real. Jesus personifies the "sinister threat" that hangs over that world, and he is appropriately more an abstract image. In his one appearance, he does not threaten Nancy, but in his absence he is identified with Satan. Faulkner uses the situation of Dilsey's illness, which puts the children in contact with Jesus, to express the view "that life inescapably involves the engagement of pain, suffering, and evil" (Hamblin 1979, 86–94).

Hamblin contends that Caddy's character provides the most pointed personification of innocence. Her inquisitiveness notwithstanding, she is consistently ignorant and naïve. By linking the name Candace with its historical reference to Ethiopian queens, Hamblin shows how Caddy becomes the queen in Nancy's story, foreshadowing her fall. As the teller is, so the female listener will become: promiscuous and pregnant. The story operates as a "microcosmic allegory of every person's initiation into tragic experience." Nancy's final solitary situation reflects not the indifference of the Compsons but the reality that each person encounters sin and death individually. When the story is interpreted as being about time, change, and the inevitable loss of innocence, the early description of a town that has been touched by modernity contributes to the thematic unity of the text. The title takes on added significance as it suggests the unavoidable aging of the children (Hamblin 1979, 86–94).

Kinney describes Quentin as "unmoved" by his observations of Nancy's beatings. Quentin's "strict limitations of sympathy are firm indications that his pity, like Jason's, is mainly self-dictated" (Kinney 1982, 12). Ferguson agrees with those who believe Quentin understands Nancy's terror although

Jason and Caddy do not, citing Quentin's increasing silence and final question as evidence of his comprehension (1991, 57).

The difference between Quentin at nine and fifteen years later has received extensive analysis. Evans Harrington suggested in an early criticism that Faulkner's use of dual narrative perspectives was a flaw. Although most critics have argued against Harrington's conclusion, his work remains an important beginning to the critical dialogue. Harrington studies narrative technique, noting that Faulkner maintains the perspective, language, and style that might be expected of a nine-year-old Quentin. He suggests that the additional layering of Quentin fifteen years later might be an error in technique because it requires opening paragraphs that "are functional only in informing the reader of the lapse of time" and differ from the style of the remainder of the story. At any rate, Harrington concludes, readers forget the older Quentin once they are into the narrative and the advantages of the youthful narrator take hold. His simple style matches the elemental emotion described; the narrative is economic and natural as the child might recall emotionally charged episodes with intervening narrative, and it makes the inclusion of the Compson family bickering reasonable. These "petty and comic" recountings, when juxtaposed to Nancy's suffering, intensify her despair and evoke a sympathetic response to her. The childish dialogues constantly reveal the children's failure to see themselves as part of her danger, even though at times they even increase it. Harrington also notes that characterization is achieved primarily by dialogue rather than description, except for the vivid descriptions of Nancy's hands, which keep in focus her "mental condition of helpless, cornered terror" (Harrington 1952, 54–58).

Frey emphasizes Faulkner's achievement in maintaining the child's perception in such images as balloons and in Caddy's follow-up question about the "watermelon" Nancy carries. Frey contends that Quentin's concern with the laundry reveals his limited understanding that Nancy is leaving but not that she is facing death (1953, 34–38). Slabey disagrees with Harrington that presenting Quentin at two different ages is an error. He describes the device as "not only justifiable but necessary." The story is "a portrait of the suicide as a young boy" that makes the later, adult reckoning of the experience essential. The dual ages of Quentin are consistent with Faulkner's belief that present time subsumes past and future. It takes Quentin fifteen years to understand Nancy's experience (Slabey 1964, 173–83).

May Brown interprets the adult Quentin's telling to represent his need "to explain and reconcile himself to that past." Brown shows how the narrative digresses subtly from the constructions of an adult to the vocabulary and syntax of a child. The first appearance of the balloon image, describing the laundry balanced on Nancy's head, initiates the narrative shift to that of the nine-year-old Quentin. Subsequently, the dialogue is simple, time shifts quickly, and the use of "he said" or similar identifications of speaker increases.

Quentin's choice of the particular event of this crisis in Nancy's life corresponds to the adult concerns Quentin reveals in *The Sound and the Fury*: "chastity, miscegenation, despair, and death." As distinguished from Caddy and Jason, who serve to emphasize irony and the racial issues, Quentin offers "clear indications of his awareness of Nancy's plight." The insensitivity of Caddy and Jason emphasize by contrast Quentin's understanding, expressed in his apparently objective narrative. The specifics of his later recollections reveal his understanding of his father's failure to act, Nancy's pregnancy and impending death (not just leave-taking), her fear, and the racial distinctions that generate much of her trouble. The shadows of the setting sun apply to Quentin as well as to Nancy in that his own "isolation and unhappiness . . . parallel Nancy's unbearable misery." The dehumanized portrait of present time parallels the dehumanized perception the white characters have of Nancy. It is Brown's opinion that the reader "feels precisely what Quentin does about Nancy's plight" (Brown 1976, 347–60). Beck believes the shift "into pure memory with a quick cinematic flow of action and dialogue is an extraordinary fictional unfolding, lucid and indeed simple on its surface, yet full of hints." The transition from adult to child in the second paragraph is supported by a "shift from impressionistic imagism to subtle effect of rhythmic and suspended sentence structure" (Beck 1976, 290–95).

Reed finds that the narrative gains greater impact by placing it within a child narrator's limited understanding and a framework of reminiscence. This outer frame contributes "atmospheric detail" by establishing a semirural setting and a time of social transition; it also establishes the family unit of the Compsons. The story, Reed argues, serves Quentin's use of the past "to inform his present." The older Quentin assumes the persona of the child, and Reed notes, "The point . . . is not that Quentin's restricted consciousness cannot see the point of the story, but that Quentin can now see everything of what, at the time, he saw almost nothing." The impact comes with the minute details on which Quentin focuses in his effort to regain, with his knowledge of how his family turned out, "that time of innocence now lost." Reed suggests that the reversion to simplistic sentence constructions represents not only the child Quentin but also the adult Quentin's effort "to get the sequence absolutely straight." Quentin lapses into his adult voice in explaining his mother's tone in calling "Jason" and his subsequent explanation of the moment and its meaning (*CS* 294). Given Quentin's knowledge of Caddy's subsequent history, his recollections of her questions function ironically in relation to that knowledge. As the example of Quentin's remembering Caddy's questions demonstrates, Reed believes the meaning of the story lies "somewhere in the contrasts and similarities between the children's arguments and the adults' concerns." Faulkner manipulates conventional narrative strategies to achieve a "very modern and indeterminate result."

Consequently, the use of reminiscence in "That Evening Sun" is an intricately interwoven tool of the text that becomes meaning (Reed 1973, 30–34).

Joseph Garrison finds the introduction of the adult Quentin an important layer of the text, but he does not believe Quentin comes to any understanding of Nancy's plight from his adult perspective. Rather, Garrison states, the story "is about a narrator who is both blinded and deceived by his cognitive and perceptual inclinations." Quentin as an adult expresses dissatisfaction in his portrayal of contemporary Jefferson because it has changed. He implies that his "present is intolerable" but his past was filled with "authentic and satisfying life experience." The reader then is to understand that by choosing such a serene recollection of what was in reality a time of horror and torment, Quentin reveals what he does not himself recognize: his own "disassociation from reality." Garrison writes, "We know that the world of his childhood was not ideal, but he does not." The reversion to the child's mentality and his emphasis on visual, external images rather than a sensitive recognition of the horror he is narrating demonstrate Quentin's failure to perceive things as they are. This condition consequently "has actually created the present-time world which he sees and which he abhors" (Garrison 1976, 371–73).

Skei describes the ironic dimension of using the child narrator to discuss such matters as race relationships, sex, death, and fear as the "most important single technical aspect . . . at least superficially." It must be remembered, however, that an adult Quentin is telling this story. His narration is of a particular memory, but when "he places it in an historical and social context, its meaning multiplies and increases." As a storyteller, the older Quentin juxtaposes Jason's fear with Nancy's. He makes a careful distinction between the white characters' reference to Nancy's dwelling as a "cabin" and the black characters' reference to it as a "house." Also the mature narrator would retell the childhood memory focusing on such matters as Nancy's hands and the Lovelady anecdote (Skei 1977, 100–05; see also Skei 1985, 199–200).

Watson seems less convinced that the adult Quentin has as yet attained a full understanding of the events described. In Quentin's narrations, though he does not understand the experiences as a child, there is a "promise" of initiation yet to come. However, Quentin's return to a child's perspective in "That Evening Sun" implies that his initiation did not fully occur and that his "maturation is also at issue" (Watson 1980, 216–17). For Carothers, the story operates as a *Bildungsroman* or a *Kunstlerroman*; hence the outcome of the conflict between Nancy and Jesus is less important (Carothers 1985, 10, 12).

Critics generally agree that the behaviors of Caddy and Jason serve as criteria against which Quentin's impressions are measured (O'Brien 1935, 331). Snell asserts that Caddy is the "most knowing" and "most observant"

(Snell 1947, 99–101). John Hermann holds that neither Quentin nor Nancy is the focus of the story. He contends that the central focus is the insight of Candace, who, at age seven, can see that the rest of the Compsons, and the other whites connected with the story, are no better than "scairy cats." Caddy's questions press both the children, especially Jason, and the adults into revealing their own egocentrisms: they all use Nancy and perceive her as less than themselves. Caddy is the only character who contends with the younger Jason. Her insistence eventually garners reprimands from both parents. Even in Quentin's narrative, which Hermann believes is a recognition and tribute to Caddy's perception, his own associative remembrance reveals that he too would like to "use" Nancy to recall a time more pleasant to him when washerwomen carried laundry on their heads. Caddy makes the more perceptive comparison of Nancy and Jesus with Mrs. and Mr. Compson, an analogy the other family members would not perceive. Quentin recognizes that Caddy "at seven had known all along how the characters of 'That Evening Sun' would turn out" (Hermann 1970, 320–23).

The three children together serve as a "Greek chorus" (Snell 1947, 99–101). Their voices serve as a choral counterpoint to Nancy's sound that is but is not singing (Bennett 1985, 341).

As Nancy's culpability remains unresolved, so too does that of the adult Compsons, particularly Mr. Compson. Frey contends that Faulkner succinctly but fully delineates Mr. Compson's "disillusionment" just as he conveys Mrs. Compson's "perfect self-absorption" (Frey 1953, 39). Some indict Mr. Compson for his failure to assist; others believe he did what was reasonable. Hagopian finds his behavior laudable. With regard to Nancy, Mr. Compson is the "only one who has any real understanding and sympathy for her plight": he escorts her, allows her to sleep in the house, and offers to take her to a neighbor's house (Hagopian 1962, 52–53). Brooks believes that although Mr. Compson does not take seriously Nancy's belief that Jesus is waiting to kill her, he does see that she is terrified and tries to help her ([1963] 1990, 334–35; see also 1971, 234). Schoenberg calls Mr. Compson a "calm and . . . reassuring presence" to the children (1977, 17).

Other critics contend that Mr. Compson fails to act in a situation where his help is needed. William Toole believes that when Mr. Compson says Jesus has left town, he is merely offering justification for his lack of action. Even though the children's father is the "finest white character" portrayed in the story, he fails to act on his responsibility to help Nancy, and the final image of the two-headed Jason, with a little head (young Jason on his shoulders) and a big one, "suggests a moral dereliction on the part of Father" (Toole 1963, Item 52). Maurice Coindreau believes the dual use of the name *Jason* in the story, as with names used more than once elsewhere in Faulkner, reflects a deliberate move by the author to add a layer of meaning (1971, 38). Given young Jason's selfishness, the correspondence is decidedly a negative reflection on Mr. Compson. Slabey asserts that Mr. Compson's failure to help Nancy signals the Compsons' "moral decay and an inability to accept responsibility for the entire family," a quality manifested in Quentin as a "negative approach to reality" (1964, 180–81).

Samway sees Mr. Compson as having helped no one in the course of the story, neither Nancy, his wife (who Quentin says believes her husband's goal is to antagonize her), nor the children. In the story, when he and the children escort Nancy to her cabin, Mr. Compson leads Quentin, Caddy, and Jason "to the threshold of a potentially evil world" that they lack the ability to understand. He "does not give them the necessary attitudes and information to cope adequately with this particular situation," and he "shows his utter lack of sympathy for her [Nancy's] plight." Samway adds that Mr. Compson is a character in whom the reader can believe because he reminds us of "people we know in everyday situations" (Samway 1985, 182–83).

Concern over the adequacy of the Compsons' response to Nancy's terror is one topic in an extensive body of criticism focusing on the social implications of the story. When asked about any suggestion of symbolism in the use of the name *Jesus*, Faulkner responded that it "was probably a deliberate intent to shock just a little." He went on to add that the name might reasonably be found among the black population in Mississippi but that his point was actually less to shock than to point out "that this Negro woman who had given devotion to the white family knew that when the crisis of her need came, the white family wouldn't be there" (*FU* 21). Many commentators reject the view that the use of the child narrator not only heightens the sense of terror but makes the text "almost purified of the racial and sexual forces that produce it" (Hagopian 1962, 50). Fisher believes that Caddy's taunting of Jason as being "scairder than niggers" introduces but does not emphasize the racial issues in the story, but this interpretation has received no further confirmation (Fisher 1960, 17).

Those who find the racial issues essential to the story make up a longer list. Beck describes the issues as possessing "vast socioethical reverberations" (Beck 1976, 296). Snell sees social criticism serving to heighten the impression of terror. The story contains Faulkner's comment on the South's mores that "have given the white man leave to use the black woman without hindrance." Jubah [Jesus], Snell comments, "has some excuse for violence" and "is a haunted man, hounded alike by his hatred of the whites who have debauched his wife, and his hatred of her for having permitted it" (1947, 100–01). Mary Orvis interprets the closing quarrel between the children as demonstrating the indifference of the white characters to the "fate of Negro servants" but also as comic relief juxtaposed to the terror (1948, 104–05). Harrington believes that the social commentary may be traced through the portrayal of Nancy's constant reference to herself as "nothing but a nigger" whose situation is "none of my fault." "Mr. Faulkner," according to Harrington, "implies that the lack of moral conscience among the South's Negroes is a result of the lack of self-respect on their part, a self-respect which the South has not helped them to gain" (1952, 58–59).

According to Hagopian, Jesus is more complex than a "pure, black villain." Nancy reports that he always shared his money with her, and she declares that she would be moved to violence if he betrayed her. He is proud but frustrated and angered by double racial standards (Hagopian 1962, 54–55). References to looking at the children having the quality of a refrain signify how Nancy's fear relates to the fact that she is both "surrounded and isolated" by white society (Baumbach and Edelstein 1968, 248–49). Charles Peavy examines Nancy's rationalization as a reflection of the lack of self-esteem among blacks who live in a society in which only whites are empowered. The failure of the jailer to believe Nancy could suffer enough to attempt suicide "illustrate[s] the white man's inability to believe in the Negro's capacity to love, hate, or suffer." Nancy's reaction is one among many examples of this attitude in Faulkner's work (Peavy 1971, 44). Elizabeth Kerr sees Jesus's redirection of his anger toward Nancy rather than Mr. Stovall as a correct reflection of social reality in which a black could expect immunity if his rage were enacted against a black rather than a white victim ([1969] 1976, 204).

George Kent studies the black woman as sexual image in Faulkner's work. He argues that the "sexual commerce between black woman and white man remained in an area tolerable to the white imagination so long as it did not include recognition of the black woman's personality and interfere or threaten to interfere with white Anglo-saxon domination." Although Faulkner does not raise "sex images far above the level of white folklore, he can occasionally explore a few of the terrible complexities." Nevertheless, the issue is frequently muted by emphasizing the "response of the white consciousness, rather than . . . the response of the victim." In "That Evening Sun" Nancy's prostitution supplements her income, but she is beaten for publicly confronting a customer and later for attempting suicide. Kent's position is that the community fails to protect her, and the Compsons fail to take her problems seriously. Her situation is presented as more complex than Compson's simplistic rebuff "that she would have no trouble if she would leave white men alone." Kent assumes that Nancy is murdered. He also believes that Faulkner develops in Nancy's dismissal of personal responsibility a clear indictment of a community as an "essential ingredient, and that it is a world that she did not have much of a part in making" (Kent 1974, 430–41).

Acknowledging the debate about the date of the narration, Kenneth Johnston offers an interesting argument for placing it fifteen years after Quentin's ninth year, his age at the time of the events. As he was born in 1889, the telling of the story would be in 1913. Although this is after Quentin's death, it is an appropriate date for the story, placing it fifty years after the Emancipation Proclamation. Thus, in Johnston's reading, it becomes an "account of the continuing bondage of the emancipated Negro in Jefferson, Mississippi." Johnston analyzes the text as an investigation of the narrow achievements of emancipation. As other critics have noted, these include Jesus's limited options of response, none of which includes retribution against the white man; the inequity that allows Compson free access to Nancy's cabin but also allows him to ban Jesus from the Compson kitchen; and Nancy's position that leaves her powerless to act on her own behalf but not able to count on her white employer to protect her (Johnston 1974, 93–100).

Paula Sunderman's analysis of "That Evening Sun" applies speech act theory (a context-dependent theoretical model) to several crucial scenes. From this she concludes that the "broader perspective" of the story is Quentin's recognition that the action of the story reveals the failed communication between the races or individual characters. Sunderman observes that Quentin's early descriptions of Nancy focus on her occupation. The images further suggest sexual promiscuity and a childish helplessness, qualities contributing to the situation that develops with her husband. When the children call Nancy from her cabin to come cook, several aspects of their relationship are revealed. They, as children, make a demand based on the cited authority of their father, while Nancy is relegated to a subservient role in both status and racial assumptions, as exemplified in the children's addressing her by her first name. Her dialect further reinforces the distinction. When she declares, "I going to get my sleep out" (*CS* 290), she reinforces the conclusion that she has used the night for social activities. At the end of the exchange, Nancy's refusal to meet the children's demands "breaks the convention that socially inferior persons should heed the order of those in positions of authority." She surprises the children; Jason ascribes it to drunkenness. Only later does Quentin retell the event as he has come to understand her "asserting her right not to come when demanded" (Sunderman 1981, 304–14).

Nancy's behavior contradicts conventional assumptions in two other episodes: with Stovall and the jailer. Her demand for payment makes public a behavior that "is condoned as long as the liaison is not made public." Further, Stovall's reputation is threatened because the exchange also reveals his lack of "Christian charity and mercy." Nancy turns the power of naming on Stovall by referring to him as "white man," a tactic in which "his personal identity is subsumed under his racial identity." Another moment when Nancy contradicts stereotyped codes of behavior is when she attempts suicide. The jailer, incapable of relating such action to a black person's personal anguish, concludes that it must be attributed to cocaine. The exploitation of Nancy extends also to her relationship with Jesus. When realizing that he cannot vent his frustration on the white man, he displaces his anger on Nancy. Nancy responds passively (evidenced by the static verbs used to describe her). Her disavowal of responsibility reflects her own reiteration of a white stereotype and the historical realities that "militate against the development of moral obligation and responsibility" (Sundermann 1981, 304–14).

The Compsons' failure to understand Nancy's situation also relates to certain white presumptions evidenced in the dialogue. Although Mr. Compson is more sympathetic than the others, he takes a paternal tone toward Nancy and chastises her for behaving in a manner that incurred Jesus's anger. His effort at reassurance bears an implicit reprimand. Then, displaying another white presumption, he suggests that Jesus has probably already taken another wife. Quentin's final question reveals not only his understanding of Nancy's fear but also his recognition that her fear is justified and his confusion over his father's unwillingness to understand. The story closes without optimism. The sun sets on Nancy's fear. Sunderman concludes, "the literary discourse shows the misapprehensions, erroneous assumptions, and implications that the characters have about each other as revealed by their speech acts" (1981, 304–314).

Dirk Kuyk, Betty Kuyk, and James Miller read "That Evening Sun" as a conjure tale commingling African and African-American traditions in a story they see as unquestionably Nancy's. The title from the blues tradition "invites the reader to think about the story in the context of black culture." Another aspect of black culture involves the image of Nancy carrying the laundry on her head. These critics argue that the tone is admiring and in no way meant to be humorous because within the African tradition, such skill represents superior intelligence and confidence. Two other qualities, belief in spiritual dualism and conjuring, operate importantly in the text. Spiritual dualism involves the ability of the spirit to separate from the physical body. Jesus maintains a spiritual presence even if he is in Memphis (or St. Louis). He wants to remain unseen and succeeds. Jesus is also a "badman" figure in the African-American tradition. He openly defies laws of white society. Further, typical of the badman as described by Daryl Dance, Jesus takes an antagonistic position toward Nancy "'for what appears to him to be her collusion with white American society to emasculate and repress him.'" Jesus is skilled with a razor and bears the scars of confrontation. He distinguishes himself as unique and uncooperative in his own community. His uniqueness is not perceived as a valuable trait but as a quality of his evil. His name, while it signals religious and moral dimensions in the story, does not represent a comparison to Jesus Christ (Kuyk, Kuyk, and Miller 1986, 33–50).

Like Jesus, Nancy also seems to act as if her physical and spiritual selves have split. She does not feel the burning of her hands touching the lamp. She is unable to swallow. Jesus has conjured Nancy. She acts like a conjured person: moaning, holding her eyes open, incapable of eating. Nancy's belief that she has protection in the Compson household stems from the belief that conjuring only works within the conjurer's race. The smell the children sense also relates to the conjuring. Further, the bone with meat, both traditionally and in this story, relates to evil and death. Nancy, consistent with the behavior of one who has been conjured, believes her death is inevitable. However, at the beginning, unlike a conjured person, Nancy resists—first within the protection of the white family, then "with the shields of her house, of fire, and of light." Eventually, however, she surrenders. These critics contend that Faulkner might have made the cultural context more explicit, but that he, like the young Quentin, narrated "an experience that Faulkner had had or heard of but did not entirely comprehend" (Kuyk, Kuyk, and Miller 1986, 33–50).

Polk believes the complex characterizations of Nancy and Jesus, including their marital difficulties, provide a "direct, frontal assault upon racial stereotypes." Nancy and Jesus do apparently love each other, but their relationship is constantly "thwarted" by circumstances that they cannot control (Polk 1987, 146–49).

Heilman believes the portrait of Nancy's fear is contrasted with but also serves to link her to Mrs. Compson, whose pretended fear is self-serving, and with the children, who have fears but proclaim that they are fearless. Other unifying elements are status issues within the family and between racial groups, played out on several levels with the adults and children (1950, 80–81). Everett applies the social deterioration widely, asserting that Nancy's experience "illuminates the moral decay of an entire society" (Everett 1969, 172).

Momberger analyzes "That Evening Sun" in the context of "The Village" section of *Collected Stories*, thus aligning himself with those who see Nancy's situation as at least partially a failure of the community. Momberger, like Heilman, discusses the parallel failures of white and black families in the story. Caddy explicitly compares the marriage partners, Mr. and Mrs. Compson and Jesus and Nancy, but remarks made by others reinforce the comparison. Twice Mr. Compson sarcastically compares himself with Jesus. Nancy mistakes the sound of Mr. Compson's approaching footsteps for Jesus's. Both marriages are estranged. Mrs. Compson has retreated to a room of her own. Jesus and Nancy are separated.

Also, the intra-family relationships are weak. Neither of the adult Compsons responds to Caddy's incessant questions; neither parent reprimands the child Jason for his behavior; the two children's bickering is rarely checked, though Nancy's behavior is constantly reproved. Quentin seems ignored by siblings and parents. In the black family it is not certain who Jesus's parents are. Aunt Rachel, unlike the maternally devoted biblical Rachel, sometimes claims Jesus as her son and sometimes does not.

The failure of the white community to help Nancy is also paralleled in the black community: Aunt Rachel does not help, and Dilsey's response is in line with the Compsons'. After initial offerings of shelter, both Mr. Compson and Dilsey dismiss their responsibility when they ask Nancy what she will do. The crucial failure of the community is that neither asks what "we" should do. As

Momberger notes, Jesus's outrage at least implies that he cares for Nancy, unlike the rest. The social norms of the community all fail her. If her relationship with Mr. Stovall is a business transaction, it is "one ungoverned by even the simplest contractual rules." The church, represented only in the person of Stovall, "has ceased to be a unifying force for compassion and love." Civil authority rises no further than concern for keeping up appearances (Momberger 1978, 23–29).

Matthews discusses the framing device (introducing or enclosing a story with a narrative distinct from the action of the main narrative) in Faulkner's fiction as a site at which the "contradictory impulses toward comprehension and evasion" are "played out." When Quentin narrates a personal experience within a frame, that frame places it in the social and historical constructs of the time. While the frame affords the possibility of greater significance, it may also "work to resist [its] own insights and identify knowledge as the realm of death." Quentin, at age twenty-four, some four years after his suicide, tells his story as a ghost (Matthews 1989, 75–83, 89).

The knowledge in "That Evening Sun" that Quentin seeks to suppress is the disintegration of codified behaviors among the races. The contradictory impulses in the story blur the boundaries between white and black and the images that reinforce those boundaries. The early image of tearing silk reflects Quentin's "sense that the town's social fabric has been rent by change." The scene of Nancy carrying the laundry bundle on her head identifies her labor as her uniform; further, the analogy of laundry to cotton bales "puts black domestic labor in its proper historical context." These images are reinforced by the white house, the white owners, and the blackened washpot, the black "tools of maintenance." Quentin's affectionate recollection hardly compensates for the fact that Nancy literally must "go down" to cross the border between white and black communities (Matthews 1989, 75–83, 89).

The children themselves seek "to maintain categories of segregation and discrimination." Their feelings are reinforced by their father's assurance that a comparison of him and Jesus is untenable and their mother's insistence that blacks could not sleep in the bedrooms. The lines of racial discrimination are emphasized; an example is Jesus's explicit recognition of the inequality that allows a white man free access to Jesus's kitchen while severely restricting Jesus's movement. Also, use of violent images such as cutting vines "underscores the fear that blacks will reverse the violence they have suffered." Nancy's question, "When you going to pay me white man?" (*CS* 291), assumes fuller import in this context.

Quentin is confronted with the unpleasant realization that the rules of engagement between the groups are changing. His people will assume new relationships with those considered beneath them. The conflict also manifests itself in images of "merging doubles." Jesus is confused with Jesus Christ, the "other Jesus." Nancy's singing is not singing; she looks but does not see; she drinks but does not swallow; she is black but carries a mulatto child. Matthews argues that the doubling may add significance to the comparable sexual behavior of Nancy and Caddy and also to the image of Nancy as a beast of burden in the story when likened to the animal Nancy in the ditch in *The Sound and the Fury*. Consideration of the racial and social implications of the text may show that Quentin's question at the end is all too literally intended: "If the South's old order of economic and racial hierarchy has been overthrown, who will do the washing?" (Matthews 1989, 75–83, 89).

Some critics, even though their arguments are significantly more limited, have sought to interpret the text in terms other than its social context. O'Connor describes the story as more than a tale of "local history of exploitation, guilt, and ignorance." He sees concern with "human frustration, white and black, at the bleakest point of hopelessness and despair" (O'Connor 1954, 68). Fisher contends that Faulkner does not locate the source of evil in the "impersonality and irritability of modern life." Rather it is a study of the "sin, fear, and hypocrisy" that is beyond the ability of the children to recognize (1960, 16–17). For Skei, the story is about "our plight, guilt, despair, lack of love; about human beings living in a world where the only thing to make life worthwhile is the co-operation and interaction with, and love for, one's fellow men." The use of local history, including racial injustice and individual failings, though valid issues in the text, should not limit the story's larger implications. These larger issues are brought in by the narrative strategy (Skei 1977, 105–06).

In his analysis of the archetypal pattern of heaven and hell in Faulkner's "That Evening Sun," Rosenman focuses on the ditch and the fear that Jesus waits in it as the core of the developing image. The ditch is hell, and Jesus is the devil lurking in it. The fear of the ditch pervades the story and heightens expectancy and suspense. It is, further, the dividing boundary between the racially segregated black and white worlds. The image of hell is enhanced by Nancy's description of the children as devils. Rosenman suggests that the popper falling into the fire may represent Nancy's own descent into hell. This reading perceives Jesus as the Antichrist, the man in whom Nancy has awakened the devil. He is symbolic of her loss of heaven. The hog-bone that Jesus presumably leaves may represent a parody of the communion wafer. Rosenman explains that another common element in the archetypal pattern is a queenlike Eve who is threatened by the presence of the devil. He points out that Nancy is no innocent in this vision, but her story to the children does include the efforts of a queen to cross the ditch safely. The message of the story is that Nancy is "forced to experience the mind and spirit-crushing revelation" that she is "'alone in the universe.'" Given that confrontation, the corollary, inscribed on the Delphic oracle, is "'Know Thyself'" as Nancy must confront, alone, the "primal depths" of her being (Rosenman 1978, 12–16).

Alma Ilacqua analyzes "That Evening Sun" as demonstrating the Calvinism in Faulkner's work. Specifically, Ilacqua argues that "Faulkner clearly projects through the aesthetics of fiction a view of order which consistently parallels the religious vision of [Jonathan] Edwards." The story's thematic concern is mankind's failure to live with love for the "other," biblical Jesus. The Compsons, in their failure to help Nancy, represent the inadequate concern for others that eventually damns the family (Ilacqua 1983, 126–30).

Taylor sees Jesus as a black Jesus as well as one who fits Faulkner's conception of blacks as an "obverse reflection" of whites. Nancy fits the exotic primitive stereotype, but she is also a believing Christian. She is struggling with the act of accepting white judgment of herself as "just a nigger" even though her husband tries to keep her away from people that perpetuate that perspective. Jesus, Nancy's husband, and mention of his name have been banned from the Compson household, but the black community manages to receive word of his return. Whites polarized good and evil into Christ (light) and Satan (darkness). Blacks could fuse both. Although whites could not perceive him as such, Nancy's Jesus could represent love and vengeance. Taylor believes the story exemplifies the understanding of the interplay between the white rituals of scapegoating and the blacks that Faulkner developed in his work. Taylor explains, "White Puritans admitted only the enlightened side of their natures; they banished their darker natures by projecting their guilt onto blacks, women, and children, then punishing that guilt vicariously." Blacks, Taylor continues, responded similarly: "They might try to avoid their own guilt, as Nancy tried to do, by accepting that dark, subhuman identity and punishing themselves. But blacks like Nancy were more likely to find they could not forget their experience of light. They had seen what happened when whites projected their guilt onto others, and because they had, they were ready to accept both qualities in themselves. That was what it meant to be able to receive the word." Nancy's Jesus is an "ironic symbol of the Word made flesh because he stood for the powers of light" (Taylor 1983, 55–59).

Although he does not employ the Christian context that Taylor uses, Peters also examines Jesus as the scapegoat of white society's effort to "purify itself." As Peters explains, "Black . . . is seen as the manifestation of the evil that should be extricated from human culture," but the white consciousness fears that the "black's feelings of humiliation and intimidation may not be so easily held below the thresholds of thought and action" resulting not in cleansing but further guilt and turmoil (Peters 1983, 87).

One measure of the complexity of "That Evening Sun" is the difficulty of separating theme from technique. Any examination of Quentin necessarily involves a discussion both of point of view and personality. In Howe's vivid description of "That Evening Sun," the story "is a triumph of indirect presentment, art by ricochet" ([1952] 1975, 267). Several critics have found that the presentation of the story requires active participation from the reader.

Heilman attributes the need for extensive reader involvement to the multiplicity of perspectives and levels of understanding (Heilman 1950, 80–81). Frey similarly argues that the irony is achieved in the discrepancy between perceptions of the central character, Nancy, Quentin's precise observations but limited understandings, and the reader's fuller understanding (1953, 34–38). Millgate believes that terror is generated in the story "in direct proportion to our growing realization that the children do not understand Nancy's plight and will do nothing to abet her scheme" ([1961] 1966 64).

The absence of Nancy's murder in the text relates to Faulkner's tactic of not portraying violent scenes. According to Joseph Flora, this "device of conspicuous silence" stimulates readers' "conceptual powers" and compels them to be "more involved in the process of moral judgment." Quentin's narration emphasizes both his identification with Jefferson, in the opening, present-time narration, and his attempt to understand the victimization of a black individual in that community. The lack of a direct portrayal of the murder is not to create multiple possibilities but because for Quentin, the portrayal simply is not necessary. Quentin does, however, carefully recreate the sounds associated with the events. His conscientiousness works to establish his reliability as narrator and to enable the reader to make more accurate judgments. The violence actually portrayed occurs in the first section, when Stovall assaults Nancy. It is her noise that provokes him. Nancy is noisy. Quentin demonstrates his acuteness to sound when he distinguishes his mother's "Jason!" as a reference to his father rather than to his brother, and when he knows which Jesus Nancy means in her wail. Nancy's "sound" that was but was not like singing becomes a motif in the story. It is contrasted with a "moment of noticeable silence" when Caddy hears someone coming. Nancy, at the close, resumes her wordless sound that is therefore "only a small space from silence." Quentin breaks his own silence with his question about the laundry. Because he does not speak to "his, the Compsons', and Jefferson's failure to have aided Nancy and to have understood Jesus," he assumes an ironic narrative stance (Flora 1982, 33, 36–40).

Laurence Perrine views "That Evening Sun" as raising questions without resolving them. He points out that the ending is "technically indeterminate"; numerous readers believe Nancy is killed while others claim the threat was only imagined, in a ratio he determines as about three-to-one. Perrine insists that whatever conclusion one holds about Nancy's fate, "it is unreasonable to think that Faulkner intended readers of the short story in 1931 to interpret it on the basis of evidence which he would not provide them until twenty years later." Perrine argues that the issue of Nancy's survival is but the climactic example of a series of uncertainties; these emphasize "ambiguities about fact and motivation" and underscore the intentionality of Faulkner's failure to resolve the conflict. Perrine examines a number of unanswerable questions in the story, unanswerable, he emphasizes, not because of Quentin's memory "but because of gaps in his knowledge." Quentin may give accurate renderings of what people said, but his accurate reporting does not necessarily "guarantee the truth of their saying." Further, Quentin has not heard everything and simply does not know everything (Perrine 1985, 295–307).

Perrine lists some twenty-one questions unanswerable from the information in the story. The Lovelady digression, for example, adds two unanswerable questions: why Mrs. Lovelady commits suicide and what happens to the child. Perrine suggests that a parallel may be intended to show how racial exploitation "causes conflict not only *between* but *within* the races." Among the other questions Perrine includes as unresolvable are Aunt Rachel's relationship with Jesus, the particular cause for Nancy's arrest, the reason for Nancy's habitual lateness to the Compsons', the paternity of Nancy's child and the status of her pregnancy after its mention early in the story (Perrine dismisses the abortion argument), and whether Jesus has actually returned. Quentin's report is at least fourth-hand—from some other black person whose source is unclear, to Nancy, to Quentin's father, to Quentin. Given these and other questions Perrine traces, he concludes that Faulkner intended for the story to end unresolved. Quentin's lack of knowledge arises in part from the separation between the white and black communities. The story is about that "gulf separating the white and black communities which is both cause and result of that fear." The personal conflict is a symptom of the "larger unresolved social conflict." For the conflict to be resolved in either direction would severely limit the story's import (Perrine 1985, 295–307).

Like Perrine, Gerlach emphasizes the importance that questionable evidence holds in the story. Gerlach includes in his comment the shifting narrative voice from more to less formal diction. He describes the child Jason's fear of the ditch as a subplot that "plays against" the main plot, "interrupting it bizarrely" and commenting ironically on it. Gerlach describes two impulses in the story: that it moves "toward an endpoint in an exaggeratedly traditional way" but also that the "vagrant sense of storytelling created by the indirect beginning may still affect the reader, diminishing the expectation of an ending." The narrator may not convey a focus sufficient to conclude in an ending, and from the perspective of Nancy's fears, delay is preferable to her assumed ending. As Gerlach points out, "The last thing Nancy wants is closure because the ambassador of closure has a razor in his mouth." The lack of closure also makes it impossible to "know whether the elder Jason Compson was reasonable." He may have been reasonable or callous; certainty simply is not available. Gerlach argues that in an attempt to find closure, some critics have relocated the focus of the story to other characters, such as Caddy. This position, he says, is untenable because Quentin's understanding is superior to Caddy's. However, one should also not assume that Quentin's question about Nancy and the laundry provides confirmation of her coming murder. The story does provide closure in its portrayal of Nancy's undoing, whether its source is real or imagined. It is a "complete depiction of social and psychological ruin." The story's lack of resolution of the conflict inclines the reader to reinvest the "energy that we put into closing a story back into the story." The "receding picture, the Compsons leaving Nancy behind," underscores Nancy's position as that of one who "bears the cost of broken social relationships while the rest of the community, white and black, sees no complicity, sees no connection between use and degradation." Quentin's question exposes the "shortsightedness fundamental to the whole social problem" (Gerlach 1985, 130–43).

Critics display a variety of attitudes regarding humor and "That Evening Sun." Sterling Brown contrasts Faulkner's treatment of a "razor-toting" black man with the more common burlesque treatment of Negroes. Although the story "is not complimentary to the Negroes," it presses for understanding of the serious consequences of razors and death. As such the story surpasses slapstick and achieves the status of literature (Brown 1931, 347, 350).

Everett finds a grim humor in the discrepancy between the understanding of the adults and the children, a humor that contributes to the ominous atmosphere of the story (1969, 171). Coburn has analyzed the humor in "That Evening Sun" from the perspective of its ties to the tradition of grim Southwestern humor. He sees Jesus as a "grotesque, seriocomic figure," and Nancy as the "suffering servant." Together they counter images of the black characters as Christ-like, patient sufferers. Jesus serves as a reminder of the biblical Jesus in his questioned parentage, his absence and anticipated return, Nancy's belief in his omniscient knowledge of her and his inevitable vengeance. He serves as a caricature of the Jesus of American Calvinism; the wish that he would disappear shadows more consciousnesses than Nancy's—the Compsons', particularly. Nancy is denied her due by the Baptist deacon Stovall on three occasions (Coburn 1974, 207–09). Nancy is a grotesque in the portrait of her carrying the laundry bundle with the black straw sailor hat perched carefully on top and in her futile and ludicrous attempts to entertain the children. Also, according to Coburn, "a bungled act of suicide . . . is potentially comic." Finally, the children's questions, posed in innocence, nullify her dismissal, based on race, of "her obligations as a moral agent." Finally, in response to their questions, she admits that "what I going to get ain't no more than mine" (*CS* 307). The horror of the tale always predominates, but it does not obliterate the comic impulse. Nancy wins sympathy; the Compsons and the other white characters "who forsake her merit contempt" (Coburn 1974, 213–16).

Only a few responses have offered extended interpretations of the story's imagery. Sunderman interprets Nancy's sitting by the cold stove as "symbolic of her inability to be warmed by human understanding." The question of whether Nancy is "through" suggests both the sense of having completed the task and of being through with living. This question is followed by Caddy's supposition that she is waiting for Jesus to take her home—a walk with her husband to the cabin but also the metaphorical possibility, as in the spiritual "Old Black Joe," when the slave is carried "home to his heavenly reward." The sign she receives from Jesus serves as another play on religious imagery associated with death (Sunderman 1981, 311–12).

Barry Sanders traces images of fire in the story. They are specifically linked to Nancy's deterioration. Sanders establishes the context of fire in religious fervor and in hellish torments, but claims that they are secularized and focused on Nancy's present existence. Initially, fire represents "life force," and its absence reveals that Nancy's "life energy is dead." This association is especially strong in the cold kitchen. The absence of Jesus from her life represents loss of life rather than loss of soul. Once Nancy states that she has awakened the devil in Jesus, the associations become reflections of the hellishness of her present condition in the cabin. When she lights the lamp, she touches it; her hand passes through the fire; the room fills with smoke, and she burns the popcorn. Like the corn, she is burned out and left for her assumed death (Sanders 1967, 69–71).

Coburn also traces the images of light and heat associated with Nancy: she "is akin to the sun of the title." She is drawn to fire; her life is a "flame in danger of extinction." She is afraid of the dark. But while the fire imagery represents at one level Nancy's urge to live, it also manifests a threat for her in its association with hellish flames. The spilled hot coffee and the name "Stovall" point to future tortures, such as the burns she experiences in the cabin. The children act as tormenting spirits. The conflicting strains of the imagery suggest an unresolved ambiguity as to whether Nancy will suffer the fires of hell or rise again like the sun. Coburn insists on the open-endedness of the text that refuses to reveal the resolution of Nancy's terror. Her story is controlled by a sense of her likely tragic fate, but it does not foreclose the comic possibility (Coburn 1974, 209–11).

Like the song from which the story takes its title, Nancy relates the setting sun to her relationship with her man. While the song links the setting sun to the lover's desertion, Nancy links it to Jesus's return. Consistent with the song, however, Nancy is not prepared to give him up. Both Nancy and the singer are jealous of a rival in St. Louis (Coburn 1974, 211–12). Johnston makes further titular associations beyond references to "St. Louis Blues." He recalls that in master–slave relationships restraints on movement by the slaves were often linked to the setting sun, at which time they were expected to be back home. Ironically for Nancy, she has lived without the restraint, but she has not received the necessary power to protect herself in the absence of the plantation setting (Johnston 1974, 98).

In addition to images that reinforce the issues and emotions of the text, Faulkner employs a short narrative digression to emphasize social concerns. For Frey, the ostensibly irrelevant story about Mr. Lovelady, his wife, and his child emphasizes Quentin's inability to understand the fact of death present in the aside and in Nancy's situation. The "matter-of-factness" of the account parallels the recounting of Nancy's situation and generates the irony in treating the two equally (Frey 1953, 36). Momberger finds two thematic links in the Lovelady episode. First, it shows that race relations in the community have been reduced to "merely economic and utilitarian" purposes. Second, it displays another failed family unit (1978, 30).

Critics have drawn contradictory conclusions in their readings of the Lovelady digression, a pattern that pervades the entire critical response to "That Evening Sun." There is consensus regarding the story's excellence, but beyond that the interpretations are widely divergent. In 1947 Snell used this story to argue that Faulkner's expertise as a short story writer exceeded his talent as a novelist, arguing that the story "succeeds so greatly in outdistancing the novel" closely related to it, *The Sound and the Fury* (1947, 96, 99). Typically, however, most critics hold the reverse to be true. It is important to maintain some autonomy for "That Evening Sun" from the related texts. Allen diminishes the story when he describes it "as an appendage; almost a footnote, to the events narrated in *The Sound and the Fury* and *Absalom, Absalom!*" (1981, 186). It is possible to enjoy a reading of the story without knowledge of those novels, and given its frequent appearance in anthologies, it is often read independently. "That Evening Sun" was the first of Faulkner's stories to be translated into Russian when it was included in a 1934 anthology, *American Short Stories of the Twentieth Century* (Inge 1984, 176; Vashchenko 1984, 196). Faulkner even made an audio recording of the story (Blotner 1974, 1758). Putzel exaggerates when he claims that the author included it "in every story collection he ever had a hand in editing" (1985, 229), but Skei is not challenged when he describes "That Evening Sun" as "one of the most inexhaustible of Faulkner's stories" (1977, 109).

## Works Cited

Adams, Richard P. 1968. *Faulkner: Myth and Motion*. Princeton, NJ: Princeton University Press.

Alexander, Margaret Walker. 1978. "Faulkner & Race." In *The Maker and the Myth: Faulkner and Yoknapatawpha, 1977*. Ed. Evans Harrington and Ann J. Abadie. Jackson: University Press of Mississippi, 105–21.

Allen, Walter. 1981. *The Short Story in English*. New York: Oxford University Press.

Barth, J. Robert. 1964. "Faulkner and the Calvinist Tradition." *Thought* 39:100–120.

Bassett, John E. [1988] 1989. "Requiem for a Nun: Revising Temple Drake." In *Visions and Revisions: Essays on Faulkner*. Ed. Bassett. Locust Hill Literary Studies No. 4. West Cornwall, CT: Locust Hill, 181–93.

Baumbach, Jonathan, and Arthur Edelstein. 1968. *Moderns and Contemporaries: Nine Masters of the Short Story*. New York: Random House.

Beck, Warren. 1976. *Faulkner: Essays*. Madison: University of Wisconsin Press.

Bennett, Ken. 1985. "The Language of the Blues in Faulkner's 'That Evening Sun.'" *Mississippi Quarterly* 38:339–42.

Benson, Jackson J. [1971] 1982. "Quentin Compson: Self-Portrait of a Young Artist's Emotions." In *Critical Essays on William Faulkner: The Compson Family*. Ed. Arthur F. Kinney. Boston: G. K. Hall, 214–30.

Bethea, Sally. 1974. "Further Thoughts on Racial Implications in Faulkner's 'That Evening Sun.'" *Notes on Mississippi Writers* 6:87–92.

Blotner, Joseph. 1974. *Faulkner: A Biography*. 2 vols. New York: Random House.

———. 1984. *Faulkner: A Biography*. 1 vol. New York: Random House.

Bradford, Mel E. 1966. "Faulkner's 'That Evening Sun.'" *CEA Critic* 28.8:1, 3.

Brooks, Cleanth. [1963] 1990. *William Faulkner: The Yoknapatawpha Country*. New Haven: Yale University Press. Reprint. Baton Rouge: Louisiana State University Press.

———. 1971. *A Shaping Joy: Studies in the Writer's Craft*. New York: Harcourt Brace.

———. 1983. *William Faulkner: First Encounters*. New Haven: Yale University Press.

Broughton, Panthea Reid. 1974. *William Faulkner: The Abstract and the Actual*. Baton Rouge: Louisiana State University Press.

Brown, May Cameron. 1976. "Voice in 'That Evening Sun': A Study of Quentin Compson." *Mississippi Quarterly* 29:347–60.

Brown, Sterling A. 1931. "The Point of View." *Journal of Negro Life* 9:347, 350.

Brown, William R. 1967. "Faulkner's Paradox in Pathology and Salvation: *Sanctuary, Light in August, Requiem for a Nun*." *Texas Studies in Literature and Language* 9:429–49.

Butterworth, Keen. 1983. *A Critical and Textual Study of Faulkner's* A Fable. Ann Arbor, MI: UMI Research Press.

Campbell, Harry Modean, and Ruel E. Foster. 1951. *William Faulkner: A Critical Appraisal*. Norman: University of Oklahoma Press.

Carothers, James B. 1984. "Faulkner's Short Stories: 'And Now What's to Do.'" In *New Directions in Faulkner Studies: Faulkner and Yoknapatawpha, 1983*. Ed. Doreen Fowler and Ann J. Abadie. Jackson: University Press of Mississippi, 202–27.

———. 1985. *William Faulkner's Short Stories*. Ann Arbor, MI: UMI Research Press.

———. 1992. "Faulkner's Short Story Writing and the Oldest Profession." In *Faulkner and the Short Story: Faulkner and Yoknapatawpha, 1990*. Ed. Evans Harrington and Ann J. Abadie. Jackson: University Press of Mississippi, 38–61.

Coburn, Mark D. 1974. "Nancy's Blues: Faulkner's 'That Evening Sun.'" *Perspective* 17:207–16.

Coffee, Jessie McGuire. 1983. *Faulkner's Un-Christlike Christians: Biblical Allusions in the Novel*. Ann Arbor, MI: UMI Research Press.

Coindreau, Maurice Edgar. 1971. *The Time of William Faulkner*. Ed. and Trans. George McMillan Reeves. Columbia: University of South Carolina Press.

Cowley, Malcolm. [1967] 1977. Introduction. *The Portable Faulkner*. Rev. ed. Ed. Malcolm Cowley. New York: Viking. Reprint. London: Penguin, vii–xxxiii.

Cox, Leland H. 1982. *William Faulkner: Biographical and Reference Guide*. Detroit: Gale Research Company.

Cullen, John B., and Floyd C. Watkins. [1961] 1975. *Old Times in the Faulkner Country*. Chapel Hill: University of North Carolina Press. Reprint. Baton Rouge: Louisiana State University Press.

Dabney, Lewis M. 1974. *The Indians of Yoknapatawpha: A Study in Literature and History*. Baton Rouge: Louisiana State University Press.

Davis, Scottie. 1972. "Faulkner's Nancy: Racial Implications in 'That Evening Sun.'" *Notes on Mississippi Writers* 5:30–32.

Davis, Thadious M. 1987. "From Jazz Syncopation to Blues Elegy: Faulkner's Development of Black Characterization." In *Faulkner and Race: Faulkner and Yoknapatawpha, 1986*. Ed. Doreen Fowler and Ann J. Abadie. Jackson: University Press of Mississippi, 70–92.

Edel, Leon. 1962. "How to Read *The Sound and the Fury*." In *Varieties of Literary Experience*. Ed. Stanley Burnshaw. New York: New York University Press, 241–57.

Emerson, O. B. 1984. *Faulkner's Early Literary Reputation in America*. Ann Arbor, MI: UMI Research Press.

Everett, Walter K. 1969. *Faulkner's Art and Character*. Woodbury, NY: Barron's Educational Series.

Faulkner, John. 1963. *My Brother Bill: An Affectionate Reminiscence*. New York: Trident.

Faulkner, William. [1929] 1987. *The Sound and the Fury. The Corrected Text*. New York: Vintage.

———. [1931] 1987. *Sanctuary. The Corrected Text*. New York: Vintage.

———. 1931. "That Evening Sun Go Down." *American Mercury* 22:257–67.

———. 1931. *These 13*. New York: Jonathan Cape and Harrison Smith.

———. 1950. *Collected Stories of William Faulkner*. New York: Random House.

———. 1959. *Faulkner in the University: Class Conferences at the University of Virginia, 1957-1958*. Ed. Frederick Gwynn and Joseph L. Blotner. Charlottesville: University Press of Virginia.

———. 1977. *Selected Letters of William Faulkner*. Ed. Joseph Blotner. New York: Random House.

———. 1987. *William Faulkner Manuscripts 6:* The Sound and the Fury. Ed. Noel Polk. 2 vols. New York: Garland.

———. 1987. *William Faulkner Manuscripts 9:* These 13. Ed. Noel Polk. New York: Garland.

Ferguson, James. 1991. *Faulkner's Short Fiction*. Knoxville: University of Tennessee Press.

Fiedler, Leslie A. 1960. *Love and Death in the American Novel*. New York: Criterion Books.

Fisher, Marvin. 1960. "The World of Faulkner's Children." *University of Kansas City Review* 27:13–18.

Flora, Joseph M. 1982. "The Device of Conspicuous Silence in the Modern Short Story." In *The Teller and the Tale: Aspects of the Short Story*. Vol. 13 of the Proceedings Comparative Literature Symposium Texas Tech University. Ed. Wendell M. Aycock. Lubbock: Texas Tech Press, 27–45.

Frey, Leonard H. 1953. "Irony and Point of View in 'That Evening Sun.'" *Faulkner Studies* 2.3:33–40.

Garrison, Joseph M., Jr. 1976. "The Past and the Present in 'That Evening Sun.'" *Studies in Short Fiction* 13:371–73.

Gerlach, John. 1985. *Toward the End: Closure and Structure in the American Short Story*. University: University of Alabama Press.

Gladstein, Mimi Reisel. 1986. *The Indestructible Woman in Faulkner, Hemingway, and Steinbeck*. Ann Arbor, MI: UMI Research Press.

Hagopian, John V. 1962. "That Evening Sun." In *Insight I: Analyses of American Literature*. Ed. John V. Hagopian and Martin Dolch. Frankfurt am Main: Hirschgraben-Verlag, 50–55.

Hale, Nancy. [1962] 1977. *The Realities of Fiction: A Book about Writing*. Westport, CT: Greenwood.

Hamb[l]in, Robert W. 1979. "Before the Fall: The Theme of Innocence in Faulkner's 'That Evening Sun.'" *Notes on Mississippi Writers* 11:86–94.

Harrington, Evans B. 1952. "Technical Aspects of William Faulkner's 'That Evening Sun.'" *Faulkner Studies* 1:54–59.

Harter, Carol Clancey. 1970. "The Winter of Isaac McCaslin: Revisions and Irony in Faulkner's 'Delta Autumn.'" *Journal of Modern Literature* 1:209–25.

Heilman, Robert B. 1950. *Modern Short Stories: A Critical Anthology*. New York: Harcourt, Brace.

Hermann, John. 1970. "Faulkner's Heart's Darling in 'That Evening Sun.'" *Studies in Short Fiction* 7:320–23.

Hogan, Patrick G. 1966. "Faulkner: A Rejoinder." *CEA Critic* 28.8:3.

Holmes, Edward M. 1966. *Faulkner's Twice-Told Tales: His Re-Use of His Material*. The Hague: Mouton.

Howe, Irving. [1952] 1975. *William Faulkner: A Critical Study*. 3d ed. Chicago: University of Chicago Press.

Hunt, John W. 1982. "The Disappearance of Quentin Compson." In *Critical Essays on William Faulkner: The Compson Family*. Ed. Arthur F. Kinney. Boston: G. K. Hall, 366–80.

Ilacqua, Alma A. 1983. "The Place of the Elect in Three Faulkner Narratives." *Christian Scholar's Review* 12:126–38.

Inge, M. Thomas. 1984. "Teaching Faulkner in the Soviet Union." In *Faulkner: International Perspectives: Faulkner and Yoknapatawpha, 1982*. Ed. Doreen Fowler and Ann J. Abadie. Jackson: University Press of Mississippi, 174–93.

Johnston, Kenneth G. 1974. "The Year of Jubilee: Faulkner's 'That Evening Sun.'" *American Literature* 46:93–100.

Karl, Frederick R. 1989. *William Faulkner: American Writer*. New York: Weidenfeld and Nicolson.

Kent, George E. 1974. "The Black Woman in Faulkner's Works, With the Exclusion of Dilsey." *Phylon* 35:430–41.

Kerr, Elizabeth M. [1969] 1976. *Yoknapatawpha: Faulkner's "Little Postage Stamp of Native Soil."* New York: Fordham University Press.

Kinney, Arthur F. 1980. "Faulkner's Narrative Poetics and *Collected Stories.*" *Faulkner Studies* 1:58–79.

———. 1982. "Introduction." In *Critical Essays on William Faulkner: The Compson Family*. Ed. Arthur F. Kinney. Boston: G. K. Hall, 1–41.

———. 1984. "'Topmost in the Pattern': Family Structure in Faulkner." In *New Directions in Faulkner Studies: Faulkner and Yoknapatawpha, 1983*. Ed. Doreen Fowler and Ann J. Abadie. Jackson: University Press of Mississippi, 143–71.

———. 1989. "The Family-Centered Nature of Faulkner's World." *College Literature* 16.1:83–101.

Kuyk, Dirk, Jr., Betty M. Kuyk, and James A. Miller. 1986. "Black Culture in William Faulkner's 'That Evening Sun.'" *Journal of American Studies* 20:33–50.

Lee, Jim. 1961. "The Problem of Nancy in Faulkner's 'That Evening Sun.'" *South-Central Bulletin* 21:49–50.

Magny, Claude-Edmonde. 1966. "Faulkner or Theological Inversion." In *Faulkner: A Collection of Critical Essays*. Ed. Robert Penn Warren. Englewood Cliffs, NJ: Prentice-Hall, 66–78.

Manglaviti, Leo M. J. 1972. "Faulkner's 'That Evening Sun' and Mencken's 'Best Editorial Judgment.'" *American Literature* 43:649–54.

Matthews, John T. 1989. "Faulkner's Narrative Frames." In *Faulkner and the Craft of Fiction: Faulkner and Yoknapatawpha, 1987.*. Ed. Doreen Fowler and Ann J. Abadie. Jackson: University Press of Mississippi, 71–91.

Meriwether, James B. [1961] 1971. *The Literary Career of William Faulkner: A Bibliographical Study*. Princeton, NJ: Princeton University Library. Reprint. Columbia: University of South Carolina Press.

———. 1971. "The Short Fiction of William Faulkner: A Bibliography." *Proof* 1:293–329.

———. 1973. "Faulkner's Correspondence with Scribner's Magazine." *Proof* 3:253–82.

Millgate, Michael. [1961] 1966. *William Faulkner*. New York: Barnes & Noble.

———. [1966] 1989. *The Achievement of William Faulkner*. New York: Random House. Reprint. Athens: University of Georgia Press. Brown Thrasher Books.

Minter, David. 1980. *William Faulkner: His Life and Work*. Baltimore: Johns Hopkins University Press.

Momberger, Philip. 1978. "Faulkner's 'The Village' and 'That Evening Sun': The Tale in Context." *Southern Literary Journal* 11.1:20–31.

Morrison, Gail Moore. 1983. "Never Done No Weeping When You Wanted to Laugh." *Mississippi Quarterly* 36:461–74.

Nilon, Charles H. 1965. *Faulkner and the Negro*. New York: Citadel.

O'Brien, Edward J. 1935. *The Short Story Case Book*. New York: Farrar and Rinehart.

O'Connor, William Van. 1954. *The Tangled Fire of William Faulkner*. Minneapolis: University of Minnesota Press.

Orvis, Mary Burchard. 1948. *The Art of Writing Fiction*. New York: Prentice-Hall.

Pearson, Norman Holmes. 1954. "Faulkner's Three 'Evening Suns.'" *Yale University Library Gazette* 29:61–70.

Peavy, Charles D. 1971. *Go Slow Now: Faulkner and the Race Question*. Eugene: University of Oregon Books.

Perkins, Hoke. 1987. "'Ah Just Cant Quit Thinking': Faulkner's Black Razor Murderers." In *Faulkner and Race: Faulkner and Yoknapatawpha, 1986*. Ed. Doreen Fowler and Ann J. Abadie. Jackson: University Press of Mississippi, 222–35.

Perrine, Laurence. 1985. "'That Evening Sun': A Skein of Uncertainties." *Studies in Short Fiction* 22:295–307.

Peters, Erskine. 1983. William Faulkner: *The Yoknapatawpha World and Black Being*. Darby, PA: Norwood.

Pitcher, E. W. 1981. "Motive and Metaphor in Faulkner's 'That Evening Sun.'" *Studies in Short Fiction* 18:131–35.

Polk, Noel. 1981. Faulkner's Requiem for a Nun: A Critical Study. Bloomington: *Indiana University Press*.

———. 1987. "Man in the Middle: Faulkner and the Southern White Moderate." In *Faulkner and Race: Faulkner and Yoknapatawpha, 1986.* Ed. Doreen Fowler and Ann J. Abadie. Jackson: University Press of Mississippi, 130–51.

Putzel, Max. 1985. *Genius of Place: William Faulkner's Triumphant Beginnings.* Baton Rouge: Louisiana State University Press.

Reed, Joseph W., Jr. 1973. *Faulkner's Narrative.* New Haven: Yale University Press.

Richardson, H. Edward. 1969. *William Faulkner: The Journey to Self-Discovery.* Columbia: University of Missouri Press.

Rosenman, John B. 1978. "The Heaven and Hell Archetype in Faulkner's 'That Evening Sun' and Bradbury's Dandelion Wine." *South Atlantic Bulletin* 43.2:12–16.

Ruppersburg, Hugh M. 1983. *Voice and Eye in Faulkner's Fiction.* Athens: University of Georgia Press.

Samway, Patrick, S.J. 1985. "Searching for Jason Richmond Compson: A Question of Echolalia and a Problem of Palimpsest." In *Intertextuality in Faulkner.* Ed. Michel Gresset and Noel Polk. Jackson: University Press of Mississippi, 178–209.

Sanders, Barry. 1967. "Faulkner's Fire Imagery in 'That Evening Sun.'" *Studies in Short Fiction* 5:69–71.

Schoenberg, Estella. 1977. *Old Tales and Talking: Quentin Compson in William Faulkner's Absalom, Absalom! and Related Works.* Jackson: University Press of Mississippi.

Skei, Hans H. 1977. *Bold and Tragical and Austere: William Faulkner's These 13: A Study.* University of Oslo Department of Literature.

———. 1981. *William Faulkner: The Short Story Career.* Oslo, Norway: Universitetsforlaget.

———. 1985. *William Faulkner: The Novelist as Short Story Writer.* Oslo, Norway: Universitetsforlaget.

———. 1992. "Beyond Genre? Existential Experience in Faulkner's Short Fiction." In *Faulkner and the Short Story: Faulkner and Yoknapatawpha, 1990.* Ed. Evans Harrington and Ann J. Abadie. Jackson: University Press of Mississippi, 62–77.

Slabey, Robert M. 1964. "Quentin Compson's 'Lost Childhood.'" *Studies in Short Fiction* 1:173–83.

Snell, George. 1947. *The Shapers of American Fiction.* New York: Dutton.

Sunderman, Paula. 1981. "Speech Act Theory and Faulkner's 'That Evening Sun.'" *Language and Style* 14:304–14.

Taylor, Walter. 1983. *Faulkner's Search for a South.* Urbana: University of Illinois Press.

Toole, William B., III. 1963. "Faulkner's 'That Evening Sun.'" *Explicator* 21:Item 52.

Trilling, Lionel. 1931. "Mr. Faulkner's World." *Nation* 133 (November 4):491–92

Tuck, Dorothy. 1964. *Crowell's Handbook of Faulkner*. New York: Thomas Y. Crowell.

Utley, Francis Lee. 1964. "Pride and Humility: The Cultural Roots of Ike McCaslin." In *Bear, Man, and God: Seven Approaches to William Faulkner's The Bear*. Ed. Francis Lee Utley, Lynn Z. Bloom, and Arthur F. Kinney. New York: Random House, 233–60.

Vashchenko, Alexandre. 1984. "The Perception of William Faulkner in the USSR." In *Faulkner: International Perspectives: Faulkner and Yoknapatawpha, 1982*. Ed. Doreen Fowler and Ann J. Abadie. Jackson: University Press of Mississippi, 194–211.

Vickery, Olga W. [1959] 1964. *The Novels of William Faulkner*. Baton Rouge: Louisiana State University Press.

Warren, Robert Penn, ed. 1966. *Faulkner: A Collection of Critical Essays*. Englewood Cliffs, NJ: Prentice-Hall.

Watson, James G. 1980. "Faulkner's Short Stories and the Making of Yoknapatawpha County." In *Fifty Years of Yoknapatawpha: Faulkner and Yoknapatawpha 1979*. Ed. Doreen Fowler and Ann J. Abadie. Jackson: University Press of Mississippi, 202–25.

Werner, Craig. 1987. "Minstrel Nightmares: Black Dreams of Faulkner's Dreams of Blacks." In *Faulkner and Race: Faulkner and Yoknapatawpha, 1986*. Ed. Doreen Fowler and Ann J. Abadie. Jackson: University Press of Mississippi, 35–57.

West, Ray B., Jr. 1952. *The Short Story in America 1900–1950*. Chicago: Regnery.

Whicher, Stephen E. 1954. "The Compsons' Nancies—A Note on The Sound and the Fury and 'That Evening Sun.'" *American Literature* 26:253–55.

Wright, Austin M. 1989. "Recalcitrance in the Short Story." In *Short Story Theory at a Crossroads*. Ed. Susan Lohafer and Jo Ellyn Clarey. Baton Rouge: Louisiana State University Press, 115–29.

*The Wilderness*

# Red Leaves

## Publication History

"Red Leaves" first appeared in the *Saturday Evening Post* on October 25, 1930, with illustrations by W. H. D. Koerner. Faulkner's story-sending schedule notes the submission date as July 24, 1930. During the next month Faulkner received $750 in payment for the story. This story was the second that the *Post* accepted from Faulkner, and the fee was increased from the $500 that Faulkner received for his first *Post* story, "Thrift." James Meriwether notes a similar pattern with Theodore Dreiser, who was paid "five hundred dollars, the usual rate for a new writer," for his first *Post* story and $750 for his second. Sometime between July 24, 1930, and August 18, 1930, apparently feeling confident about his recent successes, Faulkner wrote his agent, Ben Wasson, asking him if he might earn even larger fees. Faulkner explained that he needed money in order to make repairs on the newly purchased Bailey property (Rowan Oak) and to "get ahead and write a novel." Soon afterward the Faulkners added electricity to Rowan Oak and bought an electric stove (Blotner 1974, 664; Meriwether 1971, 174; Meriwether 1977, 461–62; Cohen 1989, 103–04).

"Red Leaves" is one of several Faulkner stories that have been frequently anthologized, though not always when Faulkner's correspondence indicates. Letters from Faulkner to George H. Lorrimer of the *Post* and to Wasson indicate that the author was asked for permission to reprint "Red Leaves" in *Blackwood's* magazine for a fee of 25 guineas. In a letter to *Scribner's* that Joseph Blotner dates "early 1930" but that Meriwether more convincingly dates at the end of that year, Faulkner cited the sum as 125 guineas. Whatever the proposed fee, the story did not appear in that British publication (*SL*, 46–47; Meriwether 1973, 261–62; Meriwether 1977, 470–72). Faulkner included a revised version of the story in *These 13* (1931) and later included that version in *Collected Stories* (1950). Malcolm Cowley included "Red Leaves" in the first section of the *Portable Faulkner* (1946). Faulkner revised a portion of the story for a prelude to "The Old People" in *Big Woods* (1955).

## Circumstances of Composition, Sources, and Influences

Hans Skei comments that the quick acceptance and rapid publication of "Red Leaves" "accounts for the lack of any textual peculiarities regarding this story" (Skei 1981, 64). Yet as with many of Faulkner's stories, dating the composition of "Red Leaves" is speculative at best, and the manuscript and typescript versions now available in the *William Faulkner Manuscripts* raise some important questions about the time of composition, particularly in relation to the writing of other stories. Skei fixes the composition of "Red Leaves" as being "around 1930" but comments that it is one of two exceptions to his observation that the short stories written around 1930 "almost exclusively deal with the recent or immediate past" (1985, 99). Also positing a 1930 date of composition, Noel Polk demonstrates a shift in perspective that Faulkner's stories underwent between the 1929 version of *Sanctuary* and the revised text of December 1930. He observes that stories composed during the beginning of that period, such as "Elly" and "A Rose for Emily," are "intense, internalized stories of repression and frustration" while stories at the late end, including "Red Leaves," are "less sexually intense, more open, more spacious, more external in their focus than the earlier stories." However, as Polk himself cautions, the submission dates on the sending schedule do not necessarily represent either the order or the time of composition of the stories listed (1985, 17, 33). There is, therefore, the possibility of alternate composition dates. Walter Taylor suggests that because of its close links to "A Justice," a related Indian story that Blotner is inclined to date in 1927, "Red Leaves" may have been written as early as 1927 (Taylor 1987, 204; Blotner 1974, Notes 82). Blotner, however, neither makes this link nor speculates on a composition date for "Red Leaves." In fact, although he does not specifically argue against an earlier composition date, he shifts his discussion of "A Justice" to the chapter "April 1930–January 1931" in his revised biography (Blotner 1984, 265–68).

Two passages deleted from the published texts of "Red Leaves" tend to support the argument for the early composition date: a "twilight" passage and an Indian name, Yo-ko-no-pa-taw-pha. In the typescript, Faulkner expands, then deletes a "twilight" passage in Part 3. Describing the slave, Faulkner writes, "He came slowly, as though he were walking in a strange place, or like a man who finds that what he thought would be a familiar place, was strange to him. He walked through what was more than twilight, since he must walk through it into what would be more than tomorrow" (*WFM 9* 169). All but "He came slowly" is then crossed out, and the magazine version contains only the shortened passage. The use of "twilight" here sounds very similar to the passage in "A Justice" where, at the close of the story, Quentin observes, "I was just twelve then, and I would have to wait until I had passed on and through and beyond the suspension of twilight" (*CS* 360). Also, in the spring of 1928, when Faulkner began the short story that would become *The Sound and the Fury*, the working title of that early draft was "Twilight" (Blotner 1974, 566). Michael Millgate has shown that the image of twilight carries significant import in the Quentin section particularly and in the novel generally ([1966] 1989, 86–87). Suggestive of a pre–1930 composition date, in the twelve-page manuscript of "Red Leaves" the second Indian is originally named "Yo-ko-no-pa-taw-fa" (*WFM 9* 139). The syllabication, according to Lewis Dabney, indicates Faulkner's experimentation with an unfamiliar word (1974, 24). If Dabney is correct, then it is possible to date the manuscript of "Red Leaves" between the composition of *Flags in the Dust*, completed in September 1927, which uses "Yocona county" (1973, 102), and the composition of *As I Lay Dying*, written in the fall and winter of 1929, which uses "Yoknapatawpha county" (*AILD* 1987, 188; see also Gresset 1985, 26, 29). Frederick Karl confirms that the fictional county is first named "Yoknapatawpha" in *As I Lay Dying* (1989, 11).

Differences in manuscript, typescript, and published versions of "Red Leaves" offer more conclusive suggestions about the way the composition process developed than when it occurred. The Indian who was to have been Yo-ko-no-pa-taw-fa becomes Louis Berry. Faulkner decided further not to name him in the opening lines of the story. Only later are he and his companion Three Basket identified by name. "Old Chief" and "the Man" become Issetibbeha and Moketubbe, Issetibbeha's father. Blotner observes that the typescript includes more information about Issetibbeha and his wife (1974, Notes 95).

Differences between the typescript and the 1930 *Post* text include added information about the New England captain and the Unitarian slaver (Blotner 1974, Notes 95). The brief glimpse of youthful disrespect for tribal custom that appears in the story is actually developed more fully in the draft (Volpe 1975, 131). The magazine version alone contains temporal references not present in either the earlier typescript or the subsequent revision for *These 13*. According to the *Post* story, the present action of the burial and hunt occur in 1840, while Doom's journey to New Orleans takes place "at the end of the eighteenth century" (*Post* 7). The revision for *These 13* (which is also the *Collected Stories* version) omits these time markers. Other time references also are changed in the published versions. Moving the steamboat across twelve miles takes five weeks in the Post story and five months in the later versions. The disappearance of the West Indian woman occurs two months after Doom's disappearance in the *Post* story (*Post* 7) and six months later in subsequent versions (*CS* 318). John Had-Two-Fathers becomes Had-Two-Fathers in *These 13* and thereafter. He is the character Sam Fathers, who is more fully described in "A Justice" and *Go Down, Moses*, although presented slightly differently in each work. Beginning with the story's appearance in *These 13*, its four-part division becomes six parts. Gilbert Muller observes that the change to six sections better controls "the pastoral pace of the narrative" and allows for a "terse and remarkably moving conclusion in the sixth and shortest section of the story" (Muller 1974, 243 n. 2).

Faulkner used portions of "Red Leaves" one final time after its appearance in *Collected Stories*. In *Big Woods* (1955), as a prelude to "The Old People," Faulkner revised sections four, five, and six of "Red Leaves"; these changes served to condense and alter the emphasis of the version in *Big Woods*. He includes a description of the enslaved headman and mentions other slaves present at the encounter between the doomed slave and the headman. The revision also described a brotherhood that had once existed between the slaves but that ended when the body servant became numbered among the dead (*BW* [101]). In the conversation between the two Indian trackers, their disdain for the "wearying work" caused by the body servant is omitted for a more succinct, "damn that Negro" and the added commentary, "Maybe Moketubbe will free them now" (*BW* [102]). Edward Holmes believes that the deletion concerning tribal politics and the problems of slaves and slave owners gives the story-as-prelude an increased "emphasis on the primitive virtues, including the respectful attitude toward life, toward death, and the ancient customs of man" (1966, 76; see also Carothers 1985, 101). The prelude omits several paragraphs at the opening of section four that had appeared in the *Collected Stories* version. These describe the body servant's inner turmoil. They are replaced with a more concise summation: "It was as though for the first time he realized his true situation, how desperate, how irrevocable, how doomed" (*BW* [103]). The prelude also departs from "Red Leaves" to describe the effects of the snakebite from the perspective of the body servant rather than as a secondhand recollection of the Indian tracker. The hunt is now presented through the eyes of the hunted, not the hunter (Ragan 1983, 307). Moketubbe's discomfort during the chase is omitted (Carothers 1985, 101). When the body servant is taken, the prelude identifies Three Basket as the Indian who finally takes him. Faulkner adds to the prelude version this parenthetical comment: "It was Three Basket, one of Issetibbeha's chief counselors and who, if Issetibbeha had had his way, would have been his successor" (*BW* [105]). As the prelude concludes, Faulkner incorporates section six unchanged from "Red Leaves." The prelude is, according to David Ragan, "designed to contribute to its [*Big Wood*'s] over-all unity" by altering the tone from elegiac to comic, while at the same time linking the slave and the wilderness in the common fate of doom (1983, 307–11).

Source studies for "Red Leaves" include examinations of Mississippi folklore and history as well as literary influences. Much of the critical response to "Red Leaves" and the other Indian tales focuses on the accurate portrayal of Faulkner's Indians that James Carothers has judged "sociologically and historically suspect" (1985, 16). Mick Gidley observes that many of their characteristics are grounded in the tradition of savagism. In "Red Leaves" they are depicted as hunters, not farmers (their slaves are their farmers); they are bound to follow the burial traditions of their ancestors, and they seem unaware of any ethical issues involved in cannibalism. It should be noted that Gidley cautions that Faulkner also countered this tradition of savagism in the creation of some of his Indian characters portrayed in other texts (Gidley 1990, 127–28). Faulkner recalled that in his own lifetime a remnant of Choctaws lived on a reservation in Mississippi, but that Mississippi Indians had been absorbed into the black and white races. He remarked further that Mississippi land records could be traced back to Indian patents (*FU* 9).

In his work on the Indian tales Dabney identified history books from which Faulkner might have gleaned his knowledge, though he concludes that "scholarship was less a source than a stimulus" for Faulkner (1974, 37). Dabney's observation is no more cautionary than Faulkner's own prior disclaimer when he said that for a writer "if it [research] don't quite fit what he wants to say he'll probably change it just a little" (*FU* 251). The Indian stories reinforce this point in their apparent use of Chickasaw and Choctaw as interchangeable terms.

Those who have not been daunted by Faulkner's disclaimer, including Dabney, have found interesting correspondences with if not recountings of Mississippi history. Ward Miner made some early connections between Mississippi history and the fictional Yoknapatawpha's beginnings. Miner describes the Indians Toby Tubby and Greenwood Leflore as having specific parallels in the Indian tales generally (1952, 20–25, 90–93). Elmo Howell searches "Red Leaves" in detail to find its facts and its fabrications. He confirms the historical accuracy of Chickasaws and Choctaws owning slaves. Regarding cannibalism, the record differs from the short story, as neither Chickasaws nor Choctaws were cannibals (Howell 1970, 293–95). Faulkner did not hesitate to confirm his play with accuracy when he was asked about the cannibalism in "Red Leaves." He responded that no record of cannibalism among the Chickasaws existed, but he conjectured, "Who's to say whether at some time one of them might not have tried what it tasted like?" (*FU*, 8–9).

Somewhat more ambiguous is Faulkner's attribution of human sacrifice to the Chickasaws. It is true that the Natchez Indians of Mississippi practiced human sacrifice in a sacramental ritual, and some Natchez survivors, when they were destroyed as a nation, joined the Chickasaws in the early eighteenth century. Nevertheless, the recorded torture of captives that Chickasaws practiced was not the human sacrifice that Faulkner portrays (Howell 1970, 296–97; Gage 1974, 27). Blotner suggests that there was an old tribal custom of burying a dead chief with his horse, dog, and body servant, a custom that Faulkner used (1974, 663). Beverly Langford also questions Howell's conclusion that the Chickasaw ritual of human sacrifice originated in Faulkner's imagination. Providing a more thorough analysis than Miner, she traces the legend that Chickasaw chief Tobba-tubby (Toby Tubby) arranged to have a slave buried with him when he died. His plans were foiled by alarmed members of the white community. Langford believes Tobba-tubby is the model for Issetibbeha and offers geographic parallels to reinforce her claim (1972, 19–24). The link with Tobba-tubby is also traced by Dabney, who observes that mixed-blood leaders were not unknown and who notes resemblances between Moketubbe's being carried on a litter during the hunt to a similar practice by the Natchez Indians. The feet of the Natchez chief, the Great Sun, were not permitted to touch the ground, and he was carried on a litter. When Great Sun died, his wives, guards, and retainer were executed (Dabney, 1974, 8, 24, 96). James Hinkle has discovered a historical study demonstrating that Faulkner's description of the medicine man's dress and action is accurate (1986, 30).

Rather than trying to find parallels between Faulkner's fictional Indians and the tribes of Northern Mississippi, Peter Beidler locates Faulkner's source in Charles Darwin's journal of his voyage on the *Beagle*, particularly the tenth chapter records of the visit to Tierra del Fuego. Captain Fitz Roy returns to Tierra del Fuego with three natives who have spent three years in England. Beidler draws several comparisons, matching the female native's name, "Fuegia Basket," with the name "Three Basket" and comparing Jemmy Button, another of the natives, with Moketubbe. Beidler suggests further that the notions of cannibalism, the victim's attempt to escape, and the story's title may also be traced to descriptions in the journal (Beidler 1973, 421–23). Although his evidence is compelling, Beidler does not investigate what is known about Faulkner's reading of Darwin. Dabney, too, sees Darwinian strains in "Red Leaves," but links he establishes focus little attention on fact pairing and more generally emphasize the sense that the capacity to endure exists in the Negro race rather than in the Indian race (1974, 99, 110; see also Polk 1981, 255–56 n. 19).

In a brief note, Richard Milum supplements historical source studies when he anchors the minor character, the Chevalier Soeur Blonde de Vitry, in the context of the Spanish Conspiracy. The two New Orleans associates of Vitry are the historical figures Baron Luis Hector de Carondelet and General James Wilkinson. This minor historical allusion, Milum suggests, "reveals a new and significant dimension of irony by reducing both de Vitry and Ikkemotubbe, not to mention the rest of Faulkner's Chickasaw tribe, to the status of minute pawns in a complex political intrigue involving the foreign policy of at least two countries" (Milum 1974a, 389–91).

Martha O'Nan posits explanations for the French roots of Doom from *du homme* and the name of the Chevalier Soeur Blonde de Vitry. Despite Cowley's concern for correct usage of *de l'homme* in the Compson "Appendix," Faulkner usually used *du homme*. O'Nan shows that du homme might be a possible if not precise construction (1970, 26–28; see also Cowley 1966, 43).

In a study that precedes much of the historical criticism, Calvin S. Brown, a professor who had been a friend of Faulkner when they were young, relates certain characteristics of the hunt motif in Faulkner's fiction to Sunday afternoon paper chases that they used to enjoy. Brown sees the fictional chases as re-creations of their adolescent games. He cites particulars of those chases to show similarities between them and the shifting point of view and the ritual nature of the stories (Brown 1966, 389–94).

Efforts to trace the literary influences discernible in "Red Leaves" have generally taken the form of listings rather than extended analyses. As with his studies of historical influences, Howell's examination of "Red Leaves" offers some of the earliest tracings of literary influences. Howell believes that most of Faulkner's Indians avoid the sentimental Noble Savage tradition in favor of more savage realism and thus follow in the tradition of Charles Brockden Brown's Hurons of *Edgar Huntly* (1799) or Robert Montgomery Bird's *Nick of the Woods* (1837). Howell adds that Sam Fathers is more nearly like "the romantic effusions of the Eastern writers" such as James Fenimore Cooper's Uncas in *The Last of the Mohicans* (1826), William Gilmore Simm's Sanutee in *The Yemassee* (1835), and the Indians in Longfellow's *Song of Hiawatha* (1855) (Howell 1967, 394–96). John Rabbetts contends that Faulkner is willing to show the potential tragedy in the natural world that Cooper did not explore. Rabbetts believes the conflict in "Red Leaves" arises in the "interaction of social pressures with natural forces" especially volatile in the temporal moment "of exploration, enslavement and conquest" (1989, 160–61).

Dabney adds that the gothic strain in "Red Leaves" follows the tradition not only of Charles Brockden Brown but also of Edgar Allan Poe. Dabney makes specific links to Conrad in the similarity between chief Doramin in *Lord Jim* and Moketubbe of "Red Leaves." This grotesque chieftain may also be a characterization drawn from recollections of Sunday comics, the "comic-strip Oriental despot rendered truly malevolent, pathetic, absurd" (Dabney 1974, 11, 24, 106). Another possible influence on "Red Leaves" and the other Indian stories is Oliver La Farge's *Laughing Boy* (1929). James Krefft supports his contention by reviewing the acquaintance between Faulkner and La Farge in New Orleans during the latter half of the 1920s. Krefft traces similarities between Faulkner's Chickasaws and Choctaws and La Farge's Navajos, pointing out the common use of the phrase "the Old People," and common thematic emphases, like the "life is motion" theme. In a note Krefft adds that they both could have been influenced by the Wallace Stevens poem "Life Is Motion" (1978, 188, 190–92).

The portrayal of the wilderness also has literary parallels. Howell sees similarities between Faulkner's wilderness and Francis Parkman's forests. He views the purpose of Faulkner's unromanticized wilderness as akin to Joseph Conrad's purpose in *Heart of Darkness*, to lift the "moral facade" and expose life "in its barest terms" (Howell 1970, 297–302).

To comparisons of the ritual of the hunt with other chases in literature must also be added Brown's biographical associations mentioned above. Dabney suggests that the hellish description of Moketubbe's tortuous ride on the litter "evokes a rare echo of Dante in Faulkner" (1974, 111). Both Dabney and Blotner attribute some influence to Sir James Frazer's *The Golden Bough*; they find the slave's flight as mirroring the physical contest of the godmen to postpone death and the unreflective participation in ritual by the Indians as enacting the diminution of ritual in the context of slavery (Dabney 1974, 97–98; Blotner 1984, 234). Blotner also suggests that Faulkner may have read stories by Lyle Saxon (1974, 663). Both Charles Peavy and Robert Funk hear echoes of Swift—from a "A Modest Proposal"—in the understated discussion of eating the slaves (Peavy 1971, 17 n. 3; Funk 1972, 340, 42). The experience of the body servant naked in the wilderness recalls Lear's existential confrontation.

Joseph Reed compares the third-person narrative strategy to Joseph Conrad's storytelling techniques. Faulkner's flexibility gives him a narrative range including "godlike omniscience," "anthropological objectivity," and the intense portrayal of the body servant's consciousness (1973, 47–48). The cryptic Indian dialogue that opens the story is generally considered to be modeled on Ernest Hemingway's method of capturing Castilian speech in English (Dabney, 1974, 102; Blotner 1984, 263). William Styron makes the specific link to Hemingway's *Death in the Afternoon*, but he adds that Faulkner's adaptation "became a grateful though individualized borrowing" (1982, 89). Lothar Hönnighausen groups "Red Leaves" with Eugene O'Neill's *Emperor Jones*. He does not argue that one influences the other; rather, he traces modernistic tendencies in both writers. In these texts they reflect the desire "to return to and probe, in black and red masks, the deep layers or archaic origins of man's consciousness and of man's culture" (Hönnighausen 1987, 200).

## Relationship to Other Faulkner Works

Faulkner introduces the Indian segment of the Yoknapatawpha community in "Red Leaves" and continues their stories in "A Justice," "A Courtship," "Lo!," and less explicitly in "Mountain Victory." Regardless of their historical inaccuracies, Faulkner's Indian stories rank among his major achievements, according to Howell. Faulkner's disregard for historical accuracy, confusing customs, irregular references to Chickasaws and Choctaws, and his generally creating a prehistoric milieu make these stories imaginative, fantastic works distinct from the other Mississippi stories. They share, he adds, the pattern of moving from "raucous sport" to "an unexpected and disturbing insight" (Howell 1967, 386–87).

"Red Leaves" has only vague links to "Lo!" Faulkner suggested that the Weddels of "Lo!" were Chickasaws like Issetibbeha and that they "may have been related by marriage, even by blood" (*FU* 261), an aside that gives impetus to Taylor's contention that the Indian tales might have become a novel (1987, 202–09). James Ferguson identifies different tonalities in the Indian stories related to the time when the stories were composed. While "Red Leaves" and "A Justice" are suffused with "complex ambiguities and wry ironies," "A Courtship," written over a decade later, possesses a "golden glow" (1991, 42).

Lionel Trilling made an early connection between "That Evening Sun," "Red Leaves," "A Justice," and "Crevasse." These four stories, Trilling argues, show Faulkner at his best because in them he "avoided social implications" and probed "some strange and hitherto unexplored setting of mind or place" (1931, 491–92).

Other early examinations of Faulkner often saw a bleak determinism in his work, and "Red Leaves" was used as evidence. In 1947, Reed Whittemore identified the body servant as one of many characters who "do what they do because they cannot do otherwise" (Emerson 1984, 183). For Robert Barth, Faulkner's major families and a number of his short fiction characters reflect a fatality, a perception of doom that negates a sense of will. Nancy in "That Evening Sun" waits passively for her fate, and the body servant in "Red Leaves" cannot will himself to live; he can only come to terms with his death (Barth 1964, 100–120).

The wilderness theme has been a point of comparison within Faulkner's work just as it has been a way to place him within the traditional American literary canon. Millgate speaks generally of the author's fiction when he observes "Faulkner's deep and almost religious sense of the permanence and richness of the land and his preoccupation with the problem of its ownership." Millgate adds that a "number of short stories, from 'Red Leaves' (1930) onwards, had demonstrated his fascination with the wilderness and with the narrative and symbolic potentialities of the hunt" ([1966] 1989, 201).

Indeed, images of hunt, flight, and pursuit provide the starting point for many critical comparisons. From this perspective, Robert Penn Warren relates "Red Leaves" to *The Wild Palms*, *The Unvanquished*, "The Bear," "Delta Autumn," "Was," and *Light in August* ([1949] 1975, 327). Millgate observes that "Red Leaves" is Faulkner's first application of the hunt theme in which a human being is the object of pursuit ([1961] 1966, 63). The body servant experiences a pattern of flight, knowledge, and acceptance like that of Joe Christmas in *Light in August* (Nilon 1965, 91; see also Pryse 1975, 133–38; Pryse 1979, 108 passim; Rabbetts 1989, 187). Brown finds similar flight motifs when the French architect flees and is tracked in *Absalom, Absalom!* and when the suitors race to the cave in "A Courtship" (1966, 390). Olga Vickery's analysis of the hunt motif divides stories into categories based on the object of the hunt: buried treasure, wild game, or human beings. Although a human being is the object of pursuit in "Red Leaves," Vickery points out that the tone is essentially comic. She contrasts this comic presentation with the absence of humor in the human hunt in "Pantaloon in Black," *Light in August*, and "Dry September" (Vickery [1959] 1964, 304). Elizabeth Kerr adds that the flight–pursuit pattern is placed in a Gothic setting and atmosphere in "Red Leaves," and Patrick Samway compares the racial character of the pursuit in *Intruder in the Dust*, "Red Leaves," and "Dry September" (Kerr 1979, 140; Samway 1980, 248). Ferguson's study of patterns in the short fiction produces an impressive list of stories concerned with initiation manifested in hunting stories. In "Red Leaves" the normal situation is reversed as the hunted man, not the hunter, undergoes an initiation when he faces his mortality (1991, 62).

Walter Slatoff examines the antithetical uses of motion and immobility that become "part of the very form and texture of experiences and events." Among the texts in which motion is essential are *As I Lay Dying*, *Pylon*, *The Unvanquished*, "Red Leaves," "The Old People," "Fox Hunt," "The Hound," and "A Courtship" (1960, 12, 24). In his study of the journey motif in *The Reivers*, Carothers notes that lack of motion in this novel and elsewhere in the fiction typically evokes Faulkner's condemnation. Carothers traces the lack-of-motion image in Moketubbe of "Red Leaves" as well as other characters in *The Reivers*, *Light in August*, *The Sound and the Fury*, "Hog Pawn," "A Rose for Emily," and "Miss Zilphia Gant" (1981b, 118–19).

Several critics have grouped "Red Leaves" with other works that examine racial issues. Charles Nilon links "Red Leaves" to "That Evening Sun," *Go Down, Moses*, "Dry September," and "Mountain Victory" in their shared use of the "lynch or crucifixion symbol." This symbol "is the means of the Negro character's victory" (1965, 33). Peavy lists the stories that include presentations of Indian slave owners as "Red Leaves," "A Justice," "A Courtship," "The Old People," and *Requiem for a Nun* (1971, 16). Dabney draws comparisons between "Red Leaves" and "Dry September" in their common focus on racial murders. Dabney argues, though not all would agree, that "Red Leaves" allows greater complexity of characterization and tragic focus than does "Dry September" (Dabney, 1974, 92). Juxtaposition, according to Kinney, becomes an important method of emphasis for Faulkner. "Red Leaves" offers an "early and condensed version" of the juxtaposition of slaves and rules seen repeatedly in his fiction. Kinney specifically mentions recurrences of the motif in *Go Down, Moses* and *Requiem for a Nun* (1978, 112).

Victor Strandberg believes that "Red Leaves" can be identified with stories in which the "Male Principle of power, violence, and freedom" motivates action. Doom, as Strandberg reads the combined information of "Red Leaves" and "A Justice," kills in order to obtain power so that he might have stature in the eyes of his white consort. (The problem of different genealogies is not resolved in this point.) Strandberg names a number of other male characters throughout the long and short fiction who demonstrate this motivation (1981, 29, 86).

Carothers examines the portrayal of a corrupted society in several stories that cut across time boundaries. He sees the societies of "Red Leaves," "Mountain Victory," and "Golden Land" beyond saving by the efforts of a hero but capable of perpetuation "by despots and tyrants" (Carothers 1981a, 264).

Another pattern is the pursuit of justice wherein *justice* is defined from a limited perspective, and in its attainment someone must commit a terrible wrong. In the case of "Red Leaves," the Indians may be able to continue their traditional rituals but at the price of human life (Ferguson 1991, 78–79). Further, the abstraction "community," when pitted against the individual, becomes destructive in such stories as "Red Leaves," "Uncle Willy," "The Tall Men," and "Dry September" (Ferguson 1991, 81–82).

Skei proposes a comparison between "Red Leaves" and "Mountain Victory," as both stories present a "treatment of a particular existential experience which transcends the limits of the story elements in the text" (1992, 69).

Recurring images also serve to connect "Red Leaves" with other fiction. The ritual greeting, "Ole, grandfather" (*CS* 335), from the body servant to the moccasin is used again in *Go Down, Moses*, though not in the same manner. Dabney interprets the greeting as totemic but matter of fact in "Red Leaves," but he believes it is invested with more symbolic import in "The Bear" (1974, 41). In a passing observation, Kerr compares the red-heeled shoes of "Red Leaves" to the "crusted slippers" carried by the child slave in *Requiem for a Nun*. Both, according to Kerr, represent Indian "corruption and degeneration" (Kerr [1969] 1976, 83; 1983, 21). Skei finds that the rats in "Red Leaves" and "Carcassonne" are "described exactly alike" (1977, 157).

Kerr points out that Faulkner frequently used seasons to reinforce the tone, mode, or action of a text. The autumnal image of "Red Leaves" is not overtly malign as it is in "Dry September" where there is a great sense that weather affects the actions of the people (Kerr 1983, 15).

Ferguson finds the technique of using a strong controlling symbol to achieve closure in a number of stories: "An Odor of Verbena," "Delta Autumn," "Dry September," and "Red Leaves" (1991, 134).

In collection, "Red Leaves" has been enhanced by its proximity to other powerful stories. Millgate suggests that in *These 13* Faulkner chose to ignore the opportunity to make obvious connections between "Red Leaves" and "A Justice," a pairing made by Cowley in the *Portable Faulkner* and later by Faulkner himself in *Collected Stories* ([1966] 1989, 261). In his study of *These 13*, James Watson observes how "Red Leaves" and "Dry September," as the first and last stories of Part II of the collection, "portray the ritual deaths of the Negro body servant and Will Mayes as extremes rather than normative conditions of the community." That one story is set in the past and the other in the present is consistent with similar temporal pairings in the collection. Watson believes that the arrangement mimics the progression of time by having the tales move from past time to present time (1980, 216, 218). Ferguson discerns a tonal variation in the second section of *These 13*. "Red Leaves" is followed by "A Rose for Emily," and together they build a horror that is relieved by the humor of the next two stories, "A Justice" and "Hair"; the lighter mood then turns somber in "That Evening Sun" and "Dry September" (Ferguson 1991, 151).

Characters who appear in these related narratives provide obvious ties between "Red Leaves" and the other Indian tales in "The Wilderness" section of *Collected Stories*, "A Justice," "A Courtship," and "Lo!" Arthur Kinney finds that the intensity of "Red Leaves" colors the subsequent Indian tales. The humor of the tales cannot completely dissolve the pervasive sense of human suffering and death. The body servant's death in "Red Leaves" is a concrete depiction that acts as a counterpoint to the spiritual deaths portrayed throughout the collection (Kinney 1980, 69–71). Ferguson sees a gradual lightening of tone in "The Wilderness" in the movement from "Red Leaves" to "Lo!" Because he sees the Indians as corrupted and certainly not noble, Ferguson does not believe that "The Wilderness" portrays positive values (Ferguson 1991, 159).

"Red Leaves" has one often overlooked feature that keeps the story at odds with the later Indian tales: in "Red Leaves" Ikkemotubbe is father of Issetibbeha and grandfather of Moketubbe. The steamboat is in place, and the Europeanization of Issetibbeha and Moketubbe results from Ikkemotubbe's earlier associations. As the Indian portion of Yoknapatawpha's history develops in later stories, Ikkemotubbe is consistently portrayed as Issetibbeha's nephew. "Red Leaves" is, of course, part of the Yoknapatawpha fabric, but its genealogical discrepancies prevent its total immersion in this part of Faulkner's work.

## Interpretation and Criticism

In 1954, William O'Connor wrote of "Red Leaves," "just what Faulkner means the story to symbolize is not completely clear"; then O'Connor suggests, "In part he must be saying that slavery disturbed, even for the Indians, the proper relationship with the land and that the tortured shadow of the Negro has hovered over Mississippi from its earliest history" (O'Connor 1954, 69). Most interpretations start with this observation of cultural impingement. During an interview in Japan, Faulkner was asked about the role of Indians and blacks "in the [Southern] tradition" (*LG* 136). He responded from a personal perspective: "They represent the dispossessed, the people who racially or ethnically have received injustice from the hands of people who were more fortunate than they, and my use of them in my work is from pity, that I believe that people should not be treated unjustly or with injustice just because they happen to be red in color or black in color" (*LG* 136). Warren believes that comments by the Indians as they pursue the slave demonstrate Faulkner's sense that slavery is the "still operative" curse on the land ([1946] 1975, 324). In the Yoknapatawpha saga, Vickery describes "Red Leaves" as well as the other Indian stories as tales that "parody the white man's follies and ways so as to counterpoint the design of the primary saga itself." In Vickery's view, "the wilderness and the vanished past form a subject of nostalgic reminiscence," and the plight of the body servant is intensified "by the essentially comic view of his pursuers moving in their decorous, stately, untroubled course" (Vickery [1959] 1964, 300).

Peavy reads an "implicit statement" indicting slavery on the grounds that it destroyed the relationship between the Indians and the land and further that it induced in the Indians a callousness also apparent in the white man's treatment of slaves (1971, 16–18).

Funk pursues this perspective in a detailed analysis of "Red Leaves." He sees the attitudes of the Indians used as "a satiric comment on the cultural effects of slavery" while the shift to the slave's point of view is movement "to an existential statement on the confrontation with death." The fundamental irony of the story is the imposition of Southern white aristocratic values on the minority Indian culture in which economic advantage is exposed as the reason for the Indian's toleration of the slavery. In creating this ironic context, Faulkner is able "to mock the actions and beliefs of Southern civilization." The more humorous portrait of the Indians contrasts with the serious handling of the black man's perspective, which comes to "stand for man's desire to cling to life." When the point of view reverts to that of the Indians, their respect for the slave's struggle serves to establish the more important aspect of the story: the struggle to survive (Funk 1972, 339–48; see also Everett 1969, 163–64).

Duane Gage sees Faulkner's Indians as a "counterpoint in race relations in the South"; "Red Leaves" focuses specifically on Indian and black relationships (Gage 1974, 32–33). Darwin Turner cautions that "conspicuously missing from Faulkner's depiction of slavery is any picture of physical brutality." Speaking specifically of "Red Leaves," he reminds us that the capture of the slave is "depicted almost as the sport of the hunt." The praise given to the slave is like that bestowed on an animal. Historically, Turner argues, Indian slave owners were kinder than white slave owners; however, Faulkner's depictions generally attribute the "major physical brutalities of slavery to Indians." The parody here is of the "White Man's Burden" (Turner 1977, 69–71). Erskine Peters also sees the story as constructing a portrait of the experience of the black man in America. Peters concludes, "This particular body servant's plight is simply a shadow of a political scheme of a much more tremendous magnitude" (1983, 93–94).

Taylor explores the implication in the story that miscegenation is the cause of Moketubbe's "genetic degeneracy." He describes Moketubbe as a symbol "of a degeneracy that might ensue when African genes were mixed with those of any other race." Although Faulkner does not fully explore this issue in "Red Leaves," miscegenation, according to Taylor, is portrayed as a result of Doom's curse upon the land when he establishes himself as owner of land and people (1983, 106, 220 n. 15).

For Skei, the nature–culture conflict forms the basis of "Red Leaves." The opening presents a strong contrast between the lives of the blacks and the Indians. He interprets slave holding among the Indians as one of the ways in which white culture infected Indian culture. "To see the clash of different worlds in 'Red Leaves' as a clash between nature and culture, one must draw attention to the fact that the story is abundant with symbols, most of which show what the white man has brought to the Indians and how useless and out of place these things are—at least until the Indians adjust to a new and different way of life, to a world where a natural life cannot be led" (Skei 1977, 56; 1985, 194–96). Carothers emphasizes that because the Indians have forfeited their "primitive innocence" in their acceptance of slavery, the world of "Red Leaves" is "a world of despair" in which "the only dignified response is the stoic acceptance of the inevitable" (1985, 76–77; see also Cox 1982, 282–83).

Although Skei develops most fully his argument for the culture–nature conflict in "Red Leaves," he adds that other concerns, such as hunt motifs and man's resistance to death in the story, "may serve to indicate its existential dimensions" (1985, 194). This view is prevalent among critics. Warren argues that the effort of the body servant in "Red Leaves" is "the human effort to find or create values in the mechanical round of experience." Warren believes that the image of the black man is drawn with pathos or heroism. He sees the fugitive slave gain "a shadowy symbolic significance" in his effort, becoming heroic as he stands as the tallest among the Indians ([1949] 1975, 320–21, 324). James Frakes and Isadore Traschen likewise see implicit in the hunt the desire for life, and in comparison with Moketubbe the slave gains heroic stature even as he remains realistic (Frakes and Traschen 1959, 43–44). Nilon also views the slave as superior to his pursuers. Despite his death, the isolated slave represents the strength of his people: "The Negro is naked except for caked mud put on his body for protection against mosquitoes. Symbolically he represents the purity of the natural man contrasted to the decay that the Indians represent in their submission to their lusts" (Nilon 1965, 43).

Howell believes the insistence of the story's sober tone emphasizes that "the inevitability of life and death bears its own somber fascination." (He miscounts the length of days of the hunt, extending the six-day ordeal to over a week.) Howell concludes that the story is about "life in general terms . . . where to eat is hardly less inevitable than to be eaten." The effect is "to shock the reader into an awareness of life" (1967, 387–89; Howell 1970, 299). Dabney insists that "Faulkner's image of black suffering is without parallel in nineteenth- or twentieth-century writing." He places this confrontation within an explicitly classical-Christian context that underscores the suffering of the black man. Though his argument is strong, Dabney may press too far when he claims that "accounts of former slaves pale before the fugitive's agony" (1974, 108, 113–15).

Edmond Volpe also concludes that "Faulkner elevates a story about cultural impingement to a terrifying existential confrontation with the reality of death." Structuring the story around the burial ritual, Faulkner stresses that the human being's ability "to contemplate its own extinction" is the human tragedy. Volpe links this pervading sense of terror with Faulkner's own inability to reconcile himself to death. Faulkner understood the slave's reaction to the snakebite as a demonstration of man's inability to accept death (Volpe 1975, 122, 130). Volpe reiterates a familiar Faulknerian observation in making his point about "Red Leaves": "Between grief and nothing, man will take grief always" (*FU* 25).

Standberg identifies the body servant as one of Faulkner's heroes, distinguished as such by his willingness to become, as Mr. Compson states in *The Sound and the Fury*, "arbiter of his own virtues." The body servant cannot avoid death and eventually accepts its inevitability (Strandberg 1981, 20–21). Mick Gidley feels the sense of inevitable doom that pervades the story. The ritualistic nature of all its actions underscores the inevitability of the outcome and gives the story its power (1990, 122–23).

With a slightly different twist, Muller examines the way in which the condemnation of slavery in "Red Leaves" combines with an existential struggle through the image of an Edenic garden. Muller argues that in casting slavery in Indian civilization, Faulkner "develops a startling conceit in which plantation culture and the institution of slavery that supported it are reduced to decadence and parody." Muller then examines how the placement of the plantation culture in a "matchless parklike forest" conveys the Edenic image. The decayed steamboat represents the degenerate plantation house but also suggests a "makeshift ark: inhabited by people and animals." This Eden becomes hellish in the hunt for the slave and unregenerate because it embraces slavery; the people "have sacrificed their territory to the devil." Muller summarizes: "They engage in a drama that is both temporal and eternal, consequently the narrative operates on two levels, as a brilliant critique on racism, and as a parable on Paradise Lost" (1974, 245–49).

According to Marjorie Pryse, "Red Leaves" is not "a study of racism or an enactment of white fears." In Pryse's reading, the ritual of the hunt "becomes epistemology" in which "Faulkner explores the search for experiential meaning which is hidden in words like *life* and *death*." Pryse emphasizes that certain characteristics in the language of the story—inscrutability, excessive negation, and masking—are indicative of the meaningless lives the Indians live. As the Indians confront the concept *death*, they explore the meaning of life, especially as this confrontation is embodied in the flight of the slave. It becomes a counterpart to Issetibbeha's dying, a means by which the Indians can understand Issetibbeha's death and "through that process of perception which Faulkner reveals as definition by negation" they may gain understanding of their own lives. Pryse argues that even for the slave, death "remains conceptual rather than experiential" until he is bitten by the snake. Pryse contextualizes much of this argument in her later examination of "marking" (stigmatizing in American fiction communities) in the works of Hawthorne, Melville, Faulkner, and Ellison (1979, 92–107, 133–38; see also Pryse 1975, 133–38).

Tatiana Morozova addresses what she perceives as the universal concerns of "Red Leaves" that has made it a story powerful across cultures. She sees the thematic polarities as a battle between God and Satan and a "clash between love of liberty and lust for power." Morozova notes that the friendship between Doom and Chevalier Soeur Blonde de Vitry raises little surprise if one considers their common villainy and mutual bond with Satan. Further, the lust for power apparent in the desire for shoes is the same obsession that is emblemized by a crown or other token of power (Morozova 1992, 279–80).

John Matthews opens a new level of interpretation of "Red Leaves" when he looks at the story in the context of magazine publication. The story's appearance in the *Post* came at a time when the magazine was enjoying the profits of advertising, which, Matthews argues, suggests a reading of the story "as a reflection on modern American society's enslavement to the principle of acquisition." The Indians are clearly "among the most sophisticated and jaded consumers in all of Yoknapatawpha," and Moketubbe represents the "utterly sated consumer" roused only by red-heeled slippers. In contrast, the body servant cannot protect himself from the Indians' urge to possess—as he is the thing possessed—and finally he cannot engage in the consumption of proffered food because he is so ill from the snakebite. Matthews concludes, "Appearing in the stuffed pages of the *Post* during the Depression, this becomes a remarkable image of the marginal man in a senselessly acquisitive society. His balked act of consumption indicts a social order—and the long history of its class and racial valences—that so extremely dooms some to surfeit and others to want" (Matthews 1992, 7, 19–21; *SL* 46–47).

The contrasting levels of language in the story have generated much discussion. Pursuing David Garnett's description of Indian dialogue as language that seems "to out-parody any parody," Howell points out that the language can be confusing at first. What becomes clear is that Faulkner's text intends for the language to be oblique. What is left unsaid becomes more important than what is said in this "narrative of ominous silence" (Garnett 1933, 387; Howell 1967, 389). For Volpe, the articulate narrative style contrasts with the unsettling dialogue that heightens emotional tension through the contrast of cultural values (1975, 125). Irony is also important in the development of the atmosphere of the tale. Frakes and Traschen point out the way thematic concerns are sharpened by irony or humor (1959, 43). Recalling Faulkner's own notion of the proximity of humor and tragedy, Dabney praises the fine balance between the two, emphasizing the incongruous and absurd details (1974, 92).

No critic has offered more praise for "Red Leaves" than Ferguson. His admiration for the work appears throughout his book-length study of the stories. He describes this story, among several others, as "technically virtually flawless." Ferguson offers an extended analysis of the selective omniscient point of view Faulkner utilizes. The story opens and closes with a dramatic rendering of the events. In the middle of the story, an omniscient narrator reveals some of the history of the tribal leaders, and we are permitted into the consciousness of the hunted body servant. Faulkner gains the effect of immersing and distancing the reader in both tragic and comic circumstances. He also alters the order of the *fabula* (the basic narrative) in his presentation. The story opens *in medias res*, moves then to the flashback of tribal history that is both panoramic and scenic, then shifts to the scene of the hunt, flashbacks through the body servant's life, and the chase and capture (Ferguson 1991, 91–93, 126–27).

The richness of imagery in "Red Leaves" has generated a list of symbol associations. Nilon matches the descriptions of the slave's breathing to his emotional state: the sound grows louder with his closeness to death. The drumming, Nilon argues, may have the practical purpose of informing the slave of the progress of events and perhaps guiding him in his flight, but the drumming intensifies as the slave's fear increases. The image of dancing demonstrates the slave's separation from the living. He cannot participate in this social activity of his people (Nilon 1965, 39–42). Volpe examines several images that help raise the slave's plight to a mythic level: images of life (especially eating) and images of death (especially smell) (1975, 126–28).

Most discussions of the title "Red Leaves" begin with Faulkner's own interpretation. Noting that it "was probably symbolism," Faulkner associated the red leaves of the title with the Indians. Their inevitable actions lead, also inevitably, to the suffocation and destruction of the black man. Their behavior was unalterable "whether they regretted it or not." Faulkner emphasized the ritual nature of the Indians' action; they were following "what the rule said" (*FU* 39, 63). Beidler links the title "Red Leaves" to autumn hostilities in Tierra del Fuego recorded by Darwin; aggression and destruction are common to both the story and its source (1973, 422–32).

Like the image of red leaves, the red-heeled slippers have not suffered for interpretations, which are fairly consistent. In Vickery's view, the shoes represent "status and authority" ([1959] 1964, 300; see also Cox 1982, 283–84). Funk sees the red-heeled shoes as an "extended metaphor for the cancerous spread of the white's influence in the Indian society." When in part five the focus returns to the Indians, the description of the slippers as "cracked," "frail and shapeless" informs the "impression of decay and thanatotic disintegration" (Funk 1972, 343, 347). Milum argues that the slippers and other relics from Europe symbolize "decadent European aristocracy"; they "are clearly leftovers, or red leaves, providing ominous historical perspective for one decadent civilization which is rapidly disappearing upon the heels of another" (Milum 1974b, 58–59). The shoes, as well as the other European artifacts, tie "old world corruption to slavery and the dynastic failure that, as always in Faulkner's work, slavery engenders" (Dabney 1974, 104). Skei likewise sees the red-heeled slippers and also the girandoles as "effective and unequivocal symbols of corruption of the Indian culture in 'Red Leaves.'" Moketubbe also operates as a symbol of "degeneration and corruption" (Skei 1985, 189, 197).

Blotner argues that the snake is a totem animal for Faulkner (1974, Note 95). Faulkner himself describes the snake of "The Bear" and "Red Leaves" as "the old grandfather, the old fallen angel, the unregenerate immortal"; he goes on to add, "The good and shining angel ain't very interesting" (*FU* 1959, 2). Funk links the snake to the serpent of Eden to remind man of his mortal and sinful nature (1972, 346–47). Dabney, however, believes that the snake of "Red Leaves" is a combination of Indian totemic and African snake cults that brought into the states a worship of the "Great Moccasin," both of which the slave could have absorbed (1974, 110–11).

Austin Wright identifies in "Red Leaves" the twentieth-century tendency toward "final recalcitrance," that is, a resistance to resolution as clarification of actions or issues raised in the text. In "Red Leaves" the body servant's recapture and impending death complete the action of the story, but the story does not conclude with an explicit understanding of the necessity of the man's death. This recalcitrance can only be resolved in "belief in the power of ritual and social pressure" the efficacy of which the reader must judge for himself or herself (Wright 1989, 124–25).

In a review of *These 13* Garnett describes "Red Leaves" as "a magnificent, a marvellous story" that opens as parody badly performed but just as "the worm sloughs its skin, [the story] spreads its wings to dry and flickers away in glory" (1933, 387). Cowley believed it to be the best of the Indian stories ([1967] 1977, 2). In 1975, Volpe argued that "Red Leaves" provides as profound a reading experience as is possible within the short story form" (1975, 122). In the same year, Irving Howe also praised the story, which he believed touched "Faulkner's most genuine themes" ([1952] 1975, 267). Literary histories continue to list "Red Leaves" not just among Faulkner's best stories but in the context of significant contributions to the short story generally (Brooks 1985, 341; Kartiganer 1988, 904; see also Brooks 1987, 119). Fourteen of Faulkner's "best" stories are gathered in a 1974 Ukrainian collection under the title *Red Leaves* (Denisova 1992, 285). A rare dissenting opinion is offered by Karl, who sees "Red Leaves" as "not particularly strong"; it is "diffuse" but "revealing" (1989, 398). More recently, Ferguson has reiterated the widespread praise of "Red Leaves," describing it as a merger of Faulkner's poetic and narrative impulses into "marvelously subtle and evocative prose" that reveals his delight in telling a tale (1991, 36, 47).

## Works Cited

Barth, J. Robert. 1964. "Faulkner and the Calvinist Tradition." *Thought* 39:100–20.

Beidler, Peter G. 1973. "A Darwinian Source for Faulkner's Indians in 'Red Leaves.'" *Studies in Short Fiction*, 10:421–23.

Blotner, Joseph. 1974. *Faulkner: A Biography*. 2 vols. New York: Random House.

———. 1984. *Faulkner: A Biography*. 1 vol. New York: Random House.

Brooks, Cleanth. 1985. "William Faulkner." In *The History of Southern Literature*. Ed. Louis D. Rubin, Jr. Baton Rouge: Louisiana State University Press, 333–42.

———. 1987. *On the Prejudices, Predilections, and Firm Beliefs of William Faulkner*. Baton Rouge: Louisiana State University Press.

Brown, Calvin S. 1966. "Faulkner's Manhunts: Fact Into Fiction." *Georgia Review* 20:388–95.

Carothers, James B. 1981a. "The Myriad Heart: The Evolution of the Faulkner Hero." In "A Cosmos of My Own": *Faulkner and Yoknapatawpha 1980*. Ed. Doreen Fowler and Ann J. Abadie. Jackson: University Press of Mississippi, 252–83.

———. 1981b. "The Road to The Reivers." In "A Cosmos of My Own": *Faulkner and Yoknapatawpha 1980*. Ed. Doreen Fowler and Ann J. Abadie. Jackson: University Press of Mississippi, 95–124.

———. 1985. *William Faulkner's Short Stories*. Ann Arbor, MI: UMI Research Press.

Cohen, Philip. 1989. "A Previously Unpublished Faulkner Letter." *College Literature* 16.1:103–05.

Cowley, Malcolm. 1966. *The Faulkner-Cowley File: Letters and Memories, 1944–1962*. New York: Viking.

Cowley, Malcolm, ed. [1967] 1977. *The Portable Faulkner*. Rev. ed. New York: Viking. Reprint. London: Penguin.

Cox, Leland H. 1982. *William Faulkner: Biographical and Reference Guide*. Detroit: Gale Research.

Dabney, Lewis M. 1974. *The Indians of Yoknapatawpha: A Study in Literature and History*. Baton Rouge: Louisiana State University Press.

Denisova, Tamara. 1992. "Faulkner and the Ukraine." In *Faulkner and the Short Story: Faulkner and Yoknapatawpha, 1990*. Ed. Evans Harrington and Ann J. Abadie. Jackson: University Press of Mississippi, 282–85.

Emerson, O. B. 1984. *Faulkner's Early Literary Reputation in America*. Ann Arbor, MI: UMI Research Press.

Everett, Walter K. 1969. *Faulkner's Art and Character*. Woodbury, NY: Barron's Educational Series.

Faulkner, William. [1930] 1987. *As I Lay Dying. The Corrected Text*. New York: Vintage.

———. 1931. "Red Leaves." *Saturday Evening Post* 203 (25 October):6ff.

———. 1950. *Collected Stories of William Faulkner*. New York: Random House.

———. 1955. *Big Woods*. New York: Random House.

———. 1959. *Faulkner in the University: Class Conferences at the University of Virginia, 1957–1958*. Ed. Frederick Gwynn and Joseph L. Blotner. Charlottesville: University Press of Virginia.

———. 1968. *Lion in the Garden: Interviews with William Faulkner 1926–1962*. Ed. James B. Meriwether and Michael Millgate. New York: Random House.

———. [1973] 1974. *Flags in the Dust*. Ed. Douglas Day. New York: Vintage.

———. 1977. *Selected Letters of William Faulkner*. Ed. Joseph Blotner. New York: Random House.

———. 1987. *William Faulkner Manuscripts* 9: These 13. Ed. Noel Polk. New York: Garland.

Ferguson, James. 1991. *Faulkner's Short Fiction*. Knoxville: University of Tennessee Press.

Frakes, James R., and Isadore Traschen, eds. 1959. "Red Leaves." *Short Fiction: A Critical Collection*. Englewood Cliffs, NJ: Prentice-Hall, 24–45.

Funk, Robert W. 1972. "Satire and Existentialism in Faulkner's 'Red Leaves.'" *Mississippi Quarterly* 25:339–48.

Gage, Duane. 1974. "William Faulkner's Indians." *American Indian Quarterly* 1:27–33.

Garnett, David. 1933. "Current Literature." *New Statesman and Nation*, 30 September, 387.

Gidley, Mick. 1990. "Sam Fathers's Fathers: Indians and the Idea of Inheritance." In *Critical Essays on William Faulkner: The McCaslin Family*. Ed. Arthur F. Kinney. Boston: G. K. Hall, 121–31.

Gresset, Michel. 1985. *A Faulkner Chronology*. Trans. Arthur B. Scharff. Jackson: University Press of Mississippi.

Hinkle, James. 1986. "The Civil War in the Apocrypha According to Faulkner." In *Faulkner and History*. Ed. Javier Coy and Michel Gresset. Salamanca: Edicions Universidad de Salamanca, 29–38.

Holmes, Edward M. 1966. *Faulkner's Twice-Told Tales: His Re-Use of His Material*. The Hague: Mouton.

Hönnighausen, Lothar. 1987. "Black as White Metaphor: A European View of Faulkner's Fiction." In *Faulkner and Race: Faulkner and Yoknapatawpha, 1986*. Ed. Doreen Fowler and Ann J. Abadie. Jackson: University Press of Mississippi, 192–208.

Howe, Irving. [1952] 1975. *William Faulkner: A Critical Study*. 3d ed. Chicago: University of Chicago Press.

Howell, Elmo. 1967. "William Faulkner and the Mississippi Indians." *Georgia Review* 21:386–96.

———. 1970. "William Faulkner's Chickasaw Legacy: A Note on 'Red Leaves.'" *Arizona Quarterly* 26:293–303.

Karl, Frederick R. 1989. *William Faulkner: American Writer*. New York: Weidenfeld and Nicolson.

Kartiganer, Donald. 1988. "William Faulkner." *Columbia Literary History of the United States*. Ed. Emory Elliott. New York: Columbia University Press, 887–909.

Kerr, Elizabeth M. [1969] 1976. *Yoknapatawpha: Faulkner's "Little Postage Stamp of Native Soil."* New York: Fordham University Press.

———. 1979. *William Faulkner's Gothic Domain*. Port Washington, NY: Kennikat.

———. 1983. *William Faulkner's Yoknapatawpha: "A Kind of Keystone in the Universe."* New York: Fordham University Press.

Kinney, Arthur F. 1978. *Faulkner's Narrative Poetics: Style as Vision*. Amherst: University of Massachusetts Press.

———. 1980. "Faulkner's Narrative Poetics and Collected Stories." *Faulkner Studies* 1:58–79.

Krefft, James H. 1978. "A Possible Source for Faulkner's Indians: Oliver La Farge's Laughing Boy." *Tulane Studies in English* 23:187–92.

Langford, Beverly Young. 1972. "History and Legend in William Faulkner's 'Red Leaves.'" *Notes on Mississippi Writers* 6:19–24.

Matthews, John T. 1992. "Shortened Stories: Faulkner and the Market." In *Faulkner and the Short Story: Faulkner and Yoknapatawpha, 1990*. Ed. Evans Harrington and Ann J. Abadie. Jackson: University Press of Mississippi, 3–37.

Meriwether, James B. [1961] 1971. *The Literary Career of William Faulkner: A Bibliographical Study*. Princeton, NJ: Princeton University Library. Reprint. Columbia: University of South Carolina Press.

———. 1973. "Faulkner's Correspondence with *Scribner's Magazine.*" *Proof* 3:253–82.

———. 1977. "Faulkner's Correspondence with *The Saturday Evening Post.*" *Mississippi Quarterly* 30:461–75.

Millgate, Michael. [1961] 1966. *William Faulkner*. New York: Barnes & Noble.

———. [1966] 1989. *The Achievement of William Faulkner*. New York: Random House. Reprint. Athens: University of Georgia Press. Brown Thrasher Books.

Milum, Richard A. 1974a. "Ikkemotubbe and the Spanish Conspiracy." *American Literature* 46:389–91.

———. 1974b. "The Title of Faulkner's 'Red Leaves.'" *American Notes and Queries* 13:58–59.

Miner, Ward L. 1952. *The World of William Faulkner*. Durham, NC: Duke University Press.

Morozova, Tatiana. 1992. "Faulkner's Short Stories in Russian." In *Faulkner and the Short Story: Faulkner and Yoknapatawpha, 1990*. Ed. Evans Harrington and Ann J. Abadie. Jackson: University Press of Mississippi, 269–81.

Muller, Gilbert H. 1974. "The Descent of the Gods: Faulkner's 'Red Leaves' and the Garden of the South." *Studies in Short Fiction* 11:243–49.

Nilon, Charles H. 1965. *Faulkner and the Negro*. New York: Citadel.

O'Connor, William Van. 1954. *The Tangled Fire of William Faulkner*. Minneapolis: University of Minnesota Press.

O'Nan, Martha. 1970. "William Faulkner's 'Du Homme.'" *Laurel Review* 10.2:26–28.

Peavy, Charles D. 1971. *Go Slow Now: Faulkner and the Race Question*. Eugene: University of Oregon Books.

Peters, Erskine. 1983. *William Faulkner: The Yoknapatawpha World and Black Being*. Darby, PA: Norwood Editions.

Polk, Noel. 1981. *Faulkner's* Requiem for a Nun: *A Critical Study*. Bloomington: Indiana University Press.

———. 1985. "The Space between *Sanctuary.*" In *Intertextuality in Faulkner*. Ed. Michel Gresset and Noel Polk. Jackson: University Press of Mississippi, 16–35.

Pryse, Marjorie. 1975. "Race: Faulkner's 'Red Leaves.'" *Studies in Short Fiction* 12:133–38.

———. 1979. *The Mark and the Knowledge: Social Stigma in Classic American Fiction*. Columbus: Ohio State University Press for Miami University.

Rabbetts, John. 1989. *From Hardy to Faulkner: Wessex to Yoknapatawpha*. New York: St. Martin's.

Ragan, David Paul. 1983. "'Belonging to the Business of Mankind': The Achievement of Faulkner's *Big Woods*." *Mississippi Quarterly* 36:303–17.

Reed, Joseph W., Jr. 1973. *Faulkner's Narrative*. New Haven: Yale University Press.

Samway, Patrick H., S. J. 1980. *Faulkner's* Intruder in the Dust: *A Critical Study of the Typescripts*. Troy, NY: Whitston.

Skei, Hans H. 1977. *Bold and Tragical and Austere: William Faulkner's* These 13: *A Study*. University of Oslo Department of Literature.

———. 1981. *William Faulkner: The Short Story Career*. Oslo, Norway: Universitetsforlaget.

———. 1985. *William Faulkner: The Novelist as Short Story Writer*. Oslo, Norway: Universitetsforlaget.

———. 1992. "Beyond Genre? Existential Experience in Faulkner's Short Fiction." In *Faulkner and the Short Story: Faulkner and Yoknapatawpha, 1990*. Ed. Evans Harrington and Ann J. Abadie. Jackson: University Press of Mississippi, 62–77.

Slatoff, Walter J. 1960. *Quest for Failure: A Study of William Faulkner*. Ithaca, NY: Cornell University Press.

Strandberg, Victor. 1981. *A Faulkner Overview: Six Perspectives*. Port Washington, NY: Kennikat.

Styron, William. 1982. *This Quiet Dust and Other Writings*. New York: Random House. Rpt. from *New York Times Book Review*, May 6, 1973.

Taylor, Walter. 1983. *Faulkner's Search for a South*. Urbana: University of Illinois Press.

———. 1987. "Yoknapatawpha's Indians: A Novel Faulkner Never Wrote." In *The Modernists: Studies in a Literary Phenomenon*. Ed. L. B. Gamache and I. S. MacNiven. Rutherford, NJ: Fairleigh Dickinson University Press, 202–09.

Trilling, Lionel. 1931. "Mr. Faulkner's World." *Nation* 133 (4 November):491–92.

Turner, Darwin T. 1977. "Faulkner and Slavery." In *The South and Faulkner's Yoknapatawpha: The Actual and the Apocryphal*. Ed. Evans Harrington and Ann J. Abadie. Jackson: University Press of Mississippi, 62–85.

Vickery, Olga W. [1959] 1964. *The Novels of William Faulkner*. Baton Rouge: Louisiana State University Press.

Volpe, Edmond L. 1975. "Faulkner's 'Red Leaves': The Deciduation of Nature." *Studies in American Fiction* 3:121–31.

Warren, Robert Penn. [1946] 1975. "Cowley's Faulkner." In *William Faulkner: The Critical Heritage*. Ed. John Bassett. London and Boston: Routledge & Kegan Paul, 314–28.

Watson, James G. 1980. "Faulkner's Short Stories and the Making of Yoknapatawpha County." In *Fifty Years of Yoknapatawpha: Faulkner and Yoknapatawpha*

*1979.* Ed. Doreen Fowler and Ann J. Abadie. Jackson: University Press of Mississippi, 202–25.

Wright, Austin M. 1989. "Recalcitrance in the Short Story." In *Short Story Theory at a Crossroads*. Ed. Susan Lohafer and Jo Ellyn Clarey. Baton Rouge: Louisiana State University Press, 115–29.

# A Justice

## Publication History

Although Faulkner tried to have this Indian story published in a magazine, "A Justice" did not appear in print until it was included in *These 13* (1931). The story-sending schedule shows that it was submitted to several magazines under various titles. It was first sent to the *Saturday Evening Post* on November 29, 1930, as "Built Fence." This date is just one month after the *Post* appearance of "Red Leaves"—only four months after that story's submission—and Hans Skei speculates that Faulkner was anticipating success with a second Indian story. The *Post* rejected the story, however, the fourth of four rejections of stories Faulkner submitted to it in the month of November 1930. Faulkner quickly forwarded the story to *Scribner's*, on December 30, 1930. The *Scribner's* submission was accompanied by a typically Faulknerian admission: "Few people know that Miss. Indians owned slaves; that's why I suggest that you all buy it. Not because it is a good story: you can find lots of good stories. It's because I need the money." (Meriwether dates this letter at the end of 1930 although Joseph Blotner dates it at the beginning of 1931.) In a letter to Faulkner, *Scribner's* referred to it as "Indians Built a Fence," and he listed the submission as "Built a Fence." *Scribner's* declined to publish the story; however, it fared no better at three other magazines: *American Mercury*, where it was submitted January 29, 1931, listed as "Built a Fence"; *Woman's Home Companion*, sent on April 11, 1931, listed as "A Justice"; and *Harper's*, submitted May 5, 1931, listed as "Justice." Blotner suggests and Skei more confidently asserts that these titles represent the same story. Noel Polk agrees with Skei but cautions that the titles may simply be different or they may "represent different versions of the same story" (*WFM 9* Introduction ix;

*SL* 46–47; Meriwether [1961] 1971, 176–80; Meriwether 1973, 261–62; Blotner 1974, 676; Blotner 1984, 268; Skei 1981, 67–68; 127 n. 254 and 255).

Faulkner included "A Justice" in *Collected Stories* (1950) and used a revised portion of it as an interlude in *Big Woods* (1955). Malcolm Cowley also included "A Justice" in the *Portable Faulkner* (1946) as the opening story of the volume. He added a few names to identify characters and to strike a balance between the opening and closing of the volume with Compson stories (1966, 48).

## Circumstances of Composition, Sources, and Influences

"A Justice" cannot be dated with certainty, but its links with other stories and *The Sound and the Fury* have led to speculation about when it was written. Blotner thinks Faulkner wrote "A Justice" and "That Evening Sun" before *The Sound and the Fury*, dating the novel "at some point in the late winter or early spring of 1928." In his biography of Faulkner, he discusses "A Justice" in the chapter "June, 1927–September, 1928." To support his choosing this early date, he observes that "A Justice" does not mention Benjy as brother to the children, Quentin, Candace, and Jason (Blotner 1974, 566, Notes 82). A number of other critics—Lewis Simpson, Estella Schoenberg, David Minter, John Hunt, and Walter Taylor—agree with Blotner's order of composition of "A Justice" and *The Sound and the Fury* (Simpson 1976, 92; Schoenberg 1977, 18; Minter 1980, 93, 283 n. 6; Hunt 1982, 369; Taylor 1987, 204). In the revised edition of *Faulkner: A Biography* (1984), however, Blotner retains the same composition dates for *The Sound and the Fury*, but he shifts the discussion of "That Evening Sun" and "A Justice" to the chapter "April 1930–January 1931," a period when it can be confirmed that Faulkner was submitting "A Justice" to magazines (1984, 265–68). James Carothers dates "A Justice" after *The Sound and the Fury* (1985, 27), but he does not specify whether his classification is based on publication date or a presumed composition date. Skei places "A Justice" in Faulkner's very productive 1930 period, but he notes that unlike most of the author's writing set at the time of this story, neither "A Justice" nor "Red Leaves" deals with the "recent or immediate past" (Skei 1985, 99). Max Putzel dates the composition of "A Justice" in 1930, shortly after "Red Leaves" (1985, 229, 312); of course, the date of composition of "Red Leaves" is also a matter of speculation. Usually, the two stories are thought to have been written close together, whether in late 1927 to early 1928 or in the 1930 period when the stories were first submitted for publication.

The order of publication does generate questions about the reappearance of Quentin as narrator. In *The Sound and the Fury*, which appeared before any of the other Quentin texts, Quentin commits suicide, but his reappearance as narrator of other stories comes in the role of a man several years older than Quentin lived to be. Schoenberg figures Quentin's age in "A Justice" to be twenty-six, though she calculates that he was twenty-one when he killed himself (1977, 18). (Others believe Quentin was twenty when he died [see Hunt 1982, 369; Matthews 1989, 71].) Thus, the speculations about order of composition become significant. Did Faulkner revive Quentin, or did Faulkner actually write the stories prior to *The Sound and the Fury*, before he perceived that Quentin was suicidal?

Evidence to date Quentin's appearance as narrator may not be available, but it is obvious that Quentin's role became increasingly important as "A Justice" developed. Simpson sees "A Justice" as the story in which Quentin's role as narrator is definitely established. By the story's end, "the scene is set for Quentin's future role as moral historian" (Simpson 1976, 92).

Because of the different titles Faulkner gave to the story and the condition of the existing manuscript, it is fairly certain that there were other drafts of "A Justice," perhaps both earlier and later, than the holograph manuscript reproduced in the *William Faulkner Manuscripts*. Skei describes the manuscript as containing "an unusually high amount of corrections and additions." He thinks it is a "relatively late one," based on "the use of paste-ons and the very fact that the title 'Built a Fence' and other similar titles on the sending schedule are presumably early titles for 'A Justice'" (1981, 68). Putzel, on the other hand, believes that it is "an early draft" because of its "numerous variants from the text published in *These 13*" (1985, 312). Whatever the place of this draft in the composition process, comparisons of the holograph manuscript with the published version show revisions that increased attention on the narrator as receiver of the tale. While the manuscript merely relates that Sam Fathers liked to "smoke and talk," the published version adds that Sam would "tell me about the old days." An extra paragraph is added to emphasize that the narrator is a willing listener: "So I would give him the tobacco and he would stop work and sit down and fill his pipe and talk to me" (*CS* 344).

The end of the story is also revised to heighten Quentin's importance. In the manuscript, Quentin responds to his grandfather's query with "I don't know, sir" (*WFM* 9 226). Then the "twilight" passage, an important Faulknerian image, closes the story with Quentin's somber affirmation that he would understand but by then Sam would be dead (*WFM* 9 227). The last image is therefore of Sam. But the published version more effectively emphasizes the narrator's twilight state of not understanding. Having described the twilight, Quentin more evasively answers his grandfather, "Nothing, sir." In this revision, the closing image is of Quentin, not Sam.

Other comparisons between the texts show refinements in the character of Sam Fathers. His name appears first in a marginal addition, and a description of him as "a clever negro carpenter" is revised to read "a clever carpenter from the quarters" (Dabney 1974, 73–74). Sam's appearance continued to evolve in subsequent works, always with the emphasis on his Indian heritage.

Between the appearance of *These 13* and *Collected Stories*, Faulkner made changes in the history of Yoknapatawpha Indians as they appeared in other works—and certain inconsistencies became evident between those texts and "A Justice." Nevertheless, Faulkner did not revise "A Justice" for *Collected Stories*. Five years later, when the steamboat section was extracted for *Big Woods*, significant deletions and additions were made to fit the overall theme and tone of that volume.

In studying *Big Woods*, David Ragan concludes that the revised interlude from "A Justice" should more accurately be described as "based upon an incident" rather than as a re-use of the story itself. Faulkner's alterations emphasize the senselessness and exploitation that are part of Doom's determination to possess the steamboat. The humor of the original tale is absent. In its place, the narrative recounts Herman Basket's memories of the months of grueling labor required to move the steamboat that make it impossible for him to sleep in the steamboat (Ragan 1983, 310–11). (Glen Johnson misreads this portion of the text and states that Doom, not Herman Basket, must go outside [1980, 250].) Carothers believes that the effect of the revision is to diminish any sense of exploitation of the slaves (Carothers 1985, 101).

The narrative of the steamboat's being brought to the plantation and made a part of the house, first detailed in "A Justice," is recounted vividly if not always consistently in several stories. When Henry Nash Smith asked the author if this was an idea gleaned from some other account, Faulkner responded that he "just invented it" (*LG* 31). He misquotes his own story, however, for the Indians, not the slaves, disappear when they learn that they will begin the task of moving the steamboat the next morning (*LG* 31; *CS* 350).

Although Smith did not uncover a historical or legendary source for Faulkner's steamboat, Elmo Howell has made several studies of sources for the Indian tales. Especially relevant to "A Justice" is his discussion of the relationship between Indians and their slaves. He notes that the Creeks and Seminoles allowed some degree of equality that led eventually to an absorption of the slave population by the Indians. More commonly, however, slaves were allowed neither to marry nor to cohabit with the Indians. After the Civil War, the Chickasaws sought racial purity by forbidding freedmen to join the Indian nation (Howell 1970, 294). Dabney, like Howell, finds historical precedent for the respect portrayed for the male slave's manhood. Yet, contradicting the line of rule in the story, Dabney indicates that among the Chickasaws rule descended in the female line (1974, 77–78, 84).

In a brief essay, Martha O'Nan examines Faulkner's use of French names, specifically Ikkemotubbe's conversion of "*du homme*" to "Doom" and his companion's name, Chevalier Soeur Blonde de Vitry. She points out that although Faulkner always used "*du homme*" he accepted Cowley's correction of "*de l'homme*" for the Compson "Appendix." O'Nan offers examples of French usage to suggest possible sources for "Soeur Blonde" and for the reasonable, if not precisely correct, use of "*du homme*" (1970, 26–28).

John Faulkner, William's brother, offers an interesting biographical connection to "A Justice." He relates Quentin's listening to Sam Fathers to times when their grandfather would take the Faulkner children to his farm. William liked to spend time listening to the stories of the black blacksmith, John Henry (Blotner 1974, 566).

"A Justice" also has literary antecedents—some predictable and some surprising. Michael Millgate calls the story a tall tale and places it in the tradition of Southwestern humor. The story is "skillfully manipulated to bring out the specifically Indian cunning and intelligence of Doom" ([1961] 1966, 63–64). Dabney also sees the influence of Southwestern humor in the suitors' competition, the magnitude of which comes from the tradition of the tall tale. The gambling, threats, counterthreats, and bargaining are also characteristics of Southwestern humor. "A Justice" borrows the stereotype of the "darky storytellers" from writers like Thomas Nelson Page and Joel Chandler Harris, but "A Justice" subverts the stereotype and enters the Indian world (Dabney 1974, 83, 79, 29).

Carothers traces a recurring trickster figure, one who "practices deceit for personal gain," in Faulkner's short fiction and novels. In "A Justice," Ikkemotubbe and Craw-ford (Crawfish-ford) are both tricksters. Faulkner, according to Carothers, is most influenced in these trickster portrayals by Mark Twain and other Southwestern humorists, as well as Shakespeare, Cervantes, and the Greek dramatists (1984, 224).

When Howell traces literary influences on "A Justice," he suggests two similarities between "A Justice" and Hemingway's work. First, Howell compares Quentin and Nick Adams as initiates to an awareness of evil. Second, "A Justice," like Hemingway's "Big Two-Hearted River," cannot be fully understood without the larger framework of the author's other texts (Howell 1967a, 151–52). Howell's claim is similar to earlier arguments by Ray B. West, Jr., and Norman Pearson that compare Quentin in "That Evening Sun" to Hemingway's Nick Adams (Pearson 1954, 61–63).

William Clark finds a possible analogue to Ikkemotubbe in Washington Irving's *Astoria* (1836). While acknowledging no specific information to demonstrate that Faulkner took Irving's work as a source, Clark sees numerous parallels between Ikkemotubbe and Irving's Blackbird, an Omaha chieftain. Both chiefs are friendly with whites, introduce white men's goods into their tribes, rule their tribes absolutely, and bring about their doom (Clark 1977, 223–225).

Faulkner reported that he was influenced in his work by the Bible, especially the narratives of the Old Testament, and that he kept a small volume of Shakespeare with him (*FU* 50, 167). Such acknowledgement sends critics to the texts to find possible influences. Walter Everett sees an analogy in Doom's naming Had-Two-Fathers and Solomon's resolution of the mothers' conflict over a child in 1 Kings 3 (Everett 1969, 147). Dabney suggests several biblical sources for themes and images in "A Justice" such as a tie to Lazarus in Doom's "let us make the steamboat get up and walk" and Doom's years in New Orleans numbering a biblical seven. Dabney also sees several Shakespearian links—Ikkemotubbe as Richard III, the division of the slaves like Lear's loss of knights, Doom's steamboat journey like Cleopatra on her barge. Dabney also compares the slow movement of the steamboat with Tamburlaine's "can ye draw but twenty miles a day" in Christopher Marlowe's *Tamburlaine* (Dabney 1974, 75, 78–81; *CS* 351). John Rabbetts contends that Faulkner and Thomas Hardy share strong affinities. The double-frame of "A Justice" represents Faulkner's affirmation, much like Hardy's, of telling tales of older times in order to understand the history and psychology of the region. Both writers reveal a particular interest in a character (in Faulkner's story it is Quentin) who has "access to both traditional and modern worlds" (1989, 62–67).

Most of these references are obscure, and the critics catalogue rather than analyze them, a method that leaves the comparisons vague and sometimes unconvincing.

## Relationship to Other Faulkner Works

It is difficult to separate interpretive comments specifically about "A Justice" from the comparative analyses relating "A Justice" to other Faulkner works. This story's relationship to other stories and novels is commonly the point of departure for critical response, much of which has to do with matching the Indian story recounted here with the variations that occur in the other Indian stories and novels such as *Requiem for a Nun* and especially *Go Down, Moses*. Edward Holmes briefly lists these associations in his study of Faulkner's re-used materials (1966, 105). Carothers does not believe that "A Justice" should actually be considered a source of *Go Down, Moses* (1985, 89). In "A Justice," Sam Fathers is a Choctaw son of Crawfish-ford. Sam, as Mick Gidley comments, is sold to the Compson, not the McCaslin, family (1990, 123). When Cowley was organizing the *Portable Faulkner*, he and Faulkner exchanged several letters about Cowley's concern over inconsistencies in the Yoknapatawpha legend. The discussion included several references to "A Justice." Faulkner's summary response was, "I realized some time ago you would get into this inconsistency and pitied you," but he did try to clarify what specifics he could. Cowley asked why the Indians in "A Justice" were Choctaw when in other stories such as "Red Leaves" the same Indians were Chickasaw. Faulkner responded, "The line dividing the Chickasaw and

Choctaw nations passed near my home; I merely moved a tribe slightly at need, since they were slightly different people in behavior." Later in the letter Faulkner returned to the point, stating that "the Indians actually were Chickasaws, or they may so be from now on. 'Red Leaves' actually were Chickasaws. 'A Justice' could have been either, the reason for their being Choctaws was the connection with New Orleans, which was more available to Choctaws, as the map herewith will explain." Faulkner then sketched a map showing the Chickasaw and Choctaw borders relative to the Tallahatchie River (Cowley 1966, 23–25, 26–27, 54; see also *SL* 207–09).

Cowley also questioned Faulkner about inconsistencies in the genealogy and chronology of this story as it compared with others. As Cowley reckoned dates, "A Justice" is told about 1900, but Sam Fathers died in 1885 or 1884. Faulkner's response confirmed his own awareness of "liberties" taken with genealogy and chronology. In the letter he established the Indian chronology as follows: Issetibbeha, father of Moketubbe, who abdicates in fear when his cousin Ikkemotubbe, Issetibbeha's sister's son, returns from New Orleans. Thus, Faulkner concludes, "Red Leaves" precedes "A Justice" in chronology. If the original family line is considered (Ikkemotubbe fathers Issetibbeha, who fathers Moketubbe), the reverse would have to be true. Dabney follows this order, placing "A Justice" first (1974, 13).

Another difference between "A Justice" and such a later tale as "A Courtship" is the change in the name of the steamboat pilot. In "A Justice," the pilot's name is David Callicoat. In "A Courtship" he is David Hogganbeck (Dabney 1974, 77). Dabney mentions that a Buster Callicot worked for Faulkner's father. The revision to Hogganbeck increases the relations between stories and novels because of the presence of the later part-Indian, Boon Hogganbeck. Another piece of information revealed in stories published after "A Justice" is that Herman Basket is Three Basket's son (Cowley 1966, 49–56). James Ferguson sees that the early tales—"Red Leaves" and "A Justice"—have more irony and ambiguity than "A Courtship," which possesses a "golden glow" characteristic of other stories written during the early 1940s (1991, 42).

The question of Sam Fathers's paternity has provided one of the main issues of critical response to "A Justice," even though it would seem that the point of the narrative is to establish just that fact. In "A Justice" Sam Fathers (Had-Two-Fathers) tells Quentin that Sam's pappy is Craw-ford (*CS 347*). In "The Old People" of *Go Down, Moses*, Sam Fathers is identified as the son of Doom (Ikkemotubbe), not Craw-ford, and the slave woman (*GDM* 165). Howell argues, "A cardinal point is that Sam is the son of Doom, the chief, and to read the story in any other way is to overlook the moral meaning that Faulkner was trying to establish." Howell believes that seeing "A Justice" as a "discrepancy" is a misreading of the text. He assumes that the lineage established in *Go Down, Moses* is correct and the implication that Crawford is the father is a cover. Further, he believes that in "A Justice" Sam Fathers knows that Doom is his father, "but because of his Indian proclivity to secrecy he keeps up the deception even when there is no occasion for doing so." The irony of the title is, therefore, that Doom has concealed his own paternity in his "just" naming of Had-Two-Fathers (Howell 1967a 149–50; Howell 1967b, 390; see also Bradford 1974, 269).

Although Skei finds some evidence in "A Justice" to support the argument that Doom is Sam's father, he is skeptical about using *Go Down, Moses* to interpret "A Justice" (Skei 1985, 315, n. 46). Indeed, not all critics read the story in "A Justice" as Doom's cover-up. Dabney disagrees with the efforts of Howell and M. E. Bradford to reconcile the discrepancies in the early story and later characterizations of Sam Fathers. He tends to see these alterations as developmental changes in the character. He shows that Sam becomes progressively more Indian in the later stories: his previously "kinky hair" becomes straight, and Doom, not Craw-ford, is his father. Dabney points out another variation that concerns Sam's mother. In "A Justice," nothing indicates that the female slave is a quadroon, though she is described as such in later versions (Dabney 1974, 74–76).

Both Blotner and Skei link "A Justice" to "The Old People" in their common focus on Yoknapatawpha's past (Blotner 1974, 1024; Skei 1981, 94). Close reading, however, reveals the discrepancies in Sam Fathers's lineage between the two stories. Dabney points out that in the *Harper's* version of "The Old People" Sam is the grandson of Doom, and the son of Had-Two-Fathers (1974, 32; *US* 202; see also Carothers 1985, 91). This version is consistent with the genealogy Faulkner provides to Cowley. Faulkner writes, "Had-Two-Fathers was the son of Doom and the slave woman in 'A Justice.' Sam Fathers was actually Had-Two-Fathers' son, and hence the *grandson* of a king" (Cowley 1966, 54). Critics like Howell do not address this variation in their argument that in "A Justice" Doom is really implied as Sam's father. Another Had-Two-Fathers exists in an early text. Though no further information is provided about the character, in the *Post* version of "Red Leaves," Had-Two-Fathers's first name is John. The name *John* does not appear in *These 13* or subsequent collections (Faulkner "Red Leaves," 62).

In scrutinizing the discrepancies between the Indian stories, especially those most closely related—"A Justice," "Red Leaves," and "A Courtship"— it is easy to lose sight of what is perhaps more important: "the number of points on which [Faulkner] remains consistent from story to story" (Taylor 1987 204). For Howell, both "A Justice" and "Red Leaves" are about the "horror immanent in the principle of life itself, which civilization tries to ignore but which is a common acceptance in the Chickasaw wilderness." He believes that "A Justice," because the narrative frame links the past to the present, possesses "an obvious moral relevance that is missing in "Red Leaves" (Howell 1967b, 390–91). For Dabney, "Doom's name indicates the imaginative unity possessed by the Indian legend." These two stories along with "A Courtship" and "Lo!" "show the paradoxes of assimilation in this dark corner of the past" (Dabney 1974, 76, 17). Victor Strandberg believes that the combined information gathered in "A Justice" and "Red Leaves" demonstrates the operative "Male Principle of power, violence, and freedom" in these characters because, as it turns out, Doom is discovered to have been motivated by his desire for a woman (1981, 29, 86). Erskine Peters reads "Red Leaves" and "A Justice" as more illustrative of the relationship of Yoknapatawpha to its black members than of the Indian population (1983, 93).

Taylor groups the Indian tales in two clusters: those that "reveal the Indians' struggle with the impact of European culture" and those that deal "with the significance of Indian culture for whites." "A Justice" joins "Red Leaves," "A Courtship," "Lo!," and "Mountain Victory" in the first group. The second group involves a "revision of both the original body of myth and its manifestations in the early stories" and includes *Go Down, Moses*, "Appendix: The Compsons," *Requiem for a Nun*, "Mississippi," and *Big Woods* (Taylor 1987, 203). Taylor suggests that the early stories had sufficient complexity to have become a novel but that the development of "the most significant portions of the stories of Ikkemotubbe and the Weddels" in *Absalom, Absalom!* and *Go Down, Moses* eliminated the need to explore the Indian characters further (Taylor 1987, 203–08).

Given the intertextuality of Faulkner's fiction, it is not surprising that "A Justice" also shares intimate ties with non-Indian stories. "A Justice," "That Evening Sun," the magazine versions of "Lion" and "The Old People," *The Sound and the Fury*, and *Absalom, Absalom!* all include Quentin Compson as narrator. Critical interest in Quentin has therefore led to a number of comparisons among these related texts. (In the revisions of "Lion" and "The Old People" for *Go Down, Moses*, Quentin is eliminated as the narrator and Isaac McCaslin replaces him as the protagonist [Hunt 1982, 370–71].)

In an early review, Lionel Trilling commented that "A Justice," like "Red Leaves" and "That Evening Sun," gained from Faulkner's "exploit[ing] emotion in some strange and hitherto unexplored setting of mind or place" and "avoid[ing] social implications entirely" (1931, 491–92).

Robert Barth asserts that fatalism defined Faulkner's main families—the Sartorises, the Compsons, and the Sutpens. Barth also finds this deterministic view in the short fiction, such as "That Evening Sun," "Red Leaves," and "A Justice," in which "that doom becomes synonymous with man himself" (Barth 1964, 100–20).

Charles Peavy itemizes the narratives in which Indians are portrayed as slave owners. They include "A Justice," "Red Leaves," "A Courtship," "The Old People," and *Requiem for a Nun*. Part of the portrait of slavery includes the black man's loss of rights as a husband in "A Justice," in an alternative version in *Go Down, Moses*, and "That Evening Sun" (Peavy 1971, 16, 18; Peters 1983, 95, 103).

Robert Slabey examines the relationship among "A Justice" and "That Evening Sun" and *The Sound and the Fury*. Both short stories employ greater complexity of sentences, more mature diction, and figurative language to distinguish the narrator's adult status. Facts in the novel about the surrey and Caddy's getting wet in the creek coincide with the details in the stories. Thematic ties link these three works and the body of Faulkner's work generally, including the father quest, adultery, and illegitimacy. Slabey sees in "A Justice" the Faulknerian attributes of subtlety in the point of view, the use of an evocative title, nonchronological time sequences, juxtaposition of events and characters in an ironic manner, and involved family history (Slabey 1964, 174–76).

Among the numerous associations between "A Justice" and "That Evening Sun," Blotner sees that "the children's activities" provide a "frame for the other story to which they would react" and concludes that in both stories Quentin responds more sensitively, especially as he gains "increasing knowledge of death" (1974, 566). Also commenting on the children, Dabney sees no tension among Jason, Caddy, and Quentin. Additionally, an innocence is present that is missing in "That Evening Sun." As companion pieces, the two stories contrast in their respective presentations of the father figure to provide protection. Although Doom does give protection to the slave, Mr. Compson cannot offer the same protection to Nancy (Dabney 1974, 73, 89). Skei sees these two stories as among the most complex of Faulkner's stories written from 1928 to 1930 (1985, 162). The two also share the "vine image" of pregnancy. In "That Evening Sun" Nancy and Jesus talk euphemistically about her pregnancy as a watermelon (*CS* 292). The same metaphor reappears in "A Justice" when Doom declares, "Any man is entitled to have his melon patch protected from these wild bucks of the woods" (*CS* 357). John Matthews suggests that the repetition of the image emphasizes "the black man's inability to get justice from the white man and his success in doing so from the red" (1989, 84).

Schoenberg discusses parallels in "A Justice," "The Old People," and *The Sound and the Fury*. These links are important because they help to establish Quentin, even if technically unnamed in the text, as the narrator of the two stories. Schoenberg argues that the narrator of "The Old People" can be identified as Quentin in part because of a reference the narrator makes to "A Justice" when he recalls Sam's telling him about his parentage. Further, we can be confident that Quentin is narrating the first and fifth sections of "A Justice" because, along with numerous other family references, he calls his siblings Jason and Caddy. In both texts they ride out to Grandfather

Compson's farm with him in the surrey. Schoenberg does comment that the children's father, not their grandfather, is driving in the novel version (Schoenberg 1977, 19, 17). Ferguson contends that the "contrast between innocence and corruption is more muted" in "A Justice" than it is in "That Evening Sun"; however, the irony may be stronger because Quentin cannot understand Sam's story. Also, Quentin's age in the frame at beginning and end are reversed in the two stories. In "That Evening Sun," the older Quentin opens and a younger Quentin closes the story. In "A Justice" the reverse happens and an older Quentin states that he did not understand at the moment what he later would (Ferguson 1991, 57–58, 112–13).

Quentin's presence is not the only similarity between "A Justice" and *Absalom, Absalom!* Dabney makes the convincing parallel between the steamboat of "A Justice" and Sutpen's mansion in the novel: the steamboat "is the comic analogue of the creation of the southern mansion in *Absalom, Absalom!*" Furthermore, "Doom's implacable will," his design for the Chickasaw plantation, prefigures Sutpen's activities at Sutpen's Hundred (Dabney 1974, 81).

Critics have identified various shared images and themes between "A Justice" and Faulkner texts that have less to do with the story's Indian element or Quentin's presence. The scene of gambling with a person as the prize anticipates the poker game in *Go Down, Moses* (Dabney 1974, 82). Quentin's recognition that understanding will come later is like Isaac's recognition that in the hunt, the chase is the beginning of an ending (Dabney 1974, 89). Peters compares the relationship between Quentin and Sam to that of Charles Mallison and Lucas Beauchamp in *Intruder in the Dust* (1983, 165). Ferguson believes that "A Justice," like "That Evening Sun," "Red Leaves," and "Spotted Horses," possesses a strong narrative revealing "Faulkner's delight in the yarn, the tale." Ferguson adds that on the whole, given the imaginative creativity involved in putting these narratives together, the Indian tales "are particularly impressive" (1991, 47, 127). Skei observes that when Faulkner's short fiction portrays an existential crisis it sometimes concerns an outsider and sometimes an individual who is suffering within the community. "A Justice" is one of a group of outsider stories including "The Hill," "Barn Burning," "That Evening Sun," and "Red Leaves" (Skei 1992, 69, 74). The black man's stomping the cock parallels Harrison Blair's trampling the fox in "Fox Hunt" (*CS* 356, 606). "Pennsylvania Station" uses the image of a preserved airplane in a manner similar to the image of Sam as a museum piece (*CS* 360, 624).

In the context of collection, "A Justice" serves to illuminate and link other texts. Millgate observes that Faulkner's arrangement of stories in *These 13* fails to exploit obvious connections between "A Justice" and "That Evening Sun" (or "Red Leaves") ([1966] 1989, 261), but Watson shows that the presence of Quentin as narrator for both short stories adds to the cyclical motion of the stories in *These 13*. Though they are not juxtaposed, "A Justice," with a twelve-year-old Quentin hearing a story from the Indian past, offers a "far past to near past" time, and "That Evening Sun," with a twenty-four-year-old Quentin telling a story of the recent past, covers a "near past to present" time. Watson comments that these two stories, as well as the other stories in Part II, "are linked in this structure by a shared time dimension or by chronologic sequence" (1980, 217–18). Leland Cox sees "A Justice" as contrasting ironically with another love story, "A Rose for Emily" (Cox 1982, 276). Pairing the stories that are grouped in the second section of *These 13*, Ferguson finds that together, "A Justice" and "Hair" focus on "love and courtship" while the preceding stories, "Red Leaves" and "A Rose for Emily," portray degradation and the final two, "That Evening Sun" and "Dry September," portray racial conflict (Ferguson 1991, 151).

Arthur Kinney discusses "The Wilderness" group in *Collected Stories*. The powerful focus in "Red Leaves" on suffering and self-indulgence is not relieved by the narrator's distance from the events described in "A Justice." The story opens with Quentin's comment on Grandfather Compson's death. Sam Fathers tells a tale filled with crime and materialism (Kinney 1980, 69). "A Justice" shares the imagery of death by water that appears in "Red Leaves," "A Rose for Emily," and "Dry September." This repetition of image works as "accretive symbolism" by which its final appearance in "Carcassonne" draws collective force and gives unity to the *Collected Stories* as a whole (Watson 1980, 213). Ferguson emphasizes the "progressive lightening of tone" in "The Wilderness" stories, with the "black comedy of 'A Justice'" moving from the "tragic spirit of 'Red Leaves,'" to the broader comedy of the subsequent stories in the section (Ferguson 1991, 159).

Clearly, "A Justice" relates to many of Faulkner's works in a variety of ways, but because we cannot make "A Justice" "fit" with what we know of the characters and chronologies of prior and subsequent works, the story is able to maintain its identity without being absorbed into the larger Yoknapatawpha saga. When, for example, Elémire Zolla rewrites the Yoknapatawpha Indian myth as if it were a cohesive narrative without acknowledging its variations, he also writes without its depth of detail and thematic complexity ([1969] 1973, 200–03). Carothers discusses this notion of autonomy versus interdependence in "With a Kindred Art," the first chapter of his study of the short stories (1985, 1–23).

## Interpretation and Criticism

The interpretive responses to "A Justice" have been largely intertextual studies. The major strains of interpretation include discussions of the themes of race, power, patriarchy, and the narrative technique used in this framed story.

Faulkner directed attention to the racial theme in his Indian tales when, in an interview in Japan, he stated that in his own work, Indians and blacks represented the "dispossessed, the people who racially or ethnically have received injustice from the hands of people who were more fortunate than they" (*LG* 136). Charles Nilon's early study of Faulkner's black characters touches only briefly on "A Justice." He links this story with "Centaur in Brass," "A Bear Hunt," and "Was" because they all mix violence against a black character with humor. In these stories, the black character is not killed; the evil in the story is revealed through the comedy (Nilon 1965, 33). Duane Gage also sees the racial theme as central to the story. Noting the tension between the frame and the internal narrative, Gage writes that the "red man and the black man compete for the love of the black woman on almost equal terms" but the "half-Choctaw child is treated as a Negro, according to the racial code of the white man" (1974, 29). Peters points out the irony in the situation that Sam, "offspring and symbol of a crucial historical predicament," is the person who holds the Compson estate intact. A blacksmith and for Quentin a teacher, Sam "is the forger of great meanings as well as of things" (Peters 1983, 95). As Kinney remarks, "There is no justice when the exploitation and possession of people are at issue" (1990, 19).

A number of commentators view the story's overall attitude as affirming a racial equality. Dabney believes that the story moves toward an image of racial justice. Even though intermarriage and cohabitation were outlawed among the Chickasaw and Choctaw tribes, miscegenation is not the motive in "A Justice" for separating Craw-ford and the woman. Dabney traces Sam Fathers's use of "nigger" and "black" in different contexts and underscores the articulation of the black man's pride for his black son, which concludes Sam's tale. Dabney presses his analysis of the racial theme further in his discussion of the sexual suggestiveness of the cockfight. Interpreting the fight as an expression of the "white man's repressed consciousness," Dabney writes, "identifying with the black man against the sexual predator, Faulkner obliquely speaks truths about the South on his Indian stage" (1974, 85–86, 75, 82).

Putzel provides an even more optimistic interpretation of the racial theme. He emphasizes the humorous tone of the internal narrative and believes "'A Justice' takes a sweeping optimistic view of man's fate," which is an early glimpse of the "author's vision of human destiny. The ultimate irony is his growing conviction that in the ongoing cycle of history justice must at last overtake racial pride, equalizing slave and conqueror, erasing indignity and quenching indignation" (1985, 237–38). One must approach Putzel's estimation with caution, however, because both his assumptions and recollections of details extend beyond the text. For example, he describes the female slave as "beautiful" and says that Craw-ford falls in love with her (Putzel 1985, 235). The story actually has nothing to say about the woman's appearance, and Craw-ford cannot be assumed to "love" her; he wants to possess her. Also there is no indication that Craw-ford and Basket murder the white men on Doom's instruction, as Putzel states (1985, 236). The conversation about the white men is strictly between Craw-ford and Basket (*CS* 351–52). Part of Putzel's argument for an optimistic reading of the racial issue is his interpretation that Sam, both Indian and black, represents races that "have adapted themselves to white bondage and survived." Yet Indian culture is clearly diminished and virtually destroyed as seen in Sam's isolation and Doom's destructive acts (Putzel 1985, 233; Polk 1981, 255–56 n. 19). As the story concludes, the image of Sam is "like something looked upon after a long time in a preservative bath in a museum"; he is dead (*CS* 360). Frederick Karl, like Putzel, believes that the racial theme in "A Justice" turns ironically on the idea of racial intermixture rather than racial pride. In this story, according to Karl, an ennobling composite racial picture is the "beginning in tentative terms of an impossible idea which grasped Faulkner's imagination: that the South eventually would become one race; that racial issues would dissolve because everyone would be black-and-white" (Karl 1989, 418).

The issue of power is another source of interpretation of "A Justice." Even though Dabney, for example, discusses the racial theme at length, he does not argue that racial equality is Doom's motivation. Dabney interprets Doom's motive as "establishing absolute power" (1974, 79). Various critics have contributed to the understanding of Doom's acquisition and display of power. Bradford identifies the central character of "A Justice" as Ikkemotubbe and the central action as "Doom's perversion of the office of Manship." Doom, Bradford tells us, is a man with a design and the power to achieve it. He lists murder, deception, and intimidation among Doom's tools. Ikkemotubbe perverts the position of chief by isolating it and himself. His absolute rule denies a "communal principle" that was formerly part of the tribe. In this reading, the fence that Herman Basket and Craw-ford must build becomes a token of Doom's role "as the *owner* . . . of his tribe and its land." The symbolic import of the fence becomes especially telling if the yellow child inside the fence is, as Bradford suggests, Doom's, not Crawford's, son. Bradford's interpretation adds significance to the "nothing" Quentin declares he and Sam were discussing (*CS* 360). Doom's alteration of tribal power from communal to individual and his realization of the monetary value of the land doom the Indian's right to the land. After Doom, "nothing" remains but the "inevitable waste which follows from bad stewardship" (Bradford 1974, 266, 269–70).

Similarly, Skei's interpretation of "A Justice" focuses on the story as a "tale of misused power, of corruption and murder." The development of this theme in the context of an Indian tribe is important, Skei believes, "because the evil acts and the desire for power seem to be by-products of culture almost forced upon the 'natural' Indians by the white men." Skei discusses this portrayal of "man's *Wille zur Macht*" in some detail. He reminds us that, in contrast to "Red Leaves," the sources and signs of corruption of Indian culture are much more ambiguous. Ikkemotubbe returns from New Orleans with evil intentions, but he had a "bad eye," a disposition toward evil, before he left. His slaves are not the first slaves on the plantation. Crawford does not hesitate to murder the white men with whom Ikkemotubbe has just bargained, and the male slave quickly threatens to kill Craw-ford in similar fashion. These are, Skei tells us, among the examples "where *pure power* . . . is used by the strongest party to force their will and wish through." Power is not only a means of gaining and keeping control but also a "treacherous and destructive road to survival." Skei argues that the portrayal of Indians here is of their inability to change in a changing world—for better or worse (1985, 160, 190–91).

Another major concern of the story is the patriarchal structure of the communities past and present. Dabney sees Sam Fathers as a mediator between the past Indian patriarchy and the present white patriarchy, represented by Quentin's portrayal of his grandfather (1974, 87). Minter writes that the Compson children in the stories and *The Sound and the Fury* are "poised at the end of childhood and the beginning of awareness." Minter argues that "In 'A Justice,' specifically as twilight descends around them and their world begins to fade, loss, consternation, and bafflement become almost all they know" (1980, 93). While this observation is certainly accurate with respect to Quentin, we do not know what Caddy and Jason might be thinking. Putzel is helpful in his perception that by linking Sam with Quentin's grandfather, Quentin can be sensitive to the respect that the two older men show for each other. Putzel also reminds us that in Quentin's mind both Sam and Grandfather Compson are associated with death (Putzel 1985, 233–34). Gidley's work on the idea of familial inheritance in the Indian stories emphasizes that Sam's story "is itself an inherited object" (1990, 123–24).

It is difficult to discuss thematic intent in "A Justice" without coming to terms with complex narrative layerings in the story. Quentin and Sam are both narrators who are telling tales that they have previously been told. Quentin establishes the frame; Sam tells the internal narrative. The result is an "ironic comedy" told in a "fluctuating first-person" (Carothers 1985, 59, 20). An early observation by Everett now seems dated and insufficient. He considers it "significant" that while this early story's "good humor centers on sexual misconduct" the narrator, Quentin, is later destroyed by what Everett describes as Caddy's "sexual immorality" (1969, 147).

Quentin's frame possesses a more somber, brooding tone. Joseph Reed explains the effect of making Quentin the narrator when he might initially seem "almost an irrelevant choice." The tactic binds the meaning of the tale to Quentin's life. The closing observation reveals Quentin's hope for perfection and his final despair. The fact that Quentin tells the story colors our response to it (Reed 1973, 23–24, 29). Millgate has observed that the presence of a filtering consciousness, such as Quentin, "whose assumptions, instincts, and sensitivities were quite different from those of the tale-teller himself," enriches the "possibility of responding to [the tale] in alternative ways." Millgate argues that "in 'A Justice,' for example, the story of Sam Fathers's birth is told in comic terms, but the presence of Quentin, brooding upon something he would understand only when he had grown older . . . effectively brings home to the reader some sense of what the events narrated must have meant in human terms to those involved, what they must still mean, in personal and racial terms, to Sam himself" (Millgate 1980, 30). Hunt believes that the humor of the internal narrative could not have been adequately told by Quentin, the narrator of the frame story, but "by shifting the burden of the narration to Sam, who has the story secondhand from Herman Basket, Faulkner assigns it to an adult temperament, to one who can relate it in a style beyond the ability of a twentieth-century young educated townsman who has no black or Indian blood." By his presence in the frame, however, Quentin "reluctantly acknowledges that he has glimpsed the formative role of violence and sexuality in historical societies" (Hunt 1982, 371–72).

Putzel sees Quentin of "A Justice" as a "Quentin redivivus," different from the Quentin of *The Sound and the Fury* in that his relationship with his brother Jason is not antagonistic. Also, Caddy does not express the compassion for him that she shows in the novel. Putzel figures Quentin as a "middle-aged" man who "is touched with no more than passing sentimentality by what had once been such potent intuitions." He describes Quentin's sense of loss of his childhood feelings: "He had felt in them then a bond with all who ever lived in the natural world. For he had seen the avatars of extinct kingdoms and cultures, if only degraded by age or poverty. And experience has merely served to rob him of the child's easy recognition of a unity no less mysterious for being no longer sentient" (1985, 230, 232). Putzel's argument would be stronger if he offered more evidence from the text. His view sees Quentin moving away from rather than toward understanding.

Skei defines Quentin's problem as trying to understand the relationship between Sam and Doom because it seems that Sam respects Doom. The narrative structure employs the "carry-over principle," shifting the bulk of the narrative to Sam. Skei reminds us that Sam is a "clever carpenter," which equals for Faulkner a good storyteller. When Sam repeats the story told to him by Herman Basket, he participates in the pattern of oral tradition. Skei adds elsewhere that by filtering the story through Quentin, the past way of life is contrasted with the modern world. Quentin is made uneasy because of the similarities in people's behavior then and now. Skei writes, "The partly ironic 'justice' in the title becomes a moral question seen from two distinctly different points of view" (Skei 1985, 161, 191–92).

Matthews defines the function of frames in Faulkner's work as typically introducing the "social and historical contexts kept at bay by the narrative's longing for purity" (1989, 74). An unframed text "often indicates a crisis transcending the determinants of history, region, and class": a framed text "involves the recontainment of that unruly material" and "promises to be the site of fuller comprehension and the point of contact between the plights of the individual characters and the historical realities that condition the narrative." Matthews concludes that "in Faulkner's texts, the frame often forecloses precisely what it promises to open." Matthews includes "A Justice" among those stories that reframe *The Sound and the Fury*. Within the structure (or stricture) of its own framed narrative, "A Justice" allows Quentin to avoid the knowledge of racial injustice that inheres in the internal narrative. Through Sam's tale, Quentin confronts the injustice of racial inequality. Yet the inability to determine whether Doom exacts justice or perpetuates another injustice is the means "by which [Quentin] can avoid comprehension"—it cannot be determined whether the black man receives justice. "Quentin," Matthews asserts, "refuses to drive the story to the point of his own discomfiture. Instead, he reserves the knowledge carried by the story to an unspecified zone associated vaguely with death." The "frames work to resist their own insights and identify knowledge as the realm of death." Quentin, by way of the frame, is able to reduce the meaning of Sam's narrative to "nothing" (Matthews 1989, 74–76, 82–89).

Given the more recent theoretical developments in interpreting narrative strategies, it is no accident that the best discussions of the narrative frame are also the more recent ones. "A Justice," like so many of the short stories, suffers from a lack of more contemporary theoretical applications. Critical response to "A Justice" tends to focus either on the tale's importance as an Indian tale or as one of Quentin's stories. In both cases, other stories receive more attention. "Red Leaves" has generated more response on the Yoknapatawpha past, and *Go Down, Moses* is the preferred point of origin for discussions about Sam Fathers. "That Evening Sun" has far surpassed "A Justice" in attracting discussion of its relation to Quentin, especially as it bears upon *The Sound and the Fury*, *Absalom, Absalom!*, and *Requiem for a Nun*. More attention needs to be directed toward this story. It is not, for example, considered in the growing body of work on Faulkner's portrayal of women, even though the female slave figures here as a pawn. Her very invisibility in the contest suggests a great deal. Those who have engaged in discussion of "A Justice" have generally been kind in their evaluation. Perhaps Dabney can be expected to be complimentary. He writes, "A classic in the adaptation of spoken narrative to print, 'A Justice' is one of Faulkner's great stories" (Dabney 1974, 72). But he is not alone. Skei, one of the most dedicated scholars of the short stories, ranks it among Faulkner's finest stories, and Ferguson counts it among those whose technical merit is "virtually flawless" (Skei 1985, 290; Ferguson 1991, 147).

## Works Cited

Barth, J. Robert. 1964. "Faulkner and the Calvinist Tradition." *Thought* 39:100–20.

Blotner, Joseph. 1974. *Faulkner: A Biography*. 2 vols. New York: Random House.

———. 1984. *Faulkner: A Biography*. 1 vol. New York: Random House.

Bradford, M. E. 1974. "That Other Patriarchy: Observations on Faulkner's 'A Justice.'" *Modern Age* 18:266–71.

Carothers, James B. 1984. "Faulkner's Short Stories: 'And Now What's to Do.'" In *New Directions in Faulkner Studies: Faulkner and Yoknapatawpha, 1983*. Ed. Doreen Fowler and Ann J. Abadie. Jackson: University Press of Mississippi, 202–27.

———. 1985. *William Faulkner's Short Stories*. Ann Arbor, MI: UMI Research Press.

Clark, William Bedford. 1977. "A Tale of Two Chiefs: William Faulkner's Ikkemotubbe and Washington Irving's Blackbird." *Western American Literature* 12:223–25.

Cowley, Malcolm. 1966. *The Faulkner-Cowley File: Letters and Memories, 1944–1962*. New York: Viking.

Cox, Leland H. 1982. *William Faulkner: Biographical and Reference Guide*. Detroit: Gale Research.

Dabney, Lewis M. 1974. *The Indians of Yoknapatawpha: A Study in Literature and History*. Baton Rouge: Louisiana State University Press.

Everett, Walter K. 1969. *Faulkner's Art and Character*. Woodbury, NY: Barron's Educational Series.

Faulkner, William. 1930. "Red Leaves." *Saturday Evening Post*, 25 October, 6ff.

———. 1931. *These 13*. New York: Jonathan Cape and Harrison Smith.

———. [1942] 1973. *Go Down, Moses*. New York: Vintage.

———. 1950. *Collected Stories of William Faulkner*. New York: Random House.

———. 1955. *Big Woods*. New York: Random House.

———. 1959. *Faulkner in the University: Class Conferences at the University of Virginia, 1957–1958*. Ed. Frederick Gwynn and Joseph L. Blotner. Charlottesville: University Press of Virginia.

———. 1968. *Lion in the Garden: Interviews with William Faulkner 1926–1962*. Ed. James B. Meriwether and Michael Millgate. New York: Random House.

———. 1977. *Selected Letters of William Faulkner*. Ed. Joseph Blotner. New York: Random House.

———. 1979. *Uncollected Stories of William Faulkner*. Ed. Joseph Blotner. New York: Random House.

———. 1987. *William Faulkner Manuscripts 9:* These 13. Ed. Noel Polk. New York: Garland.

Ferguson, James. 1991. *Faulkner's Short Fiction*. Knoxville: University of Tennessee Press.

Gage, Duane. 1974. "William Faulkner's Indians." *American Indian Quarterly* 1:27–33.

Gidley, Mick. 1990. "Sam Fathers's Fathers: Indians and the Idea of Inheritance." In *Critical Essays on William Faulkner: The McCaslin Family*. Ed. Arthur F. Kinney. Boston: G. K. Hall, 121–31.

Holmes, Edward M. 1966. *Faulkner's Twice-Told Tales: His Re-Use of His Materials*. The Hague: Mouton.

Howell, Elmo. 1967a. "Sam Fathers: A Note on Faulkner's 'A Justice.'" *Tennessee Studies in Literature* 12:149–53.

———. 1967b. "William Faulkner and the Mississippi Indians." *Georgia Review* 21:386–96.

———. 1970. "William Faulkner's Chickasaw Legacy: A Note on 'Red Leaves.'" *Arizona Quarterly* 26:293–303.

Hunt, John W. 1982. "The Disappearance of Quentin Compson." In *Critical Essays on William Faulkner: The Compson Family*. Ed. Arthur F. Kinney. Boston: G. K. Hall, 366–80.

Johnson, Glen M. 1980. "*Big Woods*: Faulkner's Elegy for Wilderness." *Southern Humanities Review* 14:249–58.

Karl, Frederick R. 1989. *William Faulkner: American Writer*. New York: Weidenfeld and Nicolson.

Kinney, Arthur F. 1980. "Faulkner's Narrative Poetics and *Collected Stories*." *Faulkner Studies* 1:58–79.

———. 1990. Introduction. In *Critical Essays on William Faulkner: The McCaslin Family*. Ed. Arthur F. Kinney. Boston: G. K. Hall, 1–57.

Matthews, John T. 1989. "Faulkner's Narrative Frames." In *Faulkner and the Craft of Fiction: Faulkner and Yoknapatawpha, 1987*. Ed. Doreen Fowler and Ann J. Abadie. Jackson: University Press of Mississippi, 71–91.

Meriwether, James B. [1961] 1971. *The Literary Career of William Faulkner: A Bibliographical Study*. Princeton University Library. Reprint. Columbia: University of South Carolina Press.

———. 1973. "Faulkner's Correspondence with *Scribner's Magazine*." *Proof* 3:253–82.

Millgate, Michael. [1961] 1966. *William Faulkner*. New York: Barnes & Noble.

———. [1966] 1989. *The Achievement of William Faulkner*. New York: Random House. Reprint. Athens: University of Georgia Press. Brown Thrasher Books.

———. 1980. "'A Cosmos of My Own': The Evolution of Yoknapatawpha." In *Fifty Years of Yoknapatawpha: Faulkner and Yoknapatawpha 1979*. Ed. Doreen Fowler and Ann J. Abadie. Jackson: University Press of Mississippi, 23–43.

Minter, David. 1980. *William Faulkner: His Life and Work*. Baltimore: Johns Hopkins University Press.

Nilon, Charles H. 1965. *Faulkner and the Negro*. New York: Citadel.

O'Nan, Martha. 1970. "William Faulkner's 'Du Homme.'" *Laurel Review* 10.2:26–28.

Pearson, Norman Holmes. 1954. "Faulkner's Three 'Evening Suns.'" *Yale University Library Gazette* 29:61–70.

Peavy, Charles D. 1971. *Go Slow Now: Faulkner and the Race Question*. Eugene: University of Oregon Books.

Peters, Erskine. 1983. *William Faulkner: The Yoknapatawpha World and Black Being*. Darby, PA: Norwood Editions.

Polk, Noel. 1981. *Faulkner's* Requiem for a Nun: *A Critical Study*. Bloomington: Indiana University Press.

———. 1985. "The Space between *Sanctuary*." In *Intertextuality in Faulkner*. Ed. Michel Gresset and Noel Polk. Jackson: University Press of Mississippi, 16–35.

Putzel, Max. 1985. *Genius of Place: William Faulkner's Triumphant Beginnings*. Baton Rouge: Louisiana State University Press.

Rabbetts, John. 1989. *From Hardy to Faulkner: Wessex to Yoknapatawpha*. New York: St. Martin's

Ragan, David Paul. 1983. "'Belonging to the Business of Mankind': The Achievement of Faulkner's *Big Woods*." *Mississippi Quarterly* 36:301–17.

Reed, Joseph W., Jr. 1973. *Faulkner's Narrative*. New Haven: Yale University Press.

Schoenberg, Estella. 1977. *Old Tales and Talking: Quentin Compson in William Faulkner's* Absalom, Absalom! *and Related Works*. Jackson: University Press of Mississippi.

Simpson, Lewis P. 1976. "Faulkner and the Legend of the Artist." In *Faulkner: Fifty Years After* The Marble Faun. Ed. George H. Wolfe. University: University of Alabama Press, 69–100.

Skei, Hans H. 1981. *William Faulkner: The Short Story Career*. Oslo, Norway: Universitetsforlaget.

———. 1985. *William Faulkner: The Novelist as Short Story Writer*. Oslo, Norway: Universitetsforlaget.

———. 1992. "Beyond Genre? Existential Experience in Faulkner's Short Fiction." In *Faulkner and the Short Story: Faulkner and Yoknapatawpha, 1990*. Ed. Evans Harrington and Ann J. Abadie. Jackson: University Press of Mississippi, 62–77.

Slabey, Robert M. 1964. "Quentin Compson's 'Lost Childhood.'" *Studies in Short Fiction* 1:173–83.

Strandberg, Victor. 1981. *A Faulkner Overview: Six Perspectives*. Port Washington, NY: Kennikat.

Taylor, Walter. 1987. "Yoknapatawpha's Indians: A Novel Faulkner Never Wrote." In *The Modernists: Studies in a Literary Phenomenon*. Ed. L. B. Gamache and I. S. McNiven. Rutherford, NJ: Fairleigh Dickinson University Press, 202–09.

Trilling, Lionel. 1931. "Mr. Faulkner's World." *Nation* 133 (4 November):491–92.

Watson, James G. 1980. "Faulkner's Short Stories and the Making of Yoknapatawpha County." In *Fifty Years of Yoknapatawpha: Faulkner and Yoknapatawpha 1979*. Ed. Doreen Fowler and Ann J. Abadie. Jackson: University Press of Mississippi, 202–25.

Zolla, Elémire. [1969] 1973. *The Writer and the Shaman: A Morphology of the American Indian*. Trans. Raymond Rosenthal. New York: Harcourt, Brace. A Helen and Kurt Wolff Book.

# A Courtship

## Publication History

In the fall of 1948 "A Courtship" appeared in the *Sewanee Review*, the only short story Faulkner published that year. Publication came six years and six rejections after Faulkner first mailed the story to his agent, Harold Ober, who, after reading the story, predicted several rejections before anyone would buy it. He wrote Faulkner: "I think you probably realize it may be a difficult story for most magazines to use." The string of rejections from high-paying magazines began with the June 8, 1942, submission to the *Saturday Evening Post*. Finally, when Albert Erskine passed the story along to John E. Palmer for the *Sewanee Review*, Palmer offered to publish it for the modest fee of $200. Faulkner must have experienced considerable satisfaction when in 1949 "A Courtship" won the O. Henry short story award, which also brought a $300 prize, and was reprinted in *Prize Stories of 1949, O. Henry Awards*. Faulkner included "A Courtship" in *Collected Stories* (1950). Undaunted by the magazine editors, when Faulkner himself judged the merits of the story for this major collection, he said, "Yes. I like this one" (*SL* 275; Blotner 1974, 1101, 1253, 1299–1300, Notes 171; Skei 1981, 101–02).

## Circumstances of Composition, Sources, and Influences

Scholars generally agree that "A Courtship" was composed in the first half of 1942. It is probably one of seven stories produced quickly for the immediate purpose of making money, an aim to which it did not contribute (Blotner 1974, 1101; Skei 1981, 101). Walter Taylor suggests that the idea and possibly a draft of "A Courtship" may have originated in the late 1920s, the earliest suggested composition date of the Indian stories "A Justice" and "Red Leaves" (1987, 204). There is little evidence to support Taylor's supposition, but Faulkner's request for a revision in the text suggests that a pre–1942 version might have existed. In 1948, when Faulkner agreed to let the *Sewanee Review* publish the story, he wrote to Ober: "Let them have the story COURTSHIP, only change the man's name from Calicoat to Hogganbeck, David Hogganbeck. I wrote that story before I had my Yoknapatawpha genealogy straightened out. The steamboat pilot, David Hogganbeck, was the grandfather of the hunter, Boon Hogganbeck, in GO DOWN MOSES. Please be *sure* that they make this change" (*SL* 268). In "A Justice," David Callicoat is the steamboat pilot Ikkemotubbe aspires to become, even to the point of assuming his name (*CS* 346–47). Faulkner's spelling of Callicoat in the story with two *l*'s and in the letter with one *l* could indicate that his instruction was merely a precaution about a six-year-old text he did not remember clearly. The carbon typescript of "A Courtship" can confidently be dated from 1942, and it uses the name "Hogganbeck" throughout, in both the complete version and the parts of story on the versos of some pages (*WFM 24* xix, 466–98). Therefore, it is curious that Faulkner would make this clarification to Ober in 1948 unless another manuscript of an earlier date did use the name Callicoat.

The published version of "A Courtship" that appears in the *Sewanee Review* and again in *Collected Stories* follows the existing typescript with only a minor revision. The words "squat at" in the manuscript are revised to "go to" in the published version (*WFM 24* 488; *CS* 373).

"A Courtship" has fewer historical references than "Red Leaves," "A Justice," or "Lo!" A. A. Hill shows how the word *plantation*, used to describe the Indian lands in "A Courtship," is a reasonable translation of Yoknapatawpha. Hill bases his translation on the meaning of several Choctaw words that are similar to the name Yoknapatawpha (1964, 82–83). In his extensive study of historical traces in the tales, Lewis Dabney observes that the marriage ritual described in "A Courtship" does not resemble the Chickasaw courtship and marriage rituals (1974, 37, 61). But one historical note that is incorporated into the story is the account of Andrew Jackson giving a United States general's coat to one of David Colbert's men after the Creek War. David Colbert was in fact an Indian of great power. Faulkner links Issetibbeha's people to Colbert by identifying the man who received the coat as Issetibbeha (*CS* 370). An account of the Colberts was available to Faulkner in the *Publications of the Mississippi Historical Society*, published in Oxford from 1900–1914 (Dabney 1974, 37).

Professor Calvin S. Brown, a childhood friend of Faulkner, has studied parallels between their adolescent chases through the woods and the manhunts that recur in Faulkner's work. According to Brown, in "A Courtship" the lengthy race to the cave by Ikkemotubbe and Hogganbeck represents a marginal use of the manhunt, and thereby suggests the challenges of endurance and strategy that characterized the childhood competitions (1966, 390; see also Dabney 1974, 61).

A more tenuous biographical assertion is Dabney's claim that Ikkemotubbe's loss of the young Indian woman parallels Faulkner's loss of Estelle to Cornell Franklin (1974, 61).

A search for literary antecedents for "A Courtship" have been more fruitful. Frank Cantrell traces various elements drawn from classical legends, seeing a resemblance between Herman Basket's sister and Helen of Troy. Like her predecessor, the Indian woman inspires larger-than-life contestants in incredible competitions. Cantrell notes further that the rivals' names are continually repeated to magnify their stature. Although Cantrell does not claim that the *Iliad* and the *Odyssey* are specific source texts for Faulkner, their epic traditions are obviously brought into "A Courtship" (1971, 289–91; see also Skei 1985, 274). Among these are the display of "elaborate, formal courtesy" that appears as a motif in the story (Cantrell 1971, 291) and what Dabney identifies as a version of a chivalric code (Dabney 1974, 58–59). Faulkner adds an air of humor when he transplants the ritual of courtly love into an American context wherein the object of the suitor has her own way (Dabney 1974, 58–59).

M. E. Bradford places the exaggerated descriptions of competitions in another tradition. He suggests that they are "in keeping with the high tradition of the Indian narratives of great feats, remembered for the instruction of the young" (Bradford 1981, 358). Faulkner also uses the wisdom of Solomon to try to soothe the wounded pride, if not hearts, of the rejected suitors. Hogganbeck does not quote Solomon directly, but he matches Ikkemotubbe's Indian wisdom with wisdom from his own tradition (*CS* 379–80). Another direct borrowing that most critics note is the use of Byron's "She Walks in Beauty." As Cantrell notes, Faulkner "adds a comic overtone" when he goes on with a slight variation: "Or she sat in it, that is, because she did not walk at all unless she had to" (1971, 290; *CS* 362). Hans Skei is correct when he suggests that Faulkner's tone is perfectly in keeping with the tone of the story if not that of the poem (1985, 321).

The story also seems to borrow from American literature in form and theme. Dabney believes that "A Courtship" "looks back to Cooper's Leather-Stocking novels, Melville's *Moby-Dick*, and Clemens's *Huckleberry Finn*, where interracial brotherhood is bound up with nostalgia for the receding frontier and withdrawal from woman and society" (1974, 57; see also Carothers 1985, 77). Dabney also links this story to the tradition of Southwestern humor, particularly Augustus Baldwin Longstreet's "The Fight" (1974, 59). Alexandre Vashchenko places "A Courtship" within a tradition of "courtship" literature in America that she traces back to the legend of Pocahontas and follows through Cooper, Longfellow, London, Hemingway, and Fitzgerald. She concludes, "in each of its reincarnations, the courtship story added new dimensions as, in time more illusions were lost and Americans were initiated into a deeper knowledge of 'doom'" (1986, 210–11).

The richness of borrowings from biblical, classical, British, and American literary traditions lends a depth to this tale that enhances and deepens the interpretive possibilities of the story.

## Relationship to Other Faulkner Works

There are few discrepancies between the details of "A Courtship" and the two other Indian stories about Ikkemotubbe. Although the narrator recalls Ikkemotubbe's leaving the plantation and returning as Doom, the recollections are brief summaries (see Holmes 1966, 102). In this story he brings eight slaves with him rather than six as in "A Justice." Ikkemotubbe is the nephew of Issetibbeha as he is in "A Justice" and the later works including *Go Down, Moses* and *Requiem for a Nun*. Chronologically, then, "A Courtship" precedes "Red Leaves" and "A Justice." Thus, in ordering the Indian stories, this "strenuous idyll" serves to "introduce and set off the tribal experience of 'A Justice' and 'Red Leaves'" (Dabney 1974, 57). James Ferguson believes the tonal quality of "A Courtship" fixes it as a much later composition. It lacks the irony and ambiguity of "Red Leaves" and "A Justice," but it shares the "golden glow" of those stories written in the 1940s. Like the other Indian stories, it is a compelling imaginative narrative (Ferguson 1991, 41–42, 127).

If Ikkemotubbe's competitor was once David Callicoat, the revision to make him David Hogganbeck further integrates this story into the larger Yoknapatawpha saga. David Hogganbeck of "A Courtship" is the grandfather of Boon Hogganbeck of "The Bear," *The Reivers*, and other stories (*SL* 203; *FU* 261). This familial line "shows the continuity and distance from the Indian stories to 'The Bear'" (Dabney 1974, 64).

The theme of brotherhood between the races is recurrent in Faulkner's fiction. Dabney finds that "A Courtship," *The Unvanquished*, and "The Fire and the Hearth" and "The Bear" from *Go Down, Moses* all treat brotherhood as an important theme. He considers Faulkner's stories dealing with Indian-black relationships much more engaging than those dealing with Indian-white relationships; "A Courtship" is particularly interesting in that it extends the idea of brotherhood into the distant past (Dabney 1974, 14, 57, 64). M. E. Bradford believes the portrayal of past relationships helps establish "A Courtship" as a counterpoint to the other Indian tales. He suggests that it stands in a normative relation to them by offering an image of Indians and whites coexisting despite their differences (Bradford 1981, 355).

"A Courtship" also shares themes and images with stories outside the Indian tales. John Longley finds its portrayal of formalized rituals similarly employed in "Shingles for the Lord" and "A Bear Hunt." These stories accomplish the difficult task of creating a comedy of manners "at the peasant level." "A Courtship" conveys an image of Chickasaw life with more success than "Red Leaves" and with greater liberty than a carefully documented historical version (Longley [1957] 1963, 115, 122). Mary Robb compares "A Courtship" to the horse-trading episode in *The Hamlet* because both amuse the reader with "someone's getting what he deserves" (1957, 30).

Walter Slatoff finds Faulkner's use of motion images, typically journeys, races, pursuits, and flights, a dominant characteristic in many works. The lengthy list includes *As I Lay Dying, Light in August, Pylon, The Wild Palms, The Hamlet, Go Down, Moses,* "A Courtship," "Red Leaves" "Fox Hunt," and "The Hound" (Slatoff 1960, 11–12).

A motif that is usually found in more serious contexts is also used in "A Courtship." Faulkner repeats in this story the image of a character's inability to drink—this time in a humorous context when Ikkemotubbe cannot drink at the eating contest. This treatment contrasts with the much more somber situations of the slave in "Red Leaves" or Rider in *Go Down, Moses* (Cantrell 1971, 291).

Charles Peavy finds slave-holding Indians not only in "A Courtship," but also in "Red Leaves," "A Justice," "The Old People," and *Requiem for a Nun* (Peavy 1971, 16). These are for the most part variations on the same fictional situation.

Ferguson likens the opening strategy in "A Courtship," characterized by a slow-paced beginning that distances the reader and emphasizes time past, to the much earlier "A Rose for Emily" and "That Evening Sun." Ferguson points out that "A Courtship" ends on the same nostalgic note that opens it, reminding the reader that it is a story of the old days (1991, 133–34, 140).

Character types familiar from Faulkner's other works also appear in this story. James Carothers ranks "A Courtship" among the trickster tales of Faulkner's later writings (1984, 226). Critics routinely compare Herman Basket's sister with Eula Varner. The descriptions are very similar for these two females who receive the unsolicited attentions of men (see Dabney 1974, 61; Bradford 1981, 356; and Skei 1985, 274, to name a few).

Vashchenko draws several important parallels between "A Courtship," "Mountain Victory," and "Delta Autumn." She observes that these stories focus on "culminating points in the history of the American South," that each story is a relatively "self-contained treatise on some aspect of the Yoknapatawpha saga never incorporated or repeated in any of Faulkner's other fictions," that they all portray unnamed, indirectly described female characters who "embody three cultures that have come together to shape the history of the New World," and that they "are enhanced by a pronounced folk effect" (Vashchenko 1986, 206–07).

Ferguson finds a homosexual element in "A Courtship," "Honor," and, most obviously, "Divorce in Naples." In the romantic triangles portrayed, the developing tensions reveal a stronger bond between the two males than between either male and the female. In these instances, the men are portrayed more positively than the woman (Ferguson 1991, 72–73).

Within the context of *Collected Stories*, the tragic tone of "Red Leaves" remains despite the comic touches in the subsequent stories including "A Courtship," in Arthur Kinney's view. Kinney also discusses "All the Dead Pilots" as a "grim extension" of "A Courtship." The courtship of the Amiens woman by John Sartoris and his rival Spoomer "mocks and degrades" the earlier courtship of Herman Basket's sister (Kinney 1980, 69–71; see also Ferguson 1991, 159).

## Interpretation and Criticism

In his review of the O. Henry award stories of 1949, Jose Yglesias praises Faulkner's narrative skill in this story of "homogenous races . . . whose inevitable conflict has a tragic issue" (1949, 76). He faults Faulkner, however, because the allegory fails. As Yglesias reads the story, "the poignancy of the relationship of the two men does not derive from their symbolic extensions; Faulkner has only told the story of an unrealized homosexual passion" (1949, 76). Although Yglesias is not as favorable to the story as most other critics, he does touch on the issues of much of the critical response to "A Courtship": interracial relationships, the nature of the relationship between Ikkemotubbe and Hogganbeck, and the success of the story at a symbolic level.

One of the recurring patterns Olga Vickery finds characteristic of Faulkner's stories is the "contest formula" that "involves some form of sexual rivalry." "A Courtship" is obviously in this class. It is also characteristic that the story maintains a comic attitude toward "the formal aspect of the contest" by competitors who are "evenly matched." Another dimension of the story formula "A Courtship" demonstrates is its emphasis on repeating patterns. Near the conclusion of the tale, Ikkemotubbe iterates a familiar experience across race and time: "Aihee. At least, for all men one same heart-break" ([1959] 1964, 302, 305; *CS* 380).

The rivalry over Herman Basket's sister that inspires such extravagant contests is not, in the opinion of most critics, the main courtship of the story. Faulkner's inability to portray successfully a romantic relationship is, in Elmo Howell's view, circumvented in "A Courtship" by the development of the relationship between Ikkemotubbe and David Hogganbeck. The tale becomes a "wistful parody of romantic love" in which the developing bond between Ikkemotubbe and Hogganbeck is really the central courtship (Howell 1967a, 310). He comments elsewhere that this appeal to brotherhood in "A Courtship" is weakened by its sentimentality (Howell 1967b, 393). Howell places this story firmly within the American tradition that in Leslie Fiedler's analysis in *Love and Death in the American Novel* presumes a superiority for the love of man for man over the love of man for woman, especially as it manifests itself in a mixed race bond (1967a, 308–14).

Dabney agrees with Howell that the real courtship is between the two men, but contrary to Howell, he contends that "A Courtship" "is conventionally masculine in feeling" and "lacks the larger subversive implications Fiedler finds in our classical fiction" (1974, 60). Frederick Karl, like Dabney, views the relationship between Ikkemotubbe and Hogganbeck as the "purest form of friendship, cemented by honorable competition and, by implication, a criterion of human behavior" (1989, 419).

Whereas the real courtship, on the evidence of the narrative, is actually between Ikkemotubbe and Hogganbeck, the real rivalry may be best defined as between men and women—in this case, men versus Herman Basket's sister, whom Howell places among the vaguely defined female characters typical of Faulkner who demonstrate the "inevitable triumph of matter over mind" (1967a, 308–14). Dabney also sees the contestants "suffering from the malady of the ideal" who lose the practical woman. Her independence "reflects the power of women through the nature which transcends societies" (Dabney 1974, 69–70).

More recent attentions to Herman Basket's sister generally prove to be more substantive. Carothers argues that Ikkemotubbe and Hogganbeck "ignore the reality of Herman Basket's sister," making no effort to know or understand her. In contrast to the courtesy and respect they show to each other, to her "they are juvenile and grotesque." Their physical efforts are contrasted to her inertia, but she renders them insignificant when she chooses Log-in-the-Creek (Carothers 1985, 77–78). Vashchenko builds on Dabney's observation that the contest over Herman Basket's sister is tied to possession of the land (Vashchenko 1986, 209; Dabney 1974, 61). Herman Basket's sister possesses those "generic categories associated with womankind": unpredictability, passivity or patience, and the inevitable power to prevail. Vashchenko reminds us that the last is also characteristic of Faulkner's depiction of the earth. She believes Faulkner raises Herman Basket's sister to a symbolic level with parallels between the young woman and the land. Herman Basket's sister, a "monumental static shape" that without effort draws men to her, is "perhaps a force of nature." She is, furthermore, a "symbol of a rite of passage—man's initiation into his mournful earthly destiny." After his initiation, Ikkemotubbe importantly becomes "Doom." The tears he sheds are for the loss of himself, his innocence, having passed by way of Herman Basket's sister into a "new sad knowledge" (Vashchenko 1986, 208–10).

In terms of the courtship, two other characters have received some attention for their roles in the wooing of Herman Basket's sister. Dabney points out that neither Ikkemotubbe nor Hogganbeck acknowledges Log-in-the-Creek's sexual potency, evidenced in his confident playing of the harmonica (1974, 69). Skei points out that the arrogance of the powerful Ikkemotubbe and Hogganbeck prevents them from even thinking the young woman might have her own idea about a marriage choice. For them, "in the masculine world where power, skill, and fighting ability count so much," Log-in-the-Creek is no competitor. Nevertheless, his one virtue, persistence, proves to be the superior trait (Skei, 1985, 274). Carothers makes an interesting analysis of Log-in-the-Creek as artist. The musician persists in playing his harmonica despite the efforts of others to thwart him. The story is a record of his success as much as it is a record of the failure of the other suitors (Carothers 1985, 78). Vashchenko notes that Log-in-the-Creek's characteristic laziness is very much like that of his soon-to-be wife, Herman Basket's sister. Unlike critics who interpret Log-in-the-Creek as a sexually symbolic name representing the defeat of Ikkemotubbe and Hogganbeck, Vashchenko interprets the name as representing a bridge: Log-in-the-Creek "seems to be not so much a husband as a tool in the hands of a woman who, in a symbolic way, transforms the obstacle in the Yoknapatawpha 'creek' into an allegorical bridge to the future" (1986, 208–09; see also Dabney 1974, 69).

Herman Basket's aunt does not receive much critical attention, but she does command respect in the story. She succeeds when Herman Basket fails to get Ikkemotubbe and Hogganbeck off the gallery. Walter Everett comments that her "genealogical snobbery" is "a slight mockery of the Southern aristocrats" (1969, 137). Little more is said about this character until Vashchenko argues that her successful hiding of Ikkemotubbe's pony "introduce[s] the theme of woman's treachery." Vashchenko concedes that as a practical matter the missing pony extends the rivalry between the contestants, but it can also be read as a symbolic deprivation of Ikkemotubbe's manhood (1986, 209–10).

The significance of the cave evokes a variety of interpretations. According to Longley, "The cave represents, of course, a great deal more than just a cave." To him, given his view of the story as a comedy of manners, going into the cave "is a descent, a plunge back into the irrational and terrible abyss of the pre-human darkness before man's struggle to create such concepts as justice, chivalry, and reverence for human life" (Longley [1957] 1963, 125). Cantrell comments that the sexually symbolic firing of the pistol in the cave is suitable imagery for the tale (1971, 292; see also Bradford 1981, 358). Dabney questions Longley's interpretation of the significance of the cave (1974, 122–23). For him, the "climax [at the cave] is a tall tale with concessions to modernity and Freud." The cave represents a "return to the womb and second birth; it correlates heterosexual initiation with the fear of death, as this strengthens the male instinct to get out alive." The description of the men's efforts to get out of the cave is of "male climax and exhaustion" that puts Hogganbeck in the role of woman. The blood that spurts from his mouth is a "vivid image of menstruation" and reinforces a fear of women that runs through the narrative (Dabney 1974, 67–68). Sharon Hult believes the story portrays the "male struggle for an ideal woman." She adds that here, unlike their use in "The Brooch," the symbols of gun and cave have a comic effect (Hult 1974, 304 n. 11).

The relationships that exist between the three suitors and the two women have received varied and complex interpretations. Given this, Howell's claim that the comedy of "A Courtship" has no association with the tragic and lacks dramatic seriousness seems an inadequate reading (Howell 1967b, 392–93). Most critics see an intricate bonding of the comic with the tragic in the story. Comic touches enhance the descriptions of Herman Basket's sister and Log-in-the-Creek as well as the competitions between Ikkemotubbe and Hogganbeck, but the tragic element appears in references to the subsequent effects of Ikkemotubbe's failure to win the woman. The story closes with Ikkemotubbe's departure on the steamboat; his New Orleans years, leading to his subsequent return to the plantation, have begun (Cantrell 1971, 289–95). Critics generally agree that Ikkemotubbe's failure to win Herman Basket's sister is the specific reason Ikkemotubbe leaves the plantation, and the comedy is unavoidably tempered by the knowledge of his cruel design when he returns (Skei 1985, 275; Carothers 1985, 78; Vashchenko 1986, 210).

Skei also contends that the comic tone is tempered by the "elements of the 'vanishing America'" that color the story (1985, 273–74). The sense of what has been lost exists not only in the character of Ikkemotubbe but also in the portrayal of what once existed. The mythic wilderness is found "sweet and pure" in "A Courtship," a story that, according to Wright Morris, elevates the frontier tradition of exaggeration "to the level of the mythic fable." He is effusive in his praise: "There is nothing in literature to compare with the fabulous courtship by David Hogganbeck and Ikkemotubbe of Herman Basket's sister, that primal and ever-receding vision of womanly loveliness." But for Morris, unlike most critics, it is both necessary that the combatants be defeated and important that defeat seem unimportant to them. He locates this wilderness without rage firmly in the American tradition (Morris 1963, 183).

For Joseph Reed, the Indian world is painted by a golden aura "somewhat tarnished by realistic detail." He asserts that Faulkner's Indians are never described when their tribal way of life is thriving and undiminished by encroachment (1973, 22). Dabney is less profuse in his praise than Morris but also sees an "evocation of radical innocence" in the Indian world as yet uncorrupted by white man's influence." To a greater degree than in his other stories, Faulkner utilizes the "noble savage" tradition in "A Courtship" (Dabney 1974, 60, 58). Carothers sees this pre-lapsarian world as important to distinguish between this time of innocence when Ikkemotubbe is still loved by his friends and the time when he is corrupted by the influence of the white man and returns as Doom (1985, 77). Karl describes this portrayal as Faulkner's "Wordsworthian belief—perhaps laced by Jefferson—that in 'lower life' a viable, livable culture can be found, and that this culture is somehow superior to the more sophisticated works of man" (1989, 418). (Karl incorrectly identifies Herman Basket's sister as Herman Basket's daughter [1989, 765n.].) Karl smells "the whiff of an Edenic past" in this portrait (1989, 418; see also Ferguson 1991, 55–56). Mick Gidley uses several examples from "A Courtship" to show the "contours of 'savagism'" in Faulkner's Indians. He cites their characterization as hunters rather than farmers and their tradition-bound courtship rituals. Gidley adds, however, that this tradition is countered by the "perceptible modulation toward simplification, elegy, and nostalgia" especially prevalent in this story's recollection of how life was in days gone by (1990, 127–28).

The sense of universal pain and the ultimate "draw" in the contest has been wrongly interpreted as a "teaching on equality, in the conventional modern sense of the term," according to Bradford. He works through a series of examples of how Ikkemotubbe and Hogganbeck recognize and accommodate their differences, pointing out that until the race for the cave, each contest gives an obvious advantage to one or the other man. Only in the race might either one prevail because in the duration of the contest, their different advantages are more equalized. Finally, in their loss to Log-in-the-Creek, another difference is seen. Hogganbeck can accept his defeat, but Ikkemotubbe cannot. As the references to the later time imply, and as the other stories detail, on his return Ikkemotubbe, now Doom, will suffer no defeat. Had Ikkemotubbe been able to make this final accommodation to defeat, Bradford continues, he might likewise have "made an accommodation with the incoming whites that would have preserved the dignity of both peoples and made of their confrontation a benefit to all." Doom's failure to accomodate to change means that the best days of the tribe are past, merely recollections present in this story that emphasizes the decayed tribal community present in other depictions of the Indians (Bradford 1981, 356–59).

Reed says that Faulkner uses an "our town" technique to gather readers into the community of the story. The speaker's first sentence is a reminiscence that includes references to the steamboat and already known Indian characters. It offers an "invitation to work upon prior knowledge, to have a comfortable feeling of recognition and familiarity" (Reed 1973, 22). Dabney sees the narrative voice as a moral mask for Faulkner, marked by nostalgia that is kept in check by the humor of the story (1974, 60). Noel Polk disagrees with Dabney, arguing that the nostalgic view belongs to the narrator but not to Faulkner (1981, 255–56 n. 19). Bradford suggests that the voice may belong to Sam Fathers as in other tales telling "how it was" to a Quentin–Ike listener (1981, 355). There is no conclusive identification of the speaker, except that he is the son of a close companion to Ikkemotubbe who passed the stories of the tribe down to his son. It is, therefore, tempting to infer that Sam is speaking. Carothers makes the easily overlooked point that the narrator "is primarily concerned with celebrating the feats of the unsuccessful rivals" (1985, 78).

One of the difficulties of dealing with "A Courtship" is that analysis often extinguishes the humor, and the broad humor often disguises the complexities of the text. Those critics who have read the text closely have found it a rich example of Faulkner's excellence. Eudora Welty, one of the judges for the 1949 O. Henry prize, judged the merits of "A Courtship" as follows: "The Faulkner story is a proper giant, of course—it is probably one of his finest Indian stories, which is enough for it to have this and any loose prizes hanging around on trees besides, for my vote. On the basis of form, Mr. Faulkner's story is matchless here, for the writing, the story, its life and world, are all one and inseparable as in none of the others" (Brickell 1949, Introduction xii). Skei ranks "A Courtship" among the better Faulkner stories written in 1942 and after (1985, 287). Cantrell believes the story has been undeservedly neglected. It is an important story because in it, "Ikkemotubbe's character is whole and fully realized, both in its comic and its tragic aspects" (Cantrell 1971, 289, 295). Vashchenko's evaluation of "A Courtship" challenges students of Faulkner to attend to this text. She writes, "A Courtship" withstands comparison to any of the major Yoknapatawpha fiction because it, among a select few of the short stories, contains "the deepest and most universal aspects of the whole saga's design" (1986, 206).

## Works Cited

Blotner, Joseph. 1974. *Faulkner: A Biography*. 2 vols. New York: Random House.

Bradford, M. E. 1981. "Faulkner's 'A Courtship': An Accommodation of Cultures." *South Atlantic Quarterly* 80:355–59.

Brickell, Herschel, ed. 1949. *The O. Henry Awards*. Garden City, NY: Doubleday.

Brown, Calvin S. 1966. "Faulkner's Manhunts: Fact into Fiction." *Georgia Review* 20:388–95.

Cantrell, Frank. 1971. "Faulkner's 'A Courtship.'" *Mississippi Quarterly* 24:289–95.

Carothers, James B. 1984. "Faulkner's Short Stories: 'And Now What's to Do.'" In *New Directions in Faulkner Studies: Faulkner and Yoknapatawpha, 1983*. Ed. Doreen Fowler and Ann J. Abadie. Jackson: University Press of Mississippi, 202–27.

———. 1985. *William Faulkner's Short Stories*. Ann Arbor, MI: UMI Research Press.

Dabney, Lewis M. 1974. *The Indians of Yoknapatawpha: A Study in Literature and History*. Baton Rouge: Louisiana State University Press.

Everett, Walter K. 1969. *Faulkner's Art and Character*. Woodbury, NY: Barron's Educational Series.

Faulkner, William. 1948. "A Courtship." *Sewanee Review* 56:634–53.

———. 1950. *Collected Stories of William Faulkner*. New York: Random House.

———. 1959. *Faulkner in the University: Class Conferences at the University of Virginia, 1957–1958*. Ed. Frederick Gwynn and Joseph L. Blotner. Charlottesville: University Press of Virginia.

———. 1977. *Selected Letters of William Faulkner*. Ed. Joseph Blotner. New York: Random House.

———. 1987. *William Faulkner Manuscripts 24: Short Stories*. Ed. Joseph Blotner. New York: Garland.

Ferguson, James. 1991. *Faulkner's Short Fiction*. Knoxville: University of Tennessee Press.

Gidley, Mick. 1990. "Sam Fathers's Fathers: Indians and the Idea of Inheritance." In *Critical Essays on William Faulkner: The McCaslin Family*. Ed. Arthur F. Kinney. Boston: G. K. Hall, 121–31.

Hill, A. A. 1964. "Three Examples of Unexpectedly Accurate Indian Lore." *Texas Studies in Literature and Language* 6:80–83.

Holmes, Edward M. 1966. *Faulkner's Twice-Told Tales: His Re-Use of His Material*. The Hague: Mouton.

Howell, Elmo. 1967a. "Inversion and the 'Female' Principle: William Faulkner's 'A Courtship.'" *Studies in Short Fiction* 4:308–14.

———. 1967b. "William Faulkner and the Mississippi Indians." *Georgia Review* 21:386–96.

Hult, Sharon Smith. 1974. "William Faulkner's 'The Brooch': The Journey to the Riolama." *Mississippi Quarterly* 27:291–305.

Karl, Frederick R. 1989. *William Faulkner: American Writer*. New York: Weidenfeld and Nicolson.

Kinney, Arthur F. 1980. "Faulkner's Narrative Poetics and *Collected Stories*." *Faulkner Studies* 1:58–79.

Longley, John Lewis, Jr. [1957] 1963. *The Tragic Mask: A Study of Faulkner's Heroes.* Chapel Hill: University of North Carolina Press.

Morris, Wright. 1963. *The Territory Ahead.* New York: Atheneum.

Peavy, Charles D. 1971. *Go Slow Now: Faulkner and the Race Question.* Eugene: University of Oregon Books.

Polk, Noel. 1981. *Faulkner's* Requiem for a Nun: *A Critical Study.* Bloomington: Indiana University Press.

Reed, Joseph W., Jr. 1973. *Faulkner's Narrative.* New Haven: Yale University Press.

Robb, Mary Cooper. 1957. *William Faulkner: An Estimate of His Contribution to the Modern American Novel.* Critical Essays in English and American Literature No. 1. Pittsburgh: University of Pittsburgh Press.

Skei, Hans H. 1981. *William Faulkner: The Short Story Career.* Oslo, Norway: Universitetsforlaget.

———. 1985. *William Faulkner: The Novelist as Short Story Writer.* Oslo, Norway: Universitetsforlaget.

Slatoff, Walter J. 1960. *Quest for Failure: A Study of William Faulkner.* Ithaca, NY: Cornell University Press.

Taylor, Walter. 1987. "Yoknapatawpha's Indians: A Novel Faulkner Never Wrote." In *The Modernists: Studies in a Literary Phenomenon.* Ed. L. B. Gamache and I. S. MacNiven. Rutherford, NJ: Fairleigh Dickinson University Press, 202–09.

Vashchenko, Alexandre. 1986. "Woman and the Making of the New World: Faulkner's Short Stories." In *Faulkner and Women: Faulkner and Yoknapatawpha, 1985.* Ed. Doreen Fowler and Ann J. Abadie. Jackson: University Press of Mississippi, 205–19.

Vickery, Olga W. [1959] 1964. *The Novels of William Faulkner.* Baton Rouge: Louisiana State University Press.

Yglesias, Jose. 1949. "Neurotic Visions." *Masses and Mainstream* 2:74–76.

# Lo!

## Publication History

"Lo!" originally appeared in *Story* in November 1934, the tenth of eleven Faulkner stories published for the first time that year. The editor said it was "one of those off-the-track Faulkners which just suits us." Faulkner was to receive the "usual rates" for the story, which probably meant $25. "Lo!" had not sold immediately on submission. Agent Morton Goldman sent the story to Alfred Dashiell at *Scribner's* with a letter dated May 10, 1934, in which he described it as a new and "successful" effort "of satire and fantasy." Dashiell responded five days later that he appreciated the reading but felt that "Lo!" was "not a magazine piece." If Goldman followed Faulkner's suggestion, before being sent to *Scribner's* "Lo!" had probably been seen by editors at the *Saturday Evening Post* and *Cosmopolitan*. "Lo!" was included in *The Best Short Stories of 1935* and the *Yearbook of the American Short Story*. It was not used again by Faulkner until he grouped it with the Indian tales in "The Wilderness" section of *Collected Stories* (1950) (which critics Dorothy Tuck and Walter Taylor list as its first publication) (*SL* 75; Meriwether 1973, 281; Blotner 1974, 854, Notes 119–20; Skei 1981, 113 n. 5; Gresset 1985, 43; Tuck 1964, 169; Taylor 1987, 203).

## Circumstances of Composition, Sources, and Influences

Although a twelve-page manuscript exists in the Rowan Oak papers, no substantive clues help to date the composition of the story (Kinney and Fowler, 1983, 331–32; Skei 1981, 81). Based on his study of Faulkner's letters to Harrison Smith and Morton Goldman, however, Joseph Blotner establishes a likely composition date as the summer of 1933 (1974, 808; see also Skei 1981, 79, 81). In a letter to Smith received July 20, 1933, Faulkner notes the recent composition of three stories that Blotner suggests are "Elly," "Lo!," and one later revised as "Love" (*SL* 72). "Lo!" is first identified by name in a letter to Morton Goldman probably from summer 1933 in which Faulkner asks Goldman to submit it to the *Post* or *Cosmopolitan* (*SL* 75). Taylor suggests that even if it were not actually written in 1927, "Lo!" may have been conceived of as early as that year, the earliest date suggested for another Indian story, "A Justice" (Taylor 1987, 203).

The versions of "Lo!" in *Story* and *Collected Stories* are virtually the same. The three minor variations include corrections of spelling or preposition usage: hyphenating fifteen-hundred-mile, correcting *on* to read *in*, and separating into two words *wood smoke*.

Although "Lo!" is not about Ikkemotubbe's people, the historical source studies for those tales also inform the background of "Lo!" Elmo Howell grounds the major premise of "Lo!" in history, noting that visits by Indian chiefs to the president of the United States were fairly common occurrences. Specifically, Howell ties Faulkner's story to two such visits by Choctaw chiefs in Mississippi: Pushmataha in 1824 and Greenwood Leflore in 1831 (Howell 1967, 253). Howell cites several parallels between Pushmataha's delegation to President James Monroe and Francis Weddel's people's journey. The U.S. government's funding of food, clothing, and housing that is a source of exasperation to the fictional president during a long stalemate in negotiations has a counterpart in Pushmataha's historical visit (Howell 1967, 255–56). Biographical detail about Greenwood Leflore also lends a historical flavor to the fictional text. When Leflore, half French and half Choctaw, journeyed to Washington, he went to complain to President Andrew Jackson about Indian agents' treatment of Indians. Despite assurances in Washington, the situation with the agents did not improve, and Leflore was discredited among the Choctaws. Faulkner himself recalled some of the story of Greenwood Leflore, who, being "wise enough to get a patented deed to his land and to take up the white man's ways," built his fortune as a cotton planter (*FU* 44). Faulkner further described Leflore's grand mansion (Malmaison) and the much embellished legend of his death when he refused to join the Confederacy (*FU* 44). Scholars agree that Francis Weddel, who built the plantation Contalmaison, is modeled after Leflore (Howell 1967, 254; Dabney 1974, 35; Blotner 1974, Notes 115). The president whom Weddel confronts is generally matched to President Andrew Jackson (Dabney 1974, 13; Karl 1989, 420). Although the president is unnamed and married in "Lo!," the recollections of the event by Saucier Weddel in "Mountain Victory" are specifically of his father's visit to President Jackson, who is named in the story (*CS* 759; Everett 1969, 152).

Lewis Dabney adds one further, more contemporary context for "Lo!" by linking this "first American fiction to describe a sit-in" to the bonus marches and mass movements of the 1930s (Dabney 1974, 43; see also Karl 1989, 419).

History was not Faulkner's only source. Dabney believes that the title and Indians of Faulkner's "Lo!" take their "point of departure" from Alexander Pope's description of Indians in "Essay on Man":

> Lo, the poor Indian! whose untutored mind
> Sees God in clouds, or hears him in the wind;
> His soul proud Science never taught to stray

Far as the solar walk or milky way;
Yet simple nature to his hope has giv'n
Behind the cloud-topt hill, an humbler Heav'n,
Some safer world in depth of woods embraced,
Some happier island in the wat'ry waste,
Where slaves once more their native land behold,
No fiends torment, no Christians thirst for gold.
To be, contents his natural desire;
He asks no Angel's wing, no Seraph's fire;
But thinks, admitted to that equal sky,
His faithful dog shall bear him company.
            (quoted in Dabney 1974, 44)

Faulkner treats Pope's natural man with irony, as evidenced by the tone of Weddel's continual reference to his people as poor and ignorant (Dabney 1974, 44). Faulkner makes another literary association himself, recalling Charles Dickens, when he describes the motley assortment of half-dressed Indians who converged on Washington: "At a glance one would have said that they had come intact out of Pickwickian England"(*CS* 382). When the President presides over the exoneration of Weddel's nephew, he reads Petrarch's Sonnets (*CS* 399).

Skei places "Lo!" in the tradition of the tall tale (1985, 213). Finally, Weddel is no "noble savage," nor is he Machiavellian, but even though James Carothers does include Weddel in his list of Faulkner's tricksters, he is as subtle a trickster as Brer Rabbit ever aspired to be (see Carothers 1984, 202–27).

## Relationship to Other Faulkner Works

Passing reference has already been made to two stories, "A Justice" and "Mountain Victory," that have important ties to "Lo!" Both "Lo!" and "A Justice" are counted with "Red Leaves" and "A Courtship" as Faulkner's Indian stories. "A Justice," "Red Leaves," and "A Courtship" typically receive more attention because of the presence of the character Ikkemotubbe and because they are more intricately woven into the fabric of Yoknapatawpha County. A definite similarity exists between Moketubbe of "Red Leaves" and Francis Weddel of "Lo!" They are both lethargic, obese, and inscrutable. Mick Gidley traces the behaviors of Faulkner's Indians that place them in the tradition of savagism. In "Lo!" the Chickasaws (not Choctaw, as Gidley once identifies them) exhibit an odd reaction to their new "white" clothing, and initially they are ignorant of the trader's motives for buying the ford. These behaviors are characteristics that demonstrate their inability to "improve" themselves and their immunity to the benefits of civilization, both qualities of savagism. Gidley makes the point that Faulkner also violates these conventions throughout the Indian tales. He also examines the "particular match" between "Lo!" and "A Justice." They both offer versions "of manipulative chiefly power, in their studied playfulness with—even inversion of—the idea of 'justice' and, of course, in their investigations of patrimony" (Gidley 1990, 127–28, 124).

Like "Mountain Victory," "Lo!" focuses on another Indian family, the Weddels. "Mountain Victory" contains the son's passing recollection of his father's trip to Washington. The trip is the focus of "Lo!" Most of the information in "Mountain Victory" complements that in "Lo!," except that Saucier Weddel describes his family as Choctaw and his father in the later story is described as Chickasaw. Faulkner was less disturbed by this kind of discrepancy than his readers often are. When Malcolm Cowley noted the shifts from Choctaws to Chickasaws, Faulkner's response, "I merely moved a tribe slightly at need," established his fairly consistent view that immediate fictional needs preempted fidelity to past text (Cowley 1966, 23–25). Blotner suggests that discrepancies between the stories "could . . . be attributed to the differences between the truth and the version of it the son would give years after his famous father's death" (Blotner 1974, Notes 115).

Strengthening his argument that the Yoknapatawpha Indians were the source of a novel never written, Taylor enlarges what is generally considered the group of Indian tales and then divides them into two subgroups. He links "Red Leaves," "A Justice," "Mountain Victory," "A Courtship," and "Lo!" as focusing on the Indians themselves while he argues that the Indian material in *Go Down, Moses*, *Requiem for a Nun*, "Appendix: The Compsons," "Mississippi," and *Big Woods* focuses on "the significance of Indian Culture for whites." Tracing the details of the two major Indian families, those of Ikkemotubbe and Weddel, Taylor argues that because the information is "not wholly necessary for the plot, [it] implies another, more complex story than the one in which it appears." Taylor traces similar alterations of the two families as their culture is influenced by white settlers: "Uniting the two plots, however, is the common theme that Europeanization, with its adjunct, the treatment of land and human beings as property, has led both families first to their aggrandizement, then to their downfall." And, as Taylor suggests, the tales offer some parallels between the families. Issetibbeha's visit to Washington in "A Courtship" could have been the same trip that is the focus of "Lo!" Taylor believes that Ikkemotubbe's friend in New Orleans named Vitry might be Francois Vidal (Francis Weddel) of "Lo!" (Taylor 1987, 203–07). This is less likely because Vitry is a white Frenchman and Weddel is half Chickasaw and half French. If chronology were ignored, Vitry might be the "French father of his from New Orleans" (*CS* 391).

Taylor might have added as an additional link between the families that in "Mountain Victory" Saucier recalls the overseer of the supplies for the trip as a full-blooded Choctaw cousin to Francis Weddel. Saucier recounts how in the "old days The Man was the hereditary title of the head of our clan; but after we became Europeanized like the white people, we lost the title to the branch which refused to become polluted, though we kept the slaves and the land" (*CS* 759). Faulkner said that Weddel's and Issetibbeha's families "may have been related by marriage, even by blood" (*FU* 261).

Although James Ferguson considers "Lo!" an "inferior" part of Faulkner's work, he praises the creative ingenuity in this as well as in the other Indian stories (1991, 46, 126–27).

The theme of land ownership that appears in "Lo!" links it to other stories. "A Courtship" opens with recollections of the time when a straight line separated the Indian land from America. Problems of encroachment mentioned in the opening of "A Courtship" are the focus of "Lo!" Floyd Watkins explores three relations to ownership that Faulkner portrays through various works: "communal ownership," "selfish aggrandizement," and "defending a reasonable quantity of property for the use of a man and his family and retainers." Watkins includes "Lo!" in his discussion of characters such as Ike McCaslin, McCaslin Edmonds, Thomas Sutpen, and the McCallums, as they appear in various works including *Go Down, Moses*, *Absalom, Absalom!*, *Requiem for a Nun*, and "The Tall Men" (Watkins 1976, 125). Skei concurs with the shared focus on property ownership in "Lo!" and *Go Down, Moses*; he notes only briefly the very different tones used in the two works in their respective presentations (Skei 1985, 221).

Charles Nilon places "Lo!" among those Faulkner stories whose black characters appear only incidentally. He includes with these "A Courtship," "A Rose for Emily," "Barn Burning," "Fox Hunt," and "Dr. Martino." The black characters in these "exist outside of or in addition to the central plot structure" (Nilon 1965, 30).

Joseph Reed believes that "Lo!" shares "overt national feeling" with the World War II stories "Shall Not Perish" and "Two Soldiers." It also represents one of Faulkner's portraits of a "sealed-off enclave" that defines social relationships seen elsewhere in *Absalom, Absalom!* (1984, 52, 99).

"Lo!" could be compared to "Mule in the Yard," "That Will Be Fine," "Afternoon of a Cow," "A Bear Hunt," and "Fool about a Horse" as stories in the tradition of the tall tale (Skei 1985, 213). Faulkner's comic tale, according to Skei, includes "bargains and deceits and lies" in which "humour has to give way to seriousness when the bargains come to involve people and destinies." Further, with the exception of "Afternoon of a Cow," Skei sees revenge as central to Faulkner's tall tales (1985, 213). Similarly, Ferguson includes "Lo!" in a lengthy list of stories exhibiting a pattern in which characters who possess a childlike innocence are able to outwit ostensibly wiser or more empowered individuals (1991, 60–61).

Another pattern that Ferguson discerns in "Lo!" is Faulkner's concern with the danger inherent in abstraction. In the case of "Lo!," "By the

People," "Point of Law," and "The Tall Men" the abstraction is *legality* (Ferguson 1991, 81).

Arthur Kinney believes that neither "Lo!" nor the other Indian tales that follow "Red Leaves" in "The Wilderness" section of *Collected Stories* relieve the suffering and self-indulgence portrayed in the opening story (1980, 69). Ferguson adds that given the degeneration of the Indian culture portrayed in these stories, the section does not offer "positive values" as contrast to the subsequent stories of "The Wasteland" (1991, 159).

## Interpretation and Criticism

Little critical attention has been paid to "Lo!" beyond source studies and its relation to other Indian tales. A narrative observation in "Lo!" articulates the ideal around which much of the criticism gravitates. When the procession of white leaders and Indians enters the Congress, the narrator observes: "So it was that behind the Speaker's desk of that chamber which was to womb and contemplate the high dream of a destiny superior to the injustice of events and the folly of mankind, the President and the Secretary stood" (*CS* 399). Paternalism, property ownership, and injustice are the thematic bases of most responses to the text.

M. E. Bradford offers the first extended discussion of "Lo!" in "Faulkner and the Great White Father." Bradford describes "Lo!" as "Faulkner's parable of misguided federalism." It is, according to Bradford, a study of the tensions between a central authority that purports to treat all its people equally and the diverse subcultures that fall under the domain of the patriarchal "Great White Father." Bradford argues that for Faulkner attention must be directed to "local justice—a justice mindful of the socio-cultural facts which locally prevail" and that the federal government must temper a uniform perspective with the recognition of human difference. Faulkner's "perspective upon the world is this combination": "a tolerant but warm humanitarianism (which recognizes the imperative *and* the true meaning of brotherhood) and a wise distrust of 'democratic dogma'" (Bradford 1964, 328–29).

Dabney's chapter on "Lo!" in *The Indians of Yoknapatawpha* presents it as the "least serious" of the Indian stories. As a "situation comedy with broad elements of farce," it suggests the Indian response to the westward movement of whites. These Indians are neither meek nor savage. They are shrewd, patronizing, and "too smart and tough to be victims" of white men's lust for land. Dabney sees "Lo!" as a text contemporary with its times—a "tall tale of how you can 'fight City Hall' written with a southerner's appreciation of the discomfiture of Washington power." Weddel is a skilled confrontationist, but the president and his staff do not become the villains of the piece though they are reduced to a level of ridiculous ineffectiveness. "Lo!" is in Dabney's view a Trojan horse story wherein the Indians invade Washington and carry the battle (Dabney 1974, 43, 49–51, 56).

The theme of property ownership generates fairly consistent critical responses. Mary Jane Dickerson understands "Lo!" to be about displacement and the "frustrating impossibility of man ever really being able to possess the land." According to Dickerson, the Indians have an "innate knowledge of the futility of the white man's effort" to profit from land ownership. The Indians also have a "basic intuition of what the white man is always up to" ([1975] 1982, 261–62). In their examinations of attitudes toward property, Melvin Backman and Floyd Watkins include "Lo!" as the demonstration of communal ownership. Watkins believes that Faulkner is being nostalgic when he occasionally indicates a longing for a communal world. The Indian tales do not picture a totally benevolent world, and the Indians after all lose the land (Backman 1966 167–68; Watkins 1976, 125–27). Although Indians laugh at fences in "Lo!," they become fence builders in "A Justice." Carothers remarks that "Lo!" explores a "sense of right relations to the land" from a different perspective than *Go Down, Moses* (1985, 20).

Pursuing Faulkner's comments to students at the University of Virginia "that the land is inimical to the white man because of the unjust way in which it was taken from Ikkemotubbe and his people" (*FU* 43), Howell argues that Faulkner's thesis is the "unjust treatment of the Indians." Howell also believes that Faulkner stresses the same vagaries of personality in his Indian portraits as in the human population generally. Howell does emphasize the sinister quality in the story as the response of people "faced with hopeless odds" that is a "latent quality in our nature which we prefer to forget" (Howell 1967, 256).

Skei observes that in most of the stories Faulkner wrote between 1933 and 1941, the protagonist suffers an injustice; there may be long-standing or sudden awareness of it, and it is frequently based on the greed or corruption of some other person or group. He includes "Lo!" with these stories, finding that here the injustice involves the whole nation (Skei 1985, 213–14).

Frederick Karl sees "Lo!" as a replaying of the Civil War in which the Yankees are outdone by the Indians (Karl 1989, 419).

There is room for more criticism of "Lo!" One could, for instance, perform a more explicit analysis of "Lo!" as a tall tale, or as a trickster tale using Carothers's work as a starting point. Investigation of language play would also be fruitful; and one might argue for a place for "Lo!" in James Watson's *William Faulkner, Letters and Fictions*. The unnamed writer of the contributors' notes for *Story* described the potential yet to be explored in the story: "It is a safe bet that anyone who reads 'Lo!' will never forget it—he will have worked too hard on it for that" ("Contributors" 1934, 4).

## Works Cited

Backman, Melvin. 1966. *Faulkner: The Major Years*. Bloomington: Indiana University Press.

Blotner, Joseph. 1974. *Faulkner: A Biography*. 2 vols. New York: Random House.

Bradford, M. E. 1964. "Faulkner and the Great White Father." *Louisiana Studies* 3:323–29.

Carothers, James B. 1984. "Faulkner's Short Stories: 'And Now What's to Do.'" In *New Directions in Faulkner Studies: Faulkner and Yoknapatawpha, 1983*. Ed. Doreen Fowler and Ann J. Abadie. Jackson: University Press of Mississippi, 202–27.

———. 1985. *William Faulkner's Short Stories*. Ann Arbor, MI: UMI Research Press.

"Contributors." 1934. *Story* 5 (November):4.

Cowley, Malcolm. 1966. *The Faulkner-Cowley File: Letters and Memories, 1944–1962*. New York: Viking.

Dabney, Lewis M. 1974. *The Indians of Yoknapatawpha: A Study in Literature and History*. Baton Rouge: Louisiana State University Press.

Dickerson, Mary Jane. [1975] 1982. "'The Magician's Wand': Faulkner's Compson Appendix." In *Critical Essays on William Faulkner: The Compson Family*. Ed. Arthur F. Kinney. Boston: G. K. Hall, 252–67.

Everett, Walter K. 1969. *Faulkner's Art and Character*. Woodbury, NY: Barron's Educational Series.

Faulkner, William. 1934. "Lo!" *Story* 5 (November):5–21.

———. 1950. *Collected Stories of William Faulkner*. New York: Random House.

———. 1959. *Faulkner in the University: Class Conferences at the University of Virginia, 1957–1958*. Ed. Frederick Gwynn and Joseph L. Blotner. Charlottesville: University Press of Virginia.

———. 1977. *Selected Letters of William Faulkner*. Ed. Joseph Blotner. New York: Random House.

Ferguson, James. 1991. *Faulkner's Short Fiction*. Knoxville: University of Tennessee Press.

Gidley, Mick. 1990. "Sam Fathers's Fathers: Indians and the Idea of Inheritance." In *Critical Essays on William Faulkner: The McCaslin Family*. Ed. Arthur F. Kinney. Boston: G. K. Hall, 121–31.

Gresset, Michel. 1985. *A Faulkner Chronology*. Trans. Arthur B. Scharff. Jackson: University Press of Mississippi.

Howell, Elmo. 1967. "President Jackson and William Faulkner's Choctaws." *Chronicles of Oklahoma* 45:252–58.

Karl, Frederick R. 1989. *William Faulkner: American Writer*. New York: Weidenfeld and Nicolson.

Kinney, Arthur F. 1980. "Faulkner's Narrative Poetics and *Collected Stories*." *Faulkner Studies* 1:58–79.

Kinney, Arthur F., and Doreen Fowler. 1983. "For the Record: Faulkner's Rowan Oak Papers: A Census." *Journal of Modern Literature* 10:327–34.

Meriwether, James B. 1973. "Faulkner's Correspondence with *Scribner's Magazine*." *Proof* 3:253–82.

Nilon, Charles H. 1965. *Faulkner and the Negro*. New York: Citadel.

Reed, Joseph. 1984. *Three American Originals: John Ford, William Faulkner and Charles Ives*. Middletown, CT: Wesleyan University Press.

Skei, Hans H. 1981. *William Faulkner: The Short Story Career*. Oslo, Norway: Universitetsforlaget.

———. 1985. *William Faulkner: The Novelist as Short Story Writer*. Oslo, Norway: Universitetsforlaget.

Taylor, Walter. 1987. "Yoknapatawpha's Indians: A Novel Faulkner Never Wrote." In *The Modernists: Studies in a Literary Phenomenon*. Ed. L. B. Gamache and I. S. MacNiven. Rutherford, NJ: Fairleigh Dickinson University Press, 202–09.

Tuck, Dorothy. 1964. *Crowell's Handbook of Faulkner*. New York: Thomas Y. Crowell.

Watkins, Floyd C. 1976. "Habet: Faulkner and the Ownership of Property." In *Faulkner: Fifty Years After* The Marble Faun. Ed. George H. Wolfe. University: University of Alabama Press, 123–37.

Watson, James G. 1987. *William Faulkner: Letters & Fictions*. Austin: University of Texas Press.

*The Middle Ground*

# Wash

## Publication History

"Wash" was first published in *Harper's* in February 1934, the same month in which "Elly," "A Bear Hunt," and "Pennsylvania Station" appeared in other magazines. Apparently, Morton Goldman handled the sale to *Harper's*, which was made on November 2, 1933, for $350. "Wash" was collected in *Doctor Martino and Other Stories* (1934) and in "The Middle Ground" section of *Collected Stories* (1950). Malcolm Cowley used "Wash" in the *Portable Faulkner* (1946), and it also appeared in the *Faulkner Reader* (1954) (Blotner 1974, 819, 825; Skei 1981, 81).

## Circumstances of Composition, Sources, and Influences

"Wash" was written in the summer of 1933, and like many of the stories Faulkner produced between 1933 and 1941, it was related to a novel he wrote later—in this instance *Absalom, Absalom!* (Skei 1981, 80–81). David Ragan remarks that the "specific motivation for the composition of 'Wash' is unclear," but Faulkner had been working on the Snopes material and the story grew from that source (1987, 5). Louis Brodsky examined the holograph drafts and typescripts of "Wash" and found that although the story underwent numerous changes, the basic elements of the plot were present from the beginning. The changes reflect Faulkner's search for an opening and an "appropriate setting and dynamically justified motivational urgency for the ending." Faulkner was not satisfied with any of the various starts focusing either on Wash in hiding or on Sutpen. He finally arrived at the opening that shows in the immediate present Sutpen's cruel rejection of Milly and his infant daughter. The effect is to reveal Wash's dilemma at once and to involve the reader in his crisis (*WFM 13*, Introduction xi; Brodsky 1984, 248–81; Brodsky 1988, 114–37). As Ragan notes, additional effects of beginning the story with Milly are to increase the tension in the account of her seduction, to alter the chronology, and to make the presentation more dramatic (Ragan 1987, 6).

Changes in "Wash" from magazine to *Doctor Martino* are minimal: the hyphen in *granddaughter* was eliminated and the adverbial form *absolutely* was adopted (*Harpers* 263, 265; *DM* 236, 240). From one collection to another,

*Collected Stories* employs standard capitalization of *Negro* (*DM* 223ff; *CS* 535ff).

Biographical traces in the fiction are limited and vague. Frederick Karl suggests that there are "glints and glimmers" of events in Faulkner's life contemporary with his writing "Wash": the death of a patriarch (Sutpen), coming so soon after the death of Murry Falkner, William's father; the murder of an infant, coming so shortly after the birth of Faulkner's own child; Wash's burning the cabin with his granddaughter's and great-granddaughter's bodies in it, coming as the writer was renovating Rowan Oak. Karl also sees the story as reflecting the author's emotional life. Faulkner, who had assumed the patriarchal role after his father's death, "was measuring the very nature of patriarchal rule" and adding to its multiple familial conflicts a racial element (Karl 1989, 504–05).

There is little substantive discussion of literary analogues for "Wash." Citing Malcolm Cowley's comparison of Faulkner and Hawthorne, Jack Stewart points out that the "symbolic stage-setting" in the opening "is certainly worthy of Hawthorne" (Stewart 1968, 589). James Carothers likens Wash's killing Sutpen to the Easterner's explanation of why the gambler kills the Swede in Stephen Crane's "The Blue Hotel," that is, the sense of being inevitably propelled into action over which one has no control and by which one gains no personal significance (1985, 37).

## Relationship to Other Faulkner Works

It is not surprising that the stature of *Absalom, Absalom!* has tended to shape the critical response to "Wash," for it is difficult to respond to "Wash" without seeing it through the larger context of the novel. Accordingly, much commentary on "Wash" is comparative.

"Wash" is only one of the stories critics have associated with the construction of *Absalom, Absalom!*. Carothers offers the most extensive list of the short works that were absorbed into *Absalom, Absalom!*: "The Big Shot," "Evangeline," "Dull Tale," and "Wash"; but Carothers affirms the autonomy of "Wash" when he comments that it, "The Hound," and "Barn Burning" "bear only superficial resemblance" to the versions that appear in the novels (1985, 127, 205).

Karl believes "Evangeline" is the "most direct source" for *Absalom*, and Ragan asserts that "Wash" may have suggested how the three stories "The Big Shot," "Evangeline," and "Wash" could be interwoven into a longer work (Karl 1989, 515; Ragan 1987, 6). While other critics are less inclined to prioritize the stories' relative contributions to the novel, they do find the origins of the longer work in the merger of these shorter narratives. Early manuscript drafts show that *Absalom, Absalom!* begins when Faulkner "took the central situation of 'Wash' and attempted to graft it onto the matter of 'Evangeline'" under the working title of *A Dark House*. The Jones woman Sutpen seduces is Wash's daughter here (Blotner 1974, 819, 828). From "Evangeline" to "Wash," Sutpen becomes a major character, "his personality appears full-bloom in 'Wash,'" and Wash's burning of his house recalls Raby's setting fire to Sutpen's mansion in "Evangeline" (Ragan 1987, 6–7).

Comparisons of the similarities and differences between "Wash" and *Absalom, Absalom!* have generated extensive, sometimes contradictory, responses. Edward Holmes cites the difficulty in pinpointing where the "Wash" narrative enters the novel text to demonstrate how thoroughly it has been integrated into the novel (1966, 84–85); Edwin Hunter indicates that the change from story to novel is "substantial" (1973, 84), while Joseph Blotner points out that some passages were brought into the novel with little or no change (Blotner 1974, 917–18). Holmes is prepared for disagreement when he asserts that "Wash Jones's story, excellent in both versions, is even better told in *Harper's* than in the novel" (Holmes 1966, 85–86).

Several studies reveal a number of specific points of divergence that distinguish "Wash" from *Absalom, Absalom!*. Some differences in the two texts involve the novel's deletion of Wash's burning the cabin down and Quentin's delay in revealing that the baby is female. Holmes points out that the story makes this fact known on the first page, without sacrificing "intensity of effect or cogency of theme" (Holmes 1966, 85–86). In "Wash" the deaths are the end of the story, but in the novel, they are "prehistoric events" that "have significance and consequences far beyond the immediate moment of their occurrence" (Carothers 1985, 37).

The particulars of characterization also reflect important differences. *Absalom* enlarges the context of "Wash" in revealing details of Sutpen's life (Minter 1992, 96). "Wash," however, shows no "design" in Sutpen's activities (Carothers 1985, 36). Harry Campbell and Ruel Foster point out how Wash's image of Sutpen in battle expands from story to novel to a "lengthier and more eloquent version" (1951, 33). As Carothers notes, in "Wash," Sutpen's wife and son (who has died in the war) are not named and are not brought into the story. Further, Sutpen's portrait in "Wash" is diminished: defeat is reflected in his near-alcoholism. In the story he is a "reeling shadow of his former greatness," but the novel emphasizes his determination to rebuild (Carothers 1985, 34; see also Ragan 1987, 7). The intensity of Sutpen's drive to father a son is not as strong in the story as it is in the novel. Richard Adams notes that the story, unlike the novel, gives facts about Sutpen without explanation. It is clear, for example, that Sutpen in "Wash" wants a male heir, but there is no attempt to explain that his desire relates to his design of a Sutpen dynasty built according to his vision of Southern aristocracy (1968, 175). In the novel Sutpen's rejection of Milly and their child is placed in the larger context of his failed "design" and more explicitly because the child is not a son. In the short story, Sutpen's rejection of the child has less to do with his desire for a son than with a general disregard for the consequences of his activities (Hunter 1973, 88; Carothers 1985, 34, 36).

Another issue that varies from story to novel is class consciousness. When Faulkner was asked about the ironic significance in having Wash Jones kill Sutpen, Faulkner agreed that being cut down by someone from the same roots as Sutpen did lend to that reading. But he added this comment about Jones: "In another sense Wash Jones represented the man who survived the Civil War. The aristocrat in the columned house was ruined but Wash Jones survived it unchanged. He had been Wash Jones before 1861 and after 1865 he was still Wash Jones and Sutpen finally collided with him" (*FU* 74–75). This interpretation applies more appropriately to the novel than to the short story because "Wash" does not reveal this characteristic of Sutpen's background. Joanne Creighton contends that the issue of class conflict is central to the Wash–Sutpen relationship in "Wash" because Sutpen cannot be distinguished from other "Southern gentlemen." The class-oriented conflict is "muted" in *Absalom, Absalom!* because Sutpen's background is known, as is the fact that Wash is "betrayed by one of his own kind" (1977, 12–14; Ragan 1987, 6). Adams likens Wash's agonizing recognition of class barriers in the short story to Rosa Coldfield's comments in the novel that express her approval of the South's defeat and her recognition that Sutpen is no gentleman (Adams 1968, 184). But for James Snead, in the novel and especially in the story, Wash "views Sutpen as the apotheosis of lower-class dreams" (1986, 110). When incorporated into the novel, the extensive parallels between Sutpen and Wash "suggest they are doubles": both are from poor white stock, both are rejected by black servants at a mansion's front door, and their tragedies are related to their female progeny (Ferguson 1991, 162).

Another contrast between the texts relates to their different narrative focuses. The story was "adjusted to the narrative technique and style of the longer work" (Skei 1981, 130 n. 20; see also Ragan 1987, 6). The dramatic structure of "Wash" contrasts with the multiple narrators of *Absalom, Absalom!* (Creighton 1977, 14). The story centers on Wash's consciousness while the novel shifts to a focus on Sutpen and Quentin Compson (Carothers 1985, 34–35). Neil Isaacs argues that Quentin assumes some of the functions Wash serves in the short story: those of "last celebrant," "incarnate *son*," and "reluctant perceiver of the changing of orders" (Isaacs 1963, 54). Hugh Ruppersburg distinguishes the use of an omniscient narrator in the short story and Mr. Compson in the novel. Ruppersburg cautions that although both texts convey similar information about Wash, the similarity should not imply that Mr. Compson's speculations in the novel are correct (1983, 93). Carothers sees some inconsistency in the lyrical tone of Wash's denouncement of Sutpen when contrasted with the level of his speech. The story can establish through the omniscient narrator the objective reality of Wash's action while in the novel it is "fabricated by the several raconteurs" (Carothers 1985, 37). Olga Scherer points out that Wash Jones "is treated monologically" in *Absalom, Absalom!* but "appears endowed with dialogic features" in "Wash" (1990, 315 n. 3).

An ostensibly minor change also carries the weight of meaning. Joseph Tuso notes that Faulkner changed the name of the mare from *Griselda* in the story to *Penelope* in the novel. The revision could be forgetfulness, but if one associates the mare with the trustworthy Penelope, wife of Odysseus, the name change contributes to "enhancing the epic quality of the novel," or as Carothers suggests, it may emphasize an "ironic contrast between Sutpen and Odysseus" (Tuso 1968, no. 17; Carothers 1985, 34; see also Hunter 1973, 86).

A lesser known version of Wash's struggle with Sutpen exists in a screenplay. According to Bruce Kawin, Faulkner's screenplay *Revolt in the Earth* was to be an adaptation of *Absalom, Absalom!*, but it required so much "condensation and simplification . . . that it might be better to call it an amplification of 'Wash'" (1977, 126–30).

Beyond its links to *Absalom, Absalom!*, "Wash" is intricately woven into Yoknapatawpha's other fiction. When Faulkner described his conception and development of *The Hamlet*, he told Cowley that he was working with "Barn Burning" and "Wash," but he rejected "Wash" as an "induction toward the spotted horse story" because he concluded it "had no place in that book at all" (*SL* 197). Michael Millgate credits Meriwether for the suggestion that "Wash" might have been linked to the Snopeses as a balance to Mink and to point out that Flem was atypical of his class ([1966] 1989, 326 n. 18). However, as Hans Skei observes, the problem Ab Snopes experiences with Major de Spain in "Barn Burning" is similar to Wash's experience with Sutpen (Skei 1985, 218; see also Moreland 1990 n. 1).

Examining behavior of characters has provided diverse comparisons among critics. Elizabeth Kerr compares Wash's murdering Milly and her infant daughter with Nancy's killing Temple's baby in *Requiem for a Nun*. Although Nancy acts unselfishly to save Temple and the other child, Wash acts from a recognition of the "illusion of caste superiority and white solidarity" (Kerr [1969] 1976, 215). Walter Taylor compares Wash's devotion to Sutpen to the loyalty old Falls shows for John Sartoris in *Sartoris* (1983, 88).

Recurring thematic interests can generate unexpected links. "Wash" fits into an extensive pattern of initiation stories. Carothers argues that "Wash," like "many of Faulkner's best stories," involves discovering evil. "Wash" is a rare text in that the moment of epiphany reveals the nature of the character both to himself and to others (Carothers 1985, 10–11). James Ferguson states that "Wash" is a story of a "terrible loss of innocence"; it is somewhat different (though not exceptional) in that the initiate is a grandfather (1991, 62). Under the category of "Love Relationships: Triangles and Wronged Women," Ferguson points out that the man in the triangle is sometimes a father figure.

Fitting this category are such stories as "Wash," "Hair," "Mountain Victory," "Dr. Martino," and "Knight's Gambit." Wash is a more traditional father figure serving his "more conventional paternal roles," as does Mr. Meadowfill in "Hog Pawn" (Ferguson 1991, 70–71).

Another way to categorize Faulkner's short fiction is to group the abstractions in them. Faulkner has much to say about the abstraction of social class, for it appears in such stories as "Victory," "Mountain Victory," "A Rose for Emily," and "Wash" (Ferguson 1991, 81). Skei points out that in the stories written between 1933 and 1941, the protagonists are victimized by "some kind of injustice, which they either have been aware of for a long time or suddenly discover in a moment of insight and revelation" (1985, 214).

Faulkner is able to present the same theme in multiple and sometimes radically opposed variations. One of these motifs is violence that ends in murder, which he developed in such different stories as "Wash," "The Hound," "A Rose for Emily," "Dry September," "Mountain Victory," *The Unvanquished*, and *Knight's Gambit* (Carothers 1985, 20–21). Olga Vickery points out that when Faulkner does not "dramatize the conclusive action" in "Wash," "That Evening Sun," "Dry September," and other texts, it serves to "intensify the dominant emotion and to project it beyond the story itself" (1964, 301).

Recalling the diversity of dwellings in Faulkner's fiction, James Watson considers "easy stereotypes of farm houses and antebellum mansions" inadequate to represent Faulkner's work. As a case in point, Watson shows how the big houses and cabins in "Wash" and "Barn Burning" evoke place but also work as counterpoint to each other (Watson 1980, 137).

Prior to the appearance of *Absalom, Absalom!*, "Wash" was recognized as a powerful short story. In collection, it regains some identity as a text independent of the novel. For reviewer Fred Marsh, "Wash" was the best story in *Doctor Martino*; Millgate considered it one of the few stories in that collection that matched the quality of *These 13* (Emerson 1984, 29; Millgate [1966] 1989, 265). Ferguson finds justice to be a thematic link in the *Doctor Martino* studies. In "Beyond," "Wash," "Elly," "Black Music," and "The Leg," the protagonists act in revolt against what they perceive to be an injustice (1991, 154).

It is somewhat surprising that "Wash" appears in *Collected Stories* because typically stories that had been revised for novels were not included. Perhaps Faulkner forgot the story's evolution; others involved in the project might have influenced the decision, or Faulkner may have felt that "Wash" remained sufficiently independent of the novel (Skei 1981, 82, 130 n. 22). Carothers believes that Faulkner's continued willingness to use "Wash" in collection "suggests both his own high regard for the story and his awareness that it is quite different from the novel version of the same events" (1985, 34). In *Collected Stories*, "The Middle Ground" section seems a miscellaneous collection, but all the stories deal with "themes of deracination and disillusion, with the loss of familiar bearings." In "Wash" the consequences are tragic, but other stories suggest comic implications. All of "The Middle Ground" stories address death, either symbolic or physical (Millgate [1966] 1989, 273–74). Arthur Kinney argues that the apparently "ramshackle" collection of stories in "The Middle Ground" is actually a "conscious, cognitive *arrangement*." The murders and suicide of the opening story, "Wash," reverberate in the murders in the closing story, "Mountain Victory," another story about hill people. Also, the "sudden recognition" and surge of passion in "Wash" return in the "more certain reaping of intrusive life" in "Mountain Victory." "Wash" is an "extraordinary index" to the despair that accrues through the collection. Wash's precarious existence as friend of Sutpen is like Monaghan's wing walking in "Honor." Kinney describes Sutpen's hatred of Milly as a "projection of his own profound despair and self-accusing anger" that appears elsewhere in the collection (1980, 72). Carothers sees "The Middle Ground" stories as "investigations of the twin themes of sex and death" but also as reflections of "Faulkner's belief that 'everyone is capable of almost anything'" (Carothers 1985, 59). Among those stories, "Wash" falls geographically with the Yoknapatawpha stories and temporally with "Mountain Victory" in the period just after the Civil War (Carothers 1985, 59). Ferguson believes only excessive ingenuity can identify order in a section where there is "no readily discernible pattern," but some parallels can be found. The opening "Wash" and concluding "Mountain Victory" both concern events after the Civil War and both involve a young girl and an older man (1991, 159).

## Interpretation and Criticism

In his review of *Doctor Martino*, William Rose Benét judges "Wash" to be "rather a melodramatic 'set-up'" (1934, 645). Benét sees the movement of the story as "dumb fealty assuming proportions of the heroic in the role of avenger" (1934, 645). Subsequent critics, including both Millgate and Hyatt Waggoner, have praised the story highly (Millgate [1966] 1989, 262; Waggoner 1959, 195). Irving Howe describes "Wash" as a "taut narrative, violent and self-contained." It shows little dependence on the novel: "But the significance of Sutpen's contempt for Milly Jones and of the ultimate rebellion, the final trace of dignity in Wash Jones—these are fully and bitterly evoked in the story itself" (Howe [1952] 1975, 265–66). Although he thinks the story is diminished by the larger context of the novel, William Van O'Connor says it "remains a masterly piece of compression, the action seeming to move inside locally accepted notions of caste but suddenly whipping about, a peripety that destroys Sutpen and elevates Wash Jones to a position of great dignity" (1954, 89). Holmes calls it "finely wrought and highly moving" (1966, 83). Skei describes it as "one of Faulkner's taut and forceful short narratives, self-contained and complete in itself despite its close relationship to *Absalom, Absalom!* (1985, 216). Karl considers "Wash" to be "tight, controlled, directed, firm"—"part of the central Faulkner vision, which is one of decline, deterioration, holding on, ultimately death" (Karl 1989, 507).

The characterization of Wash provokes some commentary, but surprisingly few comments about Sutpen relate to the qualities of the individual apart from his social context. Howe suggests that Wash feels some pride in his granddaughter's having been chosen by Sutpen ([1952] 1975, 265). For Holmes, the story is about Sutpen's inability to recognize that people want not only "economic equity but respect, and loyalty, and love." The reader feels some sympathy for Wash because he expresses "tender and gentle" concern for the progeny he is about to kill. The narrative evokes "high, tragic sorrow for Wash, for in a sense all trusting, and betrayed, and groping mankind" (Holmes 1966, 83–84). Blotner describes Wash Jones as a "malaria-ridden poor white" who undergoes a revelation that he totally misinterpreted Sutpen (1974, 819). Skei emphasizes that Wash consistently misinterprets relationships: he believes that he is superior to the blacks on Sutpen's plantation and that if God should appear on earth, God would take the image of Sutpen on his horse. Skei continues, "Jones suffers from his own illusions about Sutpen and from what Sutpen apparently understands as his aristocratic right to own and use other people." "Wash" "is mostly a story about a *situation* which develops into tragic, apocalyptic drama when Wash suddenly *sees* and understand[s] what Sutpen *is* and *does*." As the story progresses, "illusion has to give way to reality or disillusionment, and where violence is Wash Jones's only means to preserve some of the pride he has vainly and falsely asserted all his life by apotheosizing Sutpen" (Skei, 1985, 214, 216).

This explanation shows how thoroughly the characters of Wash and Sutpen are molded by the social conditions of their time and place. Their actions are best illuminated by those discussions that examine the cultural milieu Faulkner portrays. Most critics would agree with Blotner's comment that this story "of seduction and retribution" bears symbolic import (Blotner 1974, 819), for critics frequently read the story as a condemnation of Southern history and class stratification. Ward Miner believes Wash's despairing revelation represents Faulkner's belief that the lost war and deterioration of the South related directly to its failed moral code (1952, 134; see also Isaacs 1963, 47; Karl 1989, 508). For Millgate, Wash perceives Sutpen as the "supreme embodiment of all that is best in the South," which finally "cannot bring itself to recognise even the simplest human need of its inferiors, the need to be recognised as human" ([1961] 1966, 57; see also Tuck 1964, 181–82).

Using information from both "Wash" and *Absalom, Absalom!*, Shirley Callen compares Faulkner's portrayal of the relationship between planter and poor white with W. J. Cash's study of these same links in *The Mind of the South*. Callen believes Faulkner's portrayal is consistent with Cash's except that Faulkner includes a hint of resentment in Jones. Typically the poor white, Jones, affirms, honors, and obliges the planter class, identifying with it despite its inherently patronizing and derisive attitude. Through the years of their relationship, Wash acknowledges Sutpen's superiority by avoiding entrance into the mansion and by assuming an inferior pose, but during and after the war, these signs of difference begin to blur. Wash eventually gains entrance to the mansion as nursemaid to the drunken Sutpen. Nevertheless, his belief that they will become equals by Sutpen's marriage is shattered. Callen describes Sutpen's striking Wash across the face with his whip as the "classic action of an aristocrat toward a despised inferior" (Callen 1963, 24–36).

Elmo Howell comes to a different conclusion from most who study the class stratification in "Wash." He decides that it is finally an affirmation of the belief that lower classes can improve by modeling the behavior of those in a higher social rank. Howell believes "Wash" functions both to portray the complex social relations in the South and to convey "dignity to the most depraved of men." Wash authentically represents the squatter who lived on plantations. He is rare in Faulkner's work because he is a fully developed portrait of this class. Wash has some ambition and feels pride in the aura of Sutpen, but he fails to see the planter's ignoble nature. Sutpen represents the repercussion of inordinate pride as it filters from one class to another. "But," Howell adds, "the story is not a repudiation of the aristocratic concept so much as a criticism of it." Sutpen does not accept the moral responsibility incumbent on his position. The story implies that there are possibilities for good influence in the stratified society. At the end, Wash, who might have run, has at least been moved to stand up for himself. In its fullest implications beyond duties to class, the story presents a "challenge to those whom nature or fortune has placed above the average of mankind but more immediately to any man who stands in a position of trust to another" (Howell 1967, 8–12).

Stewart says that "'Wash' may be Faulkner's most concentrated parable of Southern degeneracy in the aftermath of the Civil War." Set against a "regional, historical, social, and cosmic background," interdependence among people becomes conflict that symbolizes the collapse of a feudal system and a "movement from mythical past to grim present." Faulkner builds the text around four scenes: the first three apotheosize Sutpen and the final scene portrays the apocalypse of the system. Sutpen's portraits lack a human quality; they are either bestial horse images intertwining masculine power and the power of horses or distanced deification. But as Stewart states, "The basic paradox of Sutpen's character is that, while his pose is heroic, and his appearance godlike, his responses are those of a beast." Wash's unrealistic elevation of Sutpen comes partly from his own sense of inferiority to Sutpen and partly from his racist view of superiority to the blacks on the plantation. Even the verb choices reveal the relative positions of the characters in social rank. There is an ironic parallel between Sutpen's seduction of Milly physically and

Wash mentally. When Wash finally acts, he becomes a "symbol of rootless man in rebellion against the tyrannous landowning class." Stewart concludes, "Out of the bankruptcy of the feudal order arises the apocalyptic figure of the man with the scythe, the silent, self-destroying prophet of social revolution" (1968, 586–600).

Also pursuing the issue of class stratification, Charles Peavy notes the portrayal of Wash as socially beneath the blacks at Sutpen's Hundred. Wash is reluctant to test his ground in Sutpen's house, and he resents the blacks whom he perceives as beneath him socially but who live better than he does (Peavy 1971, 19).

Sylvia Cook describes "Wash" as a story that "deals with anachronistic loyalty between poor white and landlord and explores the psychological foundations on which this loyalty is built" (1976, 51). The story reveals the paradox of a class-stratified society in which the members of the disparate groups "live in close physical intimacy." Wash's devotion to Sutpen is rooted in neither financial dependence nor gratitude for friendship but in an adoption of the "idea of Sutpen" that "fills a void in the desolate world of the poor white." Sutpen provides a sort of alter ego for Wash until, in his cruel rejection of the infant, Sutpen's real character can no longer be ignored. To an extent, though Wash has held onto a false image of Sutpen's virtue, he himself seems to be changed in the experience. He is "ennobled" in the transition from "lazy shiftlessness to courageous avenging fury." Cook adds, however, that Wash's change does not necessarily imply a "complete rejection of the class structure" (1976, 51–53).

Skei addresses the implications of Wash's continued violence after having slain Sutpen. Wash reacts not only against Sutpen but also against the social order Sutpen represents. The planter's death does not eliminate the larger problem of the structure and "all the *living* Sutpens from whom men like Wash Jones can never escape." Wash makes a decision "as if he were not only jury and judge but actually God himself" to remove himself and his kind from the earth (Skei 1985, 218).

Wesley Morris and Barbara Morris follow Cook's analysis of "Wash," agreeing that its theme is "awakening poor white class-consciousness." The Morrises see Wash as having only a limited understanding of the class oppression in which he has lived. He is more involved at a personal level in the loss of his idol. The larger message to the reader is "that such idols, regardless of personal despair, must be brought down if progress in deconstructing social injustice is to be made" (Morris and Morris 1989, 16–17).

Although starting from a slightly different perspective, Carothers and David Minter also emphasize the class stratification in the story. Examining Sutpen's "commercial seduction" of Milly, Carothers thinks the man errs in believing that Wash will maintain his subservience to Sutpen when the honor of the women of his family is involved. Wash discovers the danger of assuming the "divinity or innate superiority." Wash's murder of his granddaughter and the infant "are but the logical application of his new knowledge" (Carothers 1985, 35; Carothers 1992, 51). According to Minter, part of the bond that exists between Sutpen and Wash is that they are not female and that they are not black. The story establishes historical and social contexts more pointedly than it does psychological ones. All three main characters desire freedom from the restrictions imposed by circumstance. They want to change their past. The ending involves Wash's relinquishing the dream for himself and for his progeny (Minter 1992, 93–96).

Isaacs elevates the interpretation of "Wash" from sociological to mythic criticism. Isaacs describes "Wash" as a "form of the mythic archetype of the death of the gods." For Wash Jones, Sutpen is a horse-god. When Wash's faith system fails, he, having invested in that structure, crashes like the god does, and "purgation prepares the way for a new order to take over." It is, of course, an ironic treatment given the amoral character of Sutpen and the self-serving attitude of Wash. Isaacs points out that the opening tableau is an ironic manger setting with mother attending child in a rude shelter. Sutpen's entrance, with sunlight streaming in and Sutpen standing wide of stride, whip in hand, constitutes a parody of the adoration scene.

The rejection of human for horse then begins the chain of events that precipitates Sutpen's downfall. The image as Sutpen leaves the cabin captures the stallion, the scythe, and Wash holding the horse for Sutpen. Sutpen is Wash's god, created in Wash's image of how he imagines God would return to earth. Wash appropriately worships a horse, a symbol of power and virility, images appealing to a powerless man. Isaacs also traces the images of decay in the "rank weeds" and rusty scythe and of disorder in the "inversions and ironies." Despite the lost war, decayed house, and return of an aged Sutpen, Wash persists in deifying him. Isaacs points out that Wash's perspective contains the elements of a credo: he identifies Sutpen as a horse-god and elevates him from hero to divinity; he believes that his faith ennobles him and his faith is self-justifying. Eventually, Wash's faith collapses "through the failure of the godhead." Wash finally acts as "sacrificial priest," striking down the now defunct god. Wash sees in the posse more of Sutpen's kind. His final charge against them ends not with the portrayal of his death, but his "devotedly *wash*ing the world free of them and all they stand for" (Isaacs 1963, 47–55).

The formal characteristics of "Wash" demonstrate Faulkner's expertise in short fiction. As noted in previous discussion, one of the significant alterations of this story for the novel involved the revision of the narrative perspective. The story gives precedence to Wash's, not Sutpen's, point of view through an omniscient narrator (Millgate [1961] 1966, 57–58; Blotner 1974, 819). Ferguson describes the perspective as a limited third-person point of view that has the ability to dramatize "consciousness in the process of discovery" (1991,

98–99). Stephen Ross shows how "Wash" employs a "rhetorical hierarchy of imaged speech." Given Wash's ridicule by the black characters who see him as their inferior, his speech is "heavily stylized to lower it to its appropriate level 'beneath' black speech" (Ross 1989, 109).

The narrative structure reflects Faulkner's talent for presenting the events cohesively but in an order other than chronological. Stewart describes the temporal arrangement as "cinematic" and "cyclic," intensifying the narrative. Faulkner employs the "frozen moment" at both beginning and end. Two internal sections constitute flashbacks to the events precipitating the final crisis and serve to define the story's motivation (1968, 588–89; see also Blotner 1974, 819). (Isaacs calls the return to events leading to the birth an "old-fashioned, honest-to-goodness flashback" [1963, 48].)

Skei points out that although the story does not show sectional divisions, it has "easily discernible phases." The opening scene constitutes "one of Faulkner's marvellous frozen tableaux" that anticipates what is to come in its portrayal of Sutpen's arrogance and cynicism, the scythe, and the weeds. The central portion contains two subsections: the flashback in which Wash recalls his relationship with Sutpen, then the return to present time when Milly gives birth to her daughter. The final scene reverses the perspective—from Sutpen's view of Milly to Wash's; but Faulkner does not directly describe the violence of the murders. The "narrator moves aside and looks in another direction" (Skei 1985, 216–17). Stewart shows how Faulkner's use of oxymoron and complex rhythm in the final scene of Wash's charge on the posse intensifies the scene's effect, a passage that Karl considers representative of Faulkner at his best (Stewart 1968, 599; Karl 1989, 508).

The story also employs numerous symbolic images. The scythe recalls Father Time and Cronus's castration of Uranus to ensure regeneration of the land (Isaacs 1963, 53). It implies that Sutpen's foremost enemy is time (Adams 1968, 193). The height of the sun during the events of the story also adds symbolic import. In the dawn, Wash sees Sutpen as he really is; he kills Sutpen in full daylight, and in the sunset, Wash kills his granddaughter, presumably the infant as well, and sets fire to the cabin (Skei 1985, 217–18).

Tuso finds that Faulkner's choice of the name *Griselda* for the mare is suggestive of Chaucer's Griselda, who obliges a brutal master, comes from poor stock, like Milly, and bears a child by him (Tuso 1968, no. 17). Stewart also cites the medieval romance as emphasizing the mare's nobility. He adds that the sire's name, *Rob Roy*, comes from Sir Walter Scott's "swashbuckling hero" (Stewart 1968, 590).

The criticism discussed here shows that "Wash" merits attention as an independent text. It is unfortunate that in their story summaries, Walter Everett, Robert Kirk and Marvin Klotz, and Thomas Connolly have all omitted independent synopses of "Wash" (Everett 1969, 181; Kirk and Klotz 1963 279; Connolly 1988). Once one has knowledge of *Absalom, Absalom!*, it is nearly impossible to read "Wash" without superimposing Sutpen's fuller story on the action. But the attempt to read closely within the narrative lines of the story is worthwhile. Carothers echoes many critics when he describes "Wash" as "one of Faulkner's best stories," and Ferguson offers no exaggeration when he states, "'Wash' is, in its own right, a superlative story—moving, evocative, beautifully written" (Carothers 1985, 38; Ferguson 1991, 162).

## Works Cited

Adams, Richard P. 1968. *Faulkner: Myth and Motion*. Princeton, NJ: Princeton University Press.

Bénet, William Rose. 1934. "Fourteen Faulkner Stories." *Saturday Review of Literature* 21 April, 645.

Blotner, Joseph. 1974. *Faulkner: A Biography*. 2 vols. New York: Random House.

Brodsky, Louis Daniel. 1984. "The Textual Development of William Faulkner's 'Wash': An Examination of Manuscripts in the Brodsky Collection." *Studies in Bibliography* 37:248–81.

———. 1988. *Faulkner: A Comprehensive Guide to the Brodsky Collection*. Vol. 5 Manuscripts and Documents. Jackson: University Press of Mississippi.

Callen, Shirley. 1963. "Planter and Poor White in *Absalom, Absalom!*, "Wash," and *The Mind of the South*." *South Central Bulletin* 23.4:24–36.

Campbell, Harry Modean, and Ruel E. Foster. 1951. *William Faulkner: A Critical Appraisal*. Norman: University of Oklahoma Press.

Carothers, James B. 1985. *William Faulkner's Short Stories*. Ann Arbor, MI: UMI Research Press.

———. 1992. "Faulkner's Short Story Writing and the Oldest Profession." In *Faulkner and the Short Story: Faulkner and Yoknapatawpha, 1990*. Ed. Evans Harrington and Ann J. Abadie. Jackson: University Press of Mississippi, 38–61.

Connolly, Thomas E. 1988. *Faulkner's World: A Directory of His People and Synopses of Actions in His Published Works*. Lanham, MD: University Press of America.

Cook, Sylvia Jenkins. 1976. *From Tobacco Road to Route 66: The Southern Poor White in Fiction*. Chapel Hill: University of North Carolina Press.

Creighton, Joanne V. 1977. *William Faulkner's Craft of Revision: The Snopes Trilogy, "The Unvanquished," and "Go Down, Moses."* Detroit: Wayne State University Press.

Emerson, O. B. 1984. *Faulkner's Early Literary Reputation in America*. Ann Arbor, MI: UMI Research Press.

Everett, Walter K. 1969. *Faulkner's Art and Character*. Woodbury, NY: Barron's Educational Series.

Faulkner, William. 1934. "Wash." *Harper's* 168 (February): 258–66.

———. 1934. *Doctor Martino and Other Stories*. New York: Harrison Smith and Robert Haas.

———. 1950. *Collected Stories of William Faulkner*. New York: Random House.

———. 1959. *Faulkner in the University: Class Conferences at the University of Virginia, 1957–1958*. Ed. Frederick Gwynn and Joseph L. Blotner. Charlottesville: University Press of Virginia.

———. 1977. *Selected Letters of William Faulkner*. Ed. Joseph Blotner. New York: Random House.

———. 1987. *William Faulkner Manuscripts 13:* Absalom, Absalom! Ed. Noel Polk. New York: Garland.

Ferguson, James. 1991. *Faulkner's Short Fiction*. Knoxville: University of Tennessee Press.

Holmes, Edward M. 1966. *Faulkner's Twice-Told Tales: His Re-Use of His Material*. The Hague: Mouton.

Howe, Irving. [1952] 1975. *William Faulkner: A Critical Study*. 3d ed. Chicago: University of Chicago Press.

Howell, Elmo. 1967. "Faulkner's Wash Jones and the Southern Poor White." *Ball State University Forum* 8.1:8–12.

Hunter, Edwin R. 1973. *William Faulkner: Narrative Practice and Prose Style*. Washington, DC: Windhover.

Isaacs, Neil D. 1963. "Götterdammerung in Yoknapatawpha." *Tennessee Studies in Literature* 8:47–55.

Karl, Frederick R. 1989. *William Faulkner: American Writer*. New York: Weidenfeld and Nicolson.

Kawin, Bruce F. 1977. *Faulkner and Film*. New York: Frederick Ungar.

Kerr, Elizabeth M. [1969] 1976. *Yoknapatawpha: Faulkner's "Little Postage Stamp of Native Soil."* New York: Fordham University Press.

Kinney, Arthur F. 1980. "Faulkner's Narrative Poetics and *Collected Stories*." *Faulkner Studies* 1:58–79.

Kirk, Robert W., and Marvin Klotz. 1963. *Faulkner's People: A Complete Guide and Index to Characters in the Fiction of William Faulkner*. Berkeley and Los Angeles: University of California Press.

Millgate, Michael. [1961] 1966. *William Faulkner*. New York: Barnes & Noble.

———. [1966] 1989. *The Achievement of William Faulkner*. New York: Random House. Reprint. Athens: University of Georgia Press. Brown Thrasher Books.

Miner, Ward L. 1952. *The World of William Faulkner*. Durham, NC: Duke University Press.

Minter, David. 1992. "'Carcassone,' 'Wash,' and the Voices of Faulkner's Fiction." In *Faulkner and the Short Story: Faulkner and Yoknapatawpha, 1990*. Ed. Evans Harrington and Ann J. Abadie. Jackson: University Press of Mississippi, 78–107.

Moreland, Richard C. 1990. *Faulkner and Modernism: Rereading and Rewriting*. Madison: University of Wisconsin Press.

Morris, Wesley, and Barbara Alverson Morris. 1989. *Reading Faulkner*. Madison: University of Wisconsin Press.

O'Connor, William Van. 1954. *The Tangled Fire of William Faulkner*. Minneapolis: University of Minnesota Press.

Peavy, Charles D. 1971. *Go Slow Now: Faulkner and the Race Question*. Eugene: University of Oregon Books.

Ragan, David Paul. 1987. *William Faulkner's* Absalom, Absalom!: *A Critical Study*. Ann Arbor, MI: UMI Research Press.

Ross, Stephen M. 1989. *Fiction's Inexhaustible Voice: Speech and Writing in Faulkner*. Athens: University of Georgia Press.

Ruppersburg, Hugh M. 1983. *Voice and Eye in Faulkner's Fiction*. Athens: University of Georgia Press.

Scherer, Olga. 1990. "A Dialogic Hereafter: *The Sound and the Fury* and *Absalom,Absalom!*." In *Southern Literature and Literary Theory*. Ed. Jefferson Humphries. Athens: University of Georgia Press, 300–17.

Skei, Hans H. 1981. *William Faulkner: The Short Story Career*. Oslo, Norway: Universitetsforlaget.

———. 1985. *William Faulkner: The Novelist as Short Story Writer*. Oslo, Norway: Universitetsforlaget.

Snead, James A. 1986. *Figures of Division: William Faulkner's Major Novels*. New York: Methuen.

Stewart, Jack F. 1968. "Apotheosis and Apocalypse in Faulkner's 'Wash.'" *Studies in Short Fiction* 6:586–600.

Taylor, Walter. 1983. *Faulkner's Search for a South*. Urbana: University of Illinois Press.

Tuck, Dorothy. 1964. *Crowell's Handbook of Faulkner*. New York: Thomas Y. Crowell.

Tuso, Joseph F. 1968. "Faulkner's Wash." *Explicator* 27: Item 17.

Vickery, Olga W. [1959] 1964. *The Novels of William Faulkner*. Baton Rouge: Louisiana State University Press.

Waggoner, Hyatt H. 1959. *William Faulkner: From Jefferson to the World*. Lexington: University of Kentucky Press.

Watson, James G. 1980. "Faulkner: The House of Fiction." *Fifty Years of Yoknapatawpha: Faulkner and Yoknapatawpha 1979*. Ed. Doreen Fowler and Ann J. Abadie. Jackson: University Press of Mississippi, 134–58.

# Honor

## Publication History

"Honor" was published in July 1930 in the *American Mercury*, Faulkner's second short story to appear in a national magazine. He had sent "Point of Honor" to the *Saturday Evening Post* on March 7, 1930, but the editors had rejected the story. On March 25, Faulkner sent "Honor" to *Scribner's*, where it was also rejected. On April 22, 1930, Faulkner forwarded the story to the *American Mercury*, which accepted it; Ben Wasson may have helped in gaining this sale. "Honor" was not included in Faulkner's first collection, *These 13* (1931), but it was part of *Doctor Martino* (1934) and *Collected Stories* (1950). Movie rights to "Honor" were sold to RKO (Meriwether [1961] 1971, 173, 174, 176–79; Blotner 1974, 649–50, 655, 1219).

## Circumstances of Composition, Sources, and Influences

Critics are unable to trace prepublication developments in "Honor" because no manuscript of the story exists, but they are confident, based on similarities of titles and proximity of dates, that "Honor" and "Point of Honor" are the same story (Meriwether [1961] 1971, 173, 174; Blotner 1974, 649; Skei 1981, 61).

The only difference in the published texts of "Honor" is in the spelling of one word: *handwriting* in *American Mercury*, *hand writing* in *Doctor Martino*, restored to *handwriting* in *Collected Stories* (*American Mercury* 273; *DRM* 370; *CS* 563).

Although minimal information is available about the composition of "Honor," there are some clear biographical links between the story and the life of the author. "Honor" may reflect Faulkner's interest in the Gates Flying Circus that had intrigued him in New Orleans in 1925 and during his visits to the Memphis airport (Blotner 1974, 649). James Watson argues that Faulkner created an aviator persona that stood between the world and Faulkner and also became a way for Faulkner to write himself into his fiction, especially in the aviation stories from the early 1930s, including "Honor," "Death Drag," and "Turnabout" (1987, 4). Further, the description of uniformed students walking across campuses resembles Faulkner's experience at New Haven in 1918 (Blotner 1974, 649; 1984, 257).

## Relationship to Other Faulkner Works

In February 1933, while on MGM's payroll but working at home, Faulkner received a film adaptation of "Honor." He probably did little more than read the work already done by Harry Behn (*SL* 73; Blotner 1974, 795; 1984, 313). Bruce Kawin considers the screenplay "very fine" and suggests that it may have been abandoned because of its sexual subject matter or because, prior to its completion, *The Story of Temple Drake* received bad reviews and discouraged further efforts to produce Faulkner's fiction in film (1977, 39–40; see also Skei 1981, 75, 129 n. 298; Phillips 1988, 112–13).

The existence of the character Monaghan was not dependent on the screenplay, however, for he made appearances in prior and subsequent fiction. "Honor" focuses on the postwar aerobatic career of Monaghan, but he also appears in the World War I story "Ad Astra." Monaghan actually recalls the events of "Ad Astra" in a paragraph in "Honor," and he quotes the subadar, a character in "Ad Astra," in a context that demonstrates Monaghan's new understanding of the subadar's statement (Blotner 1974, 649). Like "There Was a Queen," "Honor" appears as a story sequel to the novel *Sartoris*. Both stories occur after the events of the novel and extend the action of particular characters from the novel (Carothers 1985, 26–27). Monaghan also appears in the later World War II novel *A Fable* (1954).

World War I soldiers and veterans continue to populate Faulkner's long and short fiction. Monaghan is clearly a character who interested Faulkner, for he fits a general type that reappears commonly in Faulkner's writing. In 1935, Aubrey Starke compared Monaghan and Bayard Sartoris, who had appeared together in *Sartoris*. They both display the "same disillusionment and bitterness" after the war (Emerson 1984, 58, 60). Like Sentry in *A Fable*, Monaghan is introduced as a hardened, tough man, and as the story unfolds, the reader learns how he came to be that way. Both men reveal some capacity for unselfish action (Carothers 1985, 18, 40). Monaghan also resembles Jock in "Death Drag," as both are drifters and casualties of war (Blotner 1974, 862).

Nancy Sederberg recognizes similarities among the older officers—Rogers in "Honor," Jock and Captain Warren in "Death Drag," and Captain Bogard in "Turnabout." They anticipate majors Hough and Fritz Goar in the first typescript of "With Caution and Dispatch." Also, the use of airplanes for both economic and entertainment purposes in "Honor" and "Death Drag" anticipates the treatment of war in both "serious and antic aspects" in "With Caution and Dispatch" (Sederberg 1985, 198). Faulkner also worked with aviator characters when he was assigned to work on an MGM script, *Flying the Mail*, that had been written by Ralph Graves and Bernard Fineman (Blotner 1974, 862).

When questioned about the assertion in "All the Dead Pilots" and "Honor" that those who fought in World War I were dead for the remainder of their lives, Faulkner responded: "They had exhausted themselves psychically . . . [author's ellipses] anyway, they were unfitted for the world that they found afterward. Not that they rejected [life], they simply were unfitted, they had worn themselves out" (*FU* 22–23). Sederberg points out that "Ad Astra," "With Caution and Dispatch," "Landing in Luck," "Honor," "Death Drag," and "Turnabout" all employ "symbolic stasis outside of time to represent a sort of psychic death-in-life" (1985, 198). Carothers identifies four characteristics apparent in Faulkner's World War I and Civil War veterans: physical disfigurement, inability to return to family and community, inability to articulate their war experiences, and inability to love. Carothers adds to the list of war-related stories already named "Dry September," "Mountain Victory," and "Barn Burning" (1987, 67–68). The suicide of White, recalled by Monaghan in "Honor," relates to the recklessness and violence Faulkner saw as characteristic of postwar aviators (MacMillan 1973, 202). And "The Lilacs," an early Faulkner poem, portrays the dispirited lost generation (Collins 1992, 122).

In *Pylon* Faulkner expresses his interest in fliers and in the fictional possibilities of a romantic triangle. Tracing the development of *Pylon* from related short stories—"All the Dead Pilots," "Ad Astra," "Death Drag," and "Honor"— Duane MacMillan asserts that while the stories do not match the novel in depth, they are demonstrably related. MacMillan identifies five themes from the stories that "reach a kind of culmination" in *Pylon*: "the 'outsider' nature of the protagonists; a belief, not in the rightness, but in the pitiableness of man; the sterility of a money-oriented society; the ironic and often understated difference between reality and unreality; and the ability of man not only to endure, but to prevail" (1973, 191, 205). William O'Connor observes that although it is obviously related to *Pylon*, "Honor" is "much more conventional in conception than the novel" (O'Connor 1954, 89–90). "Honor" and *Pylon* have thematic and narrative similarities regarding a "bizarre solution to a sexual triangle." Olga Vickery adds that the two texts may suggest sagas not developed in Faulkner's fiction ([1959], 1964; see also Millgate [1961] 1966, 52, 62; Millgate [1966] 1989, 138; Karl 1989, 409, 496).

MacMillan finds more parallels than differences in the romantic triangles involving the two flying families. In both cases, the initial motivation for maintaining the triangle is economic and the love making is portrayed in airplane imagery. The men involved in the respective triangles share similar ethical standards. Monaghan leaves the flying show to protect the honor of Mrs. Rogers, an act of unselfishness that is similar to Shumann's crashing his plan to provide for Laverne's future comfort. In the end, Shumann may be better off than Monaghan, who is destined for a living death.

The two women are very different: the personality of Rogers's wife in "Honor" is not fully delineated, and she seems rather shallow, self-serving, and incapable of understanding the comradeship between the fliers. In the longer text, Laverne is a more complex character who is less object than actor, well-integrated into the complexity of the triangle. The three characters in *Pylon* do not require a conventional solution, in which one couple emerges and one man loses, therefore increasing the possibility for "greater dramatic intensity." Additional parallels can be found in the relationships of Monaghan and the Reporter to the children, and Reinhardt's resemblance to Feinman in his concern for money (MacMillan 1973, 202–04, 207–08; see also Minter 1980, 146–47, 149). Gene Phillips finds similarities in names between "Honor" and *Pylon*: the surname *Rogers* in "Honor" appears again as the given name *Roger* in *Pylon* (1988, 113).

The character of the "self-sacrificing husband who cares only about the welfare of the wife who has betrayed him" appears before and after "Honor" (Blotner 1974, 650). Edward Holmes finds such husbands to include Howard Rogers in "Honor," Rat in *The Wild Palms*, and Roger Howes in "Artist at Home" (Holmes 1966, 105). Carothers contends that Rat Rittenmeyer is far less convincing as a sensitive though wronged husband than the men portrayed in these other fictions. Howard Rogers's behavior, like Roger Shumann's, "is grounded in coherent motivation" (Carothers 1985, 31). Hans Skei adds "The Brooch" as offering another portrayal of a loyal husband (Skei 1985, 313). Other triangles appear in "All the Dead Pilots," Spoomer-Kit-Sartoris, and in "Ad Astra," the fictitious triangle, Comyn-Bland-Bland's "wife" (MacMillan 1973, 203). James Ferguson adds "Fox Hunt" to stories that deal with the triangular conflicts of love, and he notes that these portraits relate generally to the pattern of self-abnegation prevalent in Faulkner's stories (Ferguson 1991, 36, 80–81).

Ferguson points out that in some of the stories, the triangles experience a "very curious shift in the rivalries" wherein the "real bond of affection is between the two men" as in "Divorce in Naples," "Honor," and "A Courtship." In "Divorce in Naples," the homosexual element is obvious, but it is not so apparent in the other two stories. Both, however, seem to endorse a conviction that when women intrude into the "pure and honorable world of men," trouble arises. Ferguson also compares the saving action at the end of "Honor" to the behavior of the rivals in "A Courtship" where the men prove themselves more worthy than the woman they love (1991, 72–73).

A brief list of comparisons demonstrates how completely "Honor" shares in the traits of Faulknerian lineage. Joseph Blotner compares Dr. Jules Martino in "Dr. Martino" and Saucier Weddel in "Mountain Victory" with Monaghan in "Honor" and Jock in "Death Drag." They are all being "pushed by circumstances beyond the normal boundaries of feeling" (Blotner 1974, 678, 688). Thomas McHaney traces the recurrence of the catafalque image in multiple contexts: "Honor," *Pylon, Absalom, Absalom!*, and *The Wild Palms* (1975, 32 n. 4). Cleanth Brooks believes the "theme of reckless courage" appears in "Honor" and "Death Drag" although the latter story adopts a darkly comic tone (Brooks [1978] 1990, 404).

Ilse Lind reviews critical assessments of Faulkner's portrayal of Jewish characters. Offending stereotypes appear in "Honor" and numerous short and long works, including "Death Drag" and "There Was a Queen" among the short stories (1984, 121). Carothers likens "Honor" to "That Will Be Fine" in that the effectiveness of the story depends "on the implicit rejection of the storyteller's cynicism" (1985, 107). Skei identifies a large number of early stories of a trapped, overprotected, or controlled female toward whom the narrator displays limited understanding. Included in this group are "Honor," "Mistral," "Black Music," and "Hair." These women are sometimes portrayed as possessing a "propensity for evil" as in "Honor," "Mistral," "Divorce in Naples," and "Fox Hunt" (Skei 1985, 101, 311).

Skei also places "Honor" among the stories with characters who are dreamers, typically social outsiders and losers. Often they see their dreams crushed by conventional society (Skei 1985, 102–03). In a study of the patterns of abstraction, a condition Faulkner typically treats critically, Ferguson points out that honor is one of the most abused. It appears in "Honor," "There Was a Queen," "Death Drag," "An Odor of Verbena," and "Wash" to name a few (Ferguson 1991, 81).

Both collections, *Doctor Martino* and *Collected Stories*, enlarge the comparative contexts of "Honor." "Honor" is the last story in *Doctor Martino*. Béatrice Lang believes the portrayal of the "waste world of the living dead" that opens *Doctor Martino* in "Dr. Martino" is echoed in "Honor" at the end of the collection. Also, Weddel in "Mountain Victory" realizes that war had deadened his response to life, as it had also done to the characters in "Honor" and "Death Drag" (Lang 1976, 31). Arthur Kinney sees horror as the unifying force of *Doctor Martino*. In "The Brooch," Howard is unceasingly pressed by external forces, a situation similar to the contexts of "Honor," "Mountain Victory," and "Death Drag" (Kinney 1980, 59). Ferguson suggests that Faulkner may have chosen to close *Doctor Martino* with "Honor" as a way to lessen the intensity after "Mountain Victory" and thereby achieve some sense of closure to the collection. Both of these stories offer glimpses of affirmation in the acts of courage and loyalty of the characters, but they cannot completely relieve the pessimism of the collection (Ferguson 1991, 154).

In *Collected Stories*, "Honor" appears as the second story in "The Middle Ground." Michael Millgate contends that the appearance of death, either literal or figurative, binds the stories of this section. "Honor" fits the pattern because of the psychic death of Monaghan (Millgate [1966] 1989, 274). Kinney identifies the press of "intrusive life" as a structuring theme for "The Middle Ground." Wash lives a precarious existence that corresponds to Monaghan's wing walking, and like Wash, Monaghan is insecure. Monaghan's passion then links to the subsequent story, "Dr. Martino," where the affair is "more delicate" (Kinney 1980, 72–73).

Carothers expands Millgate's analysis, saying that the theme of death is paired with sex in this section. In the "series of investigations," Faulkner seems to indicate that any person is capable of nearly every behavior (Carothers 1985, 59). Ferguson sees some patterning in the balance of the stories working from the outside toward the middle. This approach pairs "Honor" with "There Was a Queen." Both stories relate honor to tests "by sexual liaisons" (1991, 159).

## Interpretation and Criticism

"Honor" has been neglected in the corpus of critical response in part because Faulkner's war-related fiction has been marginalized by reader preference for his Yoknapatawpha texts. Also, regardless of the praise one might direct toward "Honor," its narrative milieu is not comparable to Faulkner's best short stories.

The quality of *honor* provides the thematic import as well as the titular emphasis of the story. Although critics generally agree that Howard Rogers achieves honor, they are divided about whether Buck Monaghan does. Walter Everett interprets this quality as Rogers's honorable response to his wife's affair with his friend, an honor that brings about Monaghan's defeat. Monaghan, however, lives his disconnected life because of his loss of a "sense of personal honor" (Everett 1969, 146). Blotner contends that the love affair sets the direction of Monaghan's life as a drifter. After the war, he sometimes makes a precarious living barnstorming, but he also spends time as a drifter, never able to stay for very long at any of the jobs he finds as an automobile salesman, the work he turned to after the war (Blotner 1974, 649).

Robert Harrison examines the accuracy with which Faulkner portrays airplanes and flight in his works. He points out that the hierarchy of the aviation community typically relegated wing walkers to the "unskilled or the destitute." Thus, Harrison concludes, "this clear though unspoken social distinction helps explain the moral ascendancy" of Rogers over Monaghan. The pressure of the story is morally rather than economically centered because the ethics of their profession finally unite the men in a stronger bond than the competition over Rogers's wife, whom they can destroy. Rogers's act to save Monaghan when he throws away the rope during a wing-walking act helps define Monaghan's act as "suicidal bravado, born of shame and desperation." As to the incredible save, Harrison writes, "That Rogers could have caught Monaghan in midair somewhere on the back side of a loop is physically possible, though most unlikely" (1985, 141, 144).

Skei distinguishes Monaghan's behavior as representing escape more than endurance because he does not achieve endurance in terms of adaptability and adjustability. Skei cautions that Monaghan is an unreliable narrator; he tells the story while in the process of quitting another job and may be exaggerating his misfortune in life. Still, he is a wounded war spirit whose most profound experience was the suicide of White, a card player and a flier, who killed himself because of a gambling debt to Monaghan that came of being peace-time soldiers with little else to do. Adding a different interpretation of Rogers's actions, Skei suggests that by saving Monaghan, the wronged husband exacts a "more refined revenge" than would have been achieved by letting him die because Rogers's actions recall to Monaghan the best qualities of men: honor, self-respect, and loyalty. Some ambivalence exists regarding Monaghan. He has not become the settled dead as described in "All the Dead Pilots," but it is not clear if his choice is preferable. Although he does not succumb to the avarice of Reinhardt, he must continually avoid women, which "in general shows a narcissistic approach to life." As Skei observes, Monaghan's "whole story proves that his attitude to women is superficial and prejudiced." He chooses the life of a drifter rather than be trapped by domesticity that comes with relationships with women (Skei 1985, 138–40, 177).

Both Thomas Nordanberg and Max Putzel offer sympathetic conclusions about Monaghan. Nordanberg describes the case of Monaghan as a portrait of a man trying to adjust despite the despair that had been portrayed in his character in "Ad Astra" (1983, 39). Putzel describes Monaghan as "redeemed" by removing himself from the romantic conflict. Even though his life reflects the postwar inability to adjust to civilian life, he at least maintains an ability to act with honor in the particular circumstance of a love triangle (1985, 135).

Ferguson comments briefly on the portrayal of women, stating that "Honor" contains a clear differentiation between the "clean, cold, simple world of men" and the "'hot and dirty' world of women" as well as a clear "equation of heights and masculine sexuality" (1991, 72).

Formal qualities of "Honor" are briefly considered by the critics. According to Everett, the "most salient characteristic of 'Honor' is the construction of its plot." Two stories are entwined: Monaghan's restlessness and the Rogerses' relationship. The frame story generates the internal narrative in the form of an interior monologue (Everett 1969, 146). Blotner believes the "neat ending," wherein the parents are reconciled and Monaghan is named godfather of their child, may reflect Faulkner's attempt to construct the story by the "requirements of popular fiction" (1974, 650). Brooks points out that the added element of the airplane and related danger adds intensity to the conventional love-triangle paradigm (Brooks [1978] 1990, 404). Ferguson notes that Faulkner often opened stories at the end of the *fabulae*. In "Honor," little of the story occurs in the present, as flashbacks are used to move the plot (Ferguson 1991, 129).

"Honor" is one of Faulkner's "relatively weak" stories (Ferguson 1991, 36). Nevertheless, it reflects recurring concerns in the author's collection of fiction. "Honor" also has a place in the larger set of stories portraying post–World War I dispiritedness. "Honor" should be further considered in the context of gender portrayal. The apparent condemnation of Mrs. Rogers may need to be evaluated in the context of Skei's cautionary warning that Monaghan's version of events may not be reliable.

## Works Cited

Blotner, Joseph. 1974. *Faulkner: A Biography*. 2 vols. New York: Random House.

———. 1984. *Faulkner: A Biography*. 1 vol. New York: Random House.

Brooks, Cleanth. [1978] 1990. *William Faulkner: Toward Yoknapatawpha and Beyond*. New Haven: Yale University Press. Reprint. Baton Rouge: Louisiana State University Press.

Carothers, James B. 1985. *William Faulkner's Short Stories*. Ann Arbor, MI: UMI Research Press.

———. 1987. "'I Ain't a Soldier Now': Faulkner's World War II Veterans." *Faulkner Journal* 2:67–74.

Collins, Carvel. 1992. "'Ad Astra' through New Haven: Some Biographical Sources of Faulkner's War Fiction." In *Faulkner and the Short Story: Faulkner and Yoknapatawpha, 1990*. Ed. Evans Harrington and Ann J. Abadie. Jackson: University Press of Mississippi, 108–27.

Emerson, O. B. 1984. *Faulkner's Early Literary Reputation in America*. Ann Arbor, MI: UMI Research Press.

Everett, Walter K. 1969. *Faulkner's Art and Character*. Woodbury, NY: Barron's Educational Series.

Faulkner, William. 1930. "Honor." *American Mercury* 20 (July): 268–74.

———. 1934. *Doctor Martino and Other Stories*. New York: Harrison Smith and Robert Haas.

———. 1950. *Collected Stories of William Faulkner*. New York: Random House.

———. 1959. *Faulkner in the University: Class Conferences at the University of Virginia, 1957–1958*. Ed. Frederick Gwynn and Joseph L. Blotner. Charlottesville: University Press of Virginia.

———. 1977. *Selected Letters of William Faulkner*. Ed. Joseph Blotner. New York: Random House.

Ferguson, James. 1991. *Faulkner's Short Fiction*. Knoxville: University of Tennessee Press.

Harrison, Robert. 1985. *Aviation Lore in Faulkner*. Amsterdam and Philadelphia: John Benjamins.

Holmes, Edward M. 1966. *Faulkner's Twice-Told Tales: His Re-Use of His Material*. The Hague: Mouton.

Karl, Frederick R. 1989. *William Faulkner: American Writer*. New York: Weidenfeld and Nicolson.

Kawin, Bruce F. 1977. *Faulkner and Film*. New York: Frederick Ungar.

Kinney, Arthur F. 1980. "Faulkner's Narrative Poetics and *Collected Stories*." *Faulkner Studies* 1:58–79.

Lang, Béatrice. 1976. "'Dr. Martino': The Conflict of Life and Death." *Delta* 3 (November):23–33.

Lind, Ilse Dusoir. 1984. "Faulkner's Relationship to Jews: A Beginning." In *New Direction in Faulkner Studies: Faulkner and Yoknapatawpha, 1983*. Ed. Doreen Fowler and Ann J. Abadie. Jackson: University Press of Mississippi, 119–42.

McHaney, Thomas L. 1975. *William Faulkner's* The Wild Palms: *A Study*. Jackson: University Press of Mississippi.

MacMillan, Duane. 1973. "*Pylon*: From Short Stories to Major Work." *Mosaic* 7:185–212.

Meriwether, James B. [1961] 1971. *The Literary Career of William Faulkner: A Bibliographical Study*. Princeton, NJ: Princeton University Library. Reprint. Columbia: University of South Carolina Press.

Millgate, Michael. [1961] 1966. *William Faulkner*. New York: Barnes & Noble.

———. [1966] 1989. *The Achievement of William Faulkner*. New York: Random House. Reprint. Athens: University of Georgia Press. Brown Thrasher Books.

Minter, David. 1980. *William Faulkner: His Life and Work*. Baltimore: Johns Hopkins University Press.

Nordanberg, Thomas. 1983. *Cataclysm as Catalyst: The Theme of War in William Faulkner's Fiction*. Acta Universitatis Upsaliensis. Studia Anglistical Upsaliena #49. Stockholm: Almquist and Wiksell.

O'Connor, William Van. 1954. *The Tangled Fire of William Faulkner*. Minneapolis: University of Minnesota Press.

Phillips, Gene D. 1988. *Fiction, Film, and Faulkner: The Art of Adaptation*. Knoxville: University of Tennessee Press.

Putzel, Max. 1985. *Genius of Place: William Faulkner's Triumphant Beginnings*. Baton Rouge: Louisiana State University Press.

Sederberg, Nancy Belcher. 1985. "'With Caution and Dispatch': 'Deliberate speed, majestic instancy.'" In *Critical Essays on William Faulkner: The Sartoris Family*. Ed. Arthur F. Kinney. Boston: G. K. Hall, 190–203.

Skei, Hans H. 1981. *William Faulkner: The Short Story Career*. Oslo, Norway: Universitetsforlaget.

———. 1985. *William Faulkner: The Novelist as Short Story Writer*. Oslo, Norway: Universitetsforlaget.

Vickery, Olga W. [1959] 1964. *The Novels of William Faulkner*. Baton Rouge: Louisiana State University Press.

Watson, James G. 1987. *William Faulkner: Letters and Fictions*. Austin: University of Texas Press.

# Dr. Martino

## Publication History

"Doctor Martino" was first published in the November 1931 issue of *Harper's*. Faulkner originally submitted the story to the *Saturday Evening Post* on March 5, 1931. After the *Post* turned it down, he submitted the story to *Woman's Home Companion* on March 16. On June 5, Faulkner forwarded the story to Ben Wasson. By September 1, it was again submitted to the *Saturday Evening Post*. The story went back to Wasson, and Faulkner indicates that Wasson placed it in *Harper's* for $500. The story-sending schedule lists these entries under the notations "Dr Martino" and "Martino" (Meriwether [1961] 1971, 171–72, 176–80; *SL* 50–51; Blotner 1974, 704). "Doctor Martino" was collected in *Doctor Martino and Other Stories* (1934) and as "Dr. Martino" in *Collected Stories* (1950).

## Circumstances of Composition, Sources, and Influences

Hans Skei reasons that Faulkner's decision to use "Doctor Martino" as the title story for a collection indicates the author's own regard for this story. If he was satisfied with the published text, the good feeling had not come without hard work (Skei 1981, 69).

No evidence exists to date the composition of "Doctor Martino" more specifically than March 5, 1931, the earliest date it is recorded on the story-sending schedule. Extant prepublication texts include a complete early manuscript and a partial typescript that follows the early manuscript and is possibly the first typescript prepared for magazine submissions. Joseph Blotner notes evidence in this early manuscript of marginal additions and paste-ons. Two additional incomplete manuscripts also show a great deal of revision and reconstruction as there is much reordering and pasting together of passages

(*WFM 11* Introduction viii; Blotner 1974, Notes 99). Skei does not distinguish the later incomplete manuscripts as two separate versions. He does characterize Faulkner's writing a new manuscript version from a rejected typescript as a typical practice; however, creating new manuscripts by cutting and pasting was not as common a revision technique for the author (Skei 1981, 69–70).

The content of the different versions reveals a complete revision of the opening and some alteration of the ending. Skei speculates that the "intrigues and the implied and explicit philosophical wanderings of this story . . . may explain some of Faulkner's difficulties in bringing the story to a conclusion" (1981, 69–70, 127 n. 262). Nevertheless, the basic outline of the conclusion including Jarrod and Louise's flight and Martino's death appears in all versions. Numerous additional themes and events appear in both the early drafts and published texts. The philosophy of life that Dr. Martino expounds is present in the early manuscript. In each version the question of whether Louise will ride the horse stirs the characters to action. In each text Louise breaks her engagement with Jarrod. Mrs. King's deception by returning the rabbit without Louise's knowledge appears throughout although the background story about the rabbit is expanded in the final version. And from the beginning, Martino tells Jarrod he has been conquered by a woman (*WFM 11* 1–29).

Many of the revisions relate to Hubert's appearance in the story. Originally Faulkner limits the setting to Cranston's Wells. The St. Louis and New Haven scenes are later additions. Hubert's character is fleshed out more and more in the sequence of revisions: his roots in a wealthy Oklahoma oil family are clarified, and his vanity and obtuseness are more apparent in the final version. The narrative perspective shifts almost completely to Jarrod's view. His psychology lectures are added, and the directly reported conversation between Jarrod and Martino becomes an event recounted by Jarrod to Mrs. King. Of particular interest is the alteration in the Martino–Louise relationship in the final version. In the early stages of their relationship, Martino's health temporarily improves when Louise is around. He becomes somewhat more active, taking walks away from his bench, until a heart attack nearly kills him and once again confines him to spending his summer days on the bench. In his own turn, Martino helps Louise overcome her fear of a slide and encourages her to jump from the bathhouse into the lake (*WFM 11* 1–29).

Once the text was published, Faulkner made no further revisions. The two versions differ only in a few incidental corrections. From the magazine version to the collection *Doctor Martino* one verb tense is corrected ("Dr. Martino" 737; *DRM* 20). From *Doctor Martino* to *Collected Stories* capitalization of the word *Negro* is followed throughout. More significantly, the title is changed to "Dr. Martino" in *Collected Stories*. Since then, critics have varied in their use of the different titles: "Doctor Martino" and "Dr. Martino." In the discussion that follows, "Dr. Martino" will be used unless specific reference is made to earlier published versions.

Biographical and literary source studies of "Dr. Martino" are limited. The summer resort setting, Cranston's Wells, recalls a similar resort in Lafayette Springs that the Falkners patronized (Blotner 1974, Notes 99). Frederick Karl supplements the biographical parallels of place in "Dr. Martino" with some associations between fictional characters and Faulkner's family and friends. He finds suggestions of both Faulkner and Phil Stone reflected in certain elements of Hubert Jarrod. Faulkner appears again in Jules Martino, who Karl believes represents the "magical figure of the artist who turns his bench into a throne." Louise King combines qualities of Helen Baird and Estelle Faulkner, and Alvina King's personality manifests qualities of the Oldhams (Karl 1989, 435–36).

Suggestions of literary borrowings are somewhat scarce but when offered are explained in some detail. Béatrice Lang compares the image of Dr. Martino sitting on the garden bench with the myth of renewal represented by the king in the sacred grove in Sir James Frazer's *The Golden Bough*. However, Dr. Martino is a perversion of the myth. He is replaced by Hubert Jarrod, who appropriately wins the queen, Louise King (Lang 1976, 29).

According to Arthur Kinney, Faulkner's "Dr. Martino" owes a literary debt to Henry James. Faulkner's portrayal of a character "caught metonymically in his forceful if cryptic paradigm" about being afraid and being alive seems "openly borrowed from 'The Beast in the Jungle'" (1980, 73).

The unusual, perhaps unnatural, bond between Martino and Louise recalls supernatural elements in works of Nathaniel Hawthorne and Edgar Allan Poe. More specific comparisons of particular works might reveal substantial influences of Hawthorne and Poe on Faulkner.

## Relationship to Other Faulkner Works

In 1935, Aubrey Starke linked "Dr. Martino" to the Sartoris family of Yoknapatawpha County. He pointed out that the character Lily Cranston has the same surname as Lucy Cranston, who is the mother of the Sartoris twins (Emerson 1984, 60). Most critics responding to the text of "Dr. Martino" focus on its examination of the relationship between a domineering parent-figure and a young female. "Dr. Martino" is especially interesting as an example of the conflict because two competing authority figures seek the allegiance of Louise.

Irving Malin thinks the "actual representative of authority" may be the "character most frequently met in all of Faulkner's work." Malin focuses on Martino, not Alvina King, in this role. He points out that Faulkner examines the influence of fathers on daughters as well as on sons. Malin sees in the examples of Joanna Burden, Emily Grierson, Rosa Coldfield, and Drusilla Hawk the consequence that "they become 'masculine,' distrusting normal marriage," and sublimate their sexual needs "in the affairs of men." Louise King establishes a similar relationship with Jules Martino, and she, like these other female characters, possesses an "epicene" quality (Malin 1957, 81–82).

Focusing on the importance of the mother figure, Blotner compares "Dr. Martino" and "The Brooch." Although both stories concern a "girl balked by an older woman," "Dr. Martino" offers a more complicated story than the situation of "The Brooch" (Blotner 1974, 688). Lang likens the "prismatic technique" that obscures Martino's nature to Faulkner's method in "A Rose for Emily." The portrayal of pathological behavior in which oppressive parental relationships (either father or mother) inhibit normal development also links this story to "Miss Zilphia Gant," "Elly," and "The Brooch," as well as "A Rose for Emily" (Lang 1976, 23).

Skei extends the list of stories comparable to "Dr. Martino" on the basis of an overpowering authority figure and a young woman. He finds it to be a prevalent image in the *Doctor Martino* collection generally and elsewhere in such stories as "Elly," "Miss Zilphia Gant," "Adolescence," and especially "Fox Hunt." Superficially, Louise's relationship with Martino seems much like that of Susan Reed and Henry Stribling in "Hair." Louise, however, is not so "sexually overt" as Susan. Martino's relationship with Louise has very little in common with Stribling's relationship with Susan. "Fox Hunt" and "Dr. Martino" both portray "dependent, overprotected women who are deeply troubled because of the demands of the conventional role that they have to succumb to." Skei concludes that the manipulations of people in these stories become "elements of an incessant fight for power" (1979, 15, 22 n. 2; Skei 1985, 115–16, 127–28, 160). James Ferguson identifies "Dr. Martino," "Fox Hunt," "The Brooch," and "Artist at Home" as examples of the "sophisticated tale of the triangular conflicts of modern love." The short stories frequently portray older women often involved in the romantic triangle. Ferguson finds an early example in "Frankie and Johnny" but more fully developed examples in "Dr. Martino," "Adolescence," "The Brooch," and "Elly," and more comically in "Skirmish at Sartoris" (Ferguson 1991, 36, 70).

"Dr. Martino" contains a generalized statement about female nature that has caught the attention of several critics. Skei comments that "Dr. Martino" presents a "very bad psychological understanding of how young girls tend to behave." He continues, "[T]he implied author seems to be willing to settle for an explanation where the fact that Louise is a young girl, susceptible to evil, victim and victimizer at one time, is the most decisive factor" in determining her behavior. Skei finds the assumption in "Dr. Martino" that young females are susceptible to evil to be prevalent in a number of Faulkner's tales. "Hair" and "Mistral" also convey a sense that "girls are seen as strange beings with inborn capacities for evil." This propensity is extended to women in

"Divorce in Naples," "Fox Hunt," and "Honor." Skei adds, however, that Faulkner omitted these generalizations in such stories as "Mountain Victory" and "Beyond." According to Skei, "only in stories such as 'Mistral' and 'Divorce in Naples' do these abstractions seem to have so close affinities with the central elements of the stories that their inclusion is inevitable and necessary" (1985, 116, 125–26, 311 n. 24, 30–31; see also Karl 1989, 435–36). Ferguson believes an increased objectivity in Faulkner's characterization of females helps mark his maturation as a writer. The portraits of Louise in "Dr. Martino" and other females in "That Evening Sun," "Mountain Victory," "The Leg," "Mistral," "Frankie and Johnny," and "Adolescence" all reflect "compassionate characterizations of women in difficult or impossible situations" (1991, 74). Peggy Flynn numbers Louise among the "Sister Set," that is, females who are linked with images of death (1976, 115).

Critics argue that the psychology lessons in "Dr. Martino" are reduced to meaninglessness. The lessons are filtered through the consciousness of Jarrod, who, once he meets Louise, listens in class because he senses he is "going to need psychology" (*CS* 569). When put in the position of acting, however, Jarrod argues with Louise, and she breaks their engagement; he is completely outwitted by Martino, and he is unaware until the very end that Alvina King has duped him. His psychology lessons prove to be of little value; the lesson he ponders at the conclusion is Martino's lesson. Lang believes that the psychology lessons should be dismissed, and Ferguson suggests that this scene is a case when "simple ignorance gets Faulkner in trouble" (Lang 1976, 24; Ferguson 1991, 145).

Critics make a few brief associations between the male characters in "Dr. Martino" and other fiction. Blotner compares Jules Martino to Monaghan in "Honor," Weddel in "Mountain Victory," and Jock in "Death Drag." Like these men, Martino is a "character pushed by circumstances beyond the normal boundaries of feeling" (Blotner 1974, 688). Karl finds common qualities in the Yale student Hubert Jarrod and Gavin Stevens (1989, 436). Dr. Martino also bears comparison with Uncle Willy. Both older men influence the actions of young people in ways that generate a divided response as to whether Faulkner means to portray the influence as positive or negative.

Skei traces the occurrence of death as the "result of strong emotional conflicts" in "Dr. Martino," "The Brooch," and "There Was a Queen" (1985, 214).

The formal qualities of "Dr. Martino" also invite comparative responses. Olga Vickery categorizes "Dr. Martino" as one of the "conventional stories" that relies "on plot complication and action leading to some sort of resolution" (Vickery [1959]1964, 300; see also Skei 1985, 209). Vickery might also have included it in her discussion of the contest pattern since the story raises the question of who will win Louise.

Images that assume particular importance in "Dr. Martino" have similar meanings in other works. Lang finds a recurring association of the horse with masculinity in several works including *Sartoris*, *The Unvanquished*, and "Fox Hunt" (1976, 28). The rabbit appears in Poem VII of *A Green Bough* as an image of fright; similarly, Susan Reed of "Hair" is described as a scared rabbit (Lang 1976, 33). Thomas McHaney likens Louise's rabbit to Charlotte Rittenmeyer's Bad Smell. Each is a fetish by which the woman hopes to keep evil out of her life (McHaney 1975, 80). Ferguson lists a number of stories that use "obvious controlling symbols." Louise's rabbit is one among such symbols as drought ("Dry September"), verbena ("An Odor of Verbena"), deer in several stories, hair, a brooch, and various other items (1991, 141).

Joseph Reed compares the narrative approach in "Dr. Martino" with other stories in which the narrator becomes a "faulty witness" who misinterprets events. Jarrod represents a "rather crudely handled" version of the faulty witness technique. The device is used more effectively in "Hair," "The Tall Men," and "Turnabout" (1973, 26). Reed adds that Faulkner's experimentation with narrative technique included the discovery that mixing third-person narrative strategies in "Dr. Martino" revealed "the shallowness of apparently complex substance" (1973, 55).

In her extended analysis of "Dr. Martino," Lang takes issue with Michael Millgate's assessment that the *Doctor Martino* collection offers a "miscellaneous" collection of stories (Millgate [1966] 1989, 273). Lang believes that "Doctor Martino" introduces major issues and sets the tone for the entire collection. Her inventory of issues includes the conflict between the forces of life and death. Although she argues for the victory of the life force in "Doctor Martino," Lang believes that death maintains a pervasive, accumulating influence in the collection. It appears in the guise of "the waste world of the living dead" and is contrasted with some displays of courage and affirmation of living and even suffering. The parapsychological explanation Mrs. Cranston offers about Martino is one of several examinations "of the mysteries of human nature." Sexual impulses, overbearing parents, and murder also reappear as recurring issues (Lang 1976, 31–32). Although Ferguson believes Faulkner conveys undue regard for "Doctor Martino" by using it as the opening story in *Doctor Martino*, it does introduce a concern with alienation that reappears in every other story in the collection (Ferguson 1991, 153).

James Carothers identifies the "twin themes of sex and death" as the unifying principle of "The Middle Ground" section of *Collected Stories* (1985, 59). The various analyses of "Dr. Martino" indicate how important these themes are to the story, and consequently demonstrate the story's appropriateness to Faulkner's "Middle Ground" vision. Ferguson pairs "Dr. Martino" and "Golden Land" in "The Middle Ground" because they both "focus on older people who are trying by very different means to hold on to life" (1991, 159–60).

## Interpretation and Criticism

Reed's reductive conclusion about the shallow substance of "Dr. Martino" fails to account for the complex and contradictory readings the text produces. Obvious misreadings can be corrected rather easily but differences in interpretation are not so handily resolved.

Dorothy Tuck's synopsis of the story errs slightly in asserting that Jarrod is the narrator (1964, 165). Walter Everett more accurately describes the story as "basically presented through Hubert Jarrod" but also using an omniscient narrator (1969, 139). The story is primarily but not exclusively presented from Jarrod's perspective. Tuck makes a more serious error in her claim that Louise discovers that her mother has taken the rabbit surreptitiously (1964, 165). The revelation at the conclusion is Jarrod's, not Louise's: he discovers the degree to which Mrs. King has manipulated him (Everett 1969, 139; Knieger 1972, 45). Tuck correctly places the car scene as occurring when Hubert and Louise are on the way to get married rather than after the wedding (1964, 165). Much of the criticism assumes the fact of marriage between Hubert and Louise. The implication is undoubtedly that the couple will marry, but it is not an accomplished fact of the text.

The characters of the allies Hubert Jarrod and Alvina King lend themselves to relatively easy analysis. Everett's interpretation of Jarrod is that he "seems as unaware as Mrs. King says he is" (1969, 139). Lang also emphasizes Jarrod's smugness, his lack of perceptiveness, and his at best moderate intelligence, hence Faulkner's ironic choice of his name Hubert, meaning "bright one" (1976, 30, 33 n. 14).

Mrs. King is a stereotypical "domineering, ambitious" mother (Everett 1969, 139). Lang adds some complexity to this character when she interprets Mrs. King's relationship with her daughter as ambiguous. Alvina is Martino's rival for authority over Louise, and she is in part simply jealous of his influence. She feels humiliated by it. Many of her goals for Louise are superficial and disregard Louise's own preferences. She succeeds through deception. Nevertheless, Mrs. King is the agent for Louise's entry into womanhood; she "sees to it that her daughter's initiation goes in the right direction." (Even her name, *Alvina*, reflects the ambiguity. It may mean bowels, but it also means beehive, associating her with the bee, a symbol of fertility.) A hint remains that though she and Jarrod act as allies, they will become antagonists, presumably in their own competition for Louise (Lang 1976, 29–30, 33 n. 12).

The relationship between Louise and Martino is much more complicated. Critics are divided over whether Martino's influence on Louise is liberating or destructive. An anonymous review in the *Times Literary Supplement* posed the questions that reflect two important poles of interpretation. The reviewer writes of "Doctor Martino": "That which gives the collection its title is creepy. What is the influence of the sick doctor who is keeping himself alive from the girl's vitality, living on her, and who dies immediately [when] she is withdrawn from his power? The author leaves us wondering, which is perhaps the best way to end a story of the occult" ("Doctor Martino" 1934, 618).

Everett sees the conclusion as dignifying the relationship between Martino and Louise, which provides the narrative tension. Martino, according to Everett, "uses his maturity and quiet bravery to infuse courage into Louise King," and he inspires her actions (1969, 139). Blotner understands Martino's motivation as "trying to save" Louise (1974, 688). Skei points out that Louise is being raised to be a "wife to be proud of" (*CS* 573; Skei 1985, 115). Skei also distinguishes between Louise's situation and that of Faulkner's other females under the dominance of a mother figure. Through the influence of Martino, Louise is "able to transcend her traditional role." She has adopted a belief that gives her a reason for living. Although she recognizes that her position is fragile, and "her rebellion is a weak and guarded one," Louise does not realize the extent of her mother's and Jarrod's efforts to keep her from Martino's influence. Whether she will be suppressed depends on the success of her mother's deceptions (Skei 1985, 115–16, 125). Karl likewise interprets Martino's goal as rescuing Louise "from a bourgeois, conventional experience" (1989, 435).

Another critic affirms Martino but finds Louise to be the threatening member of the relationship. Kinney describes the bond between Martino and Louise as a "delicate affair." He sees Louise as the destructive force "under the guise of life" who kills Jules when she "jolts him for once to life." The narrative unfolds in ironic contrast to Alvina King's warning that Martino is a threat to Louise's life. Martino is really more perceptive than Mrs. King. His life embodies the emptiness of both King women (Kinney 1980, 72–73).

Two critics, Malin and Lang, hold the view that Martino's relationship with Louise is unhealthy for her. Malin places his interpretation of Louise in the context of his discussion of Faulkner and Freud. The description of Louise as epicene emphasizes her psychological bond with Martino as a father-figure. Her relationship with Martino interferes with her ability to "express herself sexually with Hubert Jerrod [*sic*]." Malin reads the concluding action as Louise's rebelling against Martino and forcing herself to marry Jarrod (1957, 82).

Lang observes the way sympathy shifts in the story away from, then toward, Martino, so that in the conclusion he, not Alvina King, very nearly ends up being the sympathetic authority figure. But, Lang continues, "his role in the process of Louise King's initiation to womanhood leaves no doubts as to its negative quality" (1976, 23). The action of the text centers around Louise's initiation into womanhood. From the beginning, descriptions of Louise emphasize her sexless nature and her lack of feeling for Hubert. She must accept her own sexuality or face the alternative, her death (Lang 1976, 24–30).

Symbols are crucial to understanding Louise's choices. They reflect the incompatibility between her friendship with Martino and her engagement to Hubert. The rabbit represents her childhood and the magic that dispels her fears. The metal rabbit oxidizes as Louise passes into another stage of life. Although she puts great value in the rabbit, the proprietress sees it as a dime-store charm, and Hubert immediately detects its deterioration. When Louise realizes she does not have the rabbit, she "tacitly accepts its irreversibility as she urges Hubert to drive on." (Lang disagrees with an earlier interpretation that sees the rabbit as a symbol of fertility [1976, 33 n. 7]). The symbol of the ring counters the meaning of the rabbit. Martino's contemptuous evaluation of it compares with Mrs. Cranston's judgment of the rabbit. They are alternate choices that represent the impossibility of Louise's maintaining her relationship with both Martino and Jarrod (Lang 1976, 24–26).

Images of snakes and horses support the sexual overtones in the relationship between Martino and Louise. Crossing a snake-filled river and riding the horse represent the ambivalence in masculine and feminine roles. If Louise rides the horse, she will die or be further estranged from the role of woman. The importance of the episode justifies the intrusion of Mrs. King and Hubert, who act to save her life (Lang 1976, 26, 28).

Louise associates riding the horse with extending Martino's life. For Martino, "by retarding the girl's maturity he can maintain a relationship with her and 'feed' on her life." When Louise does leave with Jarrod, even though Martino knows she has been tricked, he dies. Lang contends that "his death thus bears out her [Mrs. King's] suspicion that Doctor Martino's hold on the girl may after all be of sexual significance." This fact seems paradoxical given the lack of overt sexuality in their relationship, but it matches the paradox of his pervasive presence despite his near invisibility and the "nonactive nature of his disturbing action." Martino is much like the dark house in which he lives, isolated and secretive. He hibernates from most of the seasonal fluctuations and from life. When he moves to the resort for the summer, his actions remain limited and screened. Martino seems to offer an affirming view of life that influences Louise and at the end even Hubert. In full, however, it proves to be another paradox of the man: it reflects an unnatural fear of death. Lang argues that "Doctor Martino never sees that death is a part of the process of life, something natural, and his fear of death must be seen as a fear of life itself" (Lang 1976, 24–30).

Louise may be facing life according to the proprietress's alternate philosophy of life: "I've come to believe it ain't very important what anybody does, as long as they are fed good and have a comfortable bed" (*CS* 573). As Lang observes, when Louise tells Hubert to drive on, she clearly surrenders, but the nature of surrender is uncertain: she could be surrendering to adulthood, she could be defeated, or both. Lang concludes, "Ultimately, Louise's surrender is to Jarrod, marriage and the true force of life. Marriage with such a young man may not be a very appealing solution, but it is for her the only alternative to death or sexlessness. The suffering and despair which accompany the surrender give the victory of life a crushing and precarious quality" (Lang 1976, 24–30).

The resort itself reinforces the "presence of death in life." Its visitors are typically older. They come to the spring for rejuvenation. They absorb themselves in the activities of the young Louise (Lang 1976, 27–28).

Skei adds another layer of interpretation over the conclusion. The power struggle in the story demonstrates that all of the characters are "incapable of either love, understanding, pity, or compassion" because people are the means to accomplishing "private and selfish needs." All four major characters use the other three. Although the ending leaves much of the tension unresolved, hysteria (Louise's) and death (Martino's) characterize the concluding images and provide an unambiguous criticism of the characters' conduct (Skei 1985, 179–80).

Ferguson considers the narrative strategy of "Dr. Martino" to be one of Faulkner's least effective uses of limited omniscience. The shift out of Jarrod's consciousness is awkward, and it does not prepare for the shift to a dramatic presentation of the confrontation between Louise and Mrs. King. The only "masterful" use of narrative strategy is the detached narration of the last scene. Overall, the effectiveness of "Dr. Martino" is "vitiated" by its point of view (1991, 89–91, 117).

Since the story's appearance, "Dr. Martino" has never received particularly high praise. In his review of *Doctor Martino*, William Rose Benét described "Doctor Martino" as "subtle, and interesting, but somehow minor for Faulkner" (1934, 645). William Van O'Connor thought that "Doctor Martino" was one of several stories in the 1934 collection that possessed "brilliant touches" but was missing "a strong commitment to theme" and seemed a "little thin and poorly conceived" (1954, 89). Everett believes the story fails in the "lack of vitality" of the characters and in the too explicit, often repeated statement of Martino's philosophy of life (1969, 139). Lang and Skei offer the most extensive examinations of "Dr. Martino," but neither suggests that the story has been unduly misjudged.

## Works Cited

Benét, William Rose. 1934. "Fourteen Faulkner Stories." *Saturday Review of Literature*, 21 April, 645.

Blotner, Joseph. 1974. *Faulkner: A Biography*. 2 vols. New York: Random House.

———. 1984. *Faulkner: A Biography*. 1 vol. New York: Random House.

Carothers, James B. 1985. *William Faulkner's Short Stories*. Ann Arbor, MI: UMI Research Press.

"Doctor Martino." 1934. *Times Literary Supplement*, 13 September, 618.

Emerson, O. B. 1984. *Faulkner's Early Literary Reputation in America*. Ann Arbor, MI: UMI Research Press.

Everett, Walter K. 1969. *Faulkner's Art and Character*. Woodbury, NY: Barron's Educational Series.

Faulkner, William. 1931. "Doctor Martino." *Harper's* 163 (November):733–43.

———. 1934. *Doctor Martino and Other Stories*. New York: Harrison Smith and Robert Haas.

———. 1950. *Collected Stories of William Faulkner*. New York: Random House.

———. 1977. *Selected Letters of William Faulkner*. Ed. Joseph Blotner. New York: Random House.

———. 1987. *William Faulkner Manuscripts 11:* Doctor Martino and Other Stories. Ed. Thomas L. McHaney. New York: Garland.

Ferguson, James. 1991. *Faulkner's Short Fiction*. Knoxville: University of Tennessee Press.

Flynn, Peggy. 1976 "The Sister Figure and 'Little Sister Death' in the Fiction of William Faulkner." *University of Mississippi Studies in English* 14:99–117.

Karl, Frederick R. 1989. *William Faulkner: American Writer*. New York: Weidenfeld and Nicolson.

Kinney, Arthur F. 1980. "Faulkner's Narrative Poetics and *Collected Stories*." *Faulkner Studies* 1:58–79.

Knieger, Bernard. 1972. "Faulkner's 'Mountain Victory,' 'Doctor Martino,' and 'There Was a Queen.'" *Explicator* 30: Item 45.

Lang, Béatrice. 1976. "'Dr. Martino': The Conflict of Life and Death." *Delta* 3(November):23–33.

McHaney, Thomas L. 1975. *William Faulkner's* The Wild Palms: *A Study*. Jackson: University Press of Mississippi.

Malin, Irving. 1957. *William Faulkner: An Interpretation*. Stanford, CA: Stanford University Press.

Meriwether, James B. [1961] 1971. *The Literary Career of William Faulkner: A Bibliographical Study*. Princeton, NJ: Princeton University Press. Reprint. Columbia: University of South Carolina Press.

Millgate, Michael. [1966] 1989. *The Achievement of William Faulkner*. New York: Random House. Reprint. Athens: University of Georgia Press. Brown Thrasher Books.

O'Connor, William Van. 1954. *The Tangled Fire of William Faulkner*. Minneapolis: University of Minnesota Press.

Reed, Joseph W., Jr. 1973. *Faulkner's Narrative*. New Haven: Yale University Press.

Skei, Hans H. 1979. "The Trapped Female Breaking Loose: William Faulkner's 'Elly.'" *American Studies in Scandinavia* 11:15–24.

———. 1981. *William Faulkner: The Short Story Career*. Oslo, Norway: Universitetsforlaget.

———. 1985. *William Faulkner: The Novelist as Short Story Writer*. Oslo, Norway: Universitetsforlaget.

Tuck, Dorothy. 1964. *Crowell's Handbook of Faulkner*. New York: Thomas Y. Crowell.

Vickery, Olga W. [1959] 1964. *The Novels of William Faulkner*. Baton Rouge: Louisiana State University Press.

# Fox Hunt

## Publication History

"Fox Hunt" was published in *Harper's*, September 1931. Prior to its acceptance, the story had undergone many rejections, a few title changes, and, most likely, additional revisions. On the story-sending schedule James Meriwether records submissions of the story to *Miscellany* as "Fox" sometime before February 5, 1930; to *Liberty* as "Fox" sometime before February 14, 1930; to *Forum* as "The Fox" sometime before March 7, 1930; to the *Saturday Evening Post* as "Fox" on December 29, 1930; to *College Humor* as "A Fox" on January 9, 1931; to *Woman's Home Companion* as "Fox-Hunt" on March 11, 1931; and by way of agent Ben Wasson to *Harper's* as "Foxhunt" on April 7, 1931. *Harper's* paid $400 for the story. Frederick Karl observes that although Faulkner tried the high-paying *Post*, *Scribner's* is noticeably absent from the list of submissions, possibly because he was "saving that valuable outlet for better stuff." The story appeared under the title "Fox Hunt," the title it retained for its subsequent appearances in *Doctor Martino and Other Stories* (1934) and *Collected Stories* (1950) (Meriwether [1961] 1971, 172; Blotner 1974, 693; Skei 1981, 58; Karl 1989, 427).

## Circumstances of Composition, Sources, and Influences

Hans Skei follows Meriwether in giving February 5, 1930, as the earliest verifiable record of the existence of "Fox Hunt." Skei suggests, however, that the undated submissions on the sending schedule might have been made prior to January 20, 1930, the date Faulkner began to keep meticulous records on submissions of his work. His conclusion is that "Fox Hunt" was written during 1929. He believes the variety of titles is less related to revisions of the story than to the convenience of shortened references on the sending schedule (Skei 1981, 57–58; Meriwether [1961] 1971, 172). Karl thinks the variations reflect "Faulkner's dissatisfaction" with the story (1989, 427). Although he does not tie revisions specifically to the various titles, Thomas McHaney argues that "revisions, perhaps not all reflected in the extant prepublication materials, were made during the submission process as the piece evolved toward a publishable story" (*WFM 11* Introduction ix).

McHaney describes differences between the typescript and the published text as "substantial" (*WFM 11* Introduction ix). An interesting omission is a section of the valet's conversation with the chauffeur. From the typescript to the published text, the valet loses an entire paragraph of criticism in which he demonstrates how "ignorance is the curse of this country" (*WFM 11* 56). While it adds a bit of humor in the exchange, it diverts the focus from the story and is omitted in published versions.

Of particular importance are three revisions that were made between the extant typescript and the published text in *Harper's*. They include sharpening the youth's comparison of Mrs. Blair and the fox, intensifying the manner in which Harrison Blair kills the fox, and describing the youth's feelings at the end of the story. The revision in the comparison of Mrs. Blair to a fox constitutes a few added words. She has just been described as having hair "like soft fire, the mass of it appearing to be too heavy for her slender neck" (*CS* 591). In the typescript, the youth says, "Just like a fox. I be durn if I see how that skinny neck . . . . You look at a fox, and you wonder how a durn little old skinny thing like that can tote all that brush" (*WFM 11* 48). In the published text the changes emphasize the youth's continued thinking about Mrs. Blair rather than his turning his attention to the nature of a fox: "Just like a fox. I be durn if I see how that skinny neck of hern . . . . Like you look at a fox and you wonder how a durn little critter like it can tote all that brush" (*CS* 592). Adding the few extra words clarifies this comparison that is central to the unfolding story.

Another refinement that strengthens this passage is the insult from her husband, Harrison Blair, that angers Mrs. Blair and turns her eyes red "then brown again like a fox" (*CS* 592). In the typescript, the youth says the insult could have come either from Harrison Blair or Steve Gawtrey (*WFM 11* 48). Since Blair's hatred of the fox has just been established, the parallel between the woman and the fox is further reinforced if the offender is Mr. Blair. As Joseph Blotner notes, in the published text, the fox is the obvious symbol for Mrs. Blair (1974, 645).

Blair's means of killing the fox is only slightly altered in the published version, but with chilling effect. All through the story, the farmers observe that Blair runs separately from the dogs and that his hatred makes him a better hunter than the pedigreed animals. In the typescript, he fends off the lunging fox with "that ere goldhead switch," but in the final version of the story, Blair kills the fox by knocking it down with his fist and trampling it to death with his boot-heels (*WFM 11* 66; *CS* 606). The revision is simple but significant in reinforcing the intensity of Blair's hatred of the fox.

The transformation of the conclusion is the most significant change "Fox Hunt" undergoes. As it evolves through the extant manuscript and typescript to published text, additional emphasis is added to the final images of Mrs. Blair and the youth. The attention to Mrs. Blair expands, then contracts, but the effect she has on the youth continues to develop. In the manuscript, after the youth looks at the cigarette-smoking Gawtrey, he looks at the "woman on the chestnut, her arms lifted and her hands busy in her hair." What follows is simply, "'She is crying,' the youth said"; then the story closes with the older man's remarks about breakfast (*WFM 11* 40). In the typescript, a description of the woman's "face of quiet and irrevocable despair" and the youth's response to his observation is added. Several attempts to describe the youth indicate his growing importance to the story. He now experiences feelings of jealousy and despair "toward the unattainable She and the still shape of that man in whom would walk forevermore the tragic and inescapable earth her ruin." The youth's voice is "harsh" and "savage"; he strikes his mule "violently" (*WFM 11* 66). In the published text, the description of the woman's despair is omitted, a final revision that concentrates the concluding impression on the youth. The youth tries to "project . . . toward that remote and inaccessible she" and "to encompass the vain and inarticulate instant of division and despair which . . . was very like rage." His mule no longer suffers as the outlet for feelings that are now expressed in savage "curses" that lack "point or subject" (*CS* 607). The effect of the revised ending is to turn the narrative into the youth's story wherein he, like numerous young male characters in Faulkner, must confront and try to assimilate the reality of one female with his idealized She.

Once published, the text underwent no further revisions other than incidental corrections. From the appearance of the story in *Harper's* to its inclusion in *Doctor Martino*, a double negative is omitted: "nobody else wouldn't have it" to "nobody else would have it" (*Harper's* 395; *DRM* 36). Unlike the prior versions, in *Collected Stories*, the words *Negro* and *Pullman* are capitalized.

Faulkner's own avid pursuit of the fox followed rather than preceded the publication of this story; therefore, few biographical connections contribute to the details of the narrative. John Faulkner, William's brother, recalls his father sharing stories of fox hunting with the boys. One particular recollection included a description of an exhausted fox wearily climbing a fence and moving across a field into the brush with a similarly exhausted hound following slowly behind it (Faulkner 1963, 15–16). Blotner notes Faulkner's use of technical phrases, indicating a knowledge of fox hunting; the author's interest in this sport would continue to grow. He suggests that Faulkner may have learned some fox-hunting lore from James Boyd, who was a Master of Foxhounds, but he indicates that their meeting in Charlottesville was in October 1931, a month after the story appeared in *Harper's*. It is likely that the character of Harrison Blair draws on Paul Rainey, who used Murry Falkner's advice about his stables and who stocked his land with foxes and pheasants for the pleasure of his guests (Blotner 1974, 645, 713–14, Notes 93; see also Blotner 1990, 17).

The literary parallels are interesting though sparse. Blotner finds suggestions of D. H. Lawrence's stories in the way "action and symbol suggest theme and technique" (1984, 255). Karl links "Fox Hunt" to Lawrence's "The Fox." He sees the "modernist" narrative technique as "Conradian and Fordian in many respects," though in "Fox Hunt" Faulkner is not so successful as either Conrad or Ford (1989, 427–28).

It is an understatement to say that John Keats's "Ode on a Grecian Urn" was important for Faulkner. One need only track its appearances in Blotner's biography to see how often it was in Faulkner's consciousness and in his texts. Michael Millgate suggests that the importance of Keats's "Ode" was that it represented "the image of motion in stasis which haunted Faulkner throughout his life" ([1966] 1989, 96). "Fox Hunt" reflects this notion in the frozen image of Mrs. Blair and Gawtrey. Together the two riders appear "with that semblance of a thrush and a hawk in terrific immobility in mid-air, . . . the man stooping, the woman leaning forward like a tableau of flight and pursuit on a lightning bolt" (*CS* 592).

David Minter believes that for Faulkner the urn in Keats's poem was "associated with life and with art—with life because it depicted love that was dreamed of yet denied, felt yet deferred; and with art because it epitomized form" (1980, 56). The youth's reaction captures this sense of denied love, not to Gawtrey, but to himself because of Gawtrey's success. In the end, the rural youth is forced to confront the discrepancy between the ideal and the actual and the irretrievability of time passed.

## Relationship to Other Faulkner Works

Keats's "Ode on a Grecian Urn" provides a link, but not an exclusive one, between "Fox Hunt" and other Faulkner works. Angry husbands, trapped females, and their various manipulations of each other are recurring concerns. Blotner likens Harrison Blair's hostility toward his wife to Plunkett's attitude toward his wife in Section V of "Drouth" ("Dry September"). Both women are portrayed as trapped (1974, 647). Skei associates Mrs. Blair with female characters such as Zilphia Gant, Elly, Emily Grierson, and Minnie Cooper who suffer from expectations of the society that they are unable to meet, the pressure of the older generation, and "their position in relation to *men.*" Setting the woman and her plight outside Yoknapatawpha might have been Faulkner's way of suggesting that the condition was not limited by geography; but even when, as in "Fox Hunt," Faulkner leaves Yoknapatawpha, he retains a Southern context for these women. They try to free themselves from the restraints of their lives, and they all fail (Skei 1985, 114–15, 127).

"Fox Hunt" is closely related to "Dr. Martino" in its love triangle and manipulations of characters. Power used to control other people and to gain personal or material advantage is another way of defining the thematic impulse of these stories. To "Fox Hunt" and "Dr. Martino" Skei adds "Elly" and "The Brooch" as stories that explore the use of power (1985, 116, 127, 160). (Incidentally, Skei describes Mrs. Blair as being from the Carolinas, but she is from Oklahoma. Harrison Blair purchases his birthplace in the Carolinas for her so that she might not be homesick for her Southern roots [Skei 1985, 310 n. 23; *CS* 593].)

James Ferguson describes "Fox Hunt," "Artist at Home," "Dr. Martino," and "The Brooch" as examples of Faulkner's "sophisticated tale of the triangular conflicts of modern love" (1991, 36). Ferguson believes the sexual imagery in "Fox Hunt" demonstrates Faulkner's gaining a greater objectivity in managing sexual themes. The imagery in this story and in other stories like "A Rose for Emily," "Dry September," "That Evening Sun," "Mountain Victory," and "The Brooch" is more subtle than in earlier stories such as "Don Giovanni" (Ferguson 1991, 37, 142–43).

Edward Holmes likens the gathering of men to observe the stables and the hunt in "Fox Hunt" to a similar experience in *Knight's Gambit*. These "poor whites" come to view stables that are much finer than their homes (Holmes 1966, 103).

In linking "Fox Hunt" to the Indian stories, Duane Gage builds his argument on the mistaken reading that Harrison Blair is an "Oklahoma oil Indian" (1974, 29–30). But Blair is not Indian. Mrs. Blair's parents became rich on Oklahoma oil, and she had a romantic attachment to a former schoolmate, a young man of Indian descent named Allen (*CS* 593, 597–98; see also Skei 1977, 180 n. 100).

Several images in the story appear in other stories in different contexts. Walter Slatoff examines Faulkner's means of portraying motion in various works "primarily around protracted physical movements such as journeys, races, pursuits, and flights." The list of examples is extensive, including "Fox Hunt," "Red Leaves," "A Courtship," "The Hound" *As I Lay Dying, Light in August, Pylon, The Wild Palms, The Unvanquished, The Hamlet* and *Go Down, Moses* (1960, 11–12).

The image of Blair trampling the fox to death with his boot-heels recalls a similar incident in "A Justice" when the black man stomps Craw-ford's fighting cock "until it did not look like a cock at all" (*CS* 606, 356). Both men's actions may be expressions of rage against competitors for their wives' affections, but the fox represents the wife Mrs. Blair whereas the cock represents the competitor Crawford.

The figure of a centaur is used in this story as well as in "Centaur in Brass." When Gawtrey and Mrs. Blair are riding side by side, they pass "like one beast, like a double or hermaphroditic centaur with two heads and eight legs" (CS 591). Similarly, Tom-Tom on Turl's back looks like a "strange and furious beast with two heads and a single pair of legs like an inverted centaur" (CS 164; see also Serafin 1983, 35).

Stephen Ross notes that when Faulkner presents black speech in ritualistic contexts such as a hunt, "he increases the density of dialect transcription," for example, with the speech of the stable boys in "Fox Hunt" and Isham in "Delta Autumn" (1989, 107).

Ferguson finds that the major patterns introduced in "Doctor Martino," the first story in *Doctor Martino*, are also pursued in "Fox Hunt": initiation and relational triangles involving a young woman. The behavior of the spouses in "Fox Hunt" introduces the motif of justice that reappears in the subsequent stories. The actions of Mr. Blair and Mrs. Blair are both a "kind of symbolic quid pro quo" (Ferguson 1991, 153).

In Millgate's analysis of *Collected Stories*, "The Middle Ground" stories all contain a death, either physical or symbolic. In "Fox Hunt," Blair's trampling the fox to death bears symbolic overtones ([1966] 1989, 273–74). Arthur Kinney, like Millgate, notes the repeated presence of death in each story of "The Middle Ground." According to Kinney, "Fox Hunt" is a vital rendering of the "newer more oblique presentations of life and death as vicarious experience" begun in "Dr. Martino." He calls the fox a "death-surrogate" (Kinney 1980, 66, 72–73). (Kinney's reference to "A Fox Hunt" as part of "The Village" section of *Collected Stories* is misleading, and the title is given incorrectly [Kinney 1980, 66].) Ferguson offers another pairing in "The Middle Ground" by linking the fourth and eighth stories, "Fox Hunt" and "My Grandmother Millard." These marriage stories respectively portray unhappy and happy resolutions to problems related to marriage (Ferguson 1991, 160).

"Fox Hunt" maintains numerous associations with other Faulkner stories and novels. The story pursues the same issues of form and content that are articulated in a variety of Faulknerian contexts.

## Interpretation and Criticism

"Fox Hunt" is one of the least discussed of the stories published in Faulkner's lifetime. It reflects many of his thematic concerns and formal techniques, but it becomes diffuse, if not defused, by attempting too much. In a 1934 review of *Doctor Martino*, Fred Marsh points out the way the fox and Mrs. Blair act as symbols of each other in the concurrent hunts in which they are the respective prizes (Emerson 1984, 29). Dorothy Tuck also emphasizes the parallel pursuits of the fox and Mrs. Blair. Tuck argues that the "story comes into sharp focus only at the very end, when the poor-white youth accidentally confronts Blair's wife after she—and the fox—have been overtaken by their respective pursuers" (1964, 166). Olga Vickery finds that the story fits comfortably in the short story pattern of the ritual pursuit of game. She responds sympathetically to Harrison Blair's actions, describing him as a "cuckolded husband" who "relieves his jealousy and mounting frustration by chasing a fox and finally killing it in a particularly brutal fashion" ([1959] 1964, 304).

Some critical reactions are explicitly focused on the portrayal of marriage in the story. Walter Everett summarizes the point of the story as a concern with "marital unhappiness" (1969, 143). Skei offers more substantive remarks about why these people are unhappy. He believes that "Fox Hunt" has a more direct preoccupation with male-female relationships and sex than Faulkner's other stories. As demonstrated by Harrison Blair, Mrs. Blair's mother, the valet, and Steve Gawtrey, manipulation and deception are the norms of behavior for controlling other people. Mrs. Blair is the victim. The question of the narrative is whether she will "be caught with her hair down," the image that represents her infidelity. Mrs. Blair cannot escape the manipulations to which she is subject. Her "prime function is to satisfy the whims of her husband." Given her circumstances, it is unreasonable to expect her to "remain untainted, faithful, innocent." When sexual attraction becomes a manipulative tool, "it serves to create hard and cruel people whose contributions to positive and meaningful human relations are utterly destructive." If the result is not actual death, it is frequently portrayed as a death of the spirit (Skei 1985, 116–17, 126, 179).

Another important pattern in "Fox Hunt" is its concern with the youth's "initiation into the world of sex." The juxtaposed hunts link sex and death, an association Faulkner often makes in his stories of initiation (Ferguson 1991, 67–68).

Everett cites the "difference between the rich and the poor" as another thematic interest in "Fox Hunt" (1969, 143). The disparity in the lives of the rich and poor portrayed in this story is less a thematic concern than a means by which to employ multiple narrative voices to tell the story. The narrators include the omniscient narrator, the grooms, the "clay-eaters," and the valet. For Everett, the distance between the reader and the central characters weakens the story's "force and realism." The farmers, valet, and chauffeur express contempt for the morning's activities (1969, 143). Blotner believes the valet's remarks, detached and cynical, add background and comic relief (Blotner 1974, 645). Skei thinks the use of different narrators "contrasts at least three worlds, three outlooks on life, three modes of understanding." The farmers see the rituals of the rich as absurd; the rich perceive seduction and adultery as insignificant. The final reaction of the young farmer to the scene of Mrs. Blair with Steve Gawtrey is important because his youth and inexperience are confronted by "unfaithfulness and adultery." Skei believes the youth's reaction is that he "tries to forget [what he has seen] at once" (Skei 1985, 117, 127).

Another aspect of the multiple narration is the contrast between country and city and also between North and South. In this story, though not always, the Southern country milieu represents a "stable and secure life" against which the city dwellers are portrayed as "rootless, dishonest, and completely estranged from the traditional values" (Skei 1985, 117, 127, 203). In Karl's estimation the narrative technique conveys the core story of Harrison Blair, his wife, and her paramour through outsiders. The reader never gets close to the main characters. The technique is "interesting" but fails to "generate interest or intensity"; "it is a technique in search of a more compelling subject" (Karl 1989, 428). Ferguson finds the narrative mode "clumsy" because it too obviously calls attention to itself as it establishes the credibility of the valet as a narrator; however, it does show Faulkner's tendency to use first-person narration in a story that is primarily a third-person text (1991, 104–05).

Faulkner's best efforts in "Fox Hunt" are superseded in other works. He creates more compelling expressions of trapped females in his other short stories and novels and more fully expressed clashes of race, class, and region. In "Fox Hunt" too many concerns compete for the reader's attention. In terms of the story's action, the valet is intricately involved in manipulating Mrs. Blair, Harrison Blair, Steve Gawtrey, and Callaghan, particularly when the valet begins to feel the pangs of a guilty conscience. However, he reveals only the vaguest reasons for his behavior, these being chiefly that he owes favors to those he helps. Also competing, if only briefly, is the nature of the relationship between the black grooms and the white farmers. The omniscient narrator consistently disparages the grooms, describing their movements as the "clever agility of monkeys" and their conversation as "mellow and meaningless and idiotic" (*CS* 587). The grooms condescend toward the white farmers who come early to watch the hunt. These "clay-eaters," as the grooms call them, have no understanding, no capacity for understanding "gempmuns." Nevertheless, as the story unfolds, the farmers, not the grooms, tell the story. The valet expresses disdain for both of these groups, a feeling related in part to their Southernness. Then, as the story concludes, we have the sense that it is not primarily an examination of the trapped female, Mrs. Blair; it is an initiation story for the youth. She, it seems, is manipulated once more. She becomes an object lesson for a young man. What becomes disconcerting is the way the youth's rage resembles Harrison Blair's rage. In the published text that anger is undirected. The reader feels that this youthful anger has not yet found its object, not that it will be dissolved. The story fails in a sense because it attempts too much and turns too late into a story of the youth's initiation.

Such criticism of "Fox Hunt" is offset somewhat by the recognition of some truly fine moments in the story. Joseph Reed judges "Fox Hunt" to fail because it is an instance where the device of the story "stands out from its substance" (1973, 56). Blotner describes "Fox Hunt" as technically ambitious, though "not a wholly successful story": it obtains a "richness . . . by filtering events through the comments and attitudes of observers" and an "immediacy of events described in progress" (1974, 645–46). Karl believes it is "not one of Faulkner's more successful efforts" (1989, 428). More recently, Ferguson has ranked "Fox Hunt" with other Faulkner stories that are not among his best but that possess "considerable merit" (1991, 36).

The finest moments in the story are in the descriptions. The subtlety of the farmers' gestures captures their understated demeanor. Harrison Blair's meanness extends beyond the context of his marriage or the hunt. That, in turn, facilitates a sympathetic rendering of Mrs. Blair, whose sense of desperation is visually "captured": "She was sitting the mare with a kind of delicate awkwardness, leaning forward as though she were trying to outpace it, with a quality about her of flight within flight, separate and distinct from the speed of the mare" (*CS* 591–92). The focus of the text, like the hunting dogs it describes, is sometimes distracted but undoubtedly bears the marks of its pedigree.

## Works Cited

Blotner, Joseph. 1974. *Faulkner: A Biography*. 2 vols. New York: Random House.

———. 1984. *Faulkner: A Biography*. 1 vol. New York: Random House.

———. 1990. "Faulkner and Popular Culture." In *Faulkner and Popular Culture: Faulkner and Yoknapatawpha, 1988*. Ed. Doreen Fowler and Ann J. Abadie. Jackson: University Press of Mississippi, 3–21.

Emerson, O. B. 1984. *Faulkner's Early Literary Reputation in America*. Ann Arbor, MI: UMI Research Press.

Everett, Walter K. 1969. *Faulkner's Art and Character*. Woodbury, NY: Barron's Educational Series.

Faulkner, John. 1963. *My Brother Bill: An Affectionate Reminiscence*. New York: Trident.

Faulkner, William. 1931. "Fox Hunt." *Harper's* 163 (September):392–402.

———. 1934. *Doctor Martino and Other Stories*. New York: Harrison Smith and Robert Haas.

———. 1950. *Collected Stories of William Faulkner*. New York: Random House.

———. 1987. *William Faulkner Manuscripts 11:* Doctor Martino and Other Stories. Ed. Thomas L. McHaney. New York: Garland.

Ferguson, James. 1991. *Faulkner's Short Fiction*. Knoxville: University of Tennessee Press.

Gage, Duane. 1974. "William Faulkner's Indians." *American Indian Quarterly* 1:27–33.

Holmes, Edward M. 1966. *Faulkner's Twice-Told Tales: His Re-Use of His Material*. The Hague: Mouton.

Karl, Frederick R. 1989. *William Faulkner: American Writer*. New York: Weidenfeld and Nicolson.

Kinney, Arthur F. 1980. "Faulkner's Narrative Poetics and *Collected Stories*." *Faulkner Studies* 1:58–79.

Meriwether, James B. [1961] 1971. *The Literary Career of William Faulkner: A Bibliographical Study*. Princeton, NJ: Princeton University Library. Reprint. Columbia: University of South Carolina Press.

Millgate, Michael. [1966] 1989. *The Achievement of William Faulkner*. New York: Random House. Reprint. Athens: University of Georgia Press. Brown Thrasher Books.

Minter, David. 1980. *William Faulkner: His Life and Work*. Baltimore: Johns Hopkins University Press.

Reed, Joseph W., Jr. 1973. *Faulkner's Narrative*. New Haven: Yale University Press.

Ross, Stephen M. 1989. *Fiction's Inexhaustible Voice: Speech and Writing in Faulkner*. Athens: University of Georgia Press.

Şerafin, Joan M. 1983. *Faulkner's Uses of the Classics*. Ann Arbor, MI: UMI Research Press.

Skei, Hans H. 1977. *Bold and Tragical and Austere: William Faulkner's* These 13: A Study. University of Oslo Department of Literature.

———. 1981. *William Faulkner: The Short Story Career*. Oslo, Norway: Universitetsforlaget.

———. 1985. *William Faulkner: The Novelist as Short Story Writer*. Oslo, Norway: Universitetsforlaget.

Slatoff, Walter J. 1960. *Quest for Failure: A Study of William Faulkner*. Ithaca, NY: Cornell University Press.

Tuck, Dorothy. 1964. *Crowell's Handbook of Faulkner*. New York: Thomas Y. Crowell.

Vickery, Olga W. [1959] 1964. *The Novels of William Faulkner*. Baton Rouge: Louisiana State University Press.

# Pennsylvania Station

## Publication History

"Pennsylvania Station" appeared in the *American Mercury* in February 1934. It was one of four stories published in four magazines that month. The printed text represented the end of a long-term evolution of a much earlier, differently titled story. Publication efforts began in autumn of 1928 when Faulkner was in New York. A letter from *Scribner's* magazine dated November 3, 1928, indicates that it was returning four stories to Faulkner, including "Bench for Two." The editor evaluated the effect of the story as follows: "I was not able to get a great deal out of 'Bench for Two,' although your device is perfectly understandable." Evidence of renewed publication efforts appeared back at Rowan Oak on the story-sending schedule when "2 Bench" was noted as submitted to the *Saturday Evening Post* on September 12, 1930. Another entry about two weeks later showed "Two on Bench" was again submitted to *Scribner's* on September 24, 1930. Neither magazine found the story suitable for publication. Joseph Blotner suspects that near the end of November 1933, Faulkner returned to the still unpublished "Bench for Two," determined to work with it once again. By November 27, Morton Goldman forwarded the revised and retitled "Pennsylvania Station" to Alfred Dashiell at *Scribner's*. The submission was the third attempt with this magazine, and again Dashiell promptly rejected the story. He recalled an early version and felt that despite its skillfulness, the story still lacked interest. Within next the month, the *American Mercury* accepted the story, paying Faulkner $200. Even though Faulkner was not completely enthusiastic about using the story, "Pennsylvania Station" was included in *Collected Stories* (1950) without any revision of the version that had appeared in the *American Mercury* (*SL* 76–77, 274; Meriwether [1961] 1971, 175, 178–79; Meriwether 1973, 256; Blotner 1974, 823–24; see also Skei 1981, 40–41). (Hans Skei indicates incorrectly that "Pennsylvania Station" was also among the stories gathered in *Doctor Martino* [1981, 82].)

## Circumstances of Composition, Sources, and Influences

Tracking variations of a story that appears under different titles is not always an easy task for Faulkner scholars. In this case, an incomplete manuscript in the Faulkner Collection at the University of Texas entitled "Bench for Two" confirms that story as an early version of "Pennsylvania Station" (Meriwether [1961] 1971, 175). Because of the New York setting, Blotner is inclined to date the story's composition from autumn 1928 when Faulkner was in New York. In fact, when Faulkner went to New York in September 1928 to work on the revisions (excisions) of *Flags in the Dust*, Ben Wasson met him at Penn Station. Blotner omits from the revised biography his speculation that the story could have been written as early as 1921 when Faulkner lived in the city for a short time (1984, 231; Blotner 1974, 582, 595).

Although, as Blotner suggests, "Pennsylvania Station" is an "uncharacteristic story" in the Faulkner canon (1984, 231), Skei considers the story characteristic of at least one trait of Faulkner's art: it is "an example of the normal practice of re-using old material, often with years between, in recurrent and numerous attempts to place the resulting stories somewhere to make some badly needed money. 'Pennsylvania Station' is indeed an extreme example, since Faulkner had to return to it so often, work so hard on it, and finally only made a small profit" (1981, 41).

The changes that finally brought the story into publication span several trials and reflect substantive alterations in the story's content. Only by degrees did it assume its shape as an "exercise in understatement in the portrayal of filial treachery and the capacity of human misery and stoic suffering" (Blotner 1974, 595). Blotner mentions that on one draft Faulkner calculated in the margin Mrs. Gihon's payments (1974, 823). The addition of the omniscient narrator came in revision of the story. The narrative idea was originally a dramatic dialogue that only later developed into the story (Carothers 1985, 71).

The partial and complete manuscripts and typescripts published in *William Faulkner Manuscripts 24* sharpen the contrast between Danny and his relatives. Danny becomes more obviously culpable for his troubles. A significant change in the narrative from typescript to published version is the addition of the note to Mr. Pinckski by which Danny gets his mother's money. The complete typescript version has Mr. Pinckski recalling that Mrs. Gihon herself came to retrieve the funds (*WFM 24* 124). Having Danny deliver a written request for a refund is a major alteration of the plot, for it confirms the reader's growing awareness that Danny is not just wild; he is criminal. Danny's forgery also provides the last measure of his mother's devotion when she claims she signed the note Danny forged and is the implied cause of her death.

Faulkner achieves the quality of understatement by omitting details from the story. Although a particular fact may no longer be explicitly stated, it can be inferred from the story. For example, an early partial typescript explains that the older man spent most of his last funds buying back the coffin his sister had selected and shown to her friends. By the conclusion of that version, he is saving a nickel for a morning cup of coffee (*WFM 24* 104). The published text lacks the detail, but the impression remains that the man never returned to Florida because he did not have enough money to do so. Another effective revision found in the published story involves a change in the way the voice on the loudspeaker is described. The effort to capture the effect of the lifeless voice on the sound system succeeds better as description than as the phonetic recreation in the complete typescript (*WFM 24* 119–20).

Another significant change in the published text is a sharpened interest in the atmosphere at Penn Station. The change in title enlarges the focus beyond the bench to the station. Descriptions of how cold the station is (indoors and out) gain importance in the published text. Conversely, much of the concern for each other displayed between the two men sharing the bench is removed from the story. In various early texts, the older man asks the young man why he does not work and how his mother is (*WFM 24* 104–05, 123). The young man seems concerned about where the older man will spend the rest of the night when they are forced to leave Penn Station. He recommends that the older man avoid the cold walk and take the subway (*WFM 24* 102–05, 125–27). The story gains from the contrast between the omniscient narrator's impersonal observations and the shared though painful concerns of the people in the inner narrative.

Blotner mentions two more early features omitted in the published text that resemble techniques of James Joyce. In a partial typescript Faulkner used dashes rather than quotation marks to introduce dialogue, and he used present tense in the italicized narrative passages (*WFM 24* Introduction xi–xii, 102–05). James Carothers finds shadows of James Joyce still discernible in the published work. In this story the reader rather than the protagonist discovers the evil present in the world. Carothers likens Faulkner's technique to Joyce's distinction between the epiphany "in which the character reveals his true nature to others" and that "in which the character reveals his true nature to himself" (1985, 10).

## Relationship to Other Faulkner Works

Both Carothers and Frederick Karl reflect on how busy 1934 was for Faulkner. A wide-ranging variety of his works were published or in progress during that year (Carothers 1985, 55; Karl 1989, 514). "Pennsylvania Station" was one of these and shares traits with texts that both preceded and followed its long-delayed appearance.

Not all of the story associations are complimentary. Joseph Reed includes "Pennsylvania Station" on his list of Faulkner's narrative failures. Like "The Brooch," "Fox Hunt," and *Soldier's Pay*, the narrative device in the story overwhelms the substance (Reed 1973, 56; see also Ferguson 1991, 106, 116). Somewhat less critical than Reed, Carothers links "Pennsylvania Station" with

"Black Music" and "Idyll in the Desert" as all being characterized by narration evolving from a conversation between an older man who has been involved with the central characters and a younger man who has not had direct contact with them (Carothers 1985, 104).

In the dramatic dialogue of an early draft of "Pennsylvania Station," Carothers sees anticipation of the narrative techniques that would later characterize *Requiem for a Nun* and *Absalom, Absalom!*. Both the young listener in the short story and Shreve have a greater perception than their narrators of the truth about the particular stories they hear. Like the locale of *Requiem for a Nun*, the story's station setting "is merely the location of a recitation of significant events long since past." Both the novel and the short story utilize an "apparently disinterested listener"—the young man in "Pennsylvania Station" and the Governor in *Requiem*. The older man demonstrates no understanding of the past events narrated, but Temple Drake comes to admit her own responsibility for some of her past actions (Carothers 1985, 71).

Carothers grants the importance of the initiation theme in Faulkner's work but argues that the author uses it in numerous variations. He places "Pennsylvania Station" in a particular group of stories in which the protagonists fail to perceive evil. Just as Georgie in "That Will Be Fine" does not recognize his uncle's true nature and Elly in "Elly" cannot acknowledge her own willfulness, the older man in "Pennsylvania Station" remains blind to his nephew's deceptions. Any such discovery is left for the reader to make (Carothers 1985, 10).

James Watson's work on letters in Faulkner's fiction includes a consideration of "Pennsylvania Station." In this story, as in several others, Faulkner uses letters "as the means of working out plots and portraying character and theme." Watson judges that "Idyll in the Desert," another story where letters help to achieve these ends, is "a marginally better letter story" than "Pennsylvania Station" (1987, 95).

Karl opens a paragraph about "Pennsylvania Station" with the comment that Faulkner is "so distant from his characteristic material we wonder at his desperation in resurrecting it." He concedes, however, that the story "makes sense" in Faulkner's complete work in its focus "upon images and metaphors of death." He connects this trait in the "Pennsylvania Station" with another story published in February 1934, "Wash" (1989, 507).

"Pennsylvania Station" and "A Justice" also share a common image, that of a preserved specimen. In "Pennsylvania Station" the motionless airplane in the rotunda looks "like a huge bug preserved in alcohol" (*CS* 624). In "A Justice" the last image of Sam Fathers is "like something looked upon after a long time in a preservative bath in a museum" (*CS* 360). The reason for repetition of the image is not necessarily because the two stories are fairly contemporaneous. The airplane does not appear in early versions of the story (*WFM 24* 102–27).

But both images convey a sense that the object or person is out of place in location or time and rendered useless by that dislocation.

The theme of dislocation links "Pennsylvania Station" to the other stories in "The Middle Ground" section of *Collected Stories*, as they all portray uprooted characters. The older and younger men are literally homeless. The story also includes a death, a consistent trait in "The Middle Ground" stories (Millgate [1966] 1989, 273). Arthur Kinney sees the focus on the sister's coffin as a sentimental treatment of the section's "presentation of life and death as vicarious experience" (1980, 73). James Ferguson expresses the opinion that the insertion of "Pennsylvania Station," "Artist at Home," and "The Brooch" between "Fox Hunt" and "My Grandmother Millard" may have weakened the unity of "The Middle Ground." However, if one pairs the stories in the section, working from the first and last toward the center, "Pennsylvania Station" and "The Brooch" strike a balance (as the fifth and seventh stories) in their common portrait of the "consequences of a stupidly unrealistic selfless devotion" (Ferguson 1991, 156, 160; see also David Dowling 1989, 156).

Even if "Pennsylvania Station" is an uncharacteristic story that remains completely independent of any Yoknapatawpha ties, it manifests numerous recognizably Faulknerian qualities, but they are not generally perceived as achieving a successful blend.

## Interpretation and Criticism

Despite Faulkner's determination to revise "Pennsylvania Station" into a satisfactory narrative, Ferguson finds the ultimate result a "dull and turgid" text (1991, 32). Carothers complains that the story relies too heavily on "sentimental and melodramatic stereotypes." He points to Mrs. Gihon as one of these—the hard-working, selfless, devoted mother of an undeserving son. Her other devotion is to her weekly payments to Mr. Pinckski, a predictably "money-grubbing undertaker." Danny is a heavily stereotyped bad boy from the streets "who combines more villainous traits than a credible character can stand." Danny's function becomes less important as an individual than as a measure by which the courage and moral conduct of his mother and uncle are judged. The omniscient narrator is the only "individual, articulate personality" to emerge from the story (Carothers 1985, 71–72).

Watson is also critical. In his evaluation of the device of letters, he finds that their pervasiveness provides much of the plot complication and resolution in "Pennsylvania Station." Because Mrs. Gihon cannot read or write, she depends on her neighbor, who, with good intentions, embellishes the letters. Consequently, Mrs. Gihon does not realize that Danny is not with his uncle in Jacksonville. Danny constantly uses the mail for self-serving ends: he fails to mail a letter, delivers the self-serving note in his mother's name, and sends a wreath by air. The uncle invents a letter from Danny to soothe his sister. Nevertheless, despite its importance to the action, Watson argues that the device of the letters is not completely successful in clearing up the opacity of the story (1987, 95).

The presentation of the forgery is also murky. The crime is only implied indirectly by the older man because he does not recognize the possibility that Danny has committed forgery. Typically, however, critics consider the fact of the forgery as the turning point in the action and as further evidence of the older man's credulity. Dorothy Tuck, for example, includes these assumptions in her synopsis of the story (1964, 173). Karl observes correctly that the brother takes care to protect his sister from full knowledge of her son's troubles (1989, 507); however, the older man himself lacks full understanding of Danny's character. Skei describes the older man's narration as his "almost desperate urge to spin a tale." In doing so, he seeks to establish his own importance through his story and to show that his present condition is the result of "bad luck and a combination of strange coincidences and circumstances." According to Skei, the man's insistence on his nephew's basic goodness and his story that "in part is fabricated by his own imagination" are efforts "to deceive himself as a means of survival" (Skei 1985, 141–42).

The older man's lack of perception is crucial to the ironic effect of the story. Not everyone is unable to see through his protective presentation of Danny. Walter Everett highlights the use of dramatic irony and ambiguity in this "pitiable" story. Guided by the young man's questions and Mrs. Zilich's actions, the reader quickly learns that Danny is the criminal authorities suspect him to be. Everett believes the story benefits from the disparity in perception because "the ironic subtleties attenuate the emotional impact and stimulate the [reader's] curiosity" (1969, 160–61). Carothers also sees the irony that originates in the contrast between the older talker and younger listener. The young listener is impatient but has no desire to hurt the older man or to be too openly critical of his obviously naïve view of Danny. Carothers adds that the contrast between the two men is compounded by the voices of the omniscient narrator, the sister, Danny, and Mr. Pinckski (1985, 70).

Everett cites some ambiguous evidence in the story to argue that Mr. Pinckski may have been less than innocently involved with Danny. Everett points out that while incarcerated in Florida, Danny claims that a man in New York has withheld some money from him, and as it turns out Mr. Pinckski's original promise not to charge interest proves untrue (Everett 1969, 161). But these unrelated details are insufficient to support Everett's argument. The information the reader does have about Mr. Pinckski functions to demonstrate his lack of genuine concern for Mrs. Gihon except as it affects his own interest earned, but that information in the story is not sufficient to determine that he and Danny were both involved in Danny's scheme to get his mother's money.

The dramatic irony created by the older man's limited understanding is enhanced by the wreath. To the older man, the wreath represents Danny's devotion to his mother. But the irony of the extravagance is that Mrs. Gihon dies just after, and by implication because of, Danny's theft of her coffin money (Everett 1969, 161).

The highly impersonal setting in which the older man relates his personal story adds significantly to the irony. Everett describes the tone of the outer narrative as "unsentimental"; Carothers describes it as "austere" (Everett 1969, 160; Carothers 1985, 70). Carothers points to the frigidity of the railroad employees, the remote voice on the loudspeaker, the image of the subway "tunneling violently" beneath the station, and the depersonalized uniformity of the homeless people as "essential details of the immediate scene." But as unattractive as the station is, it is the place of refuge from the colder world outside. This description of the station, so remote to the internal narrative but so finely drawn, "suggests the general tone of the piece" (Carothers 1985, 70; *CS* 613).

The atmosphere at the station is further emphasized because it is set in "counterpoint to the airplane in the rotunda" (Carothers 1985, 70). The image of the airplane as a preserved specimen parallels the image of the homeless people examined by the omniscient narrator's eye. These homeless people are like the airplane in that they are in an environment that renders them useless.

Skei contends that "Pennsylvania Station" is important for what it reveals about man's suffering. The narrative frame reveals that the older man's condition is repeated in the young man and in the numerous others occupying benches in the station. He believes that the urban portrait, rare for Faulkner, is more "inhuman, cold, dreary, implacable, [and] monotonous" than his countryside or village settings. The more hostile environment requires more effort to sustain the personal dreams that become even more necessary for survival (Skei 1985, 141–42).

Skei suggests that a moral could easily be extracted from this story but that it would be of the most general variety (1985, 142). Carothers finds that "Pennsylvania Station," like other pieces of Faulkner's earlier fiction, "fails because of [the author's] apparent reluctance to moralize." The story possesses an interesting contrast between the narrative and dramatic voices but it lacks a "genuine conclusion" (Carothers 1985, 69, 72).

The last image of "Pennsylvania Station" certainly lacks the energy of dramatic action or even the hint of awakened understanding in the older man. The image of time, "only two more hours till daylight," marks the dawn of a new day (*CS* 625). Presented in the same manner of understatement employed throughout the story, it represents survival for another day.

Although the older man retains a certain astonishment that he continues to survive, he does not express a wish for death. Despite the squalid conditions of his life, he would rather continue marking his time.

"Pennsylvania Station" is a story about enduring. Faulkner attempts understatement as an alternative way of portraying the desire to live that he so vividly captures in the more intense, existential moments depicted in such stories as "Red Leaves" or "Mountain Victory," stories considered better fiction. Malcolm Cowley, like many of the critics cited above, judged "Pennsylvania Station" as one of Faulkner's less successful stories (1966, 120). Faulkner himself was skeptical about its merits. When choosing his stories for *Collected Stories*, he conceded that he would be willing to omit "Pennsylvania Station" if necessary. Fortunately the story does hold its place in "The Middle Ground" of *Collected Stories*. There it serves as one of the alternate voices speaking about life and death from beyond the boundaries of Yoknapatawpha County.

## Works Cited

Blotner, Joseph. 1974. *Faulkner: A Biography*. 2 vols. New York: Random House.

——. 1984. *Faulkner: A Biography*. 1 vol. New York: Random House.

Carothers, James B. 1985. *William Faulkner's Short Stories*. Ann Arbor, MI: UMI Research Press.

Cowley, Malcolm. 1966. *The Faulkner-Cowley File: Letters and Memories, 1944–1962*. New York: Viking.

Dowling, David. 1989. *William Faulkner*. New York: St. Martin's.

Everett, Walter K. 1969. *Faulkner's Art and Character*. Woodbury, NY: Barron's Educational Series.

Faulkner, William. 1934. "Pennsylvania Station." *American Mercury* 31 (February):166–74.

——. 1950. *Collected Stories of William Faulkner*. New York: Random House.

——. 1977. *Selected Letters of William Faulkner*. Ed. Joseph Blotner. New York: Random House.

——. 1987. *William Faulkner Manuscripts 24: Short Stories*. Ed. Joseph Blotner. New York: Garland.

Ferguson, James. 1991. *Faulkner's Short Fiction*. Knoxville: University of Tennessee Press.

Karl, Frederick R. 1989. *William Faulkner: American Writer*. New York: Weidenfeld and Nicolson.

Kinney, Arthur F. 1980. "Faulkner's Narrative Poetics and *Collected Stories*." *Faulkner Studies* 1:58–79.

Meriwether, James B. [1961] 1971. *The Literary Career of William Faulkner: A Bibliographical Study*. Princeton, NJ: Princeton University Library. Reprint. Columbia: University of South Carolina Press.

———. 1973. "Faulkner's Correspondence with *Scribner's Magazine*." *Proof* 3:253–82.

Millgate, Michael. [1966] 1989. *The Achievement of William Faulkner*. New York: Random House. Reprint. Athens: University of Georgia Press. Brown Thrasher Books.

Reed, Joseph W., Jr. 1973. *Faulkner's Narrative*. New Haven: Yale University Press.

Skei, Hans H. 1981. *William Faulkner: The Short Story Career*. Oslo, Norway: Universitetsforlaget.

———. 1985. *William Faulkner: The Novelist as Short Story Writer*. Oslo, Norway: Universitetsforlaget.

Tuck, Dorothy. 1964. *Crowell's Handbook of Faulkner*. New York: Thomas Y. Crowell.

Watson, James G. 1987. *William Faulkner: Letters and Fictions*. Austin: University of Texas Press.

# Artist at Home

## Publication History

"Artist at Home" was first published in *Story* in August 1933. The title first appeared on the story-sending schedule dated March 16, 1931. Both the *Saturday Evening Post* and *Scribner's* rejected the story. After the *Scribner's* rejection, Faulkner let his agent, Ben Wasson, handle the submission. *Story* paid only $25 for stories, so although "Artist at Home" was finally published, it brought its author hardly any economic benefit. "Artist at Home" later appeared in "The Middle Ground" section of *Collected Stories* (1950) (*WFM 24* Introduction xiii; Meriwether [1961] 1971, 170, 176–80; Meriwether 1973, 267; Blotner 1974, 688–89, 693, 809; Skei 1981, 69, 70).

## Circumstances of Composition, Sources, and Influences

The first known record of "Artist at Home" is the date on the sending schedule—March 16, 1931. Two different claims can be made for the time of composition based on the story's relationship to Faulkner's life; neither can be verified by extant records. Richard Peterson suggests that the story might actually have been written during 1926, the year when it became clear that something had created a rift between Faulkner and Sherwood Anderson (1977, 21). Tony Owens supports a 1931 composition date as reflecting Faulkner's decision in the 1920s to turn from poetry to prose. Furthermore, a 1931 composition would be after his marriage in 1929 and the purchase of Rowan Oak in 1930; thus his sensibilities regarding the responsibilities of family life would have been heightened (1979, 394).

The manuscript of "Artist at Home" shows careful revision through at least two handwritten drafts prior to the typescript, including some cut-and-paste changes. There was probably only a short amount of time between the drafts. Faulkner made further changes in the story before *Story* accepted it (Blotner 1974, Notes 99; Blotner 1984, 320; Skei 1981, 70).

Several differences distinguish the published text of "Artist at Home" from the manuscript versions. First, in the manuscript, an "I" character narrates the story insisting that "you" understand. Although the "I" figure becomes only an unnamed voice in the published texts, the voice reflects a negative attitude toward women that appears in other "I" narrated stories by Faulkner (Skei 1981, 70–71). Second, the ending of the published story is very different from the manuscript. The manuscript ends with an image of the inscrutability of women rather than with the couple reunited, as in the published text (*WFM 24* 332; *CS* 646). Third, sectional divisions in the manuscript are omitted in the published versions. And finally, Anne's thoughts and words are revised including the addition of her comment on equality (*WFM 24* 320–32; *Story* 27–41; *CS* 627–46). Little was changed in the collected version. Only two minor corrections were made for it: *anymore* corrected to *any more*, and *cafe* to *café* (*Story* 27, 39; *CS* 627, 643).

The biographical ties between story and writer's life are particularly strong. Most critics assume that this story bears some relationship to Faulkner's friendship with and subsequent estrangement from Sherwood Anderson. Faulkner had already created Anderson-like characterizations in several other contexts. An earlier story, "Don Giovanni," had included an artist character named Morrison who suggested Anderson, and Anderson is an apparent model for Fairchild in *Mosquitoes* (Peterson 1977, 21; Blotner 1984, 146). In "Artist at Home," Roger Howes is identified with Anderson. Joseph Blotner says of Howes, "But for a few details, Faulkner might have been describing Sherwood Anderson at Ripshin Farm in Troutdale" (Blotner 1974, 688–89). Peterson pursues some of the more subtle criticisms of Anderson that may be implied in the story. The parallels between the fictional Howes and Anderson include the implication that Anderson, like Howe, is a man whose creative powers have diminished. Howes's success, Peterson notes, "only reveals his failure as a creative artist." Yet another parallel is that Howes profits from the story made from the events much like Anderson profited from his story about a Faulkner-like artist (Peterson 1977, 19–20; see also Blotner 1984, 277). For Arthur Kinney, the "satire on Sherwood Anderson's life at Tipton" manages to salvage "Artist at Home" "from a formulaic bathos" (1980, 73).

Some of Elizabeth Anderson's traits are found in Roger's wife, Anne. Blotner suggests that although the story expresses an intimacy beyond the relationship Faulkner had with Sherwood and Elizabeth Anderson, it may extrapolate from the actual "to what, under certain circumstances, might have been" (Blotner 1974, 688–89). Peterson adds that the portrait of Elizabeth as Anne is "unexpectedly unkind," but that Anne's protective nature probably reflects Elizabeth's inclination to shield Anderson (1977, 19).

The poet John Blair may also have some biographical parallels to Faulkner as he was when he knew the Andersons in New Orleans. Some six years before Faulkner's "Artist at Home" was published, Anderson had used a romanticized portrait of Faulkner as the protagonist of "A Meeting South." Blair's limited wardrobe recalls Faulkner's experience both in New Orleans and Europe (Blotner 1974, 688–89; Blotner 1984, 277). Peterson sees the incorporation of a self-portrait and Anderson's fictional portrait to be a parodic response to Anderson's "A Meeting South" (1977, 19).

Another indication that this story is Faulkner's response to Anderson's story is Anne's display of maternal affection toward Blair and their short-lived romance. Peterson believes that this quality parallels the scene in Anderson's story when David meets the madam Aunt Sally (Peterson 1977, 19).

Blotner contends that the first-person narrator has "near omniscience" and a "tone or rhythm" suggestive of an Anderson narrator (1974, 689). Owens makes a slightly different Anderson connection showing how the two artists, Roger Howes and John Blair, have adopted a narrow, abstracted vision of life much like Anderson's grotesques (1979, 400).

Although the likeness between Howes and Anderson is strong, Faulkner probably also drew on his own experiences as well in this portrait of the "married artist dealing with both domestic and artistic problems" (Blotner 1984, 277). Stephen Ross reads the story as an "allegory of both the success and the regret Faulkner experienced in giving up poetry for prose fiction." It is as much a story about Faulkner himself as it is a portrait of Anderson. The prose writer must symbolically kill the poet within himself so that he may "'tell/write' a story." But Faulkner treats Roger's success ironically. He is able to enjoy the financial fruits of his labor, but Blair, who creates the "more inspired" texts, achieves success posthumously. This turn of events ostensibly "affirms Blair's art and mocks Roger's." Ross believes this image matches

Faulkner's perception of himself as a failed poet working to survive financially by marketing short stories (Ross 1989, 238–39).

Critics have not looked exclusively at Anderson for literary influences. Several critics find traces of James Joyce in this story. The image of the lover in a romantic triangle standing in the rain, suffering from tuberculosis, and dying recalls the characters Michael Furey and Gretta and Gabriel Conroy in Joyce's "The Dead." M. E. Bradford terms the relationship a "grotesque allusion" to the Joyce text (Bradford 1973, 179; see also Blotner 1974, Notes 99; Carothers 1985, 73; Karl 1989, 436). Peterson suspects that at this point in Faulkner's career, his knowledge of Joyce was as yet chiefly from the remarks of people in the New Orleans circle. Thus the parody of "The Dead" may be part of "his ridicule and rejection of Anderson" who was particularly enthusiastic about Joyce's work (Peterson 1977, 21).

Additional literary influences include James Carothers's association of the story with Henry James's *The Ambassadors*. For Carothers, the story "seems often to be a deliberate inversion of James' conventions of conduct" (1985, 73). Frederick Karl sees some "intimations of Shaw's *Candida*" (Karl 1989, 436).

## Relationship to Other Faulkner Works

When placed in a relational context, the inclination to interpret "Artist at Home" as a portrait of Sherwood Anderson can be recognized as only one dimension of the story. "Artist at Home" follows an important pattern in Faulkner fiction: the paradigm of the romantic triangle. James Ferguson calls this text, "Fox Hunt," "The Brooch," and "Dr. Martino" "sophisticated tale[s] of the triangular conflicts of modern love" (Ferguson 1991, 36). Sometimes the husband and rival lover reconcile as in "Artist at Home," "Centaur in Brass," and "A Courtship" (Vickery [1959] 1964, 305). In some of the fictional triangles, Faulkner shows a degree of sympathy for the spouses, such as Drusilla and John in "An Odor of Verbena" and the Howeses in "Artist at Home" (Ferguson 1991, 71–72). Edward Holmes likens Roger Howes to Howard Rogers of "Honor" and Rat of *The Wild Palms*. In each of these texts, the wife or the lover either "honorably" reveals the affair or does not rely on the husband's domicile or money to facilitate it (Holmes 1966, 100). Carothers criticizes the improbability of the husband's supporting his wife and her lover in "The Wild Palms" but accepts as more credible the situations in "Artist at Home," "Honor," and *Pylon* (Carothers 1985, 31). Anne is victimized like the wife in "Fox Hunt," another woman "sacrificed to fulfill the desires of her husband" (Owens 1979, 409).

Carothers's complaint about the behavior of the scorned spouse relates to a portrait of self-abnegation that Ferguson identifies in "Artist at Home," "Snow," "Honor," and "Hair." In "Artist at Home," Ferguson asserts that

Howes "looks out for" Blair's interests even though Blair is infatuated with his wife (Ferguson 1991, 80).

For Owens, Roger Howes and John Blair are like other Faulkner characters whose perceptions are abstract and rigid rather than sensitive to the "complex fluctuations of experience" and who are therefore ineffectual or destructive. Others of this type are the protagonist of "The Hill" and Alec Gray in "Victory" (Owen 1979, 396–97). Owens also finds numerous links between romantic idealism and sexuality and death in Faulkner's works. Owens names *The Marionettes*, "The Hill," "Nympholepsy," and *Mayday* (1979, 395–96). Like Galwyn of *Mayday* and Quentin Compson, John fails to maintain abstraction, and he also rejects life. The deaths of all three men are related to water (Owens 1979, 407).

Hans Skei identifies dreams as a "central concept in Faulkner's short fiction." These dreams appear in numerous variations of characters trying to transcend reality, including such examples as "Beyond," "The Leg," "Black Music," and "Mountain Victory." Skei ranks "Carcassonne" as Faulkner's most eloquent fictionalization of the artist's transcending reality through art; it is much more complex than "Artist at Home," but "Artist at Home" examines how the "dream of creation also feeds on more realistic and worldly experiences" (Skei 1977, 146; 1981, 70; 1985, 103, 145).

Several critics link the formal characteristics of "Artist at Home" to similar strategies in other short stories. Olga Vickery groups "Artist at Home," "Dr. Martino," and "The Brooch" together as conventional in their reliance "on plot complication and action leading to some sort of resolution" ([1959] 1964, 300–01). The setting suggests an earlier story, "Black Music" (Blotner 1974, 688). The narrator's closing remark recalls the observation of the captain in "Crevasse" when he is exiting from the tunnel of the dead. The captain comments on the coming of summer and longer days. In both cases, there is a wasteland sense of continuation without meaning (Owens 1979, 411–12). Ferguson notes the difference between the chronology of the *fabula* and the finished work. Faulkner had used this simple strategy in early stories, like the New Orleans sketches, and he was not averse to employing it in his more mature stories also, like "Artist at Home" among others (1991, 127–28).

James Watson offers a detailed look at houses in Faulkner's fiction as they reflect characters and themes of the texts. In the case of "Artist at Home," Watson points out that the surname *Howes* reinforces an ironic distinction between *house* and *home*. This ironic rendering of names also appears in the names *Hightower* and *Barron* in other fiction (Watson 1980, 138).

Michael Millgate recognizes death as a common concern in all eleven stories in "The Middle Ground." He suggests further that the unifying principle of this section may be the "experience of upheaval and uprooting." Two stories reflect homelessness: "Artist at Home" and "Pennsylvania Station" ([1966] 1989, 273). Owens believes that concern with debasement and alienation in "Artist at Home" likens it to the fiction collected in *These 13* and also to the stories of "The Middle Ground" (1979, 399). For Kinney, "Artist at Home" fits portrayals of life and death in "The Middle Ground" "with a certain period foppishness" (1980, 73). Ferguson suggests that "Artist at Home," the middle story in "The Middle Ground," "is perhaps the most positive work in the section." The story "suggests a means of coming to terms with and transcending—if only temporarily—the tensions of human life by incorporating them into the timeless world of art" (Ferguson 1991, 160).

On the whole, the relational observations seem to achieve little more than to state the obvious or remark briefly on tangential parallels, but in doing so they at least demonstrate how this "different" Faulkner story is not really so far from those "mainstream" texts. The interpretive comments, however, show greater depth and complexity that reveal "Artist at Home" to be a challenging reading experience.

## Interpretation and Criticism

The most substantive interpretive issues in "Artist at Home" revolve around the relative importance of the romantic affair and the creation of art, with most critics identifying the real conflict to be between the men as artists rather than as lovers. Character analyses offer a helpful entry into the critical response because they begin to reveal how these three adults are constructed around stereotyped notions of "artist" and "woman" and begin to reveal the different conclusions available if one accepts these characterizations seriously or ironically.

Roger's wife, Anne Howes, generates both condemnation and praise. In Bradford's estimation, Anne "is true to her kind." She is the daughter of a minister, and she has conventional expectations of marriage and family life that conflict with Roger's artistic ambitions and his desire to nurture new artists. She embodies the concept of "home" in the story. Because Roger has not conformed to Anne's expectations and because he facilitates the growing relationship between Anne and John, she responds to the character of John Blair, whose innocence is compelling but finally limiting. There is not, Bradford observes, an implication of censure in the narrator's attitude toward Anne (Bradford 1973, 176–79). Peterson describes Anne as "shrewish" (1977, 19).

For Owens, Anne's character actually undergoes some change from her initial portrayal "as a defender of the home." Her background is traditional and her attraction to John is essentially maternal. Her realistic attitude serves as a "foil to the perverse affectations and abstractions of the artists." She can perceive and act; for example, she terminates the relationship with John when she realizes his "dangerous morbidity." Her cutting the telephone wires is a "symbolic act of severance." She laughs at John's absurd posturing in the rainstorm, but she is also compassionate. The conditional framing of adultery as something that *would not* actually achieve a closeness to John implies that their relationship has not and does not progress to sexual intimacy. Her choice of Roger over John, "obtuseness" over "solipsistic morbidity," is a pragmatic, life-affirming choice, but her rejection of the fur coat is an unexploitable "gesture of freedom" (Owens 1979, 407–09). (Blotner's one-volume biography adds a parenthetical doubt as to whether Anne and John ever engaged in sexual intimacy [1984, 277].) According to Carothers, even though Anne frets over the intrusions by the artist community, she understands that economic success is not the artist's ultimate goal. When she rejects the mink coat, she contributes to the denial of financial reward as the goal of art. However, Anne has a "lack of understanding of her own feelings, and it markedly affects the reader's response to her subsequent diatribes against Blair" (Carothers 1985, 73–74).

Anne's husband, Roger Howes, is an artist who appears to have compromised creativity in an effort to create a conventional home life but who also seems willing to compromise home for creative inspiration. Bradford comments that the "*a priori* differences in role between man and woman" are exaggerated in the intensified professional and domestic demands on Roger. Roger's profession (writer) in Anne's perspective does not validate his manhood; however, in his assumption of a somewhat conventional life, "he has imperiled the vital heart of his character" (Bradford 1973, 176–77). Blotner describes Howes as an "amiable, generous man with an unflagging desire to help other artists and an unfailing capacity for being betrayed and hurt" (Blotner 1974, 688); but the situation reveals Roger's failure both as husband and artist whose creativity has lapsed and who has come to depend on other people (Blotner 1984, 277).

Owen sees Roger's failing not as compromising art to conventionality so much as failing to integrate the respective demands of art and experience, a failure that leaves him debased and impotent. For Roger, John Blair represents his abstract definition of "artist" "with his eccentric posturing and aesthetic idealism," and Roger hopes for vicarious fulfillment in the talent he sees in John. In his effort to maintain an abstract definition of the concept *artist*, Roger debases both his art and his role as husband revealed in Anne's frustrated description: "Blind! Blind!" and in his preference for artificial, electric light (not creative light). Even his Virginia home is a middle ground between New York and Mississippi. Howes has encouraged and perhaps instigated the affair; his work "has become mere imitation of manipulated behavior" and is spoken of disparagingly in market terms. For Owens, Roger's outburst in the study reflects some conflict he feels in his choice to sacrifice his family for art (1979, 399–400, 404–06; *CS* 639).

Carothers believes that even though Howes tries to adopt the same detachment and cynicism that the narrator displays, he is not unmoved by the affair. He does express his displeasure in one outburst. Carothers states, "His love for her is genuine, but he is too sophisticated to allow himself to express it in the obvious romantic clichés." Roger would be likely to avoid clichés. Because he can recognize that Blair is not producing to the level of his capability, Roger displays his knowledge of the literary market and of art (Carothers 1985, 74).

John Blair is one "of Faulkner's many avatars of the doomed, romantic idealist" (Owens 1979, 393) constructed around the "image of Poet-as-Child" (Carothers 1985, 73). His sky-blue coat operates as a leitmotif (Ferguson 1991, 137). The poet fails "in his arrant and fatal romanticism" (Blotner 1984, 277). For Owens, Blair "is Faulkner's most ruthlessly ironic caricature of self-destructive romanticism." Blair is limited by his abstractions: his poetry about freedom and equality attends more to ideas than to people. When forced to confront the conflict between romantic ideal and physical desire, John does not fare well. He continually defines Anne as she evokes his own memories of childhood and mother. His participation is essentially narcissistic, and their relationship is "probably unconsummated." When John leaves, without an object for his "romantic idealization" and his fantasy disintegrating, he "chooses the absolute withdrawal of death." John is a diminished imitation of Shelley. As the narrator notes, it even takes less water to kill him. And the contrast to the more pragmatic Pope heightens the absurdity of John's stance in the rain (Owens 1979, 406–07).

A fourth character in the story, the narrator, is not identified. His tone is "witty" and "nonchalant," and he is a pervasive presence (Everett 1969, 132). Because Roger is accountable for facilitating the infidelity of his wife, Bradford suggests that the narrative approach must carefully avoid allowing resentment toward him. Faulkner achieves this by having the "gently mocking observer" keep the focus on artistry rather than domesticity and by the affirmation of reconciliation at the end (1973, 178).

Owens perceives the narrator as a fourth, separate identity very different from the characterization Bradford offers. He is "unsympathetic" and "unreliable," "constricted by his insensitivity and pervasive cynicism." His interpolations provide ironic juxtaposition of assumption and actuality because like the other male characters, he abstracts and stereotypes human behavior, trying to simplify complexity he does not understand. Further, he orients the focus on art rather than on the relationship between John and Anne. The narrator closes the story "with a coda of devastating irony" that recognizes a continued but meaningless existence for Anne and Roger, perhaps even a repetition of the experience of infidelity (Owens 1979, 410–11).

Carothers cautions that the narrator is unreliable but amusing. His response to John's vigil in the rain minimizes the pathos of the scene, but contrasts with the compassion apparent in Anne's laughter (1985, 74–75). Throughout the story, he shifts between past, present, and subjunctive verb tenses and makes extensive literary allusions (Carothers 1985, 72–73). Skei believes the narrator emphasizes his own idea of important concerns in the story and what is odd or questionable. Also, the narrator tries to include the reader in observing the tableaux of lovers and estranged husband (Skei 1985, 152).

An alternate view of the narrator, first suggested by Joseph Reed, is that he is in fact Howes telling his own story. Reed describes "Artist at Home" to be "perhaps as close to pure narrative experiment as any of Faulkner's other stories." The tone at the opening teases with a sense that critical judgment of the life of the writer is sure to come, but the judgment does not appear. Then, with the romantic triangle established, the narrator begins to address the reader directly, and the narrative distance narrows. Finally, the story "Artist at Home" is itself the story being written about the events unfolding. The joke is on the reader. Reed explains, "What seemed at the outset to have been rather shallow third-person satire has become the self-irony of a first-person involvement. . . . By virtue of the device of synchronous composition, the narrator in 'Artist' *is* his own subject" (Reed 1973, 41–42, 55).

Ross affirms Reed's opinion that "Artist at Home" is Roger's story and that the narrator is Roger. This voice, though unidentified, has the character of Faulkner's other communal "we"; he also shows facility with sophisticated and homey idioms, but he differs from other "community spokesmen" because he has inside access, even to the couple's bedroom. Therefore he must be Roger. This identification of the narrator as Howes helps explain the shifting verb tense: "present tense invokes, in colloquial narration at least, an immediacy of telling, while the past tense is the conventional tense of written narrative." The mingling implies a "movement into and out of telling and writing, an oscillation appropriate to Howes's role as writer and teller, as artist and gossip." Ross adds that the narrative voice undercuts the implied preference for John's poetry over Roger's prose, which would make especially good sense if Roger were narrating the story. Finally, for Ross, "Depicted telling and writing are mingled in a metanarration that becomes a self-image of the literary artist at work," which may make "Artist at Home" "Faulkner's most circular, most self-reflexive, most self-implicative text" (Ross 1989, 240–41).

More recently, Ferguson has objected to Reed's view that the story we read is Howes's story. The identity of the narrator is hard to discern, and the early omniscient voice gradually assumes a "sardonic tone" as well as the stance of a person privy to the action in the Howes household. But Ferguson points out that Howes writes a book, not a short story ("Artist at Home"). Also, Ferguson uses passages from the manuscript to show that the narrator is a "less literate individual" than Roger Howes, a Ratliff-type. According to Ferguson, even if the narrator's language is revised to a more formal style, the manuscript distinctions show that Faulkner conceived of the narrative voice as different from Howe's voice (Ferguson 1991, 114–16).

As critics disagree about the characterizations, they also have varied opinions about the theme of "Artist at Home." The one point of agreement, however, is that the story is first about artistic creation and only secondarily about marital relationships.

Walter Everett identifies the center of the story to be the "process by which literary art is created" (1969, 132). Bradford sees "Artist at Home" affirming at its core the idea of endurance in Faulkner's fiction. The conflict of the story is essentially the image of "artist as artist, set over against the artist as man," concluding that the needs of the man must give way to those of the artist. The story is comic rather than tragic because of the reconciliation, however tenuous. It is also comic because the creation of art is affirmed (even if briefly in the superior work of Blair) and "because Anne is a woman and cannot be in this way foolish without drawing Roger after her" (Bradford 1973, 175, 179–80)

Owens terms "Artist at Home" an "important work" given its "concern with the relation of art to life, with contrasting modes of perception and action, and with the modern dissociation of art and experience." The story's irony develops from the fact that both artists use the adultery (consummated or not) to inspire their art. The two men represent contrasting impulses of action, manipulation, and self-destruction. One aspect of the story is that it mirrors Faulkner's rejection of the self-indulgence and narcissism that he came to associate with aesthetic idealism. Another aspect of Faulkner's developing aesthetic was the "growing awareness of perception as a recognition of the complexity of experience." Both Roger Howes and John Blair suffer from abstract perception, as Owens notes, in their abstractions of Anne and in their attempts to treat her as category rather than an individual, a condition Owens terms "masculine obtuseness." "If there is a positive note in this story of debasement and distortion, it is this affirmation of the unpredictable complexity of experience that preserves it from artificial control" (1979, 393–99, 410).

Skei describes the story as a portrait of the "sacrificial nature of artistic creation." It is a "superficial study of what an artist may be compelled to sacrifice or cannibalize to get his work done." The titular reference to the artist's being "at home" is ironic, for he is not at home in his present inability to write. Skei continues, "The narrator . . . emphasizes the extraordinarily private and sacrificial nature of artistic creation, and also the distance there is between *life* and *art*." If the story presents a co-opting of life in art, it also affirms "life's miraculous ability to prevail in the end, if only because it outlasts all bereavement, and loss" (Skei 1981, 70; 1985, 153).

According to Karl, the story reflects the tension between a successful writer's "settled existence" and the "'real' life of the poet." One seeks return while the other seeks newness in their "forms of expression." Karl adds, "While the formulation of the idea is naive and disingenuous, it was a real conflict for Faulkner—so much of a struggle he allowed a clearly inferior piece of work to go to the *Post*, and finally to be included in *Collected Stories*" (Karl 1989, 436).

Robert Hamblin describes "Artist at Home" as a story that reveals "Faulkner's contempt for facts and documentation" as it constructs a "satirical treatment of popular notions of artists and their behavior." The story examines the relationship of fact and imagination in the writer's arsenal. Howes stops to wait for new developments in the relationship between Blair and Anne, but he also embellishes the story. The story "ridicules the notion that art is mere copying and underscores Faulkner's emphasis upon the necessity of imagination in the fictive process" (Hamblin 1989, 159–60).

For Ross, the story becomes an articulation of how one conjoins "telling and writing." It is typical of Faulkner that he would challenge the character John to "stop talking" in order to write. Blair must experience emotional depth before he can write, but these emotions lead not only to creative inspiration but also to death, which "only reinforces the special pathos and beauty of inspiration." But the issue of inspiration is more specifically involved with Howes, who also finds renewed inspiration in the affair, "specifically Anne's rejection" when she locks him out of the bedroom. Unless Roger is the narrator, he cannot finish the Blair story because he does not anticipate Anne's rejection of the gift of the fur. Finally, "The story dramatizes the triumph of the written text, which contains *both* the told story itself and the claims for a superior or more pure art as emotionally generated artifact (Blair's poem)." Through the image of Howes taking possession of both texts, Faulkner can affirm his own transition from poet to storyteller (Ross 1989, 238–42).

The comic tone that pervades the story should not be forgotten in perusing the serious thematic intent. The narrator, whether Roger or someone else, refuses in every instance, even when relating John's death, to alter the comic tone. Dorothy Tuck describes the story as "quasi-humorous" and "subtle," claiming that the conflict is "both ludicrous and critical" (1964, 160). In Everett's opinion, the "clever atmosphere" generated by the narrative voice appears as well in the conversations between Roger and Anne, and humor arises in Howes's seeming indifference to the relationship between his wife and the poet; after all, the situation does produce one good poem from the poet. The pram also provides a symbol by which the narrator maintains "critical distance, which is an integral part of this story" (1969, 132).

Carothers comments that "Artist at Home" achieves a "mock-bardic" tone (Carothers 1985, 20). Skei calls "Artist at Home" a "this-is-to-show" story, a story in which the "narrator insists that the readers must see and understand what he relates to them" (Skei 1981, 70). In "Artist at Home," Ross notes that the narrator "introduces communicative and expressive elements typical of speech into narration by addressing an implied audience." His voice is *mimetic*; it imitates talk (1989, 15, 77).

Considering the interest this story generates regarding Faulkner's portrayal of the creative endeavor, it is somewhat surprising that "Artist at Home" does not have more prominence in the short fiction. Despite their interest in the text, critics find some structural weakness in the story. Bradford locates its primary failing in its intellectual orientation; the "characters almost exist *for the sake of* their aesthetic implications (Bradford 1973, 181). Owens itemizes additional flaws: thin characterizations, undeveloped details, and a "sometimes awkward mixture of ludicrous comedy and tragic consequences" that renders the story "ambiguous and at times unconvincing." But the story is important because it reflects Faulkner's interest in the artist figure and his positioning himself with an "ironic and realistic detachment" (Owens 1979, 412). Carothers objects to the undeveloped romance between Blair and the Howe's maid, Pinkie, the use of parenthetical commentary in dialogue, the uncertain degree of intimacy between the lovers, and the obvious revelation that the new novel is about the threesome (Carothers 1985, 74). And Ferguson asserts that the ending of "Artist at Home" leaves "something to be desired." The reader is not prepared for the conclusion (Ferguson 1991, 134).

Whether or not one agrees with these assessments, "Artist at Home" is an engaging story, perhaps because it is "unique" in Faulkner's work (Skei 1985, 156)—or at least a "relative rarity" (Carothers 1985, 75). Few have been as complimentary as Everett, who writes, "The excellent manipulation of the narrator's point of view makes 'Artist at Home' one of Faulkner's most successful short narratives" (1969, 132). When trying to explain the choice of "The [sic] Artist at Home" as the second story to be translated into Russian, M. Thomas Inge speculates that it was the final affirmation of a "practical view of art" that gave the story its appeal to the Russians (Inge 1984, 176). If we resist the distance that keeps us from becoming closely involved with the characters in "Artist at Home," many of us find its puzzled identities and ironic challenges irresistible.

## Works Cited

Blotner, Joseph. 1974. *Faulkner: A Biography*. 2 vols. New York: Random House.

———. 1984. *Faulkner: A Biography*. 1 vol. New York: Random House.

Bradford, M. E. 1973. "An Aesthetic Parable: Faulkner's 'Artist at Home.'" *Georgia Review* 27:175–81.

Carothers, James B. 1985. *William Faulkner's Short Stories*. Ann Arbor, MI: UMI Research Press.

Everett, Walter K. 1969. *Faulkner's Art and Character*. Woodbury, NY: Barron's Educational Series.

Faulkner, William. 1933. "Artist at Home." *Story* 3 (August):27–41.

———. 1950. *Collected Stories of William Faulkner*. New York: Random House.

———. 1987. *William Faulkner Manuscripts 24: Short Stories*. Ed. Joseph Blotner. New York: Garland.

Ferguson, James. 1991. *Faulkner's Short Fiction*. Knoxville: University of Tennessee Press.

Hamblin, Robert W. 1989. "Carcassonne in Mississippi: Faulkner's Geography of the Imagination." In *Faulkner and the Craft of Fiction: Faulkner and Yoknapatawpha, 1987*. Ed. Doreen Fowler and Ann J. Abadie. Jackson: University Press of Mississippi, 148–71.

Holmes, Edward M. 1966. *Faulkner's Twice-Told Tales: His Re-Use of His Material*. The Hague: Mouton.

Inge, M. Thomas. 1984. "Teaching Faulkner in the Soviet Union." In *Faulkner: International Perspectives: Faulkner and Yoknapatawpha, 1982*. Ed. Doreen Fowler and Ann J. Abadie. Jackson: University Press of Mississippi, 174–93.

Karl, Frederick R. 1989. *William Faulkner: American Writer*. New York: Weidenfeld and Nicolson.

Kinney, Arthur F. 1980. "Faulkner's Narrative Poetics and *Collected Stories*." *Faulkner Studies* 1:58–79.

Meriwether, James B. [1961] 1971. *The Literary Career of William Faulkner: A Bibliographical Study*. Princeton, NJ: Princeton University Library. Reprint. Columbia: University of South Carolina Press.

———. 1973. "Faulkner's Correspondence with Scribner's Magazine." *Proof* 3:253–82.

Millgate, Michael. [1966] 1989. *The Achievement of William Faulkner*. New York: Random House. Reprint. Athens: University of Georgia Press. Brown Thrasher Books.

Owens, Tony J. 1979. "Faulkner, Anderson, and 'Artist at Home.'" *Mississippi Quarterly* 32:393–412.

Peterson, Richard F. 1977. "An Early Judgement of Anderson and Joyce in Faulkner's 'Artist at Home.'" *Kyushu American Literature* 18:19–23.

Reed, Joseph W., Jr. 1973. *Faulkner's Narrative*. New Haven: Yale University Press.

Ross, Stephen M. 1989. *Fiction's Inexhaustible Voice: Speech and Writing in Faulkner*. Athens: University of Georgia Press.

Skei, Hans H. 1977. *Bold and Tragical and Austere: William Faulkner's These 13: A Study*. University of Oslo Department of Literature.

———. 1981. *William Faulkner: The Short Story Career*. Oslo, Norway: Universitetsforlaget.

———. 1985. *William Faulkner: The Novelist as Short Story Writer*. Oslo, Norway: Universitetsforlaget.

Tuck, Dorothy. 1964. *Crowell's Handbook of Faulkner*. New York: Thomas Y. Crowell.

Vickery, Olga W. [1959] 1964. *The Novels of William Faulkner*. Baton Rouge: Louisiana State University Press.

Watson, James G. 1980. "Faulkner: The House of Fiction." In *Fifty Years of Yoknapatawpha: Faulkner and Yoknapatawpha 1979*. Ed. Doreen Fowler and Ann J. Abadie. Jackson: University Press of Mississippi, 134–58.

# The Brooch

## Publication History

"The Brooch," not published until January 1936 in *Scribner's*, existed at least as early as January 29, 1931. Submission efforts from 1931 to 1936 can be traced at least partially in the story-sending schedule, available correspondence, and extant manuscripts and typescripts.

Evidence suggests that "The Brooch" had a prior history under the name "Fire and Clock," a title on the sending schedule that James Meriwether lists as a lost story (1971, 317–18). Hans Skei argues that "Fire and Clock" is probably an early version of "The Brooch." "Fire and Clock" has its own unsuccessful submission efforts recorded on the sending schedule. All dates precede the first mention of "The Brooch" on the schedule. "Fire and Clock" was first submitted to the *American Mercury* on January 23, 1930. It was subsequently submitted to the *Saturday Evening Post* on February 6, 1930, to *College Humor* on February 14, 1930, and to *Cosmopolitan* on March 1, 1930.

It was not unusual for Faulkner to resubmit revised stories to magazines for second readings. Thus, the possibility that *College Humor* received the story twice does not diminish Skei's argument. Skei links the "Fire and Clock" title with early versions of "The Brooch" where fires and clocks are prevalent images in the text. He grants that "Fire and Clock" may be a lost story, but given Faulkner's pattern of revising and sometimes renaming unsuccessful stories, it is also reasonable to assume that the story underwent some alteration of text and title. Furthermore, Faulkner's propensity to title his stories in ways that enlighten the texts suggests "The Brooch" as the most likely story that could have carried the name "Fire and Clock" or perhaps "The Fire and the Clock." Based on this earlier date, Skei believes that "The Brooch" and two other stories, "Idyll in the Desert" and "The Big Shot," were the "first Faulkner sent out in what was to become his most sustained and consistent effort in the writing and selling of short stories" (Skei, 1981, 16, 36, 52–57, 123 n. 154; see also Skei 1979, 127–29; Meriwether [1961] 1971, 176–80; Karl 1989, 433). Skei's argument is convincing, but as he admits, no documentary evidence makes an explicit tie between the two stories. Perhaps for this reason, Joseph Blotner has acknowledged Skei's claim but has not endorsed it (1984, 274; *WFM 24* Introduction xiii).

According to his submission schedule, Faulkner first sought publication of the story titled "The Brooch" in 1931, submitting it to *Forum* on January 29, 1931, and to *College Humor* on February 13, 1931. It is fairly certain that "The Brooch" submitted in 1931 was a variant of the story published five years later. Meriwether dates an extant carbon typescript from this early period because the verso of page seven bears a notation about earnings dated January 1, 1931 ([1961] 1971, 170–71). Blotner points out that the notation was made before the sheet was re-used for the carbon copy of the story (1974, Notes 98). After the rejections in 1931, several years passed before Faulkner attempted again to publish "The Brooch." Mention of the story reappears in Faulkner's correspondence to his agent, Morton Goldman, in 1935 and it may be referred to in an earlier letter from 1934. Skei believes that a letter from Faulkner to Goldman that Blotner dates from late winter or spring of 1934 may refer to "The Brooch" rather than "Mule in the Yard" as Blotner suggests. Faulkner opens the letter, "Maybe this one will hit Cosmo." As Skei notes, it seems to complement a later reference to the "bust" he made at *Cosmopolitan* with "The Brooch"; this reference is from a letter to Goldman that Blotner dates from March 1935 (Skei 1981, 56; *SL* 79, 90). By October 1935, the proofs of the story were sent for Faulkner's review, and in January 1936, the story was finally published in *Scribner's*. Faulkner included "The Brooch" in "The Middle Ground" section of *Collected Stories* (1950).

Before "The Brooch" was adapted for television, Faulkner had tried to use it in a movie screenplay. He had been assigned to salvage several failed screenplays for the novel *The Damned Don't Cry*. He judged the title to be its strongest attribute and suggested that it might be strengthened by the incorporation of his story "The Brooch." Faulkner's revised, combined treatment was also rejected (Blotner 1974, 1164–65). Frederick Karl adds that *The Damned Don't Cry* was eventually released in 1950; however, Faulkner's treatment was not used (1989, 710 note).

Even though Faulkner could not translate "The Brooch" to the movies, it gains some distinction by being the first of his works adapted for television. It appeared on the Lux Video Theatre, April 2, 1953. Faulkner collaborated on the script with Ed Rice, an editor for the program, and Richard McDonagh, a producer-editor. The Boyd family was portrayed by Dan Duryea, Sally Forrest, and Mildred Natwick (Meriwether [1961] 1971, 48, 162). The presentation was regarded "almost unanimously" as a failure (Blotner 1974, Notes 188). A critic for the *New York Times*, Jack Gould, complained that a "bitter story of a man caught in a fatal mother complex" had become a "soap opera that dutifully met all the provisions of television's purity code" (quoted in Millgate [1966] 1989, 50). Gould's objection related to what he perceived to be a "bowdlerized" version of the original story, with a happy resolution in which the son stood up for himself, the mother agreed to stop meddling, and the couple was happily reunited (Phillips 1988, 51–52). At least Faulkner could enjoy the $1,000 he received for his effort (Blotner 1974, 1452).

## Circumstances of Composition, Sources, and Influences

If "Fire and Clock" is an early version of "The Brooch," Faulkner composed the story no later than January 23, 1930, a year earlier than "The Brooch" appeared. Several partial and complete manuscripts and typescripts titled "The Brooch" track significant developments prior to publication. It is clear that the published text evolved through numerous revisions. The Rowan Oak Papers at the University of Mississippi contain an incomplete manuscript and four incomplete ribbon typescripts of various lengths, all bearing evidence of revision. A complete early manuscript and two complete typescripts, one early and one late, are held by the University of Virginia and reproduced in *William Faulkner Manuscripts 24*. They, too, show continued effort and improvement in the story (Kinney and Fowler 1983, 327–34; *WFM 24* Introduction xiii, 246–96).

One issue of revision that is unclear is the extent to which Alfred Dashiell, editor of *Scribner's*, influenced changes in "The Brooch." In a handwritten postscript to a letter to Goldman, probably from July 1935, Faulkner asks him to return "The Brooch" so that he might rewrite it. Blotner states that Faulkner made the request "so he could rewrite it in accordance with Dashiell's suggestions" (Blotner 1974, 899). Skei follows Blotner in this claim (1981, 56–57). But alone, the letter to Goldman does not explicitly establish that influence. In the postscript Faulkner writes to Goldman, "Had letter from Dashiell at Scribner's. Send 'The Brooch' to me and I will rewrite it. Also send him 'Fool About a Horse' if he has not seen it. Will rewrite that too if necessary" (*SL* 92). The implication is that Dashiell may have suggested that an altered story would be publishable. But the vague associations in this note do not reveal the nature or degree of his influence, if any.

Dashiell probably did have some suggestions for revisions after the story was set in proofs. On October 15, 1935, an assistant editor at *Scribner's* forwarded the proofs of a story that Meriwether believes was "The Brooch." She points out Dashiell's concern over some inconsistencies in passages about "Mother" (*SL* 92; Meriwether 1973, 281–82). Early versions of "The Brooch" bear an inconsistency in the number of times Amy calls Mrs. Boyd "Mother." When Amy and Howard announce their marriage, Amy calls Mrs. Boyd "Mother for the first and the last time." Yet on the night her deception is discovered, she says "It's me, Mother" (*WFM 24* 259, 262). This contradiction is, however, corrected by a parenthetical statement that appears in the published text and in a carbon typescript that is believed to be a duplicate of the setting copy for *Scribner's* (*WFM 24* Introduction xiii). In the parenthetical remark the narrator indicates that Amy will use "Mother" on one more occasion: "That morning Amy called Mrs. Boyd 'Mother' for the first and (except one, and that perhaps shocked out of her by surprise or perhaps by exultation) last time" (*CS* 651; *WFM 24* 274).

If the carbon typescript is what Dashiell received, it is not clear what other inconsistency might have bothered him. If the carbon typescript was made after the story was published, the addition may have been made to resolve the contradiction Dashiell noted. The title page of the typescript indicates that the story was published in *Scribner's* in January 1936. Faulkner did apparently have the story typed in 1944 when he was working on the screenplay for Warner Brothers (*SL* 183). If the typescript follows rather than precedes the publication in *Scribner's*, then Dashiell may at least be credited for the parenthetical clarification.

The evidence of the manuscripts demonstrates a variety of improvements in the developing story. Faulkner changed some names in the story. Blotner notes that in the manuscript Mrs. Boyd is first named Mrs. Weddel, a surname that follows the families in the earlier story "Mountain Victory" and the later story "Lo!" (1974, Notes 98). Sharon Hult points out that additional name changes include the change from "Harry" to the more formal "Howard" from the early typescript to the late typescript. In the early typescript Martha Ross is Amy Ross, which causes some confusion with Amy Boyd (Hult 1974, 291–92 n. 3).

The narrative is more firmly controlled in the published version. The earlier version unsuccessfully mixed hints about the lost brooch and the lost key to the car. Whether Amy is exposed by a call from the garage about the car or by the lost brooch is not clear. The confusion is unnecessary and distracting (*WFM 24* 264–65).

Hult identifies more significant changes in characterization and theme in the published text. Howard shows a greater awareness of his conflict with his mother. In the "Harry" texts, he is far less sensitive to Amy's presence and needs, and he seems less conscious of his own inability to act. In the later version, Howard and Amy show much more concern for each other, even as they recognize the futility of their situation. As the text evolves, Mrs. Boyd grows more harsh and rigid. Early versions of Amy portray her as much more defiant and aggressive, especially when she accuses Harry of spying on her and challenges him to act like a man. The latest typescript and the published text reflect "more sophisticated time shifts," give greater emphasis to Howard's childhood, and record Mrs. Boyd's cruel treatment of Howard and her hatred of Amy (Hult 1974, 291–92 n. 3). Blotner sees this alteration of Mrs. Boyd as moving toward the characterization of Mrs. Compson (1974, 883).

Without doubt, the most significant revision, one probably made in 1935, was the radical alteration in the story's conclusion (*WFM 24* Introduction xiii). In the early ending, the closing scene captures Howard's despair and Amy's grief for the deceased infant. There is no indication that she will leave or that he will commit suicide (*WFM 24* 265–66). Blotner believes that in that version the "story weakened toward the end" but "achieved a powerful evocation of mood and feeling" (1974, 684; see also Hult 1974, 291–92 n. 3; Ferguson 1991, 205 n. 8). In the revision, Amy leaves and Howard commits suicide, "his tragedy set in motion years before he finally placed the pistol in his mouth" (Blotner 1974, 884).

According to Blotner, one of the most unusual characteristics of this revised version is the extended discussion of the effect W. H. Hudson's novel *Green Mansions* had on Howard at various times in his life. In earlier versions, Howard reads a book, but only in the revised ending does the book figure so prominently. Blotner points out that Howard "had read it in the same edition Faulkner owned and inscribed 'Rowan Oak 1931'" (1974, 884). Hult believes that *Green Mansions* illuminates Howard's motivations. She notes that Ernest Hemingway, like Faulkner, knew Hudson's work and included references to it in *The Sun Also Rises*; she suggests that Faulkner knew Hemingway's novel by the time he wrote "The Brooch" (Hult 1974, 291–93).

The *Scribner's* text and the *Collected Stories* text are virtually the same. Only a few incidental changes exist, the most significant being the division of one sentence into two.

Faulkner's reading of *Green Mansions* is only one of several biographical elements reflected in the text. Blotner sees several parallels in the Howard–Amy relationship and that of Faulkner and his wife, Estelle. Amy's love of dancing and Howard's inability to dance and lack of interest in it are similar to the situation with the Faulkners; Estelle, like Amy, enjoyed dancing. Also the fictional couple share with Faulkner and Estelle the tragedy of losing a child in infancy. Alabama Faulkner, born on January 11, 1931, died January 20, 1931 (Blotner 1984, 273–74). In another nine days, Faulkner listed "The Brooch" under submissions to *Forum*. According to Karl, the relationship between Howard and Mrs. Boyd recalls Faulkner's closeness to his mother, Maud Falkner (1989, 424).

## Relationship to Other Faulkner Works

Faulkner's unusual use of the novel *Green Mansions* contrasts with his more familiar creation of new twists on certain character types in "The Brooch." Mrs. Boyd, for example, is reminiscent of the much better known Emily of "A Rose for Emily," who is "wooed by a dashing outsider" (Blotner 1974, Notes 98). Other associations are more extensive and more important to the unfolding story. The abandoned Mrs. Boyd becomes one of the domineering mothers who warp the lives of their children. Blotner compares her appearance in "The Brooch" and "Miss Zilphia Gant" (1974, 683–84; see also Hult 1974, 291). Noel Polk examines this character as portrayed in the fiction from 1927 to 1931. He observes that "in Faulkner's work of this period, mothers are, almost invariably, horrible people." His list includes Caroline Compson, Addie Bundren, Mrs. Bland, Narcissa Benbow, Elly's grandmother, Mrs. Boyd, Belle Mitchell, Mrs. Gant, Zilphia Gant, Caddy Compson, and even Dewey Dell Bundren (Polk 1984, 66). (A minor correction to Polk's synopsis of "The Brooch" is that Mrs. Boyd's bedroom is downstairs, not upstairs [Polk 1984, 80; *CS* 647].)

In a separate examination of the period between the original composition of *Sanctuary* in 1929 and the rewritten text in 1930, Polk focuses on the enclosure frame that usually accompanies older women. He finds that the "image of the gray-haired old woman, repressing or repressed, or both, appears throughout the fiction of this period in various combinations with windows in which their peering faces are framed or with pillows out of which their sallow faces stare, dominant." This list incorporates many of the domineering mothers, including Mrs. Boyd of "The Brooch" and the mothers and/or grandmothers in "Elly," "A Rose for Emily," "Dry September," and "There Was a Queen" (Polk 1985, 30–32).

James Carothers also makes this comparison of "frustrated women," but he wisely cautions that the "individual treatment of these women suggests that they are considerably more than the mere types that some critics have persisted in describing." Carothers adds to the comparisons Ike McCaslin's wife in *Go Down, Moses* (1985, 20). Skei links Mrs. Boyd in "The Brooch" to a similar portrayal in "Adolescence"; at the same time he cautions that "The Brooch" is "rather peculiar" compared to other Faulkner stories and should not be used as a source for generalization. Skei notes that "The Brooch" reflects the high value placed on maternal power in a traditional society. For many women, it is their only power and can be stronger than the powers of younger women (1985, 48, 178). James Ferguson also lists this "gallery" of "'Terrible Mothers,' witches, old bitches" and adds that even Aunt Louisa in "Skirmish at Sartoris" is an interfering mother, even if her involvement is a comic manipulation (1991, 70).

Requisite to the portrayal of the domineering mother is the presentation of the child or children under her power. The daughter-in-law, Amy Boyd, is affected by Mrs. Boyd's overt cruelty and subtle manipulations. Amy herself represents one variation among numerous stories about a "girl harassed into profligacy by circumstances and an inflexible malevolent older woman"; other stories of this type are "Selvage" ("Elly") and "Hair." "Dr. Martino" similarly portrays "a girl balked by an older woman," but Blotner argues that "this was more complicated than the situation in 'The Brooch'" (1974, 683, 688). Karl likens Amy to Temple Drake (1989, 424).

Howard Boyd suffers most directly and irrevocably from his mother's domination. Hult describes Howard as a recognizably Faulknerian "sexually crippled male, tormented and bewildered (one is tempted to say, all 'Gavined' or 'Benbowed' up) by his fantasy of an ideal female." Like Quentin Compson, Howard is torn between time and timelessness. Both seek to return to "the past of his infancy by suicide" (Hult 1974, 291, 294–95). Skei takes a slightly different view and sees Howard Boyd (not Bond as printed in the text) as one male character who corresponds to the troubled female characters in Faulkner. Skei also associates Howard with various other "loyal husbands" including those in "Idyll in the Desert," "Artist at Home," and "Honor," who accept their wives' indiscretions (1985, 128, 162, 313 n. 14).

Other comparisons can be made in addition to the identification of common character traits in the stories. Olga Vickery's close study of the recurring patterns in Faulkner's short fiction identifies a "pattern of form and structure" that depends "on plot complication and action leading to some sort of resolution." She includes several stories in this group, most being non-Yoknapatawpha stories. They include "The Brooch," "Dr. Martino," and "Artist at Home" (Vickery [1959] 1964, 300–01; see also Skei 1985, 209). Ferguson points out that the structure of "The Brooch" begins *in medias res* with a "climactically disruptive situation": the phone call that initiates the events culminating in Boyd's suicide. Faulkner adopts this approach in a wide range of stories, "Red Leaves," "Dry September," and "Elly" among them. Beginning in the middle of the action, these stories also usually contain some sort of flashback or exposition to provide background to the events, as in the cases of "The Brooch" and "Elly" (Ferguson 1991, 128–29).

Joseph Reed lists "The Brooch" among the failed fiction in which the narrative "mode dwarfs the moment" and loses the author's interest. His inventory of stories that don't work counts "The Brooch" with "Fox Hunt," "Pennsylvania Station," and *Soldier's Pay* (Reed 1973, 56). Ferguson is less harsh in his judgment, suggesting that Faulkner's use of the limited third-person point of view in "The Brooch," "Elly," and "The Hound" represents the protagonist's inability to "adjust to the realities of other human beings," a failure that "dramatizes their solipsism" (Ferguson 1991, 98).

Stephen Ross uses lines from "The Brooch" to exemplify Faulkner's technique for portraying a dialogic quality of psychic voice in his fiction. A character's thoughts are often represented as several voices as in "Carcassonne," *The Wild Palms, Light in August*, and *Absalom, Absalom!* In "The Brooch" the dialogic involves Howard's intelligence speaking to his emotions (Ross 1989a, 139–40; 1989b, 168).

Skei identifies a recurring concern with the accumulation and misuse of power, particularly as it manifests itself in a need to control people and for material and personal gain. This motif is central in such stories as "Dr. Martino," "Fox Hunt," "Elly," and "The Brooch" (1985, 160).

Hult compares the use of gun and cave symbols in "The Brooch" and "A Courtship." Unlike "The Brooch," the Indian story employs these sexual symbols in a humorous manner for comic effect (Hult 1974, 304 n. 11). Ferguson places these symbols in the larger context of sexual imagery in Faulkner's short fiction. "The Brooch" reflects a more mature, subtle handling of sexual imagery also found in "A Rose for Emily," "Fox Hunt," and "Mountain Victory" (Ferguson 1991, 142–43).

In addition to noting the use of sexual imagery, Ferguson observes that Faulkner often employed "obvious controlling symbols" in his short fiction. The brooch in this story, verbena in "An Odor of Verbena," drought in "Dry September," deer in several stories, a leg, and hair are among these symbols, many of which are introduced in the titles of the stories (Ferguson 1991, 141).

In his analysis of "The Middle Ground" section of *Collected Stories*, Michael Millgate finds that "The Brooch" fits comfortably with the stories that "concern themselves with themes of deracination and disillusion, with the loss of familiar bearings." Also, like the other stories in this section, "The Brooch" contains a death (Millgate [1966] 1989, 273). Arthur Kinney also focuses on the presence of death in "The Middle Ground" stories. He notes the "sharp and resonant juxtaposition" Faulkner achieves by pairing the "sinister" story of "The Brooch" with the "romantic, distanced escapades of 'My Grandmother Millard and General Bedford Forrest and the Battle of Harrykin Creek'" (1980, 73).

Skei and Carothers also consider the placement of "The Brooch" in "The Middle Ground" section. Skei observes that the deaths in these stories are the "result of strong emotional conflict" (1985, 214). Carothers enlarges the focal emphasis adding that "The Middle Ground" stories, given their range of geographic and temporal settings, "can be understood as a series of investigations of the twin themes of sex and death" and that they also demonstrate the extremes of individual behavior (1985, 59). Ferguson adds that the late insertion of "The Brooch," "Pennsylvania Station," and "Artist at Home" in "The Middle Ground" may have disrupted the unity of the section. Nevertheless, some parallels can be found if one pairs the stories working from the outside toward the middle of the section. This strategy pairs "The Brooch" and "Pennsylvania Station," two stories "about the consequences of a stupidly unrealistic selfless devotion" (1991, 156, 160).

## Interpretation and Criticism

"The Brooch" benefits from criticism that both treats it as an individual text and sets it in the context of Faulkner's other works. This Mississippi story may or may not take place in Jefferson or Yoknapatawpha County. What goes on inside the house is more important than where the house is located. Faulkner actually omitted from the later version an aside in the early text that tells how condescending the established community was toward the "new Country Club" (*WFM 24* 254). Walter Everett gives too much emphasis to the community mind-set when he interprets the story as "pivoting on the conflict inherent in the stratified society of a Mississippi hamlet" (1969, 135–36). Although Mrs. Boyd uses Amy's background as a justification for her dislike, no evidence in the story indicates that she might have approved of any other woman for her son.

The Boyds and the dynamics of their relationships with each other are at the heart of both the story and the best criticism. Critics come to different conclusions about Howard's behavior and the degree to which he permits his mother's domination. In her synopsis of the story, Dorothy Tuck describes Howard as apparently willing to be dominated by his mother (1964, 162). Everett describes Howard as an "immature man who allows his mother to destroy his marriage and him." Amy's anguish over her "dear little baby" has an ambiguous twist. It obviously refers to the deceased child but also reflects Howard's immaturity. His identification with *Green Mansions* "delineates his loneliness, his emotional ineptitude" (Everett 1969, 135–36). Joseph Garrison argues that Howard reduces complex situations into "simple terms of cause and effect." Given his "absolutist's mentality," Howard seeks a conclusive resolution to every problem. He will not, therefore, make a commitment to Amy as long as he feels his commitment to his mother. The "them" that Howard, like his father, "cannot seem to live with" enlarges in this reading to refer not just to the women in his life, but to "tradition for tradition's sake" and "passive self-indulgence." Suicide, then, becomes the only means Howard has "of guaranteeing an absolutely final and reliable act of will" (Garrison 1974, 55–57).

Hult offers the most extensive analysis of Howard and the Boyd women. Her interpretation shows that this story, as Skei has noted, is one of Faulkner's most deliberately Freudian texts. She also discusses *Green Mansions* as a source of clues to understanding the story. Howard, living a confined life in his bedroom, contrasts with the explorer hero of the novel. In the fantasy he pursues alone in his room, he lets a third woman into his life: Rima in *Green Mansions*. Early in his life his fascination is with the ideal beauty of Rima. She represents the "perfect mother-lover for Howard Boyd." Hult concludes that "like the maiden on Keats's urn, Rima is the ever-receding goal, the virgin ideal in stasis who will never change, never become lover or Mother." In his life, Howard can never reconcile the "two female principles, the mother–lady and the wife–lover, that are merged in the novel's fantasy and his own. After Amy resumes her Saturday excursions, Howard returns to the novel. He forgoes the passages about Rima and reads about Abel's wanderings alone in the forest. Howard's reverting to this fantasy world shows him to be like his own child. Neither is able to grow up. His child's death presages his own (Hult 1974, 298–99; Skei 129). Karl's reading of the suicide is that Howard's padding the bathroom to muffle the sound of the shot is a final act of consideration for his mother. Howard commits suicide as an act of "revenge against his own impotence and against his mother's tyranny" (1989, 425).

Skei argues that the mother–son bond cannot be easily severed "because so much is invested in the parent–child relationship." He contends that the mother figure has "attained ideal dimensions." No other woman can compete with her. The security of the parent–child relationship contrasts with the danger of establishing new relationships. The influence of his mother makes it difficult for Howard to establish a mature connection with another woman even though to do so is his only means of escape from his mother's "vigilant maternity." When Howard publicly declares his relationship with Amy (spanking her), he acts like his mother, claiming ownership of this person (Skei 1985, 118–19).

Tuck characterizes Amy as "somewhat flighty" (1964, 162). Amy represents a necessary contrast to Howard's mother. She is uninhibited and not the "lady" his mother claims to be. The difference is important because it makes Howard feel autonomous and yet does not threaten his relationship with his mother (Hult 1974, 295; see also Skei 1985, 128–29). Hult also compares Amy to another woman in Howard's life: the fictional Rima in *Green Mansions*. In a sense Amy is like Rima because they are both repressed by enclosure: Rima in her hut; Amy in the Boyd house. Their differences are more crucial for Howard. With Amy, Howard must confront a real woman who exists in time and who lacks the combination of beauty, divinity, and maternal protectiveness that Rima possesses (Hult 1974, 295, 300–01).

Hult notes the way Mrs. Boyd continually acts to restrict Howard's freedom. Her "warped maternalism" is a response to abandonment by her husband and her father's death. While her stroke seems at first to suggest the possibility of Howard's liberation, it quickly becomes another more powerful means of control. Her rigidity repeats Faulkner's portrayal of rigidity in opposition to motion and change (Hult 1974, 293–95; see also Skei 1985, 119).

Sexual issues pervade the text. Hult contends that Mrs. Boyd forces Howard to choose either security or sex. In her room where time has been stopped, Howard may "return to the womb" and try to avoid death, but the cessation of time and change is death. He challenges his mother by becoming engaged to Amy, but the challenge reflects his limited success and eventual defeat. He will not succeed in bringing a sexual partner into Mrs. Boyd's house. Howard's inability to dance indicates "his psychological impotence and maternal bondage." Since he cannot win Amy in a parked car, he wins her in ritual of ownership before an audience of adults. When Mrs. Boyd gives Amy the brooch, she negates Amy's power as Howard's sexual partner. Mrs. Boyd is a constant presence, always aware of what happens in the house (Hult 1974, 294–98; see also Ferguson 1991, 143).

Howard reconciles the opposite forces of Amy and Mrs. Boyd in the erotic overtones of his suicide. Hult reads the detailed ritual of Howard's suicide as a "pathetically 'private consummation' of his marriage to Amy" where "security and sexuality merge." Significantly, he uses Amy's coverlet to make a cave, a womb, and puts the gun in his mouth. Hult concludes, "The method and the act itself of Howard's suicide is a successful fantasy, as he secures for himself in the anticipation and erotic excitement of death what he was never able to achieve in life" (Hult 1974, 304–05).

Recurring descriptions of clocks, fires, books, and brooches further indicate the importance of imagery in the story. Everett parallels the fastidiousness that drove Mrs. Boyd's husband away and the use of the heirloom brooch to defeat Amy. He understands the two clocks, one stopped by Mrs. Boyd and one stopped by Howard, to "express a rejection of an unpleasant occurrence in time" (Everett 1969, 135).

Skei suggests that even if the fire and the clock are less important symbols than the brooch, they still invest meaning in the text. The fire does not burn well, and Howard keeps poking at it. It represents the love and desire between Howard and Amy that cannot flame under Mrs. Boyd's cold maternal glare. The house is cold as the sound of the clock. Ironically, Skei notes, "Howard must *fire* his gun to escape the insoluble conflict and remain forever untroubled by time" (1981, 56).

The significance of the brooch is both literal and symbolic. It carries the narrative forward because it is the means by which Amy's lie is exposed, and its "ugliness symbolized Mrs. Boyd's unremitting hatred and intent" (Blotner 1974, 684). Hult adds that the brooch also symbolizes the inability of Howard and Amy to have a mature sexual relationship. Ordinarily a brooch is worn at the neck, securing clothing more tightly about the neck. When Amy loses the brooch, she regains her sexuality but must leave the Boyd house (Hult 1974,

298). Taking an opposing view, Karl sees the gift of the brooch as a "kind of truce" between the women rather than a weapon in their battle (1989, 425).

Little critical consideration has gone beyond the dynamics of the characters' interactions. Karl, like Reed, considers the narrative to be deficient. He believes the story lacks a distinctive voice and that this lack results in a failure of coherence. He judges the dialogue to be "awkward" and the scenes between Howard and Amy to be "clumsy, even gauche" (1989, 425). Even though "The Brooch" was originally composed much earlier than 1935, Karl includes the revised text with the stories he labels "journeyman's work" from that year, including "That Will Be Fine" and "Uncle Willy" (1989, 544). (Although he mentions the *Scribner's* publication elsewhere, Karl mistakenly indicates in one reference that "The Brooch" was not published until it was included in *Collected Stories* [1989, 542].)

Not all critics share Karl's opinions, but Faulkner might. His own comments about the stories that he planned to include in *Collected Stories* reveal his opinion of many of the texts. Of "The Brooch" (and "Monk" and "Pennsylvania Station") he wrote, "Not too good, but will be included nowhere else, and there will probably not be enough more to make a volume, provided all my pieces are to be reprinted in book form" (*SL* 274). Malcolm Cowley does not rank "The Brooch" among Faulkner's best efforts (1966, 120). Nevertheless, Garrison's work demonstrates the rich possibilities for using the story in the classroom. Hult's bias toward the text is reflected in her analysis. She believes it to be a "fascinating work warranting serious consideration" (1974, 291). And Ferguson, who does not rank "The Brooch" among Faulkner's best stories, recognizes its "considerable merit" (1991, 36). At the present time, "The Brooch" still offers suggestive possibilities for critical inquiry.

## Works Cited

Blotner, Joseph. 1974. *Faulkner: A Biography*. 2 vols. New York: Random House.

———. 1984. *Faulkner: A Biography*. 1 vol. New York: Random House.

Carothers, James B. 1985. *William Faulkner's Short Stories*. Ann Arbor, MI: UMI Research Press.

Cowley, Malcolm. 1966. *The Faulkner-Cowley File: Letters and Memories, 1944–1962*. New York: Viking.

Everett, Walter K. 1969. *Faulkner's Art and Character*. Woodbury, NY: Barron's Educational Series.

Faulkner, William. 1936. "The Brooch." *Scribner's* 99 (January):7–12.

———. 1950. *Collected Stories of William Faulkner*. New York: Random House.

———. 1977. *Selected Letters of William Faulkner*. Ed. Joseph Blotner. New York: Random House.

———. 1987. *William Faulkner Manuscripts 24: Short Stories*. Ed. Joseph Blotner. New York: Garland.

Ferguson, James. 1991. *Faulkner's Short Fiction*. Knoxville: University of Tennessee Press.

Garrison, Joseph M., Jr. 1974. "Faulkner's 'The Brooch': A Story for Teaching." *College English* 36:51–57.

Hult, Sharon Smith. 1974. "William Faulkner's 'The Brooch': The Journey to the Riolama." *Mississippi Quarterly* 27:291–305.

Karl, Frederick R. 1989. *William Faulkner: American Writer*. New York: Weidenfeld and Nicolson.

Kinney, Arthur F. 1980. "Faulkner's Narrative Poetics and *Collected Stories*." *Faulkner Studies* 1:58–79.

Kinney, Arthur F., and Doreen Fowler. 1983. "For the Record: Faulkner's Rowan Oak Papers: A Census." *Journal of Modern Literature* 10:327–34.

Meriwether, James B. [1961] 1971. *The Literary Career of William Faulkner: A Bibliographical Study*. Princeton, NJ: Princeton University Library. Reprint. Columbia: University of South Carolina Press.

———. 1971. "The Short Fiction of William Faulkner: A Bibliography." *Proof* 1:293–329.

———. 1973. "Faulkner's Correspondence with *Scribner's Magazine*." *Proof* 3:253–82.

Millgate, Michael. [1966] 1989. *The Achievement of William Faulkner*. New York: Random House. Reprint. Athens: University of Georgia Press. Brown Thrasher Books.

Phillips, Gene D. 1988. *Fiction, Film, and Faulkner: The Art of Adaptation*. Knoxville: University of Tennessee Press.

Polk, Noel. 1984. "'The Dungeon Was Mother Herself': William Faulkner: 1927–1931." In *New Directions in Faulkner Studies: Faulkner and Yoknapatawpha, 1983*. Ed. Doreen Fowler and Ann J. Abadie. Jackson: University Press of Mississippi, 61–93.

———. 1985. "The Space between *Sanctuary*." In *Intertextuality in Faulkner*. Ed. Michel Gresset and Noel Polk. Jackson: University Press of Mississippi, 16–35.

Reed, Joseph W., Jr. 1973. *Faulkner's Narrative*. New Haven: Yale University Press.

Ross, Stephen M. 1989a. *Fiction's Inexhaustible Voice: Speech and Writing in Faulkner*. Athens University of Georgia Press.

———. 1989b. "Lying Beneath Speech": Some Preliminary Notes on the Representation of Thought in 'Carcassonne.'" In *Faulkner's Discourse: An*

*International Symposium.* Ed. Lothar Hönnighausen. Tübingen: Max Niemeyer Verlag, 159–69.

Skei, Hans H. 1979. "A Lost Faulkner Story 'Fire and Clock.'" *Edda* 127–29.

———. 1981. *William Faulkner: The Short Story Career.* Oslo, Norway: Universitetsforlaget.

———. 1985. *William Faulkner: The Novelist as Short Story Writer.* Oslo, Norway: Universitetsforlaget.

Tuck, Dorothy. 1964. *Crowell's Handbook of Faulkner.* New York: Thomas Y. Crowell.

Vickery, Olga W. [1959] 1964. *The Novels of William Faulkner.* Baton Rouge: Louisiana State University Press.

# My Grandmother Millard and General Bedford Forrest and the Battle of Harrykin Creek

## Publication History

*Story* magazine published "My Grandmother Millard and General Bedford Forrest and the Battle of Harrykin Creek" in its March–April issue of 1943. In the year that passed between Harold Ober's receipt of the story on March 30, 1942, and its publication, eight magazines rejected it because, as Faulkner anticipated, they objected to the outhouse motif. Stuart Rose, editor of the *Post*, wrote to Ober, "The turning point of the story destroys it for a family magazine." Even though *Story* paid only $50 for "My Grandmother Millard," Faulkner indicated to Ober that he was glad it had been placed. Faulkner added, "I still think it is amusing." The author found another opportunity to publish "My Grandmother Millard" when he placed the story eighth in "The Middle Ground" of *Collected Stories* (1950) (*SL* 167; *WFM 24* Introduction xiv; Blotner 1974, 1099–1100, 1138; Blotner 1990, 13–14; Skei 1981, 101, 102).

A musical comedy version of "My Grandmother Millard" entitled *The Battle of Harrykin Creek* by Evans Harrington and Andrew Fox approaches the racial issues related to the Sartoris family "by way of burlesque" (Kinney 1985, 36).

## Circumstances of Composition, Sources, and Influences

The close association this story shares with the Civil War stories Faulkner wrote during the 1930s makes it tempting to date "My Grandmother Millard" from that time; however, no evidence suggests that it was written before the spring of 1942 (Blotner 1974, 1099; Skei 1985, 273). Comparative readings of the partial and complete typescripts reveal several noteworthy differences. Most important, the passage on freedom is not in the earliest typescript, and the characters are more talkative in the later versions (*WFM 24* 351–412). The differences between the magazine text and the collected version include corrected spellings and word choices: the spelling of *practiced* is corrected (*Story* 72; *CS* 673), *gatepost* becomes *gate-post* (*Story* 72; *CS* 675), *jeering* becomes *peering* (*Story* 73; *CS* 676), *trompled* is changed to *trampled* (*Story* 75; *CS* 679), *hand glass* is changed to *hand-glass* (*Story* 75; *CS* 679), *summerhouse* becomes *summer house* (*Story* 75; *CS* 680), *beautiful girl* is changed to *beautiful-girl* (*Story* 75, 86; *CS* 680, 699), *dining room* is changed to *dining-room* (*Story* 77; *CS* 684), and *tail gate* becomes *tailgate* (*Story* 81; *CS* 690).

The composition date for "My Grandmother Millard" suggests that Faulkner's story idea may have been influenced by the increasing scarcity of goods and resultant rationing during World War II. Because fuel was in such short supply, Faulkner had already had to devise a method of plowing his land in Mississippi without the aid of his gasoline-powered tractor (Blotner 1974, 1099). Old stories he had heard in his younger days also provided substance for "My Grandmother Millard." Faulkner worked into the narrative a favorite anecdote of his, that of General Early's envisioning General Wheeler in hell (Blotner 1974, Notes 152). John Cullen, a childhood friend of Faulkner's, recalls being told stories about horse thieves that may figure into the sources for "My Grandmother Millard." One was about a particularly brutal criminal named John Murrell who murdered an elderly woman. Another of his recollections concerns a Vicksburg woman who requisitioned mules from the federal troops with forged vouchers (Cullen and Watkins [1961] 1975, 66–67).

Acknowledging that Faulkner would not be especially bothered by a lack of fidelity to the facts of history, Elmo Howell compares aspects of the fiction to the historical figure Nathan Bedford Forrest. The confrontation between Forrest and U.S. General William Sooy Smith at Hurricane Creek north of Oxford actually occurred in August 1864, not April 1862. In 1862, Forrest was still relatively unknown and much less the irritant that he became in 1864 when Smith kept Forrest occupied so that Sherman could proceed with his movements south (Howell 1970, 287–90). Thomas Nordanberg believes one mention of Forrest's shrewdness as a trader refers not only to his military talents but also to his past as a slave dealer (Nordanberg 1983, 73).

John Ditsky questions whether a geographical counterpart to the fictional Hurricane (Harrykin) Creek of Yoknapatawpha County exists. He identifies references to the creek in "My Grandmother Millard" and other works including *The Reivers*. Although Ditsky cannot confirm it as a definite source, he identifies a Hurricane Creek that exists near the Tennessee state line (Ditsky 1976, 88–89).

## Relationship to Other Faulkner Works

"My Grandmother Millard" contains a good bit of silliness, but by also featuring certain personages of Yoknapatawpha County it secures the story's place in the Yoknapatawpha saga. Faulkner told Malcolm Cowley that the narrator, Bayard, is the same Bayard who narrated *The Unvanquished* (*SL* 203), and as Hans Skei points out, Bayard is recognizable both through the relatives who are named and the relationship this story has with *The Unvanquished* (1985, 273). The links this story has with *The Unvanquished* are obviously strong, even though its comic tone presents some contrast with the more sober novel (Carothers 1985, 19). M. E. Bradford believes Granny Millard's triumph, diminished as it is by the context of comic figures, is the "same *kind* of triumph" as that of Sartoris in *The Unvanquished* (Bradford 1985, 322). Skei contends that the relationship between "My Grandmother Millard" and *The Unvanquished* is essentially one of contrasts. Unlike the longer work, the story "is void of any deeper significance; it is a very simple story, broad in its outlines, based on outrageous events, and deliberately intended to evoke laughter" (Skei 1985, 273). David Dowling describes "My Grandmother Millard" as an "exhilarating cartoon version of Faulkner's preoccupations with tradition and naming in *The Unvanquished*" (1989, 156).

Because "My Grandmother Millard" is about the Sartorises, the range of stories linked through the family is long. Even though "My Grandmother Millard" has such strong ties to *The Unvanquished*, it seems to be anticipated in some of the details of *Sartoris* (Carothers 1985, 27, 44). Arthur Kinney lists the appearances of the Sartorises in *Sartoris/Flags in the Dust*, *Sanctuary*, *Absalom, Absalom!*, *The Unvanquished*, *The Hamlet*, *The Town*, *The Mansion*, "Ad Astra," "All the Dead Pilots," "With Caution and Dispatch," "A Return," "There Was a Queen," "A Rose for Emily," "Ambuscade," "Raid," "Retreat," "Vendée," "Skirmish at Sartoris," "My Grandmother Millard," "The Bear," "Knight's Gambit," "Drusilla," "Rose of Lebanon," and the film script *War Birds*. Kinney's observations point out how "My Grandmother Millard" incorporates several other prominent Yoknapatawpha families. The story includes the Compson family, and Kinney observes an important fact revealed in the story is that another important Yoknapatawpha family, the McCaslins, purchased their slaves from Nathan Bedford Forrest, who represents authority in the short story and who in real life was a notorious slave trader, a brilliant military leader, and the Imperial Grand Wizard of the Ku Klux Klan (Kinney 1984, 156; 1985, 1–2, 22).

Joseph Blotner emphasizes yet another family link made in "My Grandmother Millard." This story is related to "Knight's Gambit" because it establishes the family name of Gavin Stevens's wife. Melisandre Backus was probably the great-grandmother of the Melisandre Backus who married Gavin Stevens (Blotner 1974, 1099, Notes 152). These two stories use similar solutions for conflict resolution: marriage (Ferguson 1991, 136).

Patrick Samway finds several likenesses between "My Grandmother Millard" and *Intruder in the Dust*: both stories use young male narrators, both stories involve young boys and older women going out digging (in the novel exhuming a body, in the story burying treasure), and both stories portray an elderly woman freeing a black man (1980, 237–38).

Nordanberg compares Philip Backhouse to Saucier Weddel of "Mountain Victory." Both of these Confederate soldiers are personifications of the Southern aristocrat, but Weddel is realized as a more admirable character; Backhouse is somewhat ridiculed in the comic rendering of a "latter-day knight." In contrast to the World War I characters who are often dysfunctional in conflict and in post–war civilian life, the Civil War characters demonstrate resourcefulness and vigor. Granny Millard, Backhouse, and Forrest all act to resolve the complications that arise from the romance of Philip and Melisandre (Nordanberg 1983, 71, 104–05). Yet Nordanberg also classifies "My Grandmother Millard" with the more positive uses of war as a context generating admirable human behavior that appeared in stories after 1941, particularly the World War II stories "The Tall Men," "Two Soldiers," and "Shall Not Perish" (Nordanberg 1983, 107).

Joseph Reed points out that Faulkner portrays very little of the Civil War in his fiction. Depiction of the war is minimal in *Light in August*, *Sartoris*, and in such various stories as "My Grandmother Millard" and "Mountain Victory" (Reed 1973, 183). Faulkner himself saw the relationship of "My Grandmother Millard" to the World War II stories (*WFM 24* Introduction xiv).

Olga Vickery's work with patterns in Faulkner's short fiction recognizes a broadly varied chase pattern in which the object is a "Reluctant Lover." The "Obsessed" pursuer typically has a comic rendering when that pursuer is a male, such as Philip St. Just Backhouse, Hawkshaw in "Hair," and even Ike Snopes in *The Hamlet*. Vickery adds that the romantic comedy is treated as parody in Ike's story and in the homosexual relationship portrayed in "Divorce in Naples" (Vickery [1959] 1964, 304–05).

John Longley compares the behavior of Melisandre in "My Grandmother Millard" and Sophonsiba in "Was" ([1957] 1963, 110). Ilse Lind believes that Faulkner's interest in sexual modesty manifests itself humorously in the fiction as clashes "between the crude facts of biological life and rigidly internalized concepts which deny that life," present in "My Grandmother Millard" and "Old Man" (1978, 98).

The tactic of hiding silver had historical analogues, but it also had appeared earlier in Faulkner's fiction. Before the idea was used in "My Grandmother Millard," Mrs. Compson had successfully hidden the family silver in the outhouse (Blotner 1974, 1099). Elizabeth Kerr identifies the motif of buried treasure not only in "My Grandmother Millard," but also in *Go Down, Moses* and *The Hamlet* (1983, 233).

James Ferguson identifies three dominant patterns in the short fiction that appear also in "My Grandmother Millard." In his fiction Faulkner portrays the typically negative effect of abstraction, with concomitant tensions that "derive from the attempt to impose artificial and arbitrary formulas, axioms, conceptualizations on the complexities of human experience." This pattern appears in "My Grandmother Millard" and "A Name for the City" as a "gap between language and life." Obsessions, which are usually destined to fail, triumph typically in a comic or sentimental context such as "My Grandmother Millard" and "Thrift" (Ferguson 1991, 79, 81). "My Grandmother Millard" demonstrates justice achieved, a pattern that is extensive, though with wide-ranging variation, in the short fiction (Ferguson 1991, 76).

Ferguson compliments the *fabula*, the basic narrative, of "My Grandmother Millard" even though he believes it suffers in execution, as do the plots of *Notes on a Horsethief* and "A Name for the City." He blames the weakness on the "diminution of [Faulkner's] narrative drive" in the latter years of the author's career (1991, 127).

Hans Bungert comments that Faulkner frequently used a youthful narrator whose storytelling contributes to the comedy. Some additional stories in which this technique is employed include "Shingles for the Lord," "Uncle Willy," "Was," *The Reivers*, and most of *The Unvanquished* (Bungert 1986, 146–47). Ferguson believes that in "My Grandmother Millard," Bayard is too consciously presented as a narrator who otherwise has little place in the story. This explicit use of a viewpoint character also appears in "Skirmish at Sartoris," "Divorce in Naples," "Ad Astra," and in Chick Mallison's presence in some of the *Knight's Gambit* tales. On the whole, it is not a very effective strategy (Ferguson 1991, 110).

Bungert's study of Faulkner's humor includes examination of his use of names for comic effect. In "My Grandmother Millard," the comic complication turns on a name. Bungert notes that the change from *Backhouse* to *Backus* follows the laws of English language development (1986, 145–46).

Ferguson criticizes a "tendency toward verbosity" apparent in "My Grandmother Millard" and other later works. Ferguson suggests that the story would be better if reduced "by at least one-third" (1991, 125).

For Michael Millgate, "The Middle Ground" themes of "deracination and disillusion, with the loss of familiar bearings" receive comic treatment in the "quixotic absurdity" of "My Grandmother Millard." Like the other stories in the section, this one also portrays the theme of death, though in this case not a physical death (Millgate [1966] 1989, 273–74). Kinney believes the placement of "My Grandmother Millard" between "The Brooch" and "Golden Land" relieves the gloom of the suicidal husband with the distanced romantic comedy. Further, Granny Millard's strategies for saving silver and arranging marriage—in short, survival—serve as a counterpoint to the images of destruction in the other two stories. Granny Millard's deception contrasts with the more desperate deceptions of Mrs. Ewing in "Golden Land" (Kinney 1980, 73). James Carothers associates "My Grandmother Millard" with "Mountain Victory," which closes the section. Together these stories cover the Civil War and post–Civil War periods in this section of the collection that encompasses a wide span of years (Carothers 1985, 59). The balance Ferguson discerns in "The Middle Ground" comes in the pairing of the stories, first and last, then working toward the middle. This strategy pairs "Fox Hunt" with "My Grandmother Millard"; both deal with marriage—the former an unhappy story, the latter a marriage celebration that resolves other problems as well (1991, 160).

## Interpretation and Criticism

When Faulkner described "My Grandmother Millard" to his agent, Harold Ober, he said, "I think it's a good funny story, and I think it has its message for the day too: of gallant indomitability, of a willingness to pull up the pants and carry on, no matter with whom, let alone what" (*WFM 24* Introduction xiv; *SL* 150). The few critics who have examined this work closely affirm what Faulkner perceived to be its message for a 1942 readership. As Skei observes, despite the "humour and farcical comedy" of "My Grandmother Millard," it has serious themes as well (Skei 1985, 273).

Howell sees the appropriation of Forrest in the story to show disparate people brought together in conflict. Some details of Forrest's disreputable background give way to an admiring portrait. Despite his rustic manner and language, his deference to Rosa Millard and his courage reveal him to be a homespun gentleman and to represent the merging of various social ranks that occurred during the conflict. The story reflects an innocence of people for whom victory is assumed, a time "when there is no prescience of the tragedy lying ahead." Finally, Howell sees the story as reflecting a more relaxed attitude toward history than Faulkner's earlier uses of the war "where the Confederate cause takes on the nobility of a crusade and the tragic outcome is to him a personal anguish" (1970, 287–94).

Nordanberg agrees with other critics that Forrest is used more for his uncouth behavior than his military capabilities in order to contrast him with the genteel Rosa Millard (1983, 73). He finds that the positive rendering of war themes aligns this story with various other World War II texts (1983, 107).

Bradford sees this story as affirming values especially important for a nation at war. In "My Grandmother Millard," the Sartoris spirit serves as "prescription or example to strengthen and propel forward the entire nation" in the context of international conflict. John Sartoris explicitly tells his son Bayard and the black child Ringo that they will see a time when Southern soldiers fight to support the national interest because their desire for freedom would survive the battles lost (Bradford 1985, 318–19).

The story also suggests alternative definitions of *freedom*. Lucius presents an inadequate definition of freedom because for him it implies an abandonment of social bonds; Granny's conception of freedom incorporates a strong sense of duty and responsibility, of interdependence—though to be sure the context of these conflicting definitions remains light. Granny's rehearsals to bury the silver represent a preservation of modes of behavior and an attempt to minimize the damage brought by the enemy. The demands of civility presume to interrupt the demands of war in her summoning Forrest to the house to solve the romantic dilemma. The courtship rituals so clearly delineated for Philip and Melisandre are "roles in a conventional romantic melodrama." The issue of the name does not finally keep them apart, but it does "remind us of the distance between concept and fact, language and life." Rosa Millard disregards such abstractions as *freedom*, the "spoils of war," and the idea of "General"; and she acts pragmatically to preserve the people who come under her care. The story ends with the same activity that opened it, an action to preserve what is valuable to the family (Bradford 1985, 318–22).

Nordanberg does not completely dismiss the Civil War as subject in "My Grandmother Millard." He points out that Forrest must resolve the dilemma of Backhouse's name because the young man has become a threat to the welfare of the troops. Unable to marry his love because of his name, one that bears the history of his progenitors, Backhouse fights gallantly, willing to lose his life and his name in a fatal confrontation. His recklessness represents a threat to the other men, so Forrest's willingness to aid Millard's plan also serves to protect his troops. Ancestry, tradition, and gallantry, "all features attributed to the people of the Old South," combine in the comedy, not questioned but used as clichés. The reality of war barely touches the text. Backhouse's exploits are a more serious threat than Smith's. The resolution becomes "another example of the Southern aptitude for solving problematic situations by the creation of fictions," and the story contributes to the exaggerated tales about the Civil War. The attitude of eventual victory and an absence of criticism about the cause is accompanied by Rosa's ridicule of Lucius's hope for freedom (Nordanberg 1983, 72–74). Related to the innocence (or naïvete) of these characters is Mary Robb's observation: the flaw in Granny Millard's plan that generates "fantastic and hilarious events" is her overestimation of the enemies' chivalry (Robb 1957, 30).

The characterizations, as already noted in the case of Forrest, lend to the comic atmosphere and the thematic emphasis on valiant effort. Walter Everett describes Rosa Millard as an "admirable, stern-willed older" woman with an "acute wit." Her son-in-law, Colonel John Sartoris, is the only character not intimidated by her (Everett 1969, 155–56). Elizabeth Kerr believes that the evidence of Faulkner's females demonstrates his disapproval of the idealized Southern concept of woman. His models are many and varied but on the whole they lack genuineness. Melisandre at least has "spunk enough to overcome her humiliation" and marry Philip (Kerr 1961–62, 5, 13). Others are not so fond of Melisandre. She is, in Longley's view, a "Victorian pretending to be an aristocrat, with all of Victorian morality's morbid horror of the body and its physical functions but little else" ([1957] 1963, 110). For Howell, Melisandre's romanticisms are pointed out by her retreating into a Waverley novel and playing the dulcimer by moonlight (Howell 1970, 288).

Critics praise the humor in "My Grandmother Millard." Longley commends the "exquisitely subtle comedy" that arises from Faulkner's indirection regarding the description of Melisandre's predicament. The comedy of manners shows the development of individual characters to a point of affectation; however, common sense prevails in the end (1963, 110–14). Bungert believes the "story thrives on a contrast between romantic and realistic elements," even in the names *Melisandre* and *Backhouse*. The realistic perspective of the child also lends to the humor (Bungert 1986, 146).

According to Everett, telling the story through a boy's eyes lends the narrative a "disjointed appearance." Bayard apotheosizes his grandmother and emphasizes her ingenuity. This focus unifies the narrative that ends, back where it began, with a silver-burying drill. For the children, both Bayard and Ringo, the events unfold as a game. Digressions address such topics as freedom, Mrs. Compson's silver, and General Wheeler that typically "enrich the story, even though they impede the progress" (Everett 1969, 155–57). Blotner calls it a "contrived story" (1974, 1099).

Stephen Ross points out that "My Grandmother Millard" is one of the relatively few places in which Faulkner includes "explicit instruction" on the sound of words, a tactic that does "not constitute an important or particularly effective tool for describing speech." Bayard actually distinguishes Forrest's dialect, adding that his pronunciations are overlooked in light of his military skill (Ross 1989, 74).

The critical response to "My Grandmother Millard" is scant. Further issues might be investigated. Blotner suggests that Faulkner wrote stories even when he knew he was exploring taboo subjects (1990, 13–14). Certain elements of the text have been glossed over. For example, Louvinia, not Granny Millard, first raises the idea of the outhouse. Granny Millard ignores Forrest's recommendation that she force Melisandre to marry Backhouse and quickly end the disruption. As for the presumption that the characters are innocent of the outcome of the war, it is certain that Bayard knows, and that his knowledge affects his description of hungry soldiers and children. It may also be telling that the champagne is not saved for victory but is used for the wedding. Finally, the clock assumes symbolic import; it too is finally buried.

For Ferguson, the sentimentality in "My Grandmother Millard" "is bearable because the work, in spite of its flaws, *is* funny" (1991, 76). When choosing entries for *Collected Stories*, Faulkner affirmed this story with a simple "Yes" (*SL* 274).

## Works Cited

Blotner, Joseph. 1974. *Faulkner: A Biography*. 2 vols. New York: Random House.

——. 1990. "Faulkner and Popular Culture." In *Faulkner and Popular Culture: Faulkner and Yoknapatawpha, 1988*. Ed. Doreen Fowler and Ann J. Abadie. Jackson: University Press of Mississippi, 3–21.

Bradford, M. E. 1985. "A Coda to *Sartoris*: Faulkner's 'My Grandmother Millard and General Nathan Bedford Forrest and the Battle of Harrykin Creek.'" In *Critical Essays on William Faulkner: The Sartoris Family*. Ed. Arthur F. Kinney. Boston: G. K. Hall, 318–23.

Bungert, Hans. 1986. "Faulkner's Humor: A European View," *Faulkner and Humor: Faulkner and Yoknapatawpha, 1984*. Jackson: University Press of Mississippi, 136–51.

Carothers, James B. 1985. *William Faulkner's Short Stories*. Ann Arbor, MI: UMI Research Press.

Cullen, John B., and Floyd C. Watkins. [1961] 1975. *Old Times in the Faulkner Country*. Chapel Hill: University of North Carolina Press. Reprint. Baton Rouge: Louisiana State University Press.

Ditsky, John. 1976. "Faulkner's Harrykin Creek: A Note." *University of Windsor Review* 12.1:88–89.

Dowling, David. 1989. *William Faulkner*. New York: St. Martin's.

Everett, Walter K. 1969. *Faulkner's Art and Character*. Woodbury, NY: Barron's Educational Series.

Faulkner, William. 1943. "My Grandmother Millard and General Bedford Forrest and the Battle of Harrykin Creek." *Story* 22(March–April):68–86.

———. 1950. *Collected Stories of William Faulkner.* New York: Random House.

———. 1977. *Selected Letters of William Faulkner.* Ed. Joseph Blotner. New York: Random House.

———. 1987. *William Faulkner Manuscripts 24: Short Stories.* Ed. Joseph Blotner. New York: Garland.

Ferguson, James. 1991. *Faulkner's Short Fiction.* Knoxville: University of Tennessee Press.

Howell, Elmo. 1970 "William Faulkner's General Forrest and the Uses of History." *Tennessee Historical Quarterly* 29:287–94.

Kerr, Elizabeth M. 1961–62. "William Faulkner and the Southern Concept of Woman." *Mississippi Quarterly* 15:1–16.

———. 1983. *William Faulkner's Yoknapatawpha: "A Kind of Keystone in the Universe."* New York: Fordham University Press.

Kinney, Arthur F. 1980. "Faulkner's Narrative Poetics and *Collected Stories.*" *Faulkner Studies* 1:58–79.

———. 1984. "'Topmost in the Pattern': Family Structure in Faulkner." In *New Direction in Faulkner Studies: Faulkner and Yoknapatawpha, 1983.* Ed. Doreen Fowler and Ann J. Abadie. Jackson: University Press of Mississippi, 143–71.

———. 1985. "Introduction." In *Critical Essays on William Faulkner: The Sartoris Family.* Ed. Arthur F. Kinney. Boston: G. K. Hall, 1–40.

Lind, Ilse Dusoir. 1978. "Faulkner's Women." In *The Maker and the Myth: Faulkner and Yoknapatawpha, 1977.* Ed. Evans Harrington and Ann J. Abadie. Jackson: University Press of Mississippi, 89–104.

Longley, John Lewis, Jr. [1957] 1963. *The Tragic Mask: A Study of Faulkner's Heroes.* Chapel Hill: University of North Carolina Press.

Millgate, Michael. [1966] 1989. *The Achievement of William Faulkner.* New York: Random House. Reprint. Athens: University of Georgia Press. Brown Thrasher Books.

Nordanberg, Thomas. 1983. *Cataclysm as Catalyst: The Theme of War in William Faulkner's Fiction.* Acta Universitatis Upsaliensis. Studia Anglista Upsaliensia #49. Stockholm: Almquist & Wiksell.

Reed, Joseph W., Jr. 1973. *Faulkner's Narrative.* New Haven: Yale University Press.

Robb, Mary Cooper. 1957. *William Faulkner: An Estimation of His Contribution to the Modern American Novel.* Critical Essays in English and American Literature No. 1. Pittsburgh: University of Pittsburgh Press.

Ross, Stephen M. 1989. *Fiction's Inexhaustible Voice: Speech and Writing in Faulkner.* Athens: University of Georgia Press.

Samway, Patrick H., S.J. 1980. *Faulkner's* Intruder in the Dust: *A Critical Study of the Typescripts*. Troy, NY: Whitston.

Skei, Hans H. 1981. *William Faulkner: The Short Story Career*. Oslo, Norway: Universitetsforlaget.

———. 1985. *William Faulkner: The Novelist as Short Story Writer*. Oslo, Norway: Universitetsforlaget.

Vickery, Olga W. [1959] 1964 *The Novels of William Faulkner*. Baton Rouge: Louisiana State University Press.

# Golden Land

## Publication History

"Golden Land" was first published in the *American Mercury* in May 1935. It is not certain how many magazine editors read the story before the *American Mercury* accepted it, but it is clear that this magazine was not Faulkner's first choice. Publisher Harrison Smith encouraged Faulkner to try selling his stories to some of the high-paying magazines other than the *Post*. Since "Golden Land" was already in the hands of agent Morton Goldman, in January 1935, Faulkner asked Goldman to return the story in order to pursue Smith's connection with *Cosmopolitan*. Goldman himself apparently felt that the "flavor of perversion" in "Golden Land" might limit its suitability to *Cosmopolitan* among the better-paying magazines. In early February, Faulkner informed Smith that he had instructed Goldman to retrieve the story and forward it to Smith. After that, the story's trail is obscure. Goldman may already have sold "Golden Land" to the *American Mercury*, or Smith may not have been successful in convincing *Cosmopolitan* to buy it; at any rate, in February or early March, the lower-paying *American Mercury* bought "Golden Land." By March 9, 1935, Faulkner had already reviewed and was returning the galley proofs to the *Mercury* (Blotner 1974, 878, 881; 1984, 342; *SL* 87–90). Faulkner did not use "Golden Land" again until he included it in "The Middle Ground" section of *Collected Stories* (1950).

## Circumstances of Composition, Sources, and Influences

"Golden Land" was written in late 1934 or early 1935. In a letter to Goldman that Joseph Blotner dates from August 1934, Faulkner mentions an idea for a "good story out of California." The earliest extant reference to "Golden Land" appears in the January 1935 letter to Goldman (Skei 1981, 79–80, *SL* 84, 88).

A twelve-page manuscript of "Golden Land," part of the Rowan Oak Papers at the University of Mississippi, shows extensive revisions of the story (Kinney and Fowler 1983, 332). The opening of the manuscript begins "If he had not been 30." The published text increases Ira's age with the significant alteration "If he had been thirty." Faulkner was also dissatisfied with the concluding sentence. The manuscript ending, "'I will slug wine and live forever,' she said to herself," contrasts with the less sarcastic but more compelling "'I will stay here and live forever,' she said to herself" (Kinney and Fowler 1983, 332; *CS* 701, 726). After publication in the *American Mercury*, no changes were made in the text other than a few minor instances of added hyphenation and punctuation.

The most provocative critical responses to "Golden Land" focus on the links between the story and Faulkner's life. As Frederick Karl suggests, the story is interesting "for the shadowy way in which Faulkner illuminated a good deal about himself" (1989, 539). Some parallels are obvious. The California setting of "Golden Land," with its special emphasis on Hollywood, relates directly to Faulkner's working there. Blotner senses Faulkner's unhappiness while in California, a rather inclusive displeasure with the "terrain, the climate, the architecture, the people, their behavior, and their dress" (1974, 877–78; see also Everett 1969, 143; Skei 1981, 87; Phillips 1988, 7–8).

Critics also discern in the character portraits a variety of elements from Faulkner's life. Blotner compares the elder Samantha Ewing's longing to leave California to Maud Falkner's reaction to her Hollywood visit in 1932. He also likens Ira Ewing's visits with his mother each morning to Faulkner's visits with his mother, Maud (1974, 878). Michael Grimwood points out that like Ira Ewing, Faulkner was a heavy drinker approaching middle age, was finding himself tempted by young women, and was selling his own talent. Grimwood emphasizes that some uncertainty exists about the year in which Faulkner and Meta Carpenter began their relationship, so that as a mirror of Faulkner's own life, Ewing's adultery may be "confessional" but is more likely "prophetic" (1986, 277). Blotner dates the beginning of the affair as late 1935 or early 1936, after the appearance of the story (1984, 360–61; see also Karl 1989, 540).

Both Grimwood and Karl find parallels between the personalities of Estelle and Mrs. Ewing. Karl specifically cites bitterness and distance as common characteristics. As for the children, Grimwood notes that neither Faulkner's step-children nor his daughter Jill "shamed him," but Karl associates the estrangement between Ewing and his children with Faulkner's relationship with Estelle's children, Malcolm and Victoria, from her marriage to Cornell Franklin (Grimwood 1986, 277; Karl 1989, 540).

Grimwood finds further biographical parallels in the conflict between Nebraskan Samantha Ewing and Californian Ira Ewing, Jr., representing ambivalent impulses within Faulkner on the issues of home, family, and literary vocation. Neither Nebraska nor California represents a completely satisfying alternative. Samantha Ewing's endurance is "brittle and austere." Her desire to go home "resembles a death wish." On the other hand, Ira Ewing's flight from Nebraska is similarly self-destructive. Grimwood finds an analogy in this tension between the rural and urban world and Faulkner's own need to be in Oxford and his frequent travels away from home. He was often restless in Oxford yet eager to return when away. No "peace of place" really existed for Faulkner either in Oxford or Hollywood. Grimwood believes that the story also "testifies to a deep anxiety about marriage, paternity, and family" within Faulkner. Generational bonds are destroyed in the story. The elder Samantha Ewing discovers that she cannot maintain family traditions because her son and daughter-in-law undermine her efforts. Ewing abets the generational disintegration by using his daughter for his own materialistic ends. Although Ewing seems to find some peace when he is with his mistress, Grimwood points out that "sexual nausea permeates the story." These were current and sensitive issues in Faulkner's life at the time of composition. Even if Faulkner were as yet faithful to Estelle, he "entered imaginatively into the subject of adultery." Nevertheless, Faulkner believed in transmitting generational values and memories within the family. His concern may have been particularly acute at the time of writing "Golden Land" because Jill was a year old, and Faulkner's father had been dead about two years.

On yet another level, Grimwood suggests that the story reflects Faulkner's anxiety as an artist over the impermanence of the word. In the image of the ignited spools of film, the narrator of "Golden Land" emphasizes the fragility of the film industry and consequently, the way of life it generates. To endure in Hollywood could mean, optimistically, immortality in words. But writing for the movies also reminded him of the ephemeral nature of all of his writing. Grimwood, unlike many critics, distinguishes between Faulkner and the narrative voice of the story but adds that when speaking in his own voice, Faulkner did agree with the narrator (1986, 275–80).

Karl contends that Faulkner's view of Hollywood's "inexorable corruption" hides the issue of his own self-hatred for his participation in that milieu. Karl continues, "He is fighting off the sense he has entered a death situation" in a land that "is a wasteland, a citadel of death" (1989, 539).

Bruce Kawin compares Faulkner to the elder Samantha Ewing. Los Angeles is an "imitation world without foundation, indifferent not just to the old truths but to truth itself," but Mrs. Ewing represents the learned endurance that comes from surviving hardship with honor, courage, and pride intact. Although Faulkner resigned himself to his need to work in Hollywood, he maintained his determination to pack his own Hollywood scripts with those values. As Kawin puts it, Faulkner survived in Hollywood by "allying himself with the mother, Samantha, to save himself from the corruptions of Ira" (1990, 200–05).

The literary influences discernible in "Golden Land" come from contemporary and traditional sources. Blotner finds parallels between Ira Ewing and F. Scott Fitzgerald's Jay Gatsby (1974, Notes 122–23). Grimwood calls April Lalear the namesake of Shakespeare's King Lear and his unfaithful daughters (1986, 279). Kawin agrees, noting that Lalear is not "leer" "as in the masculine leer she wants to attract and manipulate" (1990, 200). M. E. Bradford, however, emphasizes the importance of the leer in April's life. She represents the effect of the commodification of beauty (Bradford 1965, 75). Ira's westward flight mirrors a major pattern in the American tradition and makes a particular allusion to Samuel Clemens's *Adventures of Huckleberry Finn*. The narrator explains Ira's leaving Nebraska as follows: "It was only that absence, removal, was the only argument which fourteen knew how to employ against adults with any hope of success" (*CS* 703).

Jonas Spatz uses "Golden Land" as an example of "Hollywood utopian literature because it summarizes concisely all of the elements in the New World myth." Faulkner's portrayal of Hollywood is as the "culmination of the frontier movement" that displays the achievement of wealth, pleasure, and eternal youth; however, it is corroded by a lack of courage, honor, and pride at its core. The loss of values is represented in the degrees of decay exhibited in the several generations of the Ewing family. The children are sexual deviants; the father and mother exist in an empty marriage. Ira now sees signs of his own age in his mistress. These characters are contrasted to Ewing's mother, who seeks to return to Nebraska to regain a sense of living with morality and purpose. Spatz concludes that "Golden Land" portrays the dissolution of the American dream: "The frontier dream, which began as a vision of man's regeneration in the wilderness, has ended in the denial of sin and time, and in the triumph of illusion over reality" (1969, 116–19).

Because of its unique use of a Hollywood setting, "Golden Land" may seem easier to relate to literary sources outside rather than within Faulkner's work; however, the extent to which "Golden Land" reveals itself to include those themes and characters prevalent in the Yoknapatawpha texts demonstrates the limitation of criticism based on fictional geography.

## Relationship to Other Faulkner Works

Critics have amply demonstrated just how neatly "Golden Land" fits into the body of Faulkner's fiction. James Carothers includes "Golden Land" among Faulkner's stories of the 1930s that demonstrate the "grand mixture" of themes and techniques he employed during that decade (1985, 55). Grimwood contends that the story contains "an early warning signal" of Faulkner's "growing alienation from both the personal and the cultural sources of his vocation" that characterized the years between 1935 and 1950. That tension, Grimwood adds, reappears in various manifestations in the novels of the period: *Absalom, Absalom!*, *The Wild Palms*, *The Hamlet*, and *Go Down, Moses* (1986, 280).

Specific resemblances may be drawn between characters in "Golden Land" and other fiction, even the Yoknapatawpha texts. Ira Ewing generates several comparisons. Bradford likens him to Major de Spain because both characters develop for themselves a commercial identity. Ewing is also like Thomas Sutpen in his pursuit of a design he would like to impose upon the world (Bradford 1965, 74). Sheldon Kohn disagrees with Bradford's comparison of Ewing to Sutpen, arguing that Ewing is "just another Los Angeles villain striving for respectability" without Sutpen's exceptionality (1983, 81). That desire for respectability without regard to the means of attainment likens Ewing to Flem Snopes. Blotner compares the alcoholic Ira Ewing to Jiggs in *Pylon* (1984, 342).

Critics have not identified fictional counterparts to Ira's wife and children. Numerous characters of limited social power use sex, often in destructive ways, as a means of striking back at a stifling society. In this case, however, Faulkner seems to be using sexual deviance in a stereotypical and dated way to represent corruption.

John Longley is the first of many readers to observe that "Golden Land" is the author's only fiction with a Hollywood setting (Longley [1957] 1963, 43); nevertheless, Faulkner's descriptions of Hollywood and Nebraska share common traits with other of his texts. Blotner confirms that in "Golden Land," *Pylon*, and every other reference to Hollywood, Faulkner uses the location to symbolize corruption (Blotner 1984, 342). Carothers characterizes such communities as lacking a "harmonious and sustaining order," as beyond the help of a hero figure. Among the communities in Faulkner's fiction that bear these characteristics Carothers includes the ones in "Golden Land," "Mountain Victory," "Red Leaves," *Mosquitoes*, *Sanctuary*, and *The Hamlet* (1981, 264).

In contrast, Bradford equates the portrayal of the Nebraska plains to the better known portrayal of woods in the Yoknapatawpha stories. Both offer an "objective correlative for that in man's life which is given, *a priori*, 'other,' for that with which man must come to terms in 'pride and humility'" (1965, 73).

Karl offers an analysis of "Lion" and "Golden Land" that puts them in opposition to one another. Karl suggests that they do not simply represent an ideal vision ("Lion") against a "revelation of hell" ("Golden Land"), but rather that each tempers the image presented in the other. The Edenic garden of "Lion" is a fantasy world. "Golden Land" is the location of reality, but its corruption of civilized life presents a "noisome image of what man can become" (1989, 542).

James Ferguson suggests that the shifts in the narrative perspective at the end of "Golden Land," "Dull Tale," and "Pantaloon in Black" enhance the suggestion of irony in their respective conclusions by allowing new understanding of the protagonists (1991, 102). Ferguson also groups "Golden Land" with "Crevasse," "Ad Astra," and most of the New Orleans sketches because in these the evocation of mood and revelation of theme are more important than a strongly plotted narrative (1991, 136–37).

Arthur Kinney likens the image of fire instantly destroying film to another incendiary image in "Barn Burning" (1980, 73–74). Ira's recollection of burning the rat-infested, Nebraska barn also recalls the more famous "Barn Burning" (*CS* 710). Thomas McHaney finds another use of this image in *The Wild Palms* when the tall convict's sympathy for his companion is compared to the regret he might feel over a barn burned because it had become vermin-infested (1975, 118).

Several critics trace the links among the stories gathered in "The Middle Ground" section of *Collected Stories*. Michael Millgate finds in "Golden Land" the symbolic enactment of death that appears in numerous stories in "The Middle Ground." The elder Mrs. Ewing resigns herself to a "death in life" similar to that portrayed in "Fox Hunt," "Honor," and even in the more comic portrayal of Lieutenant Backhouse in "My Grandmother Millard" (Millgate [1966] 1989, 273–74). Kinney believes that the motivations for the respective deceptions of the elder Samantha Ewing and Granny Millard are quite different. Granny Millard's "acts of preservation" are intended to counterbalance the sense of destruction in the surrounding stories of the section in which it appears in *Collected Stories*. Conversely, Mrs. Ewing "bribes her grandchildren by employing their physical hunger to satisfy her own yearning ambition to return home to Nebraska" (Kinney 1980, 73). Carothers adds that "Golden Land" contributes to the geographic diversity, the extremes of human behavior, and the conjoined themes of sex and death that characterize "The Middle Ground" (1985, 59).

Hans Skei describes the movement of the section as following an "axis of greed, corruption, and conformity," wherein "Golden Land" stands at the end toward which the Jefferson stories are headed. It contrasts with "Mule in the Yard," at the opposite end of the axis in which Mannie Hait outwits I. O. Snopes in his own greed. Moving more toward "Golden Land," both "Uncle Willy" and "That Will Be Fine" "demonstrate how the half-way agrarian county of Yoknapatawpha loses most of the positive traditional values [in] its pursuit of happiness and some elusive American dream." In "Golden Land," "Uncle Willy," and "There Was a Queen" "middle-class values, rules and regulations are presented and scrutinized through the fate of an outsider." Skei points out that although "Golden Land" is one of Faulkner's independent stories with no ties to the novels, its thematic ties show the extremes of decay in American life and also demonstrate a limited "distance from Yoknapatawpha to the Golden Land" (1985, 213–16, 219, 223; 1992, 69). Ferguson's strategy of pairing "The Middle Ground" stories from the periphery to the center pairs "Dr. Martino" and "Golden Land," both stories that "focus on older people who are trying by very different means to hold on to life" (1991, 159–60).

## Interpretation and Criticism

The critical response addressed specifically to "Golden Land" is predictable. Dorothy Tuck describes "Golden Land" as a "subtle story of success and disillusionment." Her judgment sets the general tone of subsequent interpretations (1964, 167). Bradford finds in the story the belief "that suffering, struggle, effort, and 'endurance' are necessary to the formation in man of all those traits which give life meaning and dignity"; it is a story "expressive of Faulkner's abiding agrarianism." The obvious criticism of the California Ewings' easy, superficial life is part of that theme. The elder Nebraska Ewings possessed a fundamentally religious sense of peace, including a reverence for the land and the natural process that it entails. The younger Ira rejects that relationship. He adheres to impermanent status symbols and seems terrified of aging and death. Bradford argues that the conclusion is indeterminate but "ominously suggestive" of America in transition between its "substantial agricultural roots and its uncertain urban future" (1965, 72–76). According to Walter Everett, "Golden Land" presents a "rather puritanical protest against the easy life in California" in which the "sociological commentary . . . overpowers its literary art" (1969, 143–44).

Blotner describes "Golden Land" as "impregnated with distaste and revulsion." The Ewing family is characterized by "monsters." The children have been corrupted by excess, but Ewing shows himself to be the most corrupted when he arranges to have his daughter's trial leaked to the press for his own commercial advantage (Blotner 1974, 877–78).

Skei describes "Golden Land" as a "didactic story" that possesses a "seriousness and honesty that cannot be disregarded." Skei believes Everett's judgment is too harsh and Bradford's emphasis on the story's importance somewhat overstated. The social criticism is apparent, and the theme of endurance appears here as a "kind of gospel." Nebraska life a generation back sets the norms of decency that are contrasted with the "moral anarchy" in the modern, urban California setting. Although it may be unrealistic to expect to transfer older, agrarian ways to the city, the point is that values are best conveyed in experiences of hardship and endurance. Even though Ewing's daily visits with his mother indicate some continued link to his past, he will not give up his comfort; he will not act like his father when he sacrificed his barn to rid it of rats. According to Skei, Faulkner portrays a lack of involvement and care for other humans in an environment where the measurement of success in nonhuman terms violates the law of Nature (1981, 87; 1985 227–29, 318 n. 18–22).

Most critics agree at least in part with Everett's assessment that the characters follow such stereotyped patterns they "lack credibility" (1969, 143). Some disagreement exists about the degree to which Ira Ewing recognizes his own corruption. Tuck believes he is not fully aware of the "futility" of his shallow existence (1964, 167). Bradford argues that Ewing gains some sense of his corrupted nature when he relates his own situation to his father's problem with rats in his barn. Although his father had the fortitude to burn the barn, Ewing does not have similar strength to change his life (Bradford 1965, 75–76).

According to Everett, even the elder Mrs. Ewing "is made too pitiable" (1969, 143–44). She believes that she can compensate for her dependence on her son by passing her heritage on to her grandchildren, but she is defeated in her effort by the children's parents and by the overwhelming unnaturalness of the environment in which she concedes that she will "live forever" (Bradford 1965, 74–76; *CS* 726). Kohn sees her as yet uncorrupted by life in California (1983, 82).

Kinney's rather harsh evaluation of the elder Samantha Ewing in comparison with Granny Millard is atypical. It is difficult to imagine that Voyd and Samantha (April) experience real physical hunger as Kinney suggests, but his point cannot be completely dismissed (1980, 73). The text implies a certain criticism of the elder Samantha Ewing's behavior. Her plan to raise money manifested a spirit of "pioneer's opportunism" in which "she saw neither paradox . . . nor dishonesty" but which is actually implied by virtue of raising the point in the narrative (*CS* 725). Grimwood states that the elder Samantha Ewing recognizes that she, like the rest of the family, "is damned" (1986, 277).

Ira's son's name, Voyd, reflects his most obvious quality (Bradford 1965, 75). Grimwood questions whether any other Faulkner character has a more obvious name (1986, 276). "Golden Land" is, however, enriched by imagery that is somewhat more subtly drawn than Voyd's name. Mark Winchell follows Spatz in placing "Golden Land" within the tradition of Hollywood literature. He suggests that the primary image of Los Angeles is as a horrific mutation of the Garden of Eden. The paradise of America has reached its westward limit. While the land is beautiful, the inhabitants live in a world cut off from history. Ira, for example, has relinquished his past and sees in the young people on the beach that he has no future. The elder Mrs. Ewing's presence emphasizes the horror of the dream become nightmare. Though she has the desire, she cannot flee the garden (1982, 12–17).

Kohn offers the most extensive analysis of Faulkner's use of architecture in "Golden Land." Faulkner's Yoknapatawpha fiction commonly uses houses to symbolize the lives of the people who inhabit them; therefore, it is not surprising to see him employ the same technique in this California story. As Kohn points outs, however, "the architecture motif in 'Golden Land' follows much the same line as other writers who looked at the Southern California scene around the same time." The predominant view is that the beauty and expense of the homes conceal emptiness within them. Kohn observes that Ira Ewing's occupation as real estate agent further implicates him in the deception. His wife, the daughter of a carpenter, is likewise completely enmeshed in the creation of facades. Their son, Voyd, exposes their falsity as do references about the city and the houses that constantly emphasize the deception and corruption within. These grand houses and lavish habits of living in California are compared with the more humble dwellings and modes of existence in Ewing, Nebraska. Initially, Mrs. Samantha Ewing's home in the cul-de-sac seems immune from the tainted environment, but it too is touched by the neon lights and death present in the adjacent cemetery. Kohn also believes that by setting Ira's illicit relationship in the apartment complex Faulkner intends to suggest that such relationships are as common as the units in the apartment building are numerous. Ira's failure to see the corruption described by the narrator indicts him in his complicity in the corruption. According to Kohn, Faulkner intends to demonstrate that the value of the dwelling inheres in the people who inhabit it. The homes are monuments to their owners in the most ironic sense (1983, 79–86).

Paradox serves as the basis for the values of California and deception taints the lives lived there. The images of sun, heat, and light associated with Southern California imply death, but the cold and snow of Nebraska represent life (Karl 1989, 539). Most critics agree that the use of "golden" is undoubtedly ironic. Given his argument that the Nebraska alternative is also problematic, Grimwood comments that the irony moves geographically in both directions since neither alternative offers unqualified value (1986, 279).

As measured by the numbers of critical examinations devoted particularly to one story, "Golden Land" has received more critical attention than many of the less popular stories in Faulkner's canon. Skei ranks "Golden Land" among those stories written after 1932 that demonstrate Faulkner's continued excellence in the genre even though he wrote very little short fiction after that year (1981, 34). Other critics have been less enthusiastic about the story's quality. Grimwood describes the effort as "not particularly successful" (1986, 275). Karl suggests that Faulkner was lucky that the *American Mercury* published this "second- or third-rate" story. He judges the weakness to be the unrelenting corruption of Ira Ewing without the contrast of "any redeeming force" (1989, 539). "Golden Land" may be valued most highly for its biographical traces. Blotner finds several individual passages so accurately reflective of Faulkner's life that he uses the quotations from "Golden Land" to introduce chapters of the biography.

## Works Cited

Blotner, Joseph. 1974. *Faulkner: A Biography*. 2 vols. New York: Random House.

———. 1984. *Faulkner: A Biography*. 1 vol. New York: Random House.

Bradford, M. E. 1965. "Escaping Westward: Faulkner's 'Golden Land.'" *Georgia Review* 19:72–76.

Carothers, James B. 1981. "The Myriad Heart: The Evolution of the Faulkner Hero." In *"A Cosmos of My Own": Faulkner and Yoknapatawpha 1980*. Ed. Doreen Fowler and Ann J. Abadie. Jackson: University Press of Mississippi, 252–83.

———. 1985. *William Faulkner's Short Stories*. Ann Arbor, MI: UMI Research Press.

Everett, Walter K. 1969. *Faulkner's Art and Character*. Woodbury, NY: Barron's Educational Series.

Faulkner, William. 1935. "Golden Land." *American Mercury* 35 (May):1–14.

———. 1950. *Collected Stories of William Faulkner*. New York: Random House.

———. 1977. *Selected Letters of William Faulkner*. Ed. Joseph Blotner. New York: Random House.

Ferguson, James. 1991. *Faulkner's Short Fiction*. Knoxville: University of Tennessee Press.

Grimwood, Michael. 1986. "Faulkner's 'Golden Land' As Autobiography." *Studies in Short Fiction* 23:275–80.

Karl, Frederick R. 1989. *William Faulkner: American Writer*. New York: Weidenfeld and Nicolson.

Kawin, Bruce. 1990. "Sharecropping in the Golden Land." In *Faulkner and Popular Culture: Faulkner and Yoknapatawpha, 1988*. Ed. Doreen Fowler and Ann J. Abadie. Jackson: University Press of Mississippi, 196–206.

Kinney, Arthur F. 1980. "Faulkner's Narrative Poetics and *Collected Stories*." *Faulkner Studies* 1:58–79.

Kinney, Arthur F., and Doreen Fowler. 1983. "For the Record: Faulkner's Rowan Oak Papers: A Census." *Journal of Modern Literature* 10:327–34.

Kohn, Sheldon Scott. 1983. "Ira Ewing, Jr., and His 'Monument': Architecture in Faulkner's 'Golden Land.'" *Notes on Mississippi Writers* 15:79–86.

Longley, John Lewis, Jr. [1957] 1963. *The Tragic Mask: A Study of Faulkner's Heroes*. Chapel Hill: University of North Carolina Press.

McHaney, Thomas L. 1975. *William Faulkner's* The Wild Palms: *A Study*. Jackson: University Press of Mississippi.

Millgate, Michael. [1966] 1989. *The Achievement of William Faulkner*. New York: Random House. Reprint. Athens: University of Georgia Press. Brown Thrasher Books.

Phillips, Gene D. 1988. *Fiction, Film, and Faulkner: The Art of Adaptation*. Knoxville: University of Tennessee Press.

Skei, Hans H. 1981. *William Faulkner: The Short Story Career*. Oslo, Norway: Universitetsforlaget.

———. 1985. *William Faulkner: The Novelist as Short Story Writer*. Oslo, Norway: Universitetsforlaget.

———. 1992. "Beyond Genre? Existential Experience in Faulkner's Short Fiction." In *Faulkner and the Short Story: Faulkner and Yoknapatawpha, 1990*. Ed. Evans Harrington and Ann J. Abadie. Jackson: University Press of Mississippi, 62–77.

Spatz, Jonas. 1969. *Hollywood in Fiction: Some Versions of the American Myth*. The Hague: Mouton.

Tuck, Dorothy. 1964. *Crowell's Handbook of Faulkner*. New York: Thomas Y. Crowell.

Winchell, Mark Royden. 1982. "William Faulkner's 'Golden Land': Some Time in Hell." *Notes on Mississippi Writers* 14:12–17.

# There Was a Queen

## Publication History

"There Was a Queen" was first published in the January 1933 issue of *Scribner's* magazine. An undated entry on the story-sending schedule notes a prior submission to *Scribner's* as "Through the Window." This version was returned to Faulkner with a cover letter dated July 2, 1929, in which Alfred Dashiell explained that although the story was "nearer to being publishable than most of your short pieces," the background information about Aunt Jenny overwhelmed the action of the story. Faulkner revised the work, retitled it "An Empress Passed," then changed it again to "There Was a Queen." He sent it out a second time, noting a submission to the *Saturday Evening Post* on the story-sending schedule dated August 23, 1930; it carried the abbreviated title of "Was a Queen." The story remained unsold. A September 12, 1930, notation also as "Was a Queen" indicates he sent the story to publisher Harrison Smith.

Ben Wasson received it after Smith, sometime after June 5, 1931. When Wasson tried to place Faulkner's stories, he was often effusive in his descriptions of them. His comment that "There Was a Queen" was "Faulkner at his best" might have held some sway, for he finally sold the story to *Scribner's* in November 1932. When Dashiell accepted the story, paying $300, he made no mention of the earlier rejection in 1929 (Blotner 1974, 628–29, 791; Meriwether [1961] 1971, 275–80; Meriwether 1973, 259–60, 274; Skei 1981, 50; *SL* 70–71; *WFM 11* Introduction ix). (Max Putzel errs when he states that Faulkner had to wait a year and a half for the story to be accepted [1983, 265; Putzel 1985, 251]. The period actually ran at least from *Scribner's* rejection in July 1929 to acceptance in November 1932—over three years. In another reference to the story Putzel dates the first submission as 1930 rather than 1929 [1983, 268].) Faulkner collected "There Was a Queen" in *Doctor Martino* (1934) and in "The Middle Ground" section of *Collected Stories* (1950).

## Circumstances of Composition, Sources, and Influences

No concrete evidence exists to pinpoint the original composition date for "There Was a Queen." Philip Castille speculates that it was written sometime between January and July 1929. This date would coincide with the composition of the first version of *Sanctuary*, a text related to the story both by characters and themes (1975, 309). Two parallels between the short story and the original *Sanctuary* may imply a proximity of composition dates. Saddie, who cares for the aging Aunt Jenny Du Pre, appears in the first version of *Sanctuary* and in "There Was a Queen" but is omitted in the rewritten novel, and the Snopes letters are also mentioned in the original *Sanctuary* (Kerr 1980, 16; Watson 1987, 103). Putzel believes the story was written while the Faulkners were honeymooning in Pascagoula (1985, 251). Given the dates of the marriage on June 20, 1929, and the rejection letter of July 2, 1929, the story would have been written, submitted, and rejected within a two-week period. Frederick Karl dates the composition of "An Empress Passed" in 1929 in one discussion of the story, but he later dates it in March 1930, well after the story is known to have existed (1989, 379, 417, 420).

More can be learned about the subsequent revisions of "There Was a Queen" than can be confirmed about the original composition of the story. Extant documents at the University of Virginia include a manuscript with the title "Through the Window" marked through, and the title "An Empress Passed" written in under it as the new title. A complete ribbon typescript with manuscript corrections and a carbon typescript that follows the ribbon typescript, though without the manuscript corrections, represent intermediate versions, and an untitled, incomplete manuscript probably represents the latest extant prepublication version of the story (*WFM 11* Introduction ix, xii; Skei 1981, 123 n. 134; see also Putzel 1977, 104–05). Hans Skei remarks that the development of the story from "Through the Window" to "An Empress Passed" to "There Was a Queen" was considerable, and that each title represented a different version. The number of title changes itself exceeds Faulkner's normal practice. Both "An Empress Passed" and "There Was a Queen" focus on the idea of the "passing of a Lady of Quality." Skei likens "There Was a Queen" to "Elly," another story that appears on the sending schedule in 1929. Both stories initially bear "odd" titles that are rejected for titles "more appropriate" to their stories (1981, 50, 123 n. 135). Putzel's combination title, "Through the Window an Empress Passed," is inconsistent with Faulkner's changes on the manuscript and with Putzel's own earlier description of the revised title on the manuscript (Putzel 1977, 104 n. 16; Putzel 1983, 265; Putzel 1985, 251).

Although the revised title contains a tribute to Jenny, the revised story abbreviated the recollection of her life. Dashiell's complaint to Faulkner concerned Elnora's narrative to her son about Aunt Jenny's history. It described Jenny in such a way as to show how Narcissa's actions were shocking enough to hasten the end of the older woman's life once she learned of them. In Dashiell's judgment, the digression obscured the focus of the story (Blotner 1974, 628–29).

Putzel remarks that limiting Elnora's narrative about Jenny's history is a necessary modification, but the story loses something with the alteration. Nevertheless, the affirmation of Elnora and the denigration of Narcissa remained consistent throughout the various texts (1983, 265, 268; Putzel 1985, 251). The problem of presenting the lengthy Sartoris background in the short work is improved by revision but never completely solved, according to James Ferguson. The alteration of the dialogue between Elnora and Isom to a panoramic review through Elnora's consciousness provides a more economic rendering of the information (Ferguson 1991, 124).
   Among the numerous revisions made in the various texts are several changes revolving around the characterizations of Jenny, Narcissa, and Elnora. One alteration actually results in obscuring Jenny's advice to Narcissa about what a "lady" would do with such obscene letters. In a marginal addition Jenny's comment is "I told you that a lady would be accused in public of having done something she hadn't done, before she would do that same thing hidden . . ." (*WFM 11* 110). The comment is completed in the subsequent typescript: "I told you that a lady would be accused in public of having done something she did not do, before she would do that same thing hidden in order to not be found out" (*WFM 11* 135). Another change strengthened the sense of Jenny's devotion to the Sartoris legend. In the prepublication texts, Jenny began calling Bory "Johnny" after her stroke (*WFM 11* 111, 138). In the published version, her reference to Johnny seems intentional and apart from a medical condition. In the prepublication texts Narcissa's request that Bory sit by her rather than at the head of the table is less notable as a break from Sartoris tradition. In these earlier versions, the narrative describes Bory's move to his mother's side as his taking Jenny's place at the table, which was vacant because she decided not to come to dinner (*WFM 11* 111, 139).
   One consistent quality of all the versions is Elnora's dislike of Narcissa. Her remarks are quite harsh in each version, though they differ somewhat. In the various prepublication drafts, Elnora distinguishes between Jenny's quality and Narcissa's lack of it; she adds in a remark to Isom that there will be less difference between Narcissa and whomever Bory should marry than between Jenny and Narcissa (*WFM 11* 108). Elnora also suggests that Narcissa bought bed and board with her child (*WFM 11* 116, 128). If nothing else comes to mind, Elnora remarks disapprovingly of the food choices Narcissa instructs her to prepare—"sheep fodder" in Elnora's opinion (*WFM 11*, 105).
   Elnora's identification as a half-sister of old Bayard changes slightly in terms of her awareness of her heritage. In the earliest extant manuscript, a marginal addition, "tho neither of them knew it," indicates that brother and sister were uninformed of their relationship (*WFM 11* 105). Since this manuscript most likely follows the version Dashiell read, no one can determine how the information was originally presented. The typescript reads "though

neither of them knew it, including Bayard's father, possibly" (*WFM 11* 118–19). The subsequent partial manuscript comes closest to the published version with the parenthetical explanation "tho (possibly but not probably) neither of them knew it, including old Bayard's father John" (*WFM 11* 113).

Once "There Was a Queen" was published in *Scribner's*, Faulkner made no further revisions in it. With the minor exception of a typographical error in the *Doctor Martino* text, all three texts are the same.

Biographical parallels of the Sartoris women have far fewer ties to the writer's life than the numerous demonstrable links between the Sartoris men and Falkner men. Putzel finds Faulkner's great aunt Alabama Falkner McLean to be the living model for the fictional Jenny Du Pre. Superficial correspondences include the name similarities "Alabama" reduced to "Bama" and "Virginia" reduced to "Jenny." Aunt Bama provided recollections about the Civil War and postwar years including accounts, legendary and otherwise, of Nathan Bedford Forrest. Putzel believes that Faulkner felt no risk of censure when he made an anti-Semitic remark in a personal correspondence to his Aunt Alabama and that her sentiment likely reappears in Jenny's attitude toward the agent. Still another manifestation of Aunt Bama's influence is the clash between the strength of her generation and the weakness of his wife's generation of women (Putzel 1983, 258–59; 1985, 251, 268).

Other proposed models for Jenny are literary rather than biographical. Although he does not specifically mention the portrayal of Miss Jenny in "There Was a Queen," Wyndham Lewis likens her characterization to a Dickens figure ([1934] 1987, 49). Kenneth Richardson believes that Jenny and other avatars of Faulkner's grandmother-type recall Samuel Clemens's Widow Douglas (1967, 103).

Literary references in the story relate Narcissa to the English poet George Gordon, Lord Byron. Constance Hall believes the suggestions of incestuous feelings between Narcissa and her brother, Horace Benbow, are emphasized by associating them with the British poet and his half-sister, Augusta. This correspondence is accomplished by way of Narcissa's reaction to the missing Snopes letters as described in "There Was a Queen." On her honeymoon, she feels that with the Snopes letters missing she has made love not just to her new husband but "with all men in the world at the same time." This description closely resembles Byron's wish in *Don Juan* for the assimilation of all women's mouths into one mouth, an image Horace recalls in a letter to Narcissa. Additionally, Snopes's first name is Byron, a fact more than coincidental, since Byron Snopes bears similarities to Horace and thus indirectly again associates the Benbow siblings with the poet Byron (Hall 1986, 21–22).

James Watson also finds this parallel but bases his argument on one of the letters in which Byron Snopes describes Narcissa's mouth in a way that recalls Lord Byron's description. Watson adds that this image occurs again in an even "more sexually charged context" in "Divorce in Naples" (Watson 1987, 101).

Cleanth Brooks briefly compares Faulkner's criticism of bourgeois concern for appearances, so crucial to Narcissa in "There Was a Queen," to Yeats's similar concern (1976, 147; see also Brooks [1978] 1990, 336). As the following section illustrates, these limited studies of literary analogues hardly compare to the multiple relationships examined within the body of Faulkner's fiction.

## Relationship to Other Faulkner Works

In a recent analysis of the interplay of Faulkner's short and long fiction Ferguson comments that "no great harm" comes from reading "There Was a Queen" "in the light of what one knows about *Sartoris* or *Sanctuary*, as long as one realizes that Faulkner knew that most readers of the story would probably not have read those novels." Ferguson suggests somewhat later, however, that the exposition in "There Was a Queen" is insufficient to allow the story to "work" without a prior reading of *Sartoris* or *Flags in the Dust* and possibly also *Sanctuary* (1991, 6, 132). Ferguson's comments reflect a common inability among critics to separate "There Was a Queen" from the novels. In fact, with few exceptions, most remarks about the short story are made in discussions of the novels.

The presence of surviving Sartoris family members and mention of legendary family ancestors automatically links "There Was a Queen" to a large body of Faulkner's long and short fiction. Arthur Kinney establishes the presence of the Sartoris family in "There Was a Queen," *Flags in the Dust/Sartoris*, *Sanctuary*, *Absalom, Absalom!*, *The Unvanquished*, *The Hamlet*, *The Town*, *The Mansion*, *Knight's Gambit*, *Requiem for a Nun*, "Ad Astra," "A Rose for Emily," "All the Dead Pilots," "The Bear," "With Caution and Dispatch," and the film script for *War Birds* (Kinney 1984, 156; see also Kinney 1989, 93). Relational studies, however, focus chiefly on linking the short story to *Flags/Sartoris* and *Sanctuary*, especially in the connections between the composition of the texts, narrative developments, and most especially the characterization of the three major Sartoris characters who reappear in "There Was a Queen"—Narcissa, Jenny, and Elnora.

Critics who have examined the short story's history usually place its origin after publication of *Sartoris* but before *Sanctuary*, possibly between the writing of the first and second versions of *Sanctuary*. Relational studies are enhanced by textual examinations that have produced, in addition to *Sartoris*, the original *Flags in the Dust*, and in addition to *Sanctuary* as published, the original version that Faulkner so heavily revised. All these texts have links to the story; some connections touch all the texts and some link only a particular novel to the story. Putzel sees "There Was a Queen" as a transitional story between *Sartoris* and *Sanctuary* (1983, 266). Watson also finds it noteworthy that this story comes out of the period when the Compson, Sartoris, and Benbow narratives were being written and revised. "There Was a Queen" takes up the narrative strand of the letters from *Flags/Sartoris* but supplements the text with those aspects of Narcissa's character being developed more explicitly in *Sanctuary*. In the story Faulkner adopts the "epistolary medium" present in *Flags/Sartoris* "to convey characters and themes he was setting forth by different means in *Sanctuary*" (Watson 1987, 100–101, 103).

Events in *Flags/Sartoris* precipitate the action of "There Was a Queen." The short story follows the trail of the obscene letters that Byron Snopes sent to Narcissa, then stole back from her. Irving Howe calls the story a "footnote to *Sartoris*" ([1952] 1975, 70). Michael Millgate's appraisal recognizes the "narrative continuity" between the novel and the story ([1961] 1966, 63). For Lawrance Thompson, the re-use of the Snopes letters in "There Was a Queen" possibly implies Faulkner's acknowledgement that the Snopes courtship was "inadequately fitted" into *Sartoris* (1964, 307). Other critics, it should be noted, argue that the Snopes letters illuminate Narcissa's relationships with Horace and Bayard in *Flags in the Dust* (see Watson 1987, 100–03).

Critics have made a substantial effort to find differences and inconsistencies in the various narratives. Altered chronology is here, as elsewhere in Faulkner, a characteristic difference between texts. Brooks and Haney Bell have identified inconsistent time references between "There Was a Queen" and *Sartoris*, Bayard's age in *Sartoris* and "There Was a Queen" differing by a year (Brooks [1963] 1990, 450–51). Several datable actions in the novel are referred to as having taken place some years prior to the date established in *Sartoris*, including the time when Narcissa began receiving the letters, when she lost them, Benbow's date of birth, and when Bayard and Narcissa became engaged. Bell finds the dates in the novel to be preferable. He understands the differences to be the result of a three-year gap between composition of the two texts. At the time of Bell's writing, he might not have known that the story existed in 1929, the publication year of *Sartoris* (1965, 23–26). Comparative chronologies are not facilitated by the disagreement over the time of action of the story. M. E. Bradford dates the story occurrences at about 1930 (1967–68, 122). Walter Everett uses internal evidence to place the action in June 1926, but he notes that using information in *Sartoris* would set the story in 1931 (1969, 174).

Another critical focus has been the alteration or omission of narrative action from *Flags/Sartoris* to "There Was a Queen." James Carothers calls "There Was a Queen" a sequel to *Sartoris* yet independent of the longer work in part because the Sartoris history is provided in the opening of the story. The differences in the story are as numerous as the similarities. In the story Narcissa recalls showing Jenny only one letter, but in the novel she shows her several. The letters are known to be sent from Byron Snopes in the novel, but he is only referred to as the bookkeeper in the story. Another important distinction between novel and story is that the story is almost devoid of Sartoris men. Benbow is the sole (white) male survivor, the last of the (white) Sartoris line. The novel gives a great deal of attention to Bayard's attempt to "come to terms with his family's past," but in the story, Narcissa strives "to repudiate the Sartoris traditions and values and her own past" (Carothers 1985, 42–43).

One of the main points of comparison of "There Was a Queen" to both *Flags/Sartoris* and *Sanctuary* is the characterization of Narcissa in each text. Faulkner defended the appearance of Narcissa in *Sartoris* and *Sanctuary* not as a change in the personality of the character but as the portrayal of a different aspect of her character (*FU* 9). Critics are divided as to whether Narcissa in *Sanctuary* and "There Was a Queen" is consistent with her portrait in *Flags/ Sartoris*. Several argue that the later portraits diverge significantly from Narcissa of *Flags/Sartoris*. Brooks suggests that Narcissa's character in the short story "is not necessarily the same person as her younger and earlier self." Though she receives sympathetic treatment in *Flags in the Dust*, her character deteriorates in subsequent appearances where she becomes more and more the "abject slave of mere respectability." Brooks adds that Narcissa's character may be understood as having been "psychically bruised" and disappointed by both Horace and Bayard, both "romantics" despite their differences (Brooks [1963] 1990, 109; 1990, 166–67). According to Thompson, Narcissa's serenity at the close of *Sartoris* bears "ironic significance" to the subsequent texts. She will not enjoy peace in either *Sanctuary* or "There Was a Queen" because she will be "motivated by the familiar Sartoris mannerism of self-pitying and excessive pride" (Thompson 1964, 315). Ronald Walker describes Narcissa's behavior in both "There Was a Queen" and *Sanctuary* as less "haunting" or "enigmatic" than she appears in *Sartoris* (1973, 275). Ferguson sees Narcissa's portrayal in "There Was a Queen" as the character of *Sanctuary*, not *Flags in the Dust* (1991, 34).

A number of critics argue that Narcissa's characterization is not radically changed but more fully developed from traits that were suggested if not emphasized in *Flags/Sartoris*. Olga Vickery believes the full implications of Narcissa's concern for appearance and lack of "any genuine sense of ethics" are played out in *Sanctuary* and "There Was a Queen" ([1959] 1964, 24).

Kerr finds a consistency in the characterization of Narcissa from *Sartoris* to *Sanctuary* if her behavior regarding Snopes's letters beginning in *Sartoris* and continuing in "There Was a Queen" is taken into account (1961–1962, 6–7). Bradford similarly believes Narcissa remains consistent with her previous characterizations (1967–1968, 115). Millgate suggests that given Faulkner's capacity for projective as well as retrospective references from one work to another, in *Sartoris* certain characteristics of Narcissa may have been "held back" in order to present them in *Sanctuary* and "There Was a Queen" (Millgate 1980b, 106–07).

John Bassett describes Narcissa in *Flags in the Dust* as revealing the "outlines of an emotional Southern lady who has learned to supply herself with acceptable and workable outlets for those passions" that prepare her for her subsequent behavior in "There Was a Queen" and *Sanctuary*. Unlike her husband or her brother, Narcissa "retains control," but, Bassett adds, not as a "positive standard" among Faulkner's women but as a "modern martinet and heir to Aunt Jenny" ([1981] 1989, 50). Putzel similarly traces a progressive development in Narcissa's "selfish passion for outward respectability." It exists in her earliest portrait, but by her appearance in the short story, it is a "ruthless obsession" (Putzel 1983, 266). Watson believes that the motivation for Narcissa's behavior in "There Was a Queen" is implicit in *Flags*. Her fear in *Flags* that the missing letters would disrupt her serenity and leave her vulnerable to the chance that some stranger might discover the letters reverberates in "There Was a Queen" in her confession to Jenny that she imagined herself sleeping with all men. But this remark in the short story also likens Narcissa's feelings to Horace's observation in *Sanctuary* that looking on evil brings its own corruption (Watson 1987, 100–01). Daniel Young reviews Narcissa's behavior through the three texts, finding that she "begins in overt serenity and moves through passion, fulfilment and frustration to perversity." "There Was a Queen" portrays the final act of decline of the woman who has become more and more repressed and sexless (Young 1990, 88–103).

Because of the revelation in the short story that Elnora is the daughter of John Sartoris, her character also stimulates comparisons between *Flags/Sartoris* and "There Was a Queen." Walter Taylor points out that the new information about Elnora's being a Sartoris by blood "threw the whole structure of myths that he had been building around the Sartoris and Compson families in a new light," including the diminution of John Sartoris from mythic to human dimensions. Taylor adds that if Elnora is half Sartoris, Ringo might also be, a suggestion that adds new depth to the Ringo-Bayard relationship. If, Taylor points out, Narcissa succeeds in preventing Benbow from knowing the Sartoris legends and adopting the code of the Sartoris men, then the Sartoris heritage is left to be passed through the black descendants. The parenthetical aside of the narrator questioning whether the members of the household knew of Elnora's parentage represents Faulkner's reluctance to admit the possibility that the white brother and black sister would be raised in the same household (Taylor 1983, 96–97; see also Kerr 1983, 156). Putzel also believes Elnora serves a "mediatory" role that contrasts with the "blackface bit part" she had in *Sartoris*, a change he attributes to Faulkner's growth (1983, 265). Carothers describes the change in Elnora's role, from one of the blacks portrayed in the novel as generally irresponsible to the sustainer of the household in the story (1985, 42–43).

Unlike Narcissa and Elnora, Jenny Du Pre does not change dramatically in her characterization in "There Was a Queen." Her transtextual consistency represents for some critics Faulkner's admiration for her type. Bradford finds no conflict in Jenny's behavior in "There Was a Queen" with her other characterizations (1967–1968, 115). Kerr believes that "because Aunt Jenny's virtue was genuine and she scorned conventional appearances, she is never presented ironically" in any of the works in which she appears ("An Odor of Verbena," *Sartoris*, *Sanctuary*, and "There Was a Queen") (1979, 94; see also Kerr 1978, 88).

Naturally, in the tightly woven fictional community of Yoknapatawpha, "There Was a Queen" lends itself to comparisons beyond the reappearing Sartoris family in various works. Narcissa and her relationship to the Snopes letters generate a variety of links to Temple Drake in *Sanctuary* and *Requiem for a Nun*. Bradford compares Narcissa's pleasure in the Snopes letters to Temple Drake's behavior in *Sanctuary* while she is at the bootleggers' up to the time that the rape occurs. Both women play with roles that they find enticing but frightening (Bradford 1967–1968, 118 n. 15). In Kinney's view, Narcissa's trip to Memphis emphasizes the similarity of her experience to that of Temple Drake in Memphis; both engage in hypocritical "protestations of decency" (1980, 74). Millgate believes that Narcissa's bargain for the letters in "There Was a Queen" was originally meant to serve as an "ironic counterpoint" to Narcissa's treatment of Ruby Lamar, who also gave "herself sexually to a lawyer in a somewhat better cause." He suggests that the story may have actually been meant for inclusion into *Sanctuary* and that the reference to "dead tranquil queens in stained marble" in the novel's conclusion may anticipate the story (Millgate 1980a, 28; Millgate 1980b, 98; see also Kerr 1980, 21). Watson also identifies specific associations between Narcissa and Temple in *Sanctuary*. Narcissa's lover is an agent of the law; Temple's is a gangster. Narcissa sets up her liaison, a two-night stay in a Memphis hotel; Temple is abducted and spends weeks in a Memphis brothel. Narcissa's lover is a surrogate for the letter writer just as Red is a surrogate for Popeye. Both Narcissa and Temple view themselves as the owners of their respective letters (Watson 1987, 102).

The comparisons of Narcissa and Temple extend to the latter's experiences in *Requiem for a Nun*. Edward Holmes likens the reappearance of Narcissa's letters to the return of Temple's letters in *Requiem for a Nun*, but Noel Polk contrasts Narcissa's desire to appear rather than be respectable with Temple's greater integrity, shown in her refusal "to deceive herself or her family" regardless of the disgrace such a stand would bring (Holmes 1966, 111; Polk 1981, 262–63 n. 15). Bassett compares

Narcissa's ordeal with the obscene letters to Temple's being blackmailed with compromising letters. Narcissa is allowed a "quieter redemption" in the cleansing ritual in the creek than is granted Temple (Bassett [1988] 1989, 183-84). Watson's claim that the letters in "There Was a Queen" and *Requiem for a Nun* were independently invented does not diminish the similarities found in two narratives (1987, 143).

Although the parallels are neither as strong nor as numerous as those in the Sartoris-related texts, associations between "There Was a Queen" and *The Sound and the Fury* possess a collective strength. Robert Penn Warren compares Narcissa's behavior to Mrs. Compson's in *The Sound and the Fury*. Both women reveal the shallowness of their character by letting appearance become more important than behavior; that is, they retain the letter of tradition rather than its spirit (1958, 63). Charles Nilon compares Elnora's allegiance to the Sartorises with Dilsey's devotion to the Compsons in *The Sound and the Fury*. However, Elnora, unlike Dilsey, is by her bloodline a member of the Sartoris clan, and she identifies with and accepts the Sartoris point of view. Both recognize the decline of their respective families (1965, 104–05; see also Taylor 1983, 96–97). Elnora's exclamation "Oh, Lawd" at her discovery of Jenny's death reminds Kinney of Dilsey's churchgoing (Kinney 1980, 74; *CS* 744). The purification ritual in the creek recalls an earlier scene in *The Sound and the Fury* when Quentin and Caddy wash the mud from themselves in the branch (Brylowski 1968, 77; Bleikasten 1976, 218 n. 46; Kinney 1980, 74).

Beyond the associations that can be made between "There Was a Queen" and specific works, the characterizations of Narcissa, Jenny, and Elnora can be compared to more generalized types represented broadly throughout Faulkner's fiction—with the comparisons yielding widely diverse results. Critics observing similar females will draw very different conclusions. Kerr, considering Elly and Narcissa together, finds them to demonstrate that "turmoil may exist beneath the appearance of virtue and that the 'pure young girl' may actually be a skillful hyprocrite [sic]." The image of the "pure white woman" is contradicted by the impurity beneath. Like many of Faulkner's other women, Narcissa is either self-destructive or forced to accept the cult of Southern womanhood. Narcissa's choice contrasts with the choices made by Emily Grierson, and Minnie Cooper, Elly, and Caddy Compson. Drusilla tries to avoid the female role, but she is finally compelled to accept a conventional marriage (Kerr 1961–1962, 6; [1969] 1976, 159). While Kerr reads these characters as generally representing a critical view of a restrictive code of behavior, Bradford interprets many of these same characters as "female rebels against providentially assigned status or condition." He includes Narcissa, Caddy Compson, Charlotte Rittenmeyer, Elly, Cecily Saunders, Patricia Robyn, Jenny Steinbauer, and Temple Drake (1968, 180 n. 2).

Ilse Lind looks at many of these same women in her argument that Faulkner recognized in advance of many of his contemporaries the relatively new conception of women as sexual beings. Faulkner's female characters were often portrayed in the midst of the clash of their sex drive with the repressive forces of their society. Lind names Temple Drake, Narcissa Benbow, Drusilla Hawk, and Emily Grierson as among "Faulkner's most perturbed women," whose actions reveal "thwarted or perverted drives and those aspects of their culture which, in Faulkner's view were the least wholesome—prudery, class snobbery, arrogant racism" (Lind 1978, 101).

David Miller's analysis of Faulkner's female characters divides them into the classes of "earthmothers" and "ghosts." Ghosts are noted for their sexlessness. He includes both Aunt Jenny and Narcissa (of *Sartoris* specifically) with such other ghost-women characters as Emily Grierson, Mrs. Powers in *Soldier's Pay*, Judith Sutpen, Drusilla Hawk, and Joanna Burden. These women have been or have tried to be either earthmothers or ladies but either through aging or some other circumstance they have become "ghosts." Miller does not discuss how Narcissa's sexual negotiations in "There Was a Queen" relate to his assessment (Miller 1967, 3–7).

Judith Wittenberg observes that in the Faulknerian community, there are strict limits on women's options, including access to education and economic self-sufficiency. Consequently, women use their bodies either to generate money or in place of it. The list of women in this category includes not only poor white women such as Ruby Lamar, Everbe Corinthia, Mink's wife, Laverne Shumann, and Dewey Dell Bundren, but also Narcissa Benbow and Eula Varner Snopes. Wittenberg believes that tracing the origins of the emotional and behavioral patterns of Faulkner's women generates a more sympathetic response to their mindlessness or destructiveness. Narcissa, for example, is forced by her mother's death to assume the role of mother to her brother, Horace, and to repress her own sexuality. Others whose actions are more sympathetically understood in the context of their upbringing include Cecily Saunders, Caddy Compson and her daughter, Quentin, and Eula Varner (Wittenberg [1982] 1986, 236–37, 241–42). In addition to the appearance of repressed characters, according to Watson, the "language and the psychology of sexual repression" is the same not only between "There Was a Queen" and the closely related novels, but also in the fairly contemporary stories "Elly," "A Rose for Emily," and "The Leg" (Watson 1987, 101).

Miller's grouping of both Narcissa and Jenny as sexless "ghosts" veers from the more frequent contrasts drawn between the characters. While Narcissa and her type are generally perceived as working against a traditional order, Jenny is identified as a conservator of traditional values. Although in actuality Jenny has borne no children, Richardson describes her as the first "grandmother figure" who is characterized by "*agape*, aggressive willfulness, and humanitarian purposes" and whose "function is to be a guide and instructor for youth." Her association with a garden reflects a relationship with the earth and the "chain of life." Her characterization is recreated in the later Rosa Millard and Miss Habersham (Richardson 1967, 103–09).

Brooks's analysis of Faulkner's aristocrats shows how the definition inheres in behavior rather than class. He likens the virtues of Old Bayard Sartoris, Jenny Du Pre, Rosa Millard, Uncle Buck, and Uncle Buddy to V. K. Ratliff and Lucas Beauchamp ([1978] 1990, 335). Polk's study of Faulkner's work between 1927 and 1931 reveals a recurrence of a gray-haired woman framed by a window or pillows. Jenny joins company with a varied assortment including Emily Grierson, Elly's grandmother in "Elly," and Howard's mother in "The Brooch." Polk argues that Faulkner's early title, "Through the Window," demonstrates the strength of the image (1985, 31–32).

Like Jenny, Elnora is also associated with the role of caregiver. Bradford identifies "custodianesses of the civilized life" as both white and black matriarchs such as Elnora, Jenny, Granny Millard, Miss Habersham (Miss Worsham), Judith Sutpen, Dilsey, Clytie, Molly Beauchamp, Rider's Aunt, Aunt Callie, and Louisiana. He adds that although little is known of the grandmother Ailanthia in "Elly," she too serves as a matriarch (1967–1968, 110, 138–39; 1968, 182). In a similar manner, Nilon's comparison of Elnora to Dilsey can be extended to include Clytie's loyalty to the Sutpens in *Absalom, Absalom!* (1965, 104–05). Esther Terry adds Louvinia of *The Unvanquished* to this list of matriarchal black women, a group she sees portrayed as accepting their "proscribed destiny," absolving the whites of guilt and fitting the expectations of the Southern tradition (1985, 311–12).

In addition to the caregiver role, Elnora has qualities that link her to other characters. Charles Peavy finds that Elnora's scornful estimation of Narcissa as "town trash" resembles the attitude of Weddel's servant toward the mountain people in "Mountain Victory," and the butler's disdain in "Barn Burning" and "Shall Not Perish." Peavy traces this fictional representation to condescending attitudes held by Negroes toward poor whites after the Civil War (1971, 20–21). Carothers groups "There Was a Queen" with "Dry September," "That Evening Sun," and "Elly" as stories that deal with contemporary racial attitudes (1985, 20).

Several critics have investigated the attitudes toward Jews expressed in Faulkner's fiction, attempting to learn how closely these represent the author's own opinions. Alfred Kutzik believes that Faulkner's portraits of Jewish characters were anti-Semitic prior to his depiction of Gerald David Levine in *A Fable* (1954). Until the appearance of Levine, Faulkner's prevailing Jewish character-type was an "immoral, unpatriotic, money-centered" Jew. Kutzik identifies variations of this character in "There Was a Queen," "Death Drag," "Honor," *Soldier's Pay, Mosquitoes, The Sound and the Fury, Sanctuary, Pylon, The Wild Palms, Intruder in the Dust,* and *Requiem for a*

*Nun*. Kutzik suggests unconvincingly that the Jewish lawyer in *Sanctuary* with whom Ruby Lamar has sexual intercourse in trade for legal representation for Lee Godwin may perhaps be the same character who trades the Snopes letters for sexual relations with Narcissa Sartoris (1965, 213–20). The character in "There Was a Queen" is a federal agent; no mention is made of his being a lawyer. Nevertheless, the similarity in their characterizations may reinforce Kutzik's argument of the prevailing negative stereotype.

Lind takes issue with Kutzik's conclusion that Faulkner held intense anti-Semitic feelings, particularly in the years prior to 1950. Lind does not deny the negative stereotypes of Jews in the fiction, but interprets them differently. "There Was a Queen" is one of a number of stories and novels employing a Jewish character, from the early *Soldiers' Pay* to *The Mansion*. "There Was a Queen" illustrates the anti-Semitism that existed among "Southern patricians." Jenny's animosity is portrayed as an "unchangeable, irrational condition of mind." Lind suggests that Faulkner's typical alliance with the Sartoris value system shows that the anti-Semitism present in Southern aristocrats was a familiar reality to Faulkner, but it does not necessarily reflect an endorsement of Jenny's bigotry. Lind points out that critics who see the agent's portrait as anti-Semitic assume that he does indeed approach Narcissa with the intention of sexual blackmail. It is more likely that the assumption is Narcissa's projection. There is much more evidence regarding her own "morbid sexuality" than there is any indication that the agent's original intention was something other than pursuing leads to locate Byron Snopes. Lind shows that Faulkner more than once portrayed white female characters who desired sexual liaisons with men from social groups held in contempt by their own social class. Narcissa projects onto the man the stereotype of Jewish males as "licentious and sexually sinister" (Lind 1984, 119–42). Two further points that Lind needs to address are that Jenny's anger flares not just when she sees features that lead her to conclude that the dinner guest is Jewish but also when she hears him speak and calls him a Yankee. Further, regardless of the fact that the trade of sexual relations for letters originates with Narcissa, the agent agrees and the deal is consummated.

The Memphis liaison suggests to Carothers another Faulknerian pattern. The "perilous journey" motif is specifically manifested in a trip to Memphis. One among dozens of these is Narcissa's trip to retrieve the Snopes letters. Although the journey to Memphis usually has a specific goal, the traveler typically confronts "some unexpected discoveries along the way or within the city itself" (Carothers 1981, 116–18). Since Narcissa's journey is not actually portrayed, fewer of the characteristics of the Memphis journey are described in "There Was a Queen."

Stephen Ross identifies a tendency in Faulkner's work in which "discourse habitually disengages voice from person so that individuals are taken out of themselves and implanted in a broader communal nexus defined in part by qualities given to voice 'as such,' that is, as separated from human speech as source." Both "There Was a Queen" and "Mistral" separate voice from "its human origin" (1989, 26).

Stimulated by Faulkner's expressed concern for coherence in story collections, critics often seek relationships revealed by story placement in the various collections. Although he agrees with the general critical estimate that textual integration occurs less in the *Doctor Martino* collection than in the earlier *These 13* or later *Collected Stories*, Ferguson finds that some themes emerge from the order of the stories in the second collection. A prominent theme established in the lead story "Doctor Martino" and carried throughout the collection is the "solipsistic desire to achieve justice, the need to attain some kind of quid pro quo." In "There Was a Queen" this effort manifests itself in Narcissa's trade for her letters and her subsequent cleansing in the creek (Ferguson 1991, 153–54).

More unifying features appear in *Collected Stories*. Millgate's analysis of "The Middle Ground" reveals either an actual or a symbolic death in all the stories including "There Was a Queen." He traces thematic strains of "deracination and disillusion, with the loss of familiar bearings" in these tales ([1966] 1989, 273; see also Kinney 1980, 74). The juxtaposition of "Golden Land" and "There Was a Queen" suggests a certain degree of relief in Jenny's death when viewed in the light of Mrs. Ewing's trapped existence, expressed in her poignant words of resignation at the story's end, "I will stay here and live forever" (*CS* 726).

Carothers also identifies the recurrence of death in these stories but goes further than Millgate to link it as a twin to the theme of sex also prevalent in these tales. These stories display Faulkner's belief that an individual is capable of almost any behavior (Carothers 1985, 59). Carothers does not apply these generalizations to "There Was a Queen" specifically, but given the suggestion that Narcissa's sexual negotiations cause Jenny's death, the story can easily fall into his categorization.

Skei sees the element of strong emotional conflict as a shared trait in many of the stories, "There Was a Queen" among them. There is also a sense in which "The Middle Ground" stories are figuratively the middle ground, mainstream America, middle-class values that are examined by someone from outside a defined social group (1985, 214; 1992, 69). Ferguson works with "The Middle Ground" stories by pairing the first and last, then second and penultimate, and so on, until he arrives at the middle story, "Artist at Home." This approach links "Honor" and "There Was a Queen," two stories that focus on "conceptions of honor that are tested by sexual liaisons." Looking broadly through the fictional canon, Ferguson contends that Faulkner portrays a danger present in abstractions by which "artificial and arbitrary formulas, axioms, conceptualizations" are imposed on the "complexities of human experience." "There Was a Queen," like "Death Drag," "Honor," "Wash," "An

Odor of Verbena," and numerous others, demonstrates the consequences of the elevation of the abstraction "honor" for particular characters and events (Ferguson 1991, 81, 159). As in much of Faulkner's other work, questions about family, honor, and codes of behavior reappear as the pivotal issues of "There Was a Queen."

## Interpretations and Criticism

In the decade of the 1930s, George Marion O'Donnell established the critical poles of many subsequent thematic studies when he divided Faulkner's fictional community into Snopeses and Sartorises. They represented, respectively, naturalists and humanists. O'Donnell explained that the amoral Snopeses had weakened the ethically motivated Sartorises. In a Snopes world, tradition becomes formalized into a code of behavior, thereby losing its vitality and in fact becoming "pseudo-tradition." According to O'Donnell, Narcissa's effort in "There Was a Queen" to gain possession of the letters is a "*formalization* of one aspect of her traditional morality—her pride." As such, her action is antitraditional, a Snopesish response in a Snopes world. The knowledge of it kills Jenny, who is the "embodiment of the virile tradition" (O'Donnell [1939] 1973, 85).

Critics typically follow O'Donnell in discussing the story from the antithetical poles of Jenny's and Narcissa's respective characterizations. The women share sufficient characteristics to heighten the tension of their antithetical positions in that both are widows and both have refused to remarry (Skei 1985, 170). In these comparisons, Jenny is affirmed; Narcissa is denigrated. Irving Malin, for example, compares Jenny's strength to Narcissa's weakness (Malin 1957, 38–39). Elmo Howell believes the comparison of Jenny as "quality" and Narcissa as "trash" reflects Faulkner's interest in class differentiation (1959, 18; see also Everett 1969, 173–74). Dorothy Tuck concludes that Aunt Jenny represents "pride and dignity and sense of family" lacking in Narcissa (1964, 178–79). Brooks distinguishes Jenny's confidence in "her role in life" and her "set of moral principles and a code of conduct" from Narcissa's halting inner guidance, reflected in her behavior: "uncertain, confused, and even a bit neurotic" (1983, 14–15). Although critics reach different conclusions about the import of such characterizations, they almost uniformly hold that Jenny represents family, honor, and tradition, concepts that Narcissa fails either to understand or respect.

William Rose Benét early described Jenny as "superbly drawn" in "There Was a Queen" (1934, 645). Malin views Jenny as one of Faulkner's "sweet-sour old women" for whom the author has great respect. She is strong willed but in a positive way, because her age prevents her from using her sexuality "to destroy men." Malin finds a "Cassandra-like strain" in Jenny because she sees (even if she is reticent to admit it) the doom of the family (1957, 38–39).

For Bradford "There Was a Queen" is an exemplary text by which to understand Faulkner's attitude toward women. He argues that Faulkner presents as an admirable paradigm the "women who followed after, gave themselves to, and sustained an older social ideal, that of the family and clan culture of the old South." Jenny fits this model because she perpetuates the Sartoris family even while she remains "undeluded by the vainglories of the men." Her loyalty is secure because it is the "idea of Sartoris" that "provides her with a place and secures her dignity therein." Jenny fails to see Narcissa's lack of quality until their final conversation because, as an adherent of the code herself, she assumes that Narcissa's choice to become a Sartoris unquestionably includes the assumption that she will accept the "especial obligations" of that position (Bradford 1967–1968, 106–39).

Richardson describes Jenny's "chief characteristic" as a "prim and firm morality that is a perpetuation of the past glory of Southern womanhood." She contributes to but also diminishes the Sartoris myth in which she senses destructiveness (Richardson 1967, 104–05). Kerr argues that the dishonor of Narcissa's behavior is too great for Aunt Jenny to bear ([1969] 1976, 122). Karl counts Aunt Jenny as the "sole direct survivor" of the Sartoris family, apparently discounting the generations represented by Benbow and Elnora, both also present in "There Was a Queen." Putzel points out that although Jenny's obvious rudeness to the as yet unidentified guest in her home is hardly characteristic of a "great lady," the real manifestation of her stature is in her reserved response to Narcissa's confession (1983, 267).

Karl discusses the anti-Semitism present in Aunt Jenny's reaction to the dinner guest as part of her inability to escape the past. He adds, however, that she is "redeemed by her relationship to the past." Karl believes her reaction represents a value system that Faulkner affirms. She equates the "Yankee Jew" with an older, much hated man, the reformer who emerged in the South during the Reconstruction period whose values contrast with the honor of the Sartoris men. When she learns that Narcissa willingly sleeps with this enemy, Jenny dies. Karl believes Jenny's perspective reflects Faulkner's own (1989, 421).

Those who venture into a criticism of Jenny's character often use her treatment of the dinner guest as an entree into a negative analysis of the older woman. Bernard Knieger believes that Jenny's response demonstrates "less than admirable behavior" that Faulkner portrays in a critical light (Knieger 1972, Item 45). Castille is even harsher when he interprets Jenny's invalid condition as a reflection of her outmoded moral code. Her behavior toward the dinner guest, the federal agent, demonstrates the degeneration of her values into "supercilious rudeness and blind intolerance." Castille believes this incident is important in revealing how dated her views are, just as the dismissal by Elnora's children of the story of Jenny's journey and the Sartoris legend shows how the importance of these family tales has diminished in the changed world (1975, 311–15).

Polk points out that Jenny "is frequently and unexplainably querulous, rude, impatient, intolerant, and downright mean." She is also nihilistic, her humor is biting, and she enjoys the "sensational" stories in her afternoon paper. Polk suggests that she lives a vicarious existence to replace the one that was denied her. The relationship of her death to learning of Narcissa's Memphis liaison with the FBI agent involves "her adamant and self-righteous disapproval," but, Polk asserts, it may also entail some envy (1984, 77–79).

Skei contends that although Faulkner may have admired the qualities apparent in such characters as Jenny, she and others like her were from a different time and special war-generated circumstances. Jenny is admirable because she embodies traditional values, has endured difficulties, and "has become an anachronism without complaining." Skei tempers the view of Jenny as an ideal woman devoted to maintaining family and community. He points out that by defining herself as a Sartoris she has imposed limitations that curtailed her choices and narrowed the influence she might otherwise have had. Modern women faced new demands and needed new social patterns in order to be "useful, respected, full members of society." The delicate balance is to maintain the best traditional values without inhibiting newer, also positive values. According to Skei, Jenny would never choose Narcissa's means of resolving the threat because Jenny has accepted an assigned role with a "fixed code of behavior." She has given up herself to the demands of the Sartoris clan. Skei suggests that some caution should be imposed in assigning a causal link between Narcissa's Memphis trip and Jenny's death. Her age and fragile condition would make her death at this time not unexpected, even without an external shock (Skei 1985, 128, 169–72, 204, 314 n. 27).

Even if some critics doubt Narcissa's role in Jenny's death, her behavior has elicited exceedingly harsh judgments. Most of these readers assume that she displays a narcissistic attitude reminiscent of her name and evolving from her understanding—or misunderstanding—of honor and respectability. Although Benét approved of Jenny's characterization, he thought Narcissa's behavior was unconvincing even though "crucial" to the story (1934, 645). William O'Connor describes the story as a "satiric treatment of Narcissa Benbow's willingness to sacrifice her honor for her reputation" (1954, 89).

Edmond Volpe sees Narcissa's using her body in trade for the letters as "fulfilling the desire that originally prevented her from destroying them" ([1964] 1989, 147). For Bradford, Narcissa is not self-sacrificing like Jenny but "self-preoccupied and self-possessed." Her dislike of men stems from the threat they pose to her "dreamy self-absorption." She herself poses a threat to the family in the manner in which she intends to raise Benbow—without allegiance to the family (hence not named after a Sartoris). Narcissa's preference is to retreat from life, and she believes that for the letters to be out in the world again shatters the self-enclosed world she has created. Bradford views her washing in the creek as "her sole concession to the reality of her misdeed; but her pleasure in it serves only to certify to the reader the depravity of her conception of respectability as sanctuary" (1967–1968, 106–39).

Floyd Watkins also asserts that Narcissa's seeming almost to treasure and enjoy the letters as she receives them indicates her eventual "loss of virtue" played out in "There Was a Queen" (1971, 179). Panthea Broughton also sees Narcissa acting out codified behavior that carries no significant meaning. She sits in the creek with Bory as a "rite of absolution" that "will wash her clean of sin," expecting "that the mere repetition of a gesture will be sufficient to allay difficulties." She fails to understand what Jenny sees, the "absurdity, as well as the amorality, in Narcissa's actions" (Broughton 1974, 81–82).

Brooks counts Narcissa as "no aristocrat at all"; she is "completely in thrall to bourgeois respectability." Narcissa chooses the act of fornication that will remain private rather than risking public innuendo that the letters might generate (Brooks 1976, 147). (One should recall that this is precisely opposite to Jenny's specific recommendation for action as it appeared in prepublication versions.) Narcissa sets the meeting with the agent in Memphis rather than in Jefferson to, as she professes, protect Jenny and Bory from embarrassment. Her "lack of sensibility" is more explicit in this self-serving declaration of concern to Jenny than in the actual rendezvous itself. The shock to Jenny of hearing about such behavior is fatal (Putzel 1983, 266–67).

Sherrill Harbison describes Narcissa as having "exposed the underbelly of her character" by her actions in the story (1985, 301–02). Young believes that Narcissa's sexual relationship with the federal agent is an attempt to cancel out her feeling as a younger woman that the letters constituted a violation by many men, a violation that she both desires and fears. The perverse logic of the act matches her act of cleansing when she sits in the creek (1990, 102-03). Ferguson does not see the confession as a purging of her guilt, nor does he believe that her sitting in the creek suggests much more than "an almost *literal* need to cleanse herself of the dirt of the 'Yankee Jew.'" Her confession is too casual to admit "deep-lying moral concern."(Ferguson 1991, 144).

Some readings are less critical of Narcissa if not in fact sympathetic to her. Kerr cannot be classed as a sympathetic reader with such judgments of her as "Faulkner's most complete portrait of the spurious 'ideal' Southern girl and woman" or as the "counterfeit image of pure Southern womanhood," a role to which Narcissa conforms voluntarily. Kerr distinguishes "quality" as a reflection of character, not class. Narcissa comes from a "good family," so she is not merely an affront to a class. In fact, Kerr attributes the end of the (white) Sartoris line to Narcissa's character (Kerr [1969]1976, 122; 1983, 133–34, 168, 289). Nevertheless, Kerr's analysis of the destructive nature of the ideal of Southern womanhood and the harm that comes to those who rebel introduces an alternative means by which Narcissa's actions may be understood (1961–1962, 6–8; see also Kerr 1979, 85, 94; Wagner, Black, and Harrington 1977, 147–49). (Bradford calls Kerr's reading of "There Was a Queen "exasperating" [1967–1968, 113 n. 10].) Sally Page classifies Narcissa as a "sexually thwarted" female who cannot easily love a man. She adds that "there is every indication that Narcissa views sex as something repulsive and that her natural sexual drives have been repressed." Her embrace of Bayard after the automobile ride and her response to Snopes's letters reveal the conflict within Narcissa (1972, 38).

Castille offers the most positive reading of Narcissa's character. He interprets her gaining stature as the new head of the Sartoris household as the "fundamentally affirmative" movement of the story. She is, in Castille's interpretation, one of Faulkner's females who "instinctively possess a sense of practical ethics that enables them in a thoroughly amoral way to accomplish what they will." Given the circumstances of the situation Narcissa acts expeditiously to retrieve the letters. Castille does not deny her "hypocrisy and selfishness," but he contrasts her pragmatism with the Sartorises' escapism and Horace's ineffectual idealism. Narcissa takes her stand as head of the household before Jenny's death is known. At the dining table, she seats her son at her side, a clear departure from previous Sartoris tradition (Castille 1975, 307–15).

Carothers points out that the story itself does not reflect a unified judgment of Narcissa. Although Elnora considers her to be "town trash," Jenny expresses a "seeming acquiescence" to Narcissa's character. Even if Narcissa lacks "quality," it is clear that Sartoris "quality" is limited. Sartoris quality includes an inability "to cope with life's disgusting alternatives" and a reactionary response by family members to draw into themselves. Narcissa acts matter-of-factly to resolve her dilemma, then enacts the cleansing and confessional rituals to absolve herself of any taint from her actions (Carothers 1985, 43–44). Watson points out that given the way in which in *Sanctuary* the courtroom display of the corncob used in the rape of Temple Drake generated "obscene speculation," it is no wonder that Narcissa would act so radically to keep the letters from public view (1987, 102–03).

Some clarification should be made regarding the issue of the Memphis assignation. Narcissa, according to her own recounting of the story, suggests that the trade of letters for sex is based on her belief that "men are all about the same, with their ideas of good and bad. Fools" (*CS* 741). Bradford makes the observation that Narcissa bargains with the agent for return of the letters and that his original intention was not to solicit her (1967–1968, 133); numerous critics have implied otherwise. In 1984 Watson wrote that Narcissa "submits to sexual blackmail," but in his later work makes the point that the rendezvous is directed by Narcissa (1984, 242; 1987, 102). Watson's reference is not exceptional but rather exemplary of the critics' sometimes inaccurately understood point of origin of the offer. It is important in understanding Narcissa's character to remember that she, not the agent, first makes the proposal.

Readers' judgments of Narcissa necessarily come by way of acceptance or rejection of Elnora's obvious hatred of the woman. Typically, critics interpret Elnora's views as those meant to be embraced. Nilon defines Elnora as a "point-of-view character" by whose opinions the reader is to understand the story. Her loyalty is a loyalty to the past Sartorises, and she explains the demise of Sartoris "quality" as its inability to perceive and defend itself against "unquality" (Nilon 1965, 104–05). Bradford sees her role enhanced by the revelation of her own Sartoris blood to that of a "peculiarly prescient and judicious spokesman or representative of her white family." Her voice is "normative and choric." That her children do not understand her reflects their similarity to Narcissa and her confused values. Elnora's concern reaches beyond Jenny's life to the survival of the Sartoris family that she, like Jenny, has worked to sustain (1967–1968, 122). Everett believes Elnora's opinions are supported by the action of the story (1969, 173–74). She understands the concept of "honor" as well as Aunt Jenny and better than Narcissa (Weisgerber [1968] 1974, 26).

Just as some readers see Elnora as expounding the correct view of Narcissa, many see Benbow's character as evidencing the Sartoris family's decline. Benbow is last seen as a bachelor in the air force in "Knight's Gambit" and *The Town*. There is a sense that Benbow represents both a movement away from the Sartoris nature and the end of the family. In Everett's view Benbow's role as a Sartoris child seems diminished (Everett 1969, 174). Castille argues that when Narcissa takes her stand as head of the household, before Jenny's death is known, and seats her son at her side, she makes a clear departure from previous Sartoris tradition (1975, 307–15).

Hall also believes the story concludes with the dark picture of the demise of the Sartoris family. Even Jenny's self-sacrifice has not been enough to maintain it. Hall believes that Narcissa's moving Benbow (Bory) from the head of the Sartoris table to a seat at her side indicates that she will raise him to fill the role Horace (Hory) once filled in her life. In combination with references to him elsewhere, Benbow, heir to both Benbows and Sartorises, appears to be doomed (Hall 1986, 33).

Bradford, however, offers a dissenting, affirmative view of Bory. The child's slow obedience to his mother in her effort to "unman him" suggests that he may survive as a Sartoris despite his mother's failure to understand his role as the Sartoris heir. The story concludes with some hint of reassurance in Bory's assumption of the male Sartorises' lack of need for other people. Whether Bory is "trash" like his mother "raises the question of family honor in connection with family continuity," issues that Bradford contends are inseparable for Faulkner (1967–1968, 122, 136–37).

Few critics have examined the formal qualities of the story, but among those who have, Ferguson has indicated that its action is largely unbelievable. He contends that the twelve-year lapse between the theft and reappearance of the letters is unlikely. It is not probable that the letters would reappear or that the agent would continue to pursue the bookkeeper, Byron Snopes. Further, although Ferguson believes Narcissa would make the sexual trade for the letters, she would not tell Jenny about her negotiations. Even if Narcissa lacks the sensitivity to judge the effect of her confession on Jenny, she would not make the confession because of her "strong sense of propriety" (Ferguson 1991, 144).

As the prepublication texts amply proved, Faulkner revised repeatedly to achieve a satisfactory perspective from which to tell the story. Ferguson's analysis of the third-person point of view in "There Was a Queen" is that it is handled ineffectively. The shifts from Elnora's voice to Jenny's voice then to a "dramatic perspective" of Narcissa's confessional scene are "halting, uncertain, inconsistent, lacking in focus" (1991, 89).

Bradford speaks more positively of the story's development. He discerns a thematic transition from section to section. Bory, for example, is the topic of conversation at the close of Section II and the opening of Section III. This critic also identifies particular images that reinforce theme. Bradford interprets the jasmine and the glass panes as representatives of Jenny's perpetuation of a continuity across land and time. They represent the female's "order-bringing errand into the wilderness" and the "validity and the vitality of her tradition." In contrast, Narcissa's white attire represents a falsification rather than perpetuation of tradition. Jenny's insistence on talking about the jasmine when Narcissa begins to tell about her Memphis trip sets a "specific historical and ethical context for their forthcoming exchange." Bradford compares Bory to the jasmine and glass panes; he is the surviving repository of the Sartoris line (1967–1968, 121, 128–30).

In his discussion of Faulkner's sensual descriptions, Maurice Coindreau similarly observes that the "odor of jasmine and the dying glimmers of the stained-glass windows are, for Miss Jenny, her whole past and her ancestral glory" (1971, 39). For Putzel, the closing sensory appeal to the smell of flowers is a tribute to the deceased lady (1983, 267). In a less affirming interpretation, Polk describes Jenny's narrow, leaded glass window as very closely associated with her—Jenny, who moves in with old Bayard, becomes as much a part of his inheritance as the window is (1984, 77–78).

The title of the story is typically perceived as a tribute to Jenny (see Richardson 1967, 104–05). A line in *Sartoris* indicates that Jenny was treated deferentially, like a queen (Kerr 1983, 38). Everett describes the story as tracing the passing from the idea that "there *was* a queen" to "there *is* a queen"

(1969, 174). Skei believes the operative word in the title is *Was*, indicating that for all Jenny's positive traits, her type is a thing of the past, a fact that "had better be accepted as a necessary part of a world at change" (1985, 169–70).

Perhaps the most interesting element, the one that offers the greatest potential for further commentary, is the role of the letters in the story. The obscene letters themselves are more fully revealed in *Flags in the Dust* and when discussed by critics are typically placed within that context. John Matthews discusses the letters as they suggest the novel's consideration of the complexities of writing. The letters provide a "veil of words" through which the writer enjoys a paradoxically anonymous intimacy and the reader enjoys the "erotic secrets of language." Byron's visit to Narcissa's bedroom and subsequent assault of Minnie Sue, however, emphasize the "frustration that language can never present the thing itself." Once the letters reappear in "There Was a Queen," Byron's "mad 'courtship' of Narcissa is consummated" albeit with the federal agent. She retrieves the letters because their existence represents the "fragmentation of herself as a written subject, her lost sense of property and propriety" (Matthews 1982, 54–56).

In a separate study, Matthews juxtaposes the letters with Saddie's reading a fashion magazine. Once the letters are lost, they are public property, and they, like the magazine, like Faulkner's publications, can repeatedly generate and satisfy desire and can possibly "leave traces of the desires, emotions, identifications, and gratification" (1992, 11–13).

Another facet of Matthews's study is that "There Was a Queen" reflects the ability of the short story in the marketplace to encourage the "emergence of heterogeneity." Within the text, Jenny and Elnora clash with new ideas and former distinctions that are obscured or proved ambiguous. Matthews notes that "categories threaten to collapse into each other," and younger voices, like Isom's, neither discern nor oblige difference (Matthews 1992, 13–16).

Wittenberg identifies as a quality of Faulkner's female characters that they sometimes lack language, the Logos being "predominantly a male possession." Jenny is one notable exception to this generalization in that she "is both vocal and interested in words." Wittenberg describes Jenny's voice in *Flags in the Dust* as nearing the narrator's voice. Other women who "author" their own pasts include Rosa Coldfield, Mrs. Hines, Drusilla Hawk, Linda Snopes Kohl, and Charlotte Rittenmeyer ([1982] 1986, 243–44). Wittenberg does not pursue "There Was a Queen" specifically in this context, but because the voices of Elnora, Jenny, and Narcissa provide contrasts, and because Narcissa must use her body to buy someone else's words, Wittenberg's observation finds substantiation in this story.

In his extended study of letters in Faulkner's fiction, James Watson examines the way letters become "familiar tools for telling stories" especially in the period from 1925 to 1929. They are prevalent in both the long and short Sartoris fiction although they operate in a variety of relationships to the particular texts. In "There Was a Queen," Watson sees the "enigmatic durability of written experience in letters" as the "generative force in the writing of the story" (1987, 75, 92, 100). The centrality of the letters to the story involves the way they distinguish Jenny's and Narcissa's different attitudes, and how they "shape Narcissa's sexual attitudes and guide her sexual activity." She is strongly affected by her role as receiver of the letters, feeling that she has marked the letters with her rereading them and assuming a relationship with the sender, even though he is anonymous, an assumption confirmed by the agent's belief that she might lead him to the man. Watson explains that Narcissa seeks to claim the "written image of herself" in the letters. Her trade of her body for the letters makes the vicarious experience of the letters real. Watson notes that the man with whom she has intercourse is an "agent." Furthermore, because Narcissa considers herself socially superior to both the letter writer and the agent, they become the "carnal Everyman" that she imagined with her in her marriage bed (Watson 1987, 101–02).

Pamela Rhodes offers an alternative reading of the actions in "There Was a Queen." Rhodes examines the power of gazing in Faulkner's texts, showing how gazing implies violation. Thus, Snopes's gaze violates Narcissa and consequently the class boundaries that should separate them. Her feeling that she has become partner to many men "makes her 'wild'" because of the "social diversity of the men who actually 'know' her." Her nightmare is a social nightmare. Rhodes concludes, "To Elnora and Miss Jenny, certain of their social categories, custodians of the plantation values, Narcissa is, indeed, the trash which lets chaos in" (1989, 87).

The cumulative evidence of these discussions of people and texts suggests how urgent and understandable Narcissa's need is to retrieve the letters. The way in which the text of the letters defines her selfhood aligns the importance of the letters with the intimate nature of her trade for them. It becomes a trade of equal value, not a sacrifice of true value for false value. Narcissa acts, finally, to take control of her text.

There is no way, and perhaps no need, to reconcile the critical disagreement regarding "There Was a Queen." Howe believes that the story reveals "Faulkner in his aspect of traditional Southerner" ([1952] 1975, 263). Yet Kerr contends that Faulkner's point is not to affirm a Southern code but to expose its shallowness. Bradford speaks at greatest length on the story, yet his interpretation is "exasperatingly" outdated by his belief that the story operates as the "epitome" of Faulkner's understanding (and apparently his own) of the "social implications of women's practice or avoidance of the appropriate business of their sex, endurance or failure to endure." The text defers in most instances to the reader's ideology according to which he or she might sympathize either with Jenny's or Narcissa's means of defining self.

## Works Cited

Bassett, John E. [1981] 1989. "Shifting Conflict in *Flags in the Dust.*" In *Vision and Revisions: Essays on Faulkner*. Ed. Bassett. Locust Hill Literary Studies No. 4. West Cornwall, CT: Locust Hill, 35–54.

———. [1988] 1989. "Heir and Prototype: Original and Derived Characterizations in Faulkner." In *Vision and Revisions: Essays on Faulkner*. Ed. Bassett. Locust Hill Literary Studies No. 4. West Cornwall, CT: Locust Hill, 181–93.

Bell, Haney H., Jr. 1965. "A Reading of Faulkner's Sartoris and 'There Was a Queen.'" *Forum* 4.8:23–26.

Benét, William Rose. 1934. "Fourteen Faulkner Stories." *Saturday Review of Literature*, 21 April, 645.

Bleikasten, André. 1976. *The Most Splendid Failure: Faulkner's The Sound and the Fury*. Bloomington: Indiana University Press.

Blotner, Joseph. 1974. *Faulkner: A Biography*. 2 vols. New York: Random House.

Bradford, M. E. 1967–1968. "Certain Ladies of Quality: Faulkner's View of Women and the Evidence of 'There Was a Queen.'" *Arlington Quarterly* 1.2:106–39.

———. 1968. "Faulkner's 'Elly': An Expose." *Mississippi Quarterly* 21:179–87.

Brooks, Cleanth. [1963] 1990. *William Faulkner: The Yoknapatawpha Country*. New Haven: Yale University Press. Reprint. Baton Rouge: Louisiana State University Press.

———. 1976. "William Faulkner and William Butler Yeats: Parallels and Affinities." In *Faulkner: Fifty Years After The Marble Faun*. Ed. George H. Wolfe. University: University of Alabama Press, 139–58.

———. [1978] 1990. *William Faulkner: Toward Yoknapatawpha and Beyond*. New Haven: Yale University Press. Reprint. Baton Rouge: Louisiana State University Press.

———. 1983. *William Faulkner: First Encounters*. New Haven: Yale University Press.

Broughton, Panthea Reid. 1974. *William Faulkner: The Abstract and the Actual*. Baton Rouge: Louisiana State University Press.

Brylowski, Walter. 1968. *Faulkner's Olympian Laugh: Myth in the Novels*. Detroit: Wayne State University Press.

Carothers, James B. 1981. "The Road to The Reivers." In "A Cosmos of My Own": *Faulkner and Yoknapatawpha 1980*. Ed. Doreen Fowler and Ann J. Abadie. Jackson: University Press of Mississippi, 95–124.

———. 1985. *William Faulkner's Short Stories*. Ann Arbor, MI: UMI Research Press.

Castille, Philip. 1975. "'There Was a Queen' and Faulkner's Narcissa Sartoris." *Mississippi Quarterly* 28:307–15.

Coindreau, Maurice Edgar. 1971. *The Time of William Faulkner*. Ed. and trans. George McMillan Reeves. Columbia: University of South Carolina Press.

"Doctor Martino." 1934. *New York Times Literary Supplement*, 13 September, 618.

Everett, Walter K. 1969. *Faulkner's Art and Character*. Woodbury, NY: Barron's Educational Series.

Faulkner, William. 1933. "There Was a Queen." *Scribner's 93* (January):10–16.

———. 1934. *Doctor Martino and Other Stories*. New York: Harrison Smith and Robert Haas.

———. 1950. *Collected Stories of William Faulkner*. New York: Random House.

———. 1959. *Faulkner in the University: Class Conferences at the University of Virginia, 1957–1958*. Ed. Frederick Gwynn and Joseph L. Blotner. Charlottesville: University Press of Virginia.

———. 1977. *Selected Letters of William Faulkner*. Ed. Joseph Blotner. New York: Random House.

———. 1981. *Sanctuary: The Original Text*. Ed. Noel Polk. New York: Random House.

———. 1987. *William Faulkner Manuscripts 11*: Doctor Martino and Other Stories. Ed. Thomas L. McHaney. New York: Garland.

Ferguson, James. 1991. *Faulkner's Short Fiction*. Knoxville: University of Tennessee Press.

Hall, Constance Hill. 1986. *Incest in Faulkner: A Metaphor for the Fall*. Ann Arbor, MI: UMI Research Press.

Harbison, Sherrill. 1985. "Two Sartoris Women: Faulkner, Femininity, and Changing Times." In *Critical Essays on William Faulkner: The Sartoris Family*. Ed. Arthur F. Kinney. Boston: G. K. Hall, 289–303.

Holmes, Edward M. 1966. *Faulkner's Twice-Told Tales: His Re-Use of His Material*. The Hague: Mouton.

Howe, Irving. [1952] 1975. *William Faulkner: A Critical Study*. 3d ed. Chicago: University of Chicago Press.

Howell, Elmo. 1959. "Colonel Sartoris Snopes and Faulkner's Aristocrats A Note on 'Barn Burning.'" *Carolina Quarterly* 11.3:13–19.

Karl, Frederick R. 1989. *William Faulkner: American Writer*. New York: Weidenfeld and Nicolson.

Kerr, Elizabeth M. 1961–1962. "William Faulkner and the Southern Concept of Woman." *Mississippi Quarterly* 15:1–16.

———. [1969] 1976 *Yoknapatawpha: Faulkner's "Little Postage Stamp of Native Soil."* New York: Fordham University Press.

———. 1978. "The Women of Yoknapatawpha." *University of Mississippi Studies in English* 15:83–100.

———. 1979. *William Faulkner's Gothic Domain*. Port Washington, NY: Kennikat.

———. 1980. "The Creative Evolution of Sanctuary." *Faulkner Studies* 1:14–28.

———. 1983. *William Faulkner's Yoknapatawpha: "A Kind of Keystone in the Universe."* New York: Fordham University Press.

Kinney, Arthur F. 1980. "Faulkner's Narrative Poetics and Collected Stories." *Faulkner Studies* 1:58–79.

———. 1984. "'Topmost in the Pattern': Family Structure in Faulkner." In *New Directions in Faulkner Studies: Faulkner and Yoknapatawpha, 1983*. Ed. Doreen Fowler and Ann J. Abadie. Jackson: University Press of Mississippi, 143–71.

———. 1989. "The Family-Centered Nature of Faulkner's World." *College Literature* 16.1:83–102.

Knieger, Bernard. 1972. "Faulkner's 'Mountain Victory,' 'Doctor Martino,' and 'There Was a Queen.'" *Explicator* 30:Item 45.

Kutzik, Alfred J. 1965. "Faulkner and the Jews." *Yivo Annual of Jewish Social Science* 13:213–26.

Lewis, Wyndham. [1934] 1987. *Men Without Art*. London: Cassell. Reprint. Santa Rosa, CA: Black Sparrow.

Lind, Ilse Dusoir. 1978. "Faulkner's Women." In *The Maker and the Myth: Faulkner and Yoknapatawpha, 1977*. Ed. Evans Harrington and Ann J. Abadie. Jackson: University Press of Mississippi, 89–104.

———. 1984. "Faulkner's Relationship to Jews: A Beginning." In *New Directions in Faulkner Studies: Faulkner and Yoknapatawpha, 1983*. Ed. Doreen Fowler and Ann J. Abadie. Jackson: University Press of Mississippi, 119–42.

Malin, Irving. 1957. *William Faulkner: An Interpretation*. Stanford, CA: Stanford University Press.

Matthews, John T. 1982. *The Play of Faulkner's Language*. Ithaca, NY: Cornell University Press.

———. 1992. "Shortened Stories: Faulkner and the Market." In *Faulkner and the Short Story: Faulkner and Yoknapatawpha, 1990*. Ed. Evans Harrington and Ann J. Abadie. Jackson: University Press of Mississippi, 3–37.

Meriwether, James B. [1961] 1971. *The Literary Career of William Faulkner: A Bibliographical Study*. Princeton, NJ: Princeton Universtiy Library. Reprint. Columbia: University of South Carolina Press.

———. 1971. "The Short Fiction of William Faulkner: A Bibliography." *Proof* 1:293–329.

———. 1973. "Faulkner's Correspondence with Scribner's Magazine." *Proof* 3:253–82.

Miller, David M. 1967. "Faulkner's Women." *Modern Fiction Studies* 13:3–17.

Millgate, Michael. [1961] 1966. *William Faulkner*. New York: Barnes & Noble.

———. [1966] 1989. *The Achievement of William Faulkner*. New York: Random House. Reprint. Athens: University of Georgia Press. Brown Thrasher Books.

———. 1980a. "'A Cosmos of My Own': The Evolution of Yoknapatawpha." In *Fifty Years of Yoknapatawpha: Faulkner and Yoknapatawpha 1979*. Ed. Doreen Fowler and Ann J. Abadie. Jackson: University Press of Mississippi, 23–43.

———. 1980b. "Faulkner's First Trilogy: Sartoris, Sanctuary, and Requiem for a Nun." In *Fifty Years of Yoknapatawpha: Faulkner and Yoknapatawpha 1979*. Ed. Doreen Fowler and Ann J. Abadie. Jackson: University Press of Mississippi, 90–109.

Nilon, Charles H. 1965. *Faulkner and the Negro*. New York: Citadel.

O'Connor, William Van. 1954. *The Tangled Fire of William Faulkner*. Minneapolis: University of Minnesota Press.

O'Donnell, George Marion. [1939] 1973. "Faulkner's Mythology." In *William Faulkner: Four Decades of Criticism*. Ed. Linda Welshimer Wagner. East Lansing: Michigan State University Press, 83–93.

Page, Sally R. 1972. *Faulkner's Women: Characterization and Meaning*. Deland, FL: Everett/Edwards.

Peavy, Charles D. 1966. "Faulkner's Use of Folklore in The Sound and the Fury." *Journal of American Folklore* 79:437–47.

———. 1971. *Go Slow Now: Faulkner and the Race Question*. Eugene: University of Oregon Books.

Polk, Noel. 1981. *Faulkner's* Requiem for a Nun: *A Critical Study*. Bloomington: Indiana University Press.

———. 1984. "'The Dungeon Was Mother Herself': William Faulkner: 1927–1931." In *New Directions in Faulkner Studies: Faulkner and Yoknapatawpha, 1983*. Ed. Doreen Fowler and Ann J. Abadie. Jackson: University Press of Mississippi, 61–93.

———. 1985. "The Space between Sanctuary." In *Intertextuality in Faulkner*. Ed. Michel Gresset and Noel Polk. Jackson: University Press of Mississippi, 16–35.

Putzel, Max. 1977. "Faulkner's Short Story Sending Schedule." *Papers of the Bibliographical Society of America* 71:98–105.

———. 1983. "Faulkner's Memphis Stories." *Virginia Quarterly Review* 59:254–70.

———. 1985. *Genius of Place: William Faulkner's Triumphant Beginnings*. Baton Rouge: Louisiana State University Press.

Rhodes, Pamela E. 1989. "'I Remember Them Letters': Byron Snopes and Interference." In *Faulkner's Discourse: An International Symposium*. Ed. Lothar Hönnighausen. Tübingen: Max Niemeyer Verlag, 77–89.

Richardson, Kenneth E. 1967. *Force and Faith in the Novels of William Faulkner*. The Hague: Mouton.

Ross, Stephen M. 1989. *Fiction's Inexhaustible Voice: Speech and Writing in Faulkner*. Athens: University of Georgia Press.

Skei, Hans H. 1981. *William Faulkner: The Short Story Career*. Oslo, Norway: Universitetsforlaget.

———. 1985. *William Faulkner: The Novelist as Short Story Writer*. Oslo, Norway: Universitetsforlaget.

———. 1992. "Beyond Genre? Existential Experience in Faulkner's Short Fiction." In *Faulkner and the Short Story: Faulkner and Yoknapatawpha, 1990*. Ed. Evans Harrington and Ann J. Abadie. Jackson: University Press of Mississippi, 62–77.

Taylor, Walter. 1983. *Faulkner's Search for a South*. Urbana: University of Illinois Press.

Terry, Esther Alexander. 1985. "For 'blood and kin and home': Black Characterization in William Faulkner's Sartoris Saga." In *Critical Essays on William Faulkner: The Sartoris Family*. Ed. Arthur F. Kinney. Boston: G. K. Hall, 303–17.

Thompson, Lawrance. 1964. Afterword. In *Sartoris*. By William Faulkner. Signet Classic. New York: New American Library, 304–16.

Tuck, Dorothy. 1964. *Crowell's Handbook of Faulkner*. New York: Thomas Y. Crowell.

Vickery, Olga W. [1959] 1964. *The Novels of William Faulkner*. Baton Rouge: Louisiana State University Press.

Volpe, Edmond L. [1964] 1989. *A Reader's Guide to William Faulkner*. New York: Noonday. Reprint. New York: Octagon Books.

Wagner, Linda Welshimer, Victoria Fielden Black, and Evans Harrington. 1977. "Faulkner and Women." In *The South and Faulkner's Yoknapatawpha: The Actual and the Apocryphal*. Ed. Evans Harrington and Ann J. Abadie. Jackson: University Press of Mississippi, 147–51.

Walker, Ronald G. 1973. "Death in the Sound of Their Name: Character Motivation in Faulkner's Sartoris." *Southern Humanities Review* 7:271–78.

Warren, Robert Penn. 1958. "William Faulkner." In *Selected Essays*. Ed. Warren. New York: Random House, 59–79.

Watkins, Floyd C. 1971. *The Flesh and the Word: Eliot, Hemingway, Faulkner*. Nashville: Vanderbilt University Press.

Watson, James G. 1984. "'But Damn Letters Anyway': Letters and Fictions." In *New Directions in Faulkner Studies: Faulkner and Yoknapatawpha, 1983*. Ed. Doreen Fowler and Ann J. Abadie. Jackson: University Press of Mississippi, 228–53.

———. 1987. *William Faulkner: Letters and Fictions*. Austin: University of Texas Press.

Weisgerber, Jean. [1968] 1974. *Faulkner and Dostoevsky: Influence and Confluence*. Trans. Dean McWilliams. Athens: Ohio University Press.

Wittenberg, Judith Bryant. [1982] 1986. "William Faulkner: A Feminist Consideration." In *Modern Critical Views: William Faulkner*. Ed. Harold Bloom. New York: Chelsea House, 233–45.

Young, T. Daniel. 1990. "Narcissa Benbow's Strange Love/s: William Faulkner." In *American Declarations of Love*. Ed. Ann Massa. New York: St. Martin's, 88–103.

# Mountain Victory

## Publication History

This story was first published as "A Mountain Victory" in the *Saturday Evening Post* on December 3, 1932, with illustrations by Albin Henning. The *Post* originally accepted the story on October 9, 1930, but for reasons unknown, and unusual for the magazine, it held the story, already set in type, for over two years. Faulkner, however, did not have to wait two years for the fee. In correspondence from Phil Stone to Myrtle Demarest, dated October 31, 1930, Stone tallies Faulkner's success with the *Post* as four stories sold, the first for $500, the subsequent three for $750 each. "A Mountain Victory" was the fourth of this group. It was revised and retitled "Mountain Victory" for *Doctor Martino and Other Stories* (1934). The *Doctor Martino* text was used unchanged in *Collected Stories* (1950) (Meriwether 1977, 461–62 n. 3, 468–70).

## Circumstances of Composition, Sources, and Influences

Hans Skei describes the publication history of "Mountain Victory" as "complicated, interesting, and revealing" (1981, 64). That description applies equally well to the composition of the story. "Mountain Victory" first surfaces in the flurry of efforts listed for 1930 on the story-sending schedule. Although Noel Polk cautions that dates on the sending schedule do not represent composition dates, in this case, a close relationship may exist. Polk suggests that "Mountain Victory" may come from the later end of the period between spring 1929 and fall 1930 because it is more externally focused than stories from the beginning of that period (1985, 17, 33). Walter Taylor includes

"Mountain Victory" among the Indian tales that may have existed in some form as early as 1927 (1987, 203–04). This story, like "A Justice," identifies its Indians as Choctaws, but this association may be based more on the relationship it bears to the Choctaw Greenwood Leflore than a temporal association with "A Justice."

Even if the composition date cannot be positively established, it is certain that numerous revisions of the story took place between its first submission and publication. "Mountain Victory" demonstrates Faulkner's willingness to revise work at the direction of editors. Faulkner's story-sending schedule shows two submission dates to *Saturday Evening Post*, September 24, 1930, and October 4, 1930. Although the September date is crossed out, the October date is circled—Faulkner's means of recording acceptance. Based on a letter from Faulkner to the *Post*, James Meriwether thinks it likely that the September submission was rejected and returned to Faulkner with a suggestion for revision and resubmission (1977, 468). The letter of acceptance from the *Post*, dated October 9, 1930, implies that the editors had seen the story before. It reads: "The clearer motivation that you have introduced into 'A Mountain Victory' fixes everything up nicely. Weddel's course of action is now quite understandable. It is an unusually strong story, and we shall be glad to use it in The Post" (Meriwether 1977, 468–69; see also Skei 1981, 65). By the end of the month, however, when the *Post* forwarded proofs of the story, a new request to shorten the text was made. Again, Faulkner obliged by deleting "one unnecessary chapter" and by offering to omit additional words if needed (Meriwether 1977, 470). Skei makes an important point about the prescribed revisions: "His revisions of 'A Mountain Victory' were done because the *Post* asked for them, while the nature and the quality of the changes and the improvements they represent have to do with Faulkner's growing awareness of the demands of the genre and his growing sophistication as an artist" (1981, 14).

Extant manuscripts available in *William Faulkner Manuscripts* are easily identified from the pre–*Post* publication work. Both the holograph and typescript are titled "A Mountain Victory," and they contain the chapter that Faulkner deleted for the *Post* (*WFM 11* Introduction xi). Another typescript at the University of Texas Humanities Research Center is a later version used as setting copy for the 1934 *Doctor Martino* text. Faulkner did not restore the omitted chapter in this version (*WFM 11* Introduction xi; Skei 1981, 65). Before the "lost" chapter became available in *William Faulkner Manuscripts*, Meriwether published it separately; he argued that it did have a functional place in the *Post* text (1979, 481).

When Faulkner included "Mountain Victory" in *Doctor Martino*, he revised the story for a final time, according to Skei, "considerably yet insignificantly." Skei adds that this story was only one of two previously published stories to be revised at all (1981, 65). Among the revision is the use of heavier dialect to portray Jubal's speech. A typical example is the revision from "'That's water,' the negro said. 'What are you bringing me water for?'" to "Dat's water. Whut you bringing me water fer?" (*Post* 7; *DRM* 324). Another change is that the daughter speaks directly to Weddel, something she does not do in the *Post* version (*Post* 42; *DRM* 336). Generally, the conversations between Hule and Weddel are slightly more developed. Even so, there is some disagreement about when Hule decides to help Weddel. Dorothy Tuck's synopsis of "Mountain Victory" implies that Hule makes his decision to help Weddel before the morning of the ambush (1964, 171). Bernard Knieger disagrees with Tuck's argument that Hule is not initially part of the ambush plan. He cites evidence that strongly implies that Hule actually leads Weddel and Jubal into the ambush and only at the last moment makes a futile and fatal attempt to foil the plans of his father and brother (1972, Item 45). M. E. Bradford follows Knieger in arguing that Hule's decision to aid Weddel comes only after he has failed to convince Weddel to marry his sister (1987, 381). Faulkner did not revise the story again after *Doctor Martino*. Whatever ambiguities existed in that version have remained.

Faulkner's use of an eastern Tennessee rather than a Yoknapatawpha setting is a distinguishing characteristic of this story. The fact that staunch Unionists lived in the Tennessee mountains lends an air of historical accuracy to "Mountain Victory." Elmo Howell identifies pockets of Union sympathizers located in eastern Tennessee and throughout the Confederacy and cites evidence to show that Union support existed in areas much closer to Faulkner's actual Mississippi home. Faulkner did not have to move Weddel from Mississippi in order to present conflicting loyalties in a postwar setting (Howell 1962, 251–59). He could, however, exploit the greater public awareness of eastern Tennessee sympathizers.

The Mississippi associations that do exist in the fiction also have historical links. Saucier is part of the fictional Weddel family described in this story and in "Lo!" It is generally agreed that Francis Weddel, Saucier's father, is modeled on Greenwood Leflore, a Mississippian, half-French, half-Choctaw. Leflore traveled to Washington on behalf of the Choctaw people, became an extremely successful cotton planter, and built a grand mansion, Malmaison (Howell 1967, 254; Dabney 1974, 35; Blotner 1974, 13). Faulkner himself was known to retell the legendary tales about Leflore's life (*FU* 44).

The change of milieu for "Mountain Victory" has also prompted critics to look for literary analogues. Cleanth Brooks believes that Faulkner was influenced by Irvin S. Cobb, a popular writer of short stories in the early twentieth century. Cobb's story of a Confederate veteran returning from Virginia who is killed in the Tennessee mountains corresponds to the general plot outline of "Mountain Victory" (Brooks 1973, 385; [1978] 1990, 375–76). According to John Inscoe, "Faulkner owed much to current literary and historical treatments of the Appalachians," particularly in his portrayal of violently prejudiced mountaineers. Inscoe wrongly credits Brooks's work to Irving Howe, but he identifies three works about Appalachia that Faulkner inscribed for his library in September 1932 as possible source texts for "Mountain Victory" and *Absalom, Absalom!* They were George Washington Harris's *Sut Lovingood*, which numerous critics cite as an important influence on Faulkner, and two contemporary novels, Emmett Gowen's *Mountain Born* (1930) and Grace Lumpkin's *To Make My Bread* (1932). Although he does not claim that Faulkner knew these studies, Inscoe also mentions two nonfiction studies about the Southern Appalachians that were available: Horace Kephart's *Our Southern Highlanders* (1913 and 1922) and John C. Campbell's *The Southern Highlander and His Homeland* (1921) (1987, 249–52). Although Inscoe may correctly apply this argument to *Absalom, Absalom!*, he is incorrect in using the September 1932 inscription date as a point of reference for any influence on "Mountain Victory." This story was accepted by the *Post* two years earlier, in October 1930, not in October 1932, as Inscoe claims. He acknowledges that the inscription date does not necessarily mean the acquisition date (1987, 250 n. 13). Thus, except for the 1932 Lumpkin novel, it is arguable that these works influenced "Mountain Victory."

## Relationship to Other Faulkner Works

"Mountain Victory" does not draw on a Yoknapatawpha setting, but it is specifically linked to a Mississippi context and other Yoknapatawpha stories. Similarly, "Mountain Victory" is not specifically an Indian story, but it maintains a family identity with that group of tales. For this reason, Edward Holmes should have included it in his listing of characters and episodes repeated in Faulkner's novels and stories (see Holmes 1966, 99–115).

Saucier Weddel relates a family history that ties him to Francis Weddel of "Lo!" Although "Mountain Victory" precedes "Lo!" in publication, it follows "Lo!" in the chronology of the Weddel family. According to Taylor, the insertion of this detailed material about the Weddels into "Mountain Victory" is "not wholly necessary for the plot" and "implies another, more complex story than the one in which it appears." This observation is part of Taylor's larger argument that the Indian materials had sufficient complexity to become a novel (1987, 205, 207; see also Gidley 1990, 127–28). As early as 1954, William Van O'Connor made a passing remark that "Mountain Victory" would most certainly be included if the "Ikkemotube saga ever reaches the form of a novel" (1954, 89). The number of times some variant of the name Weddel appeared in manuscripts or published works is an interesting complement to such speculation. Faulkner used the name *Weddel* in the manuscript of "The Brooch" then changed it to *Boyd*, and in the manuscript of "Knight's Gambit," Charles Mallison is originally named Charles *Weddell*. Faulkner did know a man named Jimmy Weddell, who has a fictional counterpart Matt Ord in *Pylon*, and a character Grenier Weddel appears in *The Town*. These are very loose associations in the fiction, hardly sufficient to support an argument for a planned novel. Further, the Weddel line would have come from someone other than Saucier because he does not return home to continue the lineage.

Bradford compares Saucier to that character's father, Francis, in their similar appearance and patriarchal attitudes. He points out an important difference in that Saucier's world is aristocratic and lacks a distinct Indian culture (Bradford 1987, 372). These similarities are more important than the variation in "Lo!" in which Faulkner describes the Weddels as Chickasaws rather than as Choctaws as they are in "Mountain Victory." Skei finds the nature-culture opposition prevalent in the Indian tales (sometimes expressed in terms of old versus new) also present in this tale. In "Mountain Victory" this contrast demonstrates "that humanity and compassion and a deep understanding of the life and time of man are not only products of a modern conscience" (Skei 1985, 204).

Polk lifts the Weddel family background material from "Mountain Victory" to demonstrate his belief that Faulkner did not create his Indians to sentimentalize noble savages and the loss of their Edenic wilderness (1981, 255–56 n. 19). Saucier Weddel explains to the mountain family that his Europeanized family line lost the title of "Man," but they retained the land and slaves. The Man, on the other hand, held title but lived as an "upper servant" (*CS* 759). Polk believes the Indians are "of a piece with his reiterated conviction, fundamental in his fiction, that the test of maturity in a human being is the ability to cope with a changing world" (1981, 255 n. 19).

"Mountain Victory" also relates to war stories, both to Faulkner's other Civil War tales and to the stories of World Wars I and II. The comparisons focus on characters who resemble Weddel. Thomas Nordanberg suggests a likeness between Civil War combatants Saucier Weddel and Philip Backhouse in that they are both abstracted personifications of the Southern aristocrat. But Weddel is different from another Civil War veteran, John Sartoris, because at least initially Sartoris continues the violence of war in a postwar setting. Weddel, to his own peril, refuses to engage in further violence against former enemies; ultimately, and at the cost of his life, John does likewise. Nordanberg sees these Civil War veterans as significantly different from the World War I veterans because they are able to act on their "concern for home and family" (1983, 71, 82–83, 104–05).

Unlike Nordanberg, many critics see strong similarities between Weddel and the dispirited veterans of World War I. Joseph Blotner compares Weddel to Monaghan in "Honor"; they both find themselves glad to learn they can still be afraid (1974, 669). They are, like Dr. Martino of "Dr. Martino" or Jock in "Death-Drag," "pushed by circumstances beyond the normal boundaries of feeling" (Blotner 1974, 688; see also Lang 1976). James Carothers argues that in Faulkner's fiction the veterans of the Civil War and World War I are typically disfigured, unable or unwilling to be comfortable again in the family or community they enjoyed before the war, unable to articulate the meaning the war has had for them, and unable to love. Weddel and Ab Snopes of "Barn Burning" are examples from the Civil War, and World War I veterans with these traits are present in "Victory," "Ad Astra," "Honor," "Death Drag," "All the Dead Pilots," "The Leg," and "Dry September" (Carothers 1987, 67–68).

Lewis Dabney likens Weddel to Bayard Sartoris in that he sees both characters as ready to die (1974, 36). Bradford disagrees with Dabney's comparison. Bradford argues that Weddel exhibits "no conventional *angst* behind his conduct on this last day of his life," and that he has actually rediscovered a reason to live (1987, 379). John Rabbetts makes a particular comparison between Sartoris and Weddel. Both characters are pictured in a moment before sleep as thinking, trying to comprehend their situations. Rabbetts sees a similar portrayal of Isaac McCaslin in "Delta Autumn" (1989, 236 n. 90).

Stephen Ross makes the same associations Rabbetts does, but broadens the scope. Ross finds in Faulkner's fiction similar depictions of "meditative moments" wherein the character is reclining, in a moment just before sleep or death. Ross finds this portrayal links Bayard Sartoris and Weddel with such other characters as Darl Bundren, Gail Hightower, Mink Snopes, Horace Benbow, and the protagonist of "Carcassonne." For the "Carcassonne" character, Mink Snopes in *The Mansion*, and Weddel in "Mountain Victory," the thoughts are treated "explicitly as a form of writing, as visualizable words 'appearing' silently in the mind" (1989, 137, 144).

Additional character comparisons focus on the mountain family. Tuck likens Hule to Sarty Snopes in "Barn Burning." Both boys must choose between loyalty to the father and recognition that the father is wrong (1964, 171; see also Bomze 1983, 9–10). Lewis Leary identifies the Grier child in "Two Soldiers" as presenting another portrait of loyalty (1973, 136–37). Hule's choice constitutes a moral decision, the making of which involves great anguish. The circumstances include in this story, as well as in most of the others named here, an attempt to achieve justice from one person's perspective that implies "terrible wrongs" in the enactment of that justice (Ferguson 1991, 78, 174).

The brother-sister relationship is also familiar in Faulkner. As Skei notes, this aspect of "Mountain Victory" is shared by a number of stories and, of course, *The Sound and the Fury* (1985, 48, 304, n. 35). Alexandre Vashchenko also sees a familiar pattern in the sister and Hule. They are "Faulkner's favorite pair, a woman and a boy who, in their sensitivity to truth, attempt to save the world; who understand and perceive so much, while others are not merely blind, but possessed by evil" (1986, 212). Vashchenko likens them to characters in *Intruder in the Dust* (1986, 212).

James Ferguson recognizes a recurring pattern of sympathy for females caught in impossible circumstances. The mountain girl in "Mountain Victory" is trapped much like the females in "Frankie and Johnny," "Adolescence," "That Evening Sun," and "Dr. Martino" (1991, 74). Further, the girl is part of a romantic triangle (of sorts) in which the object of her affections is an older man, a pattern repeated with diverse outcomes in "Hair," "Wash," and "Dr. Martino." Faulkner is more subtle in handling the sexual imagery in this story than he is in some early pieces. The story is comparable in its effectiveness to "A Rose for Emily," "Fox Hunt," and "The Brooch" (1991, 70, 142). (Ferguson suggests that the many characters whose limbs are "lost, maimed, and injured," as is the case with Weddel in this story, may represent, in a Freudian interpretation, "fear of castration" [203 n. 11]).

The presence of intense, racially motivated hatred ties "Mountain Victory" to a substantial portion of Faulkner's work. In a review of *Doctor Martino*, William Rose Benét made the early connection between "Elly" and "Mountain Victory" in their common technique of blurring the racial identity of a character (1934, 645). Charles Peavy groups several texts around the portrayal of post–Civil War black characters expressing disdain for poor whites: "Mountain Victory," "Barn Burning," "Shall Not Perish," and "There Was a Queen" (1971, 21).

Erskine Peters believes that the characterization of Jubal in "Mountain Victory" is one example of "callous and inept racial portraiture" present in Faulkner's work. Other examples of failed representations of black being include characterizations in *Soldier's Pay*, *Sartoris/Flags in the Dust*, *Go Down, Moses,* and *The Unvanquished*. Peters is particularly critical of the portraits of the "servile valet" in "Mountain Victory" and *The Unvanquished* (Peters 1983, 38, 45).

Vashchenko links "Mountain Victory" to "A Courtship" and "Delta Autumn." She sees a folk characteristic in these fairly autonomous pieces and is especially interested in their female characters, who collectively portray the three racial strains forming the New World—white, black, and Indian (1986, 206–07). Inscoe compares "Mountain Victory" to *Absalom, Absalom!* Both stories portray Southern mountaineers' first experiences with race that "are traumatic to the white characters involved and drive them to drastic actions." Inscoe believes these texts indicate Faulkner's interest in the "unique brand of racism" of Southerners whose lives did not share the "biracial character of the rest of the South" (1987, 244). Both Peavy and Frederick Karl see similarities in Saucier Weddel's mistaken racial identification and the later exploration of this issue in *Light in August* (Peavy 1971, 37; Karl 1989, 420). Ferguson notes that the mountain dwellers' tendency to perceive of race in abstract terms leads to destructive consequences like those that follow most abstractions presented in Faulkner's fiction (1991, 81).

The racial theme is reinforced by a recurring image Charles Nilon finds associated with black characters in Faulkner's fiction. Nilon ranks "Mountain Victory" among those stories that possess "the lynch or crucifixion symbol." He associates Jubal's death with the deaths of black characters in "Red Leaves," "That Evening Sun," "Dry September," and sections of *Go Down, Moses*. Even if the death is not actually portrayed, its association with crucifixion "is the means of the Negro character's victory" (1965, 33).

In his study of the Faulkner hero, Carothers observes that the hero cannot save the community if the community is "debased, corrupted, or depraved." He cites "Mountain Victory," "Golden Land," "Red Leaves," *Mosquitoes*, *Sanctuary*, and *The Hamlet* as portraying communities that cannot be bettered; they do continue to survive, however, "perpetuated by despots and tyrants" (Carothers 1981, 264).

Carothers sees the implied death of Jubal in "Mountain Victory" as an example of "a characteristic Faulkner practice, that of creating deliberate ambiguity regarding the facts of death." Since the actual death of Jubal is not described, it is not absolutely certain. Carothers includes Nancy in "That Evening Sun," Elly in "Elly," the father and brother of Sarty Snopes in "Barn Burning," the protagonist of "Carcassonne," George in "The Leg," Gail Hightower in *Light in August*, and Mink Snopes in *The Mansion* with Jubal in the list of characters whose deaths are implied but not confirmed (1984, 219). Ferguson notes that many of Faulkner's stories end with a protagonist or antagonist dead, including "Mountain Victory," "There Was a Queen," "Red Leaves," and *Mayday* (1991, 136).

In a 1934 review of *Doctor Martino*, Fred Marsh paired "Mountain Victory" and "Wash" as "exceptional stories of the Reconstruction" as men faced the "havoc," "hatreds," and "demoralizations" of that postwar period (Emerson 1984, 29). Ferguson recognizes common themes from the collection that appear in "Mountain Victory" to include alienation, initiation, and justice (quid pro quo). He speculates that Faulkner did not end *Doctor Martino* with "Mountain Victory" because the volume needed "some diminution of intensity in order to achieve effective closure" (1991, 154).

In the context of *Collected Stories* several critics argue that "Mountain Victory" holds a pivotal position in the order of stories. The significance of placement in *Collected Stories* in "The Middle Ground," as Michael Millgate notes, is that all the stories contain either a physical or symbolic death ([1966] 1989, 273). Similarly, Arthur Kinney describes the ambush in the story as a "fitting perspective for life in Faulkner's stories" (1980, 74). "Mountain Victory," of course, contains the physical deaths of at least Hule and Weddel.

Joann Bomze argues that "Mountain Victory" works as a thematic link in *Collected Stories*. Images of conflict, loss, displacement, and transcendence evolve in the sections from "The Wasteland" to "Beyond." As the culminating story in "The Middle Ground," it concludes a series of failed visions with a story about the "triumph of vision." Furthermore, because the "plot of the story pulls together characters, settings, and circumstances from all over *Collected Stories*, it unifies all the preceding sections of the collection and introduces the "concept of self-transcendence" that is central to the final part, "Beyond" (Bomze 1983, 9–11).

Skei also traces a related theme through "The Middle Ground" and "Beyond" stories: their presentation of "existential crisis situations." In "The Middle Ground" stories, "middle class values, rules and regulations are presented and scrutinized through the fate of an outsider" whose "estrangement is the result of a society which has forgotten all the important values . . . the old verities of the heart." To these stories, Skei would also add this thematic kinship with "The Hill," "Uncle Willy," "Barn Burning," "Red Leaves," and "That Evening Sun." Other stories that "compassionately defend" the "old verities of the heart" include "All the Dead Pilots," "The Tall Men," and "Shall Not Perish" (1992, 69). Ferguson pairs "Wash" and "Mountain Victory" as the framing stories for "The Middle Ground." They share common post–Civil War settings , and both concern relationships between a young girl and an older man (1991, 159).

The numerous associations that can be made between "Mountain Victory" and so much of Faulkner's fiction indicate the complexity of this story. More comparisons could be made. It is possible, for example, to speculate on a link between this story and *The Sound and the Fury* given the proximity of publication acceptances, if not composition. Fruitful comparisons could be drawn between Weddel and Quentin around their concepts of honor, family, and self-sacrifice. Also intriguing would be a study linking the title of *The Sound and the Fury* not only to the fuller quotation from Shakespeare's *Macbeth* but also to Weddel's "soliloquy": "Contalmaison. Our lives are summed up in sounds and made significant. Victory. Defeat. Peace. Home. That's why we must do so much to invent meanings for the sounds, so damned much" (*CS* 766).

## Interpretation and Criticism

In the early development of criticism on "Mountain Victory," Irving Howe's observations established the general paths of interpretation. Howe saw reflected in "Mountain Victory" two particularly strong traits of Faulkner's writing. First, Weddel's stop at the mountain home demonstrates clashes between life-styles. Second, the story examines the "way an encounter between strangers can overwhelm their lives" (Howe [1952] 1975, 264).

Critical points of entry into the story generally revolve around Faulkner's treatment of the Southern myth, the Civil War, racial tensions, and individual crises. All of these touch at least superficially on Howe's early observations.

Critics use "Mountain Victory" both to demonstrate and to deny that Faulkner surrendered to the power of the Southern myth. Howell considers Faulkner's motivation for locating this story outside the borders of Yoknapatawpha to be a preservation of an idealized antebellum South. He asserts, "By going to East Tennessee for his story he was able to make his point and still keep intact his idealized view of the South which pervades all his work." "Mountain Victory" "takes a wistful look at the civilization that might have been if the South had prevailed." Weddel represents an idealized Southern portrait; Vatch symbolizes the treacherous alternative, and Hule demonstrates the reforming influence that Weddel's presence offers. Howell concludes that "Faulkner's chauvinism" in his portrayal of the South was not meant to gloss historical fact but to provide a medium for presenting loyalty, courage, honor, and pride (1962, 26, 253–54, 260–62). Dabney's view is that Faulkner possessed a tarnished rather than glimmering vision of antebellum South. According to Dabney, the use of a fictionalized Greenwood Leflore and his plantation, Malmaison, is "brought in for color" and suggests that Faulkner possessed an "initially stale vision of the Old South" that "contributed to [his] interest in the Mississippi Indians" (1974, 35–36).

War also dominates the text. Walter Everett considers the "tension existing between Confederate and Union partisans immediately after the Civil War" to be the theme of "Mountain Victory." This sectional animosity is complicated by differences in economic backgrounds, the interest Hule and his sister have in the stranger, and the obligation of Southern white to black (Everett 1969, 155). The war is not only that conflict recently ended, but the war being waged inside the mountain cabin.

Blotner notes the "aura of violence" that pervades the mountain household in this straightforward narrative. Although Weddel's death seems more and more inevitable, Faulkner maintains a "mood of ominous suspense" (Blotner 1974, 669). Nordanberg believes that the setting indicates Faulkner's recognition of the heterogeneousness of the South. Vatch's animosity toward Weddel originates in Weddel's being a member of the plantation aristocracy that is antithetical to the mountain regions and that has cost the mountain communities so dearly during the war. Vatch also bears deep psychic wounds of the war, experiences that haunt his dreams. Weddel, however, has dismissed old animosities and his code of honor obliges him not to act with hostility toward his hosts. The conclusion of the story reenacts in the characters of Vatch and Weddel the outcome of the war in which the Union (Vatch) defeats the South (Weddel). "Mountain Victory" expresses Faulkner's admiration for the qualities of Weddel but also are understanding of the perspective of the mountain people (Nordanberg 1983, 66–70).

Offering a very different reading from Nordanberg's high estimation of Weddel's character, Jacques Pothier believes that Weddel "has decided that he does not have to come to terms with the words which make history, that he is free of the burden of meaning." Weddel declines to address the "failure of the father" and simply plans to return home (1986, 191–93).

For Vashchenko the conflicting forces of hatred and love provide thematic intensity, and the "relationship between Saucier Weddel and the unnamed white girl is the key which unlocks the meaning of the story." It is through the girl that we learn about Weddel's character. She is, for example, profoundly affected by Weddel's generosity in using his coat lining as shoes for Jubal. Although other family members are wary of the stranger, she accepts him totally. She is the first to introduce the idea of being unvanquished and claiming victory in defeat when she tells her father: "You can whip me, but you cant whip him" (*CS* 763). Vashchenko believes that in these attitudes the girl is much like Weddel, and in her longing for freedom she is very different from Jubal. She represents the "road not taken." The enmity caused by prejudice, class stratification, and violence cuts across regional boundaries in this text. Likewise, the similarities between Weddel and the girl also ignore social boundaries. Vashchenko asks whether the girl might also represent the "prospect of spiritual union between the warring parties" (1986, 211–14).

It is not possible to read this story perceptively without acknowledging the issue of racial prejudice that Faulkner raises in the text. In his study of Faulkner's use of Indian characters to emphasize race relationships, Duane Gage includes a brief consideration of "Mountain Victory." Gage notes the particular irony of Weddel's being mistaken for a black man by Vatch and his family, an irony heightened when Weddel himself recognizes the source of the family's hostility: "So it's my face and not my uniform. . . . And you fought four years to free us, I understand" (*CS* 751; Gage 1974, 30). Dabney also believes Faulkner sensed the "subversive possibilities" of Weddel's being mistaken for a black man. He interprets the "lushly glamorized" Weddel and the "stereotyped comic black servant" as Faulkner's use of "conventional southern mythology" in which the black man is portrayed as the white man's burden (Dabney 1974, 36).

Peavy takes seriously the affection shown in the relationship between Weddel and Jubal. Peavy supports the believability of the fictional portraits by citing anecdotes of masters and slaves together in the war (1971, 26–27) (Darwin Turner does not discuss "Mountain Victory," but his comments on the portrayal of the black man as a burden in Faulkner are applicable to this story [Turner 1977, 62–85].) Bradford also believes Faulkner makes use of irony in having a half-French, half-Indian represent the Southern planter's "slavocracy" (1987, 373). (Bradford must be describing Francis Weddel. Saucier's mother's race and nationality are not identified, except that she must not have been black given Saucier's denial of being black. He reveals only that his father met her while in Washington to see President Jackson [*CS* 759].) Bradford argues that the interpretation of Jubal as a burden "undervalues the affection which links him to Saucier" (1987, 376; see also Bradford 1974, 270 n. 7).

According to Inscoe, the central focus of the story is the racial theme. The mountain people are attracted yet repelled, fascinated but contemptuous of the black man. They confront for the first time the notion of biracial union: it is taboo. The dynamics of racial conflict in the story provide, according to Inscoe, "the most basic explanation for its violent denouement" (1987, 246). Frederick Karl sees in this story Faulkner's continuing interests in miscegenation, racial identity, and master-slave relationships. Given the portrayal in this story and elsewhere in his fiction, Karl believes Faulkner does not see the destructiveness of noblesse oblige (1989, 420).

Although they do not discount the sectional or racial conflicts presented in "Mountain Victory," some critics interpret Weddel's individual victory as the prevailing theme of the text. Bomze considers the action of "Mountain Victory" to be "simultaneously triumphant and apocalyptic" in its "effort to sustain vision in the face of defeat." The willful self-sacrifice of both Weddel and Hule is an act of freedom. Weddel achieves victory over inaction when he discovers he has not lost the ability to be afraid. Hule's death is also a victory by association with Weddel. His choice is "between family loyalty and an emerging moral consciousness" (Bomze 1983, 9–10).

Bradford's reading complements Bomze's in its interpretation of Weddel. Vatch and Weddel are alike in their "mutual antipathy," and it is clear from each family member's response to Weddel that conflict is inevitable. Bradford suggests that the father joins Vatch in the ambush for two reasons. First, he must not lose face in the eyes of Vatch. Second, he is insulted by Weddel's refusal to leave by the specified deadline. But it is the way in which Weddel responds to the hatred that is unmistakably manifested toward him that determines the story's focus. Weddel is described early on as incomplete, but rediscovery of fear completes him, and though he cannot escape his death, he dies "intact." Vatch, on the other hand, is last seen withdrawing once more "to deal with his enemies only from a great remove, down the protective barrel of his gun" (Bradford 1987, 374–81).

Skei's understanding of "Mountain Victory" follows much the same argument as the interpretations of Bomze and Bradford. He argues that Faulkner's best stories distinguish themselves in their presentation of an existential experience. He explains that "they present experience, episodes, critical situations, which are not of the everyday type, which are not controlled and tempered by society, rules and conventions, which somehow elude us in normal daily life, but which may be seen as more basic, more primitive, and perhaps more *genuine* than the experience relayed in stories of action and event in a society of men and women, at a given time and in a specific place, from which the stories never take off." Skei suggests that in Faulkner's stories the existential experience may involve a choice of values that extend beyond the individual. Also, these moments of insight may be quickly lost; they may manifest only a "vague feeling" or a "foreboding of knowledge." In "Mountain Victory" the conflict of enemies, racism, and class hatred are superseded by the existential struggles of several characters (Skei 1992, 64–65, 71–74).

Weddel's reasons for not trying harder to save his own life linger through the story and after its conclusion. His actions are complicated by the necessity of also having to choose whether to save Hule and the girl. They, too, long for a less violent, barren world, and they attach their dream to Weddel. (In an earlier study, Skei describes the daughter as a "pathetic and helpless" dreamer, a type reappearing in Faulkner's work. Her dream, one she shares with her brother, Hule, is "of a less harsh, less barren world . . . where girls wear shoes"; the presence of this dream "adds a touch of human frailty, helplessness, and desire to the story [1985, 103, 118].) Weddel, however, is better prepared to make significant life choices. When forced to choose between several unsatisfactory courses of action, Weddel finds that he is able to make a morally satisfying decision. Unlike others among Faulkner's alienated characters, Skei argues, Weddel possesses an ethical system that he tests and finds valid (1992, 71–74).

Commenting on the organizational structure of "Mountain Victory," Ferguson notes that it follows a more conventional ordering of events, but it also presents an original, engrossing story that represents Faulkner's "delight in storytelling." The opening generates the tension that will pervade the story until the powerful closing scene of violence. Ferguson recognizes some weakness in the story in the unnecessary repetition of *quizzical* and *motionless* (1991, 127, 129, 133, 134, 139).

Benét recognized early the power of "Mountain Victory." He described it as "the most natural and absorbing of narratives" (1934, 645). Howe considered it Faulkner's best Civil War writing ([1952] 1975, 264). Malcolm Cowley wanted Faulkner to transpose the final two sections of *Collected Stories*. Not least among his reasons was his sense that "Mountain Victory" would provide a strong conclusion to the collection (Cowley 1966, 119). Skei ranks it "among the best Faulkner ever wrote" (1992, 71). Faulkner sustains the ominous intensity of the encounter not only with the more obvious movements of the plot but even in the most subtle delineations of the least significant characters. When, for example, the father orders the girl from the room, the mother's confused response underscores the pervading oppressiveness of her mountain life: "Me to go back? the mother said to the floor" (*CS* 761). If, as Weddel suggests, "our lives are summed up in sounds and made significant," perhaps this is why Jubal is so needfully verbose and, at the other extreme, the mountain family is so laconic (*CS* 766). The victory of this story goes not only to Weddel but also to Faulkner.

## Works Cited

Benét, William Rose. 1934. "Fourteen Faulkner Stories." *Saturday Review of Literature*, 21 April, 645.

Blotner, Joseph. 1974. *Faulkner: A Biography*. 2 vols. New York: Random House.

Bomze, Joann. 1983–84. "Faulkner's 'Mountain Victory': The Triumph of 'The Middle Ground.'" *CEA Critic* 46:9–11.

Bradford, M. E. 1974. "That Other Patriarchy: Observations on Faulkner's 'A Justice.'" *Modern Age* 18:266–71.

―――. 1987. "A Late Encounter: Faulkner's 'Mountain Victory.'" *Mississippi Quarterly* 40:373–81.

Brooks, Cleanth. 1973. "A Note on Faulkner's Early Attempts at the Short Story." *Studies in Short Fiction* 10:381–88.

―――. [1978] 1990. *William Faulkner: Toward Yoknapatawpha and Beyond*. New Haven: Yale University Press. Reprint. Baton Rouge: Louisiana State University Press.

Carothers, James B. 1981. "The Myriad Heart: The Evolution of the Faulkner Hero." In *"A Cosmos of My Own": Faulkner and Yoknapatawpha 1980*. Ed. Doreen Fowler and Ann J. Abadie. University Press of Mississippi, 252–83.

―――. 1984. "Faulkner's Short Stories: 'And Now What's to Do.'" In *New Directions in Faulkner Studies: Faulkner and Yoknapatawpha, 1983*. Ed. Doreen Fowler and Ann J. Abadie. Jackson: University Press of Mississippi, 202–27.

―――. "'I Ain't a Soldier Now': Faulkner's World War II Veterans." *Faulkner Journal* 2:67–74.

Cowley, Malcolm. 1966. *The Faulkner-Cowley File: Letters and Memories, 1944–1962*. New York: Viking.

Dabney, Lewis M. 1974. *The Indians of Yoknapatawpha: A Study in Literature and History*. Baton Rouge: Louisiana State University Press.

Emerson, O. B. 1984. *Faulkner's Early Literary Reputation in America*. Ann Arbor, MI: UMI Research Press.

Everett, Walter K. 1969. *Faulkner's Art and Character*. Woodbury, NY: Barron's Educational Series.

Faulkner, William. 1932. "A Mountain Victory." *Saturday Evening Post*, 3 December, 6ff.

―――. 1934. *Doctor Martino and Other Stories*. New York: Harrison Smith and Robert Haas.

―――. 1950. *Collected Stories of William Faulkner*. New York: Random House.

―――. 1959. *Faulkner in the University: Class Conferences at the University of*

*Virginia, 1957–1958*. Ed. Frederick Gwynn and Joseph L. Blotner. Charlottesville: University Press of Virginia.

———. 1987. *William Faulkner Manuscripts 11: Doctor Martino and Other Stories*. Ed. Thomas L. McHaney. New York: Garland.

Ferguson, James. 1991. *Faulkner's Short Fiction*. Knoxville: University of Tennessee Press.

Gage, Duane. 1974. "William Faulkner's Indians." *American Indian Quarterly* 1:27–33.

Gidley, Mick. 1990. "Sam Fathers's Fathers: Indians and the Idea of Inheritance." In *Critical Essays of William Faulkner: The McCaslin Family*. Ed. Arthur F. Kinney. Boston: G. K. Hall, 121–31.

Holmes, Edward M. 1966. *Faulkner's Twice-Told Tales: His Re-Use of His Material*. The Hague: Mouton.

Howe, Irving. [1952] 1975. *William Faulkner: A Critical Study*. 3d ed. Chicago: University of Chicago Press.

Howell, Elmo. 1962. "William Faulkner and Tennessee." *Tennessee Historical Quarterly* 21:251–62.

———. 1967. "President Jackson and William Faulkner's Choctaws." *Chronicles of Oklahoma* 45:252–58.

Inscoe, John C. 1987. "Faulkner, Race, and Appalachia." *South Atlantic Quarterly* 86:244–53.

Karl, Frederick R. 1989. *William Faulkner: American Writer*. New York: Weidenfeld and Nicolson.

Kinney, Arthur F. 1980. "Faulkner's Narrative Poetics and *Collected Stories*." *Faulkner Studies* 1:58–79.

Knieger, Bernard. 1972. "Faulkner's 'Mountain Victory,' 'Doctor Martino,' and 'There Was a Queen.'" *Explicator* 30:Item 45.

Lang, Béatrice. 1976. "'Dr. Martino': The Conflict of Life and Death." *Delta* 3:23–33.

Leary, Lewis. 1973. *William Faulkner of Yoknapatawpha County*. New York: Thomas Y. Crowell.

Meriwether, James B 1977. "Faulkner's Correspondence with *The Saturday Evening Post*." *Mississippi Quarterly* 30:461–75.

———. 1979. "An Unpublished Episode from 'A Mountain Victory.'" *Mississippi Quarterly* 32:481–83.

Millgate, Michael. [1966] 1989. *The Achievement of William Faulkner*. New York: Random House. Reprint. Athens: University of Georgia Press. Brown Thrasher Books.

Nilon, Charles H. 1965. *Faulkner and the Negro*. New York: Citadel.

Nordanberg, Thomas. 1983. *Cataclysm as Catalyst: The Theme of War in William Faulkner's Fiction*. Acta Universitatis Upsaliensis. Studia Anglistica Upsaliensia #49. Stockholm: Almquist & Wiksell.

O'Connor, William Van. 1954. *The Tangled Fire of William Faulkner*. Minneapolis: University of Minnesota Press.

Peavy, Charles D. 1971. *Go Slow Now: Faulkner and the Race Question*. Eugene: University of Oregon Books.

Peters, Erskine. 1983. *William Faulkner: The Yoknapatawpha World and Black Being*. Darby, PA: Norwood.

Polk, Noel. 1981. *Faulkner's* Requiem for a Nun: *A Critical Study*. Bloomington: Indiana University Press.

———. 1985. "The Space between *Sanctuary*." In *Intertextuality in Faulkner*. Ed. Michel Gresset and Noel Polk. Jackson: University Press of Mississippi, 16–35.

Pothier, Jacques. 1986. "History and Family Stories in Faulkner from *Absalom, Absalom!* to *The Mansion*." In *Faulkner and History*. Ed. Javier Coy and Michel Gresset. Salamanca: Edicions Universidad de Salamanca, 181–95.

Rabbetts, John. 1989. *From Hardy to Faulkner: Wessex to Yoknapatawpha*. New York: St. Martin's.

Ross, Stephen M. 1989. *Fiction's Inexhaustible Voice: Speech and Writing in Faulkner*. Athens: University of Georgia Press.

Skei, Hans H. 1981. *William Faulkner: The Short Story Career*. Oslo, Norway: Universitetsforlaget.

———. 1985. *William Faulkner: The Novelist as Short Story Writer*. Oslo, Norway: Universitetsforlaget.

———. 1992. "Beyond Genre? Existential Experience in Faulkner's Short Fiction." In *Faulkner and the Short Story: Faulkner and Yoknapatawpha, 1990*. Ed. Evans Harrington and Ann J. Abadie. Jackson: University Press of Mississippi, 62–77.

Taylor, Walter. 1987. "Yoknapatawpha's Indians: A Novel Faulkner Never Wrote." In *The Modernists: Studies in a Literary Phenomenon*. Ed. L. B. Gamache and I. S. MacNiven. Rutherford, NJ: Fairleigh Dickinson University Press, 202–09.

Tuck, Dorothy. 1964. *Crowell's Handbook of Faulkner*. New York: Thomas Y. Crowell.

Turner, Darwin T. 1977. "Faulkner and Slavery." In *The South and Faulkner's Yoknapatawpha: The Actual and the Apocryphal*. Ed. Evans Harrington and Ann J. Abadie. Jackson: University Press of Mississippi, 62–85.

Vashchenko, Alexandre. 1986. "Woman and the Making of the New World: Faulkner's Short Stories." In *Faulkner and Women: Faulkner and Yoknapatawpha, 1985*. Ed. Doreen Fowler and Ann J. Abadie. Jackson: University Press of Mississippi, 205–19.

# Index of Faulkner's Works

*Absalom, Absalom!*, 10, 12, 13, 15, 16, 58, 97, 98, 99, 100, 161, 175, 176, 224, 225, 227, 228, 240, 269, 274, 275, 276, 277, 284, 291, 309, 327, 350, 352, 358, 379, 387, 388, 389, 390, 391, 392, 394, 398, 405, 414, 435, 460, 468, 478, 480, 491, 497, 498, 508, 518, 521
   *Dark House, A*, 389
"Ad Astra," 147, 178, 209, 403, 404, 405, 407, 467, 469, 480, 490, 519
"Adolescence," 99, 222, 223, 224, 226, 281, 414, 415, 458, 521
"Afternoon of a Cow," 253, 379
"Al Jackson," 156
"All the Dead Pilots," 76, 209, 210, 367, 403, 404, 405, 408, 468, 491, 520, 523
"Ambuscade," 467
"Appendix: The Compsons 1699–1945," 208, 274, 324, 346, 350, 378
"Artist at Home," *440–53*, 68, 147, 159, 405, 414, 426, 436, 459, 460, 500
*As I Lay Dying*, 10, 11, 14, 16, 34, 35, 47, 65, 75, 102, 103, 144, 175, 183, 211, 212, 224, 225, 239, 280, 321, 328, 338, 366, 426, 458, 497, 520

"Barn Burning," *3–32*, 34, 36, 37, 41, 47, 66, 68, 69, 70, 75, 77, 78, 105, 155, 161, 180, 212, 228, 254, 262, 275, 282, 283, 352, 379, 388, 391, 404, 481, 498, 520, 521, 522, 523
"Bear, The," 46, 57, 159, 210, 274, 281, 327, 329, 336, 365, 468, 491
"Bear Hunt, A," *54–64*, 69, 102, 146, 159, 160, 166, 253, 274, 280, 354, 365, 379, 387
"Beyond," 229, 392, 415, 444

"Big Shot, The," 388, 454
*Big Woods*, 55, 56, 57, 58, 59, 60, 61, 62, 280 319, 322, 338, 343, 345, 350, 359, 378
"Black Music," 144, 147, 213, 229, 392, 406, 435, 444
"Brooch, The," *453–66*, 99, 104,144, 224, 226, 229, 241, 248, 262, 405, 406, 414, 415, 426, 434, 436, 443, 444, 471, 498, 518, 521
   "Fire and Clock," 453, 455
   "Fire and the Clock, The," 454
"By the People," 35, 47, 254, 379–80

"Carcassonne," 15, 16, 228, 329, 353, 444, 460, 520, 522
"Centaur in Brass," *154–69*, 35, 58, 60, 105, 147, 178, 213, 252, 254, 255, 262, 285, 354, 427, 443
*Collected Stories of William Faulkner*, 3, 4, 5, 11, 16, 17, 28, 32, 33, 37, 38, 41, 43, 44, 47, 52, 55, 57, 59, 62, 65, 68, 69, 70, 71, 73, 74, 77, 78, 79, 80, 81, 87, 104, 105, 109, 111, 112, 114, 118, 125, 127, 135, 142, 143, 145, 147, 148, 149, 150, 151, 152, 154, 155, 158, 161, 162, 165, 166, 167, 169, 171, 172, 173, 178, 179, 189, 192, 193, 195, 200, 204, 205, 206, 212, 213, 215, 216–17, 218, 221, 222, 226, 227, 229, 233, 235, 237, 241, 243, 244, 245, 246, 249, 250, 253, 254, 256, 258, 260, 262, 263, 266, 267, 270, 272, 274, 277, 283, 284, 285, 286, 288, 294, 299 301, 302, 307, 311, 319, 320, 321, 322, 329, 330, 338, 343, 344, 345, 347, 351, 352, 353, 355, 359, 362, 363, 364, 367, 373, 375, 376, 377, 379,

*Collected Stories of William Faulkner* (*continued*)
  380, 382, 387, 388, 392, 400, 402, 406, 409, 411, 412, 415, 418, 419, 421, 422, 423, 424, 425, 426, 427, 429, 430, 431, 432, 435, 436, 438, 439, 440, 441, 446, 450, 452, 454, 456, 457, 458, 460, 465, 466, 467, 474, 475, 476, 477, 479, 481, 483, 485, 487, 496, 500, 505, 511, 515, 519, 522, 523, 525, 526, 528
  "Beyond," 523
  "Country, The" 1, 16, 17, 37, 43, 48, 59, 65, 69, 77, 78, 161
  "Middle Ground, The," 384, 387, 392, 393, 406, 416, 427, 436, 439, 440, 444, 445, 454, 460, 466, 471, 476, 481, 482, 487, 500, 522, 523
    "Village, The," 85, 87, 105, 147, 161, 162, 179, 213, 229, 237, 241, 246, 254, 255, 260, 262, 263, 285, 286, 310, 427
  "Wasteland, The," 46, 380, 523
  "Wilderness, The," 317, 330, 353, 375, 380
  "Courtship, A," *362–74*, 36, 57, 58, 104, 159, 326, 327, 328, 330, 348, 349, 350, 377, 378, 379, 405, 426, 443, 460, 521
"Crevasse," 327, 442, 481

"Death Drag" ("A Death Drag"), *204–20*, 16, 47, 102, 105, 160, 162, 179, 229, 285, 402, 403, 404, 405, 406, 415, 498, 501, 519, 520
"De Gaulle Story, The" (screenplay), 36, 46, 68
"Delta Autumn," 36, 46, 66, 68, 76, 274, 327, 329, 366, 427, 521
"Divorce in Naples," 147, 178, 212, 367, 405, 406, 415, 469, 470, 490
*Doctor Martino and Other Stories*, 55, 161, 204, 206, 213, 218, 221, 226, 227, 229, 234, 235, 245, 387, 388, 392, 393, 400, 402, 406, 409, 411, 412, 414, 416, 420, 421, 422, 424, 427, 430, 487, 490, 4500, 511, 515, 517, 521, 522
"Don Giovanni," 426, 441
"Dr. Martino" ("Doctor Martino"), *411–422*, 47, 97, 103, 146, 178, 213, 226, 281, 379, 391, 404, 405, 425, 426, 431, 442, 443, 458, 459, 481, 518, 520
  "Dr Martino," 411
  "Martino," 411
"Drusilla," 467
"Dry September," *169–203*, 15, 47, 95, 96, 97, 98, 99, 100, 101, 102, 103, 104, 105, 112, 133, 144, 145, 146, 147, 148, 160, 213, 225, 226, 227, 229, 240, 254, 262, 280, 281, 282, 283, 284, 328, 329, 330, 353, 392, 404, 416, 425, 426, 458, 459, 460, 4956, 498, 520, 522
  "Drouth," 145, 169, 170, 189, 425
"Dull Tale," 66, 212, 388, 481

"Elder Watson in Heaven," 102
"Elly," *221–37*, 15, 97, 98, 99, 105, 144, 176, 179, 213, 241, 281, 285, 320, 375, 387, 392, 414, 425, 426, 435, 458, 459, 460, 488, 496, 497, 521, 522
  "Salvage," 221, 222
  "Selvage," 144, 221, 222, 459
"Evangeline," 99, 227, 387, 388

*Fable, A*, 11, 16, 46, 47, 66, 76, 210, 212, 280, 403, 498
*Father Abraham*, 154, 157
*Faulkner in the University: Class Conferences at the University of Virginia, 1957–1958*, 11, 28, 33, 34, 41, 89, 106–07, 119, 122, 135, 206, 213–14, 218, 279, 297, 311, 323, 327, 333, 335, 336, 338, 346, 359, 365, 373, 376, 379, 381, 382, 390, 400, 402, 409, 493, 511, 517, 529
*Faulkner Reader, A*, 40, 386
"Fire and the Hearth, The," 15, 159, 240, 365
*Flags in the Dust*, 44, 46, 66, 97, 99, 101, 206, 209, 224, 250, 258, 321, 338, 433, 491, 492, 493, 494, 508, 521
"Fool About a Horse," 7, 10, 12, 36, 253, 379, 455
"Fox Hunt," *422–31*, 104, 120, 161, 176, 226, 281, 283, 328, 352, 366, 379, 405, 406, 414, 415, 416, 434, 436, 443, 459, 460, 471, 521
  "Fox," 422
  "Fox, A," 422

"Fox-Hunt," 422
"Foxhunt," 422
"Frankie and Johnnie," 226, 281, 414, 415, 521

*Go Down, Moses*, 11, 14, 36, 57, 58, 68, 99, 100–01, 158, 160, 182, 226, 227, 240, 241, 253, 274, 281, 282, 283, 321, 328, 329, 347, 348, 349, 350, 351, 352, 358, 359, 363, 365, 366, 378, 379, 381, 426, 458, 470, 480, 498, 521, 522
"Go Down, Moses," 66, 281
"Gold Is Not Always," 160, 178
"Golden Land," *476–86*, 224, 240, 241, 253, 262, 329, 416, 471, 500, 522
*Green Bough, A*, 416

"Hair," *142–53*, 47, 58, 102, 104, 105, 144, 162, 173, 174, 212, 213, 226, 228, 283, 285, 320, 353, 392, 406, 414, 416, 443, 459, 460, 469, 521
*Hamlet, The*, 3, 4, 6, 7, 8, 9, 10, 12, 13, 15, 16, 35, 36, 55, 57, 67, 76, 91, 100, 103, 144, 155, 158, 162, 180, 226, 228, 241, 253, 366, 391, 426, 468, 469, 470, 491, 497, 522
  "Peasants, The," 3
"Hand Upon the Waters," 254
"Hill, The," 12, 87, 282, 352, 444, 523
"Hog Pawn," 101, 328, 392
"Honor," *402–11*, 104, 144, 147, 204, 206, 208, 209, 210, 211, 213, 367, 393, 415, 443, 459, 481, 498, 500, 501, 519, 520
  "Point of Honor," 402
"Hound, The," 6, 7, 103, 161, 177, 213, 229, 328, 366, 388, 392, 426, 459

"Idyll in the Desert," 101, 147, 212, 223, 225, 228, 435, 454, 459
*Intruder in the Dust*, 14, 16, 37, 58, 66, 98, 159, 171, 177, 181, 182, 210, 274, 275, 283, 328, 352, 469, 498, 521
"Justice, A," *342–62*, 12, 58, 59, 104, 105, 148, 159, 178, 240, 254, 265, 267, 268, 274, 277, 278, 282, 283, 320, 321, 326, 327, 328, 329, 330, 363, 365, 366, 375, 377, 378, 381, 426, 435, 516

"Built Fence," 342
"Built a Fence," 342, 344
"Indians Built a Fence," 342

*Knight's Gambit*, 15, 45, 47, 103, 144, 210, 392, 426, 470, 491
"Knight's Gambit," 178, 211, 271, 392, 468, 469, 506, 518

"Landing in Luck," 87, 209, 402
"Leg, The," 15, 16, 47, 99, 209, 226, 228, 229, 281, 392, 415, 444, 460, 497, 520, 522
"Liar, The," 144
"Lilacs, The," 403
*Light in August*, 11, 14, 15, 35, 58, 65, 75, 97, 98, 100, 101, 102, 115, 146, 159, 180, 181, 182, 227, 228, 240, 279, 282, 284, 327, 328, 366, 414, 426, 444, 460, 469, 497, 508, 520, 521, 522
"Lion," 11, 57, 68, 274, 278, 350, 481
*Lion in the Garden: Interviews with William Faulkner 1926–1962*, 330–31, 338, 345, 354, 359
"Lizards in Jamshyd's Courtyard," 7, 35, 99, 104, 154, 155, 156, 160, 161, 178, 254
"Lo!," *375–83*, 47, 67, 76, 160, 253, 326, 327, 330, 350, 363, 456, 517, 518
"Love," 36, 375

*Mansion, The*, 10, 15, 35, 37, 67, 76, 155, 156, 180, 210, 228, 239, 240, 274, 468, 491, 499, 508, 520, 522
*Marble Faun, The*, 160
*Marionettes, The*, 226, 444
*Mayday*, 96, 443, 521
"Miss Zilphia Gant," 87, 88, 95, 96, 97, 98, 99, 101, 102, 103, 144, 174, 175, 224, 225, 226, 228, 233, 328, 414, 425, 458
"Mississippi," 350, 378
"Mistral," 144, 212, 226, 227, 281, 406, 414, 415, 500
"Monk," 463
"Moonlight," 142, 144, 178
*Mosquitoes*, 96, 144, 210, 225, 274, 441, 480, 496, 497, 498, 522
"Mountain Victory" ("A Mountain Victory"), *515–30*, 12, 15, 16, 47,

"Mountain Victory" (*continued*)
66, 75, 99, 103, 104, 146, 212, 213, 226, 227, 228, 281, 326, 328, 329, 350, 366, 376, 377, 378, 391, 392, 403, 404, 405, 414, 425, 438, 443, 455, 459, 468, 470, 479, 497

"Mr. Acarius," 11, 68

"Mule in the Yard," *248–59*, 36, 41, 45, 155, 156, 158, 159, 160, 161, 178, 229, 240, 241, 379, 453, 480

"My Grandmother Millard and General Bedford Forrest and the Battle of Harrykin Creek," *466–76*, 36, 46, 66, 76, 99, 155–56, 228, 274, 427, 436, 460, 481

*Mythical Latin-American Kingdom Story* (screenplay), 240

"Name for the City, A," 35, 160, 470

*New Orleans Sketches*, 68, 87, 94, 254, 481

*Notes on a Horsethief*, 470

"Nympholepsy," 226, 444

"Odor of Verbena, An," 12, 211–12, 329, 406, 416, 443, 460, 495, 501

"Old Man," 14, 469

"Old People, The," 274, 319, 322, 328, 348, 349, 350, 351, 366

"Pantaloon in Black," 159, 177, 182, 254, 281, 282, 284, 328, 481

"Pennsylvania Station," *432–40*, 227, 262, 352, 387, 444, 459, 460, 461, 464
  "Bench for Two," 432, 433
  "2 Bench," 432

"Point of Law, A," 15, 47, 380

*Portable Faulkner, The*, 26, 87, 125, 204, 207, 218, 278, 319, 329, 343, 347, 387

*Pylon*, 100, 146, 159, 178, 206, 208, 209, 210, 237, 240, 328, 366, 404, 405, 426, 443, 480, 497, 498, 519

"Race at Morning," 36, 45, 46, 47, 61, 68, 254

"Raid," 274, 468

"Red Leaves," *319–41*, 12, 47, 58, 99, 100, 101, 104, 105, 148, 160, 176, 177, 178, 179, 182, 229, 240, 254, 281, 282, 284, 343, 347, 348, 349, 350, 352, 353, 356, 358, 359, 363, 365, 366, 367, 377, 378, 380, 426, 439, 459, 480, 522, 523

*Red Leaves* (Ukranian collection), 337

*Reivers, The*, 11, 37, 57, 66, 228, 239, 240, 253, 283, 328, 365, 468, 470, 497

*Requiem for a Nun*, 12, 15, 35, 101, 144, 160, 210, 225, 240, 274, 275, 278, 279, 280, 287, 328, 329, 347, 350, 358, 365, 366, 378, 379, 391, 435, 491, 496, 498–99

"Retreat," 274, 468

"Return, A," 467

*Revolt in the Earth* (screenplay), 391

"Riposte in Tertio," 10

"Rose for Emily, A," *87–141*, 13, 16, 17, 58, 135, 144, 145, 147, 148, 160, 161, 162, 169, 173, 174, 175, 176, 178, 179, 212, 213, 217, 225, 226, 227, 228, 229, 233, 241, 255, 275, 280, 281, 282, 283, 285, 286, 320, 328, 330, 353, 366, 379, 392, 414, 425, 426, 444, 458, 460, 468, 491, 496, 497, 521

"Rose of Lebanon," 468

*Sanctuary*, 10, 11, 12, 15, 16, 35, 97, 98, 99, 100, 101, 144, 146, 156, 175, 176, 179, 180, 210, 225, 226, 228, 240, 279, 280, 281, 282, 284, 311, 320, 435, 458, 459, 468, 480, 488, 491, 492, 493, 494, 495, 496, 497, 498, 499, 505, 511, 520, 522

*Sartoris*, 44, 45, 46, 47, 50, 65, 66, 75, 97, 102, 105, 156, 211, 225, 228, 250, 258, 261, 282, 391, 403, 416, 468, 469, 491, 492, 493, 494, 495, 497, 498, 507, 521

*Selected Letters of William Faulkner*, 3, 4, 6, 7, 10, 28, 33, 38, 41, 44, 53, 54, 55, 57, 60, 62, 65, 69, 70, 71, 74, 75, 81, 135, 155, 167, 200, 207–08, 218, 221, 235, 237, 245, 246, 249, 251, 256, 258, 260, 266, 267, 269, 270, 275, 312, 319, 334, 338, 342–43, 348, 359, 362, 365, 373, 375, 382, 391, 400, 403, 409, 411, 421, 432, 439, 455, 456, 464, 465, 466, 468, 471, 474, 475, 476, 477, 485, 487, 511

"Sepulture South: Gaslight," 261

"Shall Not Perish," *73–83*, 12, 14, 17, 34, 46, 48, 59, 65, 66, 67, 68, 69, 271, 379, 469, 498, 521, 523

"Shingles for the Lord," *32–43*, 11, 14, 17, 45, 47–48, 65, 68, 69, 77, 160, 161, 241, 252, 253, 254, 283, 366, 470

"Skirmish at Sartoris," 274, 414, 458, 468, 470

"Smoke," 142, 144, 145, 147

"Snow," 46, 76, 147, 212, 227, 271, 443

*Soldier's Pay*, 96, 99, 101, 161, 175, 209, 210, 211, 225, 240, 434, 459, 497, 498, 499, 521

*Sound and the Fury, The*, 14, 16, 97, 99, 100, 101, 103, 144, 149, 180, 183, 210, 212, 224, 225, 226, 227, 228, 261, 267, 268, 269, 272, 274, 275, 276, 277, 278, 279, 280, 284, 286, 291, 294, 303, 309, 311, 321, 328, 333, 343, 344, 350, 351, 356, 357, 358, 457, 458, 459, 496, 497, 498, 520, 523

"Spotted Horses," 7, 8, 26, 35, 154, 155, 156, 160, 161, 177, 178, 211, 249, 252, 253, 254, 267, 270–71, 352

*Story of Temple Drake, The* (film), 403

"Sunset," 104, 177

"Test Pilot" (book review), 209

"Tall Men, The," *43–54*, 16, 36, 37, 59, 66, 67, 68, 75, 76, 177, 212, 240, 254, 329, 379, 380, 469, 523

"That Evening Sun," *267–316*, 11, 12, 13, 14, 15, 36, 58, 70, 103, 104, 105, 145, 148, 161, 176, 177, 179, 180, 213, 217, 227, 228, 229, 240, 241, 254, 255, 262, 265, 327, 328, 330, 343, 346, 350, 351, 352, 353, 358, 366, 415, 426, 498, 521, 522, 523

"Never Done No Weeping When You Wanted to Laugh," 268, 269, 270, 271

"That Evening Sun Go Down," 268, 269, 270, 271, 271, 276

"That Will Be Fine," *260–67*, 14, 36, 68, 179, 227, 239, 240, 241, 255, 283, 285, 379, 406, 435, 464, 481

"There Was a Queen," *487–515*, 12, 66, 75, 98, 99, 103, 156, 160, 176, 178, 210, 211, 224, 227, 228, 241, 254, 403, 406, 407, 415, 458, 468, 482, 521, 522

"Empress Passed, An," 487, 488

"Through the Window," 487, 488, 498

"Was a Queen," 487

*These 13*, 67, 87, 89, 104, 105, 135, 142, 143, 147, 151, 152, 169, 171, 173, 179, 186, 200, 245, 267, 269, 270, 271, 272, 274, 284, 285, 286, 311, 319, 321, 329, 330, 336, 342, 344, 345, 349, 352, 353, 359, 392, 402, 445, 500

*"A Rose for Emily" and Other Stories*, 87

"Thrift," 66, 160, 211, 319, 469

"Tomorrow," 9, 12, 76, 104, 146, 178

*Town, The*, 9, 36, 45, 66, 67, 76, 154, 155, 156, 157, 158, 159, 162, 165, 166, 167, 180, 210, 212, 240, 249, 251, 252, 253, 255, 258, 274, 468, 491, 506, 519

"Turnabout" ("Turn About"), 47, 68, 206, 209, 210, 213, 401, 402, 403

"Two Soldiers," *64–72*, 12, 14, 34, 36, 46, 59, 73, 74, 75, 76, 77, 379, 469, 520

"Uncle Willy," *237–48*, 11, 14, 36, 37, 47, 68, 105, 177, 178, 179, 213, 229, 253, 255, 262, 283, 285, 329, 464, 470, 481, 482, 523

*Uncle Willy and Other Stories*, 245

*Uncollected Stories of William Faulkner*, 10, 28, 87, 135, 152, 222–23, 235, 246, 266, 349, 359

*Unvanquished, The*, 9, 10, 11, 13, 37, 46, 58, 68, 97, 99, 101, 103, 156, 160, 198, 225, 262, 274, 327, 328, 365, 392, 416, 426, 468, 470, 491, 496, 497, 498, 508, 521

"Vendee," 10, 274, 467

"Victory," 103, 104, 105, 392, 444, 520

"Waifs, The," 156, 158

*War Birds* (screenplay), 206, 468, 491

"Was," 36, 37, 41, 60, 159, 178, 182, 183, 252, 253, 327, 354, 470

"Wash," *387–401*, 6, 12, 15, 27, 103, 104, 146, 156, 161, 229, 283, 405, 434, 500, 520, 521, 522

"Wild Palms," 159
*Wild Palms, The* , 35, 65, 75, 98, 101, 144, 175, 178, 210, 225, 226, 262, 274, 327, 366, 404, 426, 443, 460, 480, 481, 496, 498, 508
*William Faulkner Manuscripts 6:* The Sound and the Fury, 279, 312
*William Faulkner Manuscripts 9:* These 13, 88, 89, 135, 142, 143, 152, 170, 200, 204, 218, 267, 269, 270, 312, 320, 321, 338, 342, 344, 360
*William Faulkner Manuscripts 11:* Doctor Martino and Other Stories, 205, 206, 218, 222, 235, 412, 421, 423, 424, 431, 487, 488, 489, 490, 511, 516, 529
*William Faulkner Manuscripts 13:* Absalom, Absalom!, 387, 400
*William Faulkner Manuscripts 15:* The Hamlet, 3, 4, 6, 28
*William Faulkner Manuscripts 21:* The Town, 249, 250, 258
*William Faulkner Manuscripts 24: Short Stories*, 33, 34, 44–45, 53, 73, 74, 81, 363, 373, 433, 434, 436, 439, 440, 441, 452, 454, 455, 456, 457, 461, 465, 466, 467, 469, 471, 475
*Wishing Tree, The*, 280, 283, 284
"With Caution and Dispatch," 210, 403, 404, 468, 491

"Yo Ho and Two Bottles of Rum," 160

# General Index

Achilles, 5
Adams, Richard P., 5, 27, 252, 256, 257, 274, 309, 389, 390, 398, 399
African, 300
African-American, 300
Albuquerque, New Mexico, 110
Alexander, Margaret Walker, 287, 309
Allen, Charles A., 107, 121–22, 133
Allen, Dennis W., 120–21, 133
Allen, Walter, 91, 93, 117, 133, 194, 199, 309
*American Magazine*, 3
*American Mercury*, 142, 143, 154, 155, 169, 204, 237, 245, 260, 267, 269, 270, 271, 342, 402, 432, 453, 476, 477, 484
*American Short Stories of the Twentieth Century* (Russian collection), 309
Amos, 274
Anderson, Elizabeth Prall, 442
Anderson, George, 158–59, 166, 252, 257
Anderson, Sherwood, 94, 143, 223, 238, 441, 442, 443
  "Adventure," 94
  "Book of the Grotesque, The," 94
  "Meeting South, A," 442
  *Winesburg, Ohio*, 94
Arensberg, Mary, 130–31, 133
Armour, Richard, 133

Bache, William, B., 143, 151, 171, 172, 173, 188, 194, 195, 199
Backman, Melvin, 8–9, 27, 100, 133, 145, 151, 181, 199, 381, 382
Bainter, Fay, 73
Baird, Helen, 412
Bal, Mieke, 25
Balzac, Honoré de, 273

Baptist, 36, 307
Barber, Marion, 94, 133
Barnes, Daniel R., 91, 133
Barnett, Ned, 238
Barr, Caroline (Callie), 207
Barth, J. Robert, 100, 133–34, 282, 309, 327, 337, 350, 359
Bassett, John E., 158, 166, 182, 199, 255, 257, 280, 309, 494, 495–96, 510
Baudelaire, Charles, 172
Baumback, Jonathan, 298, 310
Bavaria, 5
Beardsley, Aubrey, 172
Beck, Warren, 4, 7, 9, 11, 27, 276, 283, 291–92, 294, 297, 310
Behn, Harry, 403
Beidler, Peter G. 324, 335, 337
Bell, Haney H., Jr., 492, 510
Benedict, Ruth, 23
  *Patterns of Culture*, 23
Benét, William Rose, 217, 227, 234, 393, 399, 420, 501, 503, 510, 521, 527, 528
Bennett, Ken, 272, 273, 296, 310
Benson, Jackson J., 272, 310
*Best Short Stories of 1935, The*, 375
*Best Short Stories of 1936, The*, 260
Bethea, Sally, 288–89, 310
Bezzerides, Albert, 3
Bible, 172, 274, 346, 347. *See also* Amos, Garden of Eden, Isaiah, Jesus, Lazarus, Solomon, Tobias
Bird, Robert Montgomery, 325
  *Nick of the Woods*, 325
Black, Victoria Fielden, 505
*Blackwood's*, 319
Blake, William, 93–94, 111, 274
  "Nurse's Song," 274
  "Sick Rose, The," 93–94, 111

Blake, William (*continued*)
  *Songs of Innocence and of Experience*, 274
Bleikasten, André, 35, 41, 103, 134, 180, 199, 496, 510
Blotner, Joseph, 3–4, 6, 8, 9–10, 11, 27, 32, 33, 34, 35, 36, 38, 41, 43, 44, 45, 46, 50, 51, 52, 54, 55, 56, 57, 58, 60, 62, 65, 66, 67, 68, 70, 71, 73, 74, 75, 78–79, 80, 87, 88, 89, 93, 133, 134, 143, 144, 145, 146, 151, 154, 155, 156, 157, 160, 162, 165, 167, 169, 170, 171, 172, 173, 176, 179, 180, 182, 183, 195, 199, 204, 205, 206, 207, 209, 210, 211, 212, 213, 215, 217–18, 221, 222, 223, 226, 234, 237, 238, 239, 240, 246, 248, 249, 250, 252, 256, 257, 260, 261, 262, 263, 265, 267, 268, 269, 270, 271, 272, 277, 279, 280, 284, 309, 310, 319, 320, 321, 323, 326, 336, 337, 342, 343, 346, 349, 351, 359, 362, 363, 372, 375, 376, 378, 382, 387, 389, 394, 397, 398, 399, 402, 403, 405, 407, 408, 409, 411, 412, 413, 414, 415, 418, 420, 422, 423, 424, 425, 428, 430, 432, 433, 434, 439, 440, 441, 442, 443, 444, 446, 447, 451, 454, 455, 457, 458, 459, 463, 464, 466, 467, 469, 470, 473, 474, 476, 477, 480, 482, 485, 487, 488, 510, 517, 519–20, 524, 528
Blount, Emily, 90
Blythe, Hal, 112, 134
Bodkin, Maud, 274
  *Archetypal Patterns in Poetry, Psychological Studies of Imagination*, 274
Bomze, Joann, 520, 522–23, 526, 528
Bonner, Thomas, Jr., 142, 151, 155, 167, 237, 246, 260, 265
Booth, Wayne C., 149
Boston, Massachusetts, 270
Bowdry, Dave, 272
Bowen, James K., 18–19, 27
Boyd, James, 424
Bradbury, Ray, 274
  *Dandelion Wine*, 274
Bradford, M. E., 5, 11, 17, 24, 27, 35, 41, 45, 48, 49, 50, 51, 52, 65, 70, 71, 75, 79, 81, 223, 224, 225, 230, 233, 234, 289–90, 310, 349, 355, 359, 366, 370, 371, 372, 380, 382, 443, 445, 446, 447, 449, 451, 468, 472, 474, 479, 480, 482, 483, 485, 492, 493, 495, 502, 503–04, 505, 506, 507, 508, 510, 517, 519, 520, 525, 526, 528
Bradley, Dean F. W., 33
Brehm, George, 54
Brer Rabbit, 377
Brevda, William, 51, 53
Brickell, Herschel, 372
Bride, Sister Mary, 113, 134
Brodsky, Louis Daniel, 36, 41, 46, 52, 68, 71, 102, 134, 387, 399
Brooks, Cleanth, 8, 19, 27, 34–35, 36, 41, 78, 81, 91, 94, 95, 96, 97, 101–02, 103, 107, 110, 113–14, 117, 118, 126, 129, 133, 134, 158, 167, 177, 183, 195, 199, 209, 215, 218, 275, 276, 281, 282, 288, 296, 310, 336–37, 405, 408, 409, 491, 492, 493, 498, 501, 504, 510, 517, 518, 528
Broughton, Panthea Reid, 281, 310, 504, 510
Brown, Calvin S., 56, 246, 250, 257, 325, 326, 327, 337, 364, 372
Brown, Charles Brockden, 90, 325
  *Edgar Huntly*, 325
Brown, May Cameron, 275, 276, 293–94, 310
Brown, Sterling, A., 272, 286, 307, 310
Brown, Suzanne Hunter, 13, 27, 131–32, 134
Brown, William R., 279, 310
Browning, Robert, 92, 94
  "Porphyria's Lover," 92, 93
Brylowski, Walter, 496, 510
Buie, Marie, 74
Bungert, Hans, 17, 27, 36–37, 41, 239, 246, 470, 473, 474
Burduck, Michael L., 117, 134
Burnett, Whit, 64–65
  *Time to Be Young*, 65
Burr, Raymond, 73
Bush, Ad, 55, 56, 238
Butterworth, Keen, 280, 310
Byron, George Gordon, Lord, 364, 490
  *Don Juan*, 490
  "She Walks in Beauty," 364

Cable, George Washington, 92, 223
  "Jean-ah Poquelin," 92
  "Madame Delicieuse," 223

Cackett, Kathy, 6, 21, 27
Cagney Productions, 65
Caldwell, Erskine, 172
   "Saturday Afternoon," 172
California, 240, 253, 477, 482, 483, 484.
   *See also* Hollywood, Los Angeles
Callen, Shirley, 394–95, 399
Calvinism, 100, 304, 305
Campbell, Harry Modean, 100, 121, 134, 278, 310, 389, 399
Campbell, John C., 517
   *Southern Highlander and His Homeland, The*, 518
Cantrell, Frank, 364, 366, 370, 372, 373
Cantwell, Robert, 75, 81, 102–03, 134, 155–56, 167, 186, 250, 257, 286
Carey, Glenn O., 180, 187, 199
Carondelet, Baron Luis Hector de, 324
Carothers, James B., 6, 10, 11, 14, 15, 17, 19, 21, 26, 27, 28, 35, 36, 37, 38, 39, 40, 41, 49, 51–52, 55–56, 57, 59, 61, 62, 66, 67, 68, 71, 75–76, 78, 81, 98, 99, 101, 103, 114, 134–35, 144, 145, 146, 150, 151, 155, 156, 157, 162–63, 167, 176, 179, 180, 181, 182, 186, 187, 188, 199, 208, 218, 224, 226, 227, 228, 233, 234, 238, 239, 240, 246, 250, 252, 253, 254, 255, 256, 257, 261, 262, 264, 266, 270, 271, 274, 276–77, 279–80, 284, 289, 295, 310, 322, 328, 329, 332, 337, 343, 345, 346, 347, 349, 353, 356, 359, 365, 366, 368, 369, 370, 371, 372, 373, 377, 381, 382, 388, 389, 390, 391, 392, 393, 396–97, 399, 403, 404, 405, 406, 407, 409, 416, 420, 433, 434, 435, 436, 437, 438, 439, 443, 446, 447, 448, 450, 451, 458, 460, 464, 468, 471, 474, 480, 481, 485, 492–93, 494, 498, 499, 500, 505, 510, 520, 522, 528
Carpenter, Meta, 477
Cash, W. J., 394
   *Mind of the South, The*, 394
Cassandra, 502
Castille, Philip, 487, 502, 505, 506, 510
CBS, 3, 64
   Lux Video Theatre, 73, 453
Cervantes Saavedra, Miguel de, 250, 346
   *Don Quixote*, 207
Charlottesville, Virginia, 425
Chatto and Windus, Ltd., 245
Chaucer, Geoffrey, 398

*Canterbury Tales, The*, 398
Chesnutt, Charles Waddell, 95
Chickasaw, 56, 57, 323, 325, 326, 327, 345, 347, 348, 349, 352, 354, 363, 366, 377, 378, 519
Chilton, Bob, 238, 239
Chilton, Top, 238
Choctaw, 323, 325, 326, 347, 348, 354, 363, 376, 377, 378, 516, 517, 519
Christianity, 23, 241, 333
Churchill, Winston, 5
China, 27, 40, 52, 78
Civil War, 4, 10, 12, 17, 46, 77, 79, 119, 189, 345, 381, 390, 393, 395, 404, 467, 469, 471, 472, 473, 490, 498, 519, 521, 523, 524, 527. *See also* Gettysburg
Clark, William Bedford, 346, 359
Clemens, Samuel (Mark Twain), 5, 95, 155, 223, 238, 242, 243, 250, 346, 364, 479, 490
   "Celebrated Jumping Frog of Calavares County, The," 155
   *Huckleberry Finn*, 5, 238, 242, 243, 364, 479
Clements, Arthur L., 113, 135
Cobb, Irvin S., 95, 517
Coburn, Mark D., 274, 307, 308, 311
Cofield Collection, 90
Cohen, Philip, 319, 337
Coindreau, Maurice Edgar, 112, 133, 135, 169, 296, 311, 507, 511
Colbert, David, 363
College Hill, Mississippi, 89
*College Humor*, 422, 453, 454
*Collier's*, 204
Collins, Carvel, 404, 409
Collins, Jimmy, 209
   *Test Pilot*, 209
Columbus, Mississippi, 260
Commins, Saxe, 60
Connolly, Francis, 216, 218
Connolly, Thomas E., 166, 167, 240, 246, 255, 258, 398, 399
Conrad, Joseph, 5, 223, 325, 326, 425
   *Heart of Darkness*, 325
   *Lord Jim*, 325
   *Nigger of the "Narcissus," The*, 5
"Contributors," 381, 382
Cook, Sylvia Jenkins, 23–24, 28, 50, 52, 396, 399
Cooper, James Fenimore, 325, 364, 365
   *Last of the Mohicans, The*, 325

540  *General Index*

*Corporal Eagan*, 205
*Cosmopolitan*, 3, 248, 375, 453, 454, 476
*Country Gentleman*, 3
Cowley, Malcolm, 6, 7, 26–27, 28, 77, 81, 87, 155, 167, 204, 207, 258, 275, 278, 311, 319, 324, 329, 336, 337, 343, 345, 347–48, 349, 359, 378, 382, 388, 391, 439, 464, 468, 527, 528
Cox, Leland H., 14, 15, 18, 20, 28, 288, 311, 332, 336, 337, 353, 359
Crane, John K., 145, 151, 171, 174, 184, 186, 196, 199
Crane, Stephen, 388
 "Blue Hotel, The," 388
Creek, 345, 363
Creighton, Joanne V., 8, 28, 156, 157, 158, 166, 167, 249, 251, 252, 258, 390, 399
Crichton, Kyle S., 154, 162, 249, 267
Cronus, 398
Cullen, John B., 74, 81, 89, 135, 238, 246, 272, 311, 467, 474

Dabney, Lewis M., 56, 62, 176, 199, 277, 278, 311, 321, 323, 324, 325, 326, 328, 329, 333, 335, 336, 338, 344, 345, 346, 347, 348, 349, 350, 351, 352, 354, 355, 356, 358, 359, 363–64, 365, 366, 368, 369, 370, 371, 372, 373, 376, 377, 380, 382, 517, 520, 524, 525, 528
*Damned Don't Cry, The*, 454
Daniels, Edgar F., 184, 185, 186, 187
Dante Alighieri, 172, 192, 326
 *Inferno*, 172, 192
Darwin, Charles, 324, 335
 *Voyage of the Beagle*, 324, 335
Dashiell, Alfred, 87, 179, 204, 221, 248, 249, 375, 432, 455, 456, 487, 488, 489
Davidson, Donald, 44
Davis, Robert Gorham, 143, 173
David, Scottie, 288, 290, 311
David, Thadious M., 272, 311
Davis, William V., 127, 135
Defoe, Daniel, 93
 *Moll Flanders*, 93
Delta Council, 36, 37
Demarest, Myrtle, 514
Denisova, Tamara, 337, 338

Dessner, Lawrence Jay, 172, 193, 200
Devlin, Albert J., 45, 51, 52
Díaz-Diocaretz, Myriam, 99
Dickens, Charles, 92, 94, 223, 377, 490
 *David Copperfield*, 93
 *Great Expectations*, 92–93, 95
 *Little Dorrit*, 93
Dickerson, Mary Jane, 381, 382
Dickinson, Emily, 90
Ditsky, John 468, 474
Dixon, Thomas, 95
Dobkowski, Michael N., 210, 218
"Doctor Martino" (review), 418, 421, 511
Dolch, Martin, 113
Doran, Leonard, 121, 135
Dostoevsky, Fyodor, 223
Douglas, Ellen, 184, 200
Dowling, David, 38, 41, 47, 52, 186, 200, 436, 439, 468, 474
Duryea, Dan, 455
Dreiser, Theodore, 319
Duvall, John N., 12, 15, 28, 112, 135, 146, 150, 151, 175, 180, 200

Early, James, 57, 62
Edel, Leon, 275, 287, 311
Edelstein, Arthur, 298
Edwards, C. Hines, Jr., 91, 93, 135
Edwards, Jonathan, 304
Eliot, T. S., 94, 172, 192
 *Waste Land, The*, 94, 172, 192
Ellison, Ralph, 177, 334
Emancipation Proclamation, 298
Emerson, O. B., 10, 28, 146, 152, 155–56, 167, 186, 193, 200, 206, 218, 286, 311, 327, 338, 392, 399, 403, 409, 413, 421, 428, 430, 522, 528
Endres, Karen, 228
Erikson, Erik, 108
Erskine, Albert, 362
Europe, 336, 442
Everett, Walter K., 35, 38, 39, 41, 50, 51–52, 58, 60, 61, 62, 69, 70, 71, 74, 78, 79, 81, 123, 135, 145, 148, 150, 151, 152, 166, 167, 176, 186–87, 194, 195, 200, 217, 218, 230, 234, 242, 246, 255, 258, 264, 265, 266, 290, 301, 307, 311, 331, 338, 347, 356, 359, 369, 373, 376, 382, 398, 399, 407, 408, 409, 417, 418, 420,

421, 428, 430, 437, 438, 439, 447, 449, 450, 451, 461, 463, 464, 473, 475, 477, 482, 483, 484, 492, 501, 506, 507–08, 511, 524, 528

Falkner, John Wesley Thompson (J. W. T., grandfather), 4, 260, 346, 490
Falkner, Maude Butler (mother), 207, 457, 477
Falkner, Murry Charles ("Jack," brother), 44, 207, 218, 272
Falkner, Murry Cuthbert (father), 207, 261, 388, 425
Falkner, Sallie Murry (grandmother), 260
Falkner, William Clark (great-grandfather), 260, 274
  *White Rose of Memphis, The*, 274
Falkner, William Henry, 260
Faulkner, Alabama (infant daughter), 457
Faulkner, Estelle Oldham Franklin (wife), 222, 223, 364, 413, 457, 477, 478
Faulkner, Howard, 185, 186, 187–88, 195, 200
Faulkner, Jill (m. Summers, daughter), 3, 478
Faulkner, John (brother), 44, 272, 311, 346, 424, 430
  "Good Neighbors," 44
  *Men Working*, 44
Faulkner and Yoknapatawpha Conference 1984, 238
Ferguson, James, 11, 12, 16, 17, 18, 19, 26, 27, 28, 33, 34, 36, 37, 40, 42, 44, 46, 47, 49, 53, 58, 59, 62, 66, 67, 68, 69, 71, 76, 78, 81, 87–88, 99, 102, 103–03, 105, 106, 132, 135, 143, 146, 147, 148, 152, 156–57, 160, 162, 165–66, 167, 171, 176, 177, 178, 179, 193, 194, 195, 200, 205, 211–12, 213, 217, 218, 226, 229, 235, 238–39, 240, 244, 245, 246, 254, 256, 258, 262, 264–65, 266, 268, 271–72, 277, 280, 281, 282, 283, 284, 285, 286, 291, 292–93, 312, 327, 328, 329, 330, 335, 337, 338, 348, 352, 353, 358, 360, 365, 366, 367, 371, 373, 379, 380, 382, 390, 391–92, 393, 397–98, 400, 405, 406, 407, 408, 409, 414, 415, 416,
420, 421, 426, 427, 428, 429, 430, 431, 434, 436, 439, 443, 444, 445, 447, 448, 451, 452, 457, 458, 459, 460–61, 463, 464, 465, 469, 470, 471, 474, 475, 481, 482, 485, 489, 491, 493, 500, 501, 504, 507, 511, 520, 521, 522, 523, 527, 529
Fetterley, Judith, 109–10, 112, 135
Fiedler, Leslie A., 10, 28, 238, 246, 291, 312, 368
  *Love and Death in the American Novel*, 368
Fielden, William, 33
Fineman, Bernard, 403
Fisher King, 5
Fisher, Marvin, 13–14, 18, 19, 28, 282–83, 291, 297, 303, 312
Fitzgerald, F. Scott, 6, 224, 365, 479
  *Great Gatsby, The*, 6, 479
  *Tender Is the Night*, 224
Flaubert, Gustave, 274
Flora, Joseph M., 172, 197, 200, 273, 305, 312
*Flying the Mail* (screenplay), 402
Flynn, Peggy, 144, 152, 225–26, 235, 415, 421
Foote, Horton, 3
Ford, Arthur L., 183, 185, 195, 200
Ford, Ford Madox, 425
Forrest, Nathan Bedford, 467, 469, 490
Forrest, Sally, 454
*Forum*, 87, 88, 89, 160, 221, 422, 454, 457
Foster, Ruel E., 100, 121, 134, 278, 389
Fowler, Doreen, 170, 201, 237, 247, 249, 258, 260, 266, 375, 383, 455, 465, 477, 485
Fox, Andrew, 466
  *Battle of Harrykin Creek, The*, 466
Frakes, James R., 332, 335, 338
France, 169
Franklin, Cornell, 222, 223, 364, 478
Franklin, Malcolm, 478
Franklin, Phyllis, 18, 23, 29
Franklin, Victoria, 477
Frazer, Sir James, 172, 326, 413
  *Golden Bough, The*, 172, 326, 413
Frazer, Winifred L., 190, 198, 200
Frierson, Em, 89–90
Frierson, Sally Wyatt, 89
Frenchmen's Bend, Mississippi (fictional), 16, 34, 67, 80

Freud, Sigmund, 16, 47, 92, 96, 110, 212, 370, 418
Frey, Leonard H., 273, 274, 288, 293, 296, 305, 308–09, 312
Friedman, Alan Warren, 15, 29
Fuentes, Carlos, 94–95
*Aura*, 94–95
Funk, Robert W., 326, 331, 336, 389

Gage, Duane, 60, 63, 323, 331, 338, 354, 360, 426, 431, 525, 529
Garber, Frederick, 185, 186, 187, 188, 190, 191, 200
Garden of Eden, 21, 195, 333, 336, 371, 481, 483
Garnett, David, 334–35, 336, 338
Garrison, Joseph M., Jr., 124, 135, 295, 312, 461, 464, 465
Gates Flying Circus, 402
Genette, Gerard, 25
Gerlach, John, 117, 135, 273, 274, 306–07, 312
Gerstenberger, Donna, 185, 186, 187, 188, 190, 191, 200
Gettysburg, Battle of, 16
Gidley, Mick, 322–23, 333, 338, 347, 356, 360, 371, 373, 377–78, 382, 518, 529
Gladstein, Mimi Reisel, 176, 200, 289, 312
Going, William T., 122, 125, 126, 136
Gold, Joseph, 5, 14, 29, 47, 76, 92–93, 120, 136, 240, 243, 246, 261, 264, 266
Goldman, Morton, 54, 55, 248, 249, 260, 375, 387, 432, 454, 455, 476, 477
Gothic fiction, 90, 91, 92, 114, 130, 328
Gould, Jack, 455
Gowen, Emmett, 518
*Mountain Born*, 518
Graves, Ralph, 403
"Great Moccasin" (worship of), 336
Great Sun (Natchez chief), 324
Gregory, Eileen, 240, 247
Gresset, Michel, 209–10, 211, 216, 218–19, 321, 338, 375, 382
Griffin, William J., 194, 200
Grimwood, Michael, 4–5, 10, 14, 16, 29, 44, 47, 49, 53, 55, 56, 63, 477, 478, 479, 480, 483, 484, 485
Gump, Andy, 207
Gwin, Minrose C., 99–100, 136

Haas, Robert, 44, 77
Hadley, Charles, 14, 25, 29, 262, 263–64, 266
Hagopian, John V., 90, 113, 114, 122, 126, 127, 136, 207, 209, 214, 215, 216–17, 219, 272, 275, 287, 296, 297, 298, 312
Hale, Nancy, 289, 312
Hall, Constance Hill, 227, 235, 490, 506, 511
Hall, Joan Wylie, 5, 29
Hamblin, Robert W., 274, 292, 312, 450, 452
Hamby, James A., 18–19, 27
Handy, W. C., 273
"St. Louis Blues," 272, 274, 308
Hannah, Barry, 238, 247
Happel, Nikolaus, 115, 122, 125, 136
Harbison, Sherrill, 504, 511
Hardy, Thomas, 347
*Harper's*, 3, 154, 342, 349, 387, 389, 411, 422, 423, 424, 425
Harrington, Evans B., 293, 297–98, 312, 466, 505
*Battle of Harrykin Creek, The*, 466
Harris, George Washington, 518
*Sut Lovingood*, 518
Harris, Joel Chandler, 95, 346
Harrison, Jane, 190
Harrison, Robert, 74, 81, 207, 209, 210, 211, 214, 216, 217, 219, 238, 247, 407, 409
Harter, Carol Clancey, 281, 312
Hashiguchi, Yasuo, 48, 49, 51, 53
Hawthorne, Nathaniel, 5, 90–91, 94, 127, 172, 177, 334, 388, 413
*House of the Seven Gables, The*, 90–91, 95
*Scarlet Letter, The*, 127, 172
"White Old Maid, The," 91
Hayes, Ann L., 180, 200
Hays, Peter L., 90, 136
Heilman, Robert B., 287, 301, 305, 312
Helen of Troy, 91, 364
Heller, Terry, 90–91, 116–17, 136
Hemingway, Ernest, 172, 273, 326, 346, 365, 457
"Big Two-Hearted River," 346
*Death in the Afternoon*, 326
"Indian Camp," 172
"Killers, The," 273
*Sun Also Rises, The*, 457

Hendricks, William O., 127–28, 136
Henning, Albin, 514
Hermann, John, 295, 312
Hiles, Jane, 19–20, 29
Hill, A. A., 363, 373
Hinkle, James, 89–90, 136, 324, 339
Hochman, Baruch, 25, 29, 93, 111, 136
Hoffman, Daniel, 7, 10, 29
Hogan, Michael, 25, 29
Hogan, Patrick G., 290, 313
Holland, Norman N., 108–09, 114–15, 129, 136
Hollywood, California, 477, 478, 479, 480, 481
Holmes, Edward M., 8, 29, 35, 42, 47, 53, 57, 63, 75, 81, 96, 101, 136, 144, 152, 156, 157, 165, 166, 167, 174, 175, 200, 208, 219, 239, 240, 242, 247, 251, 252, 255, 258, 261, 262, 266, 275, 279, 313, 322, 339, 347, 360, 365, 373, 389, 393, 394, 400, 405, 410, 426, 431, 443, 452, 495, 511, 518, 529
Homer, 364
  *Iliad*, 364
  *Odyssey*, 364
Hönnighausen, Lothar, 326, 339
Howard, Leon, 268
Howe, Irving, 18, 20, 29, 119, 121, 136, 162, 163, 167, 187, 194, 201, 208, 214, 215, 216, 217, 219, 268, 286–87, 291, 304, 313, 336, 339, 393, 394, 400, 492, 509, 511, 518, 523–24, 527, 529
Howell, Elmo, 11–12, 22–23, 29, 39, 42, 44, 45, 48, 49, 50, 53, 66, 71, 76, 81, 97, 107, 112, 113, 136, 323, 325, 326, 332–33, 334–35, 339, 345, 346, 348–49, 360, 368, 370, 373, 381, 382, 395, 400, 467, 468, 471–72, 473, 475, 501, 511, 517, 524, 529
Hudson, W. H., 456
  *Green Mansions*, 457, 458, 461, 462
Hult, Sharon Smith, 370, 373, 456, 457, 458, 459, 460, 461, 462, 463, 464, 465
Hume, Captain Jack, 89
Hunt, John W., 58, 63, 268, 313, 343, 344, 350, 357, 360
Hunter, Edwin R., 7, 29, 156, 157, 167, 251, 258, 389, 390, 391, 400

Hunter, William B., Jr., 126–27, 136
Hurricane Creek, 467

Ilacqua, Alma A. 304, 313
Inca, 56
Inge, Thomas, 143, 152, 173, 201, 309, 313, 451, 452
Inscoe, John C., 517–18, 521, 526, 529
Irvin (barnstormer), 207
Irving, Washington, 238, 346
  *Astoria*, 346
  "Rip Van Winkle," 238
Isaacs, Neil D., 390, 394, 397, 398, 400
Isaiah, 196

Jackson, Andrew, 363, 376
Jackson, Mississippi, 239
Jacksonville, Florida, 435
Jacobs, John T., 119, 137
James, Henry, 94–95, 223, 413, 443
  *Ambassadors, The*, 443
  *Aspern Papers, The*, 94–95
  "Beast in the Jungle, The," 413
Japan, 70, 330, 354
Jazz Age, 214
Jefferson, Mississippi (fictional), 35, 37, 44, 79, 80, 105, 106, 112, 115, 117, 118, 124, 143, 145, 146, 160, 161, 162, 165, 170, 173, 174, 176, 177, 184, 186, 187, 189, 190, 192, 195, 208, 211, 217, 238, 239, 241, 246, 252, 261, 285, 295, 299, 305, 371, 461, 481, 504
Jenkins, Lee Clinton, 180, 201
Jesus Christ, 26, 185, 292, 304, 307
  Crucifixion, 191
Jewett, Sarah Orne, 90, 95
Jie, Tao, 78, 81
John Henry (blacksmith), 346
Johnson, C. W. M., 118, 137
Johnson, Glen M., 345, 360
Johnson, Ira, 172, 173, 201
Johnston, Kenneth G., 16, 29, 298–99, 308, 313
Jones, Tommy Lee, 9
Joyce, James, 434, 443
  "Dead, The," 443

Kane, Harnett T., 90
  "Emily and the Baron," 90

Karl, Frederick R., 3, 29, 34, 35, 42, 43, 46, 49, 52, 53, 57, 61, 69, 71, 78, 81, 87, 95, 99, 137, 172, 174, 187, 188, 201, 207, 208, 214, 215, 219, 223, 234, 235, 241, 245, 247, 256, 258, 262, 263, 265, 266, 272, 313, 321, 337, 339, 355, 360, 368, 371, 373, 376, 381, 382, 388, 394, 398, 400, 404, 410, 413, 415, 418, 421, 422, 423, 425, 429, 430, 431, 434, 435, 437, 439, 443, 449–50, 452, 454, 457, 459, 462, 464, 465, 477, 478, 481, 484, 485, 488, 502, 511, 521, 526, 529
Kartiganer, Donald M., 8, 29, 337, 339
Kawin, Bruce F., 3, 29, 178, 201, 391, 400, 403, 410, 479, 485
Keats, John, 93, 172, 425, 462
  "Ode on a Grecian Urn," 93, 425
Kelly, Captain Colin P., Jr., 74
Kempton, Kenneth Payson, 123, 137
Kent, George E., 298, 313
Kephart, Horace, 517
  *Our Southern Highlanders*, 517
Kerr, Elizabeth M., 10, 12, 13, 29, 35, 42, 44, 45, 50–51, 52, 53, 65, 71, 75, 80, 81, 97, 98, 106, 137, 175–76, 177, 179–80, 182, 183, 186, 201, 225, 227, 230, 235, 239–40, 242, 247, 261, 266, 281, 298, 313, 328, 329, 339, 391, 400, 470, 473, 475, 488, 493, 494, 495, 496, 502, 504–05, 507, 509, 511–12
Kindermann, Wolf, 211, 219
Kinney, Arthur F., 17, 26, 30, 34, 37, 42, 47, 48, 53, 57, 59, 63, 68, 71, 75, 77–78, 79, 80, 82, 98, 105, 137, 144, 152, 161–62, 168, 170, 175, 181, 185, 201, 213, 219, 229, 235, 237, 241, 243, 247, 249, 255, 256, 258, 260, 262, 266, 268, 274, 276, 286, 292, 313, 328, 330, 339, 353, 354, 360, 367, 373, 375, 380, 383, 393, 400, 406, 410, 413, 418, 421, 427, 431, 436, 440, 442, 445, 452, 455, 460, 465, 466, 468, 469, 471, 475, 477, 481, 483, 485, 491, 495, 496, 500, 512, 522, 529
Kirk, Robert W., 166, 168, 255, 258, 398, 400
Klotz, Marvin, 166, 168, 255, 258, 398, 400

Knieger, Barnard, 417, 421, 502, 512, 517, 529
Kobler, J. F., 122, 137
Koerner, W. H. D., 319
Kohn, Sheldon Scott, 480, 483, 484, 485
Krefft, James H., 325, 339
Kurtz, Elizabeth Carney, 123, 137
Kutzik, Alfred, J., 210, 219, 498, 499, 512
Kuyk, Betty M., 300–01, 313
Kuyk, Dirk, Jr., 300–01, 313

La Farge, Oliver, 325
  *Laughing Boy*, 325
Lafayette County, Mississippi, 33, 50, 55, 56, 74, 89, 90
  airport, 206, 207
Lafayette Springs, 412
Landeira, Ricardo López, 94–95, 137
Lang, Béatrice, 103, 137, 213, 219, 226, 235, 406, 410, 413, 414, 415, 416, 418–20, 421, 520, 529
Langford, Beverly Young, 323–24, 339
Lawrence, D. H., 223, 425
  "Fox, The," 425
Lazarus, 347
Leary, Lewis, 8, 12, 30, 66, 71, 119, 137, 520, 529
Leflore, Greenwood, 323, 376, 516, 517, 524
Lee, Jim, 287–88, 313
Levitt, Paul, 94, 137
Lewis, R. W. B., 21
  *American Adam, The*, 21
Lewis, Wyndham, 489, 511
*Liberty*, 221, 421
Lincoln, Abraham, Gettysburg Address, 74
Lind, Ilse Dusoir, 98, 137, 205, 206, 207, 210, 215, 217, 219, 226, 235, 253, 257, 258, 406, 410, 470, 475, 497, 499, 512
Lisca, Peter, 7, 30
Littler, Frank A., 120, 123, 137
London, England, 110
London, Jack, 365
*Long Hot Summer, The*, 9
Long, Elizabeth, 129, 137
Longfellow, Henry Wadsworth, 325, 365
  *Song of Hiawatha, The*, 325
Longley, John Lewis, Jr., 36, 38, 42, 61,

63, 366, 369–70, 374, 470, 473, 475, 480, 486
Longstreet, Augustus Baldwin, 365
   "Fight, The," 365
Lorrimer, George H., 319
Los Angeles, California, 240, 479, 483
Lumpkin, Grace, 513
   *To Make My Bread*, 518
Lupack, Barbara Tepa, 110, 137

McCormick, John, 65
McDermott, John V., 192, 201
McDonagh, Richard, 455
MacEwen, George, 238
McGlynn, Paul D., 125–26, 138
McHaney, Thomas L., 4, 45, 53, 56, 63, 65, 72, 75, 82, 205, 405, 410, 416, 421, 423, 481, 486
McLean, Alabama Falkner (aunt), 490
MacMillan, Duane, 208–09, 215, 219, 404, 405, 410
Magalaner, Marvin, 120, 138
Mager, Gus, 143, 173
   *Hawkshaw the Detective*, 143, 173
Magny, Claude-Edmonde, 278, 284, 313
Malin, Irving, 11, 18, 30, 97, 107, 138, 174, 180, 184, 201, 225, 230, 231, 235, 413–14, 418, 421, 501, 502, 512
Mallarmé, 172
Manglaviti, Leo M. J., 269, 270, 313
Marcel, Gabriel, 18
Marlborough, Duke of, 5
Marlowe, Christopher, 347
   *Tamburlaine*, 347
Marsh, Fred, 392, 427–28, 522
Massachusetts, 110. See also Boston
Matthews, John T., 160, 165, 166, 168, 178–79, 198, 201, 254, 255, 256, 257, 258–59, 269, 278, 302–03, 314, 334, 339, 344, 351, 358, 360, 508, 512
Mellard, James M., 92, 93–94, 111, 130, 138
Melville, Herman, 5, 177, 332
   *Moby-Dick*, 5
Memphis, Tennessee, 206, 207, 238, 242, 261, 300, 402, 495, 499, 503, 504, 505, 507
Mencken, H. L., 269, 270
Meriwether, James B., 3, 8, 30, 73, 82, 87, 138, 142, 152, 154, 162, 168, 169, 170, 201, 204, 219, 221, 222, 235, 249, 259, 267, 314, 319, 339–40, 342, 343, 360, 375, 383, 391, 402, 410, 411, 421, 422, 423, 431, 432, 433, 440, 452, 453, 454, 455, 456, 465, 487, 512, 515, 516, 529
Methodist, 36, 39
Metro-Goldwyn-Mayer (MGM), 403
Miller, David M., 497, 513
Miller, James A., 300–01, 313
Millgate, Michael, 6, 7, 8, 9, 14, 16–17, 18, 24–25, 30, 36, 37, 42, 47–48, 53, 59, 63, 67, 70, 72, 77, 78, 82, 88, 89, 96, 101, 103, 104, 105, 121, 138, 147, 152, 154–55, 156, 159, 161, 165, 168, 170, 171, 173, 174, 176, 179, 180, 181, 194, 195, 201–02, 208, 209, 212, 213, 219–20, 255–56, 259, 276, 278, 280, 283, 285, 305, 314, 321, 327, 329, 340, 346, 352, 357, 360–61, 391, 392, 393, 394, 397, 400, 404, 406, 410, 416, 421, 425, 427, 431, 436, 440, 444, 452, 455, 460, 465, 471, 475, 481, 486, 492, 493–94, 495, 500, 512–13, 522, 529
Milton, John, 5
   *Paradise Lost*, 5
Milum, Richard A., 324, 336, 340
Miner, Ward L., 44, 49–50, 53, 56, 63, 323, 340, 394, 400
Minter, David, 4, 30, 35, 42, 208, 220, 268, 314, 343, 356, 361, 389, 396–97, 401, 405, 410, 425, 431
*Miscellany*, 421
Mississippi, 23, 56, 193, 260, 323, 324, 326, 376, 461, 467, 517, 518. See also College Hill, Columbus, Jackson, Pascagoula, Ripley, Yalobusha County
Mitchell, Charles, 5, 20–21, 30
Momberger, Philip, 105, 138, 147, 152, 161, 168, 179, 202, 213, 220, 229, 235, 241, 247, 254–55, 259, 263, 266, 276, 284, 285, 286, 292, 301–02, 309, 314
Monroe, James, 376
Montenyohl, Eric L., 132, 138
Moore, Janice Townley, 195–96, 202
Moreland, Richard C., 4, 8, 13, 22, 30, 57, 63, 391, 401

Morozova, Tatiana, 334, 340
Morris, Barbara Alverson, 12, 30, 46, 49, 51, 53, 396, 401
Morris, Wesley, 12, 30, 46, 49, 51, 53, 396, 401
Morris, Wright, 370, 371, 374
Morrison, Gail Moore, 268, 269, 270, 314
Mortimer, Gail L., 97, 100, 138, 161, 168, 197–98, 202, 253, 259
Mottstown, Mississippi (fictional), 261
Muller, Gilbert H., 107–08, 138, 321–22, 333, 340
Murrell, John, 467
Murry, Emily Holcombe (great-grandmother), 260
Murry, John Young (great-grandfather), 260
Myres, W. V., 38–39, 42

Natchez, 323, 324
National Recovery Administration (NRA), 238
Native Americans. See Chickasaw, Choctaw, Creek, Natchez, Navajo, Seminole
Natwick, Mildred, 455
Navajo, 325
Nebeker, Helen E., 115, 126, 138
Nebraska, 479, 480, 481, 482, 484
Neilson, Mary Louise, 89
New Haven, Connecticut, 402, 412
New Orleans, Louisiana, 324, 325, 347, 348, 356, 370, 378, 402, 442, 443
New York, New York, 433
  Penn Station, 433
*New York Times*, 455
Nicholson, Norman, 223, 235
Nicolaisen, Peter, 161, 168
Nicolet, William P., 26, 30
Nilon, Charles H., 60, 63, 80, 82, 117, 138, 159–60, 163, 164–65, 166, 168, 172, 176, 182, 187, 202, 227, 230, 236, 272, 281, 282, 288, 289, 314, 327, 328, 332, 335, 340, 354, 361, 379, 383, 496, 498, 506 513, 522, 529
Nobel Prize, 75
Nordanberg, Thomas, 46, 49, 50, 53, 67, 70, 72, 76, 78, 79, 80, 82, 408, 410, 468, 469, 472, 473, 475, 519, 524, 530

Ober, Harold, 3, 4, 6, 32, 43, 64, 65, 73, 74, 362, 466, 471
O'Brien, Edward J., 272, 273, 287, 295, 314
  *Short Story Case Book*, 272
O'Connor, William Van, 96, 106, 138–39, 145, 151, 152, 185, 202, 208, 214, 215, 220, 278, 303, 314, 330, 340, 393, 401, 404, 410, 420, 421, 503, 513, 518, 530
O'Donnell, George Marion, 23, 501, 513
Odysseus, 390
O. Henry. See Porter, William Sydney
O. Henry Memorial Award, 3, 6, 362, 367
  *Prize Stories of 1949*, 362, 372
Oklahoma, 412, 426
Oldham family, 223, 413
"Old Black Joe" (spiritual), 308
O'Nan, Martha, 324, 340, 345–46, 361
O'Neill, Eugene, 326
  *Emperor Jones, The*, 326
Ono, Kiyoyuki, 70, 72, 234, 236
Orvis, Mary Burchard, 297, 314
Owens, Tony J., 441, 442, 443, 444, 445–46, 447, 449, 451, 452
Owsley, F. L., 48
  *Plain Folk of the Old South*, 48
Oxford, Mississippi, 44, 56, 65, 74, 89, 155, 207, 238, 239, 250, 261, 364, 467, 478
  Confederate Monument, 74
  Homer Duke House, 90
*Oxford Eagle*, 4, 171

Page, Sally R., 96, 97–98, 114, 139, 144, 145, 150, 152, 174–75, 178, 184, 189, 191, 195, 202, 225, 230–31, 236, 240, 247, 253, 257, 259, 505, 513
Page, Thomas Nelson, 346
Pagliacco, 207
Palmer, C. B., 193
Parkman, Francis, 325
Palmer, John E., 362
Pascagoula, Mississippi, 488
Patton, Nelse, 171
PBS *American Short Story* series, 3, 9
Pearson, Norman Holmes, 269, 271, 273, 276, 291, 314, 346, 361
Peavy, Charles D., 12, 30, 75, 82, 298, 314, 326, 328, 331, 340, 350–51,

General Index 547

361, 366, 374, 396, 401, 498, 513, 521, 525, 530
Penelope, 391
Perkins, Hoke, 282, 314
Perrine, Laurence, 305–06, 314
Perry, Menakhem, 128–29, 139
Persephone, 108
Peters, Erskine, 181, 182, 188, 191, 202, 227, 236, 281, 284, 304, 314, 331–32, 340, 350, 352, 354, 361, 521, 530
Peterson, Richard F., 441, 442, 443, 445, 452
Petrarch, Francesco, 377
Petry, Alice Hall, 127, 139, 223–24, 228, 231–32, 233, 234, 236
Pharaohs, 56
Phillips, Gene D., 3, 9, 30, 403, 405, 410, 455, 465, 477, 486
Pikoulis, John, 8, 12–13, 30, 57, 63
Pilkington, John, 171, 179, 202, 227, 236
Pitavy, François, 10, 30, 87, 96, 97, 101, 139, 145, 146, 152–53, 174, 175, 180, 181, 202
Pitcher, E. W., 290, 314
Pocahontas, 365
Poe, Edgar Allan, 89, 91, 92, 94, 325, 413
  "Cask of Amontillado, The," 91
  "Fall of the House of Usher, The," 91, 92
  "To Helen," 91
Polk, Noel, 7, 12, 15, 16–17, 30, 31, 98–99, 111, 139, 143, 170, 174, 175, 176, 180, 181, 186, 202, 224, 226, 231, 233, 234, 236, 238–39, 242–43, 244, 245, 247, 269, 279, 301, 315, 320, 324, 340, 342, 355, 361, 372, 374, 458, 465, 495, 498, 503, 507, 513, 515, 519
Pope, Alexander, 376–77
  "Essay on Man," 376–77
Porter, Minnie, 171
Porter, William Sydney (O. Henry), 95, 143
Portland, Oregon, 110
Pothier, Jacques, 525, 530
Powers, Lyall H., 13, 31
*Prairie Schooner*, 239
Prometheus, 5
Protestantism, 242, 282
Pryse, Marjorie, 176–77, 186, 189, 202, 333–34, 340

*Publications of the Mississippi Historical Society*, 364
Pushmataha (Choctaw chief), 376
Putzel, Max, 41, 42, 88, 104, 120, 124, 139, 155, 165, 168, 171, 185, 186, 194, 202, 204, 217, 220, 269, 277, 309, 315, 343, 344, 354–55, 356, 357, 361, 408, 410, 487, 488, 489, 490, 491, 494, 502, 504, 507, 513
Pyramus, 224

Quick, Ad, 74
Quick, Sulton, 74

Rabbetts, John, 95, 139, 250, 259, 261, 266, 325, 327, 340, 347, 361, 520, 530
Ragan, David Paul, 59, 61, 322, 341, 345, 361, 387, 388, 389, 390, 401
Rainey, Paul, 424
Ransom, John Crowe, 94
  "Emily Hardcastle, Spinster," 94
*Red Book*, 3
Reed, Joseph W., Jr., 10, 14, 15, 25, 26, 31, 34, 39, 40, 42, 47, 53, 56, 58, 63, 67, 68, 72, 76, 77, 82, 102, 123–24, 139, 145, 146, 148, 149, 153, 177, 179, 193, 202, 240, 243–44, 245, 247, 254, 256–57, 259, 262, 263, 266, 282, 283, 288, 294–95, 315, 326, 341, 356–57, 361, 371, 372, 374, 379, 383, 416, 417, 421, 430, 431, 434, 435, 440, 448, 452, 459, 464, 465, 469, 475
Rhodes, Pamela E., 508, 512
Richardson, H. Edward, 274, 315, 506
Richardson, Kenneth E., 490, 497–98, 502, 513
Ripley, 56, 260
Riveriere, Baron Henry Arnous de, 90
RKO Studio, 204, 402
Robb, Mary Cooper, 366, 374, 473, 475
Rogalus, Paul 188, 202
Rose, Stuart, 466
Rosenman, John B., 274, 303, 315
Ross, Danforth, 95, 100, 120, 139
Ross, Stephen M., 14, 25, 26, 31, 61–62, 99, 139, 158, 168, 228–29, 236, 264, 266, 398, 401, 427, 431, 442–43, 448, 450, 452, 460, 465–66, 473–74, 476, 499, 514, 520, 530

Rowan Oak, 143, 170, 237, 260, 319, 387, 431, 440, 454, 456
Ruppersburg, Hugh M., 102, 139, 239, 247, 265, 266, 283, 315, 390, 401
Russia, 27, 309
Ruzicka, William T., 15, 16, 31, 37, 39, 42

St. Francis of Assisi, 225
St. Louis, Missouri, 412
Samway, Patrick H., S.J., 58, 64, 159, 168, 177, 203, 268, 276, 297, 315, 328, 341, 469, 476
Sancho Panza, 207
Sanders, Barry, 308, 315
Sardis Reservoir, 65
Sartoris, Brenda, 24, 31
Saturnalia, 191
*Saturday Evening Post*, 3, 32, 33, 43, 44, 54, 55, 64, 70, 73, 74, 80, 142, 143, 154, 204, 248, 319, 321, 334, 342, 349, 362, 375, 402, 411, 422, 432, 440, 450, 451, 466, 476, 487, 515, 516, 517
Saxon, Lyle, 326
Scherer, Olga, 390, 401
Scherting, Jack, 100–01, 110–11, 113, 117, 122–23, 139
Schoenberg, Estella, 58–59, 64, 226–27, 236, 279, 296, 315, 343, 344, 351–52, 361
*Scribner's*, 87, 88, 142, 145, 154, 162, 169, 170, 171, 179, 204, 205, 206, 221, 222, 248, 249, 267, 319, 342, 375, 402, 422, 432, 440, 453, 455, 456, 457, 464, 487, 490
Schyfter, Sara E., 130–31, 133
Scott, Sir Walter, 473
Sederberg, Nancy Belcher, 210, 220, 403, 404, 410
Seminole, 345
Serafin, Joan M., 160–61, 168, 224, 236, 253, 259, 427, 431
*Sewanee Review*, 362, 363
Shakespeare, William, 5, 93, 250, 274, 346, 347, 479, 523
  *Antony and Cleopatra*, 347
  *King Lear*, 274, 347, 478
  *Macbeth*, 5, 523
  *Othello*, 5
  *Richard the Third*, 347
  *Romeo and Juliet*, 122

Shaw, George Bernard, 443
  *Candida*, 443
Sherman, William Tecumseh, 468
Shenton, Edward, 60
Shiroma, Mikio, 118, 139
Simms, William Gilmore, 325
  *Yemassee, The*, 325
Simpson, Lewis P., 343, 344, 361
Skaggs, Merrill Maguire, 9, 26, 31
Skei, Hans H., 3, 6, 8, 12, 19, 24, 31, 32, 33, 34, 35, 39–40, 41, 42, 43, 46, 48, 53, 54, 55, 59, 60–61, 62, 64, 65, 67, 68, 69, 70, 72, 73, 75, 76, 78, 79, 80, 82, 87, 88, 89, 94, 95, 96, 99, 103, 111, 114, 120, 124–25, 133, 139, 142, 143, 144, 145, 146, 148, 149, 150, 153, 154, 155, 157, 160, 161, 163, 169, 170, 174, 176, 177, 178, 179, 184–85, 189, 191–92, 194, 195, 198, 203, 204, 207, 208, 211, 212, 217, 220, 221, 224, 226, 228, 231, 233, 234, 236, 237, 239, 240–41, 243, 244–45, 247, 248, 249, 253, 254, 256, 259, 260, 261, 262, 264, 265, 266–67, 270, 271, 272, 273, 275, 280, 281, 282, 284–85, 288, 291, 295, 303, 309, 315, 320, 329, 332, 341, 342, 343, 344, 349, 351, 352, 355–56, 357, 358, 361, 362, 363, 364, 366, 369, 370, 372, 374, 375, 377, 379, 381, 383, 387, 390, 391, 392, 393–94, 396, 398, 399, 401, 403, 405, 406, 407–08, 409, 410, 411, 412, 414–15, 418, 420, 422, 423, 425–26, 428, 429, 431, 432, 433, 437, 438, 440, 441, 444, 448, 449, 450, 451, 452–53, 454, 455, 458, 459, 460, 461, 462, 463, 464, 465, 466, 471, 474, 475, 481, 482, 483, 484, 486, 487, 488, 500, 501, 503, 508, 514, 515, 516, 519, 520, 523, 526–27, 530
Skinner, John L., 130, 140
Slabey, Robert M., 268, 273, 275, 276, 277, 278, 279, 287, 289, 291, 293, 297, 315, 351, 361
Slatoff, Walter J., 120, 140, 212, 220, 328, 341, 366, 374, 425, 430
Smith, Albert C., 4
Smith, Harrison, 375, 476, 487
Smith, Henry Nash, 345
Smith, William Sooy, 467–68

*General Index* 549

Snead, James A., 67, 72, 176, 203, 390, 401
Snell, George, 91, 121, 140, 272, 286, 289, 295–96, 297, 309, 315
Solomon, 364
South (the American), 11, 17, 48, 60, 91, 94, 106, 108, 110, 112, 113, 115, 118, 119, 120, 128, 129, 191, 192, 194, 195, 196, 223, 227, 230, 232, 286, 297, 298, 303, 330, 331, 355, 367, 369, 389, 394, 426, 429, 468, 472, 473, 498, 499, 502, 509, 524
Southwestern humor, 34, 56, 57, 95, 155, 250, 251, 261, 307, 346
Spatz, Jonas, 479, 483, 486
Spenser, Edmund, 5
  *Faerie Queen, The*, 5
Stafford, T. J., 101, 117–18, 140
Starke, Aubrey, 146, 206, 403, 413
Starke, Catherine, 95, 140
Stein, William Byshe, 5, 20, 31
Stevens, Aretta J., 91, 140
Stevens, Wallace, 325
  "Life Is Motion," 325
Stewart, Jack F., 172, 192, 203, 388, 395–96, 398, 401
Stewart, James T., 92, 140
Stewart, Randall, 92
Stockton, Frank, 95
Stone, Edward, 90, 91, 92, 97, 123, 140
Stone, James, 55, 56
Stone, Phil, 413, 515
Stoneback, H. R., 27, 31, 40–41, 42, 52, 54, 78, 82
Stonum, Gary Lee, 7, 31, 35, 43, 57, 64, 239, 248
*Story*, 73, 221, 222, 375, 376, 381, 440, 441, 466, 467
Stowe, Harriet Beecher, 274
  *Uncle Tom's Cabin*, 274
Strandberg, Victor, 98, 111, 114, 140, 328–29, 333, 341, 350, 362
Stribling, T. S., 143
Stronks, James, 91, 140
Styron, William, 326, 341
Sullivan, Ruth, 112, 115–16, 140
Sullivan, Walter, 115, 140
Sunderman, Paula 299–300, 307–08, 315
Sundquist, Eric J., 181, 203
Suratt, Hugh Miller, 55
Swift, Jonathan, 326
  "Modest Proposal, A," 326

Swinburne, Algernon Charles, 172
Széky, Annámaria, 173, 174, 175, 180, 184, 187, 188, 190, 203

Tallahatchie River, 348
Taylor, Tom, 143, 173
  *Ticket of Leave Man, The*, 143, 173
Taylor, Walter, 57, 64, 182, 184, 185, 203, 281, 282, 315, 320, 327, 332, 341, 343, 349, 350, 362, 363, 374, 375, 378–79, 383, 391, 401, 494, 496, 514, 515–16, 518, 530
Tefs, Wayne A., 109, 129, 140
Tennessee, 468, 524. *See also* Memphis
Terry, Esther Alexander, 498, 514
Thompson, Lawrance, 492, 493, 514
Thoreau, Henry David, 44
  *Civil Disobedience*, 44
Thisbe, 224
*Times Literary Supplement*, 417–18
Toby Tubby (Tobba-Tubby, Chickasaw chief), 323, 324
Tobias, 95
Toole, William B., III, 296, 316
Toomer, Jean, 198
  *Cane*, 198
Transcendentalism, 44
Traschen, Isadore, 332, 335
Trilling, Lionel, 5, 21, 31, 106, 118, 140, 286, 316, 327, 341, 350, 362
Trojan horse, 381
Trowbridge, John, 95
Tuck, Dorothy, 59, 64, 78, 82, 122, 140, 148, 153, 156, 169, 180, 203, 224, 236, 242, 244, 248, 261, 267, 275, 277, 279, 291, 316, 375, 383, 394, 401, 417, 422, 428, 431, 437, 440, 450, 453, 461, 462, 466, 482, 483, 486, 501, 514, 517, 520, 530
Tulane University Library (William B. Wisdom Collection), 142, 155, 237, 260
Turner, Darwin T., 331, 341, 525, 530
Tuso, Joseph F., 391, 398, 401
Tuttleton, James W., 145, 150, 153
"Twa Corbies, The," 273
Twain, Mark. *See* Clemens, Samuel

Underwood Company, 26
University of Mississippi (Rowan Oak Papers), 74, 223, 237, 260, 375, 455, 477

University of Texas, 433
University of Virginia, 88, 170, 381, 455, 489
Uranus, 398
Utley, Francis Lee, 272, 287, 316

Vashchenko, Alexandre, 27, 31, 309, 316, 365, 366–67, 368–69, 370, 372, 374, 520–21, 525, 530
Verlaine, Paul, 172
Vickery, John B., 172, 190–91, 203
Vickery, Olga W., 8, 31, 44, 54, 59, 64, 65, 72, 75, 82, 125, 140, 146, 148, 153, 159, 169, 173, 182, 197, 203, 214, 220, 228, 236, 283–84, 316, 327–28, 331, 336, 341, 367, 374, 392, 401, 404, 411, 415, 422, 428, 431, 443, 444, 453, 459, 466, 469, 476, 493, 514
Vidal, Gore, 3
Volpe, Edmond L., 5, 10, 11, 19, 20, 26, 31, 49, 54, 120, 189–90, 203, 208, 209, 220, 222–23, 232–33, 234, 236, 238, 240, 242, 248, 321, 333, 335, 336, 341, 501, 514

Waggoner, Hyatt H., 27, 32, 41, 43, 179, 192, 203, 252, 253, 259, 393, 401
Wagner, Linda Welshimer, 88, 140, 212, 220, 505, 514
Walker, Ronald G., 492, 513
Warren, Robert Penn, 91, 107, 113, 118, 134, 281, 316, 327, 331, 341, 496, 514
Washington, DC, 376, 377
Wasson, Ben, 204, 221, 319, 402, 411, 422, 433, 440, 487
Watkins, Floyd C., 7, 8, 32, 66, 72, 74, 76, 81, 82, 89, 127, 135, 140, 246, 272, 379, 381, 383, 467, 504, 514
Watson, James G., 15, 17, 32, 77, 78, 83, 99, 103, 104, 105, 112, 140–41, 142, 147, 153, 161, 169, 178, 179, 194, 203, 206, 208, 220, 228, 236, 241, 249, 255, 259, 283, 284, 286, 295, 316, 329–30, 341, 352–53, 362, 381, 383, 392, 401, 402, 411, 435, 436, 440, 444, 453, 488, 490, 491–92, 494, 495, 496, 497, 505, 508–09, 514
Watson, Judson D., III, 145, 149, 153

Weaks, Mary Louise, 123, 141
Weber and Fields, 215
Weddell, Jimmy, 518
Weisgerber, Jean, 50, 54, 505, 513
Weiss, Daniel, 172, 182–83, 191, 203
Welty, Eudora, 239, 372
  "Lily Daw and the Three Ladies," 239
Werner, Craig, 282, 316
West (American), 6, 79
West, Ray B., Jr., 48, 54, 103, 118–19, 141, 273, 289, 291, 316, 346
W. G. Lassiter Paving Company, 89
Whicher, Stephen E., 268, 278–79, 316
Whitefield, George, 34
Whittemore, Reed, 327
"Wife of Usher's Well, The," 273
Wilde, Oscar, 172
Wilkins, Sallie Murry (cousin), 272
Wilkinson, James, 324
Wilson, Charles Reagan, 34, 40, 43
Wilson, G. R., Jr., 126, 141
Wilson, Gayle Edward, 5, 23, 32
Wilson, James, 20
Winchell, Mark Royden, 93, 141, 482, 485
Winslow, Joan D., 196, 203
Wittenberg, Judith Bryant, 208, 220, 229–30, 237, 497, 508, 515
Wolfe, Ralph Haven, 184, 185, 186, 187, 203
*Woman's Home Companion*, 142, 204, 342, 411, 422
Woodward, Robert H., 125, 141
Wordsworth, William, 371
Works Project Administration (WPA), 35, 36, 44, 50
World War I, 10, 44, 46, 70, 76, 185, 206, 208, 209, 210, 214, 403, 404, 409, 467, 519
World War II, 17, 46, 67, 70, 74, 76, 77, 379, 403, 467, 469, 472, 519
Wright, Austin M., 131, 141, 198, 203, 273, 316, 336, 342

Yalobusha County, Mississippi, 261
*Yearbook of the American Short Story, The*, 260, 375
Yeats, William Butler, 491
Yglesias, Jose, 367, 374
Yocona County, 321

Yoknapatawpha County, Mississippi (fictional), 10, 12, 13, 16, 17, 35, 37, 44, 55, 56, 59, 60, 65, 75, 89, 106, 144, 148, 150, 173, 179, 182, 208, 239, 241, 251, 253, 261, 262, 275, 277, 280, 323, 326, 330, 331, 334, 345, 347, 349, 350, 353, 358, 363, 367, 372, 377, 378, 391, 393, 407, 426, 436, 439, 451, 468, 469, 479, 480, 482, 484, 495, 517, 518

Yo-ko-no-pa-taw-fa, 321
Yo-ko-no-pa-taw-pha, 320
Yoshizaki, Yasuhiro, 101, 141, 240 248
Young, Thomas Daniel, 7, 8, 494, 504, 515

Zender, Karl F., 5–6, 11, 21–22, 32
Ziegler, Heide, 36, 43, 241, 248, 253, 259
Zolla, Elémire, 353, 362